Criminal Investigation

In Search of the Truth

Criminal Investigation
In Search of the Truth

Bill Van Allen
Georgian College of Applied Arts and Technology

Toronto

Library and Archives Canada Cataloguing in Publication

Van Allen, Bill
    Criminal investigation : in search of the truth / Bill Van Allen.

Includes bibliographical references and index.
ISBN 0-13-197271-5

    1. Criminal investigation—Textbooks. I. Title.

HV8073.V35 2006   363.25   C2005-906475-7

ISBN 0-13-197271-5

Vice-President, Editorial Director: Michael J. Young
Senior Acquisitions Editor: Ky Pruesse
Executive Marketing Manager: Judith Allen
Developmental Editor: Patti Altridge
Production Editor: Charlotte Morrison-Reed
Copy Editor: Anne Borden
Proofreader: Jonathan Dore
Production Manager: Wendy Moran
Composition: Laserwords
Photo Research: Sandy Cooke
Art Director: Julia Hall
Cover and Interior Design: Anthony Leung
Cover Images: BrandX Pictures/Alamy

7 8 9   11 10 09

Printed and bound in Canada.

To the victims of violent crimes everywhere, who did nothing to contribute to their own victimization other than by their mere presence. They did not deserve what happened to them and, unfortunately, they did not always find the justice they deserved.

And to the men and women who are dedicated to preventing crime and to detecting and apprehending criminals. Yours is an honourable profession, often conducted under adverse circumstances. You can make a difference in the lives of others. Never give up searching for the truth. The answer is there, waiting to be discovered.

WVA

Brief Contents

Contents

Chapter 4   **Interviewing Witnesses and Victims**   **83**

Introduction

With the technological innovations of the past several decades, criminal investigation is an exciting field to be in. As science and the law continue to provide investigators with additional tools with which to fight crime, criminal investigation will remain the most continually evolving field of law enforcement.

One thing that never ceases to amaze me, however, is the manner in which police investigations continue to be depicted by the majority of Hollywood feature films, television series and various other works of fiction. While the lone hero or heroine single-handedly breaking the case, against all odds, unquestionably makes for good entertainment, this overworked scenario bears no resemblance to the reality of modern criminal investigation.

Teamwork and coordination are what successfully resolves most criminal investigations; teamwork and coordination between investigators, investigative units, police agencies, forensic analysts, medical professionals and prosecutors. In fact, there is no place for any individual with a private agenda in modern-day police work. Nor is there any place for lack of ethics, incompetence, and a lack of dedication or a failure to employ a methodical approach to each and every case requiring an official examination into its circumstances.

Is it possible to teach criminal investigation? The short answer is, certainly it is possible. In fact, learning how to properly conduct an investigation is an absolute necessity. Why is it then that some investigators seem more capable than others? Were the best investigators born with some innate ability to investigate and to solve crimes? Or did they just have the benefit of expert role models and mentors who taught them the necessary skills? Perhaps they began investigating with an above average understanding of human behaviour and through a process of trial and error, guided by mentors, or combined with a self-learning program, they honed their investigative skills to a high degree. Good investigators are made—sometimes they are self-made—but they are never born.

There are expert and inexpert practitioners in all professions. Think about it; have you ever taken your automobile for repairs and been less than satisfied with the results? Have you ever been disappointed by the incompetence of a member of the medical or legal profession? If you haven't personally experienced one of these frustrations, you probably know someone who has. So it is with police officers in general, and with criminal investigators in particular. There are good and bad in every profession.

To achieve success as an investigator requires a life-long commitment as a student of crime in general, and of law, offenders, and investigative best practices. An investigator needs to constantly strive to improve their knowledge of the law, the correct application of forensic science, human behaviour, investigative methods and a host of sub-specialties to remain both current and effective in this very challenging area of police work. There is no magic in conducting a proper criminal investigation—in fact, there never was any. An investigation, simply defined, is nothing more than a search for the truth that involves the collection of evidence and the gathering of information regarding the circumstances of an incident.

Should you regard this simple definition as an oversimplification, I admit that investigations can often be extremely complicated. A complex investigation typically involves many units of one or more law enforcement agencies, forensic sciences and a variety of disciplines. A straightforward or non-complex investigation might be conducted by a single investigator, without any expert resources. The common features of any investigation, regardless of its relative complexity are the component functions of evidence collection and the gathering of information—nothing more and nothing less.

Another point that astounds me is the scarcity of Canadian textbooks on the subject of criminal investigation. This disturbing shortage became self-evident when I became involved in the education of students aspiring to careers in the criminal justice system after I retired from a 30-year career with the Ontario Provincial Police involving a primary focus on criminal investigation.

After several years of observing investigative practices across Canada, North America, Europe and abroad, I can confidently state that Canada takes a back seat to no other nation in the field of criminal investigation. Canadians have led the way in many innovative aspects and, in my opinion, will continue to do so. The Violent Crime Linkage Analysis System (ViCLAS) and the Rigel computer system used in geographic profiling, both of which will be discussed in further detail, are only two examples of Canadian innovation in the field of criminal investigation.

That isn't to say that every investigation ever conducted in Canada has been totally without its flaws. On the contrary, there has been a litany of high-profile cases throughout the last several decades involving contentious or wrongful convictions involving persons such as Steven Truscott, David Milgaard, Donald Marshal, Guy Paul Morin, and Thomas Sophonow, among others.

Public opinion once held the criminal justice system to be infallible. The findings of the police and criminal courts were implicitly trusted by the public at large. (Sher 2002) With each allegation of investigative bungling and miscarriage of justice, public confidence in the ability of the criminal justice system has been irreparably shaken. The result has been unprecedented media and judicial scrutiny of police investigations and investigative practices.

As damaging as it is to lose public confidence in law enforcement, there is an even greater loss when victims of crimes are denied justice. As investigators, we owe it to the victims of crimes and to those individuals charged with offences to do the best possible job we can to ensure the interests of justice are met—for everyone concerned.

Throughout this book, you will find many quotations preceding the relevant subject matter. Some of these quotations are contemporary, while some are several hundred years old and some are from the Bible. I am not a religious person and include these philosophical, behavioural and biblical references only to demonstrate that this vast body of knowledge of human behaviour has been widely known for centuries and is no less applicable in today's modern, highly technical world.

This book represents the lessons I have learned both experientially and from a collection of some of the finest investigators, coroners, prosecutors, judges and other justice professionals in Ontario and across Canada whom it was my privilege to meet and on occasion, to work with.

The lessons I learned from them all was that the police have a heavy responsibility to seek only the truth and to let justice be dispensed by the courts. The modern investigator must strive to see justice done, rather than try to win cases—at any cost.

This book attempts to answer many of the questions that I had as a young investigator. It is a way of sharing the benefit of my experience in the hope that it will answer similar questions for students and, at the same time, allow me to continue to expand my knowledge in the field of criminal investigation.

Because technology and the law continually evolve, I believe it is impossible for anyone to know everything about conducting criminal investigations—learning is a lifelong process

Bill Van Allen, Orillia

SPECIAL FEATURES:

Decimal Numbering System:

- The content of this text is structured utilizing a uniform system of subordinate decimal numbering, which is consistent with legislation students are exposed to throughout the Police Foundations Program, such as the frequently referenced Criminal Code and various other statute laws. This allows the student to navigate between topics and subtopics in a systematic manner and serves as an introduction to the process of deductive reasoning used during an actual criminal investigation.

Major Case Management Manual:

- This is the first text to reflect the investigative best practices contained in the Ontario Major Case Management (MCM) Manual, mandated January 1, 2005 by the Police Services Act, for use by all Ontario police services in the investigation of serial predator crime. The recommended procedures contained in this text, mirror the strong focus on interdisciplinary coordination and investigative excellence recommended by judicial reviews such as the Bernardo Investigation Review - Report of Mr. Justice Archie Campbell (Campbell Report 1996) and the Commission into Proceedings Involving Guy Paul Morin (Kaufman Report 1998). These two judicial reviews critically addressed investigative and procedural deficiencies that occurred during recent, high-profile investigations and effectively changed the way major crime is investigated in Canada. The MCM methodologies recommended in this text can easily be adapted to the circumstances of any criminal case to ensure that the investigation is conducted in a systematic and ethical fashion.

Boxed Inserts

- Investigative Relevance boxes provide students with practical advice on procedures and concepts that relate to an investigation. Drawn from the author's vast experience as a police officer, these boxes give aid on what to consider or be aware of in specific investigative situations.

- Proper Investigative Procedure boxes offer tips on correct techniques highlighting small but critical items that police officers may not immediately think of but could greatly impact the integrity of the investigation.

- Investigative Hypothesis boxes supply students with an excellent visual of a deductive equation or linear hypothesis derived from a crime scene.

Reality-based Situations

- Actual investigations recounted to emphasize what happens in actual police investigations based on the author's experiences.

Photos/Crime Scene Drawings

- Photos provided by the author of criminal investigative techniques and procedures. Figures of grid search patterns and crime scene drawings give students excellent visual aids for conducting a proper investigation.

Investigative and Case Management Forms

Includes a representative sampling of examples of frequently used investigative and case management forms, which were developed by investigators from a variety of police services over the last several years.

SUPPLEMENTS:

The following instructor supplements are available for downloading from a password-protected section of Pearson Education Canada's online catalogue (vig.pearsoned.ca). Navigate to your book's catalogue page to view a list of those supplements that are available. See your local sales representative for details and access.

Instructor's Manual: This manual, available in PDF format, includes learning objectives for each chapter, a brief chapter outline and a lecture plan to supplement the PowerPoint slides.

Test Item File: Available in Microsoft Word format, this comprehensive test bank features multiple-choice and true-false questions with references to text page numbers, level of difficulty, and skill level.

PowerPoint Presentation: The slide presentations complement the material located in the Instructor's Manual highlighting pertinent topics in each chapter.

Acknowledgements

I am sincerely grateful to all those who have so generously assisted, guided and inspired me, sometimes unknowingly, both throughout my career and during the writing of this book. Without the contribution made by each of you in your own way, this book would never have happened.

First and foremost, without the support and tolerance of my wife, Emily, I would never have been able to successfully pursue my career-long passion for criminal investigation. Your sacrifice of our time together during the writing of this book and your encouragement did as much to sustain me as your frequent deliveries of snacks, meals, coffee and tea to "the office". I'm sorry that I wasn't always there for you when you needed me to be. Thank you for realizing how important both my career and this project were to me and for standing by me.

I had the privilege, during my policing career, to serve with so many dedicated and knowledgeable police officers that I could not possibly mention them all. Some of the many who inspired me with their knowledge and personal standards of excellence include past and present members of the O.P.P. Criminal Investigation Branch: Detective Inspectors Jack Welsch, Dennis Olinyk, Bob Adams, Jim Hutchinson, D/C/Supt. Dave Crane, among others. Special thanks is extended to retired O.P.P. D/Superintendent C.F. (Bud) Brennan for teaching me the principles – and benefits – of major case management and to retired D/C/Supt. Wayne C. Frechette for your continuous faith and confidence in my abilities.

A great number of other police officers influenced and supported me during my career, including my coach officer, PC Maurice Lapointe; D/Const. Ian Rooke; Sudbury O.P.P. Crime Unit members D/Sgt. Tom Wright; D/S/Sgt. Morgan Pitfield and D/Const. Steve Easton and my brother, D/Sgt. Jim Van Allen who generously shared his vast knowledge regarding behavioural crime scene analysis.

I am indebted for the assistance and support of the following dedicated police officers from across Ontario who were at various times involved with the Campbell Report Implementation Project, including: D/Chief Mike Boyd, Toronto P.S.; D/Chief Ron Bain, Peel Regional P.S.; Chief Gary Nicholls, Niagara Regional P.S.; Chief Vince Bevan, Ottawa P.S.; Chief Ean Algar, Halton Regional P.S.; Supt. Gary Beaulieu, Niagara Regional P.S.; D/Inspector Gary Parmenter O.P.P.; Deputy Chief Roger Mortimore, Windsor P.S.; D/Sgt. Rick DeFacendis and Detective David Jarvis, Peel Regional P.S.; Inspector Dan McMullan, Durham Regional Police; D/Sgt. Douglas Conley, York Regional P.S. and Inspector John Van der Lelie, Halton Regional P.S.

My thanks also to those who taught me the importance of interdisciplinary cooperation, including Dr. James Cairns and Dr. Bonita Porter, Deputy Chief Coroners for Ontario; Dr. James Young, former Chief Coroner of Ontario; Dr. Jerry Melbye, University of Toronto (Erindale Campus), Dr. Dean Knight, Wilfred Laurier University, Dr. Peter Collins, Clark Institute of Psychiatry, Mr. Gus Bradley, Pathologist's Assistant, Sudbury Regional Hospital – St. Joseph's Health Centre (formerly the Sudbury General

Hospital); The Late Mr. Barry Bleinkinsopp, Pathologist's Assistant, Office of the Chief Provincial Pathologist, Toronto and Mr. Mike Cwihun, formerly of the Ministry of the Solicitor General, Integrated Justice Information and Technology Division.

The highlight of my policing career was my six-year secondment to the Ministry of the Solicitor General (now the Ministry of Community Safety and Correctional Services) during which time I served as the Project Director of the Campbell Report Implementation Project. At various times throughout this difficult assignment I was able to rely on the continuous support and guidance of Standards Officers Morah Fenning; Lisa Sabourin and Jeeti Sahota of the Policing Services Division. You three ladies have done more to support law enforcement and to assist victims of violent crimes than you will ever know.

My gratitude is extended to Ms. Lisa Sabourin, Ministry of Community Safety and Correctional Services, Policing Services Division. You inspired me with your writing expertise and by your example helped me to develop my own. You offered encouragement and convinced me that I had a message worthy of being passed on to others. I can never repay you for your contribution to the Major Case Management Project or for your direct inspiration for the writing of this book.

My thanks also go out to those who assisted me during my research for this book including Dr. William Lucas, Regional Coroner, Bracebridge; Gail Hussey, Georgian College Library, Orillia Campus, Jeeti Sahota, and Gloria Taylor, Ministry of Community Safety and Correctional Services, Policing Services Division, Toronto. Thanks to the able and supportive staff of Pearson Education including Ky Pruesse, Acquisitions Editor. Special thanks to Patti Altridge, Associate Editor, for your editorial advice and support. Your patience with a first-time author was greatly appreciated. I enjoyed dispelling certain television myths while responding to your in-depth queries.

My sincere thanks are extended to my family; my mother, Edna, my late father, Bill and my sisters, Jane and Lori. To my son, Bill Jr., I wish you every success in your future marketing career and hope that you find the same personal satisfaction in your chosen field that law enforcement gave to me. Opportunity awaits you. You have the necessary qualities to excel at whatever you set your mind to. Never quit and never stop learning.

To my brother, D/Sgt. Jim Van Allen, Criminal Profiling Unit, O.P.P. Behavioural Sciences Section, you continue to be a source of inspiration and advice to me. May you continue to make a difference in your quest to educate police officers and in your untiring and selfless pursuit of dangerous offenders. Your "behind the scenes" contribution to the effective investigation of violent, high-profile crime in Ontario and abroad has made you legendary in law enforcement circles. I am honoured to be your brother.

To my daughter, Provincial Constable Jennifer Van Allen, O.P.P. Southern Georgian Bay detachment, I have every confidence that you will continue to distinguish our family name in law enforcement for many years to come. I am proud that you chose law enforcement as your profession and wish you a career as varied and fulfilling as mine was. May the lessons contained in this book complement your outstanding talents and the work ethic that you have demonstrated during the early stages of your policing career. You will always be my greatest contribution to law enforcement – I owe you so much.

To my students, both past and present, at Georgian College Barrie and Orillia campuses, thank you for providing me with an outlet to impart my experiences and for encouraging me through your enthusiasm to write this textbook.

You are the future of law enforcement and the future looks very bright.

Bill Van Allen, Orillia, 2005

Criminal Investigative Function

" . . . then you shall inquire and make search and ask diligently . . . "

Deuteronomy 13:14.

Learning Outcomes

After reading this chapter, students should be able to:

- Relate the process of **deductive reasoning** involved during the investigative process to the objectives of an investigation.
- Differentiate between various types of police investigations.
- Explain the phenomenon and danger of **tunnel vision.**
- Describe the various steps involved in the investigative process, considering the significance of victim–offender relationships.
- Analyze the factors that can cause investigations to fail.
- Give examples of the requirements and qualities of an investigator.

1.1   WHAT IS AN INVESTIGATION?

In-ves-ti-gate [L investigatus, pp. of investigare in – in + vestigare – to track, trace]: To search or inquire into; make a formal or official examination of.

Funk & Wagnall's Standard College Dictionary (Canadian Edition)

An investigation may be conducted into the circumstances of a wide variety of events, incidents or situations and may include investigations of offences or crimes. On occasion, a thorough investigation into certain allegations will reveal that no actual event or wrongdoing ever occurred.

At the mere mention of the word "investigation," most people immediately think of police investigations, however, various professions conduct investigations of one form or another on a daily basis. Members of the medical profession conduct investigations every time they attempt to diagnose a patient's illness. Journalists conduct investigations when covering news stories. Employers conduct background investigations prior to hiring employees. Financial institutions and credit card companies conduct credit checks and other forms of inquiries to assess whether or not a loan or credit applicant constitutes an acceptable risk. While these examples may differ greatly in complexity, their goal, as in a police investigation, is to arrive at the truth.

It is beyond the scope of this textbook to cover every imaginable type of investigation in detail, however, all investigations can be said to involve similar basic principles. The focus of this textbook will deal primarily with investigations into allegations of crimes conducted by the law enforcement profession.

1.2   TYPES OF POLICE INVESTIGATION

Police investigations typically fall into one or more of the following categories:

- Incidents that involve either a known violation of statute law, or an allegation of a violation of statute law.

For example, a citizen reports that his or her residence has been broken into and several expensive personal items of property have been stolen, or a uniformed officer witnesses an armed **robbery** occurring, while on patrol, and takes appropriate enforcement action. A citizen might report that a relative has not been heard from for several days and disappeared under circumstances which would lead to the suspicion of the involvement of foul play.

- Situations that may afford evidence of a planned or intended crime.

A citizen might report having observed a suspicious vehicle and occupants in the vicinity of the residence of a neighbour, who is known to be away on vacation, and request the police check it out. In so doing, the investigator might determine that although no crime has been committed, the vehicle is stolen and its occupants have lengthy criminal records for property offence **convictions** and are also in possession of burglary tools. A confidential police **informer** may come forward with information relating to a group of known criminals conspiring to commit criminal acts such as break enter and **theft** at a commercial business sometime in the future.

- Proactive or reactive investigations arising from a potential threat/risk situation.

This category includes a wide variety of examples: missing persons not involving foul play, such as chronic adolescent runaways; domestic disputes that have not escalated to personal violence against any of the participants; or bomb threats. The case may involve large public gatherings with a potential to become unruly or disruptive, or the management of a situation that, if left unchecked, might result in widespread damage or injury to the public such as a paroled high-risk sexual offender moving into a new neighbourhood or suspected terrorist activity.[1]

- Circumstances prescribed by statute (e.g., *Coroner's Act*, or *Highway Traffic Act*).

---

[1] Arcaro (2004).

Certain situations require mandatory investigation, such as the in-custody death of an inmate of a correctional institution or police lock-up, or the accidental personal injury collision between a motor vehicle and a pedestrian. Even though traffic investigation may or may not be included under the umbrella of "criminal investigation," the investigative methodology is virtually the same. Perhaps a citizen reports that upon returning home from work, they discovered their recently diagnosed, terminally ill spouse has taken his or her own life in their home and has left a **suicide** note explaining his or her actions. None of these incidents necessarily involve the commission of any offence or crime.

- Instances involving an event, transaction, claim of loss, damage or civil liability.

Many occurrences are reported to the police as possible crimes and require investigation to establish whether or not a breach of statute law has occurred. An example of this would be white-collar crime such as fraud or insider stock market trading. While police investigations are not primarily concerned with establishing civil liability, the results of a police investigation are often relied upon in subsequent civil actions to determine levels of civil liability, if any, in order to award appropriate damages to a plaintiff in a civil court action.

1.3 OBJECTIVES OF AN INVESTIGATION

A police investigation may be simple and of short duration or it may be complex and drawn out. Regardless of whether it is straightforward or difficult, it is best accomplished in a systematic and methodical way. Any investigation, from the simplest to the most difficult, involves the following investigative objectives.

1.3.1 To Seek the Truth

Regardless of the circumstances of any matter under investigation, the objective of any police investigation is to search for the truth. To arrive at the truth is not always easy to achieve, as different participants in an event may have substantially different views as to exactly what occurred. Victims will view the crime, their involvement in the crime, and the impact the crime has upon their lives one way. Offenders, witnesses, and police investigators may each have very different perceptions of the event and how it occurred, all influenced by the varied nature of their involvement in the event.

Subsequently, during the course of any investigation, there may be many different versions of the "truth" according to the individual perspectives of the participants involved in any single event and the relative importance it holds for them. The misperception of the "facts" of a case, can even be witnessed at the prosecutorial stage – the prosecution alleging one set of facts and the defence putting forth a different set of facts, or at the very least, a different interpretation of the same facts.

Regardless of the various perceptions of the incident or event, or the "facts," there can only ever be one truth. And the truth is certain. Truth cannot be manufactured, nor can it be altered or reshaped; it may be mistaken by those who perceive it, but the real truth is always close at hand, just waiting to be revealed.

The worst and most common mistake that can be made during an investigation is when an investigator, believing they know what the truth is, sets out with pre-conceived notions or beliefs with little or no regard for any evidence he or she may find that contradicts their "theory." This all too common phenomenon is referred to as "tunnel vision."

Arguably, the best definition of tunnel vision that exists was rendered by The Honourable Mr Justice Fred Kaufman, a former Justice of the Quebec Superior Court, in his 1998 report on the Commission on Proceedings Involving Guy Paul Morin. Justice Kaufman defined tunnel vision as: "[A] single-minded and overly narrow focus on a particular investigative or prosecutorial theory, so as to unreasonably colour the evaluation of information received and one's conduct in response to that information."[2]

Mr Justice Kaufman's succinct definition of tunnel vision, simply stated, warns investigators of the danger of making up one's mind before all of the facts of a case are known. Improper or inaccurate interpretation of evidence can result in investigators focusing on conclusions that are not supported by the evidence in a case. To form a "theory" that is not substantiated by the known facts of a case can often cause investigators to distort or misrepresent the facts and take inappropriate action due to their distortion of the facts.

Investigators, operating out of a mindset of an honest but mistaken belief, sometimes attempt to make the evidence fit a particular and erroneous theory, rather than allowing the existing evidence to simply tell the story. Tunnel vision creates several potentially dangerous ramifications for an investigation. A fundamental principle of criminal investigation is: "Let the evidence TELL the story, ... don't make the evidence FIT the story."

Tunnel vision allows offenders to escape apprehension, it results in victims' accounts of their victimization being mistakenly evaluated as false allegations and, perhaps most importantly, can potentially result in innocent persons being unjustly accused, or worse, imprisoned for crimes they did not commit, while the true offender avoids detection and continues to re-offend.

The cure for tunnel vision is deceptively simple. Always embark upon every investigation with an open mind. Assume that evidence, in any form, is legitimate until it is either corroborated (verified, supported or strengthened) by an independent piece of evidence, or it is proved to be false. Just because evidence doesn't fit the investigator's theory of the crime doesn't mean that it can be discounted. An investigator does not have the luxury of "picking and choosing" which portion of the evidence he or she relies on merely because it happens to agree with the "theory of the day."

Recognize that evidence, such as witness statements or physical evidence in the form of documents or **trace evidence**, is vulnerable unless it can be independently corroborated. At the same time, be mindful that direct (witness) evidence may be false, either due to the faulty perception of the witness or through an intentional attempt to deceive, or at the very least might be exaggerated. Physical evidence may have been deliberately altered, or may have been placed by someone in an intentional effort to mislead an investigation (see Chapter 6.19: Staged Crime Scenes, p.167).

To the extent possible, an investigator must never rely completely upon evidence that is unsupported by corroborative evidence, or upon evidence that clearly disagrees with any previously gathered evidence, in order to establish the facts of the case. If contradictory evidence is corroborated, it might well indicate to a cautious investigator that the previously accepted facts of the case are possibly flawed, providing him or her with

---

[2]Kaufman (1998), p. 479.

ample justification to investigate further for the purpose of clearing up the obvious and important discrepancy.

The investigative phase is the proper time to clear up discrepancies between pieces of evidence. To allow unexplained discrepancies between evidence to proceed to the prosecution phase, merely to "let the courts sort it out," is to invite the creation of "reasonable doubt" as to the guilt of the **accused**, resulting in an **acquittal**.

To knowingly conceal a piece of contradictory evidence from the prosecutor, defence, and the court, in favour only of evidence that supports a particular investigative theory, amounts to wilful non-disclosure, a serious investigative misconduct and an inexcusable breach of police ethics. To do so, at best, will properly result in an acquittal; at worst, it will result in a loss of the investigator's integrity and may also incur civil liability for the investigator's police service.

For an investigator to knowingly fabricate or plant false evidence, to knowingly give perjured testimony, or to condone any of these acts in order to obtain a conviction, is to commit an unspeakable breach of ethics for someone who has sworn to uphold the law.

More important than the moral and ethical implications of such actions, any investigator engaging in such actions commits serious criminal offences rendering them totally unsuitable and unworthy of a career in law enforcement.

It is only through a systematic and methodical evaluation of the evidence gathered during an investigation that the "facts" of the case are accurately established. According to Weston and Wells, in *Criminal Investigation: Basic Perspectives*: "Evidence may tend to prove a fact, or may be sufficiently strong to compel a conclusion of fact, or may be just strong enough to create a reasonable doubt."

An investigator must take the evidence he or she uncovers during an investigation as it is found, whether the evidence goes for, or against, the case. It must be weighed on its own merits and evaluated accordingly. Then, and only then, will the truth be discovered.

Two simple principles of criminal investigation need to be kept in mind at all times. First, "Things are not always what they appear to be," and second, "Just because someone says 'It's so', doesn't make it so."

1.3.2   Gather All Evidence and Relevant Information Utilizing Lawful Methods

A competent and ethical investigator gathers all relevant evidence and information, which may be either admissible or inadmissible evidence, such as **hearsay evidence,** utilizing only lawful methods. There is no excuse for an investigator to "bend the rules" either merely for the sake of convenience, or to ensure the conviction of an accused person by fabricating or tampering with evidence. There was a time when evidence, regardless of how it was obtained, was admissible. It is as the result of past abuses that we now face very stringent limitations on how evidence may be legally obtained during police investigations. Types of evidence and rules of admissibility will be discussed in detail in Chapter 2 of this textbook.

It is to your advantage to demonstrate a genuine respect for the rights of all individuals through following proper procedures, for example obtaining judicial pre-authorization in the form of a search warrant, except in emergency situations where it may be impracticable to do so or where otherwise explicitly authorized by law. It is crucial for you to develop the reputation of an investigator whose actions are above reproach among your peers, local prosecutors, the judiciary, and the defence bar.

Such a reputation gains the respect of your superiors that you can be trusted to accomplish a complex investigation without tarnishing the image of your police service. You will even find that many offenders will respect you because you treated them fairly. The benefits may come back to you in ways that you might never have imagined, such as through increased cooperation or by their providing you with information on future or past crimes.

1.3.3   Prove the "Facts in Issue"

The **facts in issue** of any case are those essential elements of a specific offence that must be proven to form the basis for a finding of guilt in court. This is referred to as a *prima facie* case, which establishes sufficient proof that, if not contradicted, will result in a conviction or finding of guilt. In addition to the facts in issue, it is always necessary to prove the following fundamental elements in any criminal offence:

- Identity of the accused;

- Date of the alleged offence;

- Location of the alleged offence (municipality and judicial district);

- *Mens Rea* (Latin = guilty mind, or required degree of criminal intent); and

- *Actus Reus* (Latin = guilty act, an act prohibited by law).

In proving *mens rea* or criminal intent, it should be pointed out that specific offences differ in the degree of intent that is required to be proven. An offence such as Cause Disturbance requires only the identity of the accused, date, and location, plus evidence of one of the acts prohibited by s. 175(1) Criminal Code (hereafter CC), in order to obtain a finding of guilt. It need not be proven that the accused intended to cause a disturbance, making this offence one of absolute liability.

The offence of Unlawfully Causing Bodily Harm [s. 269 CC] requires only that the bodily harm caused to a person be unlawful (i.e., a deliberate act prohibited by federal or provincial statute). It must only be proven that the accused committed a deliberate act whether or not they intended to cause the bodily harm, making this a general intent section.

Offences such as **Assault** [s. 265(1) CC], Theft [s. 322(1) CC], Possession of Property Obtained by Crime [s. 354(1) CC], and **Murder** [s. 229 CC] all require that it be proven that the accused possessed the specific intent to commit the offence charged. An examination of these sections will contain the words or phrases "knowingly" or "with intent," making them part of the facts in issue that are required to be proven.

In proving the *actus reus*, it is always necessary to refer to the relevant offence under investigation to determine the individual "facts in issue" of the section of the statute. Take, for example, the offence of Sexual Assault Causing Bodily Harm [s. 272(1)(c) CC], which comprises the following facts in issue:

- *Everyone (regardless of gender) who, in committing a sexual assault* [assault is defined in s. 265(1) CC as the intentional application of force to another person, without their consent, directly or indirectly – the definition of sexual assault is found in the Supreme Court decision of *R. v. Chase* which states that an assault as described in s. 265(1) CC "in circumstances of a sexual nature such that the sexual integrity of the victim is violated"[3]].

- *causes bodily harm to the complainant (victim)* [bodily harm is defined in s. 2 CC as "any hurt or injury to a person that interferes with the health or comfort of the person and that is more than merely transient or trifling in nature"].

1.3.4 Prove the Identity of the Involved Offender(s)

When speaking of proving the identity of the accused, there is no need to prove that the **defendant's** name is actually John Smith or Jane Smith, as the case may be. A defendant may be charged and convicted under an assumed name, providing they answer to that name in court. A person may even be charged under the name of John Doe or Jane Doe if their actual identity is unknown. Proving the identity of the accused refers to establishing the defendant as being the person criminally responsible, beyond a reasonable doubt, of the commission of the alleged offence.

A criminal charge may be proven as the result of the evidence, but if the identity of the accused as the person who committed the offence remains in doubt, there should not be a finding of guilt. Where there is ample evidence as to the actual identity, that is to say the involvement of the accused, but the offence is not proved beyond a reasonable doubt, an acquittal, or finding of not guilty is, similarly, the appropriate **verdict**.

A finding of guilt cannot be made without first establishing the identity of the accused responsible for the commission of the offence beyond a reasonable doubt, which is not to say beyond any doubt. If the guilt of every accused had to be established beyond any doubt, there would never be a conviction for any crime that was not captured on videotape. "Beyond a **reasonable doubt**" means to a high degree of moral certainty.

Beyond a reasonable doubt is the standard of proof in our criminal courts used to establish criminal culpability (guilt). It is a different, and far higher standard than both the **balance of probability** burden of proof used in civil court to establish a person's civil liability in suits involving claims of loss or damage, or the standard of reasonable grounds (see next section) necessary for a peace officer to formulate the basis of belief necessary to either make an arrest or to lay a charge before the courts.

The identity and guilt of an accused person may be established by several means, including:

- direct evidence (the testimony of a witness);

- a **confession** of guilt;

- **real evidence** (e.g., **physical evidence** in the form of **DNA**); or

- **circumstantial evidence**, such as fingerprints, or other circumstances that provide reasonable grounds for believing the basis of a fact, or that are consistent with the guilt of the accused and inconsistent with any other rational conclusion.

---

[3]*R. v. Chase* (1987) 2 S.C.R. 293, 37 C.C.C. (3d) 97, 59 C.R. (3d) 193 6:0

It is rare, but not unheard of, to have an accused person brought before the court whose identity is either unknown or is in doubt. If the accused refuses to provide a true identity or if he or she supplies an identity that is known or believed to be false, they can be tried under the suspected false name they provide, or as a "John" or "Jane Doe." What does not change is the burden of proof that rests with the Crown to prove that the person standing charged before the court is the same person who committed the offence alleged in the circumstances in which the crime is alleged to have been committed.

1.3.5   Establish Grounds Upon which to Effect an Arrest and/or Lay a Charge or to Further the Investigation

After having confirmed that a breach of statute law has occurred, the investigator must use the same grounds (reasonable grounds) to formulate the basis of belief necessary to obtain a search warrant to further the investigation or to make an arrest or lay a charge. Reasonable grounds is defined as a set of facts or circumstances that exceeds mere suspicion, and which, if true, would lead an ordinary, prudent, and cautious person to have a strong belief as to the identity of the accused, and/or as to a **suspect** having committed a breach or violation of statute law.

Reasonable grounds may be obtained through the correct interpretation of physical evidence or from witness evidence gathered during the investigative process in any number of ways that will be discussed in the following chapters. Reasonable grounds to effect an arrest do not automatically give the peace officer the reasonable grounds necessary to lay a charge. Once an arrest has been made, the peace officer is not required to lay a charge and, in many cases, may decide not to charge at that time, if at all.

Subsection 495(1) CC reads:

"A peace officer may arrest without warrant;

(a)   a person who has committed an indictable offence or who, on reasonable grounds, he [or she] believes has committed or is about to commit an indictable offence;

(b)   a person whom he [or she] finds committing a criminal offence; or

(c)   a person in respect of whom he [or she] has reasonable grounds to believe that a warrant of arrest or committal, in any form set out in Part XXVIII in relation thereto, is in force within the territorial jurisdiction in which the person is found."

An officer may have reasonable grounds to effect a lawful arrest in a situation where a credible witness indicates that a certain person committed a specific crime. If sufficient reasonable grounds exist upon which to make the arrest, the arrest is lawful. The investigator must now make a decision as to whether or not to lay a charge against the prisoner.

While the legal standard of reasonable grounds for making the arrest and laying a charge are apparently the same, the officer would be unwise to lay a charge and commence judicial proceedings if there wasn't enough evidence to realistically meet the burden of proof beyond a reasonable doubt in court.

An arrest might be necessary to establish the identity of a suspect or to prevent the continuation of an offence. **Common law** and **case law** grant peace officers the legal authority to search prisoners and the area immediately surrounding them for:

1. evidence;

2. weapons; or

3. tools of escape.

All may provide some evidence that the prisoner is the person responsible for the commission of the offence under investigation, or might either injure or escape from the arresting peace officer(s).[4]

Paragraph 503(1)(a) CC requires that a person arrested, without warrant, must be brought before a justice within 24 hours of being arrested. This allows the police to hold the prisoner for up to 24 hours, at which time either a charge must be laid, or the accused must be released unconditionally.

If the case is weak, and sufficient evidence to meet the standard of proof beyond a reasonable doubt is lacking, or is unlikely to be found, it would be better to release the prisoner and continue the investigation. Even if there is a possibility that the suspect might flee the jurisdiction in which the offence was committed, it would be reckless to lay a charge based upon insufficient evidence that would not withstand judicial scrutiny in a criminal proceeding.

If, at the time of the arrest, sufficient reasonable grounds exist upon which to lay a charge, a peace officer may solemnly affirm or swear to "an information" in Form 2 (see Part XXVIII CC) in any of the circumstances described in sections 504, 505 or 788 CC. The laying (affirming or swearing) of an information marks, " . . . the commencement of criminal proceedings."[5]

1.4   BASIC INVESTIGATIVE SEQUENCE

According to the lifestyle theory of criminology, advanced by Lawrence Cohen and Marcus Felson in 1979, " . . . crime is likely to occur when a motivated offender and a suitable victim come together in the absence of preventative measures." To take any one of these variables out of this very simple equation, the crime will simply not occur. If neither a "motivated" offender, such as a mugger in need of money, nor a "suitable" victim, such as an elderly woman carrying a purse are present, the crime will not happen. If a uniformed police officer or some other "preventative measure" is in the vicinity of a "motivated" offender and a "suitable" victim, there would still be little likelihood of the crime taking place.[6]

---

[4]*Gottschalk vs. Hutton* (1921), 17 Alta. L.R. 347, 1 W.W.R. 59, 66 D.L.R. 499, 36 C.C.C. 298; *R. v. Storrey*, (1990), 1 S.C.R. 241; *Cloutier v. Langlois* (1990) 1 S.C.R. 158, 53 C.C.C. (3d) 257, 74 C.R. (3d) 316; *R. v. Caslake* (1998) 1 S.C.R. 51, 121 C.C.C. (3d) 97, 155 D.L.R. (4th) 19.

[5]*R. v. Southwick, ex p. Gilbert Steel Ltd.* (1968) 1 C.C.C. 356, 2 C.R.N.S. 46 (Ont. C.A.).

[6]Schmalleger & Volk (2005).

Unfortunately, crime is very much a part of our everyday life and likely always will be. The *Police Services Act* of Ontario[7] mandates all Ontario police services to maintain the capability to address the inevitable problem of crime that occurs within their respective jurisdictions, and reads:

> "Adequate and effective police services must include, at a minimum, all of the following police services:
>
> 1. Crime prevention.
>
> 2. Law enforcement.
>
> 3. Assistance to victims of crime.
>
> 4. Public order maintenance.
>
> 5. Emergency response. 1997, c. 8, s. 3."

1.4.1   A Brief History of Policing

Policing, as we know it today, is still a relatively recent historical development that has only been with us for some 200-odd years. Prior to the Middle Ages, the responsibility for enforcing the laws of the land and for bringing offenders to justice rested with the citizenry itself, who had banded together for their own protection in towns and villages. Following the Norman invasion of England in 1066, sheriffs were appointed by kings and were made responsible for law enforcement within appointed jurisdictions.

During the 1700s in London, England, author Henry Fielding established a body of men known as the "Bow Street Runners," who were responsible for law enforcement and crime prevention within the city. In 1785, William Pitt, the British prime minister, put forth a bill to create a police service for the City of London with a mandate similar to the Bow Street Runners. Pitt's bill was eventually withdrawn due to strong opposition from those who felt that such an organization could be used to strengthen an already unpopular government.

During the Industrial Revolution, private police forces were established to ensure security of the shipping and commerce that occurred along the waterfront area of the River Thames. These forces were very successful in dealing with crime and were officially taken over by the City of London in 1800.

Only as recently as 1829 did Sir Robert Peel, a British politician, successfully propose legislation that created a model of a police force that present-day Canadian police services are modelled after. Peel also successfully proposed a division of responsibility between the police (the detection and prevention of crime) and the courts (the prosecution of crime), that remains virtually unchanged in Canada today.

The current business practices of police services in dealing with crime vary widely across Canada. In police services too small to maintain dedicated investigative units, uniformed members investigate crimes at all levels. Larger police services maintain specialized investigative units comprising plainclothes detectives. All are investigators regardless of their rank or the organizational structure of their respective police service.

---

[7]*Police Services Act*, R.S.O. 1990, c. P.15, s. 4(2).

Public and judicial scrutiny place extremely high demands on the police to investigate crime in an effective and efficient manner. Now, more than at any previous time, any peace officer charged with the responsibility of investigating crime must possess the appropriate degree of training and experience to deal with the specific crime to which he or she is assigned.

1.4.2   Classifications of Crimes

In Canada, crimes that are reported to the police are classified into categories of violent crime, property crime, and crimes against public order, according to the Uniform Crime Report (UCR). Statistics Canada (StatCan) reports Canadian national crime statistics by total incidents per category and rates per 100 000 of the population.

The classification of Violent Crime includes personal crimes of violence such as **Homicide** [which is interpreted as **Culpable Homicide**, including murder, manslaughter, and infanticide, as defined in subsection 222(4) of the *Criminal Code* rather than the true *Criminal Code* definition of Homicide that includes the killing of a human being by any means, directly or indirectly, as defined in subsection 222(1) CC]. Also included under the classification of crimes of violence are the offences of attempted murder, all levels of assault, all levels of sexual assault, other sexual offences, robbery, kidnapping, abduction, and other crimes of violence.

The classification of Property Crime includes the offences of breaking and entering, motor vehicle thefts, thefts (of property both over and under $5 000 in value), possession of stolen property (over and under $5 000), mischief (over and under $5 000), fraud and other criminal offences. Public order offences include morality offences such as prostitution and gaming (gambling) offences, arson, offensive weapons, and disturbing the peace. Drug offences, other federal statutes and criminal traffic offences are reported separately.

Canadian crime statistics are considered to be significantly under-reported, due to the fact that many crimes, perhaps more than half of the total number of all crimes, are never even reported to the police.[8] UCR statistics also report only the most serious offence that occurs in a series of crimes. If a murder occurred as part of a series of related offences that included an attempted murder, a robbery, assorted thefts and weapons offences, the reporting police service is required to report only the most serious offence, which would, of course, be the murder. Therefore, if the murder was only one of ten crimes in the series of offences, nine criminal offences will remain unreported.

1.4.3   Known-Offender/Unknown-Offender Crimes

Crimes reported to the police can be classified in one of two categories. Either the identity of the offender is known to the victim, witnesses or through having been apprehended by police at or near the scene of the crime at the time of the initial report, or the identity of the offender is not known. Cases in which the identity of the offender is known are by far the more common of the two and the easier of the two to investigate. However, as previously discussed, just because the identity of the offender is known, his or her

---

[8]Schmalleger & Volk (2005).

identity as the person responsible for the commission of the alleged offence must still be proved in court.

The investigation of a "known offender" crime does not end merely because the offender has been identified. Even when the offender is known or when the offender has been apprehended following the offence, the investigation must diligently pursue all evidence, whether it is **inculpatory** (against the accused) or **exculpatory** (in favour of the accused) in nature.

In addition to establishing the identity of the person responsible for the commission of the offence under investigation, it is the responsibility of the investigator, in both known and unknown offender cases, to establish the following information in relation to the alleged crime (the *actus reus*):

- the offence(s), if any, involved one or more breach(es) or violation(s) of statute law which must be specified by statute and section.

- the offence(s) occurred in a certain location that the investigator must establish with as much specificity as possible. When alleging the location of offence on a Form 2 *Criminal Code* information, the location need only be specified by township, town, or city and judicial region or district, which may be the same location or a different location from that originally reported to the police. Municipal street addresses are not required on a Form 2 information.

- the manner and circumstances in which the alleged crime occurred whether or not they are the same as or different from those originally reported.

1.4.4   The Investigative Process

In a laboratory, the scientist utilizes inductive reasoning, involving the observation of particular instances, such as laboratory experiments, to test a general hypothesis or scientific principle. The police investigator, on the other hand, utilizes the process of deductive reasoning. Through the examination of general information from a variety of sources, the collection of available physical evidence, and **interviews** of witnesses, the investigator employs the processes of logical inference, reasoning, event reconstruction combined with the appropriate application of forensic science, and analysis to arrive at a particular conclusion.

Police investigations can be either reactive or proactive in nature. Typically, a reactive police investigation is initiated as the result of a "call for service" or complaint from a member of the public, for example a theft, robbery or assault. A proactive investigation is generally one that is conducted without a crime having occurred or without having received a complaint or allegation from the public. A proactive investigation may be initiated to target a known or suspected individual or criminal group to obtain intelligence regarding the nature of their activities, or for the purpose of gathering evidence upon which to base a prosecution or to justify further investigative efforts. Such cases often involve undercover operations or interception of private communications.

Whether the offender is known or unknown at the time of the initial receipt of a complaint, or upon initiating a proactive investigation, all police investigations involve the following steps.

1.4.4.1 Gathering of Information

Information may be gathered from a wide variety of sources that will be discussed in detail in Chapter 2, including, but in no way limited to:

- Victim and witness interviews
- Non-witness interviews and canvasses
- Police informants or **agents**
- Victim background information
- Suspect background information
- Tips from the public
- Police records
- Telephone and utility records
- Financial institution and credit card records
- Government records
- Employment records
- Car rental, hotel / motel records
- Airline, train and other transportation records
- Medical records
- Records of retail purchases
- As a result of conducting static, mobile, or electronic surveillance

1.4.4.2 Collection of Evidence

"I see a pattern, but my imagination cannot picture the maker of that pattern."

Albert Einstein, U.S. (German-born) physicist (1879-1955)[9]

The types and collection of physical evidence will be discussed in further detail in Chapter 2. The sources of physical evidence, including trace evidence, are numerous and varied in nature. The following list of potential sources of physical evidence should not be considered, by any means, to be exhaustive:

- From the suspect's person (his or her body) and clothing at the time of arrest
- From the victim's person and clothing
- From the search of any type of **crime scene**
- From the interior of vehicles involved in the commission of the offence
- From the victim's or suspect's residence
- Evidence discarded by the suspect
- Through the execution of search warrants

---

[9]Albert Einstein quote retrieved January 24, 2005 from www.bartleby.com

- Through forensic analysis of data on computer drives
- As a result of an effective **interrogation** of a suspect or accused person
- As a result of conducting static, mobile, or electronic surveillance

1.4.4.3 Reconstruction of Events

Through the methodical analysis of the information gathered and physical evidence collected, it is essential for the investigator to reconstruct the events of the incident in order to gain a full understanding of the manner and circumstances of the event under investigation. Very few crimes occur in a spontaneous or random manner. Offenders generally plan their crimes, sometimes in painstaking detail. Offenders must often take certain steps to prepare for the crime, recruiting accomplices and obtaining the tools or equipment necessary to carry out their criminal plan.

It would be impossible to convince a judge or jury of how a crime or non-criminal event occurred without a thorough knowledge of the reconstructed events, solidly supported by the evidence of the case. A theory of how the crime might have happened that is based upon conjecture and supposition invites the creation of reasonable doubt that, if successfully created, will always be resolved in favour of the accused.

The use of a time line is extremely useful to graphically illustrate the time and date of known events in chart form. The time line is helpful in confirming or refuting **alibi** evidence to establish that a particular **person of interest** or suspect either did or did not have the opportunity to commit the offence under investigation. See Figure 1.1.

Making the effort to prepare a time line will also ensure that discrepancies between witnesses' accounts are identified and make certain that no piece of information in a known temporal context is overlooked. Many times a properly prepared time line will assist in identifying weaknesses in the case and other areas that require further investigation.

1.4.4.4 Analysis of Findings

"Now, what I want is facts. Facts alone are wanted in life."

— Charles Dickens, British author and playwright (1812-1870)[10]

There would be nothing more pointless than to embark upon a large-scale investigation into an event or a crime without ever conducting a proper analysis of the findings of the case. Inadequate information management systems or, even more inexcusable, not having any information management system whatsoever, invites a situation in which vital pieces of information become lost or overlooked.

A thorough analysis of the findings of the investigation is necessary to establish the true facts of the case. Remember, it is always the truth that we strive to establish. Allowing an investigation to become overwhelmed by the information and evidence collected can result in the significance of certain evidence not being recognized. Lack of analysis or inadequate analysis of the findings of an investigation can also result in investigative leads not being generated that might have identified crucial pieces of evidence, thereby weakening a case – sometimes fatally.

---

[10]Charles Dickens quote retrieved April 26, 2005, from www.bartleby.com

FIGURE 1.1 | Example of an Investigative Timeline

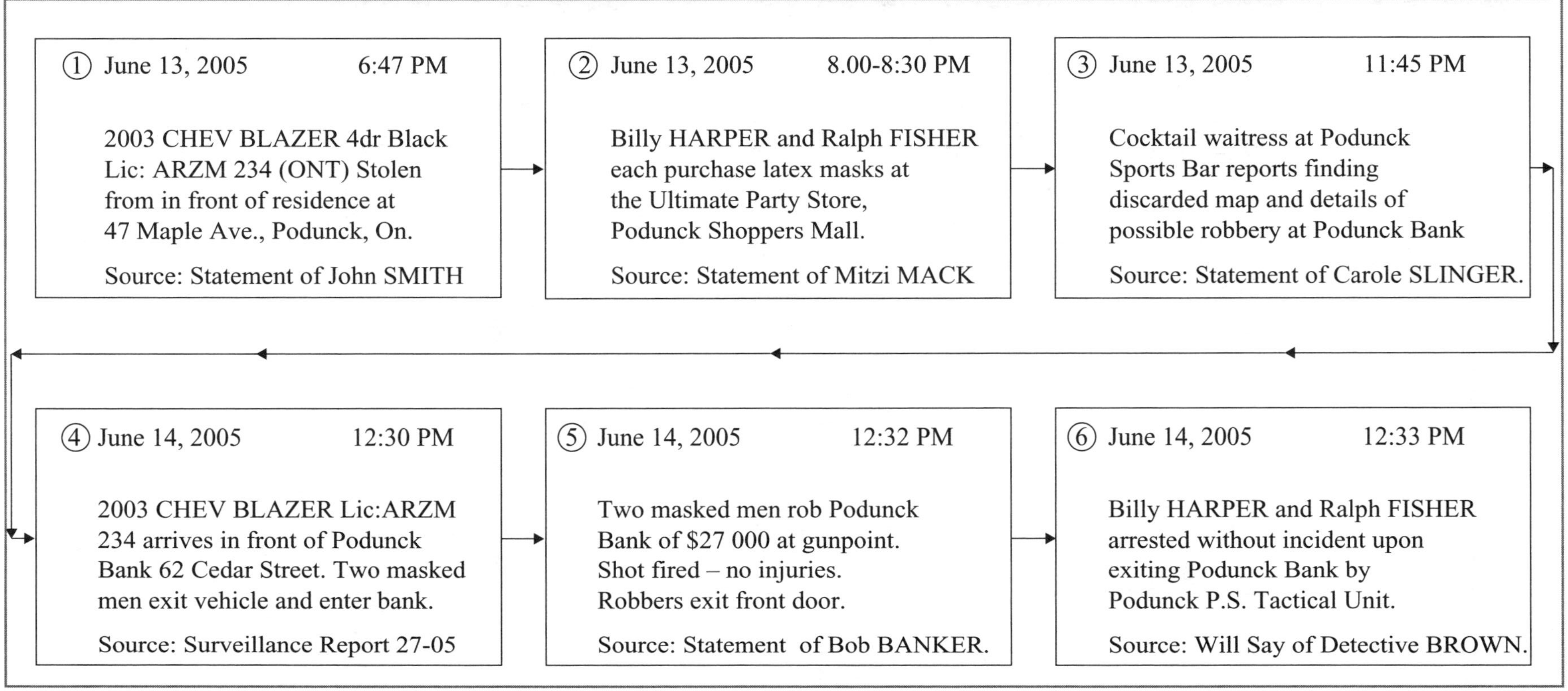

① June 13, 2005   6:47 PM

2003 CHEV BLAZER 4dr Black
Lic: ARZM 234 (ONT) Stolen
from in front of residence at
47 Maple Ave., Podunck, On.

Source: Statement of John SMITH

② June 13, 2005   8.00-8:30 PM

Billy HARPER and Ralph FISHER
each purchase latex masks at
the Ultimate Party Store,
Podunck Shoppers Mall.

Source: Statement of Mitzi MACK

③ June 13, 2005   11:45 PM

Cocktail waitress at Podunck
Sports Bar reports finding
discarded map and details of
possible robbery at Podunck Bank

Source: Statement of Carole SLINGER.

④ June 14, 2005   12:30 PM

2003 CHEV BLAZER Lic:ARZM
234 arrives in front of Podunck
Bank 62 Cedar Street. Two masked
men exit vehicle and enter bank.

Source: Surveillance Report 27-05

⑤ June 14, 2005   12:32 PM

Two masked men rob Podunck
Bank of $27 000 at gunpoint.
Shot fired – no injuries.
Robbers exit front door.

Source: Statement of Bob BANKER.

⑥ June 14, 2005   12:33 PM

Billy HARPER and Ralph FISHER
arrested without incident upon
exiting Podunck Bank by
Podunck P.S. Tactical Unit.

Source: Will Say of Detective BROWN.

1.4.4.5 Formation of a Conclusion

"There really aren't many coincidences in life. And to call coincidence after coincidence after coincidence a coincidence is just plain stupid."

– Ed Sulzbach, FBI Profiler.[11]

When all of the evidence is known, the analysis of the findings leads to the formation of a logical conclusion. The analysis of the findings employing the correct use of reasoning and common sense are required to arrive at a defensible and properly supported conclusion. A conclusion might be made concerning the validity of the original complaint – either a reported crime did, or did not, occur.

Conclusions might range from the sufficiency of reasonable grounds to charge a certain individual or to terminate an investigation where all investigative avenues have been exhausted. It is at this stage of the investigative process that tunnel vision, as previously described, must be guarded against at all costs.

It is sometimes helpful to obtain the opinions of other investigators involved in the investigation, or the assistance of expert resources. If appropriate, medical practitioners, coroners, Crown Attorneys or superior officers might be consulted to establish consensus to arrive at certain crucial conclusions. The old adage, "Many heads are better than one," lends itself well to the field of criminal investigation. An investigator with an inflated ego, who fails to seek the advice and counsel of others to confirm the validity of certain conclusions, does a great disservice to the investigation as a whole.

1.4.5   Victim–Offender Relationships

Except for certain seemingly motiveless crimes, committed by offenders suffering from some form of mental disorder by which they may be judged to be "Not Criminally Responsible on Account of Mental Disorder," the overwhelming majority of crimes are committed for one of the following motives:

Greed (or gain)

- Theft

- Robbery

- Fraud

- **Arson** for fraudulent insurance purposes

- Extortion

- Kidnapping for ransom

- Drug trafficking

- Enterprise crime committed by criminal organizations

---

[11]Ed Sulzbach quoted in Cornwell (2003).

Sex

- Sexual Assault, Sexual Exploitation, Invitation to Sexual Touching
- Indecent exposure
- Trespassing at night
- Gross Indecency
- Bestiality, etc.

Even though sexual crimes are considered to be motivated by the offender's primary need to exert power and control over their victim(s), sex is the vehicle used by the offender to control, humiliate and cause pain in order to accomplish their purpose.

Revenge

- Murder
- Attempted murder
- Assault
- Threatening
- Arson
- Mischief to Private Property
- Criminal Harassment, etc.

After examining the offences listed above and considering the reasons that most, if not all, of these offences are committed, a simple but extremely significant conclusion can be drawn regarding victim–offender relationships. Far more people are victimized by persons who are known to them or with whom they share some form of connection or association. Statistically, you have a greater chance of being victimized by an intimate partner, family member or other relative, co-worker, neighbour or acquaintance than you do at the hands of a total stranger.

Statistics Canada has published the following victim–offender relationship statistics for homicides that occurred in Canada during 2003:

- 51 percent of all homicides were committed by acquaintances of the victim.
- 34 percent of all homicides were committed by family members.
- 14 percent of all homicides were committed by strangers, and, perhaps the most striking statistic of all,
- 64 percent of all female homicide victims were killed by a person with whom they had previously shared a relationship, either by marriage or dating.[12]

These statistics are of little importance to the investigator when the offender in a given case is known and the relationship between the victim and the offender is self-evident. The significance of these statistics is anything but trivial in unknown offender cases when attempting to identify the person responsible for the crime. While

---

[12]Statistics Canada: *The Daily*, July 28, 2004 and September 29, 2004.

detailed victim–offender relationship statistics aren't available for other crime categories, experience with known-offender crimes and solved unknown-offender crimes indicates that the vast majority of other crimes are also committed by offenders with a familial relationship or previous relationship to the victim or the location of the crime.

The known statistics relating to victim–offender relationships, combined with considerable experience and personal knowledge dealing with past crimes, have a significant impact on certain assumptions which can be made during the investigation of a case in which the offender is unknown.

First, always assume, until it can be conclusively proved to be the result of a false allegation, that the reported crime occurred in the manner in which it was reported.

Next, strongly consider the possibility that the crime which, until you can prove to the contrary, did occur, may have been committed by a family member of the victim, such as a spouse, parent, sibling, child or other relative.

- Family members are known or are easily identified and often reside at or near the same location as the victim.

- Family members usually have intimate knowledge of the victim, their habits, patterns, lifestyle, wealth, possessions, business and personal affairs, giving them a distinct advantage over most acquaintances and strangers.

- Family members who may benefit from the crime or who have a motive to commit the crime are often easily identified, through the assistance of other family members.

- Family members with solid alibis are often quickly and easily eliminated from suspicion.

Subsequent to the elimination of family members and relatives, the investigator should then consider the possibility that the offender may be an acquaintance of the victim.

- Offender may have shared a previous relationship with, or may have previously dated or attempted to date the victim.

- Offender may be a close friend of the victim.

- Offender may be a co-worker, business partner, client, or neighbour of the victim.

- Offender may be a close friend or acquaintance of a family member or relative of the victim.

- Offender may be otherwise known to the victim.

- Offender has previously visited the victim or the scene prior to the incident. The offender may have posed as, or actually been, a customer at the place of business where the victim is employed, or may have "cased" the scene during the planning stage of the crime.

The final consideration for an investigator is the possibility that the offence was committed by a stranger.

- As demonstrated in the example of homicide statistics, only 14 percent of all homicides in Canada in 2003 were committed by strangers. Statistical probability alone indicates that the preliminary investigative effort should be concentrated on those closest to the victim in the vast majority of cases.

- Criminal investigation is not conducted "by the numbers" or according to any rigid checklist. It is highly likely that in certain cases, evidence of the potential involvement of a stranger might be greater than in others – for example non-familial child abductions – thereby justifying the immediate concentration of investigative effort on the assumption of the involvement of a stranger regardless of the general statistical probability of stranger involvement. Nevertheless, those persons closest to the victim should be eliminated at the earliest practicable stage of any investigation.

- Nor is it recommended that all of these steps be necessarily followed in exact sequence or in strict isolation from each other. Teams of investigators are routinely assigned to simultaneously concentrate on the elimination of family members and acquaintances while others investigate the possibility of involvement of a stranger. The timely and conclusive elimination of family members and acquaintances, however, can lend credence to the commission of the crime by a stranger and allow the officer in charge to confidently focus all investigative efforts on identifying a stranger as the person responsible for the crime.

1.5 FACTORS THAT CAUSE INVESTIGATIONS TO FAIL

In my opinion, there is no such thing as a "perfect crime." Yet, it is an unfortunate fact of life that a good many investigations fail. What is tragic is that many investigations fail before they even get off the ground. Why would a police service allow the expenditure of precious police resources on an investigation that was doomed to fail? Let's look at some of the unfortunate but avoidable reasons why some investigations fail to reach a successful conclusion.

1.5.1 Unclear Goals and Objectives

An investigation must have clearly defined goals and objectives to be successful. They may be simple and relatively straightforward in nature, however, there needs to be a clear sense of what the investigation is intended to accomplish. Establishing goals and objectives may be obvious in a reported crime of personal violence. The goals and objectives would merely be to verify the circumstances of the event, gather all relevant evidence and identify and prosecute the person(s) responsible for the crime.

Establishing goals and objectives might not be so simple in a proactive investigation into an organized break and enter ring or a criminal enterprise organization such as an outlaw motorcycle gang or large-scale drug trafficking ring. Some investigations can, if allowed, take on a life of their own to the extent that the later stages of an investigation no longer resemble what the investigation originally intended to accomplish.

That is not to say that, once set, the goals of an investigation can never be changed. It is obvious that if an allegation is proven to be false, or if a case is subsequently linked to an unsolved series of crimes in different police jurisdictions, the original goals and objectives of an investigation will be altered dramatically.

Even if the goals and objectives aren't immediately evident at the commencement of an investigation, there needs to be a plan developed at the earliest opportunity, formal or otherwise, as to what the investigation is intended to accomplish, to ensure that the investigation remains focused and on track. Clear goals and objectives are vital in determining an investigative strategy. Clearly defined goals and objectives are also necessary to know when to terminate an investigation that has exhausted all possible investigative avenues.

1.5.2   Inadequate Resources

It is an unfortunate fact of modern life that police resources are often inadequate and under-funded in most, if not all, police organizations. And, unfortunately, there is no better way to guarantee the failure of an investigation than to fail to commit adequate human and physical resources to any investigation once it is undertaken.

Insufficient equipment, such as vehicles and facilities, or insufficient funding for costly investigative techniques, overtime and travel can cause an investigation to be unsuccessful. The assignment of insufficient numbers of investigators, or worse, inexperienced or unskilled investigative staff, can cripple an investigation from the outset. An arrangement needs to be arrived at that balances the dedication of already scarce resources with the efficient management of those resources, once they have been committed to an investigation.

It is not uncommon for human and physical resources to be scaled down following the commencement of an investigation. Once any investigation becomes stabilized and focused, a core team carries on, ideally, until the successful conclusion of the case. This may mean that a police service must prioritize which investigations will be conducted and also underscores the value of partnerships between police services for the purpose of combining investigations where feasible to do so, to share resources in the solving of common enforcement problems.

Now more than ever, when the integrity of every police service is determined by its ability to solve major crime, there is a clear and convincing need to ensure that costly investigations are properly resourced. To do anything less is a great disservice to the public, whom we are sworn to protect.

1.5.3   Unclear or Non-existent Chain of Command

Every investigation needs to have one person clearly responsible for the command and control of all aspects of the investigation. This fundamental principle increases in importance in direct proportion to the complexity of an investigation. Investigators must know exactly to whom they report and whom to inform of important information obtained during the course of any investigation.

The officer in charge of the case must have all relevant information at his or her disposal in order to form intelligent investigative strategies. The officer in charge, or Case Manager, is accountable to the executive level of the involved police service(s) and to prosecutors involved in the case, if any. In addition to other possible aspects of the investigation, the Case Manager is also responsible to the investigative team for the provision of adequate resources, leadership, direction, and to establish systems to regulate the management of crime scene examination, forensic issues, victim issues, media issues, and information management issues.

An investigative team becomes an organizational unit within a police service, even if only temporarily. The integrity of that organizational unit must be respected while it exists. The reporting of valuable information by an investigator to someone other than the case manager or someone delegated by them, would constitute grounds for disciplinary action or removal from the investigative team. It is no less inappropriate for a police manager, not directly involved in the investigation, to attempt to influence any aspect of the investigation or a member of the investigative team.

That is not to say that an investigative team answers to no one. In fact, it is quite the contrary. Every case manager is responsible to, and needs to report to, his or her accountable police executive(s) to ensure that they are regularly and properly informed regarding the status and progress of the investigation. The efforts of any investigation must be kept consistent with the overall goals, objectives, and budgets of the involved police service(s).

Where the costs of a complex investigation exceed the normal operating budget of a police service, the responsibility then falls to senior police management to obtain the necessary extraordinary funding to continue the investigation based upon the justifications provided by the case manager. To ensure the success of any investigation, the case manager must be responsible for the day-to-day operations of the investigation and accountable for the overall conduct of the investigation. It is the prerogative of senior management to decide when to terminate any solved or unsolved investigation.

1.5.4   Haphazard Approach

A focused and methodical approach is vital during any investigation. If an investigation is allowed to remain unfocused, with no clear investigative strategy, it is usually not long before it runs completely off the tracks. Leads and evidence must be properly evaluated and prioritized while formulating a plan as to how the investigation will be conducted.

The formulation of a proper investigative strategy is sometimes easier said than done, especially during the initial stages of a complex case. Even though the focus of an investigation may change as new facts are verified, it is nonetheless crucial to establish a proper plan of the conduct of an investigation as soon as possible, which is best done in consultation between the officer in charge and the experienced members of the investigative team.

Failure to develop and follow a plan results in investigators running off chasing unproductive leads and can quickly drive up the costs of an investigation that goes nowhere. The need to develop a clear investigative strategy points to the necessity of conducting regular briefings involving the entire investigative team so that everyone is aware of the plan in order to be aware of how their respective roles impact the assignments of other investigators and the investigation as a whole.

Investigative assignments must be consistent with the overall investigative plan and be clearly communicated to the personnel that are assigned to carry them out. A large group of investigators cannot be relied upon to automatically know what needs to be done. There may be times when a sensitive piece of information might have to be confined to one segment of the investigative team on a "need to know" basis, even temporarily. This practice is usually counterproductive and results in frustration and resentment among those members of the investigative team that are kept in the dark.

1.5.5   Failure to Follow-up Leads

While the need to follow-up investigative leads may seem obvious, time and time again unsolved investigative case files have been found to contain leads that, had they been followed-up, might have pointed directly to the person responsible for the commission of the offence under investigation. Unfortunately, the causes of this investigative cancer are many. Either the lead never makes it to the attention of an investigator responsible for generating investigative assignments, or the significance of the lead is not recognized for what it is.

A lack of investigative resources or an ineffective information management system may lead to a faulty prioritization of the information that is then relegated to the "back burner" or is soon overlooked and forgotten completely. The failure to follow-up leads can result from inexperience, incompetence or downright laziness and neglect.

Whatever the reason, the results become a foregone conclusion. Failure to follow-up any lead may guarantee that the offender continues to avoid apprehension, or if they are identified, the case against them may be weakened, perhaps irreparably. The result of failing to follow-up a lead that would have exonerated an accused can lead to a life being ruined and considerable civil liability against both the involved police service and investigative personnel.

Unless a lead can be positively and conclusively discounted as being irrelevant to the investigation, it needs to be fully investigated and eliminated.

1.5.6   Failure to Exhaust All Avenues of Investigation

As with failing to follow-up leads, all practicable investigative avenues, such as electronic surveillance, searches, canvasses, or public appeals, must be explored and exhausted during the course of an investigation. Some investigative techniques may be discounted due to exorbitant costs or organizational financial constraints, while some may be deemed impracticable for other reasons of hardship such as distance or unavailability.

Where practicable, however, there is no excuse for leaving "any stone unturned." Think about the last time you misplaced your car keys. You found them in the last place you looked, didn't you? If you hadn't looked in that last place, you would never have found them and you'd still be a pedestrian. If a certain investigative avenue would further the objectives of an investigation, it is unconscionable to ignore it on the basis of cost or convenience.

To terminate an investigation prematurely, without having exhausted all possible and practicable avenues of investigation, is to "leave stones unturned," any one of which might conceal the solution to the crime under investigation.

1.5.7   Terminating the Investigation before the Objective is Achieved

There is no such thing as a perfect crime. A bold statement, perhaps, but every crime should be considered solvable. Why then is there no shortage of unsolved crimes? We have already examined some of the reasons why cases remain unsolved. If inadequately resourced, they are doomed to fail before they begin. An inadequate or non-existent chain of command can similarly doom an investigation. If leads and investigative avenues aren't followed up, the answer may still be out there and just wasn't discovered.

If an investigation is abandoned prior to its objectives being achieved, it can remain unsolved until new, or perhaps even previously known, information surfaces or public pressure forces the re-opening of a case. Sometimes the case will remain unsolved forever, guaranteed by the death of witnesses or the degradation of their memories of the case due to the passage of time.

Many police services frequently express the position that an unsolved case is never considered "closed" and often that explanation successfully deflects public or media criticism for the time being. Some investigations seem to be driven only by the amount of media coverage that they receive. Once a story falls from the interest of the local media, it sometimes drops in priority for the involved police service.

The point is, while there are financial and operational limits as to what a police service can reasonably be expected to accomplish, to terminate an investigation before the objectives have been achieved is to close a book before the final chapter has been written. It is far more difficult, and costly, to preserve and re-examine the results of a cold case investigation than it may have been to solve it in the first instance.

1.6 REQUIREMENTS OF AN INVESTIGATOR

Not every police officer has the aptitude to be a good investigator. Some officers are just naturally better suited for some duties rather than others. I have compiled the following list of attributes that I observed in many of the finest investigators that I encountered throughout my career – attributes that any aspiring criminal investigator would do well to imitate.

1.6.1 Knowledge of Statute and Case Law

First and foremost, an investigator requires an above-average knowledge of laws, both statute laws and case law. One cannot expect to enforce the law if one does not know what the law is. Not all law in the field of criminal investigation comes from statute law such as the *Criminal Code*. Much of the law that impacts upon the field of criminal investigation comes in the form of case law (previous court decisions that, by the **rule of precedent,** bind lower courts facing similar situations in the future).

The law of search and seizure is one of the most continually evolving areas of criminal law that face criminal investigators. As well, investigators must be aware of case law decisions that impact on any specialized area of investigation they are assigned to, such as homicide, drugs, robbery, surveillance, etc.

An investigator needs to develop a lifelong interest in the law and remain aware of current case law decisions and amendments to statute law to be effective in the field of criminal investigation.

1.6.2 Knowledge of Investigative Techniques and Best Practices

The knowledge of investigative techniques and "best practices" (practices that are universally recognized as the most correct and proper methods or techniques within any given profession) is also gained over the long term in the form of self-education, seminars, either formal or in-service training courses, practice and experience. Criminal investigation is a rapidly changing field, considering the recent advances in forensic science in general and in DNA technology in particular during the past decade alone.

Relying on obsolete investigative methods and techniques using the excuse, "That's the way we've done it for the last 20 years; I see no good reason to change now," is no longer acceptable. A popular trial strategy currently being employed by defence lawyers, who are faced with insurmountable evidence against their client, is to attack the police investigation. This was never more apparent, nor successful, than in the 1996 trial of the *People of the State of California v. Orenthal James (O.J.) Simpson.*

BOX 1.1	Investigative Relevance

Investigative "best practices" and professional manuals are studied by defence lawyers and are referred to during their **cross-examination** of police officers on the witness stand. If a certain investigative technique was known and available but, without good reason, was not utilized, a defence lawyer can easily cast doubt on the integrity of the investigation and allow the conclusion to be drawn that the police either didn't care enough to do their jobs, or, "If they screwed that up, what else did they screw up?" The end result? Ask the prosecutors and investigators from the O.J. Simpson case.

1.6.3 Ability to Apply Knowledge of Law and Investigative Techniques

All of the knowledge in the world doesn't make a good investigator. Effective investigators have the expert knowledge of law and investigative techniques, and the ability to relate that knowledge to actual situations. An expert investigator has a well-developed sense of exactly what constitutes an offence and knows what evidence he or she will require to prove his or her case.

An expert investigator knows which investigative method will have the highest probability of success and in which sequence to employ various techniques to avoid the risk of destroying evidence. The expert investigator is proficient in a number of skills, including interviewing, interrogation, detecting deception, collecting evidence, how to work as part of a highly skilled team, the writing of reports and search warrants, case preparation and how to properly testify in court.

These skills are not developed by attending training courses or by reading investigative manuals late at night in bed. These skills are developed through years of experience, trial and error, modelling oneself after successful investigators and honing one's own skills in the trenches. Criminal investigation can be learned, but it is learned in the field during the middle of the night, perhaps the second night without sleep. It is learned in the autopsy studio, while conducting field interviews, in the interrogation room, the crime scene and inside a courtroom – not just inside the classroom or within the covers of a book. Investigative ability is learned mostly through practice and experience.

1.7   THE QUALITIES OF AN INVESTIGATOR

The following is a list of qualities that I have observed in the most successful criminal investigators I have known. Some investigators were stronger in some areas than they were in others. Certain investigators excelled in all of the following areas. Some of these qualities are instinctive and some may be developed – but all are found in the "best of the best."

1.7.1   Motivation

A good investigator demonstrates a sincere interest in all aspects of his or her job and continually strives to improve himself or herself. A good investigator is highly motivated and always strives for success. Criminal investigation requires working long, hard hours, sometimes under very stressful circumstances. Lack of interest leads to lack of results.

1.7.2   Attention to Detail

An investigator must be just as methodical in his or her approach to problem-solving as he or she is in processing a crime scene or preparing his or her case. There is no place in investigations for a disorganized approach, either in note taking, conducting an interview, or maintaining an information management system for the case file.

Without a methodical approach at all times, important details become lost or overlooked. Attention to detail is essential for success as an investigator. Information received must be recorded accurately in notes, reports, search warrants and court documents. An investigator must be absolutely fastidious in his or her approach to and documentation of all aspects of his or her investigations. (See Chapter 3: Note Taking and Report Writing.)

1.7.3   Common Sense and Good Judgement

Common sense has been described as "the least common of all of the senses." An investigator must be a good judge of people – all people. Knowing what makes people "tick" is an invaluable asset for any investigator.

The level of understanding of human behaviour and day-to-day life, in a variety of circumstances, is what makes some investigators excel over their colleagues in the field of criminal investigation. Unfortunately, common sense cannot be taught – it can sometimes be developed through life experience, but you won't find common sense on the shelf of a library.

Good judgement involves intuitiveness (the ability to anticipate events before they occur) and good decision-making skills. In short, it involves knowing when to act and instinctively knowing what to do when it is time to act.

1.7.4   Decisiveness and Perseverance

" . . . never, never, never give in."

Winston S. Churchill, British prime minister (1874-1965)
Excerpt from a speech to schoolchildren at
Harrow School (October 9, 1941).[13]

An effective investigator demonstrates self-confidence in his or her ability to make decisions to commit to a course of action. It is not enough just to make a decision to commit to a course of action. A good investigator also has the tenacity to continue on, even in the face of adversity.

1.7.5   Sincerity and Empathy

"People may not remember exactly what you did, or what you said, but they will always remember how you made them feel."

Unknown

The investigator must always demonstrate a professional sincerity and empathy, regardless of whom they may be dealing with. Sincerity helps establish trust with victims, witnesses and even suspects and accused persons, and will result in a higher level of co-operation from them.

Empathy involves identifying with other people and the trauma they have undergone and the emotions they may be experiencing at the time. Put yourself in the shoes of the other person, whether he or she is a victim or a suspect, and imagine what would be most important to you in that position.

Except in rare cases where an aggressor can become a victim, victims don't ask to be victimized, nor do they deserve their victimization. They may feel threatened or may be grieving. By your professional attitude and demonstrating empathy for them, you build a rapport with them that will earn their gratitude, respect and trust.

Much has been written regarding the post-crime secondary victimization of victims as the result of their involvement with the criminal justice system. Never contribute to re-victimizing a victim. Empathize with victims and, to the extent that you are able to, help them feel safe and assist them to start healing and rebuilding their lives.

Even suspects deserve to be treated with professionalism and dignity. You don't empathize with suspects for what they may have done, but you can empathize with them for the position that they now find themselves in. Helping them deal with a first-time or subsequent arrest, when they may be in the position of losing their job or family or facing the prospect of societal disgrace or a term of imprisonment can, in many cases, help to gain their trust, respect and co-operation.

In the circumstances of our jobs as investigators, we tend to see people at their absolute worst. Always remember that everyone deserves to be treated with professionalism and dignity at all times, regardless of the circumstances they find themselves in.

---

[13]Winston Churchill quote retrieved April 19, 2005, from www.bartleby.com

SUMMARY

- Police services are required to conduct proactive and reactive investigations into a wide range of circumstances that may or may not involve the commission of an offence or violation of the law.

- A police investigation may be straightforward or complex; it may or may not involve a crime, and the identity of the offender may be known or unknown.

- In all cases, utilizing the process of deductive reasoning, investigators apply the same basic principles to every investigation, namely: gathering information; collecting evidence; reconstructing events; analyzing investigative findings; and forming conclusions.

- It is crucial that an investigator possess the correct level of knowledge and experience, commensurate with the complexity of the task he or she is assigned to investigate.

- The appropriate level of knowledge results from a lifelong process that combines formal training, self-education and experience.

- Participants in a crime, including victims, witnesses, offenders and even investigators, may all have very different perspectives of the incident under investigation and the impact the event had upon them.

- These differing perspectives may result in skewed or erroneous versions of the events and facts of the case.

- The investigator is responsible for sorting through all available evidence to differentiate between truth and fiction and individual belief from fact, in order to arrive at a conclusion that is properly supported by the total evidence.

- Following proper procedures and "best practices" (using only lawful methods) the ethical investigator gathers all the evidence, both for and against a suspect or defendant, and fairly presents the evidence in a court of law.

- An experienced investigator knows that he or she has no personal stake in the outcome of any case. Investigating is never a win or lose proposition.

- It is the responsibility of a court of competent jurisdiction to deliver justice. It is the task of the investigator to investigate, thoroughly and fairly – to seek the truth.

DISCUSSION QUESTIONS

1. On the basis of statistical probability and past experience, certain inferences may be made regarding victim–offender relationships in the early stages of an investigation. These inferences may assist the investigator in focusing his or her investigative efforts to eliminate certain categories of persons from suspicion. What would be an

example of a case that might tend to suggest the involvement of a relative and what would be an example of a case that would tend to suggest the involvement of a stranger? Why?

2. A female complainant reports that during the previous month she has observed her estranged spouse follow her to her workplace every morning and follow her back to her residence every evening. On more than one occasion, she has observed him sitting across the street in his vehicle, presumably watching to see if any other men visit her. Due to previous incidents of domestic violence that ended their marriage and his possession of firearms, the complainant fears for her personal safety. The complainant pleads for you to help her. Has an offence been committed? If so, what are the facts in issue that must be proven? If an offence has been committed, can an arrest be made or are there any other investigative steps that could be taken to strengthen your case? If yes, what are they?

3. It is important that any investigator assigned to a case possesses the appropriate level of training and experience to conduct that investigation. List the requirements and qualifications for an investigator assigned to investigate a break-in at a service station. How do they differ from the requirements and qualifications of an investigator assigned to a sexual assault involving an unknown offender? Why?

WEBLINKS

www.statcan.ca/

Statistics Canada. Statistics on criminal offences in Canada compiled from Uniform Crime Reporting (UCR) returns submitted by Canadian police services.

http://laws.justice.gc.ca/en/index.html

Department of Justice, Government of Canada. Selected Federal statutes and links to sites of case law databanks.

www.e-laws.gov.on.ca/home_E.asp?lang=en

Government of Ontario. Provincial statutes and associated regulations.

www.pearsoned.ca/crimcjpolicing/glossary0.html

Pearson Education Criminology, Criminal Justice and Policing Online Glossary of Terms and Concepts.

www.canlii.org/index_en.html

Canadian Legal Information Institute. Federal and provincial statutes and case law database.

Chapter 2

Evidence

"Justice delayed is justice denied."

William Gladstone, British prime minister (1809-1898).[1]

Learning Outcomes

After reading this chapter students should be able to:

- Explain what is meant by the term **presumption of innocence.**
- Differentiate between various types of evidence, and give examples of each type.
- Give examples of different potential sources of evidence.
- Explain what is meant by the **Hearsay Rule.**
- Explain **Locard's Exchange Principle** and describe the significance of this doctrine as it relates to the transference of trace evidence during the commission of a crime.
- Summarize the concept of the **chain of continuity.**

2.1   INTRODUCTION

We are very fortunate to live in a free and democratic society that places a high value upon the rights of individuals. The presumption of innocence is one such right that is firmly entrenched in subsection 11(d) of the *Canadian Charter of Rights and Freedoms*, which reads:

"Any person charged with an offence has the right to be presumed innocent until proven guilty according to law in a fair and public hearing by an independent and impartial tribunal."[2]

---

[1]William Gladstone quote retrieved November 23, 2003, from www.quotationspage.com

[2]*Canadian Charter of Rights and Freedoms*, Being Part 1 of the *Constitution Act*, 1982, Enacted by the *Canada Act 1982 (U.K.)* c. 11; proclaimed in force April 17, 1982, 11(d).

The phrase "presumed innocent until proven guilty according to law" means, as discussed in Chapter One, that every accused person is considered to be innocent of any offence they are charged with until they are proven guilty beyond a reasonable doubt in an open and impartial court. This presumption (something that is presumed to be true) protects all persons in Canada (not just Canadian citizens) and is ingrained in our law to prevent the wrongful conviction of innocent persons. Unfortunately, as the record shows, Canadian courts are not infallible and have, on occasion, convicted innocent people.

Although it can be argued that this **irrebuttable presumption** of law results in far more guilty people being found innocent than innocent people being convicted, your attitude as investigators must be that even one wrongfully convicted person is one too many. As stated at the end of Chapter One, "an experienced investigator should know that he or she has no personal stake in the outcome of any case. Investigating is never a win or lose proposition." Any decision, especially a verdict made by a court, is beyond the control of the investigator. Every wrongfully convicted person, however, is proof of a failed investigation – the truth was not discovered.

2.2   PROVING THE "FACTS IN ISSUE"

In Canada, the responsibility for the administration of justice in criminal matters lies with the Crown (the Crown = the government). The Attorney General of each province is responsible for the overall administration of justice (not including law enforcement) within their respective provinces. Crown Attorneys and Assistant Crown Attorneys bear the day-to-day responsibility for the administration of justice within their respective jurisdictions.

In any criminal proceeding, whichever party alleges a fact bears the burden of proving that fact. When an accused person pleads guilty to an offence that he or she is charged with, the prosecutor reads into court a statement of facts (a synopsis of the evidence almost always prepared by the investigating officer) that has been stipulated (agreed upon) by the defence. If the defence substantially agrees with the facts of the case, as read by the prosecutor, and if the evidence is sufficient to prove all of the facts in issue of the charge(s), the judge may then find the accused guilty and sentence the accused accordingly.

Where an accused person enters a plea of not guilty, the burden of proving the accused's guilt rests with the Crown. The **trier of fact** must be persuaded of the guilt of the accused beyond a reasonable doubt before convicting an accused person. In trials held in a court composed of a judge sitting without a jury, the judge is the trier of fact. In a court composed of a judge and jury, the jury assumes the role of the trier(s) of fact.

All accused persons are protected by the presumption of innocence and the burden of proving the guilt of all accused persons rests with the Crown; therefore, it is always the Crown that must produce sufficient evidence to convince the trier of fact of the guilt of the accused in criminal proceedings. Where does the evidence come from that is used to convince the trier of fact of the guilt of an accused person?

The responsibility for the investigation of crime (including the identification and apprehension of offenders, gathering of evidence, etc.) is that of the investigative agency having jurisdiction where the alleged crime occurred. It is the responsibility of the individual investigator to be familiar with various types of evidence and the rules of evidence. The investigator needs to recognize what evidence is either for or against the accused when it is encountered, and to utilize the proper methods to gather it to ensure its eventual admissibility in court.

Always remember, we don't investigate and gather evidence for the purpose of convicting people. We investigate and gather evidence in order to seek the truth. The responsibility for the determination of guilt or innocence is solely that of the trier of fact in a criminal proceeding.

The Crown's burden of proving the guilt of an accused is no simple task. Not all evidence collected during an investigation will be deemed to be admissible. In all trials, it is the duty of the judge, using a complex set of rules, to determine the admissibility of every piece of evidence, whether or not he or she is the trier of fact. Evidence does not prove the facts of a criminal case – the facts of the case are determined by the trier of fact after careful evaluation and an impartial interpretation of the evidence.[3]

2.3   CLASSIFICATIONS OF EVIDENCE

In this section, we will examine the various types of evidence that are commonly encountered during a criminal investigation. Evidence can be generally classified into one of four categories:

1. *Direct evidence* – the sworn (or affirmed)[4] oral testimony of a victim, witness, or accused person of which they have direct, personal knowledge.

2. *Real evidence* – physical evidence. For example, a tangible item such as a firearm or article of clothing.

3. *Circumstantial evidence* – a detail or circumstance (or a series of circumstances) that is consistent with the guilt of the accused and inconsistent with any other rational explanation. Circumstantial evidence does not directly prove a fact but may be used to infer one or more facts in a criminal proceeding. For example, the fact that the accused's vehicle received a parking ticket near the scene of a crime approximately two hours before the crime occurred does not prove the guilt of the accused but may be used to infer that the accused was present at the location and is guilty of the offence, as charged.

4. *Hearsay evidence* – the oral testimony of a witness that is third person in nature and not from the witness's direct knowledge. For example, this could be something that the witness heard spoken by another person who is not called to testify, which the witness then repeats.

---

[3] Weston & Wells (1997).

[4] *Canada Evidence Act*, R.S., c. E-10, s. 14(1).

2.4 TYPES OF EVIDENCE

As mentioned in the previous chapter, evidence – whether direct, real, hearsay or circumstantial – may be discovered in many forms during the course of an investigation. The different types of evidence commonly encountered include, but are not limited to:

- Direct evidence (statements) from victims and witnesses
- Admissions and confessions (of accused persons)
- Documentary evidence (see Section 2.5: Sources of Evidence)
- Fingerprints
- Weapons
- Ballistics
- Tool marks
- Patterned evidence
- Blood spatter
- Biological evidence (bodily fluids, DNA, etc.)
- Hair / fibre
- Handwriting
- Soil
- Paint chips
- Insects
- Glass
- Footwear impressions
- Tire mark impressions
- Poisons
- Chemicals

2.5 SOURCES OF EVIDENCE

The possible locations where evidence may be located will be determined by the circumstances of the crime under investigation and its discovery will only be limited by the imagination of the investigator(s). Some common sources of evidence include:

- Victim and witness interviews
- Neighbourhood canvasses
- Public appeals
- As a result of an effective interrogation of a suspect or accused person
- Through the execution of search warrants

- From the suspect's person (his or her body) and/or clothing at the time of arrest

- From the victim's person and/or clothing

- From the victim's or suspect's residence

- From the search of any type of crime scene

- Police informants or agents

- **Expert evidence** (and other **opinion evidence**)

- Victim background information

- Suspect background information

- Physical evidence discarded by a suspect or accused

- Seized contraband

- Tips from the public (e.g., Crime Stoppers, telephone hotlines, etc.)

- Police records

- Employment and education records

- Telephone and utility records

- Financial institution and credit card records

- Government records (driver's licences, vehicle registration, birth records, taxation, passports, employment insurance, land titles, military, etc.)

- Car rental agency records

- Hotel / motel / hostel records

- Airline, train, and other transportation records

- Medical records

- Records of retail purchases

- Internet service provider (ISP)

- Information / evidence gathered as a result of conducting static, mobile, or electronic surveillance

- Forensic analysis of data on computer drives

2.6 DIRECT EVIDENCE

When investigating an alleged crime, an investigator should never assume any facts of the case. An investigator only determines the facts of the case after collecting and evaluating the various types of evidence in their totality. Generally, direct evidence is by far the most commonly encountered evidence during the course of police investigations. Direct evidence is the oral testimony of witnesses who are allowed to testify to matters they have perceived through one of the five senses (sight, sound, taste, smell, and touch).

The practical techniques of obtaining information from participants involved in any event – whether they are victims, witnesses, persons of interest, suspects, or accused persons – is covered in detail in Chapters 4 and 5. However, no meaningful discussion of evidence in this chapter would be possible without an examination of the significance of direct evidence to any police investigation and subsequent criminal proceeding.

The interview of a witness (the term "witness" includes victims) will result in a statement that is either handwritten, audio taped or videotaped, depending on the circumstances of the case and the departmental policy of the agency involved. The objective of interviewing a witness is to gather all the information, either admissible or inadmissible, that the witness has about the case under investigation.

Because of the rules of evidence that determine admissibility, a witness may not be allowed to testify in court about each and every piece of information contained in his or her statement. This is of no concern to an investigator during the investigative phase. All available information must be gathered in order to determine what is of actual relevance to the investigation.

By collecting a witness's knowledge about the events in statement form, the investigator accomplishes several goals, namely:

- Investigators create a permanent record of the witness's knowledge. The account may be added to or changed, if necessary, in the form of subsequent statement(s), all of which will be used to determine the reliability of the witness's information.

- They compile the witness's information in a form that can be evaluated and utilized by the police, prosecutor, and the defence.

  - Police use it for investigative purposes.

  - Prosecutors use it to determine what a witness can testify to.

  - The defence uses it for purposes of cross-examination and to identify possible defence witnesses.

- They create a formal account of the information a witness provided at a specific time. It may used by the witness to refresh his or her memory prior to testifying. It may also be used by the party who calls the witness as a basis upon which to cross-examine the witness in court, in the event the witness provides conflicting information at a later time and is declared adverse by court.[5]

The investigator will use the information gathered in a statement (whether it be that of a witness, a suspect or an accused) for several investigative functions, including:

- to assess the relevance of the information to the investigation;

- to evaluate the credibility of the information;

- to compare the information against other known facts of the case;

- to determine whether or not the information gathered corroborates any previously known information or is being learned for the first time;

- to determine whether or not the information changes the focus of the investigation;

---

[5]*Canada Evidence Act*, R.S., c., E-10, s. 9(1).

- to determine whether or not the information requires further investigation;

- to determine whether or not the information can be used for any other investigative purpose (such as a basis for **reasonable grounds** to obtain a search warrant, obtain an authorization for an order to intercept private communications, or to make an arrest or lay a charge, etc.); and

- to determine whether or not the information proves one or more facts in issue.

2.7 REAL EVIDENCE (PHYSICAL EVIDENCE)

Physical evidence is generally considered to be more reliable than the direct evidence of witnesses. The simple reason for this belief is because physical evidence is a tangible item that isn't subject to any normal human frailties such as bias, mistaken perception, emotion, motive or intentional deception.

This is not to say, however, that physical evidence is necessarily reliable 100 per cent of the time. Physical evidence may be fabricated (such as a forged document) or planted (placed) at a crime scene for the purpose of misleading a police investigation.

2.8 CONTINUITY OF EVIDENCE

Continuity of evidence, often referred to as the "chain of continuity," involves the systematic management of physical evidence to ensure the safety and integrity of each individual item. There could be no better choice than the analogy of a "chain" in relation to the continuity of physical evidence. As in the case of a real chain, the chain of continuity must remain unbroken to be of any purpose or value. Similarly, the chain of continuity, just like the chain described in the age-old adage, "is only as strong as its weakest link."

The chain of continuity tracks the movement of pieces of evidence to prove that a particular item was in a specific place at a specific time in a particular condition and tracks all persons who handled or controlled the item at any given point in time. Continuity begins the very moment that an item is discovered and ends, either when the "chain" is broken (meaning the item is lost or continuity of the item is lost due to the inability to account for exactly where, or in whose possession an item was at any given time), when the item is released (returned to its lawful owner), or when it is destroyed or otherwise disposed of.

Should the piece of evidence become altered or contaminated in any way, as often does occur during many forensic testing processes, continuity should provide an adequate explanation of when and how this occurred, and who was in possession of the item at the time. What this proves is that incriminating evidence, such as hair or fibres found on a victim's clothing that implicate a defendant in a certain crime, were present at the time of the item's discovery and were not placed there at any time after the item's discovery. Continuity also proves to the court that the exhibit has not been mistaken for, nor could it have been replaced with, another piece of evidence.

In order to prove continuity of a particular piece of evidence, all persons who handled the evidence and any movement of the evidence must be recorded in an acceptable manner. Evidence must be preserved by packaging it in a suitable container at the time of collection to avoid contamination. The person who initially seizes a piece of evidence must label the item (either the item itself or the package containing the item) with a concise description of the item including the time, date, location of discovery, and his or her name.

Once collected and documented, evidence must be placed in secure storage with restricted access while awaiting forensic examination or production in a court of law. Secure storage facilities for certain types of evidence may require special considerations (e.g., climate control to prevent decomposition or suitable biohazard precautions). Evidence must always be suitably protected from the possibility of cross-contamination by other evidence. In matters of handling, packaging, and storage of evidence, when in doubt consult a **forensic identification** officer, the manual *Laboratory Guide for the Investigator,* or the appropriate section of the Centre of Forensic Sciences, Toronto.[6]

To maintain the chain of continuity, every subsequent person who handles or receives a piece of evidence must also document the time and date the item came into their possession, the person from whom the item was received, any action taken by them in relation to the item, and the date, time, and person to whom it was given subsequently. It is not sufficient merely for each person to individually record their respective involvement in relation to a particular piece of evidence. The investigator in charge of the case, or another member designated for this specific purpose, must maintain a permanent master record of continuity regarding all pieces of evidence relevant to the case.

The need to maintain continuity of evidence does not necessarily end at the closure of the investigation, regardless of whether the case is solved or unsolved. A solved case usually results in some form of court proceedings, which may, in turn, result in one or more appeals before all judicial recourse is exhausted. If continuity of evidence is properly maintained on a "cold case," the evidence can still be used to prove a case in the event that new information surfaces, even years later.

Unfortunately, there are still no standardized policies covering how long evidence must be retained in police custody. Individual police services are left to maintain their own evidence and records retention policies and schedules. In many police services, under the guise of "housekeeping," an ill-advised practice is to dispose of evidence and related police reports at the first available opportunity.

During an actual investigation, new information came forward in relation to an eight-year-old unsolved sexual assault involving an 18-year-old female victim. Upon inheriting the case, I found that the continuity of the biological evidence and victim's clothing had been lost several years before. Not only had the continuity of the evidence been lost, but the exhibits themselves had simply "vanished into thin air" with absolutely no record having been made of their last known whereabouts or disposal.

The defendant in that case eventually pleaded guilty to Aggravated Sexual Assault and received a 13-year prison sentence, based upon the reliable identification of the accused by the victim and considerable evidence that was otherwise purely circumstantial. For the victim, justice was eventually served, but this case would have been infinitely easier to prove had the biological evidence provided a positive DNA match to the

---

[6]Horton (2000).

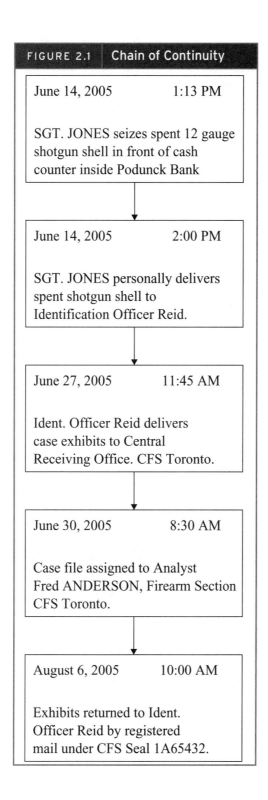

FIGURE 2.1 | Chain of Continuity

June 14, 2005   1:13 PM

SGT. JONES seizes spent 12 gauge shotgun shell in front of cash counter inside Podunck Bank

June 14, 2005   2:00 PM

SGT. JONES personally delivers spent shotgun shell to Identification Officer Reid.

June 27, 2005   11:45 AM

Ident. Officer Reid delivers case exhibits to Central Receiving Office. CFS Toronto.

June 30, 2005   8:30 AM

Case file assigned to Analyst Fred ANDERSON, Firearm Section CFS Toronto.

August 6, 2005   10:00 AM

Exhibits returned to Ident. Officer Reid by registered mail under CFS Seal 1A65432.

accused. The case could easily have been lost due to the unidentified officer who, for unknown reasons, disposed of the evidence.

Over the past decade, in cases where the continuity of evidence was properly maintained, several wrongfully convicted persons have been exonerated and released from prison after deoxyribonucleic acid (**DNA**) testing of exhibits proved that they could not possibly have committed the offence for which they were imprisoned. Such was the case in the 1984 murder of nine-year-old Christine Jessop, of Queensville, Ontario, resulting in the overturned conviction of Guy Paul Morin.[7]

The need to maintain continuity of evidence in solved cases was never more apparent than in the controversial 1959 conviction of 14-year-old Steven Murray Truscott for the murder of his 12-year-old classmate, Lynne Harper. Although paroled from Collins Bay Penitentiary since 1969, Truscott has, for over 40 years, steadfastly maintained his innocence.[8]

Had the original evidence collected from the crime scene been properly preserved, current DNA technology, which did not even exist in 1959, might have been successful in resolving the ongoing mystery of Truscott's guilt or innocence. With the potential benefits resulting from the imminent advent of future technology, the financial burden of warehousing evidence of cold-case crimes seems trivial compared with ensuring that justice is available for victims and convicted persons alike.

2.9   LOCARD'S EXCHANGE PRINCIPLE

"When any two objects come into contact, there is always a transference of material from each object onto the other."

Dr. Edmond Locard, French criminologist (circa 1928).

Dr. Edmond Locard is universally credited with having developed this principle, during the early 20th century, that explains how physical evidence (real evidence) is transferred from one source to another. Locard's Exchange Principle laid the very foundation for modern crime-scene examination and forensic scientific examination.

Stop for a moment and consider that the very instant you entered the room where you are sitting now and reading this passage, some transference of trace physical evidence occurred. As you entered, every surface of the room that you came into contact with (including the floor, walls, and furniture) left some trace of themselves upon your shoes, clothing, hands or skin. At that same instant, and for as long as you remain in this room, you continue to deposit some trace evidence of yourself upon the room (e.g., foreign material from your shoes, footwear impressions, your fingerprints, hair, fibres from your clothing, bodily fluids, etc.).

The transference of material that occurred might have been significant, depending on the duration of your presence in the room and your relative level of activity while inside the room; or it may be so small as to be invisible to the naked eye. The detection of this double transference of evidence might be so minute as to require the use of examinations such as utilizing a luma-lite, laser, microscopic examination, microspectrophotometry (MSP) or thin-layer chromatography (TLC) to confirm its presence.

Regardless of how small the transference of trace evidence was, or how rapidly it might disappear once you leave the room, what is important is that you accept that

---

[7]Kaufman (1998).

[8]Sher (2002).

this double transference of trace evidence did occur. In order to be a successful investigator, you must accept that it is virtually impossible for any two surfaces to come into contact without leaving some trace on each other. As an investigator, once you totally and unconditionally accept the validity of Locard's Exchange Principle, you will be confident of the presence of trace evidence and you will be motivated to search for it.

2.9.1   Trace Evidence

Trace evidence is a very broad term that is applied to small quantities of various types of physical evidence transferred from the source onto another surface. Trace evidence is used to infer associations between the location where the evidence is found and the source where the evidence originated. (Some examples are rug fibres found on the clothing of a victim that are related back to an accused's vehicle or residence, or microscopic blood spatter transferred from a victim onto a suspect's clothing). Trace evidence is, generally, circumstantial evidence at a trial.

Trace evidence is very fragile in nature. A single hair or fibre may only be laying on the surface where it is found and might easily be dislodged by wind, human carelessness, or destroyed by environmental causes with the passage of time. Trace evidence is very easily overlooked – but unless it has already been dislodged or destroyed through natural causes, it will still be there.

2.9.2   Double Transference of Trace Evidence

A double transference of trace evidence is what occurs when the two surfaces come into direct contact with each other, as explained by Locard's Exchange Principle. Trace evidence from surface number one is transferred onto surface number two. In this type of evidence exchange, we could expect, for example, in the case of a single motor vehicle collision involving a car and a lamp post, there would be traces of paint transferred from the car to the lamp post and conversely, traces of paint from the lamp post on the car.

The greater the degree of contact and the greater the force involved, the greater the likelihood of a double transfer. A double transference, as in the above example, is proof of direct contact between the two involved surfaces.

2.9.3   Single Transference of Trace Evidence

Two objects don't necessarily have to come into to direct contact with each other for transference of trace evidence to occur. Often, an object in close proximity to another will pick up airborne trace evidence of the other object through the effects of air movement, gravity or the laws of physics.

During a crime of personal violence involving the use of a blunt instrument, blows from the weapon will often cause a loss of blood from the victim. Repeated blows will result in the surface of the weapon contacting the victim, projecting blood from the victim by way of impact or centrifugal force onto another surface, (such as the walls, or ceiling of the room, or perhaps onto the assailant him or herself). The greater the velocity of the weapon, the farther the trace evidence of the victim's blood will be projected.

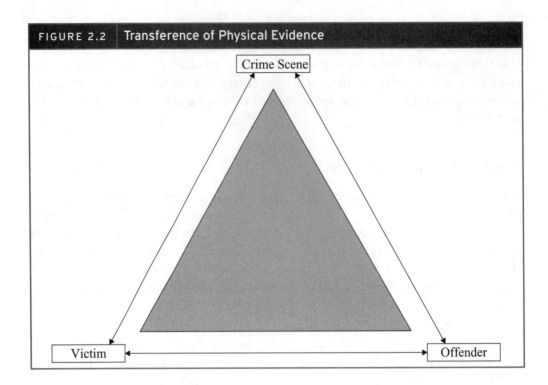

FIGURE 2.2 | Transference of Physical Evidence

The surface upon which the blood is projected, was never in direct contact with the victim – but the transference of evidence still occurred.

The diagram above illustrates how trace evidence may typically be transferred during the commission of a crime.

There may be trace evidence transferred by a victim (such as hair or fibres, fingerprints or footwear impressions) to the scene itself, and the scene may deposit evidence upon a victim (such as soil, botanical matter, paint, etc.). The victim may transfer trace evidence onto the offender (such as hair, fibres, blood, etc.) and may in turn have trace evidence from the offender transferred onto them (hair, fibres, bite marks, bodily fluids, etc.). Likewise, an offender may transfer trace evidence to a crime scene (footwear impressions, fingerprints, tool marks, bodily fluids, etc.) and trace evidence from the scene will be transferred to the offender (dust, paint, soil, botanical material, fragments of glass, etc.).

As you can see, there are any number of potential ways in which trace evidence can be transferred during the commission of a crime. The successful detection of trace evidence is limited only by the investigator's ability to locate and preserve it.

2.10 CIRCUMSTANTIAL EVIDENCE

*"**Circumstance** n. a fact, occurrence, or condition, esp. (in pl.) the time, place, manner, cause, occasion, etc., or surroundings of an act or event."*

– The Concise Oxford Dictionary 9th Edition.

For the purposes of this text, I suggest the following definition of circumstantial evidence:

A detail or circumstance [or a series of them] that is consistent with the guilt of the accused and inconsistent with any other rational conclusion. Circumstantial evidence does not directly prove a fact, but may be used to infer one or more facts in a criminal proceeding.

Circumstantial evidence differs substantially from the direct evidence of an eyewitness who has personal knowledge of an event. For example, victims through portions of their testimony may prove the facts in issue of a case, such as by proving that a crime did occur (*actus reus*) and may even help to identify the person responsible for the commission of the crime. Circumstantial evidence also differs greatly from real (physical) evidence used to prove facts of the case (such as ballistic evidence from a bullet recovered from a victim's body, or at a crime scene, that is used to prove that a particular firearm was the firearm used in a crime, to the exclusion of all other firearms).

Circumstantial evidence can be a single fact or a series of facts (or circumstances) that can be indirectly used to infer another fact, without directly proving it. For example, a man is accused of an armed robbery of a bank. Circumstantial evidence might show that an accused, who has no visible income or means of support, made several large cash purchases shortly after the time of the alleged robbery. These facts would be circumstantial evidence that could be used to infer that he had robbed the bank.

There is a public perception, largely fuelled by the media (shared by some lawyers and, unfortunately, by a number of police officers) that circumstantial evidence is somehow weaker than other types of evidence. Post-trial media interviews of disgruntled defence lawyers and convicted persons often leave viewers with the impression that because a conviction was based largely upon circumstantial evidence that it is somehow less reliable than a case based upon eyewitness testimony.

The resulting perception that circumstantial evidence is less trustworthy than other forms of evidence really couldn't be further from the truth. Consider, for a moment, that a court of law makes no distinction whatsoever between the weight (i.e., importance or credibility) attached to either direct evidence or circumstantial evidence. Consider also, that certain eyewitness testimony might be totally unreliable, making circumstantial evidence considerably superior in a majority of cases.

If you consider that finding an accused's fingerprints at the scene of a crime does not positively prove their guilt and only establishes circumstantial evidence of their presence at the scene, you may come to appreciate that circumstantial evidence doesn't deserve the bad reputation that it has received in the media. Given the choice, I'll take a circumstantial case – hands down – every time.

BOX 2.1	Investigative Relevance

Scenario: Following a fiercely contested divorce settlement, an estranged wife is found shot to death in her apartment. There are no eyewitnesses to her murder. The ex-husband's fingerprints are located within the deceased's apartment, which he never shared with his ex-wife. Ballistic evidence indicates the make, type, and calibre of firearm involved but the murder weapon is not recovered. Circumstantial evidence now becomes absolutely vital to the investigation. Evidence is discovered that the victim's ex-husband had previously made threats of death to the victim both during and after the couple's divorce proceedings.

The investigation reveals that the ex-husband previously owned a firearm similar to the weapon used to murder his ex-wife

---

BOX 2.1	(Continued)

but had reported the firearm stolen about six months prior to the murder. On the evening of the murder, a vehicle owned by the ex-husband received a ticket for a parking infraction only one mile away from the scene of the murder.

The ex-husband matches the general physical description of a man seen running away from the apartment building around the time of the murder and he has no alibi for his whereabouts at the time of the murder. Now let's analyze the individual facts of the case:

INDIVIDUAL FACTS

INDIVIDUAL FACTS	PROOF OF GUILT
Acrimonious divorce	Not proof of ex-husband's guilt for murder
Ex-husband's fingerprints found at apartment	Only circumstantial evidence of ex-husband's presence at the scene at some previous time – not proof of guilt for murder
Prior death threats by ex-husband	Not proof of ex-husband's guilt for murder
Ex-husband's known ownership of a firearm similar to that used in the murder	Not proof of ex-husband's guilt for murder
Reported theft of firearm six months prior to ex-wife's murder	Not proof of ex-husband's guilt for murder
Ex-husband matches physical description of unknown male seen running from the scene around the time of the murder	Not proof of ex-husband's guilt for murder
Ex-husband's vehicle receives parking ticket	Not proof of ex-husband's guilt for murder
Ex-husband has no alibi for his whereabouts at the time of the murder	Not proof of ex-husband's guilt for murder

EVALUATION OF THE CIRCUMSTANTIAL EVIDENCE IN TOTALITY

- Bitter divorce proceedings
- Prior death threats
- Previous ownership of firearm
- Recent report of theft of the firearm
- Physical description match to person fleeing murder scene
- Parking ticket one mile from scene on the evening of the murder
- No alibi for whereabouts

None of these facts, individually, prove anything. However, when viewed together, they form a chain of circumstances that, if true, are consistent with the guilt of the ex-husband for the murder of his ex-wife (and inconsistent with his innocence). The court might use this evidence to infer the husband's guilt for his ex-wife's murder.

2.10.1 Consciousness of Guilt

"The wicked flee when no one pursues, but the righteous are as bold as a lion."

– Proverbs 28:1.

You may wonder why several quotations in this textbook have been taken from the Bible. No one familiar with me would describe me as being either particularly religious, or known for quoting biblical passages. What is significant about the relevant quotations from the Bible is that their subject matter, relating to human behaviour, is neither new nor innovative by any stretch of the imagination. These concepts have been common knowledge for many centuries and are no less relevant today than in the simpler times in which they originated.

When an investigator is attempting to identify the person responsible for a crime, it is sometimes helpful to examine circumstantial evidence relating to the post-offence conduct of a suspect. Where incriminating post-offence behaviour exists, the investigator should not hesitate to investigate it thoroughly and to include the findings in the court brief given to the Crown Attorney.

After reading the opening quotation for this topic, you might ask, "Why would a person flee when nobody is pursuing them?" The simple answer, known since biblical times, is **consciousness of guilt**. Suspects know that they are guilty before anyone else does and flight from a crime might well be indicative of guilt and an attempt to escape responsibility for something only they know they have committed. The two most common circumstances of post-offence behaviour that might be useful in proving consciousness of guilt are fleeing the scene of a crime[9] and the destruction, concealment or fabrication of evidence.[10]

If an accused flees the scene immediately after committing a crime, and the trier of fact is satisfied, beyond a reasonable doubt, that the accused's flight was motivated by their consciousness of guilt rather than by any other reason (e.g., fleeing the scene of a murder due to fear of being apprehended as a parole violator is not conclusive proof that the flight resulted from consciousness of guilt for the murder), the evidence may have probative value that may be used to infer the guilt of the accused.[11]

In the 1994 Supreme Court *Arcangioli* decision[12] the court stated, "...[E]vidence of the accused's flight was a factor to be considered in reaching their verdict but that this evidence was not conclusive *as innocent people sometimes flee the scene of a crime*" (emphasis added). In *Arcangioli*, the accused had admitted to being involved in an assault earlier that same evening. The Supreme Court held that *Arcangioli's* flight from the scene of the later stabbing was "equally consistent" with fleeing from the assault and, for that reason, was not definite proof of his involvement in the stabbing.

2.11   HEARSAY EVIDENCE

Hearsay evidence is the oral testimony of a witness that is not as the result of the direct knowledge of the witness and is third person in nature (i.e., the witness heard something spoken by another person and then repeats it in court). Hearsay evidence is generally held to be inadmissible, as the truthfulness (reliability) of the evidence cannot be assessed by the court nor does it present the accused with the opportunity to confront or cross-examine his or her accuser. For example, a witness would not be allowed to testify that a friend of his told him that the accused stole a certain car if the witness testifying didn't have any direct, personal knowledge of the facts of the alleged theft.

---

[9]*R. v. White* (1998) 2 S.C.R. 72.

[10]*R. v. Jacquard* (1997) 1 S.C.R. 314.

[11]*R. v. Menard* (1998) 2 S.C.R. 109.

[12]*R. v. Arcangioli* (1994) 1 S.C.R. 129.

2.11.1   Hearsay Rule

"The long-standing evidentiary rule is that hearsay [evidence, under most circumstances] cannot be used in court. Rather than accepting testimony based upon hearsay, the trial process asks that the person who was the original source of the hearsay information be brought into court to be questioned and cross-examined. Exceptions to the hearsay rule may occur, [for example spontaneous utterances, dying declarations, admissions or confessions, business records, or when there are sufficient indicators of the statement's reliability and the evidence must be admitted due to circumstances of necessity, such as] when the person with direct knowledge is dead or is otherwise unable to testify."

– Pearson Education, Online Glossary of Terms.

In 1978, the Supreme Court of Canada characterized the "Hearsay Rule" as follows:

"It is settled law that evidence of a statement made to a witness by a person who is not himself called as a witness is hearsay and inadmissible when the object of the evidence is to establish the truth of what is contained in the statement; it is not hearsay and is admissible when it is proposed to establish by the evidence, not the truth of the statement, but the fact that it was made."[13]

The hearsay rule means that if the person who made the original statement is not called to court as a witness and the statement is repeated by another witness to establish the truth of the statement (e.g., "John shot Frank") the statement will be declared hearsay and will be inadmissible. If the statement is introduced merely to prove that the statement was made and not as proof of the fact that John actually did shoot Frank, the statement will not be hearsay and will be admitted.

2.11.2   Exceptions to the Hearsay Rule

It isn't long, as with most rules (good or otherwise), before situations occur that cause exceptions to the rule to arise. This is certainly the case with the hearsay rule. There are several exceptions to the hearsay rule that allow hearsay evidence to be admitted. Some of the traditional exceptions to the hearsay rule include:

- "Dying declarations": If a victim was intentionally injured and had identified his or her assailant to any witness, prior to succumbing to his or her wounds, the witness who was told the identity of the assailant by the victim would be able to testify as to the victim's statement without having any personal knowledge of the attack. Obviously, the unfortunate victim must expire for there to even be a dying declaration, otherwise the surviving witness would be available to testify in court him or herself.

- Admissions or confessions made by an accused person to any witness, especially to a **person in authority**, admitting full or partial guilt in a crime may be admissible as evidence if under the confessions rule the statement can be proven,

---

[13]*R. v. O'Brien* (1978) 1 S.C.R. 591.

beyond a reasonable doubt, to have been made voluntarily and be free from threats or inducements.

- **Spontaneous utterances**: Unanticipated, unsolicited, incriminating verbal statements made by a suspect or person in custody to a witness (especially a police officer) admitting or confessing some responsibility for the crime under investigation, prior to the administering of the standard caution. The caution should be administered to the suspect or prisoner as soon as possible after such a statement is made. A spontaneous utterance is one exception to the hearsay rule as witnesses are permitted by the courts to testify as to such statements they heard being made by an accused. The situation of a spontaneous utterance made by a prisoner to a police officer is specifically addressed in Rule # 5 of the Judge's Rules in Chapter 5.

- "*Res Gestae* statements": A statement made by an accused person that is so closely related to the offence as to form part of the offence, made in the hearing of any witness. For example, an assailant armed with a baseball bat, while approaching an unarmed victim, utters the threat, "I'm going to break every bone in your body." A witness hearing that statement could testify as to the threat, from which the guilt of the accused and the intent (*mens rea*) of the accused to commit the offence could be inferred by the court.

- "Undenied accusations made in the presence and hearing of the accused." A witness at the scene of a homicide hears another person say to the accused person, who is found standing over the lifeless body of a victim, "You killed him!" The witness would be allowed to testify regarding the statement made (by another person) to the accused if the accused did not respond to the accusation. It is presumed that an innocent person, when faced with such an accusation, would ardently deny their involvement in the crime.

- "Business records" that are made in the normal course of business may be admitted as an exception to the hearsay rule, in that the records are admitted into evidence without the necessity of the person(s) who made the record(s) having to testify. This situation usually occurs in relation to the records of financial institutions, where it is common to secure cancelled cheques, account statements, credit documents, etc. to prove a case. The law in relation to the introduction of business records into evidence may be found in ss. 30(1)–(12) of the *Canada Evidence Act*.[14]

- Section 715 of the *Criminal Code* provides that the "prior testimony" of a witness that was given in evidence that was taken (audio or videotaped) during the investigation of the charge against the accused or at a previous trial or preliminary inquiry into the charge may be admitted into evidence if the witness:[15]

  – refuses to be sworn (or affirmed), or

  – refuses to testify, or

  if it can be proven on oath that the witness is either:

  – dead, or

  – has since become insane, or

---

[14]*Canada Evidence Act*, R.S., c. E-10, ss. 30(1), 30(2).

[15]*Criminal Code*, R.S. 1985, c. C-46, s. 715.

– is so ill that he is unable to travel or testify, or

– is absent from Canada,

unless the accused proves that he did not have the full opportunity to cross-examine the witness at the time the testimony was given. Testimony given at a previous trial or during the investigation of a charge may also be entered into evidence in the prosecution of the accused for another offence.

- "Prior Inconsistent Statements": If at trial a witness recants (denies or challenges) an earlier statement they made to the police, the original statement may be entered into evidence. In the K.G.B. decision,[16] the Supreme Court specified certain conditions in which it will regard the prior inconsistent videotaped statement of a witness as reliable. These conditions include warning the witness about possible prosecution for perjury, administering an oath or solemn affirmation to the witness, videotaping the interview in its entirety, a *voir dire* to assess the reliability of the statement and a full opportunity for cross-examination. The police service investigating an offence, at least in serious cases, would be well advised to adopt the Supreme Court's criteria (as described in Chapter 4) when interviewing potentially hostile witnesses who might possibly recant their testimony at a later date.

- Any investigation in which the complainant or other witness might not be available to testify at trial. These situations might include a witness who is moving to a location outside the jurisdiction of the court (e.g., out-of-country) or a victim or witness who is suffering from an injury or terminal illness and may succumb to his or her illness or injury prior to trial. The interview may be admissible in evidence as an exception to the hearsay rule if the court finds that it is "necessary" to do so due to the unavailability of the witness.[17]

- Any investigation in which the child victim or witness is too young (under the age of 14 years) to provide sworn evidence at trial.[18]

Recently, Canadian courts (including the Supreme Court of Canada) have taken a much less stringent approach to admitting hearsay evidence where it is considered both "reliable" and "necessary" to do so.

2.12 CORROBORATION

When an independent piece of evidence or an independent fact confirms and supports another piece of evidence or fact, it is corroborating evidence. Corroborative evidence strengthens the belief in the related evidence and has the effect of enhancing its credibility due to its independent (i.e., different) and material (i.e., relevant) nature.

If similar or supporting material information comes to light from independent sources, it is held to be more likely to be true. The Supreme Court of Canada has ruled, "Before evidence can be treated as corroborative, it must be found to be admissible."[19]

---

[16]*R. v. KGB* (1993) 79 C.C.C. (3d) 257 S.C.C.

[17]*R. v. Smith* (1992) 2 S.C.R. 915.

[18]*R. v. Khan* (1990) 2 S.C.R. 531.

[19]*R. v. B(CR)* (1990) 1 S.C.R. 717.

There are certain offences in the *Criminal Code* that require corroboration (i.e., do not permit an accused to be convicted on the evidence of a single witness). These uncommon offences include:

- Treason s. 47(3) CC;

- Perjury s. 133 CC; and

- Procuring a feigned (false) marriage s. 292(2) CC.

Corroboration, in the form of recent-complaint evidence, was formerly an essential element of certain sexual offences and judges were previously required to warn juries (or themselves) of the danger of convicting an accused on the single evidence of a witness, especially that of a child witness. Fortunately, those sections of the *Criminal Code* dealing with recent-complaint evidence and mandatory warnings have been repealed.[20]

2.13 BEST EVIDENCE RULE

The **best evidence rule** requires that the best possible evidence available be presented to the court. If an original of a document is available, unless otherwise provided by law, a copy is not acceptable as evidence. The best evidence principle also applies to situations such as wounds to living or dead victims where healing or burial renders photographs of injuries the best evidence. Photographs of items which, due to their size, would be impracticable to produce in court might also be considered the best evidence possible.

Where original records could be admitted as evidence but the originals are required for business purposes (such as municipal by-laws, or the records of a municipality or other corporation, records of financial institutions, etc.) a certified copy[21] is admissible. Before a copy of a government book or document is admitted into evidence, the party who produces the copy must give the party against whom the copy will be produced "reasonable notice" of his or her intention to introduce a copy of the record. The notice required to be given to the party against whom the record will be produced must not be less than seven days.[22]

In these days of computerized technology, it is becoming more and more common to resort to electronic documents as evidence. There is an onus (obligation) on the part of any person wishing to enter an electronic document to first satisfy the court of the authenticity of the document.[23] These specific instances will be further covered in Chapter 13: Courtroom Procedures.

2.14 PLAIN VIEW SEIZURE RULE

In certain situations, incriminating evidence will be encountered inadvertently by the police in circumstances that make it absolutely impracticable to obtain a search warrant.

---

[20]*Criminal Code of Canada*, R.S. 1985, c. C-46, s. 275, s. 659.

[21]*Canada Evidence Act*, R.S., c. E-10, s. 24(b), s. 29, s. 30.

[22]*Canada Evidence Act*, R.S., c. E-10, s. 28(2).

[23]*Canada Evidence Act*, R.S., c.E-10, s. 31.1.

A "common law" doctrine permits the warrantless seizure of inadvertently found evidence in circumstances that make it entirely impracticable to obtain a search warrant.

Three conditions must exist for a "plain view" seizure to be considered valid:

1. The police officer must be lawfully positioned.

   The police must have a legal right to be where the viewing of the evidence occurs. An example of this may occur when a police officer is serving a summons at a private residence. When the occupant opens the door, the officer observes a large quantity of marijuana being processed on the kitchen table in plain view of the front door. The officer had a legal right to be at the residence.

2. The finding of the evidence must be inadvertent. Using the above scenario, if the officer was not expecting to find the marijuana, and was not actively searching for it, the find would be held to be inadvertent.

3. The evidence must implicate the accused in some criminal activity. In this case, the marijuana would most certainly implicate those persons having actual possession of the narcotic for the purpose of trafficking and plain view seizure would be valid.[24]

Sec. 489(2) of the *Criminal Code* embodies the **Plain View Seizure Rule** in situations where a peace officer is lawfully positioned whether executing a search or not. Peace officers may seize, without warrant:

1. anything obtained by the commission of a criminal offence;

2. anything used in the commission of a criminal offence; or

3. anything that will afford evidence of a criminal offence.

Any such evidence seized is required to be treated in the same manner as if it had been seized under the authority of a search warrant.[25]

2.15   DOCTRINE OF RECENT POSSESSION

Section 359(1) of the *Criminal Code* provides an important tool to prove *mens rea*, or guilty knowledge on the basis of similar fact evidence where an accused is charged with a designated offence under section 342 (theft, forgery of credit card) or section 354 (possession of property obtained by crime) or section 356(1)(b) (possession of property stolen from the mail). Evidence that property found in the accused's possession that was stolen within the previous twelve months may be introduced as proof that the accused knew the property relating to the charge before the court was, in fact, stolen.

Section 360(1) of the *Criminal Code* provides that evidence of *mens rea* may also be introduced for the designated offences under section 354 (possession of property obtained by crime) or section 356(1)(b) (possession of property stolen from the mail) by way of previous convictions. Similar fact evidence that the accused was convicted, within the previous five years, of an offence involving theft or possession of property

---

[24]*Controlled Drugs and Substances Act* 1996, c. 19 s. 5(2).

[25]*Criminal Code* R.S. 1985, c. C-46, s. 489.

obtained by crime may be introduced as proof that the accused knew that the property relating to the charge before the court was unlawfully obtained.[26]

2.16 ADMISSIBILITY OF EVIDENCE

As was previously stated, not all evidence will be deemed to be admissible during a criminal proceeding. If the evidence is material (relevant) to the proceeding, it will be admitted, providing there is no reason in law to exclude the evidence. Not all rules of evidence are codified in legislation, although some may be found in the *Criminal Code, Canada Evidence Act*, and the *Canadian Charter of Rights and Freedoms*. Many legal authorities relating to the **exclusion of evidence** are found in "case law."

While it is beyond the scope of this textbook to provide a definitive study on all rules of evidence, this section will attempt to cover many of those circumstances in which evidence may be deemed inadmissible.

2.16.1 Freedom against "Unreasonable" Search and Seizure

Many of the basic rights and freedoms afforded to persons in Canada under the *Canadian Charter of Rights and Freedoms* deal specifically with the rights of individuals with respect to fundamental justice and the rules of evidence. As such, investigators need to be familiar with the rights granted to individuals under the Charter and consider their conduct in selecting the correct method for gathering evidence during an investigation.

In addition to individual rights, such as the right to be informed of the reason for an arrest, the right to legal counsel, the right to remain silent, and the freedom against self-incrimination, one of the most common *Charter* rights (as guaranteed by Section 8) is the " . . . right to be secure against unreasonable search and seizure."[27]

The 1984 Supreme Court decision of *Hunter v. Southam Inc.* upheld the widespread and long-established criminal and common law search requirement of prior judicial authorization, in the form of a valid search warrant, in all cases where it is practicable and feasible to do so. Warrantless searches have generally been held by the Supreme Court of Canada to be *prima facie* unreasonable, meaning that evidence obtained during a warrantless search is initially considered to be inadmissible unless the Crown can prove that the seizure was necessary and that to obtain a search warrant would have been impracticable under the circumstances of the case.[28]

The requirement of judicial pre-authorization recognizes that society's interests, including that of effective law enforcement, on occasion outweigh the rights of the individual but places the responsibility on the Crown to demonstrate that the need to enforce the law and to gather evidence did outweigh the individual's rights. Prior judicial authorization, in the form of a search warrant, will only be granted when credibly based probability (reasonable grounds) replaces suspicion.

---

[26]*Criminal Code*, R.S. 1985, c. C-46, ss. 359(1), 360(1).

[27]*Canadian Charter of Rights and Freedoms*, Being Part 1 of the *Constitution Act, 1982*, Enacted by the *Canada Act 1982* (U.K.) c. 11; proclaimed in force April 17, 1982, s.8.

[28]*Hunter v. Southam Inc.* (1984), 2 S.C.R. 45, 14 C.C.C. (3d) 97, 11 D.L.R. (4th) 641.

Investigators should always adhere to the following recommendations during the course of their duties:

1. Always utilize the most cautious (most reasonable and least-intrusive) investigative strategy possible under the circumstances.

2. To the extent possible, when engaging in any investigative action not involving prior judicial authorization, always follow the precise intent of any available legal authority for your actions.

3. Always ensure that a search warrant is obtained, if required.

Section 8 *Charter* violations will not always result in the exclusion of evidence, but they will be held to be *prima facie* unreasonable. If evidence is put before the court resulting from a warrantless search (not otherwise authorized by statute or by search warrant), the court will automatically hold the search to be "unreasonable" unless evidence to the contrary establishes the "reasonableness" for having done so. Fortunately, the *prima facie* unreasonableness of warrantless searches does not apply to searches of suspects incident to (resulting from) an arrest.[29]

The Crown has the opportunity to lead further evidence that the investigator(s) acted in good faith and to prove the circumstances that made the search both necessary and "reasonable." **Exigent circumstances** (emergency circumstances) may make it impracticable to obtain a search warrant if waiting for a search warrant would have resulted in the loss, removal or destruction of evidence. Always thoroughly document all circumstances that require the seizure of evidence that are not authorized by a search warrant.

According to the (1987) Supreme Court decision of *R. v. Collins*, for a search to be considered reasonable:

- The search must be authorized by law (including warrantless search authorities).

- The law itself must be reasonable.

- The manner in which the search was conducted must be reasonable.[30]

Even in situations when a statute does provide an authority to conduct warrantless searches, police officers should only resort "to its availability [in] situations in which exigent circumstances make it impracticable to obtain a warrant."[31] Unless the circumstances of a given situation require immediate action to preserve life or to prevent the imminent loss, removal or destruction of evidence, or where the opportunity exists to obtain a search warrant – always get a warrant!

2.16.2 Opinion Evidence

Generally, witnesses who are called to testify in court are not allowed to express personal opinions. As has been previously stated, witnesses are called to court to testify regarding matters they have perceived through one of their five senses. It is the role of the trier of fact – not witnesses – to draw inferences from the evidence and form opinions. For

---

[29]*R. v. Golden* (2001) 3 S.C.R. 629.

[30]*R. v. Collins* (1987) 1 S.C.R. 265, 33 C.C.C. (3d) 1, 56 C.R. (3d) 193.

[31]*R. v. Grant* (1993) 3 S.C.R. 223.

example, a witness's opinion that an accused intended to commit the offence he or she is charged with is both irrelevant and without basis (i.e., not based on an observed fact). For these reasons, the witness's opinion would be considered inadmissible. The intent (*mens rea*) of the accused must be inferred from the evidence at trial.

Non-expert witnesses may be permitted to testify about matters requiring issues widely considered to be universal knowledge, such as the speed of a moving vehicle or the effects of intoxication by alcohol on an individual.

> **Question: "Witness, in your opinion, was the accused [or another witness] intoxicated by alcohol?"**
>
> *Answer: "The way he was stumbling, slurring his speech, smelling of liquor and vomiting, I would say that he was intoxicated. Yes." or*
>
> **Question: "Witness, in your opinion, was the red car travelling in excess of the posted speed limit?"**
>
> *Answer: "That location is a 100 km/h zone and I was driving at the speed limit. When the red car went past me, it had to be doing at least 140 km/h."*

Expert witnesses are permitted to express opinion evidence on matters that require special knowledge or training. An expert witness must be qualified as an expert each and every time they testify; regardless of the number of times they have been qualified in the past. Quite often the party, other than the party calling the witness, will stipulate the expert's qualifications on the basis of an examination of his or her credentials or prior knowledge of his or her status as an expert in a particular field.

The Crown and the defence are limited to calling five expert witnesses each before having to obtain the permission of the presiding judge to exceed that number.[32]

Expert witnesses may include professionals such as physicians, pathologists, forensic scientists, or engineers. Often police officers are qualified as experts on the basis of special training and expertise, such as breathalyzer technicians, fingerprint examiners, traffic accident reconstructionists and criminal behavioural profilers, to name a few.

2.16.3 Similar Fact Evidence

Evidence of previously proven acts committed by the accused might be admissible in court in certain strict situations in an effort to prove the identity of the accused (i.e., that the accused is the person who committed the offence for which he or she is charged). Similar fact evidence can be highly prejudicial to the accused, and for that reason, the courts have exercised extreme caution when attempting to strike the appropriate balance between the **probative** value and the potential **prejudice** to the accused (any negative impact on the fairness of the trial).

The test as to whether or not similar fact evidence will be admitted is that the evidence of previous acts must be so remarkably similar (virtually identical) to the offence(s) charged as to allow the trier of fact to infer the guilt of the accused for the charge(s) before the accused.

---

[32]*Canada Evidence Act*, R.S., c. E-10, s. 7.

2.16.4 Character Evidence

Character evidence is any evidence that would tend to establish the likelihood of the accused to behave in a certain manner (that he or she did or did not commit the offence for which he or she is charged). The general rule of evidence regarding character evidence is that the Crown may not introduce evidence of bad character unless it is relevant to an issue at trial (e.g., motive, to counter a defence of lack of intent, credibility of the accused, etc.) or if the defence puts the accused's good character into issue.[33]

According to the 1993 Supreme Court decision of *R. v. B. (F.F.)*, "Evidence which tends to show bad character or a criminal disposition on the part of the accused is admissible if (1) relevant to some other issue beyond disposition or character, and (2) the probative value outweighs the prejudicial effect."[34]

BOX 2.2	Investigative Relevance

An accused is on trial for a sexual assault in which it is alleged that he broke in through an unlocked second storey apartment patio door. During the trial, evidence is produced that the offender wore a full-faced rubber Halloween mask to conceal his identity and, while armed with a knife, forced the victim to engage in nonconsensual sexual intercourse after tying the victim's hands with strips of cloth torn from her own pillow case. During the crime, the victim was also forced to recite certain scripted dialogue at the urging of the offender. No DNA evidence was recovered at the scene.

Evidence is introduced regarding a prior offence of sexual assault the accused was tried and convicted for eight years before. The previous attack involved the accused climbing up to the second storey balcony of an apartment building and forcing the lock on the patio door to gain entrance. In the previous assault, the accused, who had disguised his face with a Halloween mask, was armed with a butcher knife and bound the victim's hands with her nightgown which the accused cut off using the knife. The previous victim was forced to speak the same words at the direction of the accused and, according to the victim, the attacker had put on a condom before forcing sexual intercourse upon her.

In this situation, there are a number of comparable facts between the previous incident and the current trial that the court could find so similar as to logically infer the identity and guilt of the accused.

Additionally, section 666 *Criminal Code* permits that when an accused introduces evidence of good character at any time during a trial (e.g., through the testimony of another witness or by his or her own testimony) the Crown may then introduce evidence of the previous conviction of the accused for any offence, even an offence committed after the offence for which the accused is on trial. Under this section, the Crown is limited to producing ("leading") evidence only of previous convictions and not evidence of other acts of misconduct for which the accused was not convicted.[35]

---

[33]*Lewis v. The Queen* (1979) 2 S.C.R. 821.

[34]*R. v. B(FF)* (1993) 1 S.C.R. 697.

[35]*Criminal Code*, R.S., 1985 c. C-46, s. 666.

"An accused does not put his character in issue merely by denying his guilt and repudiating the allegations against him, nor by giving an explanation of matters which are essential to his defence. However, he may not, without putting his character in issue, assert expressly or implicitly that he would not have done the acts alleged against him because he is a person of good character."[36]

"Where an accused in **examination-in-chief** testified that he had never been convicted nor arrested he put his character in issue."[37]

2.17 EVIDENCE OBTAINED BY CONSENT

There are many instances in which a person of interest, a suspect, or even an accused may **consent** to allow the police to conduct a search or examination that would otherwise require a search warrant. In the 1992 Ontario Court of Appeals decision of *R. v. Wills*, Mr Justice J. A. Doherty defined the six necessary conditions that, on a balance of probabilities, must exist to constitute a valid consent search:[38]

1. The person giving the consent actually stated, or implied (not verbally stated, but in some other way insinuated) their consent to the search or examination.

2. The consent must be given by someone with the right to do so (e.g., a guest in someone's house couldn't legally consent for the police to search the owner's house in their absence).

3. The consent must have been given voluntarily (not coerced or obtained by threat, etc.).

4. The person giving the consent must be aware of the nature of the police conduct they are being asked to consent to. Example: "Mr Smith, we would like you to provide samples of your handwriting that will be compared to the forged document, to determine whether or not you are the person who wrote it."

5. The person giving the consent must be aware of their right to refuse to permit (or withdraw their consent for) the police to conduct the search or examination. Example: "Mr Smith, we would like to search your car for evidence of the bank robbery. As you are aware we would normally need a search warrant to do that but you have indicated that you want to co-operate with the investigation and let us examine your car without a warrant – is that correct? You are aware that you have the right to refuse to give us permission to search your car – is that correct?"[39]

6. The person giving the consent was aware of the potential consequences of giving their consent. Example: "Mr Smith, you have indicated your intention to provide a voluntary DNA sample in regards to the sexual assault investigation we are conducting. You are aware that if the sample you provide identifies you as the person responsible for this offence that you will be charged with (Sexual Assault) and the sample you provide will be used as evidence in court – is that correct?"

---

[36]*R. v. McNamara* (1981), 56 C.C.C. (2d) 193 (Ont. C.A.).

[37]*R. v. Morris* (1979) 1 S.C.R. 405, 43 C.C.C. (2d) 129, 91 D.L.R. (3d) 161.

[38]*R. v. Wills* (1992), 70 C.C.C. (3d) 529 (Ont. C.A.).

[39]*R. v. Lewis* (1998), 122 C.C.C. (3d) 481, 13 C.R. (5th) 34 (Ont. C.A.).

It is strongly recommended that, where possible, prior to conducting a "consent search," an investigator take the time to explain the elements of consent (as per the Wills decision – see p.53 fn.38 – on a departmental form if your agency has such a pre-printed form) and obtain the consenter's signature. Investing a small amount of preparation can go a long way to proving to the court that, where charges are laid against the individual, the accused's consent was an **informed consent**.

Where the person being requested to consent to a search or other police action is a young person, they must also be advised of the special protection afforded to them under the *Youth Criminal Justice Act*[40] (their rights to counsel and to have a parent or another adult present). In serious cases, it would be unwise to proceed on the sole consent of a young person without also attempting to obtain a parent or guardian's consent in writing, if practicable to do so.[41]

2.18 ABANDONED EVIDENCE

There are times when a seizure by the police is not considered a search. One of those times includes when a suspect or accused voluntary provides a sample or thing voluntarily to the police. Another example is when a person abandons physical evidence that is then recovered by the police. Evidence, such as a mucous- or blood-stained tissue, discarded by an individual (even one who is in custody) may be seized without warrant by the police for investigative purposes. The courts have held that when an individual discards property, they relinquish their privacy interest in that item and forfeit any **reasonable expectation of privacy**.[42]

The same principle of abandonment holds true for when investigators conduct a warrantless seizure of a person's trash left at the curb for pick-up. Courts have held that seizure of abandoned garbage does not breach an individual's privacy interest as the individual can no longer claim any reasonable expectation of privacy.[43]

2.19 EVIDENTIAL TEST OF PROBATIVE VALUE V. PREJUDICE

In determining whether or not to admit a certain piece of evidence at trial, the presiding judge must weigh the probative value. The probative value means the evidential value of the evidence and its ability to afford proof of a fact of a case. The probative value of the evidence must be weighed against any possible prejudice, which is the potential harm or injury that might be caused to the fairness of the trial to the extent that it causes a distortion of the events in the mind of the trier(s) of fact. Only if the probative value outweighs the prejudice to the accused will the evidence be admitted.

It could be said that every piece of incriminating evidence has probative value and causes some potential harm to the accused but probative evidence doesn't necessarily

---

[40] *Youth Criminal Justice Act*, S.C. 2002, c. 1, ss. 1-165 and Schedule, in force April 1, 2003.

[41] *R. v. Stillman* (1997) 1 S.C.R. 607.

[42] *R. v. Stillman* (1997) 1 S.C.R. 607.

[43] *R. v. Krist* (1995) 100 C.C.C. (3d) 58, 42 C.R. (4th) 159, 103 W.A.C. 133 (B.C.C.A.).

create prejudice for the accused. The presence of the accused's DNA at the scene of a violent crime has probative value that helps to establish the guilt of the accused and is entitled to be given the weight that it deserves.

It is only when the prejudice resulting from the admission of the evidence creates an unjustifiable effect on the fairness of the trial that causes an imbalance when judged against its probative value, that the evidence will be excluded. In his book *The Law of Evidence,* University of Ottawa law professor David M. Paciocco defines prejudice as the effect of evidence that "...has a tendency to be given more weight than it deserves."[44]

2.20 WITNESS COMPETENCY AND COMPELLABILITY

For either a Crown or defence witness to testify, he or she must be deemed to be both **competent** and **compellable**. "Competence" simply means the legal appropriateness or suitability of a witness to be heard on matters relating to the trial. A witness may be competent but not compellable. A spouse is always a competent witness for the defence and is generally an incompetent witness for the Crown (with certain exceptions as discussed later).[45]

The competency of a witness to testify may also be affected by their age (under 14 years) or mental capacity. Prior to such a witness testifying, the court must conduct an inquiry to determine whether or not the witness understands the nature of swearing an oath or solemn affirmation; and whether or not the person is able to communicate (not necessarily orally) his or her evidence.[46]

Whether or not a witness is compellable means the degree to which a Crown or defence witness can be legally forced to testify. For example, a spouse is not compellable to disclose any communication made to him or her by his or her spouse during their marriage except for specified sexual offences involving children, sexual assaults, abandonment or abduction of children, bigamy and polygamy offences (or attempts to commit those offences).[47]

A legally married spouse may not be compelled to disclose any communication made to him or her during the marriage unless the marriage was legally dissolved[48] by his or her spouse. This protection is not afforded to "common law" marriages.[49] A spouse is always competent and compellable for the Crown against his or her spouse on charges of:

- Causing death by criminal negligence;

- Causing bodily harm by criminal negligence;

- Murder;

---

[44]Quoted. in Euale, Martin, Rock & Sadek (1998).

[45]*Canada Evidence Act,* R.S., c.E-10, s. 4(1).

[46]*Canada Evidence Act,* R.S., c.E-10, ss. 16(1)(a)(b).

[47]*Canada Evidence Act,* R.S., c.E-10, ss. 4(2).

[48]*R. v. Marchand* (1980), 55 C.C.C. (2d) 77, 115 D.L.R. (3d) 403 (N.S.C.A.).

[49]*R. v. Jackson* (1981), 61 C.C.C. (2d) 540, 23 C.R. (3d) 4 (C.A.),

- Manslaughter;

- Infanticide;

- Attempted murder;

- Accessory to murder;

- Level I Assault;

- Level II Assault;

- Level III Assault; or

- Unlawfully causing bodily harm,

where the victim involved in the charge is under the age of 14 years.[50]

Any Crown or defence witness may be compelled to attend court under the legal authority of a **subpoena** (Form 16 CC) or a **warrant for a witness** (Form 17 CC). A subpoena is an order issued by the court that commands a witness to appear at a stated time and place to give evidence concerning the charge before the court. Under the terms and conditions of the subpoena, the witness may also be required to bring to court certain specified items or documents, relevant to the offence, which are in his or her possession.[51]

A witness could legally attend court voluntarily to give evidence; however, it is strongly recommended that a witness be served with a subpoena prior to each and every court appearance. In the event that a witness simply forgets to attend or takes ill and is hospitalized, an affidavit of proof of service of the subpoena allows for the issuance of a warrant for a witness and the granting of an adjournment of the proceedings to another date.

A warrant for a witness may be issued by a justice where it has been made likely that a Crown or defence witness will not attend court unless compelled to do so, is evading service of a subpoena, or was served with a subpoena and failed to attend court as required. Other warrants for witnesses exist in Form 18 CC and Form 20 CC, respectively, to apprehend witnesses who have absconded (fled the jurisdiction of the court) or are about to abscond, or to commit them to jail for a specified period for refusing to be sworn (or affirmed) or to give evidence.

2.21 PRIVILEGE

Privilege is another reason why certain evidence may be declared inadmissible in court. Privilege is immunity against forced disclosure that is granted to certain evidence made under circumstances of assured confidentiality, such as spousal communication, attorney-client privilege, etc.

2.21.1 Self-Incrimination

Privilege also extends to the protection against self-incrimination granted to a witness under the *Charter of Rights and Freedoms* while testifying. Unlike motion picture and

---

[50]*Canada Evidence Act*, R.S.C. 1985, c. C-5, s. 4(4).

[51]*Criminal Code*, R.S. 1985, c. C-46, ss. 698, 699, 705.

television courtroom scenes in which the witness refuses to testify at all, "on the grounds that my answer may tend to incriminate me" (under the Fifth Amendment to the United States Constitution), a witness in a Canadian court proceeding can be obliged to testify, but may object to answering individual questions if the answer would incriminate him or her in a criminal offence. Unlike in the United States, a Canadian court may instruct the witness to answer the question; however, nothing that the witness testifies about may be used as evidence against the witness in any future proceeding,[52] except on a charge of perjury. [53]

2.21.2 Spousal Communications

The privilege afforded to spousal communications afforded by s. 4 of the *Charter of Rights and Freedoms* has been previously touched upon. The law will not force a spouse to testify as to things said to him or her by his or her (legally married) spouse. The law places a higher value on the sanctity of marriage and the greater need to protect existing marriages.[54]

The privilege may be claimed by the spouse who originated the communication, as opposed to the spouse who received the communication. If any part of the spousal communication is disclosed to a third party, including a child of the family old enough to testify, the spousal communication privilege is lost. However, the communication to a third person would be protected by privilege if that third party was an attorney.

2.21.3 Solicitor-Client Privilege

The privilege afforded to communications between a client and his or her lawyer reflects the need to protect such communications for a client to be absolutely free to consult and instruct his or her lawyer in order to be able to make full answer and defence to the charge(s) against him or her.[55] Solicitor–client privilege extends beyond the actual communications between the client and the lawyer and also protects "work product" made by the lawyer as the result of privileged communications (such as notes, reports, memoranda, etc.).[56]

Solicitor–client privilege covers all communications between a prisoner and an attorney, including those in a police lock-up, correctional institution and any similar conversations that may be electronically intercepted, as in the case of a wire-tap. Solicitor–client privilege does not exist when the communication involving a lawyer is in furtherance of a criminal act or under the public safety exception where there is a clear and imminent risk of serious bodily harm or death to an identifiable person or group.[57]

---

[52]*R. v. Nöel* (2002) 3 S.C.R. 433.

[53]*Canadian Charter of Rights and Freedoms*, Being Part 1 of the *Constitution Act, 1982*, Enacted by the *Canada Act 1982* (U.K.) c. 11; proclaimed in force April 17, 1982, s. 13.

[54]*R. v. Hawkins* (1996) 3 S.C.R. 1043.

[55]*R. v. McClure* (2001) 1S.C.R. 445.

[56]*R. v. Brown* (2002) 2 S.C.R. 185.

[57]*Smith v. Jones* (1999) 1 S.C.R. 455.

2.21.4 Crown (Police-Informer) Privilege

This complex issue will be discussed in further detail in Chapter 9 dealing with Informant Management; however, with certain exceptions the Crown has the privilege of concealing the identity of any person who supplies confidential information to a police officer about the charge before the court. Courts have historically recognized the valuable information provided to the police by confidential informants in the administration of justice.[58]

2.21.5 Case-by-Case Privilege

Privilege may also be claimed by an accused in instances involving communications with certain professionals such as physicians, psychiatrists, psychologists, therapists, members of the clergy[59] and journalists. This privilege, as the name suggests, is not absolute. The admissibility of the incriminating evidence will be determined on a case-by-case basis.

SUMMARY

- The presumption of innocence is an irrebuttable presumption of law that states that every accused person is considered to be innocent of any offence he or she is charged with until he or she is proven guilty beyond a reasonable doubt in an open and impartial court.

- The trier of fact must be persuaded of the guilt of the accused, beyond a reasonable doubt, before convicting an accused person.

- Evidence does not prove the facts of a criminal case – the facts of the case are determined by the trier of fact after careful evaluation and an impartial interpretation of the evidence that is collected by the police service having jurisdiction.

- Evidence can be classified as either direct, hearsay, real or circumstantial.

- The chain of continuity tracks the movement of pieces of evidence to prove that a particular item was in a specific place at a specific time in a particular condition and tracks all persons who handled or controlled the item at any given point in time.

- Dr. Edmond Locard, a twentieth-century French criminologist, is credited with developing Locard's Exchange Principle to explain the transference of physical evidence at crime scenes. "When any two objects come into contact, there is always a transference of material from each object onto the other."

- Trace evidence is a very broad term that is applied to small quantities of various types of physical evidence transferred from the source onto another surface.

- Hearsay evidence is generally held to be inadmissible, as the truthfulness (i.e., reliability) of the evidence cannot be assessed by the court, nor does it present the accused with the opportunity to confront or cross-examine his or her accuser.

[58]*R. v. Leipert* (1997) 1 S.C.R. 281.

[59]*R. v. Gruenke* (1991) 3 S.C.R. 263.

- Exceptions to the hearsay rule may occur, such as: spontaneous utterances; dying declarations; admissions or confessions; business records; or when there are sufficient indicators of the statement's reliability and the evidence must be admitted due to circumstances of necessity, such as when the person with direct knowledge is dead or is otherwise unable to testify.

- Investigators need to be familiar with the rights granted to individuals under the *Charter of Rights and Freedoms,* and consider their conduct in selecting the correct method for gathering evidence during an investigation.

- Only when the probative value outweighs the potential prejudice to the accused will the evidence be admitted at trial.

- For either a Crown or defence witness to testify, they must be deemed to be both competent and compellable.

- Privilege is one reason why certain evidence may be declared inadmissible in court. Recognized circumstances of privilege include: self-incrimination; spousal incompetence; solicitor–client privilege; Crown (police–informer) privilege; and various case-by-case instances that may involve physicians, psychiatrists, clergy, therapists and journalists.

DISCUSSION QUESTIONS

1. A police officer responds to a single-vehicle rollover involving injuries. Upon arrival ambulance attendants are removing an unconscious male occupant from the wreck and bring your attention to a bag of money, a ski mask and a replica handgun inside the car. You are aware that a bank was robbed one hour ago in a city about 80 kilometres away. A check of Canadian Police Information Centre (CPIC) database reveals that the vehicle involved in the collision was reported stolen two days earlier. What legal authority do you have to seize the items without a search warrant? What three conditions must be met before such a seizure would be considered legal?

2. The body of a female victim is found in her second-storey apartment by her landlord after co-workers report that she failed to show up for work for two consecutive days. Efforts to contact her had been unsuccessful. The only door to the apartment was locked from the inside but the patio door was unlocked and slightly ajar. You find the victim lying on her bed with her nightclothes ripped and lying beside her. Her wrists and ankles are bound with rope that an unknown offender presumably brought with him to the scene. The victim's eyes and mouth are covered with duct tape. Evidence indicates that the victim was sexually assaulted and manually strangled. What types of trace evidence might you reasonably expect to encounter and conduct examinations for? What is the scientific principle that deals with the transference of physical evidence from one source to another?

3. While interviewing witnesses to an armed robbery, a bystander informs you that he didn't see it himself but, according to his friend who left the scene before the arrival

of police, the robbers fled in a black 4-door sedan with the letters ADRS in the licence plate number. Can the witness being interviewed subsequently testify about the involvement of the described vehicle in the armed robbery? Why (or why not)?

WEBLINKS

www.mpss.jus.gov.on.ca/english/pub_safety/centre_forensic/ forensic_links.html

Government of Ontario, Ministry of Community Safety and Correctional Services. Centre of Forensic Sciences. Services provided and related links.

www.rcmp.ca/fls/home_e.htm

Royal Canadian Mounted Police. Forensic Laboratory Services. Directory of regional RCMP forensic laboratories and services provided.

www.nddb-bndg.org/main_e.htm

Government of Canada. National DNA Databank. Case histories, statistics and related legislation.

Chapter 3

Note Taking
and Report Writing

"The report of my death has been greatly exaggerated."

Mark Twain, U.S. Author (1835-1910).

Written in response to an erroneous report
of his death by an English newspaper in 1896.[1]

Learning Outcomes

After reading this chapter, students should be able to:

- Differentiate between the nature and purpose of note taking and report writing.
- Explain the various factors that impact upon a person's ability to take notes.
- Explain the various physical characteristics used to describe persons, vehicles and property.
- Describe the accepted procedure for correcting an error made while writing notes.
- Distinguish between the use of first-person and third-person reporting and when to use the 12-hour or the 24-hour clock system when reporting.
- Describe the elements of a **Crown brief**.

3.1 NOTE TAKING V. REPORT WRITING V. CROWN BRIEFS

Note taking, report writing and the preparation of Crown briefs are fundamental police procedures that involve committing observations and facts to writing but are very different in their nature and purpose. Note taking involves the creation of a permanent record by an individual officer to be used for investigative purposes and as an *aide-mémoire* to refresh – not replace – the investigator's independent recollection of an event, an activity or an observation. Proper investigative notes provide precision and detail to an investigator's testimony in court and enhance the officer's credibility as a witness.[2]

---

[1] Mark Twain quote retrieved April 26, 2005, from www.bartleby.com

[2] Martin (2005).

Report writing also creates a permanent record, but one that is meant to provide an overview of the findings of an investigation. Investigative reports convey information concerning one or more aspects of a case to whomever may subsequently read it, be they other investigators, supervisors, or external police agencies and non-police agencies.

The Crown brief is a document that combines all of the findings and evidence of the case to be used as the basis for prosecuting offenders when charges have been laid and to provide disclosure of the case to the defence.

Note taking is an ongoing process that begins when the offence is first reported and continues contemporaneously during (at the time of) the investigation. Reports are submitted initially to officially document the occurrence and may be supplemented at regular intervals or milestone events such as the laying of charges, court disposition and other material developments in a case.

An investigator will maintain notes continually throughout an investigation at stages when it may still be difficult to sort out fact from fiction. Report writing usually occurs at times during the investigation when the facts of the case have been more accurately established. Investigative notes can and often do serve as a foundation for investigators when compiling police reports and Crown briefs.

Note taking is largely handwritten in police-issued notebooks, but report writing, while being anything but standardized across Ontario, is evolving from handwritten, paper-based format into electronic, "fill-in-the-blank" formats that are part of most larger police services' records management systems (RMS).

What note taking and report writing have in common is the need for absolute accuracy. Once created, your notes and reports become official police records created during a police investigation and, as such, both can be subject to being produced in court or released to the public under freedom of information legislation. Never write anything in your notes or in a report that you cannot substantiate as fact or that you don't want to be made public in court. I am not suggesting that information which might "harm a case" should not be disclosed. The only information that shouldn't be disclosed is privileged information such as the identity of a confidential informer or inappropriate information.

3.2   NOTE TAKING

Note taking skills rank highly among the essential skills that an investigator needs to develop in order to be successful in the field of criminal investigation. The accuracy of your notes will reflect your attention to detail. The completeness of your notes will reflect your thoroughness, and the overall consistent quality of your notes will reflect upon your credibility as an investigator.

Your notes should be written in a bound book with sequentially numbered pages. Some police services allow investigators to maintain separate notebooks for complex, major investigations; otherwise, only one notebook should be maintained at one time. Most issued notebooks contain a cover page upon which the officer enters similar information to the following:

1. name;

2. rank;

3. badge number;

4. police service, unit or detachment;

5. handcuff serial number;

6. sidearm serial number;

7. date of first entry; and

8. date of last entry

Notebook entries, to the extent possible, should be made chronologically, using only black or blue ink. If noteworthy information is recalled out of sequence, it should be identified as a late entry. Every line and every page of an issued notebook should be either written on, or crossed out with a single line and initialled to prevent an entry from being written in afterward. Pages must never be removed from a police notebook – for any reason. Notes made during each individual tour of duty should be separated in the manner prescribed by your police service – typically separated by date.

Once a notebook entry is made, it must never be altered or amended in any way. Errors made at the time of writing in a notebook should be struck through with a single line and initialled. To show that the correction was made at the time of the writing of the notes, the correct information should be written in following the strike-through, not above or below it.

Notes must always be made at the time of the observation/event, or as soon afterward as practicable. In any event, investigative notes must be completed before going off duty. Copies of the notebook entries for police witnesses should also be collected during the investigation and included in the Crown brief for disclosure purposes (see Chapter 13: Courtroom Procedures).

3.2.1 What Information should I Record in my Notes?

It simply isn't possible to capture every detail regarding every aspect of an event or case in your notes. Some factors that impact an individual's ability to take notes include:

1. *Perception* – No two people will perceive every detail or event the same way. An individual must perceive a detail through one of the five senses for it to register in his or her consciousness.

2. *Memory* – You can only document details that are recalled from memory. The better your memory is, the more you can recall and the more complete your notes will be.

3. *Time constraints* – It is only possible to document so much information in a given period of time.

4. *Volume of information* – It is only possible to record limited amounts of information. The sheer volume of facts or details may require that the information be paraphrased or summarized.

5. *Natural selectivity* – One individual may deem a certain fact to be noteworthy, while another individual will deem the same information to be unimportant and consciously decide not to record it.

6. *Anticipation of importance* – Through experience, an investigator may recognize the significance of a certain detail or contentious piece of information and ensure that he or she duly documents it.

3.2.2   Information in Relation to Persons

Fully identify each person who is a complainant, victim, witness, person of interest, suspect and accused person including:

1. full name, including details of identification used to confirm his or her identity, if any;

2. any known alias(es) (other names by which he or she is known, including nicknames);

3. gender (male or female);

4. date of birth;

5. current address, including street name, house and apartment, and municipality;

6. telephone number, including area code (home and business);

7. injuries or physical and emotional condition, if relevant;

8. physical description, including height, weight, hair and eye colour;

9. a description of distinguishing marks, scars, tattoos, etc., if relevant; and

10. a detailed description of his or her clothing and condition, if relevant.

The need to include the above information differs for various individuals and is driven by the nature of their roles in the case. There is usually no need to record the physical description etc., of a witness or of an uninjured victim. All of the above information would be relevant in relation to a suspect or person being charged or placed under arrest.

3.2.3   Information in Relation to Vehicles

Fully identify vehicles that are relevant to an investigation, including:

1. year of manufacture;

2. make and model;

3. colour(s);

4. body style (2 door, 4 door, SUV, convertible, pickup, etc.);

5. licence number, including province/state and year;

6. registration and insurance particulars, if relevant;

7. any damage or distinguishing features, if relevant; and

8. detailed description of items or evidence contained in the vehicle, if relevant.

3.2.4 Information in Relation to Property

Fully identify any stolen, recovered or seized item or property that is relevant to an investigation, including:

1. nature of the item;

2. physical description, including size and colour(s);

3. model and serial numbers; and

4. physical condition, including damage or distinguishing features.

Items should be distinguished from any other similar items in the manner we will examine in Section 7.13.1: Labelling of Evidence.

3.2.5 Observations, Activities and Information

The remaining information that is recorded in an investigator's notebook pertains to: what they saw, heard, smelled or touched (what they learned); what they did; and/or what they were told. It is recommended that investigators record as much information as possible in their notes as it is not always obvious in the early stages of an investigation what will become relevant.

An investigator should include all details of the receipt of a dispatch to an occurrence, such as: the time, date, nature and the reported location of the call; contact information of the complainant; and the identity of the dispatcher, if known. During my career, I would typically include my location when I received the dispatch, the route I had taken to the scene, and my time of arrival.

The remaining details of an officer's notes will vary with the circumstances of the occurrence and the personal style of the investigator. Thorough notes should include summaries of relevant conversations with persons at the scene, anything they tell you in connection with the investigation, and your observations at the scene. Record the identity of witnesses at the scene and the results of field interviews conducted with them.

Record details of the location of physical evidence, description of stolen property, seized items and the physical description of any fleeing suspect(s). If an arrest is made, full particulars of the suspect should be recorded, even if he or she is well known to you. The times and circumstances regarding your compliance with sections 10(a) and 10(b) of the *Charter of Rights and Freedoms* relating to notifying a prisoner of the reason for the arrest and of his or her rights to counsel and the standard caution to a prisoner should be precisely recorded.

Record the description of the suspect's clothing and any statements made by him or her. Details of injuries to both witnesses and suspects should also be noted in detail. Anything seized without warrant from a suspect, incident to arrest or under the Plain View Seizure Rule, should also be described in your notes.

3.2.6 A Picture is Worth a Thousand Words

Investigators often include sketches or diagrams of significant items of evidence or crime scenes for investigative purposes and to refresh their memory while testifying.

Diagrams included in a police notebook are rough, not-to-scale diagrams, but should, where possible, include accurate measurements and compass orientation. As with any other writings in a notebook, once a diagram has been drawn, it should never be altered or amended.[3]

I have used diagrams or sketches in my notes to depict the scene of a break and enter to show the location of the point of entry, the location of footwear or tire impressions, the route taken by the person(s) responsible, and the location of any other physical evidence. I have used diagrams to depict the location of a body and other items of evidence during sudden death investigations, including the description and location of wounds to victims.

One of the most significant sketches I ever included in a notebook was the sketch of a footwear impression made in snow, which was located outside the scene of an alleged prowler who had attempted to break and enter the residence of a woman who was home with her two young children. The person responsible for the offence, who had evidently intended to commit a sexual assault on the woman, was arrested a short distance away and was found to be wearing boots with a distinctive horizontal bar pattern.

The suspect's left boot had a distinctive striation (scratch or gouge) on the heel that was clearly visible in the footwear impressions found in the snow. We arrested the suspect for attempted break and enter of a dwelling house with intent to commit an indictable offence and his footwear was seized as evidence, incident to his arrest.

Due to circumstances beyond my control, I was unable to have a forensic identification officer attend the scene to photograph or cast the footwear impression. The only way for me to record the evidence at the scene was to sketch a diagram of the footwear impression found there.

I sketched my observations of the footwear impression depicting the precise number of bars in the pattern of the sole, the length, width of the impression, and the precise location of the striation. Measurements were also taken to the corner of the house so that I could accurately state where the impression had been located.

At the trial, the simple sketch in my notebook, which was entered as an exhibit, served to establish the nexus (the link or connection) that placed the accused at the scene and corroborated my testimony. The accused was convicted and was sentenced to a term of imprisonment. The interest shown by the trial judge in my simple notebook sketch demonstrated the significance he attached to its evidential value and the importance the diagram played in his reaching a verdict of guilt.

See the references to creating notebook sketches or diagrams in Chapter 6.9: Crime Scene Security Scenario and Chapter 6.14.4: Recording the Crime Scene.

3.2.7   Who Said What?

In court proceedings it is vital to be able to testify precisely what an individual stated to you during an investigation. As an investigator, you should record what a person tells you, verbatim (in his or her exact words). If, for example, during an assault investigation a suspect stated under caution, "I punched him in the head twice – he asked for it," the investigator should record the individual's exact words as the statement constitutes an

---

[3]Turpin (2002).

exception to the hearsay rule and, if deemed to be admissible, may be used as evidence. If the officer paraphrased the suspect's statement as: "Suspect admitted to striking victim twice in head," any evidential value of the statement is lost because it is no longer in the words of the person who spoke it.

Normally, an officer wouldn't be allowed to repeat what a victim or witness stated as such statements are not exceptions to the hearsay rule, except in circumstances where the statement can be shown to be reliable and its introduction into evidence is deemed necessary. Prior inconsistent statements of witnesses may be entered into evidence through hearsay testimony, but only if the witness's verbatim statement can be repeated.

Every individual's role in a case isn't always obvious in the early stages of the investigation. Alleged victims of staged crimes may become suspects or accused. Co-operative witnesses can turn into hostile witnesses. Get into the habit of recording everyone's verbal statements in your notes as you would write their interview statements. If it is important enough for the individual to say it, it is important enough for you to write it down – verbatim.

3.2.8 Use of Inappropriate Language

The use of slang or other inappropriate language in official police documents and records, including notes and reports, is neither desirable nor acceptable. The professionalism of your notes will be enhanced if you avoid the use of slang. Even though certain words have become common in our language, such as "kids," the proper word to use is "children." We are not "cops"; we are "police officers." The suspect was not "drunk," he was "intoxicated." The accused did not have "booze" in his possession, he had "liquor." Slang should only appear in your notes if it is contained in a direct quotation of a person involved in the investigation. If they say it, write it down – if you say it, write it correctly.

Refrain from using derogatory terms to describe individuals in your notes. Always remember that any person with a genuine interest in the case stands a very good chance of obtaining copies of your notes should they apply under your police service's freedom of information policy.

Writing profanity in your notebook is perfectly acceptable, but only when it forms part of a direct quotation from an individual and should then be identified as a quote. Statements made by individuals involved in the case should be recorded verbatim, including the profanity.

BOX 3.1	**Proper Investigative Procedure**

Avoid using phrases in your notes such as one that I actually observed in a police notebook: "The suspect was acting weird." This phrase constitutes a conclusion on the part of the officer, but contains no useful terms of reference to allow anyone who didn't observe the behaviour in question to understand what the writer intended to convey.

Compare that phrase to the following example: "Suspect shouting incoherently – did not respond appropriately to questions I put to him. His moods changed rapidly, from serious to laughing for no reason, to sobbing within the space of a minute. Suspect breathing rapidly and sweating profusely. His shirt was undone in the front with

---

BOX 3.1	(Continued)

the shirt-tail hanging out of the waistband of his pants on the right side only. Suspect was wearing a running shoe on his right foot. On his left foot, he wore only a sock. No evidence of odour of an alcoholic beverage noted on suspect's breath."

The second example paints a picture that allows the reader to understand exactly what behaviour the officer actually observed. From the second description it is safe to conclude that there are reasonable grounds to believe that the individual in question is either suffering from a medical condition such as hypoglycemia or from a mental or emotional disorder, or is perhaps under the influence of a drug. In any event, the behaviour described is indicative of an individual who requires immediate medical attention.

3.2.9   Economy of Language and Use of Short Forms

The use of proper contractions and acronyms is quite acceptable for report writing, but when writing your notes, the rules are even more relaxed. You may use any short forms or abbreviations for words that you wish to save time. Your notes are made primarily for your own use and you will develop your own style of note taking and your own short forms for commonly used words. Some typical short forms used by officers when note taking – not report writing – include:

Accused	acc, or Δ
Address	addr
Assault Causing Bodily Harm	Assault CBH
Black	blk
Blue	blu
Brown	brn
Building	bldg
Business	bus
Constable	Const, or PC
Detachment or Detective	det
Driver or Doctor	dr
Green	grn
Highway	hwy
Inspector	Insp
Motorcycle	m/c
Northbound	N/b
Passenger	pass
Residence	res
Sergeant	Sgt
Southbound	S/b
Station	stn
Suspect	susp
Therefore	∴
Vehicle	veh

Victim	vic
White	wht
With	$\overline{w}$
Witness	wit
Yellow	yel
Young Offender	YO

Your notes should be specific and thorough, yet concise. Include all details that are relevant to the case, using normal conversational language. Police work, like other professions, has its own unique terminology. Police jargon, such as that used on police television programs, continually crops up in the notes of students and junior officers. A very common example is "I proceeded to search the accused," when to say "I searched the accused" precisely describes the action in a more concise fashion.

Proceeding to do something means that you commenced the action but doesn't enlighten the reader as to whether or not you successfully completed the action. When writing notes or reports, speak as you would in normal conversation. If you don't "proceed to grocery store" when you are off-duty, don't do it in your notes either. I don't believe that anyone "proceeds" to do anything until he or she becomes involved in a police-related activity. Keep your language professional – but keep it real.

3.2.10 If it Looks like a Duck, and Walks like a Duck – It's a Duck

As no two people perceive things in exactly the same way, it is not surprising that officers will have slightly different recollections regarding an incident or an observation. In an attempt to be overly specific, officers can unwittingly create discrepancies between their testimony and that of other officers or witnesses.

I once testified at an armed robbery trial in which three individual police officers separately testified that the suspect vehicle they had observed at various locations, as it was allegedly fleeing from the scene of the robbery was: beige, tan, and bronze in colour, respectively. The pickup truck in question was brown.

The owner of the truck knew it was brown, the registration certificate described the truck as brown, and both the accused and his attorney knew that the truck was brown. Counsel for the defence, however, created reasonable doubt by making it appear to the jury that the officers were either mistaken or had observed different vehicles. Try to be as specific as possible in your descriptions but keep it simple and call things as they are – brown is brown. If it looks like a duck, and it waddles like a duck and it quacks like a duck....

Now, if you honestly believe the duck that you observed was in fact a North American Bald Eagle, don't be influenced by anyone just because he or she says they saw a duck – it is what you perceived it to be. But, if you attempt to describe the duck you saw, don't describe it as, "a plumed, web-footed, billed, waterfowl of the genus *Anatinae*" – it's just a duck.

3.2.11 Eliminate Investigator Bias

"[W]rongful conviction[s] have resulted from ... pressure on law enforcement officials to resolve the case either because it is high profile or

because of resource or other institutional factors. That pressure in turn triggers and justifies a bias known ... as 'tunnel vision' ... that causes police investigators to select evidence to build a case for the conviction of their chosen suspect while suppressing or ignoring information and interpretations that point away from guilt."[4]

Dianne Lee Martin (1945-2004),
Professor of Criminal Law, Osgoode Hall Law School,
York University, Toronto.

You will recall the previous introduction of the concept of tunnel vision, as defined by Mr Justice Fred Kaufman, in Section 1.3.1: To Seek the Truth. In this latest quotation, the late Professor Dianne Martin offered a plausible explanation for some unintentional causes of systemic (institutional) tunnel vision. When improper selectivity, suppression or ignorance of evidence occurs, for any reason, it is also referred to as **investigator bias**.

Investigator bias must, of necessity, creep into investigative notes, police reports and Crown briefs. For investigator bias to occur during investigations involving more than one officer, it almost always requires that investigators collaborate when preparing their notes and reports.

The very instant that collaboration occurs, the investigation fails – the victim is failed, the suspect is failed, and the public interest is failed. When two or more investigators collaborate on their notes for the purpose of synchronizing their testimony, one or more of them may adopt facts that they have no independent recollection of. An investigator who falsely testifies in court to facts he or she has no personal knowledge of commits the offence of perjury.

No two police officers will document their notes of any event in the same way, nor should an individual officer's notes be influenced by anyone else, including another police officer. Your notes should reflect your own personal observations or information that was provided to you by someone else – notes of your observations should never reflect someone else's observations.

Canadian courts are well aware of the opportunity and the potential temptation by police officers to collaborate during the preparation of investigative notes and are vigilant for evidence of such collaboration. Never fall into this destructive trap. No case is so important that an investigator must knowingly lie to secure a wrongful conviction – especially when the consequences of doing so may result in the actual offender remaining at large.

BOX 3.2	Investigative Relevance

On the morning of a preliminary hearing involving a charge of murder, a junior officer was called to the witness stand and swore an oath that the evidence he was about to give would be the truth, the whole truth and nothing but the truth. When the Crown Attorney commenced his examination-in-chief of the officer, the constable admitted that his notes pertaining to the investigation had been falsified. The officer had falsified

---

[4]Martin (2005).

BOX 3.2	(Continued)

his notes on the instructions of a superior officer, for the purpose of implicating the accused.

The case was immediately adjourned while an investigation was conducted into both officers' activities – the senior officer for allegedly attempting to obstruct justice and the junior officer for allegedly following an illegal order. The officers had collaborated on certain aspects of their notes, even though the junior officer had allowed himself to be coerced into doing so. Both officers had sacrificed all credibility by falsifying police records. At least the junior officer took steps to prevent perjuring himself, due to his attack of conscience.

3.2.12 Permission to Refer to Notes in Court

An investigator who is testifying in court may, with the permission of the judge or justice, refer to their notes for the purposes of memory if the notes were made at the time of the investigation and if those notes have not been altered or amended in any way since the time they were written. During examination-in-chief by the Crown Attorney, you should testify from memory to the extent possible. At some point you will have to refer to your notes to refresh your memory of a specific time or other detail, at which point you would ask the judge or justice:

Officer: "Your Honour [or Your Worship], may I refer to my notes for the purpose of refreshing my memory?"

Justice: "When were your notes made, Officer?"

Officer: "At the time of the investigation, Your Honour [Worship]."

Justice: "Were your notes made during the same tour of duty?"

Officer: "Yes, Your Honour [Worship], they were."

Justice: "Have your notes been altered or amended in any way since that time?"

Officer: "No Your Honour [Worship], they have not."

Justice: "Very well, Officer. Proceed."

Officer: "Thank you, Your Honour [Worship]."

During cross-examination, defence counsel may ask you if you have reviewed your notes prior to testifying. If in fact you did read over your notes prior to court – everyone should, every time they testify – answering "Yes" only demonstrates that you took steps to prepare yourself prior to testifying.

Your notes are subject to disclosure and defence counsel is entitled to review them. If there is any information in your notes that would identify a confidential informer or undercover police officer, or would jeopardize an ongoing unrelated investigation, that information should be edited out by photocopying your notes to obscure the privileged information with a black felt pen, prior to being disclosed.

3.3 REPORT WRITING

Depending on the level of implementation of computer technology within a police service, the method of writing internal reports concerning general occurrences will include one of the following.

1. Paper-based handwritten reports:

    Such a reporting system usually includes a multi-page snap set form with multiple copies that are forwarded to various departments or bureaux within the police service. An investigator selects the appropriate first page from an assortment of choices including: General Occurrence Report; Missing Person Report; or Homicide/Sudden Death Report; and adds generic supplementary pages, as required.

    Paper-based systems were formerly the most common police reporting system but are steadily being phased out by one of the following types of computerized reporting systems:

2. Computerized Interactive Forms:

    Computerized reporting is intended to speed up the process of report writing for patrol officers. From a menu screen, an investigator selects which type of report he or she wishes to submit and inputs the data directly into pre-determined fields. The report is then reviewed by a supervisor who approves the content and enters it into the records management system database or returns it to the submitting officer for necessary revision.

    Some police services provide electronic systems that allow police officers to dictate their reporting information to a stenographer who inputs the information into the reporting system. If a dictation system is available, this type of reporting works well, depending on the keyboarding skills of police officers and the number of dedicated workstations for investigators to use at busy shift-change periods.

3. Computerized "Smart Form" Reporting:

    "Smart forms" are similar in many respects to interactive forms but are superior. Data entered into any field of a smart form is automatically populated (transferred or shared) into similar fields of related reports.

    This means that if a dispatcher handles a call for police service, he or she assigns an incident number and type in the details of the caller, address, time, etc. Using smart form technology, the information automatically populates the identical fields of the report the investigating officer is required to submit and minimizes double data entry for the officer.

    The officer then completes the remainder of the report and, again, relevant information is automatically populated into other required forms and reports to prevent the officer from keying identical information into multiple reports.

Police reports serve a variety of purposes. Reporting information on a variety of offences is compiled monthly and is submitted to Statistics Canada. Crime statistics are also used internally by police services to conduct records analysis for budgeting, scheduling, program evaluation purposes and plotting crime trends.

Occurrence reports must provide all known information on the case in the event that another officer is reassigned to the case, or develops information that can solve the case, or is assigned to a similar case that is in some way connected to the original offence. In cases of financial loss, aggrieved parties or insurance companies may acquire copies of police reports for civil purposes.

3.3.1 Tombstone Information

Police reports must all contain the unique information to distinguish it from other similar occurrences or crimes. **Tombstone** information refers to the distinctive details that identify the following:

1. Incident or occurrence number.

   These are specific to the police service and are generated sequentially by year.

2. Time, date, and location of occurrence (if known).

   Occasionally it is only possible to fix a range of time, such as "between 0001 hrs and 0430 hrs Sunday, May 1, 2005." Sometimes it may only be possible to estimate a range of dates, such as "between the dates of December 1–3, 2004."

3. Type or nature of occurrence.

   These are classified by type of occurrence reported or what crime can be proven; for example "Break, Enter and Theft – Dwelling House or Assault Level II."

4. Name, address and telephone number of the person who reported it.

   This is important information to gather at the time the initial report is received. The complainant may be a victim, a witness, an otherwise uninvolved person or may even be the person responsible for the offence. Securing his or her contact information allows investigators to interview the complainant to ascertain his or her degree of involvement in the case, if any.

5. Name, date of birth (DOB), address and telephone number of victim(s).

6. In the event of a death occurrence, details must be recorded regarding the notification of next-of-kin. Note which surviving family member of the deceased was officially notified of the death, by whom and when. The identity of a deceased person should never be released to the media until the surviving family has been personally notified of the death.

7. Investigating Officer.

   Contact information should include name, rank, badge number and unit.

3.3.2 Narrative Summary

Regardless of which reporting system is used by a police service, the investigating officer is still required to complete a narrative summary of the occurrence in every report. At this stage, the officer's notebook entries made during the investigation will provide the necessary information to describe the relevant circumstances of the occurrence and the investigation that was conducted.

The written narrative or summary of a report must attempt to accurately answer all possible questions to provide the reader with a clear sense of what occurred. The narrative of a report must remain factual and contain only information that can be verified.[5]

The simplest way to construct a narrative of an occurrence is to compile all of the required information in advance and explain the event(s) under investigation in chronological form answering the Who?, What?, When?, Where?, Why? and How? of the case. The 'Why?,' or the explanation of the offender's motive for a crime, isn't always evident,

---

[5]Turpin (2002).

nor are they required in a police report or a Crown brief. But if there is evidence or some factual basis for motive, those details ought to be included in the narrative.

A narrative summary of a police report should be written in the past tense and should refer to all persons in the third person or by his or her proper name and title. The accused, John Smith, should never be referred to as anything other than by John Smith or as "the accused." For brevity of reporting, multiple references to the victim of a crime may refer to his or her role as "the victim."

All references to times in investigative notes and police reports, other than Crown briefs, should be stated in the 24-hour time system. For example:

	12 Hour System		24 Hour System
Midnight	12:00 a.m.	-	0001 hrs
	1:00 a.m.	-	0100 hrs
	2:00 a.m.	-	0200 hrs
	2:27 a.m.	-	0227 hrs
Noon	12:00 p.m.	-	1200 hrs
	1:00 p.m.	-	1300 hrs
	2:00 p.m.	-	1400 hrs
	4:30 p.m.	-	1630 hrs
	11:59 p.m.	-	2359 hrs

3.3.3   Objectivity in Police Reporting

Objectivity can be described as an investigative mindset that is based purely on observable facts and is not influenced by the investigator's personal prejudices or emotions.

To the extent that it is possible to do so, you should always strive to reflect objectivity rather than expressing your own subjective beliefs or feelings in your investigative notes and reports. If the details of a case cannot be independently verified, they should be qualified as being either speculative in nature or the opinion or theory of the author.

As an investigator, you should never allow your personal views on any subject to distort the reporting of the circumstances of an incident or draw unsubstantiated conclusions relating to the evidence of a case. If certain information doesn't add any particular value to the notes or report, its relevance should be questioned and the information should be deleted.

Unverified facts from personal observations, which can't be proven but which are material to the investigation, should be properly described; for example, if you discover unconfirmed bloodstains at a crime scene, it is proper to describe them in terms which can be verified, for example, "a brownish stain, resembling blood, was located at..." The rule of thumb to be followed is: if you can't prove a fact, don't name it – describe it.

If facts are received from another source, such as from a witness or a confidential informer, which are either unverified or can't be proven, that information should be qualified as such. It is proper to say that any fact or element of a case that has not yet been proven in court has been "alleged." Describing a fact as "alleged" indicates an attitude of objectivity on the part of the author even where evidence exists to verify the allegation.

An offence, an action, or a verbal statement by a person may be alleged. For example:

"The alleged robbery was committed while the accused was on parole."

"The accused allegedly disposed of the stolen property by selling it."

"It is alleged that the accused stated, 'Hand over the money, or I'll shoot.'"

Even where the stated fact forms part of the Crown's case, referring to the crime, action or statement in this manner in the above examples reveals that while the author may or may not believe the allegation to be true, he or she still acknowledges that the subject of the allegation has not been proven guilty beyond a reasonable doubt.

3.3.4 Confidentiality of Information

All police and civilian employees of a police service swear an oath of secrecy prior to their appointment and are required not to disclose any information that they receive by reason of their employment, except as may be required for law enforcement purposes. There are times when it will be necessary to submit a report but to restrict the dissemination of information to a select group of individuals. Some instances that might require the restriction of information in a police report include:

1. intelligence information – confirmed or unconfirmed information that a named or unnamed individual or an organization is involved either in ongoing criminal activity or a reported or unreported crime;

2. information that would tend to identify a confidential informer or agent;

3. information that would tend to identify an undercover police officer;

4. information regarding a sensitive law enforcement matter, such as a wiretap, that, if released, could jeopardize an ongoing investigation; and

5. information alleging a criminal wrongdoing involving a member of any police service that, if released, could jeopardize an investigation of the allegation.

BOX 3.3	Investigative Relevance

The rule of thumb for protecting information is that if I provide information to you that I wouldn't want you to disclose to anyone else, the responsibility is on me to inform you of that at the time. Sensitive information should be clearly designated as confidential, in accordance with the reporting policies of the individual police service.

Police services have restricted file designations for reports which are only maintained in certain secure physical locations and are only accessible to employees with a certain level of security clearance. Restricted intelligence files are exempted from release under Freedom of Information legislation.

3.4 CROWN BRIEFS

In my opinion, the most important "report" an investigator will write is a "Crown brief." The Crown brief is a compilation of the findings and evidence of a case that is used as the basis for prosecuting an offender charged with an offence. It is easy to assume that by the time your case gets to court, everyone will share your intimate knowledge about it. Without the primary investigator's exposure to the case, other officers, prosecutors and defence attorneys must rely on the Crown brief to learn the facts of an investigation.

The Crown brief should contain all information about the crime, the witnesses, the investigation and evidence – not just evidence that implicates the accused. I recommend preparing a brief of an investigation prior to archiving an unsolved case, to assist investigators should new information be discovered to justify any future re-opening of the case.

With experience, individual investigators develop their own personal styles regarding their construction of Crown briefs. Departmental policy might influence certain aspects of Crown brief preparation for investigators from different departments; however, I will describe the format of Crown briefs commonly used by investigators across Ontario that I used successfully throughout my career.

The success or failure of a Crown brief is judged by the completeness and accuracy of the facts it contains. The ease or difficulty with which a reader locates relevant information in a Crown brief is the result of the investigator's experience, organizational skills and skills in preparing the brief – even if the information appears in multiple locations for ease of reading.

3.4.1 Crown Brief Format

Crown briefs for non-complex criminal cases are several pages in length while others may comprise several volumes and thousands of pages. Some Crown briefs are prepared as separate, stand-alone documents while others are electronically generated by a police service's computerized records management system. While Crown briefs vary in size, with few exceptions, most use the following format and contain the following information:

3.4.2 Cover Page

The purpose of the cover page is to identify the accused, the charge(s), and the officer in charge of the case. At a glance, the cover page tells a busy Crown Attorney that this is the correct brief that was prepared on a particular charge or dealing with a particular accused person.

The cover page of a Crown brief usually displays the name and logo or crest of every law enforcement agency involved in the investigation. The name of the accused is stated as *R. v. John Doe* (the "R." is a contraction for "Regina," the Latin word meaning "the Queen" – who is our head of state. If and when Her Majesty Queen Elizabeth II is succeeded by a male heir, the "R." will signify "Rex," the Latin word for "the King." The letter "v.," which precedes the name of the accused, is a contraction for "versus," meaning "against," signifying that the subject matter of the Crown brief is a court proceeding between the state and the accused in accordance with our adversarial court system. References to all court proceedings, including case law citations, are cited in this manner.

All charges against the accused that are contained in the Crown brief are listed, complete with section number(s) and statute(s), following the accused's name. The investigating officer's name and contact information as well as that of the case manager, if they are different, are included at the bottom of the cover page.

3.4.3 Index

As with any book, the index contains references that assist the reader in locating any particular element by page number. The index may be broken down into headings and sub-headings depending on the circumstances of the case and the need to organize the information for ease of retrieval. Witnesses might be listed according to the sequence of events or by their significance to the case if they are few in number. Witnesses are usually listed alphabetically if there is no other way to distinguish one from the other, or they can also be listed alphabetically in relation to each charge about which they may give evidence.

Witnesses may be listed alphabetically if they were part of one large group at a particular location or event, or separated as police or civilian witnesses. If witnesses are categorized in any way, an overall master witness list should also be created. Such lists are used by court staff, prosecutors and police to ensure that no witness is overlooked.

I recommend that witnesses be listed in alphabetical order to avoid the appearance that the investigator ranked the witnesses by importance to the case. A short factual description of the witness can be included following the witness's name to provide some significance of his or her involvement, such as "Doe, John – victim Count # 1," or "Smith, Fred, Co-worker of the accused," or "Doe, Jane – Constable # 11814 – [Your Police Service], Investigating Officer."

All items of evidence should be catalogued in the court brief. As in the case of witnesses, items of evidence may also be categorized if it would add value to the organization of the Crown brief and assist readers with comprehending and retrieving information contained in the brief. Other items found in the index would point the reader to elements such as the synopsis of the investigation or the accused's criminal record, if any.

3.4.4 Information / Remand / Release Documents

Always include a true copy of the information used to press the relevant charges against the accused person. Doing so removes ambiguity (any possible misunderstanding) regarding the allegation(s) against the accused and allows the prosecutor to view and, if necessary, correct any technical deficiencies in the wording of the charge or the section number or statute prior to court.

Include copies of remand warrants and/or release documents to provide a history of the accused's court appearances and accurate information concerning time spent in custody or concerns reflected by the conditions placed upon an accused at the stage of interim release.

3.4.5 Main Page

The Main Page – which may actually be multiple pages in complex briefs – contains more detailed information regarding the accused, the charges and the victim(s). The information about an accused should include all charges, and personal information such as date of birth, aliases, if any, his or her address and whether or not the accused has a record of criminal convictions.

If a criminal record is included, the page of the Crown brief where it may be found should also be noted. Even if information regarding the location of the accused's criminal record is also to be found in the index, duplication of information such as this in a

Crown brief is not unusual. Remember that we are trying to make it as easy as possible for the reader to locate relevant information.

3.4.6 Witnesses

Every statement provided by a witness should be included in the Crown brief and should be typewritten and double-spaced, depending on your departmental policy and the severity of the charge. Multiple statements that contain discrepancies in testimony may be used by the Crown or the defence to cross-examine witnesses.

A document known as a **Will Say** should be prepared for each witness to condense the content of their statement(s) and to summarize the testimony it is possible for them to give if called upon to do so. A Will Say should include information that describes each witness's role in a case, his or her observations, any statements made by an accused person in his or her presence, and any physical evidence associated with the witness. The following example of a Will Say describes the involvement of a police officer, other than the investigating officer, who played a relatively minor role in an investigation:

Will Say Statement of:

Smith, John, Constable # 8657 – [Your Police Service]

Constable Smith will say:

– That he has been a member of [Your Police Service] since July 17, 1987 and holds the rank of Police Constable;

– That on Sunday, May 8, 2005, he was on duty between 7:00 a.m. and 7:00 p.m. and was assigned to uniform patrol conducting general law enforcement duties;

– That at 12:36 p.m., May 8, 2005, he was dispatched to assist with an armed robbery investigation at the Super-Go Service Station, situated at Elm Street at Johnson Avenue;

– That upon his arrival at 12:39 p.m., May 8, 2005, he was assigned to establish and maintain a security perimeter around the premises which he did, utilizing yellow crime scene tape.

– That he created and maintained a crime scene security log, recording the names and times of all persons entering and leaving the perimeter.

– That at 2:15 p.m. he observed a single spent bullet casing in the parking lot of the Super-Go Service Station, which he brought to the attention of Identification Officer Susan Parker, who photographed and measured the location of the shell casing before taking it into evidence.

– That he was relieved by Sergeant Roberts at 6:45 p.m., May 8, 2005 and had no further involvement in this case.

3.4.7 Synopsis

The purpose of the synopsis in a Crown brief provides readers with an abbreviated, chronological overview of the facts of an occurrence and the subsequent investigation. The synopsis of a case does not have to include every piece of information or evidence but should briefly describe the event, the participants, and the involvement and extent of any loss, damage or injury that was incurred.

Whether a synopsis is 1 page in length, or 30 pages, or more depends on your departmental policy, local court practices and the investigating officer's personal preference. I recommend beginning the synopsis with details of the actual victimization, followed by any relevant events involving the participants, the report to the police and subsequent action taken, including seizure of evidence, arrest, etc.

The synopsis of a Crown brief will serve as the basis for a Crown Attorney to introduce evidence in the event of a guilty plea, if the facts contained in the synopsis have been substantially agreed upon by both the Crown and the defence. The synopsis must contain enough evidence to establish a *prima facie* case in order to obtain a conviction. The entire synopsis should be written in the third-person – "He did …," "She said …," "They went …," etc., and should be in the past tense, as if telling a story.

3.4.8   Exhibits

Every piece of physical evidence, including videotapes, audio tapes and photographs should be listed for disclosure and prosecution purposes. If an up-to-date exhibit register is maintained during the investigation, a copy of it might adequately serve the purpose. Exhibits should be described in detail including when, where and how they came into the possession of the police, who seized the item, and the continuity. For example:

Number	Item	Date	Location	By Whom Seized	Continuity
1	21 cm. black handled serrated steak knife. Make: U/k Reddish coloured stains on blade.	1:37 a.m. May 9/05	NW corner parking lot, Good Times Bar, 123 Smith St., Your Town	PC BROWN	BROWN JONES CFS JONES
2	Men's black leather jacket, size: 40R with cuts to left sleeve and back	2:05 a.m. May 9/05	Room #2, Emergency Ward, Your General Hospital	Detective JONES	JONES CFS JONES

3.4.9   Criminal Record

The record of the accused's previous criminal convictions should be included in the Crown brief for the Crown prosecutor to ensure that the information is brought before the court at the time of sentencing in the event of a conviction. The criminal record, if any, may either be a photocopy of the record returned from the Royal Canadian Mounted Police (RCMP) or may be a typewritten reproduction.

The complete criminal record, including acquittals, discharges and outstanding charges that have yet to be adjudicated should be provided to the Crown Attorney for information purposes and for disclosure. The Crown Attorney should be aware of the full extent of the criminal background of the accused in order to make informed decisions as to the appropriateness of interim release and for sentencing recommendations. At the time of conviction, the judge is provided only with the actual previous convictions for sentencing purposes.

3.5 REPORTING PROFESSIONALISM

Every written police communication should be easily understood and, to the extent possible, should leave no questions unanswered in the mind of the reader. Verbs in police reports should consistently be stated in the past tense. Even though you may be writing your notes as the events are occurring – by the time your report is read or you testify in court, those events will be in the past.

Except for confidential police informers, the names of involved persons should be stated as their full proper names. Take the time to determine the correct name of involved persons and refer to them by their correct names rather than commonly used nicknames. For example, a witness commonly known as "Zeke" should first be referred to by his or her legal name "Ezekiel JOHNSON (aka: Zeke)" and thereafter by "JOHNSON." If more than one involved person shares a surname, they can be distinguished by adding their initials after the surname, such as "ROBERTSON, W." and "ROBERTSON, T."

Many police services require that surnames of involved persons be capitalized in reports, for example: John DOE. Some police services require that surnames be placed before the person's given name, for example: DOE, John. Be guided by matters of departmental policy and local practice when submitting reports and Crown briefs.

When referring to yourself in your notes or in a report, other than a Crown brief, or when preparing your own statement, always refer to yourself in the first person – "I," "me," "my," "mine," etc. When referring to yourself in a Will Say statement or a Crown brief synopsis, you should refer to yourself in the third person, for instance "Constable Smith arrived at the scene at 8:37 a.m."

Spelling and grammar in notes and reports reflect the professionalism of the writer. Documents such as notes, reports, memoranda and Crown briefs that are full of spelling errors create the impression that the investigator may be deficient in his or her investigative skills and written communication skills. If the investigator didn't take the time and effort to check his or her spelling, did the investigator check his or her facts?

If you feel that your written communication skills could be improved, I recommend that you start by developing a reading program to enhance your writing abilities. If your spelling skills are weak, keep a dictionary or thesaurus handy and make use of Spell Check or similar functions of software applications to identify and correct spelling and grammatical errors.

Reading any type of professional document, especially those similar to the type you will be writing, will give you a sense of the proper construction or format to be used. Read Crown briefs and reports prepared by experienced investigators to observe the type of information that was included and the manner in which it was expressed.

While reading books, magazines or newspapers pay attention to the sentence and paragraph structure – not just the content. Compare the two sentences for clarity:

1. "He arrested him and brought him to his car."

2. "At 0247 hrs., May 9, 2005, at the intersection of Main Street and Park Street, PC BROWN placed the accused, David THOMPSON, under arrest for Assault with a weapon and returned the suspect to the police cruiser."

In the first sentence, it is clear that someone arrested somebody for something and took him or her to a car. The second sentence identifies the participants of the event, clearly states when, where and why the arrest occurred, and indicates that the suspect was taken into custody. The first sentence answers the question, What?, while the second sentence provides answers to Who? What? When? Where? and Why?

Neatness and professionalism also includes not submitting a report or a Crown brief with coffee or food stains on the pages and taking time to proofread the document for errors. In fact, an investigator should always attempt to have someone else proofread his or her reports and Crown briefs prior to submitting them. A fresh eye might pick out a mistake – if you didn't catch it the first time, there is a higher probability that you won't catch a mistake the second time reading it.

SUMMARY

- Note taking involves the creation of a permanent record by an officer that is used for investigative purposes and as an *aide-mémoire* to refresh the investigator's independent recollection of an event, an activity or an observation. Proper investigative notes provide precision and detail to an investigator's testimony in court and enhance the officer's credibility as a witness.

- Report writing creates a permanent record that is meant to provide an overview of the findings of an investigation. Investigative reports convey information concerning one or more aspect of a case to other investigators, supervisors, or external police agencies and non-police agencies.

- Crown briefs combine all of the findings and evidence of the case to be used as the basis for prosecuting offenders when charges have been laid and to provide disclosure of the case to the defence.

- Notebook entries should be chronological and be written only in black or blue ink.

- Write on every line and every page of an issued notebook, or cross out with a single line and initial blank lines or pages to prevent an entry from being written in afterward.

- Once a notebook entry is made, it must never be altered or amended in any way. Errors made at the time of writing in a notebook should be struck through with a single line and initialled.

- Write your notes at the time of the observation/event, or as soon afterward as practicable. In any event, investigative notes must be completed before going off duty.

- Include sketches or diagrams of significant items of evidence or crime scenes for investigative purposes and to refresh your memory while testifying.

- Record in your notes exactly what a person tells you, verbatim (in his or her exact words).

- The use of slang or other inappropriate language in official police documents and records, including notes and reports, is neither desirable nor acceptable, except when quoting a witness.

- Never allow your personal views on any subject to distort the reporting of the circumstances of an incident or draw unsubstantiated conclusions relating to the evidence of a case.

DISCUSSION QUESTIONS

1. The nature and amount of personal information recorded about an individual in your notes will be driven by his or her role in the occurrence. Explain why you might record more information about certain classes of individuals than others in your investigative notes.

2. Explain what is meant by the verbatim recording of a statement made by an individual. When is it beneficial to record statements of individuals verbatim? Think of some examples of such situations.

3. Describe situations in which it would be proper to restrict the dissemination of a police report. How does an investigator accomplish this? What are the benefits of restricting the dissemination of a police report?

 ## WEBLINKS

www.pearsoned.ca/crimcjpolicing/glossary0.html

Pearson Education Criminology, Criminal Justice and Policing Online Glossary of Terms and Concepts.

http://dictionary.law.com/

Law.com web-site. Free dictionary of legal terms.

www.legal-explanations.com/index.htm

Legal Explanations.com website. Free explanations of legal terms and concepts.

Chapter 4

Interviewing Witnesses and Victims

"The most serious obstacle to obtaining information is the interviewer."

Avinoam Sapir,

Founder of the Laboratory for Scientific Interrogation

Phoenix, Arizona.[1]

Learning Outcomes

After reading this chapter, students should be able to:

- Distinguish between an interview and an interrogation and explain the various classifications of persons each technique is applied to.

- Explain what is meant by the **"90–10 Rule"**.

- Outline the structure of an investigative interview and give examples of the goals and objectives of the various phases of the P.E.A.C.E. model.

- Analyze the difference between **open-ended** questions and **leading** questions.

- Summarize the significance of the Supreme Court decision of *R. v. KGB*.

- Analyze the benefits of videotaping and audio taping statements.

4.1   INTRODUCTION

The importance of interviewing as the primary method of gathering information during the course of all police investigations cannot be overstressed. It is not an understatement, in the least, to characterize interviewing as the "backbone" of every successful investigation. An investigator may be expert in the drafting of search warrants or may be very knowledgeable regarding case law and statute law, but if he or she has poorly developed interviewing skills, his or her cases will not be as strong as the investigator who successfully gathers every available piece of relevant information from victims and witnesses.

---

[1]Sapir (2000).

When the so-called "big break" in a case comes, or when the crucial piece of physical evidence is located, it quite often only corroborates the direct evidence (testimony) of a witness. Interviewing witnesses justifiably consumes the majority of effort expended during an investigation, as much of the evidence gathered during the course of an entire investigation is obtained by interviewing witnesses. Proficiency in interviewing is the hallmark of the successful investigator.

Some witnesses may be reluctant to share their full knowledge with an investigator for any number of reasons that will be discussed during this chapter. Some witnesses may give an account of an event that is either intentionally or unintentionally false. During any investigation, investigators must take their witnesses as they find them. Whatever the witness says in his or her account of the event remains the witness's account, whether or not that account is mistakenly or deliberately false.

This chapter gives the investigator some insight into how to prepare for an interview, and the recommended structure and techniques for conducting interviews. The following chapter will deal with conducting interrogations and detecting indications of deception.

The main goal of any interview or interrogation is to obtain a written or an electronically recorded statement from the subject being questioned – interviewing and interrogation are merely the various techniques applied by investigators to different situations involving different classes of individuals. A clear distinction must be drawn between an interview and an interrogation because they are different in nature, and different legal rules apply to each.

4.1.1   "Interview" Defined

For the purposes of a police investigation, "interview" means a conversation conducted with a person from whom information is sought, relating to the event under investigation. "The purpose of [an] interview is to gather information to determine whether an offence has been committed, to identify the individual[s] responsible for the commission of the offence and/or to obtain evidence which may assist in the investigation/prosecution."[2]

An interview may result in the taking of a statement, either in writing or by audio or video recording if it is determined that the subject being interviewed has relevant knowledge of the case under investigation. Interviews are conducted with various categories of persons, including victims, witnesses, non-witnesses, persons of interest and, to a smaller degree, suspects and accused persons.

A victim (complainant) is the person who has suffered loss or damage, or against whom a crime has been committed. It is often through the victim's testimony that direct evidence of the *actus reus* (guilty act or prohibited act) is introduced in court. A victim may or may not be able to provide testimony concerning the identity of the person responsible for the event/crime and/or testimony relating to the criminal intent (*mens rea*), if any, of the offender(s).

---

[2]Ministry of Community Safety and Correctional Services Ontario: *Major Case Management (MCM) Manual* (undated), p. 40.

A witness is a person who has perceived some information relating to the event under investigation through one or more of his or her five senses (sight, hearing, touch, smell or taste). Every surviving victim is, of necessity, a witness. A witness, other than a victim, may provide testimony relating to one or more issues, such as the identity of an offender, the *actus reus* or the *mens rea*, if any.

When we think of a witness, we usually think of someone testifying in court, but a witness in an investigation means anyone with relevant information, whether or not a charge is laid, and whether or not he or she is ever called upon by either the prosecution or the defence to testify in court. Every police officer involved in an investigation is also a witness.

A non-witness is one of many different types of people who may be interviewed during the course of an investigation, while attempting to identify witnesses or gather information. The results of a non-witness's interview may reveal that he or she is not a victim, nor did he or she perceive any information relevant to the event under investigation. For example, perhaps the non-witness was not in the area at the time that the event occurred or, if the non-witness was present, he or she was totally unaware of the event and did not perceive any relevant information.

A person of interest is "a person whose background, relationship to the victim or the opportunity to commit the offence may warrant further inquiry but [at that time] no other grounds exist to suggest culpability [criminal liability, blameworthiness] in the commission of the [event(s) being investigated]."[3]

For example, the owner of a business is found murdered inside his or her business premises. Everyone connected with that business (such as management, employees, business associates, etc.) by virtue of their connection to the victim or their association to the location of the murder, would all be considered to be persons of interest. This is due to the possibility of their opportunity to commit the crime even though no evidence exists, at that time, to suggest that any of them are guilty of the offence. Any grounds for believing in their involvement in the incident under investigation falls below the standard of credibly based suspicion.

Several persons of interest may require elimination from suspicion during the course of the investigation. Their elimination from suspicion is accomplished largely through the interviewing/questioning process and through establishing and verifying their alibis. A person of interest is never considered to be a suspect, nor should he or she ever be officially identified as such.

A suspect is "a person of interest [whom] investigators [reasonably] believe [has a degree of] culpability in the commission of the offence[s] [being investigated] based on the evidence [linking the person to the crime]."[4] It is important to distinguish between persons of interest and suspects, as persons of interest are interviewed, while suspects can either be interviewed or interrogated. The distinction depends on the individual circumstances of the case and the objectives involved in dealing with the specific person, either to obtain additional information from him or her (interview) or to obtain an **admission** or confession to a crime (interrogation).

---

[3]Ontario Major Case Management Manual. (Oct 1, 2004), p. 10.

[4]Ibid.

A suspect may once have been a person of interest, against whom incriminating evidence became known at some point during the investigation, shifting at least a partial focus of the investigation onto him or her. Perhaps a suspect may come to the attention of the investigation through a different avenue of inquiry. The most important distinction between persons of interest and suspects is that a suspect, once declared as such, requires total and conclusive elimination from suspicion, to the extent that his or her elimination is possible.

It is never wise to take an accused person to court while one or more other known suspects have not been eliminated. To do so allows for the creation of reasonable doubt that a suspect other than the accused may have actually committed the crime. The key factor to declaring someone to be a suspect is the degree of incriminating information linking the person to the crime and not merely the possibility that he or she might have committed the crime.

While there may be some incriminating evidence against a suspect, it may fall short of the standard of reasonable grounds to arrest or to lay a charge. It may be practical to interview suspects under caution, if they are co-operative, in an attempt to gather additional information about their knowledge of the case. To a certain degree, interviewing and interrogation both include the element of questioning.

An accused is a person against whom a charge has been laid. Once before a court of law, an accused may alternatively be referred to as a defendant. An accused person is interrogated until he or she fully admits guilt regarding the offence they are charged with, at which time his or her formal statement is taken (either in writing or recorded on audio or videotape) under caution.

An accused may be interviewed (always under caution) to obtain information regarding the offence with which he or she is charged (e.g., if the accused wishes to implicate other person(s) involved in the offence). Accused persons may also be interviewed as a witness in regard to their knowledge of a related or unrelated offence that they did not commit.

Investigators should always exercise considerable caution when obtaining witness statements from accused persons, as they sometimes falsely implicate others in crimes that they themselves committed to attempt to avoid prosecution, to reduce the number of charges, or to receive a more lenient sentence for the offence they are charged with.

4.1.2 "Interrogation" Defined

The subject of interrogation and the legal requirements of questioning suspects and accused persons will be dealt with in detail in Chapter 5. Interrogation means the formal examination of a suspect or an accused person by questioning. The interrogator (an investigator conducting an interrogation) is no longer in the information-gathering stage of the investigation and is attempting to obtain an admission (a partial admission of a fact or an acknowledgement of guilt) or confession (a full acknowledgement of guilt) from the suspect or accused to establish his or her culpability in the matter under investigation.

4.2   DIFFERENCE BETWEEN INTERVIEWING AND INTERROGATION

There are numerous differences between the techniques used to conduct either an interview or an interrogation.

4.2.1   Nature of Questioning

An interview is non-accusatory in nature as the interviewer is attempting to obtain as much information from the witness, person of interest or suspect as possible, about the incident(s) under investigation. The interviewer is still in the information-gathering stage of the investigation. Interviews are usually conducted both before and after the laying of any criminal charges.

In an interrogation, the officer is no longer concerned with information-gathering and is attempting to obtain an admission or confession from a suspect or an accused. The interrogator should leave no doubt in the subject's mind that the person being interrogated is responsible for either committing the offence or had direct or indirect involvement in its commission. For this reason, victims, witnesses and persons of interest are never interrogated. Interrogations usually precede the laying of criminal charges against a suspect.

4.2.2   Administering the Standard Police Caution

When conducting an interview, there is no legal requirement to caution a witness or person of interest. A suspect or an accused should always be administered the standard police caution to warn them that they are not obliged to give a statement but that anything they say may be used in court, even though there may not be sufficient reasonable grounds upon which to arrest them or upon which to lay a charge.

4.2.3   Advising of Right to Counsel

A police officer is never legally obligated to advise a witness of his or her right to consult with legal counsel. Witnesses will not usually have any reason to consult with a lawyer prior to being interviewed, nor will they wish to have an attorney present during their interview, although it sometimes does occur. Should a witness ever wish to consult with counsel prior to an interview, he or she should always be permitted to. If the witness insists on having an attorney present during his or her interview, it is advisable to oblige the witness's request, rather than to forego the opportunity to interview him or her.

An individual being interrogated (i.e., suspect or accused) should always be advised of his or her right to counsel (whether or not he or she is under arrest) and must be afforded the opportunity to consult with a lawyer, should he or she wish to do so, prior to the interrogation to ensure the admissibility of any subsequent statement.

Prior to or during an interview or an interrogation, a subject may ask, "Do I need a lawyer?" It is recommended that your response should be to the effect, "I'm not able to answer that for you. If you think that you might need a lawyer, then you probably do."

Never recommend any specific attorney to a subject. Always allow the subject to select an attorney either from a telephone directory or from a prepared list of local lawyers.

BOX4.1	Investigative Relevance

The request to consult with or to be represented by counsel made by any subject being questioned, whether he or she is a witness, or is under suspicion, does not (contrary to popular belief) automatically imply anything about the subject (e.g., guilt, innocence or reliability, etc.) other than that the subject wishes to exercise his or her right to legal counsel.

4.2.4 Questions Posed During Interviews and Interrogations

During an interview, the interviewer must ask only open-ended questions and refrain from the use of leading questions to avoid influencing the witness's account of the incident(s) under investigation. The witness may be asked follow-up questions to clarify ambiguities or to attempt to have the witness expand upon his or her account.

During an interrogation, the suspect or accused should not be cross-examined by the interrogator regarding the statement he or she provided; however, clarifying questions may be posed to the suspect or accused for the purpose of clearing up any ambiguity in his or her statement.

4.2.5 Recording of the Statement

During an interview, one technique is to ask the witness a series of questions to assess the scope of his or her knowledge of the incident under investigation, prior to the formal taking of a statement, either in writing or through audio or videotape. The alternative is to proceed directly with the handwritten or electronically recorded statement. The normally handwritten statement should always be audio taped or videotaped if the witness is related or is closely associated to the suspect or accused, and there is any possibility that the witness may later recant his or her statement.

An interrogation should always be audio or videotaped (from beginning to end) where the equipment is available and where it is practicable to do so. The taking of a statement following an interrogation may be handwritten; however, the entire process should also be either audio or videotaped to prove to the court that the statement was voluntary.

4.2.6 Voluntariness of Statement

No witness, person of interest, suspect or accused is ever obligated to consent to being interviewed or interrogated. Normally, the Crown is not required to prove the voluntariness of a witness statement. However, the voluntariness of the statement of an accused must always, first, be proven to be voluntary prior to it being admissible as evidence.

4.3 WITNESS INTERVIEWS

As previously stated, proficiency in the art of interviewing witnesses is one of the most valuable tools an investigator requires. It is from this segment of the investigation that the majority of information is gathered that will assist in bringing the case to a successful conclusion. To be effective in this field of investigation, the investigator must have a basic understanding of human behavioural characteristics, maintain a positive attitude and remain ever mindful of the nature and extent of human frailties.

A witness interview is markedly different from an interrogation of a suspect or an accused person. During an interview, the interviewer is free to ask any question of a witness regarding the investigation being conducted. A witness is not administered a formal statement caution and the interviewer is free to seek as much information as possible from the witness in order to assist him or her in the investigation of the offence.

The principal rule of interviewing is, however, that at any time an interview may turn into an interrogation. An example of this would be during the interview of a person of interest or of a suspect, during which the subject tells one or more obvious lies or discloses information that, in the opinion of the investigator, only the actual offender would know. During every interview, always act in a professional manner and treat the individual being interviewed with respect and dignity at all times.

Special categories of witnesses, such as the developmentally challenged, child victims, people with learning disabilities and anyone in need of particular consideration, will require special considerations and must be dealt with using extra care. There will be times when, encountering such a witness, an investigator will have to seek the guidance of an interviewer (e.g., a Children's Aid case worker) who is specially trained in conducting interviews with these types of witnesses. If such expertise is available in your area, do not hesitate to avail yourself of it.

If any witness requires the services of an interpreter or a support person, as in the case of a sexual assault victim accompanied by a support person or trauma counsellor, do not hesitate to involve such persons, if these services are available in your area.

4.3.1 Principles of Memory

For a witness to reliably and accurately recall an incident or event, it must first have been committed to his or her memory. There are two main categories of memory: **episodic memory** (i.e., a witness's memory of an event) and **procedural memory**, such as the repetitive learning of a skill (e.g., children learning the alphabet or learning to tie their shoes). For the purposes of investigative interviewing, we are more concerned with episodic memory, being the manner through which witnesses recall incidents.

In order for an event to register in a witness's memory, the event must initially create an impression (i.e., a memory trace) through perception involving one or more of their five senses. This is referred to as the memory acquisition, or encoding process. If an event fails to make an impression and register in the witness's memory, the witness will not have any reason to recall it, nor will he or she likely be able to recall it successfully, without the assistance of questioning.

The next process that impacts on a witness's memory is the retention or storage of the memory trace, and whether it was committed to short-term memory or to long-term memory. Human beings have the ability to store only six to eight items in short-term memory, and then only for a matter of minutes. Most memory loss occurs within minutes (e.g., looking up a telephone number in a telephone book, using it once, and having to look it up a second time) unless the memory trace becomes stored in long-term memory.

The human mind has the ability to retain extremely large numbers of memory traces in long-term memory. Think of all of the addresses, names, telephone numbers, details and vocabulary that you are able to recall from memory. Whether or not a witness is able to recall significant details, however, has much to do with their intention to remember the details of the event.[5]

If the witness is aware that something noteworthy is about to occur, he or she will be more attentive to the specific details of the incident. Similarly, if there is a perception on the part of the witness that there will be a need to remember the event (e.g., for subsequent investigative or court purposes) he or she will more likely be motivated to recall the details of the event.

A witness may have been able to commit a memory trace to long-term memory through "rehearsing" it (i.e., repeating it to him or herself) if the witness was not in a position to commit it to writing at the time of the event. Another process that assists witnesses in committing certain details to memory is through associating the detail with a previously known memory.

BOX 4.2	**Proper Investigative Procedure**

If a witness is able to record information in writing at or shortly after the time of the incident, such as the licence number of a suspect vehicle, etc., the actual writing should	be signed and dated by the witness and seized as evidence, whether it is on a scrap piece of paper, cigarette package or in any other form.

Not all witnesses have good memories and yet it is sometimes possible, through effective and repetitive questioning, to have a witness accurately recall facts they perhaps didn't realize they had committed to memory or might have merely forgotten. The key to "tapping" into a witness's memory is to find the appropriate association (e.g., the association between time and place, or time and the witness's activities) to trigger the memory of the idea, if in fact there is a memory of it.

4.3.2 Factors that Affect Memory

Memory will decay as the result of a lengthy "retention interval" (i.e., the passage of time between the acquisition/encoding process and the actual retrieval of the memory). Memory may also degrade through the process of natural selectivity. We experience many things throughout our life and tend to remember only those things that we believe are important to us at the time.

---

[5]Hopper (2003).

A witness's memory may be affected by their emotional state at the time of the incident or through impairment by alcohol, drugs or even fatigue. Memory may be impaired or totally destroyed as the result of a head injury, creating **amnesia** (a temporary or permanent loss of memory). In neurological cases involving trauma to the brain, be guided by the advice of medical experts.

4.3.3 Leading Questions

One way to alter a witness's memory is to influence their memory through the asking of "leading questions." A leading question is one where the very question itself suggests the answer to the question. For example, "How fast was the car going?" – implies that the car was, in fact, travelling at a high rate of speed; or, "Was the car that you saw a black one?" – implies to the witness that the car was, in fact, black in colour.

In the November 2003 issue of *American Psychologist*, Dr. Elizabeth F. Loftus, a renowned researcher on the topic of implanted memory for over 30 years, is quoted as stating: "In fact, leading questions are only one way to distort memory." Dr. Loftus goes on to say, "Related studies showed that memory could become skewed with various techniques that fed misinformation to unsuspecting [subjects]."

Several studies have shown many instances of interviewers and psychotherapists "implanting memory" in witnesses by supplying him or her with false information. When people are confronted by an authority figure, they may either become susceptible to wanting to do what is expected of them or not wanting to appear to remember things differently from others. Always remember, it is the witness's version of the event that we want to obtain – anything else is unacceptable.

Implanted memory is also seen when witnesses, at a crime scene, are not separated prior to being questioned. If the witnesses are allowed to speak to each other regarding their perception of the incident or event, or are allowed to hear the responses of other witnesses, it is virtually guaranteed that witnesses, including police officers, may begin to combine elements of other witness's stories into their own accounts. They may often begin to believe the revised "facts" as if they had witnessed the event in a different way.

4.3.4 Witness Suggestibility

In many cases, it will become necessary to interview child witnesses or witnesses with learning disabilities or developmental handicaps, etc. The investigator must remember that many young children have very active imaginations but very little life experience. Young children tend to embellish stories and may be very susceptible to wishing to please, or appear knowledgeable to, adult authority figures. "[Y]ounger children's memories tend to be less reliable than older children's, and older children's memories tend to be less reliable than adults'. [T]his does not mean that children's memories are too unreliable for accurate testimony in legal proceedings."[6]

The same basic rules of interviewing apply to children as to adults. Both adults and children may be suggestible to some degree but extra caution must be exercised as children are even more suggestible than adults and tend to give responses influenced by what they believe the interviewer wants or expects them to say.

---

[6]Lowenstein (2004).

- Ask only open-ended questions (i.e., those questions that minimize the possibility of suggestion to the subject being interviewed). Open-ended questions call for a more thorough and complete answer (e.g., "Can you describe what the car looked like?" or, "Can you describe what clothing the person was wearing?" etc.)

    – Who...? "Who was there when you arrived?"

    – What...? "What colour was the car?"

    – Where...? "Where were you standing at the time?"

    – When...? "When did you finish work for the day?"

    – How...? "How did the man enter your house?"

- Avoid the use of leading questions, (i.e., questions that suggest or invite a specific answer).

    – "Who was there? Was Mary there?"

    – "What threats did the person make to you?"

    – "Where did he hit you? In the face?"

    – "When did the person start robbing the store?"

    – "How fast was he driving the car?"

An investigator is never required to necessarily accept the witness's first answer to any question until the investigator is certain that no additional information is forthcoming or the witness remains steadfast in the details of his or her account. Sometimes, a witness's vague memory of an event can be enhanced, allowing him or her to accurately recall additional details when he or she is asked the same question more than once or in different ways. This issue will be addressed in more detail during the discussion of interviewing techniques.

4.4   THE "90-10 RULE"

The interviewer must always bear in mind the "90–10 Rule," which means that during an interview, the individual being interviewed should do 90 per cent of the talking, while the interviewer does no more than 10 per cent of the talking. After all, the interviewer should be attempting to gather information – a difficult thing to do when the interviewer is doing most of the talking, instead of vice versa. The "90–10 Rule" is substantially reversed during an interrogation, as the interrogator is no longer seeking information, but is attempting to obtain an admission or confession from a suspect or accused person.[7]

4.5   PRINCIPLES OF INTERVIEWING

You will not become an expert interviewer as the result of reading this chapter on interviewing, or any of several books dedicated to the subject of interviewing. Interviewing

---

[7]Sapir (2000).

skills are learned by constant practice and by continually striving to improve the necessary skills that need to be developed on the path to becoming a competent interviewer. Expect that you will make mistakes – and that's all right – providing that mistakes are learned from and are not repeated.

Following every interview, in addition to evaluating the validity of the information obtained, a competent interviewer should always critique his or her performance during the interview. What could have been done differently or better? What lessons were learned? What will you do differently next time? Self-evaluation and self-improvement are desirable traits in a professional interviewer.

The interviewer should approach each and every interview with an open mind. Our personal reactions to people, as individuals, greatly influence our judgment about what they have to say to us. Every victim, witness and person of interest deserves a fair hearing.

An interviewer is never permitted to impose his or her own personal values or beliefs upon any subject being interviewed. Listen carefully to every subject being interviewed and respond to him or her impartially and without prejudice. Information obtained during an interview should always be tested against what the interviewer already knows or can be reasonably established.

The interviewer needs to strike the appropriate balance between accepting, at face value, what the witness says (unless it contradicts previously known information that has already been confirmed) and being mindful that some witnesses may intentionally or selectively withhold information, for any number of reasons, from their account. There are, of course, other persons who intentionally attempt to deceive an interviewer.

An effective interviewer is skilled in obtaining all possible information from subjects, recognizing where sensitive information may have been omitted and recognizing signs of possible deception. Always bear in mind the rule that "just because someone says it's so, doesn't make it so."

One common mistake made by interviewers who are unsuccessful in obtaining all possible information from the subject of an interview is in not asking the right questions. Knowledge of the facts in issue of the offence under investigation will ensure that relevant witnesses are asked questions that will reveal evidence to prove the offence in court. Another common mistake made is assuming that a subject of an interview or an interrogation will not be willing to speak to you.

Until the subject absolutely refuses to talk (i.e., refuses to answer or requests to speak to a lawyer before answering any questions) the interviewer should assume that everyone will be willing to speak to him or her. In fact, according to Avinoam Sapir, founder of the Scientific Content Analysis method, "The more the [interviewer] expects the subject to talk, the higher the probability is that the subject *will* talk" (emphasis added).

Generally, human nature indicates that people readily respond better to people whom they trust and respect. Consider persons whom you have known in your past (e.g., teachers, peers, or employers who you respected and for whom you gave a far greater effort than those who did not earn your respect). This same principle holds true for interviewing. An interviewer will be far more successful if he or she can gain the trust and respect of the subject being interviewed.

It may be an extremely difficult thing for a victim or witness to reveal intimate or shocking details of his or her victimization (e.g., a sexual assault) to a total stranger, especially to an authority figure. An interviewer who takes the time to establish a professional rapport with the witness and is respectful of his or her situation and who demonstrates a sincere interest in the witness's account will be far more effective than one who appears distant, unsympathetic, uninterested or uncomfortable with what he or she has to say.

Two words of caution must be injected at this point. First, prior to interviewing potential witnesses at a crime scene, or shortly after a crime has occurred, separate all parties at the earliest possible opportunity to minimize the likelihood that they will compare their stories and adopt the details of another's version. Second, unless it is absolutely unavoidable, never interview a potential witness in the presence of another potential witness.

In the early morning hours of December 24, 1990, 14-year-old Tammy Lynn Homolka suddenly collapsed into respiratory arrest at her St. Catharines, Ontario residence. Her parents and one older sister were upstairs in the house, asleep at the time. Tammy Homolka could not be revived and was pronounced dead 18 minutes after her arrival at St. Catharines General Hospital. The incident involving Tammy had occurred in the presence of another older sister, Karla, and Karla's fiancé, Paul Bernardo. The coroner later concluded that Tammy Homolka's death was due to "natural causes."

It is now known that Karla Homolka and Paul Bernardo had secretly drugged Tammy with the sedative Halcion, and had both sexually assaulted the 14-year-old, videotaping much of the incident. Upon the arrival of police, Karla Homolka and Bernardo were questioned together and were able to compare their stories, knowing what the other was saying to the authorities.

"It has been suggested that someone should have ensured that Bernardo and Homolka were kept separate and apart before the interview. There is no directive that requires that all witnesses involved in a sudden death (or any investigation for that matter), particularly family members, should be separated. It may or may not be prudent to do so and it cannot be stated categorically that it is an error not to do so, particularly when they have already been together before the arrival of the police."[8]

Had Homolka and Bernardo been separated, however, upon the arrival of the police, even though they had been together for some time "before the arrival of the police," each would *not* have known what the other was saying to the investigators. There might also have been the chance that investigators could possibly have detected discrepancies between their accounts. The point to be made here is, by questioning Homolka and Bernardo together, the investigators compromised their ability to detect possible signs of deception in the accounts of the persons now known to be responsible for Tammy's death.

It did not become known, until the re-investigation of Tammy's death (once Bernardo had been identified as the Scarborough Rapist, a series of brutal sexual assaults that occurred in Toronto between 1987 and 1990, and as the prime suspect in the 1991–1992 abductions and murders of Leslie Mahaffy and Kristen French), that Bernardo had originally informed two ambulance attendants of a 15–20 minute delay between the time

---

[8]Campbell (1996) p. 75.

that Tammy collapsed and the time that the incident was reported. Bernardo and Homolka intentionally omitted this detail during their subsequent account to police to avoid raising further suspicion. Unfortunately, the two ambulance attendants were not interviewed by police during the initial investigation.

"Even if further checking had led [the assigned investigator] to question Homolka and Bernardo more closely, it is difficult to say that the result would have been different. He had no evidence against them, and no leverage to work with. It is purely speculative to suggest that further questioning of either Bernardo or Homolka would have revealed the truth about Tammy's death."[9]

It is not the intent of this book to criticize anyone. It would be grossly unfair, knowing now that Bernardo was responsible for sexually assaulting 18 women and killing 3 women, in three different police jurisdictions, to sit back, armed with information not known to the original investigators, and criticize their actions – because we weren't there. It is, however, strongly recommended that when persons (e.g., two emergency services professionals) are known to have had contact at the scene with individuals involved in a serious occurrence, they should always be interviewed.

Had the discrepancy regarding the times between Tammy's collapse and the 9-1-1 call become known earlier, even though at the time no evidence existed against Bernardo or Homolka, the mere awareness of the discrepancy might have raised a certain amount of suspicion. Discrepancies in a subject's account of an event might indicate a high probability of deception, as the details could be fabricated and do not come from actual memory. Every word spoken by a person of interest or a suspect can be significant to the investigation. Possible indicators of deception will be discussed in Chapter 5.

One of the best ways to establish initial rapport with witnesses is to ask them how they wish to be addressed. The witness may be asked, "May I call you [John or Mary]?" Otherwise, address the witness formally as "Mr," "Mrs," "Ms.," etc. Most people like to be called by their name and doing so will personalize the experience for them while maintaining a professional approach.

First impressions created by the interviewer by presenting a well-groomed appearance and courteous but professional manner will help set the stage for obtaining a full and complete account from a co-operative witness. Always display confidence during an interview – never give the appearance of being uncertain or confused. Again, always be courteous, respectful and treat every witness with dignity, regardless of their social standing, background or lifestyle.

4.6 STRUCTURE OF THE INVESTIGATIVE INTERVIEW

Every person from whom information is sought during the course of an investigation should be interviewed. Investigators may speak briefly to a large number of people in order to determine the person(s) from whom formal statements should be obtained. Many investigators have their own personal preferences in interview styles. The following is the structure that I used very successfully over the course of a 30-year policing career.

---

[9]Ibid., p. 90.

4.6.1   Field Interviews

The initial contact with many victims and witnesses is in the form of a **field interview** by an investigator or a first responding police officer. A field interview involves the preliminary questioning of a victim, witness or bystander at or near the scene of a crime to identify the participants of an event and to determine the essence of their involvement in the incident under investigation. Field interviews differ from investigative interviews in purpose, duration and the amount of planning and structure involved in them.

The information obtained during a field interview is recorded, at a minimum, in point form in the officer's investigative notebook and possibly also in the form of a brief written statement (if time permits). Field interviews determine the significance of a subject's involvement and may require re-interview by an investigator at a later time and date, in the form of a formal investigative interview for the purpose of obtaining a full statement from the witness.

4.6.2   Investigative Interviews

It is essential that investigative interviews be conducted in a methodical manner. Except for the initial field interview of witnesses and bystanders at the scene of a crime, investigative interviews should be structured in a manner similar to that described in the comprehensive P.E.A.C.E. model, developed by the National Crime Faculty, Bramshill, England.

The mnemonic (a device used to aid in remembering things) P.E.A.C.E. stands for:

Planning and Preparation;

Engage and Explain;

Account, Clarification and Challenge;

Closure; and

Evaluation.

4.6.3   Planning and Preparation

The success in obtaining complete, reliable and accurate information from any interview will increase in direct proportion to the amount of planning and preparation that occurs in advance of the actual interview, to the extent that it is possible to do so. Because of time constraints or sheer operational demands, it may not always be possible to plan every interview to the extent discussed.

Even if a witness at a crime scene is only subject to a preliminary field interview at the time of first contact with investigators, some degree of planning will benefit any proposed re-interview of the witness at a later time. Where the opportunity to plan and prepare for an interview does exist, the interviewer will do well to adhere to as many of the following considerations as possible.

Regardless of the number of interviews to be conducted during an investigation, an interviewer should carefully define the objectives of each interview based on the anticipation of what a particular witness might be able to say. For example, consider whether it is likely that the witness may provide evidence of: one or more of the facts in issue, (the *actus reus* - what occurred); the *mens rea* (the criminal intent, if any, of the person[s] responsible); or the ***modus operandi*** (how the offence, if any, was committed). The interviewer should ask himself or herself the questions, "Why is it necessary to interview this witness?," and "What information is it possible to obtain from this witness?"

The next question the interviewer should ask him or herself is, "Why interview this particular witness at this time?" Witnesses should be interviewed with some plan in mind based upon a methodical approach to the appropriate sequencing of all interviews. "Is this the correct time to interview this witness or do I need more information concerning the event(s) before interviewing this witness?" As no two investigations are exactly the same, it isn't possible to provide a checklist or guidelines that would apply to every possible situation.

To the extent possible, assemble whatever information is known about the case under investigation prior to the interview of any witness. The interviewer should know as much as possible about the case before speaking to any witness. Review (and verify) all available information from police reports, photographs of the crime scene and discussions with other investigators, etc.

Along this same line, it is essential that an investigator know as much information as possible about the background of the witness prior to engaging him or her in an interview. Is the witness associated with the suspect in any way? What is the witness's occupation? Does the witness have a criminal record? Has the witness been previously interviewed during this investigation and, if so, what was said by him or her at that time?

Where is the best location to conduct the interview? You may wish to conduct important interviews at a police station where absolute privacy can be assured, and with the availability of audio or video recording equipment. A police station represents a far more controlled environment for an investigative interview free from interruptions of other family members, such as young children, and time constraints. It also restricts the number of people who can overhear (and then later repeat) what the witness disclosed to the investigation.

If possible, you might allow the witness to choose the time and place of the interview, within reason, as he or she may not wish to be interviewed in close proximity to family, co-workers or associates. Some witnesses might not even want their friends and associates to know that they are being interviewed by the police.

Privacy is of the utmost concern in any interview, but if a vulnerable person (e.g., a young child, sexual assault victim, or a developmentally challenged person) prefers to have a support person accompany him or her it is recommended that these wishes be respected. If a witness requires a translator, arrangements should be made in advance to have a qualified and competent translator present. "The victim of a sexual assault shall be asked if he or she would prefer to be interviewed by an officer of a particular gender if [a qualified officer of that gender is] available."[10]

---

[10]Ministry of Community Safety and Correctional Services: *Ontario Major Case Management (MCM) Manual* (Oct 1, 2004), p. 38.

4.6.4 Engage and Explain

Assume now that the planning and preparation phase of an interview is complete and the witness has been contacted, has agreed to speak with you, and has attended your police service for the purpose of being interviewed. This may be your first meeting with the witness, or you may be dealing with someone with whom you have had prior dealings.

This is the rapport building phase of the interview in which you have the opportunity to establish an atmosphere of cooperation with the witness. The interviewer should always shake hands with the witness and introduce any other police officer who will be participating in the interview. You might offer the witness refreshment, such as coffee, etc., if available, or direct him or her to a restroom, if needed, to avoid interrupting the momentum of the interview once it begins. If the witness is under emotional stress or is under the influence of an intoxicating substance, you may need to consider postponing the interview until the witness is in a proper state of mind.

Acknowledge the witness's cooperation by attending the interview location to assist with the investigation. As previously stated, establish how the witness prefers to be addressed or called. Spend a moment conversing with the witness. Your inquiries about the witness's background should have given you some information to ask about, such as his or her family, occupation, etc. If nothing else, make some comment about the weather or ask about any concerns he or she might have to help put the witness at ease. It is not sufficient for an interviewer to merely act sincere – the interviewer must be sincere.

Explain the purpose of the interview to the witness, even if the reason may seem obvious to you. Explain to the witness why he or she is being interviewed, and how the interview will be conducted. Inform the witness that what he or she says will be written down or request the witness's permission to make an audio or videotape of the interview, if it is your intention or departmental policy to do so. Explain to the witness that at the end of his or her account you will ask clarifying questions, if needed, following which, he or she will be given the opportunity to review and make changes to the interview before being asked to sign his or her statement. Finally, ask the witness if he or she is ready to begin.

4.6.5 Account, Clarification and Challenge

Whether the witness's statement is to be hand-written, audio taped or videotaped, begin by recording: the date; location of interview; full names of all persons present; any other personal information, including the witness's date of birth, address and contact telephone numbers; and the start time of the interview. At the conclusion of the interview, the end time should also be recorded. "Where the subject of the interview has relevant information pertaining to the investigation, a written statement, at a minimum, shall be obtained."[11]

If the interview is to be recorded on audio tape or videotape, the witness must be advised that the interview is being recorded. "Consent of the subject is not required, but if the person objects to the interview being [electronically recorded], the interviewer may decide whether to continue the interview without the aid of the videotape."[12] The

---

[11]Ministry of Community Safety and Correctional Services: *Ontario Major Case Management (MCM) Manual* (undated), p. 40.

[12]Ibid.

interviewer should always give strong consideration to electronically recording interviews with child witnesses, any witness who may later retract his or her statement, and those of any person(s) in custody.

It is at this crucial stage of the interview that the subject's uninterrupted account, in his or her own words, is obtained. If the statement is being hand-written, record the words of the witness verbatim (in exactly the same words). In the case of a hand-written statement, if the subject uses vulgar or profane language, it should be written down exactly as the witness stated it.

If the subject relates conversation he or she had with another person, the written statement should contain the exact words spoken by each party in quotation marks. For example, if a victim states, "…then he pulled out a revolver and said he was going to kill me," the witness should be asked for the exact words spoken (especially by offenders) which would be written as, "…then he pulled out a revolver and said, 'I'm going to kill you.'" Quotes attributed to people, if recalled, should be written in the first-person singular. Even if the statement is being audio taped or videotaped, the witness should be asked to state the exact words that he or she heard – and not be allowed to paraphrase them.

The interviewer must exercise the 90–10 Rule during the interview and listen intently to what the subject is saying. Many subjects will ask, "Where would you like me to start?," at which point, the interviewer may reply, "Wherever you wish," or, "Start from the time you got up that morning," or "from the time you got off work," or "from the time you left your house," etc.

Brief questions may be asked to assist the subject from time to time. However, remember that it is the subject's account of the incident that you are trying to obtain and the subject should be allowed to give his or her version of the event. Never ask more than one question at a time and allow the subject being interviewed an adequate period of time to give his or her response before asking another question.

The interviewer must never display shock or surprise in response to any detail, no matter how bizarre or horrific it might seem, or to any otherwise unexpected new piece of information that the subject may disclose during the interview. Always remain professional, composed, focused and interested in what the subject has to say.

Encourage the subject to continue his or her uninterrupted account by using both verbal and non-verbal prompts, such as, "Go on," "Continue," "Uh-hum," "Then what happened?," etc.,) until they stop, at which point they will usually indicate they are finished with words such as, "And that's about it, I guess."

Most subjects tend to give incomplete or edited answers and may leave out important details or may arrange them in the wrong sequence. As the subject gives his or her uninterrupted version of the events, make note of points that you wish the subject to expand on. Once the subject has finished his or her uninterrupted version, the interviewer may now ask questions to expand and clarify the subject's account and sequence of the event. Always allow the subject the opportunity to consider his or her answers to every question. Long pauses don't necessarily indicate deception on the part of the subject. The subject may be legitimately recalling details from memory or may be formulating his or her response.

When formulating a question to pose to a subject, it is important to "mirror" the subject's own language (except the use of profanity or derogatory or racial slurs, if any, unless it is to repeat actual conversation spoken during the course of the event under investigation). For example, if the subject refers to people as "guys," so should you. If the subject uses a particular manner of speech, providing it is not offensive, using the same language will demonstrate to the witness that what he or she has to say is important and that you are not being judgmental of them.

During the clarification phase, it is quite proper to ask a subject, "Earlier in your statement, you said, 'I left work at the usual time and went home.' What else can you tell me about that?" The interviewer is attempting to establish what is meant by the usual time, the location of his or her workplace, the subject's method of transportation, who else might have accompanied him or her, the subject's route, any stops the subject may have made along the way and his or her time of arrival home. Clearly, from the subject's initial response, there is additional information that can be obtained.

During the clarification phase of the interview, the interviewer must ensure that he or she has obtained answers to, at a minimum, all of the following points:

- Where, exactly, was the subject when he or she perceived the information?

- What was the distance between the subject and the event he or she perceived?

- What were the prevailing weather conditions at the time?

- What were the lighting conditions at the time?

- Where there any visual obstructions between the subject and the event (that might have obscured the witness's line of sight)?

- Was any of the information perceived by the subject previously known to him or her (e.g., the identity of either the victim or the person responsible for the incident)?

- How long has it been since the subject perceived the incident?

Do not focus strictly on what the subject observed visually. Remember to ask the subject if he or she perceived any information by using his or her other senses. Never interrupt a pause before a response is given by asking another question. If a question is important enough to ask, it is equally important to wait for the subject's response. If you ask any question, listen carefully to the subject's response to ensure that the response he or she gives answers the question that was asked. If the subject's response didn't answer the question that was asked, merely ask it again (and again, if necessary) until a proper response is obtained.

It may assist a subject if you ask him or her to recall certain additional details during the interview about his or her activities before, during and following the event that may have had little, if anything, to do with the incident under investigation. These details may assist the subject, months or years later, while refreshing his or her memory from his or her statement, to make associations to help put the incident into context and recall important or forgotten details from his or her long-term memory.

For example, if the subject was watching television, what program was on? Was anyone else present with the subject? What was the purpose of his or her car ride on the way to the location where he or she became a witness to the event? Demonstrating this type of attention to detail may help to convince the subject that you are diligently seeking all possible information and may prompt him or her to include details they believed were too insignificant to discuss.

If the subject has stated anything that is inconsistent with known details of the case (e.g., the **corroborated** evidence of other witnesses) it may be necessary to "challenge" the subject's version. It may be that the subject is deliberately withholding information or is intentionally providing false details of the event. A challenge to any information stated by the subject should come at a late stage of the interview, once you have the main account provided by the subject committed to writing/recording.

One technique of clarifying a subject's statement is to have the subject draw a sketch of the location where the event occurred and mark relevant locations of acts or movements of participants at crucial times. If time permits, a (not to scale) drawing should be prepared in advance and provided to the subject for this purpose. This technique is particularly useful when interviewing multiple subjects (individually, of course) who witnessed the same event. Once the individual subject makes his or her notations on the diagram, it should be signed and dated by both the subject and the interviewer and appended to the subject's statement to refresh the subject's memory if he or she is required to testify in court.

All challenges to anything a subject has stated should be conducted in a non-accusatory manner to avoid losing the relationship of trust that was established during the "engage and explain" phase of the interview. The interviewer should merely attempt to establish if there is any reason why certain witnesses viewed all or part of an event differently from the subject of the interview; and the subject may indeed have an explanation to offer. Perhaps the subject may correct what he or she previously stated or may even add additional details to what he or she has already stated.

If the subject being interviewed is a person of interest, even if he or she has not been cautioned, it is quite permissible for the interviewer to put "The Question" to him or her (e.g., "Did you take the money?", "Did you kill Jane?", etc.) Once "The Question" has been asked, the interviewer, including any police officer participating in the interview, is never allowed to be the first one to speak and break the silence.

The subject's reaction to the question and his or her next response may be absolutely critical in determining whether the witness is being truthful or deceptive. A refusal to answer the question or hanging his or her head, followed by a long pause, may indicate that this is the appropriate time for the interviewer to change tactics and move into an interrogation. The subject's next response might be a full confession that requires him or her to be cautioned but may be instrumental in solving the case – and only because somebody asked "The Question."

A recommended question to ask a subject at the end of the interview is, "Except for those questions that I have asked you, is there anything else you can tell me?" Or, simply, "Is there anything else you can tell me that I haven't asked you?" Some subjects may possess valuable information and may not volunteer it, simply because, "You didn't ask me that."

4.6.6 Closure

The "closure" phase has been reached when the interviewer has determined that the objectives of the interview have been achieved and no further possible information can likely be obtained at that time. The main purpose of the closure phase is to achieve consensus as to what information was stated during the account, clarification and challenge phase of the interview.

If, at any time during the closure phase, it appears that the subject has recalled additional information, or the interviewer thinks of an additional line of inquiry, the interviewer should automatically revert to the "account, clarification and challenge" phase to include the additional information in the subject's statement. If the subject's statement was taken down in writing, it would be at this stage of the interview that the subject should be invited to read his or her statement or, alternatively, the interviewer should read the statement to the subject.

If the subject elects to read aloud his or her own statement, he or she might be asked to read a passage aloud to prove fluency in the language in which the statement was written. It is recommended that a subject always be asked, "Now that you have read your statement [or had your statement read back to you], is there anything you wish to add, change or delete?"

Should the subject wish any changes be made, the relevant words or passage should be struck out with a single line strike-though that is then initialled by both the subject and the interviewer. The correction should then be made to the subject's satisfaction. If the subject adopts his or her statement, the subject should be requested to sign his or her statement as well as every page in the margin and initial any strike-throughs resulting from inadvertent mistakes made by the interviewer during the writing of the statement.

Subjects should then be informed, to the extent possible, what will happen next. In unsolved cases, it might only be said that the investigation will continue. The subject may be advised that if required to testify as a witness in court at a later date, he or she will be contacted in advance. Always "leave the door open" to the possibility that the subject may be re-contacted should additional information be required and make every effort to obtain his or her agreement to be re-interviewed, if necessary.

Conversely, the subject should be made to feel welcome to contact the investigator in the event he or she recalls additional information that was not included in his or her previous statement. The subject should be provided with the name and contact number of an investigator for that purpose. It is sometimes problematic, when a case reaches court, to have multiple statements from the same subject, especially when discrepancies are involved between the accounts. Remember that YOU did not create the discrepancies. YOU are not the trier of fact in the case. Leave that responsibility up to the judge or the jury, as the case may be. You are only charged with the task of seeking the truth.

4.6.7 Evaluation

"When you've eliminated the impossible, whatever remains, however improbable, must be the truth."

Sherlock Holmes.[13]

Once the official interview has been concluded and the interviewer and subject have parted company, the information obtained from the interview needs to be evaluated in terms of whether or not any new information was obtained and the effect, if any, the

---

[13]Sherlock Holmes quote from *The Sign of Four* by Sir Arthur Conan Doyle (1859-1930). Quoted in Darden 1996.

interview has had on the investigation as a whole. Is the information obtained consistent with the previously known details of the case? Does the information create any conflicts with previously obtained information that now need to be verified and/or resolved?

Was any new information obtained during the interview that changes the focus of the investigation or presents new avenues of investigation to follow-up, such as previously unknown witnesses that now need to be interviewed, or physical evidence that may require the issuance of a search warrant, etc.? The information obtained must be evaluated in terms of accuracy, sufficiency, credibility and reliability.

Is the information obtained accurate (i.e., consistent with other known facts of the case)? Is the information obtained sufficient (i.e., enough information of sufficient detail)? Is the information credible (i.e., could the subject's account believably have occurred in the manner in which the subject related it during the interview)? Is the subject's account reliable (i.e., trustworthy and free from factors, such as intoxication or bias motivated by self-interest, which would render his or her version of the event questionable)? Can the details of the subject's account be verified by independent sources or other previously known information?

It is useful to summarize the witness's statement (when preparing a court brief) in a separate document referred to as a Will Say statement. A Will Say is a point form summary prepared to assist the Crown Attorney and the defence quickly to review the main points of testimony that a witness is capable of testifying to and includes any evidence, in any form, regarding any of the facts in issue of the case (e.g., verbal statements by a suspect that the witness overheard, and any physical evidence that the witness has knowledge of).

Multiple statements by a single witness may be consolidated into a single Will Say statement. In addition to forming an essential part of the court brief, the Will Say may also assist the investigative function by summarizing lengthy statements in a "quick-reference" format.

"Where an electronically recorded statement is not transcribed [written or typed word-for-word], a detailed written summary of the relevant information from the interview shall be [prepared]."[14]

4.6.8 Indexing

Depending on the case load of the investigator(s) assigned to a case, the gravity of the offence under investigation and the volume of statements obtained, the Case Manager should strongly consider the need to have relevant information from witness interviews (and tips from the public) indexed in some retrievable form. If the case is a Major Case criteria offence (e.g., homicides and attempts; sexual assaults and attempts, etc.) as defined, for instance, in the Ontario Major Case Management Manual[15], all statements should be entered into the MCM Database using the standard case management software, *Xanalys Investigation Manager*™ (formerly known as *PowerCase*™) by Xanalys LLC. Information entered into the MCM software may then be indexed and researched.

---

[14]Ministry of Community Safety and Correctional Services: *Ontario Major Case Management (MCM) Manual* (Oct. 1, 2004), p. 38.

[15]Ibid., p. 7.

When case management software is not used to organize the large volumes of information that are collected during a complex investigation, it is only a matter of time before crucial pieces of information become lost in the vast collection of statements and someone asks the inevitable question, "Which witness mentioned the red truck?" The solution is simple – the evidence must be indexed. It is of no use to an investigation to have vital information yet not be able to manage it, retrieve it and analyze it.

One simple form of indexing is to have a designated indexer work through each and every statement, extracting important or potentially important items such as names, addresses, telephone numbers, vehicles, etc., and document them. If resources are scarce, a manageable (but time-consuming) method is to record these items on ordinary index cards, which can be searched as needed. Indexing will be discussed in further detail in Chapter 12: Major Case Management.

4.7   UNCO-OPERATIVE WITNESSES

While the majority of witnesses interviewed during the course of an investigation will usually be co-operative, it would be a mistake to assume that this will always be the case. Certain witnesses may be hesitant or reluctant to co-operate with the investigation for a number of possible reasons.

The person being questioned as a possible witness may actually be the person responsible for committing the offence under investigation, or may be **party to the offence**. This individual will obviously attempt to avoid self-incrimination. The subject being interviewed may be related to or be associated with a known or unknown suspect (e.g., a friend, family member or relative, etc.) and he or she may be unco-operative with investigators in an attempt to protect the suspect.

Genuine witnesses or individuals making false allegations of crimes may appear to be co-operative but, if motivated by revenge, may either falsely implicate someone in a crime or knowingly embellish the details of a crime. Witnesses may not wish to co-operate with an investigation due to a reluctance to become involved in the case or an unwillingness to testify in court.

Finally, victims may disclose the details of their victimization incrementally until they trust that the interviewer will believe everything they have to say. The witness may not wish to discuss the case at all, purely due to the sensitive and embarrassing nature of the details of the event (e.g., having been the victim of a sexual assault).

Unless the subject absolutely refuses to be interviewed, the interviewer must attempt to persuade him or her from their "unwilling" stance to a position where the subject is willing to co-operate with the investigation. While there are no hard and fast rules of how to accomplish this feat, it underscores the importance of establishing a rapport with the subject, maintaining a professional confidence in adverse situations and the need to convince the subject of the interviewer's genuine interest in seeking the truth.

Be confident. Be professional. Be persistent. Don't be discouraged by a subject's initial unwillingness to co-operate, and above all, don't ever be hesitant to ask the relevant questions that need to be answered.

4.7.1   KGB Statement Guidelines[16]

In the case of *Regina v. KGB*, (the name of the accused, a **young offender**, is identified only by his initials to protect his identity) four young men were involved in a fight with two other men. During the course of the fight, the accused pulled a knife and fatally stabbed one of the men before fleeing the scene with his three friends. Two weeks later, KGB's three friends, each accompanied by a parent, were interviewed separately on videotape by the police. In each of their statements, they indicated to the police that KGB had made statements to them acknowledging responsibility for the stabbing. Based largely on the three videotaped statements, KGB was arrested and charged with second-degree murder.

During the trial, the three youths recanted their videotaped statements and testified that they had lied to the police about the confessions made to them by KGB. Under existing common law, the prior inconsistent statements of the witnesses could only be used to challenge their credibility but could not be used as proof that KGB had actually confessed to the stabbing. In the absence of other evidence, the trial judge acquitted KGB, a decision that was upheld by the Ontario Court of Appeal.

In February 1993, the Supreme Court of Canada overturned the acquittal and ordered a new trial. The Supreme Court stated that the three prior inconsistent statements could be used as evidence of proof of the truth that KGB was the person who had caused the fatal wound to the victim, if the new trial judge determined that the statements were sufficiently "reliable" and "necessary."

4.7.2   KGB Statement Taking Procedures

In the *KGB* decision, the Supreme Court specified certain conditions in which it will regard as reliable the prior inconsistent videotaped statement of a witness. These conditions include warning the witness about possible prosecution for perjury, administering an oath or solemn affirmation to the witness, videotaping the interview in its entirety, a *voir dire* to assess the reliability of the statement and a full opportunity for cross-examination. The police service investigating an offence, at least in serious cases, would be well advised to adopt the Supreme Court's criteria when interviewing potentially hostile witnesses who may recant their testimony at a later date.

The following procedures should be adopted by investigators when interviewing witnesses:

- The witness should be invited to give a videotaped statement to the police. The videotape should show a visual image of the witness and as many of the other participants in the interview as possible. The videotape should have a time-date stamp feature that accurately and continuously displays the time and date. The video camera should be on when the parties enter the interview room.

- The principal investigator should state the time, date and location of the interview, verbally identify him or herself and the other parties to the interview, including the Justice of the Peace (or Commissioner) and the witness. Each party

---

[16]*R. v. KGB* (1993), 79 C.C.C. (3d) 257 (S.C.C.).

present should be asked to state their name in an audible manner to assist with voice identification.

- The principal investigator should ask each participant to acknowledge that the statement is being videotaped and audio taped and that they consent to the recording. This can be done by stating:

    "I would ask that each of you acknowledge that you understand that this statement is being videotaped and audio taped and that you consent to such a tape being made."

- The principal investigator should remind the witness of the nature of the offence(s) being investigated and the significance of the statement being made in terms of the police investigation by stating words to the following effect:

    "As you are aware we are investigating _____. As part of our investigation into that offence we would like to interview you. Your statement is an important part of our investigation. We would like to speak to you about this offence on videotape and under oath (or solemn affirmation) and that is why we have asked you to come here today."

- The justice or commissioner should explain to the witness the potential for prosecution in the event of a false statement. Sections 137 CC Fabricating Evidence, s. 138 CC Offences Relating to Affidavits, s. 139 CC Obstructing Justice, and s. 140 CC Public Mischief, should be explained to the witness in such a way that the witness understands the significance of the statement being made and the need to be truthful. The witness should also be told that the statement he or she makes may be used as evidence at a subsequent trial should the witness recant. The justice or commissioner might use the following warning:

    "As the police have explained, your statement to them is an important part of their investigation. You should understand that it is a serious criminal offence to make a false statement to the police, to wrongly accuse someone of a crime, or to cause the police to enter into an investigation of another person. You should also understand that it is a serious offence to make an affidavit that is false. If you later give sworn evidence that is different from what you swear to today, that could be another offence. Your statement today might be used against you if you are ever charged with one of these offences. Do you understand this caution?"

- If the witness doesn't understand the warning, the principal investigator (not the justice or commissioner) should attempt to explain the offences to the witness. If the witness still does not understand, the investigator, where practicable to do so, should inquire whether or not the witness wants to speak to someone (e.g., legal counsel) before continuing.

- Once the person has acknowledged an understanding of the seriousness of making a false statement, one of the investigators should explain that he or she wishes to take a sworn statement and that if the witness changes his or her statement before or during the trial, the Crown Attorney may be allowed by the judge to use the videotaped statement as evidence at that trial.

- After all of these warnings, the witness should be sworn by the justice or Commissioner. The witness should be asked to swear (or solemnly affirm) the truth of the statements he or she is about to make. A Bible should be used if an oath is to be administered. The oath or solemn affirmation should be in the following terms:

    "Do you, _____, swear (or solemnly affirm) that the evidence that you shall give on this investigation shall be the truth, the whole truth and nothing but the truth, so help you God?" (Omit "So help you God" if the witness is affirming).

- The videotaped interview should then proceed. The camera angle should show the face of the witness and the proximity between the witness and the interviewer. To the extent possible, the conduct (including gestures) of all parties to the interview should be captured on the recording.

- The interview should be concluded by asking the witness if there is anything that he or she would like to say for the record, noting that the earlier oath continues to apply.

    "You know that what you have told us has been under oath. Is there anything that you want to change? Is there anything else that we should know to understand your statement fully?"

Use only new sealed video and audio tapes. After an hour, stop the recorder (never pause the recorder) insert a new tape, press "Record" and resume the interview. At the conclusion of the interview, remove tape(s), make copies of the tapes to serve as your "working copies." Seal the "master tapes" (originals) and preserve continuity as evidence.

4.8 BENEFITS OF ELECTRONICALLY RECORDING INTERVIEWS

Videotaping allows an investigator to produce a permanent visual and sound record of the entire interview in court to allow the trier of fact (the judge or jury as the case may be) to view the actual circumstances and content of the interview to assess the reliability and voluntariness of the statement. The demeanour of all participants at the time of the interview may be viewed to remove any doubt of police misconduct and to allow the court to observe the behaviour of the witness during the interview to evaluate his or her reliability (credibility).

Not all witness interviews are required to be videotaped or audio taped; however, there are certain times when the practice of videotaping is recommended.

- Videotaping is recommended in any investigation in which there is a high probability that the victim or witness could recant (withdraw or deny) his or her previous statement (e.g., domestic abuse situations or other instance in which the witness is related to or is a close associate of the suspect).

- Videotaped interviews are also recommended in any investigation in which the witness is in custody on a related or unrelated offence (See Section 9.1.4: The In-custody Informer).

- During any investigation of an offence listed in s. 715.1 CC involving a complainant or witness under the age of 18 years at the time of the offence (if the video is made within a reasonable time after the alleged offence), the use of videotaped interviews is recommended. The videotape of the victim or witness's description of the acts may be admissible in evidence if the complainant or witness adopts the contents of his or her statement, while testifying.

- Investigators are advised to videotape interviews in any investigation of an offence listed in s. 715.2(1) CC in which the complainant or other witness might have difficulty communicating his or her evidence by reason of a mental or physical disability. The interview must also be made within a reasonable time after the alleged offence and must be adopted by the witness while testifying.

- For any investigation in which the complainant or other witness might not be available to testify at trial, investigators should videotape interviews. These situations might include a witness who is moving to a location outside the jurisdiction of the court (e.g., Europe or Asia, etc.) or a victim or witness who is suffering from an injury or terminal illness and may succumb to the illness or injury prior to trial.[17] The interview may be admissible in evidence as an exception to the "hearsay rule" if the court finds that it is "necessary" to do so due to the unavailability of the witness.

Interviews should be videotaped for any investigation in which the child victim or witness is too young (i.e., under the age of 14 years) to provide sworn evidence at trial.[18]

SUMMARY

- Interviewing is the primary method of gathering information during the course of all police investigations and is the backbone of every successful investigation.

- An interview is conducted with a complainant (victim), witness, person of interest and sometimes with a co-operative suspect.

- In terms of legal requirements and actual procedure involved, an interview is different from an interrogation of a suspect or an accused person, which is to obtain an admission or confession regarding the offence(s) under investigation.

- Always remember that, at any time, an interview may turn into an interrogation.

- Memory can be either episodic or procedural.

- During an interview, the subject being interviewed should do 90 per cent of the talking, while the interviewer does no more than 10 per cent of the talking.

- Self-evaluation and self-improvement are traits of a professional interviewer.

---

[17]*R. v. Smith* (1992) 2 S.C.R. 915.

[18]*R. v. Khan* (1990) 2 S.C.R. 531.

- An investigative interview should be structured on the basis of the "P.E.A.C.E." model, incorporating the following stages:

  Planning and Preparation;

  Engage and Explain;

  Account, Clarification and Challenge;

  Closure; and

  Evaluation.

- Unless a subject absolutely refuses to be interviewed, the interviewer must attempt to persuade the subject from his or her unwilling stance to a position where the subject is willing to co-operate with the investigation.

- The 1993 Supreme Court decision in *Regina v. KGB* provided comprehensive guidelines for the videotaping of witnesses in criminal cases.

DISCUSSION QUESTIONS

1. What are the differences between the objectives of an interview and those of an interrogation? Which categories of persons is each technique employed with during an investigation?

2. One sure way to influence a witness's memory is through the asking of leading questions. What is an example of a leading question? What influence might the use of leading questions have on a witness who is asked one or more leading questions during an investigative interview?

3. Why is it desirable to separate witnesses who are being interviewed, whenever it is practicable to do so?

4. You are an investigator assigned to conduct interviews of 10 witnesses in regards to a cold-case homicide investigation where urgency is no longer an immediate concern. List the steps you will take in planning your interviews. By what process will you prioritize the order in which each witness will be interviewed?

 ## WEBLINKS

www.lexum.umontreal.ca/index_en.html

University of Montreal, Faculty of Law.
Supreme Court of Canada decisions and links to other case-law databases.

www.ontariocourts.on.ca/

Website maintained by the Judge's Library. Guide to Ontario Courts including selected judgments of the Ontario Court of Appeal.

www.natcom.org/ctronline/nonverb.htm

Com Resources Online. Links to various resources relating to nonverbal communication.

www.geocities.com/marvin_hecht/nonverbal.html

Nonverbal Communication Research webpage with links to various associations and works in the field of nonverbal communication.

Chapter 5

Interrogation of Suspects

"Unless a man feels he has a good enough memory, he should never venture to lie."

Michel Eyquem de Montaigne, French philosopher (1533-1592).[1]

Learning Outcomes

After reading this chapter, students should be able to:

- Explain the objectives of an interrogation.

- Give examples of the necessary elements of planning an interrogation.

- Explain the significance of the Judges' Rules as they relate to the questioning of **suspects** by police officers.

- Apply the legal requirements of administering the statement **caution** and an individual's rights under subsections 10(a) and 10(b) of the *Canadian Charter of Rights and Freedoms.*

- Explain the use of **Proxemics** (i.e., the study of personal space as it relates to ordinary human relations) during an interrogation.

- Give examples relating to the detection of deception from verbal and non-responses of the subject being interviewed or interrogated.

5.1 "INTERROGATION" DEFINED

As discussed in the previous chapter, the main goal of any interview or interrogation is to obtain a written or electronically recorded statement from the subject being questioned – interviewing or interrogation comprise the various techniques applied by investigators to different situations involving different classes of individuals.

Interrogation means the formal examination of a suspect or an accused person by questioning. The primary objective of an interrogation is to obtain an admission or confession from the suspect or accused to establish his or her guilt in the matter under investigation. Interviews are conducted with various categories of persons, including

---

[1]de Montaigne quote retrieved December 29, 2004, from www.home.tele2.ch/kuljo/quotes_by_keyword/memory

victims, witnesses, non-witnesses, persons of interest and, to a smaller degree, suspects and accused persons.

For review purposes, the basic differences between an interview and an interrogation are listed in the following sections.

5.1.1 Nature of Questioning

An interview is non-accusatory in nature as the interviewer is attempting to obtain as much information as possible from the witness, person of interest or suspect, about the incident(s) under investigation. The interviewer is still in the information-gathering stage of the investigation. Interviews may be conducted both before and after the laying of any criminal charges.

The interrogator is no longer concerned with information-gathering and directly accuses the subject being questioned of the crime under investigation. An interrogation is the process by which an attempt is made to obtain a confession of guilt, an admission of a relevant fact, or an alibi concerning the subject's whereabouts at the time of the offence.

Unlike an interview, an interrogation is accusatory in nature. By accusatory, it is not meant that the interrogation is either mentally or physically oppressive or abusive in any way. The accusation is made in a calm, professional and firm manner. The interrogator should leave no doubt whatsoever in the subject's mind that he or she believes the subject is responsible for either having committed the offence being investigated or for having had direct or indirect involvement in the commission of the offence.

For this reason, victims, witnesses and persons of interest are never interrogated; they are interviewed. Interrogations, in most cases, precede the laying of criminal charges against a suspect.

5.1.2 Administering the Standard Police Caution

When conducting an interview, there is no legal requirement to caution a witness or person of interest. A suspect or an accused should always be administered the standard police caution to warn them that they are not obliged to give a statement but that anything they say may be used in court, even though there may not be sufficient reasonable grounds upon which to either arrest the suspect or accused, or to lay a charge.

5.1.3 Advising of Rights to Counsel

A police officer is never legally obligated to advise a witness of his or her rights to consult with legal counsel. An individual being interrogated (i.e., suspect or accused) should always be advised of his or her rights to counsel (whether or not he or she is under arrest) and must be afforded the opportunity to consult with a lawyer, prior to the interrogation, should he or she wish to do so, to ensure the admissibility of any subsequent statement.

Prior to or during an interview or an interrogation, a subject may ask, "Do I need a lawyer?" It is recommended that your response should be to the effect that "I'm not able to answer that for you. Do you think you need a lawyer?" (Or, "If you think that you might need a lawyer, then you probably do.") Never recommend any specific attorney to a subject. Always allow the subject to select an attorney either from a telephone directory or from a prepared list of local lawyers.

The request to consult with or to be represented by counsel made by any subject being questioned, whether he or she is a witness or is under suspicion, does not, contrary to popular belief, automatically imply anything about the subject (e.g., guilt, innocence or reliability, etc.) other than that he or she wishes to exercise the rights to legal counsel.

5.1.4 Questions Posed During Interviews and Interrogations

During an interview, the interviewer must ask only open-ended questions and avoid using leading questions to preclude any possible influencing of the witness's account of the incident(s) under investigation. The witness may be asked follow-up questions to clarify any vague or uncertain details or to attempt to have the witness expand upon his or her account.

During an interrogation, the suspect or accused may be asked any nature of question regarding the account of their knowledge (if any) of the incident. The suspect or accused should be questioned concerning discrepancies in their account of the events, or regarding any discrepancies between their account and other known facts of the case.

Following an interrogation, if a confession is not received, the interrogator may wish to take a written or electronically recorded cautioned statement from the subject. Once a suspect or accused is in the process of providing a cautioned statement, he or she should not be cross-examined by the interrogator regarding the statement he or she provides; however, clarifying questions may still be posed to the subject for the purpose of clearing up any uncertainties in the details of his or her statement.

5.1.5 Recording the Statement

During an interview, one technique is to ask the witness a series of questions to assess the scope of their knowledge of the incident under investigation, prior to the formal taking of a statement, either in writing or through audio tape or videotape. The alternative is to proceed directly with the handwritten or electronically recorded statement. The normally handwritten statement should always be audio taped or videotaped if the witness is related to or is closely associated to the suspect or accused, and there is any possibility that the witness may later recant their statement.

An interrogation should always be audio taped or videotaped (from beginning to end) where the equipment is available and where it is practicable to do so. A handwritten statement may be taken following an interrogation; however, the entire process should also be either audio taped or videotaped to assist with proving the voluntariness of the statement in court.

5.1.6 Voluntariness of Statement

No witness, person of interest, suspect or accused is ever obligated to consent to being interviewed or interrogated. Normally, the Crown is never required to prove the voluntariness of a witness statement. However, the voluntariness of the statement of an accused must always, first, be proven to be voluntary prior to it being admissible as evidence in a *voir dire* (see Section 5.7.2: Admissibility of Statements by Suspects / Accused Persons).

5.2   WHO DO WE INTERROGATE?

As discussed in the previous chapter, the important distinction between interview and interrogation is that victims, witnesses, non-witnesses, persons of interest and, to a certain degree, co-operative suspects and accused persons are interviewed to gather information regarding the offence(s) and event(s) under investigation. Suspects and persons accused of criminal offences are interrogated when attempting to obtain an admission or confession of guilt regarding their involvement in the crime.

For the purposes of review, a person of interest is: "A person whose background, relationship to the victim or the opportunity to commit the offence(s) [may warrant] further investigation but [at that time no other grounds exist] to suggest culpability [i.e., criminal liability, blameworthiness] in the commission of the [event being investigated]."[2] For example, the owner of a business is found murdered inside his or her business premises. Everyone connected with that business (e.g., management, employees, business associates, etc.) by virtue of their connection to the victim or their association to the location of the murder, would all be considered to be a person of interest, due to the possibility of their opportunity to commit the crime even though no evidence exists, at that time, to suggest that he or she is guilty of the offence.

Several persons of interest may require elimination from suspicion during the course of the investigation. Their elimination from suspicion is accomplished largely through the interviewing process and through establishing and verifying their alibis. A person of interest is not considered to be a suspect, nor should he or she ever be officially identified as such.

A suspect is: "A person of interest [whom an investigator reasonably believes may possess a degree of culpability] in the commission of the offence(s)[being investigated] based on the evidence [linking the person to the crime]."[3] It is important to distinguish between persons of interest and suspects, as the former are interviewed and the latter are interrogated, although both processes, to a large degree, involve the element of questioning.

A one-time person of interest, against whom incriminating evidence becomes known at some point during the investigation, may develop into a suspect when at least a partial focus of the investigation shifts onto him or her. Perhaps a suspect may become known to the case through a different avenue of investigation. The most important distinction between persons of interest and suspects is that a suspect, once declared as such, requires total and conclusive elimination from suspicion, to the extent that elimination is possible.

It is never wise to take an accused person to court while one or more other known suspects have not been eliminated from suspicion. To do so allows for the creation of

---

[2] Ministry of Community Safety and Correctional Services: *Ontario Major Case Management (MCM) Manual* (Oct. 1, 2004),. p. 10.

[3] Ibid.

reasonable doubt that a suspect other than the accused may have actually committed the crime instead of the accused. The key factor in declaring someone to be a suspect is the degree of incriminating information linking the person to the crime and not merely the possibility that he or she might have committed the crime.

An accused person is one against whom a charge has been laid. Once before a court of law, an accused is alternatively referred to as a defendant. A person is interrogated once there is some incriminating evidence against him or her or when they have been charged with a criminal offence even though that evidence may fall short of the standard of reasonable grounds upon which to base an arrest or upon which to lay a charge. An accused person who is questioned to gain information regarding an offence for which he or she is not considered responsible, is interviewed as a witness – not interrogated as an accused.

5.3   WHY DO WE INTERROGATE?

In the investigator's search for the truth, one potential source of information that is often overlooked is the suspect or accused. There is a sometimes a curious reluctance on the part of some investigators to interrogate suspects, in all but the most serious of cases. Many times an investigator will pass up the opportunity to attempt to obtain a possible admission or confession from a suspect or accused on the belief that "They'll probably just deny it anyway or they'll only refuse to even talk to me," or "As soon as I try, they'll just want to talk to a lawyer."

Neither of these (nor any other possible excuse) justifies the passing up of an opportunity to gather evidence of any crime under investigation. As investigators, we go to great lengths to gather evidence at crime scenes. Why then is it not just as worthwhile to attempt to gather information from every possible source, including the person suspected or accused of the commission of the crime under investigation?

Interrogating suspects is an art in itself, involving unique interpersonal dynamics between the interrogator and the subject being interrogated. These skills are developed only through considerable training and experience. There are many occasions in which the situation calls for the assignment of the most qualified interrogator available to question a suspect in a major case investigation, such as serial sexual assault, robbery, homicide, etc.

Perhaps the resources of your police service are limited and you might not have access to a local expert interrogator. Maybe the resident "expert" in a larger or adjacent police service is unavailable or the timing is such that an interrogation must be done right away. If there is no investigator better suited than you available for the task of conducting the interrogation, then roll up your sleeves – you're about to interrogate the suspect.

As you ponder how to deal with your profusely sweating hands and forehead, the herds of butterflies in your stomach and your increasing sense of panic and impending doom, just take a few deep breaths and stop for just a moment to calmly analyze the situation. What is the downside of conducting the interrogation, should absolute necessity require you to do so? As you will see in the following chart (all other things being equal), your investigation might possibly benefit from having attempted an interrogation, rather than if you had not tried at all.

TABLE 5.1	Possible Outcomes of an Interrogation
Possible Outcome	*Effect*
• Suspect/accused refuses outright to speak to interrogator	• Neutral effect
• Suspect/accused requests to consult a lawyer and, on the advice of legal counsel, elects to remain silent	• Neutral effect
• Suspect/accused requests to consult a lawyer and, contrary to the advice of counsel, decides to give a statement (–it happens)	• Positive effect. Your suspect will either truthfully deny his or her involvement in the offence under investigation, falsely deny his or her involvement and may even offer an alibi which can later be proven, or be proven to be false.
• Suspect/accused provides an admission or confession under caution	• Positive effect. You may have solved the investigation, identified additional evidence or, at a minimum, committed the subject to an account of events in a permanent record that might be extremely valuable should the suspect/accused provide a different account of events at a later time.

There is an adage in law enforcement that describes the following conversation between a young police officer and an older career criminal, following his release from prison:

Police Officer: "Did you do what they say you did?"

Suspect: "Yes."

Police Officer: "Why didn't you ever tell anyone?"

Suspect: "Nobody ever asked me."

The moral of the story is self-evident. "It's always better to ask the question and risk learning the answer than to never to ask the question and not ever find the answer."

5.4   WHEN DO WE INTERROGATE?

Subject to certain legal requirements that will be discussed later in this chapter, an interrogation of a suspect may occur at any time during an investigation. The interrogation of a suspect may occur either before they are in police custody (i.e., pre-arrest) or after an arrest has been made. The interrogation of a suspect who is not yet in police custody may occur at any time that an individual or group of individuals becomes at least a partial focus of the investigation and certain evidence exists implicating him or her in the crime (whether or not reasonable grounds exist upon which to make an arrest or upon which to lay a charge).

An accused (i.e., a person against whom a charge has been laid) may be interrogated at any time after his or her arrest, prior to his or her conviction in court.

The decision as to whether or not to interrogate such person(s) may have to be assessed against the possible risk of their destroying evidence once they become aware that they are suspected of the offence under investigation. If the possible destruction of evidence is not, however, a consideration, there may be no valid reason for not attempting an interrogation. As previously discussed, several possible outcomes may result from the questioning of an out-of-custody suspect – all of which might quite easily further the investigation. With odds like this in your favour, why not take the opportunity to question every suspect? The possible favourable outcomes include:

- The suspect may exonerate him or herself and provide an alibi that can be verified by way of further investigation, thereby clearing him or herself of suspicion in the case.

- The suspect may deny his or her responsibility and provide a false alibi that might be proven to be false.

- The suspect may provide an admission to some part of the incident and/or provide certain details regarding previously unknown avenues of investigation.

- The suspect may fully confess his or her involvement in the offence under investigation.

- The suspect, once aware that he or she is formally suspected, might be prompted into attempting to destroy evidence of the crime (under the watchful eyes or ears of police surveillance, of course) or may even be prompted to pass on details of his or her involvement in the crime to friends or associates. The probability that relevant information will eventually come to the attention of the investigation is directly proportional to number of people who have knowledge of it.

5.5   OBJECTIVES OF AN INTERROGATION

The main goal of an interrogation is to attempt to determine the subject's complete involvement, if any, in the case under investigation. An interrogation may also indicate the involvement and possible identity of accomplices (e.g., parties to the offence, accessories, co-conspirators, etc.) in the crime(s).

As previously discussed in Chapter 1, every criminal offence comprises facts in issue, being the essential **elements of an offence** that must be proven before a finding of guilt is possible. The overall goal of an interrogation is, ideally, to obtain a full confession from a guilty subject (i.e., obtain a written or verbal acknowledgement of the subject's involvement that proves all of the facts in issue of the offences).

If a full confession is not obtained, it is possible and quite common for a suspect or accused to provide an admission. An admission is a partial acknowledgement of a suspect's involvement in the crime(s) under investigation that might prove one or more (but not all) of the facts in issue. An admission may be either written or verbal.

An admission might only provide an acknowledgement of one or more elements of the case (e.g., knowledge of the victim, location, or events). An admission may provide an acknowledgement that the alleged offence occurred but in some way the subject alleges legal justification for his or her actions. Some examples are a sexual offence which the subject admits did occur, but claims the victim consented to the act, or a homicide in which the subject admits to intentionally causing the death of the deceased, but asserts that he or she acted in self-defence.

An admission might also provide valuable circumstantial evidence of the subject's involvement, such as certain skills necessary to commit the crime (e.g., welding skills – if the offence includes a safe attack involving the use of oxy-acetylene welding equipment, etc.). An admission may be obtained in which the suspect admits that he or she was at the location where the offence was committed but denies any involvement in the offence. Even though an admission is less than a full confession, the interrogation should still be considered successful because you will end it with more information than you had when you began.

Finally, even if neither an admission nor a confession are obtained, the subject might still provide a denial of his or her involvement in the case under investigation and may or may not provide an alibi (i.e., a claim or proof that when the offence occurred, the subject was in a different location and therefore could neither have participated in, nor been responsible for the alleged crimes). Whether or not a subject who denies his or her involvement in a crime provides an alibi, a denial is still valuable if, on the basis of independent evidence, the denial can be proven to be false.

5.6 PLANNING AND PREPARATION FOR AN INTERROGATION

If planning and preparation are important prior to interviewing a victim or witness – and, without a doubt, they are – planning and preparation for the interrogation of a suspect or accused is doubly important. Witnesses can usually be expected to be somewhat co-operative with the police. There are no harmful consequences for them that result from being interviewed (except perhaps that of being required to testify in court).

A suspect or accused person who confesses his or her guilt to an interrogator, however, is virtually guaranteed to be punished and, in the case of a first-time offender, he or she must also bear the stigma that goes along with being charged with a serious criminal offence. All clear-thinking, rational offenders generally seek to avoid punishment and usually won't be eager to admit their guilt.

A guilty suspect or accused may very well agree to be questioned by the police in an attempt to persuade investigators of his or her innocence. Few suspects, though, enjoy the experience of an interrogation enough to consent to a second one. Always interrogate on the assumption that in all likelihood you will only have one opportunity to conduct the interrogation – so, even if it's your very first interrogation, make it count!

Once an interrogation begins, the interrogator is locked into a "battle of wits" with the suspect or accused and must establish and maintain an advantage of superiority at all times concerning knowledge of the case, attitude and control of the interrogation. The interrogator must never back down from the subject being interrogated.

The steps involved in organizing the questioning of a suspect or accused are very similar in nature to the planning and preparation prior to the interview of a witness, and include the following issues.

5.6.1   Knowledge of the Case

"Know the enemy and know yourself; in a hundred battles you will never be defeated. When you are ignorant of the enemy but know yourself, your chances of winning or losing are equal. If ignorant both of the enemy and of yourself, you are sure to be defeated in every battle."

Sun Tzu, Chinese General (6th century BC)[4]

It makes little sense to interrogate a suspect about a crime that he or she may or may not have been involved in unless the interrogator is fully aware of all available information regarding the crime prior to the interrogation. Never try to deceive or attempt to trick a subject whom you are interrogating. If the person you are interrogating is in fact the person who committed the crime or someone who was even present at the time the crime was committed, he or she will already know more about the case than you do and will immediately realize that you are bluffing. The following are examples of information that, if available, would give the investigator a sound knowledge of the case prior to commencing an interrogation:

- details from all police reports of the occurrence under investigation;

- details from any relevant witness and suspect statements;

- personal conversations with other investigators working the case; and

- knowledge of the crime scene through the viewing of photographs and/or from personally viewing the crime scene, if possible.

In addition to knowing the facts of the case, an investigator should attempt to gather as much background information as possible relating to the subject to be interrogated including:

- Personal history of the suspect or accused;

- Record of any previous criminal convictions;

- Details of any previous offences he or she was involved in;

- Modus operandi used in the commission of previous offences;

- Motives for committing previous offences;

- Results of any previous interrogations (e.g., successful or unsuccessful – subject confessed only when implicated by physical evidence, etc. What worked and what didn't work with the suspect on previous occasions? Is a rational or emotional approach likely to be more effective?);

- Whether the suspect has previously provided an alibi. If so, has it been fully investigated and proven to be false?;

- Suspect's lifestyle (e.g., use of alcohol, non-prescription drugs, sexual orientation, etc.);

---

[4]Hanzhang (2000).

- Family history (e.g., parents, siblings, relationships with them, etc.);

- Employment history (e.g., long-time employment or sporadic?);

- Friends and associates (e.g., criminal affiliations or law-abiding, etc.?);

- Institutional records from previous incarcerations; and

- Personal information (e.g., previous and current relationships, education, financial history, medical history, current medications that may affect his or her behaviour or responses to questioning, hobbies or aversions, etc.).

5.6.2   Timing of the Interrogation

The interrogator must choose both the optimum time and location in which to conduct every interrogation. The interrogator must be fully prepared to conduct the questioning of the subject. If all available information regarding the case under investigation has not been analyzed; or if the suspect's alibi has not been fully investigated, consideration should be given to rescheduling the interrogation to increase the possibility of success.

The interrogator must also determine whether or not any additional investigation (e.g., witness interviews or forensic testing) needs to be carried out prior to the interrogation. Could conducting the interrogation at this point of the investigation result in any potential loss or destruction of physical evidence as the result of the suspect learning that he or she is under suspicion? If so, is this really the best time to conduct the interrogation?

5.6.3   Location, Location, Location

Interrogations occur in police stations rather than in the suspect's residence due to the obvious need to be able to control the environment at all times. Always select a room in which to conduct the interrogation, keeping in mind the need to strike the appropriate balance between privacy and security. The interrogation room should be one that is equipped with video recording capability and free from interruptions.

If possible, the room should be near a restroom to avoid any accidental contact between a suspect and uninvolved personnel, should the subject require a break during the interrogation. Always have an adequate stock of supplies (e.g., audio or videotapes, statement forms, writing implements, etc.) on hand before you begin.

The Case Manager should also consider whether there is any possible advantage in **propping** the route into an interrogation room or the room itself. Propping involves the strategic placement of artifacts intended to be observed by the suspect to impress upon the suspect the gravity of the offence and the strength of the evidence against him or her. Propping may include conspicuous signage, photographs, wall-charts and file cabinets bearing the suspect's name on the drawer-fronts, etc. Case Managers have even displayed mannequins dressed to resemble a victim in homicide cases.

I once intentionally orchestrated the transport route of a prisoner to include driving past the crime scene while the transport officer (who was also assigned to conduct the interrogation) asked a prepared script of questions to coincide with the location. The combination of the significant location in conjunction with the pointed line of questioning proved to be very effective.

5.6.4 Privacy

You wouldn't want to share extremely personal information about yourself in a room full of people or in a noisy room full of distractions – would you? Neither will your suspect. Privacy does not guarantee obtaining a confession, but it creates an environment that promotes the sharing of sensitive personal information, (e.g., an admission or confession). The interrogation room should be conspicuously posted indicating that an interrogation is in progress, to warn other personnel against entering the room.

The suspect must be afforded absolute privacy when consulting with legal counsel, either in person or by telephone.

5.7 LEGAL INTERROGATION REQUIREMENTS

The legal rules for interrogating suspects and accused persons are considerably stricter than for interviewing witnesses. Investigators must be guided by current best practices and case law in their attempt to obtain confessions from person(s) suspected of, or known to have been directly involved in, the commission of criminal offences.

Investigators involved in conducting interrogations should be familiar with the Judges' Rules, which have been replicated in the following section. The Judges' Rules appear at the beginning of most police-issued notebooks and serve as a checklist for police officers involved in questioning people during investigations.

5.7.1 The Judges' Rules

In October, 1912, the judges of the King's Bench Division in England prepared a set of rules for the guidance of police officers in interrogating prisoners and suspects. These rules are not considered to have the force of law, but are still commonly referred to and provide a useful summary of the legal rules of questioning.

It is of no benefit to any investigation, nor does it provide any relief whatsoever to the victim of a crime, should evidence gathered during an investigation be subsequently rejected at trial by the presiding judge because the police officer(s) disobeyed the rules (i.e., violated a suspect or accused's *Charter* rights).

RULE No. 1:

"When a police officer is endeavouring to discover the author of a crime, there is no objection to his [or her] putting questions in respect thereof, to any person or persons whether suspected or not, from whom he [or she] thinks useful information may be obtained."

There are no restrictions as to the number or type of questions that a police officer, including other persons in authority, may ask of witnesses, non-witnesses, persons of interest or suspects from whom they believe information may be obtained, "whether [the person is] suspected or not" of the crime under investigation.

Once a police officer considers the individual to be a suspect (i.e., "A person of interest [whom an investigator reasonably believes may possess a degree of culpability] in the commission of the offence(s)[being investigated] based on the evidence [linking the person to the crime]"[5]), and believes that a charge against the suspect is possible, whether or not the suspect is in custody at the time of questioning, it is strongly recommended that the caution, which is discussed further in Rules 2 and 8, be administered prior to initial questioning or to further questioning if grounds to arrest or charge are formed during the course of the initial questioning.

The administering of the caution in this case discharges a legal obligation on the part of the investigator and demonstrates to the court an attitude of fairness and respect for the rights of the individual being questioned.

RULE No. 2:

"Whenever a police officer has made up his [or her] mind to charge a person with a crime, he [or she] should first caution the person before asking any question or further questions as the case may be."

The caution referred to reads as follows: "You [are charged / will be charged / may be charged] with [the offence under investigation]. Do you wish to say anything in answer to the charge? You are not obliged to say anything unless you wish to do so, but whatever you say may be given in evidence. Do you understand?"

In this situation, there is either a strong possibility, or an absolute certainty that the suspect will be charged. Although this rule states that the police officer should first caution an individual "whenever a police officer has made up [his or her] mind to charge a person with a crime…" the wording implies that once a police officer has reasonable grounds to charge or even arrest an individual, the caution should be read to him or her, whether or not the individual is arrested or charged at that time.

The benchmark for administering the caution is not merely the act of arresting or the laying of a charge – it is the formation of reasonable grounds upon which to arrest or to lay a charge. A police officer who has formed reasonable grounds to arrest or charge any individual, but does not actually charge or arrest him or her, is not relieved of the responsibility for cautioning that individual.

RULE No. 3:

"Persons in custody should not be questioned without the usual caution first being administered."

A "person in custody" means any individual who has been arrested, on the charge under investigation, either with or without warrant, or is incarcerated for any previous related or unrelated offence. A "person in custody" also includes any person who has merely been detained, whether or not they have been charged with any offence, if the person subjectively believes that his or her liberty has been removed – meaning that they feel they are not free to leave the officer, the police cruiser or the police station, etc.

Prior to any questioning of individuals in such circumstances, the standard caution, described in Rules 2 and 8, must be given before questions are asked of the prisoner. The test conducted by a court to determine the state of mind of the suspect at the time of questioning is referred to as the "objective test."

---

[5]Ministry of Community Safety and Correctional Services: *Ontario Major Case Management (MCM) Manual* (Oct. 1, 2004), p. 10.

In determining whether or not a person is being "detained," a police officer should be able to honestly answer the question, "If the subject was to walk away from me now, would I let him or her go?" If the answer is, "Yes, I would," it is the subjective belief of the police officer that the subject is not being detained. Regardless of the officer's subjective belief, a court may still determine the existence of a subjective belief the individual was being "detained" if, in the mind of the subject, they believed that they were not free to leave the custody of the police officer.

In the case of a suspect who is invited to a police station for questioning, it is recommended that the suspect be explicitly reminded that he or she is not under arrest and is free to leave whenever he or she wishes to. From experience, innocent parties will remain as they wish to be co-operative, while guilty suspects will most often also remain, in an effort to convince you of their innocence. In the case of audio taped or videotaped statements, repeated cautioning and reminders to out-of-custody suspects that they are not under arrest and are free to leave, remove considerable doubt about the voluntariness of the statement and the possibility of any subjective belief on the subject's part that they were under detention.

RULE No. 4:

"If the prisoner wishes to volunteer any statement, the usual caution should first be administered."

Rule 4 refers to a person in police custody, such as a person who has been placed under arrest or is being detained, or at any other time during the investigation or while during their subsequent incarceration, who volunteers to give the police a statement, either inculpating (i.e., admitting) or exculpating (i.e., denying) him or herself, in regards to the crime for which he is in custody, or for any other offence. Any such prisoner should be administered the standard caution, referred to in Rules 2 and 8, and *Charter* rights to legal counsel[6] before being questioned.

RULE No. 5:

"A statement made by a prisoner before there is time to caution him, is not rendered inadmissible by reason of no caution being given to him, but in such cases, [the caution] should be given as soon as possible."

Rule 5 refers to what is known as a "spontaneous utterance," such as any statement, usually an admission or confession, made by an individual before the investigator has the opportunity to administer the standard caution. Take, for example, the following conversation between an investigator, upon arriving at the scene of an alleged homicide, and a suspect who walks out of a house with a knife (after the officer relieves the suspect of the knife, of course):

Police Officer: "What happened here?"

Suspect: "I killed her. I caught her cheating on me with the next-door neighbour."

---

[6]*Canadian Charter of Rights and Freedoms*, Being Part 1 of the *Constitution Act*, 1982, enacted by the *Canada Act* 1982 (U.K.); proclaimed in force April 17, 1982 s. 10(b).

> **Question: Using the formation of reasonable grounds as the threshold for administering the statement caution, is the officer required at this time to advise the individual of his right not to answer questions and of the possibility that anything he does say may be given in evidence, quite possibly against him?**

> *Recommended Answer: I suggest that the officer is on the verge of "reasonable grounds" but is not quite there. The officer still cannot answer the following questions: Who has been killed? When was the person killed? Where is he or she now? Now let's consider the following conversation:*

Police Officer: "What happened here?"

Suspect: "I killed her. I caught her cheating on me with the next-door neighbour."

Police Officer: "Who did you kill?"

Suspect: "My wife, Lucy Smith."

Police Officer: "When did this happen?"

Suspect: "Twenty minutes ago. Just before I called 9-1-1."

Police Officer: "Where is your wife now?"

Suspect: "She's in the bedroom; I'll take you and show you."

At this point, the officer has sufficient "reasonable grounds" upon which to legally arrest the individual for the alleged second-degree murder of Lucy Smith. Prior to asking the suspect any further questions, the police officer is now required to administer the usual caution. The failure to administer this suspect the caution would render any subsequent statements made by the prisoner inadmissible at trial. The remainder of the conversation should be:

Police Officer: "I am placing you under arrest for the second-degree murder [as no evidence of planning and deliberation exists at this time that would justify arresting for first degree murder] of Lucy Smith. Do you wish to say anything in answer to the charge? You are not obliged to say anything unless you wish to do so, but whatever you say may be given in evidence. Do you understand?" [Followed by advising the suspect of his rights to counsel under section 10(b) of the *Charter of Rights and Freedoms*.[7]]

The arrested suspect should be searched, handcuffed and placed into a police cruiser, under constant guard, in the event he might blurt out any further incriminating statements after having now been cautioned – but should not be interrogated until the decision to do so is made by the Case Manager. Under no circumstances should the suspect be allowed to return inside to the alleged crime scene, and his clothing should be seized at the earliest opportunity (see Chapter 6: Crime Scene Investigation).

---

[7] *Ibid.*

RULE No. 6:

"A prisoner making a voluntary statement should not be cross-examined, and no questions should be put to him except for the purpose of removing ambiguity in what is said."

A cross-examining type question would be one that seeks to investigate further into what has been said by the suspect in custody. Questions may be asked to clear up certain issues, such as obtaining the surname of a person referred to only by his or her first name in the statement. If the suspect refers to an incident having occurred at a certain time of day, for example, "I went to work at eight o'clock," the investigator is free to ask the suspect, "Do you mean eight o'clock in the morning or eight o'clock in the evening?"

Take only the information that the suspect offers in his or her statement. If a part of the statement is held to be inadmissible, any evidence located near that portion of the inadmissible statement might also be deemed inadmissible.

When a suspect finishes his or her statement, the investigator may always ask, "Is there anything else you wish to tell me?," but should not ask questions about what the suspect has said except for the purpose of clarification.

RULE No. 7:

"When two or more persons are charged with the same offence, and statements are taken separately from them, the police should not read these statements to the other person(s) charged, but each such person(s) should be furnished with a copy of the said statement. Nothing should be said or done by the police to invite a reply. If the person(s) charged desire to make a statement in reply, the usual caution [referred to in Rules 2 and 8] should be administered."

A statement made by a suspect in custody is evidence only against that suspect and not against any other suspect or co-accused. Where an investigation has shown that more than one person committed the crime under investigation and one or more of the accused persons has provided a statement incriminating himself, or denying criminal responsibility and blaming other persons, the other suspect(s) should only be provided with a copy (never with the original) of the first suspect's statement.

The additional suspect(s) referred to in the statement should be given the opportunity to read what the first suspect said regarding his or her involvement in the offence under investigation. The investigator in this case should not make any comments to the second suspect about the statement, nor should he or she encourage the second suspect to make any statement regarding the crime under investigation. If the second suspect does make a verbal response, the standard caution should be administered prior to the taking of any statement.

RULE No. 8:

"The caution should be in the following words: 'You are arrested on a charge of _____. Do you wish to say anything in answer to the charge? You are not obliged to say anything unless you wish to do so, but whatever you say may be given in evidence. Do you understand?'"

The caution, previously referred to in Rule 2, is the standard police caution which is used throughout most of Canada. The caution should be read by the arresting officer directly from a caution card, which is issued by most police services, or from the wording contained in most police notebooks.

If asked by defence counsel for the exact words that were used when administering the caution to the accused, the officer, with the permission of the court, may refer to the caution card or to the wording in his or her notebook to recite the exact wording that was used at the time of the arrest.

RULE No. 9:

"The statement made in accordance with the above rules should whenever possible be taken down in writing and signed by the person making it, after it has been read to him and he has been invited to make any corrections he may wish."

A statement made to the police by a suspect or accused person may be taken down in writing or recorded electronically, or both. If the statement is handwritten, it should be read back to the suspect or accused by the officer. The suspect or accused may be invited to read the statement aloud to assure the officer that the suspect or accused is fluent in the language the statement was taken in. The officer may, alternatively, read the statement back to the individual.

Spelling, grammar and content corrections should be initialled by the suspect or accused providing the statement, by the interrogating officer and by any witness officer(s). The margin of each and every page of the statement should also be initialled or signed by the suspect or accused providing the statement, and by the interrogating and witnessing officer(s).

On the last page of the statement, the suspect or accused should be requested to write his or her signature. All officers involved in the taking of the statement must also sign the statement form, including the end time of the statement. If the suspect or accused refuses to sign the statement, the interrogating officer should include words to the effect, "accused or suspect refused to sign". The interrogating officer should then place his or her signature, rank and badge number and end time on the statement.

The Judges' Rules were first established prior to the invention of audio and video recording equipment. More and more, modern courts expect the police to record statements of accused persons to assist them in assessing the voluntariness of the statement, where recording equipment is available and where it is practicable to do so. The benefits of audio and videotaped statements were discussed previously in Chapter 4: Interviewing Victims and Witnesses.

5.7.2   Admissibility of Statements by Suspects / Accused Persons

Under the legal maxim known as the **confession rule** any statement made by a suspect or accused to a person in authority must be proven to have been made voluntarily and be free from threats or **inducements** by the Crown, beyond a reasonable doubt before it can be admitted into evidence. A person in authority is defined as "any person formally involved at any stage of the investigation, arrest, detention, examination or prosecution of a person suspected or charged with an offence, and whom the accused believes to have such authority."[8]

---

[8]*R. v. Wells* (1998) 2 S.C.R. 517.

In addition to police officers, the term "person in authority" is applied any person(s) involved at any stage of the investigation, arrest, incarceration, examination or prosecution of a person suspected or charged with an offence that, by virtue of his or her position, could be deemed to have any potential power or influence over the suspect or prisoner and whom the suspect believes holds such power. Peace officers, jailers, educators, parents of young offenders and members of the medical profession have all been considered to be persons in authority.

"Fear of threat" includes the use or threatened use of physical force or other form of oppression, or threats of any kind made by the police against either the individual or any third party, such as a spouse, child, family member, intimate partner, etc., of sufficient seriousness as might either cause a guilty person to confess or an innocent person to confess to a crime he or she did not commit. The use or threatened use of force by a police officer against any individual for the purpose of extorting a confession, or to compel them to do anything they have a legal right to refrain from doing, is not only a violation of their *Charter* rights, an inexcusable breach of police ethics – it is a serious criminal offence.

A statement made by a suspect or accused may also be rendered inadmissible if it was obtained under oppressive circumstances, such as depriving a prisoner of sleep, food or drink for a lengthy period of time. The courts have long recognized that an innocent person may confess to a crime they did not commit just to end such oppressive behaviour by his interrogator(s). Courts take a dim view of confessions obtained under such conditions and of the police officers who resort to such archaic and unlawful techniques.

Inducements are also referred to in court as any "promise of favour" and/or "hope of advantage." Persons in authority are not permitted to bargain with a suspect or accused in exchange for a confession. An example of an inducement would be to say to a prisoner, "In return for a confession, we will do [a certain thing] for you."

The voluntariness of a confession must be proven beyond a reasonable doubt during a voir dire. A *voir dire* is a hearing within a trial outside the presence of a jury (if a jury is sitting for the trial) to determine the admissibility of any evidence, in this case the confession. The person giving the statement also needs to be aware of the consequences of the statement he or she made being used as evidence, usually against him or her. The requirement for laying the groundwork to establish voluntariness of a statement is a responsibility that rests with the person in authority who obtains the statement, although such evidence is introduced in court by the Crown Attorney.

Even if the statement is determined to have been made consciously, the accused might still be found to have not had the knowledge of the consequences of making the statement by reason of a psychological condition[9] or due to intoxication, and the statement may be ruled inadmissible. In the 1986 Supreme Court of Canada decision of *Clarkson v. The Queen,* the court ruled that: "Absent any urgent reason compelling the police to act immediately to gather evidence, the interrogation [of a woman intoxicated by alcohol charged with murdering her husband], at a minimum, should have been delayed until the accused was in a condition to properly exercise her s. 10(b) [Charter] rights [to retain and

---

[9]*R. v. Whittle* (1994) 2 S.C.R. 914.

instruct legal counsel] or appreciate the consequences of waiving it.... If the mind operated sufficiently to make a conscious statement but could not have the knowledge of the consequences of making it, the evidence should as well be excluded."[10]

5.7.3   Cautioning and Charter Rights

The standard police caution is read or recited to the individual by the person in authority, prior to questioning, and begins to discharge the Crown's burden of proving the voluntariness of a statement.

BOX 5.1	Read v. Recite - A True Story

The choice of reading the caution from a department-issued card or reciting it from memory may not be as simple as it seems. A now deceased RCMP officer once related an incident in which he had obtained a confession from a suspect after having recited the caution, rather than reading it from his issued caution card. During the *voir dire* to determine the admissibility of the statement, the officer was required by defence counsel to recite the caution during his testimony – no less than 47 times.

Had the officer made the slightest deviation in wording in any single recitation, defence counsel might have been able to make a case that the caution actually administered to the accused was something different than the recommended caution, and attempted to create doubt regarding the proper taking of the confession. In this case, the officer successfully recited the correct wording of the caution in each of the 47 occasions and, presumably, the statement was admitted into evidence.

While the ability to recite the caution and **supplementary caution** from memory definitely gives an investigator the appearance of knowledge, experience and professionalism, relying on memory may result in a situation in which the officer is required to prove to the court the integrity of the caution administered from memory. Simply stated, if your memory isn't up to the task, or you prefer not to be subjected to the pressure of unnecessary cross-examination, read the caution from your department-issued card that is provided to you for that purpose. The recommended caution is repeated once again below:

"You (are charged / or will be charged / or may be charged) with (the offence under investigation). Do you wish to say anything in answer to the charge? You are not obliged to say anything unless you wish to do so, but whatever you say may be given in evidence. Do you understand?"

The purpose of administering the caution is first to help to prove that a statement given was made voluntarily by reason of informing the individual that he or she was considered a suspect or was being charged for a specified offence. Second, the caution informs the suspect or accused that any statement provided may be repeated in evidence in court.

If a suspect or accused was arrested or previously dealt with by any person in authority other than the interrogator, it is then necessary for the interrogator to administer the secondary caution to the prisoner to minimize the effect of any threat or inducement that

---

[10]*Clarkson v. The Queen* (1986) 1 S.C.R. 383.

may have been made by the previous person in authority. The wording of the secondary caution is to the effect:

"If you have spoken to any police officer, or to anyone with authority, or if any such person has spoken to you in connection with this case, I want it clearly understood that I do not want it to influence you in making any statement. Do you understand?"

The offence under investigation must be accurately specified to suspect or accused. If, for example, a suspect was arrested on a charge of Aggravated Assault or Attempted Murder, and during the interrogation, the victim dies as a result of his or her injuries, the suspect or accused should be immediately cautioned on the charge of first or second degree murder and re-informed of his or her rights to legal counsel.[11]

It is necessary to re-caution the suspect after he or she has already been cautioned for the original offence, because of the greater consequences in the form of increased penalty that will follow for the suspect or accused to now give a statement for the more serious offence. The interrogator must always create an environment that is free from threats, oppression, and inducements, documenting all of the conditions under which the statement was obtained if the interrogator wishes to be able to use any resulting statement as evidence in court.

There are two main dangers of obtaining an inadmissible confession. If the statement is determined not to have been made voluntarily, or is shown to have resulted from some other form of breach of the accused's *Charter* rights, the statement will, in all likelihood, not be admitted as evidence. Also, any evidence obtained as a result of the tainted statement may also be declared inadmissible using the analogy of the "fruit of the poison tree." Where the root source of the evidence is tainted, so may any derivative evidence be excluded, unless to fail to admit it would tend to bring the administration of justice into disrepute (See Chapter 13: Courtroom Procedures).

5.7.4 Informing of Rights: Reason for Arrest and Rights to Legal Counsel

Subsection 10(a) of the *Canadian Charter of Rights and Freedoms* states: "Everyone has the right on arrest or detention to be informed promptly of the reasons therefore."[12]

Certainly, any person who is under arrest or detention must be advised of the reason for his or her arrest as soon as is practicable to do so (e.g., "I am Constable Smith, a police officer with the _____ police service. I am placing you under arrest for Theft over $5 000").

Subsection 10(b) of the *Canadian Charter of Rights and Freedoms* states: "Everyone has the right on arrest or detention to retain and instruct counsel without delay and to be informed of that right."[13] The literal effect of s. 10(b) is that only persons who have been arrested or detained are legally required to be advised of his or her rights to counsel. In addition to being informed of his or her rights to counsel, the Supreme Court of Canada has also ruled that arrested or detained persons must also be advised of the existence and availability of legal aid.[14]

---

[11]*R. v. Black* (1989) 2 S.C.R. 138, 50 C.C.C. (3d) 1, 70 C.R. (3d) 97.

[12]*Canadian Charter of Rights and Freedoms*, Being Part I of the *Constitution Act*, 1982 Enacted by the *Canada Act* 1982 (U.K.) c.11; proclaimed in force April 17, 1982 s. 10(a).

[13]*Ibid*, s. 10(b).

[14]*R. v. Brydges* (1990), 1 S.C.R. 190, 53 C.C.C. (3d) 330, (1990) 2 W.W.R. 220.

In Ontario, an officer might use the following wording to discharge his or her responsibilities under s. 10(b) of the Charter:

"It is my duty to inform you that you have the right to retain and instruct counsel without delay. You have the right to telephone any lawyer you wish. You also have the right to free advice from a Legal Aid lawyer. If you are charged with an offence, you may apply to the Ontario Legal Aid Plan for legal assistance. 1-800-265-0451 is a toll free number that will put you in contact with a Legal Aid Duty Counsel lawyer for free legal advice right now. Do you understand? Do you wish to call a lawyer now?"

An out-of-custody suspect who voluntarily attends a police station for questioning does not have to be advised of his or her 10(b) *Charter* rights prior to being questioned.[15] Nor, should it be noted, is there anything in law that prevents him or her from being advised of his or her rights to consult an attorney prior to questioning, at any time. Nor is it ever a mistake for a police officer to inform such a person that he or she has the rights to legal counsel. In my opinion, doing so only indicates to the court an abundance of good faith and respect for the rights of the individual on the part of the investigator – something that will never be held against you in court – especially if you are successful in obtaining an admission or confession.

Once an arrested person has indicated a desire to consult legal counsel, it is the duty of the police to immediately cease questioning the individual until the prisoner has had a "reasonable opportunity" to consult counsel.[16]

Reasonable opportunity is not clearly defined, but is not the same as the "single phone call" criminals are allowed in the movies and television. In reality, if a prisoner is required to make several calls to contact a lawyer, he or she must be permitted to do so – in privacy.[17]

It must also be noted that except in the case of a young person, who has the right to contact a parent or other adult, legal counsel is the only person a detained prisoner has the legal rights to contact. He or she does not have the legal right to telephone a friend, criminal associate, girlfriend, boyfriend or anyone other than legal counsel.

Furthermore, a detained person is required to exercise a certain degree of diligence in his or her efforts to contact counsel. If a detained person unsuccessfully attempted to contact legal counsel, he or she must be permitted another opportunity. Should a prisoner refuse to attempt to contact counsel after having been given the opportunity by the police to do so, the police have the right to continue with the questioning or their investigation of the individual.[18]

The *Canadian Charter of Rights and Freedoms*[19] guarantees individuals in Canada certain fundamental rights, including freedom from self-incrimination (i.e., the right to remain silent). Once a suspect or accused has indicated his or her intention to remain silent, all attempts to question or interrogate him or her do not necessarily have to cease.

---

[15]*R. v. Hawkins* (1993), 2 S.C.R. 157, 79 C.C.C. (3d) 576, 20 C.R. (4th) 55.

[16]*R. v. Manninen* (1987), 1 S.C.R. 1233, 34 C.C.C. (3d) 385, 58 C.R. (3d) 97; *R. v. Ross*, (1989), 1 S.C.R. 3, 46 C.C.C. (3d) 129, 67 C.R. (3d) 209.

[17]*R. v. Whitford* (1997), 115 C.C.C. (3d) 52, 141 W.A.C. 97, 196 A.R. 97 (C.A.), leave to appeal to S.C.C. refused 117 C.C.C. (3d) vi, 46 C.R.R. (2d) 397n.

[18]*R. v. Smith* (1989), 2 S.C.R. 368, 50 C.C.C. (3d) 308, 71 C.R. (3d) 129.

[19]*Canadian Charter of Rights and Freedoms*, Being Part 1 of the *Constitution Act*, 1982, enacted by the *Canada Act* 1982 (U.K.); proclaimed in force April 17, 1982.

The Supreme Court of Canada has held that continued questioning of a suspect or accused who has consulted (or has had a reasonable opportunity to consult) legal counsel, short of denying the suspect or accused the right to choose to remain silent does not necessarily breach the right to silence. This is providing that the suspect is not coerced into making a statement nor deprived of the choice to remain silent.[20] It is recommended that in such cases, investigators proceed with an abundance of caution and document their actions thoroughly and accurately.

The Supreme Court has also held that where the subject being questioned by police elects to exercise his or her section 10(b) *Charter* rights to counsel,[21] ("...unless any urgent reason compels the police to act immediately to gather evidence"[22]) all questioning must cease until the subject has had a reasonable opportunity to contact legal counsel. The phrase, "unless any urgent reason compels the police to act immediately," implies that the Supreme Court might be, in certain circumstances of extreme emergency, somewhat sympathetic to a police interrogation that violates the suspect's rights to silence and to retain and instruct legal counsel.

BOX 5.2	Investigative Relevance
It is recommended that extreme caution be used by an investigator to intentionally deny any suspect his or her rights to silence and to counsel on the basis of urgency, at the time of questioning. It is	strongly suggested that any attempt to do so should be made only in the most dire of circumstances (e.g., to do so could be justified on the basis of the need to save a person's life, etc.), if at all!

5.8 PROXEMICS

Proxemics: The study of socially conditioned spatial [distance] factors in ordinary human relations.

Concise Oxford Dictionary, 9th Edition.

The concept of Proxemics, founded by anthropologist Edward T. Hall, plays a significant role in the day-to-day interpersonal relationships between human beings. We all have clearly defined personal comfort zones that we consciously or sub-consciously guard against intrusion by those who are not welcomed. While these recognized distances may differ slightly from one culture to another, the following chart describes the social distances commonly used in normal everyday relationships in the West and indicates the nature of normally acceptable activities that occur within them.

---

[20]*R. v. Hebert* (1990) 2 S.C.R. 151.

[21]Canadian Charter of Rights and Freedoms, Being Part I of the Constitution Act, 1982 Enacted by the Canada Act 1982 (U.K.) c.11; proclaimed in force April 17, 1982 s. 10(b).

[22]*Clarkson v. The Queen* (1986) 1 S.C.R. 383; *R. v. Manninen* (1987), 1 S.C.R. 1233.

TABLE 5.2	Proxemics	
Zone	Distance	Explanation
Public	3.6 metres +	The minimum distance maintained between a public speaker and an audience. The tone of voice used at this distance must be sufficiently loud to allow the speaker to be heard by the listener(s).
		The distance between the speaker and listener is non-threatening. Due to the lack of privacy, no secrets are exchanged at this distance. The topic of conversation is of a general and impersonal nature.
Social - Consultative	1.2 – 3.6 metres	The distance most people maintain while conversing with acquaintances or strangers in a typical social setting. The tone of voice used at this distance is one of normal conversation.
		The distance between the speaker and the listener presents no physical threat to the listener; however, there is little chance of any personal information being exchanged, again, due to a lack of privacy.
Personal - Casual	45 cm – 1.2 metres	Only trusted friends and family members are usually allowed into this personal comfort zone of approximately one arm length or less. The tone of voice used at this distance is at or below one of normal conversation.
		This distance promotes privacy and encourages a suspect or accused person to confess.
Intimate	15 – 45 cm	The distance reserved only for close family members and loved ones. Tones of voice are at or slightly above a whisper.
		A suspect will be the most likely to confess when the interrogator can enter and remain in this comfort zone, free from resistance. The interrogator must use a subdued, compassionate tone of voice, consistent with the normal communication that occurs in this zone, and maintain a sincere, concerned expression for the suspect's situation.

Source: http://members.aol.com/doder1/proxemi1.htm

5.8.1   The Use of Proxemics During an Interrogation

The use of Proxemics during an interrogation involves the interrogator, or lead interrogator if more than one officer is involved, alternately moving in and out of the suspect's personal-casual zone (45 cm – 1.2 metres). The objective of "invading" the suspect's personal space is to induce anxiety for the purpose of establishing psychological domination over the suspect. Moving closer to the suspect, who is unable to move away or defend his or her personal space, will eventually result in the interrogator's acceptance in the suspect's intimate zone and will promote the desired interaction (i.e., the receiving of the suspect's confession).

The interrogator should sit in an office chair, equipped with casters (wheels), while the suspect should be provided with a stationary chair (without wheels or armrests) to sit in.

The interrogator's moveable chair allows the interrogator to roll in (and out) of the suspect's personal-casual and intimate zones as the need or opportunity arise.

It is recommended that the interrogator commence the interrogation by maintaining a distance of between 1.2 to 3.6 metres (social-consultative zone) from the suspect. There should not be any physical or psychological barriers (e.g., a desk or table) between the interrogator and the suspect. This distance allows the interrogator to study the subject's normal body language patterns in response to routine, non-threatening questions while under the minimal stress of being questioned at a police station.

As the interrogation progresses, the distance between the suspect and interrogator can alternately be increased or decreased. As the interrogator moves closer to the subject, the subject's stress will increase, while backing away provides the suspect with a certain degree of relief. The interrogator can also synchronize the movement toward the suspect with the asking of vital questions. As the subject's stress level increases, the interrogator should continuously observe the suspect for verbal and nonverbal responses that may indicate deception.

People rarely, if ever, divulge closely guarded secrets at distances of less than 1.2 metres, or one arm's length. An interrogator can benefit from the use of Proxemics by gaining access to the suspect or accused person's intimate zone, as it is in this zone that the sharing of personal and intimate information most easily occurs.

5.9   THE FIVE STAGES INVOLVED IN A CONFESSION

In 1969, Dr. Elisabeth Kübler-Ross (1926–2004) is credited with having developed the theory that terminally ill patients progress through a five-stage transitional process progressing through denial, anger, bargaining, depression and acceptance. To a certain extent, victims of crime also experience the same five stages in attempting to cope with their victimization.[23]

During an interrogation, a suspect or accused person may also demonstrate the identical five stages in response to the interrogator's questioning:

- *Denial:* "Of course I didn't do that."

- *Anger:* "How dare you even accuse me of this?"

- *Bargaining:* Attempts at compromise to gain their freedom. "I didn't take it, but I'd pay back the money if that would help clear this matter up."

- *Depression:* Sadness as the full impact of the strength of the case against them inevitably leads to the realization that they have been caught. Perhaps mixed with guilt. The subject becomes quiet, their posture slouches and their head may hang down to their chest. They may sigh heavily or even weep openly.

- *Acceptance:* The subject will appear less emotional, calm and even relieved as they are no longer under the stress of lying to convince the interrogator of their innocence.

---

[23]Schmalleger & Volk (2005) p. 254.

5.10   TECHNIQUES OF INTERROGATION

"Sin has many tools, but a lie is the handle which fits them all."

Oliver Wendell Holmes Jr, US jurist, (1841-1935).[24]

The interrogator's demeanour is of vital important during an interrogation. The goal is to establish and maintain a psychological advantage at all times over the subject being interrogated. Always be professionally attired (whether in business suit or a neatly pressed and polished uniform). Remember that you are trying to gradually reduce the subject's resistance to your entering his or her intimate zone to encourage the subject to share the "secret" of their guilt (if, in fact, they are guilty) with you – you don't wish to seem repulsive to them in any way. You must appear to the suspect to be a professional law enforcement officer who is worthy of receiving his or her confession. A suspect will never want to lose any contest as important as this will be to them to anyone who does not convey a professional and authoritative presence.

5.10.1   Attitude

The interrogator must develop the mindset that by the time the interrogation is finished, he or she will be certain of whether or not the subject interrogated did or did not commit the offence under investigation. The interrogator should indicate to the suspect the belief that based on the evidence gathered during the investigation, there is no doubt whatsoever in the interrogator's mind that the suspect is the person who committed the offence.

The interrogator must never be overwhelmed by the seriousness of the allegation the suspect has allegedly committed, regardless of how distasteful the subject matter may be. The interrogator must remain highly motivated, regardless of how fatigued or hungry he or she may be. If you are tired, the suspect is probably tired also. When you feel that you can't continue, challenge yourself to continue for just another ten minutes, then another, then another. Somebody always has to be the first one to give up.

Most physical altercations are lost not on the basis of strength or fighting ability. They are lost when one of the involved combatants becomes the first to quit. Never be the first person to quit, either in a physical contest or in an interrogation.

5.10.2 Minimization Techniques

A useful strategy is to minimize the gravity of the suspect's actions and the consequences by assuring the suspect just how many people commit the same type of act every day. The offence might be compared to similar scenarios (real or imagined) to convince the suspect that, in your experience, his or her offence is relatively minor. The suspect may need to be reassured that his or her family will understand what he or she has done and will be forgiving. Their boss, their neighbours and the judge will understand too.

---

[24]Oliver Wendell Holmes quote retrieved November 23, 2003, from www.quotationspage.com

The suspect's role might be downplayed to make it easier for the suspect to admit to his or her guilt. Perhaps the crime could be blamed (at least partially) on the victim, (e.g., "Well, it's their fault for leaving all that money lying around," or "You only hurt him – it's not like you killed anyone," or "They could have saved a lot of trouble by putting in a good alarm system.")

If the suspect continues to deny the allegation, hold your hand up with your palm facing them in the international stop sign (i.e., you don't want to hear any more of their lies) and continue by reminding them of the evidence against them. Then try another approach that will be easier to confess to.

5.11 NON-VERBAL COMMUNICATION (BODY LANGUAGE)

"To acquire knowledge, one must study; but to acquire wisdom, one must observe."

Marilyn vos Savant, American author (b.1946).[25]

Research tells us that during average conversation, a mere 7 per cent of all communication is verbal, while an additional 38 percent of communication comprises information transmitted through verbal tones and the remaining 55 per cent is communicated through facial expressions. These statistics are extremely significant to a law enforcement officer tasked with gathering information from persons in the investigation of crimes.

We rely on the words people speak to us every day regarding any number of subjects but the words spoken amount to only 7 percent of the total information that is available to us. By relying solely on the words spoken by a witness, suspect or accused, an interrogator might easily overlook indicators of reliability or possible deception in the subject's tone, facial expressions and gestures that are either consistent or inconsistent with the words he or she is saying.

It is far easier for some people to tell a lie intentionally than it is for others. Some people lie better simply because they are more experienced at it. Some people lie well out of necessity (if they need to escape a threatening situation). It is far more difficult, however, for someone to control their body language, which may be communicating the true state of their thoughts and emotions while their spoken words convey a totally different message.

A seated person may smile warmly while they are speaking to you, yet cross their arms and or legs in a defensive posture indicating a desire to protect their personal space. A person being interviewed or interrogated may lean forward in their chair, aligning their body to the closest door, in the classic sprinter's stance, indicating an unconscious desire to get away.

What you must remember is that considerable caution must be exercised whenever you are attempting to determine reliability or deception from assessing a subject's body

---

[25]Marilyn vos Savant quote retrieved September 16, 2004, from www.members.aol.com/nonverbal2/nvcom

language. Just being questioned by the police can be very stressful, even for a witness, resulting in the same gestures, due to transient nervousness, as are indicated by guilty persons.

More than mere experience is necessary to be able to assess a person's body language reliably. Gestures, expressions and changes in tone of voice are significant only if they deviate from the subject's normal patterns or if they occur every time a sensitive question is posed to them.

5.12   INDICATORS OF DECEPTION

"False words are not only evil in themselves, but they infect the soul with evil."

Plato (427 - 347 BC).[26]

Regardless of how capable a judge of character you think you are, the detection of deception through a subject's verbal cues and nonverbal cues is a complex and highly subjective process. Contrary to popular belief, reluctance on the part of a subject to maintain constant eye contact with the interrogator is not (necessarily) proof of deception unless eye contact is broken every time the subject is asked a direct question. None of the verbal and nonverbal indicators represent a hard and fast rule for detecting deception.

The skilled interrogator never relies merely on one word, one facial expression or a single gesture to formulate an opinion as to whether or not the subject is being deceptive. Rather, deception should only be inferred from verbal responses, expressions and gestures that are observed in conjunction with each other (referred to as clusters) and which deviate from the subject's normal speech and behavioural patterns that are established during normal conversation with the subject prior to the questioning commencing in earnest.

5.12.1   Verbal Indicators of Deception

Changes in a person's tone, rate of speech and every word spoken by them can be useful to assess their reliability during questioning. It is vitally important to listen carefully to every word spoken by a person being interviewed or interrogated and, sometimes more importantly, what the subject didn't say. When the subject being interrogated doesn't answer a direct question, either the person didn't understand the question or it is very possible that the subject is being deceptive.

A subject, when asked a direct question, may respond with a long and rambling explanation that avoids the issue being discussed. An interrogator should ensure that every issue is dealt with before moving on to the next issue. If the subject did not answer the question – ask yourself, "Why didn't they answer the question?," and ask it again (and again if you have to).

---

[26]Plato quoted from *Dialogues, Phaedo*. Quote retrieved November 23, 2003, from www.quotationspage.com

A subject may also attempt to avoid giving direct answers to sensitive questions by altering the verb tenses of his or her answers:

Officer: "Did you take the money from the cash register?"

Subject: "I would never do that."

At first glance, the response appears to be a denial to the question and an unwary interrogator might move on. Examine the question and answer closely and you will notice that the question was asked in the past tense while the subject's answer is in the conditional tense. The person could possibly be honest and be stating that they would never steal money (implying that they didn't on the date in question, either) – but they didn't answer the question that was asked. The interrogator still doesn't have an answer to the question and would make a mistake by moving on without asking the question again.

A subject may avoid giving a direct answer to a question by responding with a question of his or her own:

Officer: "Did you take the money from the cash register?"

Subject: "Who, me?" (or, "Why would I take the money?")

Innocent people will respond directly and forcefully when accused of crimes they didn't commit, but a guilty person will either stall for time, avoid the issues or will over-emphasize a negative response.

If the subject adds certain phrases to his or her response to attempt to persuade the interrogator of his or her honesty (by adding, for instance, honestly, truthfully, to be perfectly honest, to tell you the truth, honest to God, or I swear on my mother's grave), the response that follows will be highly suspect.

5.12.2 Non-verbal Indicators of Deception

"A worthless person, a wicked man, goes about with crooked speech, winks with his eyes, scrapes with his feet, points with his finger...."

Proverbs 6:12-13.

Since ancient times, it has been widely recognized that a person's thoughts and emotions speak as loudly as their words. The naturalist, Charles Darwin, founder of the theory of evolution, believed that "[r]epressed emotion almost always comes to the surface in some form of body motion." Human biology has equipped modern humanity with an internal defence mechanism referred to as the "fight or flight" response.

Whenever we find ourselves faced with a situation that we perceive to be either threatening or harmful to us, our body produces adrenalin, our muscles tense up, our pulse quickens and we breathe more rapidly in preparation for possible physical exertion necessary to defend ourselves. Our earliest human ancestors relied on these involuntary physiological responses to stand and fight a perceived threat, or to flee from it.

Even today, we experience the "fight or flight" response when faced with any potentially threatening situation. While standing on a street corner or sitting restfully in an armchair, upon hearing the backfire of a car engine, the vast majority of us will instantaneously spring to our feet or tense up in preparation to defend ourselves or to run away from a possible threat to our physical safety.

These same responses are demonstrated by guilty people being questioned. If their "secret" (their guilt) is discovered, they may potentially face the loss of their liberty, their employment or their family and could be labelled as a criminal. Having to relate a false account of an incident or of their whereabouts places guilty offenders under the additional stress of having to fabricate lies to cover their tracks and having to recall those lies they have previously told – which is infinitely harder than a truthful person finds relating facts that come from actual memory.

A person's eyes are said to be the "window to the soul." A guilty person may avert eye contact by pretending to yawn, picking imaginary lint off their clothing or by frequently looking at their watch. People who turn their gaze away and look away to a clock, close their eyes or cover their eyes with their hands are uncomfortable facing up to the accuser (or "seeing" the truth of what they have done). Occasional glancing away during conversation is perfectly natural, unless it immediately follows every time a direct question is asked.

A guilty person may attempt to convince you of his or her innocence by maintaining continuous eye contact with you. No one ever maintains eye contact 100 percent of the time – it's not considered to be polite to stare at someone. Be aware of the person who never lets his or her eyes lose contact with yours; they could be trying to intimidate you with their excellent (but excessive) eye contact. The interrogator must confidently meet the gaze of the person and not be the first one to look away to avoid giving up any psychological advantage of superiority.

A person's mouth may become very dry as the result of nervousness (or deception) or they may occasionally bite or lick their lips. They may smile inappropriately in efforts to conceal their true emotions. If, when asked a sensitive question, they bring their hand to their head or nose, or if they cover their mouth when asked a direct question – their answer will quite possibly be deceptive.

A person's posture demonstrates a great deal about his or her comfort and confidence in normal situations. Sometimes people in social settings demonstrate positions of dominance and subordination that are easily visible through body language. A person may unconsciously bend forward at the waist – symbolically lowering him or herself – when being introduced to a person whom he or she admires. A person may instinctively stand taller and exhibit grooming actions when an attractive person passes by. A person who is depressed or defeated will hang his or her head, slump the shoulders, sigh and make open-handed motions indicating a "why bother?" attitude.

An open posture with the arms unfolded and legs uncrossed, using open-handed gestures away from the centre of the body usually indicates a relaxed, confident and honest demeanour. Closed-handed gestures, crossing arms and legs, and continual shifting of weight indicate nervousness and possibly defensiveness. The interrogator must attempt to assess what, if anything, is being communicated by certain postures, especially if they occur repeatedly at significant times during the interrogation.

A person's hands held in front of him or her with the fingers interlaced in a "steepled" position is usually considered to be an expression of honesty, but if the hand goes to the person's head, nose or mouth when asked a direct question, that could indicate deception. Physiological responses of deception can also be detected if the interrogator is watchful.

A subject's face may go red as his or her blood pressure increases, their face or hands may begin to perspire or their breathing may become more rapid due to stress.

Nonverbal indicators that are observed in conjunction with verbal indicators may be considered reliable indicators of deception. Once again, these rules are not to be considered as proof of deception – only indicators of possible deception. The key is to look for indicators that deviate from the subject's normal behaviour patterns and analyze why they are occurring.

5.13   CLOSURE

By the end of the interrogation, you will either have arrived at a confession (in which case you will possibly be taking the suspect into custody) or you will have taken the interrogation as far as you possibly can for the time being and will have to release the suspect unconditionally. Whether it is the former or the latter option, it is important to remain professional and to treat the suspect with dignity.

If, after receiving a confession, reasonable grounds exist upon which to arrest, make certain to comply with all legal requirements. If the suspect is co-operative following the interrogation, the interrogator should accompany the suspect to any possible re-enactment of the offence or to retrieve hidden evidence at location(s) known only to the suspect (**a show and tell statement**). The interrogator should remain involved to maintain the rapport established during the interrogation and to reduce the number of officers involved with the suspect for court purposes.

If no confession has been obtained, you must maintain a professional rapport with the individual in the hope that he or she may agree to a second interrogation, if necessary. Remind him or her that the investigation will continue and always demonstrate confidence, stating that, "It is only a matter of time until we have the evidence we need to solve this case and we may have to contact you again." Thank him or her for coming in and leave an impression in the individual's mind that you are even more convinced of his or her guilt than you were before.

SUMMARY

- Interrogation is the process by which an attempt is made to obtain a confession of guilt, an admission of a relevant fact, or an alibi concerning the whereabouts of a suspect or accused at the time of the offence.

- The primary objective of an interrogation is to obtain an admission or confession from the suspect or accused to establish his or her guilt in the matter under investigation.

- Unlike an interview, an interrogation is accusatory in nature.

- An admission is a written or verbal partial acknowledgement of a suspect's involvement in the crime(s) under investigation that might prove one or more (but not all) of the facts in issue of an offence.

- A confession is a written or verbal acknowledgement of a suspect's involvement in the crime(s) under investigation that proves all of the facts in issue of the offence(s).

- The legal requirements involved in questioning a person suspected of a crime are far different from those when questioning a victim or witness (e.g., advising the suspect of his or her rights to counsel and his or her right to remain silent.)

- In 1912, English judges prepared a set of rules for the guidance of police officers in interrogating prisoners and suspects. The Judges' Rules have no force in law, but are still commonly referred to and provide a useful summary of the legal rules of questioning.

- Under the Confession Rule, any statement made by a suspect or accused to a person in authority must be proven to have been made voluntarily and be free from threats or inducements beyond a reasonable doubt by the Crown before it can be admitted into evidence.

- The use of Proxemics (socially conditioned spatial [distance] factors) plays a significant role in the day-to-day relationships between human beings and can be utilized to advantage during an interrogation.

- The interrogator must maintain a professional air of confidence and indicate to the suspect that there is no doubt of his or her guilt in the matter under investigation.

- The use of minimization techniques is one strategy to convince a suspect that his or her crime(s) are less serious, in an attempt to gain a confession.

- An interrogator must establish what a subject's normal behavioural patterns are and be observant for clusters of verbal and nonverbal indicators of deception.

- A subject being interrogated should at all times be treated fairly, professionally and with respect for his or her individual rights, regardless of the nature of the offence(s) under investigation.

DISCUSSION QUESTIONS

1. How is the nature of questioning different between an investigative interview and an interrogation? What are the differences in the legal requirements upon a police officer when conducting an investigative interview and an interrogation?

2. Why is it always beneficial to attempt to interrogate every suspect or accused person? What are the five possible outcomes of every interrogation?

3. What requirements must be met according to the Confession Rule before a statement of a suspect or an accused person may be admitted as evidence in court? What steps may be taken by a police officer to ensure that the requirements of the Confession Rule are satisfied?

WEBLINKS

www.canlii.org/

Canadian Legal Information Institute. Federal and provincial statutes and a searchable case law databank.

http://dictionary.law.com/

Law.com. A searchable database of legal terms and definitions.

www.apa.org/

American Psychological Association. Includes a searchable database of resources relating to the detection of deception.

Chapter 6

Crime Scene Investigation

"If you want to catch something, running after it isn't always the best way."

Lois McMaster Bujold, American author (b.1949).[1]

Learning Outcomes

After reading this chapter students should be able to:

- Explain what is meant by a crime scene, giving one example each of the three criteria that fulfill the definition provided.
- Explain Locard's Exchange Principle and its significance to the field of crime scene investigation.
- Summarize the **burning bridges theory** of crime scene investigation.
- Summarize the responsibilities of the first officer at a crime scene.
- Design and execute an appropriate search plan for searching an imaginary crime scene.
- Create a scale crime scene diagram, depicting a mock crime scene and the locations of exhibits consistent with instructions provided.
- Explain what is meant by a **staged crime scene** and the significance, if any, of evidence of staging with respect to establishing a victim–offender relationship.

6.1   WHAT IS A "CRIME SCENE" ?

"Crime scene" means any location where one or more of a series of events involved in the commission of a crime occurred, including:

1. Any location where a crime was actually committed, e.g.:

   - the branch office of a bank that is victimized by an armed robbery;

   - the scene from which the getaway vehicle was stolen.

   These are the traditional examples of crime scenes due to their obvious connections to the crime itself.

---

[1]Bujold quote retrieved November 23, 2003, from www.quotationspage.com

2. Any location where evidence of the crime is located, e.g.:

- the suspect in an aggravated assault with a weapon flees the location where the crime was actually committed and throws the weapon into a ditch, making the ditch a crime scene;

- the stolen money and the disguise worn during the commission of an armed robbery are located at the suspect's residence, making it a crime scene.

Both are examples of crime scenes due to the connection they provide to the crime and/or the offender.

3. Any a location where evidence of the crime is known to have been previously located, e.g.:

- a suspect transports the body of a homicide victim in the trunk of an automobile from the location of the crime to a remote location where it is disposed of, making the automobile a crime scene as it could yield physical evidence linking it to the victim, crime and offender.

Any of these crime scenes are capable of providing a link between the victim(s), the crime, and the offender(s).

Crime scenes need not be restricted only to buildings such as residences, office buildings or commercial institutions, although many times crimes do occur in such locations. In addition to physical structures, I have examined crime scenes in fields, forested areas and even underwater locations where evidence of a crime had been disposed.

Imagine embarking on a one-month tour of Europe without an itinerary of routes to travel, destinations or places of interest that you intend to visit. At the end of your vacation, you would certainly have seen some parts of Europe, but while the trip may not have been a total loss, you probably wouldn't have made the most of your time or taken advantage of a perhaps once in a lifetime opportunity.

Crime scenes are somewhat similar because you have only one opportunity to examine them correctly. There are many benefits to having a systematic plan to follow so that you maximize the time, effort and resources expended to achieve the strongest possible result. The ability to examine a crime scene methodically and effectively is one of the most important factors that distinguish great investigators from mediocre investigators. For a discussion of how to devise a crime scene plan, see Section 6.12.

When you examine the following examples please note the distinction between a cursory examination and the methodical and effective examination of a crime scene.

Example # 1:   A police officer responds to the scene of a break enter and theft at a business premises. He or she examines the crime scene by quickly walking through the scene, making few notes or observations and drawing hasty conclusions about the nature and events of the crime or clues regarding the identity of the offender. Upon returning to his or her police station, the officer notes in a report, "No evidence found." Such a search as this, by any definition, could not be described as either methodical or effective. In this example, the investigator made no effort to reconstruct the events of the crime nor to identify and collect evidence that might have led to the identification of the person(s) responsible for the break and enter. Unfortunately, this is a true story.

Example # 2: Investigators respond to an alleged break and enter of a dwelling house. The lone female occupant states that an unknown offender entered her residence and sexually assaulted her. A methodical examination of the interior and exterior of the residence is conducted. The scene is extensively photographed. Areas of the residence are dusted for fingerprints. It is noted that the telephone line has been disabled within the residence.

A careful, preliminary examination of the crime scene is unsuccessful in locating any biological evidence of a sexual assault. The investigators conclude that the complaint is a false allegation and close their investigation as unfounded. While this crime scene examination could be described as methodical, it was by no means effective.

Due to a faulty reconstruction of events of the crime, due largely to misperception of the evidence, this investigation failed to confirm the crime as it was reported by the complainant and had no hope of identifying the person responsible. The offence did occur, exactly as the victim related it. This actual case involved a serial rapist who went on to victimize several more women before he was eventually apprehended.

Example # 3: Investigators respond to a crime scene involving the double homicide of two females who were stabbed repeatedly inside their own residence. The crime scene was carefully examined and documented. It was noted that several items had been moved, presumably by the offender(s), after the murders to give the appearance that the homicide had occurred in a different manner (see Section 6.19: Staged Crime Scenes).

Based on the evidence from the crime scene, the investigation resulted in a former boyfriend of one of the women and another man being arrested and charged with first degree murder. This is an example of a crime scene search that was both methodical and effective. This crime scene examination demonstrated a correct interpretation of the evidence, resulting in an effective reconstruction of the events and identification of the persons responsible. This is also a true story.

6.2 OBJECTIVES OF CRIME SCENE INVESTIGATION

Most, but not all, crimes investigated by the police will have one or more known crime scenes. Crime does not occur in a vacuum; all crimes occur at some location or other. Accordingly there must, of necessity, always be a crime scene; however, due to steps taken by the offender to conceal the circumstances of the offence, the location of the crime scene may not be known for some time, if at all. For example, if a woman is reported missing by her parents who suspect that she met with foul play at the hands of her intimate partner and if homicide is indeed involved, the location of the crime scene might be unknown at the time of the initial report.

For the purposes of this chapter, let's simplify matters and say that for all of our "crimes" we will have distinct crime scenes. Let's take a look, then, at the various objectives involved in the investigation of crime scenes.

Goals and Objectives:

- to confirm that a crime (or an event requiring investigation) has occurred;

- to confirm that a crime occurred in the manner in which it was reported;

- if a crime has occurred, to identify the appropriate criminal charge;

- identify the victim(s) (if not successfully concluded through other methods);

- identify the person(s) responsible for the event or crime;

- arrest and charge the person(s) responsible, where legal authority exists to do so;

- identify and interview possible witnesses to the event or crime;

- reconstruct the events, assessing all available evidence, to determine the true facts of the crime or event;

- collect information and gather evidence necessary to prove the facts in issue of the crime (*actus reus*); and

- document the circumstances of the event/crime and present them fairly in the appropriate judicial or quasi-judicial proceeding (e.g., criminal court, Coroner's Inquest, tribunal, etc.).

Of course, police officers do far more than just these stated objectives during the course of an entire investigation, such as ensuring adequate support for the victim, etc. However, for the purposes of this chapter we will confine our discussion of responsibilities to those that relate directly to the examination of the crime scene itself.

6.3 THE BURNING BRIDGES THEORY OF CRIME SCENE INVESTIGATION

Picture yourself walking across a wooden bridge that crosses a river. Once on the far side of the river, you set fire to the bridge, destroying it completely. You will never be able to return to where you started in the exact same manner as you did when you first crossed. Of course, you might decide to return to the other side of the river by boat, or perhaps by building another bridge or even by finding a shallow location to wade back across. But, you can never return to where you started in the exact same manner if you "burn the bridge" behind you!

And so it is with crime scene investigation. Every time anything is done at a crime scene, it represents another "bridge" burned. Whatever has been changed can never be restored to its original condition. If an exhibit is moved, it can never be put back in exactly the same place. If "contamination" of the crime scene occurs, for example through exposure to environmental factors (wind or precipitation) or the introduction of foreign material or trace evidence, not connected to the crime, the crime scene can never be restored to its original condition. Still more bridges burned!

Why is the burning bridges theory relevant to crime scene investigators? All crimes are committed by offenders. Any "trace evidence" left by the offender and physical evidence of the crime(s) will be strongest immediately following the crime. At the precise time the crime scene is initially discovered by either a civilian witness or by the police, the crime scene is as close as possible to the same condition that it was at the time of the actual crime (ruling out any possibility of environmental or other form of contamination having occurred since the crime).

The "chain of continuity" (for each piece of evidence) must be proven from the time of its initial discovery, throughout the entire investigative process until such time that it is entered as an exhibit in court (see Section 2.8). The integrity of each piece of evidence, including any conclusion that can be drawn from it, relies upon meticulous documentation from the time of the exhibit's discovery, subsequent handling of it and throughout all the steps taken to prevent contamination until its admission in court. It is not sufficient to know that a firearm was discovered in a certain room of a certain house. Its precise location within the room must be proven – it could make the difference between proving suicide or homicide.

"Bridges" must eventually be burned during the processing of crime scenes. Evidence must ultimately be gathered (moved and handled) sooner or later. We now know, however, that when evidence is moved from its original location, yet another bridge is burned. To the extent possible, the solution to successfully working around the Burning Bridges theory is to preserve evidence as we find it, that is, through photographing, videotaping, creating crime scene diagrams and taking thorough and accurate written notes before the bridge is burned.

The proper gathering of evidence and processing of crime scenes is a necessary function of law enforcement. In accomplishing this, we satisfy the "best evidence rule" and are able to reproduce the evidence located at the crime scene (in writing, electronically, on video or through the use of still photography) that we couldn't otherwise bring into the courtroom. It is the unauthorized changes to the crime scene that diminish the integrity of the evidence and decrease the chances of successfully proving the crime.

All evidence located at a crime scene may still be challenged in court; however, a properly processed and meticulously documented crime scene will stand up to the most rigorous judicial scrutiny. The lesson to be learned in relation to crime scene examination, as with crossing every bridge that you intend to burn behind you, is that you have only one chance to do it correctly.

6.4   EXHIBIT V. EVIDENCE

The confusion, if any, between these two terms results from the fact that both terms are applied to individual pieces of physical evidence in one manner during the investigative phase and another way during the prosecution phase. To clear up any possible confusion in the mind of the reader as to the terms "exhibit" versus "evidence" in the context of an investigation, items of evidence (again, using the example of physical evidence) are located at crime scenes. Evidence is anything that is material (relevant) to the investigation. Evidence may be admissible or inadmissible in court or it may never be introduced at court (as in the case of an unsolved investigation), but it always remains evidence.

During a judicial proceeding, once evidence is declared admissible by the presiding justice, it is then considered an exhibit and is numbered sequentially (or lettered) as an exhibit for either the Crown or the defence. You will also hear the term exhibit applied to physical evidence located at a crime scene during the investigative phase. We have Exhibit Control Officers, investigators who track pieces of physical evidence on Exhibit Registers, and we discuss proper exhibit management.

The term "exhibit" was likely adopted by police from the court usage on the incorrect assumption that all pieces of physical evidence would eventually be entered as exhibits in court. With our current strict rules of evidence, we now know that not all evidence will be entered as exhibits in court. The two terms have become so universally applied by law enforcement officers that they are considered synonymous for all intents and purposes. Accordingly, I will refer to pieces of evidence as exhibits in relation to both the investigative and prosecutorial phases.

6.5   THE DANGERS OF "TUNNEL VISION"

In Chapter 1, we discussed the concept of tunnel vision as it relates to police investigations, generally. While an investigation may fall victim to tunnel vision at any stage, an investigation is particularly vulnerable during a crime scene examination phase. Awareness of the potential danger of falling victim to tunnel vision is so crucial for investigators that a brief passage from Chapter 1 is repeated at this point.

To refresh the reader's memory, Mr Justice Fred Kaufman defined tunnel vision as:

"[A] single-minded and overly narrow focus on a particular investigative or prosecutorial theory, so as to unreasonably colour the evaluation of information received and one's conduct in response to that information."[2]

Mr Justice Kaufman's succinct definition of tunnel vision, simply stated, warns investigators of the danger of making up one's mind before all of the facts of a case are known. Improper or inaccurate interpretation of evidence can result in investigators focusing on conclusions that are not supported by the evidence in a case. By forming a theory that is not substantiated by the known facts of a case, investigators may distort or misrepresent the facts and take inappropriate action due to their distortion of the facts.

Investigators operating out of a mindset of an honest, but mistaken, belief sometimes attempt to make the evidence fit a particular and erroneous theory, rather than allowing the existing evidence to simply tell the story. Tunnel vision creates several potentially dangerous ramifications for an investigation. A fundamental principle of criminal investigation is to "Let the evidence TELL the story … don't make the evidence FIT the story."

Remember Example # 2 (Section 6.1) that dealt with the serial rapist who broke into houses and sexually assaulted the female residents? Although it is difficult to believe that several well-intentioned, professional investigators could have misinterpreted (or disregarded) an abundance of physical evidence that corroborated the victim's story (tunnel vision), I will now share with you that the identical situation occurred in no less than three other cases dealing with the same offender – all between two adjacent police jurisdictions.

Had the offender in this case been identified and apprehended shortly after the initial offence, it is a virtual certainty that the other women in this case would never have been victimized. This reason alone should be ample incentive for any investigator to zealously guard him or herself against falling into the tunnel vision trap. Unfortunately, these

[2]Kaufman (1998), p. 479.

are not isolated incidents. Regrettable examples of tunnel vision can be found in many instances in a variety of locations. Don't ever let this happen to you!

BOX 6.1	Investigative Relevance

Guarding yourself against tunnel vision is only half the battle for a professional investigator. When you observe tunnel vision occurring (and unfortunately you will), never be afraid to stand up and say something about it, or else you too will become tainted by the stigma of tunnel vision. If you don't stand up for your own beliefs, at the very least, stand up to tunnel vision on behalf of the victim.

Investigate every case as the victim has reported it until you can satisfy yourself beyond a reasonable doubt that the event could not possibly have occurred in the manner in which it was reported.

And always remember (especially at crime scenes) to "Let the evidence TELL the story … don't make the evidence FIT the story."

6.6   LOCARD'S EXCHANGE PRINCIPLE

If the passage from Chapter 1 dealing with tunnel vision was worth repeating (and believe me, it *is* that important), let's also do a quick review on Locard's Exchange Principle, which was first discussed in Section 2.9. It is vital to us, as crime scene investigators, to appreciate the significance of this scientific principle that explains the transference of physical evidence because it is at crime scenes that this transference occurs. To refresh the student's memory, this scientific principle states:

"When any two objects come into contact, there is always a transference of material from each object onto the other."

Dr. Locard did not state that a transference of material "might" occur. If two objects come into direct contact with each other, a transference "will" occur. A transference of material "might" still occur even if there is no direct contact, but it is fundamentally impossible for two objects to come into contact with each other without leaving a trace of themselves on each other. The lesson learned is that science tells us that the evidence is there – the investigator only has to find it.

Once you accept Locard's Exchange Principle as irrefutable, the significance of the following diagram, illustrating how trace evidence may typically be transferred during the commission of a crime, becomes self-evident when speaking about crime scene investigation.

There may be trace evidence transferred by a victim (e.g., hair or fibres, fingerprints or footwear **impressions**) at the scene and the scene may deposit evidence upon a victim (e.g., soil, botanical matter, paint, etc.). The victim may transfer trace evidence onto an offender (e.g., hair, fibres, blood, etc) and may in turn have trace evidence from the offender transferred onto them (e.g., hair, fibres, bite marks, bodily fluids, etc.). Likewise, an offender may transfer trace evidence to a crime scene (e.g., footwear impressions, fingerprints, tool marks, bodily fluids, etc.) and trace evidence from the scene will be transferred to the offender (e.g., dust, paint, soil, botanical material, fragments of glass, etc.).

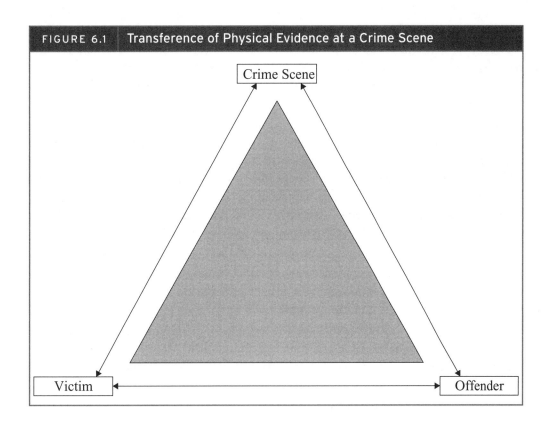

FIGURE 6.1 | Transference of Physical Evidence at a Crime Scene

As you can see, there are any number of potential ways in which trace evidence can be transferred during the commission of a crime. The successful detection of trace evidence is limited only by the investigator's ability to locate and preserve it.

If the above diagram doesn't look familiar, the student may wish to re-read Chapter 2, dealing with evidence. More will follow regarding of techniques how to search for trace evidence later in this chapter.

6.7 RESPONSIBILITIES OF THE FIRST OFFICER AT A CRIME SCENE

The initial actions taken by the first officer at the crime scene will profoundly impact the final outcome of any investigation. Upon arriving at a chaotic crime scene, the responsibilities of the first officer can sometimes seem overwhelming and intimidating. One thing is certain about crime scenes – no two are exactly the same. It isn't possible to examine two crime scenes in the same way due to the different dynamics involving the participants of the event, the circumstances of the locations themselves and the varying circumstances of the crimes.

It is possible, however, to provide some standardized guidelines for responding to crime scenes that are based upon recognized best practices in the field of criminal investigation. The primary duty of the first officer is to **secure the crime scene**. By securing the scene we mean the continuous stabilization and protection of the crime scene against entry by unauthorized persons and against "contamination" until a methodical and effective examination of the scene can occur.

Without making the job of the first officer at a crime scene even more difficult than it already is, his or her responsibilities commence the very moment he or she initially receives the call or dispatch. "En route to the scene, the route taken and any [observations] regarding fleeing vehicles, suspect(s) and potential witnesses shall be [documented in the officer's notebook]."[3]

As a patrol officer, and later as a criminal investigator, when responding to a serious occurrence, I always ran through a mental checklist of the tasks that I might expect to encounter and assessed how I might prioritize my responses and what actions I might take upon my arrival. If a crime allegedly involved a firearm, I might encounter shell casings, other ballistic evidence and gun-shot residue (GSR). If it was a crime of violence, I would have to ensure that I seized both the victim's and the offender's clothing. In the case of a sexual offence, I might have to employ a Sexual Assault Kit, if appropriate.

I subsequently drafted procedures for my police service dealing with the responsibilities of the first officer at a crime scene and collaborated in the drafting of "Initial Crime Scene Functions" contained in the original (undated) *Ontario Major Case Management (MCM) Manual*, which is no longer in print.

While the current MCM manual applies specifically to designated criteria offences (e.g., homicides, sexual assault, non-familial abductions, etc.), the principles of the initial crime scene minimum investigative standard, which is reproduced in part below, apply universally to crime scenes of every description:

"The following shall be conducted, as required:

(a)   record [the] exact time of [your] arrival;

(b)   ensure the placement of vehicles does not interfere with evidence;

(c)   direct other arriving personnel with respect to parking to preserve footwear/ tire impressions and trace evidence;

(d)   record full details of all persons present at the scene upon arrival and any actions taken [by them] prior to [your] arrival;

(e)   assess the situation and request any necessary assistance for scene/victim/ prisoner security;

(f)   make appropriate notifications to other personnel [e.g., supervisor, investigators, forensic identification officers, etc];

(g)   enter the scene, noting the route taken to perform a cursory search for victim(s), suspect(s) and weapon(s);

(h)   discard, move or touch nothing unless evidence is of a short-lived nature;

(i)   in death/serious injury cases, unless rigor mortis, decapitation, decomposition or transection is present [or unless the body is grossly charred by fire or the head or torso of a pulse-less and non-breathing patient is open with a gross outpouring of the brain or internal organs], death shall not be [presumed];

(j)   in death cases, consider having the Coroner [or other medical doctor] pronounce death at the scene;

---

[3]Ministry of Community Safety and Correctional Services: *Ontario Major Case Management (MCM) Manual* (undated), p. 46.

(k)   ensure ill/injured persons receive immediate care as required;

(l)   where practicable, if a victim is transported from the scene, remain with the victim to record any statements and maintain continuity of the victim and his/her clothing;

(m)   keep exhibits (e.g., short-lived evidence, evidence received from third parties) separate to avoid contamination;

(n)   record details and times in relation to all persons attending and leaving the scene;

(o)   record details of the physical scene (e.g., victim position and description, lighting conditions, doors and windows unlocked or locked, etc.) and prevailing conditions, including weather and note anything unusual such as odours, vehicles nearby, etc;

(p)   establish one route in and out of the scene to be followed by all persons attending the scene;

(q)   allow only persons who are absolutely essential, such as the Coroner, fire and ambulance personnel, to enter a major scene prior to the arrival of forensic identification personnel;

(r)   record any alterations made out of necessity at the crime scene;

(s)   establish an adequate scene perimeter and clearly mark special areas to be protected;

(t)   if necessary, cover deceased persons exposed to public view using a device such as an emergency blanket or forensic tent, while taking reasonable precautions to prevent contamination;

(u)   record all relevant events such as time of pronouncement of death, notification of next-of-kin, etc.;

(v)   protect obvious evidence at outdoor scenes to prevent possible contamination and if in danger of removal by onlookers, mark [the] location, seize [the] items and record details;

(w)   record whatever conditions exist [if any] that necessitate emergency seizure of evidence without a [search] warrant;

(x)   prohibit a suspect who has been removed from a scene from re-entering the scene unless approval is received from the [officer-in-charge];

(y)   leave nothing behind at a crime scene; do not use toilets/sinks;

(z)   prohibit [the] use of the telephone inside a crime scene except in emergency situations; and

(aa)   where persons of interest are present at the crime scene that involves a firearm, seek the informed consent of all persons to submit to a gun shot residue (GSR) test."[4]

---

[4]Ministry of Community Safety and Correctional Services: *Ontario Major Case Management (MCM) Manual* (undated), pp. 46-47.

6.8   CONTAMINATION OF THE CRIME SCENE

"[W]e even find our own officers' cigarette butts [at crime scenes]."

Alleged comment of a forensic identification officer [whom I choose
not to identify] during a meeting between the police, the Crown Attorney
and a representative of counsel for the defence on December 10, 1985
during the prosecution of Guy Paul Morin for the murder of Christine Jessop.[5]

I seriously doubt that the officer alleged to have made the above statement ever intended that such a statement would ever become enshrined as part of Mr Justice Kaufman's official report of his examination of the controversial investigation and prosecution of Guy Paul Morin. Unfortunately, police officers can sometimes become careless and complacent when proper crime scene procedures break down. Chewing gum wrappers, cigarette butts, coffee cups, and food packages have all been left strewn about by officers who either don't know any better or who "just don't get it!"

Imagine the following exchange between an investigator and a defence lawyer during a trial:

Defence: Officer, we are looking at a photograph of the scene of the homicide that depicts the location of the murder weapon. Did you take this photograph?

Officer: Yes, I did.

Defence: Officer, I direct your attention to the bottom right corner of the photograph. What is that object?

Officer: It's a pizza delivery box.

Defence: And what is the significance of the pizza box, Officer?

Officer: I was hungry?

Defence: Oh, so it is your pizza box in the photograph?

Officer: Yes it is.

Defence: And what are these objects in the bottom left corner of the photograph?

Officer: Coffee cups.

Defence: I count six coffee cups. What is the significance of the coffee cups?

Officer: We were thirsty?

Defence: Whose coffee cups are they?

Officer: Well, one is mine, but I'm not sure which one it is and I don't know whose the other cups are.

Defence: Officer, you don't know who left those cups at the murder scene?

---

[5]Kaufman (1998), p. 61.

I think, by now, you may begin to appreciate the purpose of this line of questioning being developed by counsel for the defence. The defence (in just a few short minutes) has cast doubt on the integrity of the crime scene and thus on the integrity of each piece of physical evidence found there. The defence is laying another foundation for the creation of reasonable doubt by implying that someone, other than the accused may have left a coffee cup at the crime scene and may have committed the murder.

Possible Outcomes:

- Impression created in the mind of the trier of fact: the police are incompetent, the investigation is flawed, consequently, why should I/we believe anything that the police tell us about this investigation?

- Reason: the crime scene and physical evidence have lost all integrity and the officer has lost all credibility.

- Result: reasonable doubt which will be resolved in favour of the accused.

- Verdict: Not guilty.

Locard's Exchange Principle can be your best friend at a crime scene, but it can also be your worst enemy. It not only explains how physical evidence might be transferred through the direct contact of objects during the commission of a crime, it also explains how **contamination of evidence** might occur after a crime scene has been discovered. Remember that it is not only the victim and offender(s) who leave traces of their presence at a crime scene.

Any persons or things that were there before the crime, or are introduced to the crime scene after the crime (including police officers) also leave traces of their presence. Because Locard's Exchange Principle applies equally to all persons and all locations, it highlights the need to exercise caution to protect a crime scene from contamination – even from ourselves.

BOX 6.2	Proper Investigative Procedure

Disposable latex gloves are excellent for keeping your fingerprints on your fingers, where they belong. When you are finished with them, put them into your pocket and take them from the crime scene with you. Criminals also use latex gloves – that sometimes yield fingerprint impressions – and you don't want yours to be collected as evidence.

Another topic that is related to the issue of contamination is the inadvertent destruction of evidence. The following is a true story. I was once assigned to supervise the scene of an alleged triple homicide until the assigned investigator could arrive, some time later. The crime scene was a single family dwelling in a rural community, situated at the end of a long country driveway so as not to be visible from the roadway.

I parked my vehicle on the shoulder of the main roadway and identified myself to the uniformed Sergeant on point duty at the end of the driveway who duly recorded my particulars and my time of entry into the crime scene. I walked along the side of the winding driveway (not on it) examining the surface for possible tire or footwear impressions, or physical evidence that may have been discarded by an offender while departing the residence.

Upon my arrival at the residence, I observed no less than one unmarked police vehicle and four marked cruisers parked in the driveway; the same driveway that the offender, in all probability, had used to arrive at and depart from the crime scene. The officers had unnecessarily involved themselves in the chain of continuity of the crime scene and might have been required to testify regarding their attendance at the scene. Also consider the potential loss of physical evidence caused by five vehicles unnecessarily driving over it.

All officers, including high-ranking officers, who attend crime scenes, should serve some bona fide (genuine or legitimate) purpose by their presence. Curiosity seekers only increase the risk of contamination and possible destruction of evidence at crime scenes.

On occasion, the ego of an otherwise well-intentioned superior officer (with no legitimate reason to be at the crime scene) may get in the way of his or her common sense and he or she might insist on entering a crime scene – even when challenged by a junior uniformed patrol officer who has been assigned to guard the scene. The most effective way to deal with such a situation is to politely inform the individual that upon entering the scene, he or she automatically becomes involved in the chain of continuity and will be considered a witness. If the individual still insists on entering, do not put your career in jeopardy – document his or her entry and let him or her deal with the consequences of these misguided, ego-driven actions.

BOX 6.3	Investigative Relevance
If you expect a court of law to believe that you meticulously examined and documented the crime scene, carefully preserving the chain of continuity of each piece of physical	evidence that will be used to prove the guilt of an accused person beyond a reasonable doubt, you must carefully guard against all forms of contamination.

6.9   CRIME SCENE SECURITY SCENARIO

Picture yourself arriving at a crime scene involving a shooting, situated in a downtown business area of a large city. The scene is an outdoor parking lot of a night club. Upon your arrival, you observe a crowd of 80–100 people standing around. An adult male is lying on the paved surface of the parking lot, conscious, but apparently gravely injured. Women are screaming. A group of four males is involved in a physical altercation. You observe several bullet casings lying on the ground but do not see a firearm.

At the sight of the police arriving, people begin to quickly depart the location in their vehicles. A large, verbally abusive male approaches you and demands that you "do your job and get these people out of my parking lot – right _____ now!" You are faced with a situation in which witnesses (and perhaps even the suspect) are leaving and the probability of destruction of physical evidence is very high. Now, as honestly as possible, answer the following questions.

Question # 1: Do you still want to be a police officer?

Question # 2: How would you begin to deal with the described situation?

A wise and experienced investigator once passed on this pearl of wisdom that I will share with you. Whenever you are faced with a situation in which things are happening too quickly for you to control, "slow things down." Another accomplished investigator recommended that when there seem to be too many tasks that simultaneously require your attention, simply "do them in bite-sized chunks."

"Great!" you say. "I just paid _____ dollars for this textbook and the best advice I get is to 'slow things down' and do things 'in bite-sized chunks?'" Did something like that just run through your mind? If it did, stop for a minute and consider the utter simplicity and truthfulness of the previous two pieces of advice.

"Slowing things down" means to take control of the crime scene and not let the crime scene take control of you. Police officers take control by stabilizing the events and the participants, if any, to prevent any given situation from worsening. You can't even begin to protect a scene that is out of control, so order must first be re-established as soon as practicable.

The first officer needs to quickly assess the situation and prioritize his or her actions. Common sense and good judgement are key assets for the first officer at a major crime scene. If you arrived with one or more other officers, your duties will be infinitely easier. Someone, usually the senior officer on-site, assumes control of the crime scene and issues instructions to the other officers. Never automatically assume that everyone knows exactly what to do.

You can't eat a seven-course meal all at once – you eat it one bite at a time. Doing things in "bite-sized chunks" at a crime scene merely recognizes that all problems can't be solved at the same time. You must identify the priorities and handle tasks individually (not necessarily one at a time – multi-tasking is also a desirable asset for the first officer at the scene – but on a priority basis).

Let's examine your priorities. Prior to even exiting the patrol vehicle, you should request that your dispatcher obtain the assistance of how many additional officers might be necessary to help manage the scene. If assistance is available, you can delegate certain tasks to them to relieve the pressure while you handle other issues.

Never feel as if you have to do everything yourself. If you need help, ask for it. Next, if events at that location have been chaotic for a while, don't expect them to de-escalate within 30 seconds of your arrival, but begin stabilizing matters as soon as possible. At this time you would instruct your dispatcher to make any appropriate notifications to persons such as your supervisor and Identification Officers, if required, and confirm the requirement of an ambulance, if needed. (Assistance requested – notifications made – job one: done.)

Your primary responsibility is the preservation of life.[6] Therefore, your first priority will always be to respond to the injured and to keep others from being injured. Request that emergency medical services be dispatched to the location immediately. Apply first aid

---

[6]*Police Services Act*, R.S.O 1990, c. P.15, s. 1.

to stop bleeding, maintain an open airway and prevent shock. (Caring for the injured – job two: done.) You're well on your way to stabilizing this crime scene.

How do you deal with the irate owner who is demanding that you "do your job"? I suggest that you precisely follow his advice and "do your job." Ask him his name, and in a professional (but firm) manner instruct him to wait at a location (perhaps inside the building) to allow you to deal with the situation before speaking to him. If he continues to be disruptive, adopt a more direct and firmer (but still professional) approach and instruct him to leave the area. (Owner removed from area – job three: done – are you starting to feel more in control?)

Although the screaming female bystanders constitute a distraction, they are a very low priority. Focus your next attention on the group of males involved in the altercation. One of them may possibly be responsible for the incident that you are responding to. Once they have been separated and identified, things have sufficiently calmed down enough for you to start to piece things together. You determine that half the group are acquaintances of the suspect while the other half are associated with the victim. (Combatants separated – job four: done.)

One officer (assuming that there is more than one present) should begin to secure the scene (i.e., to restrict further access to and from the location) by establishing check-points at entrances and exits, or at least by placing yellow crime scene tape around the enter area to establish a perimeter. Anyone whose vehicle is parked inside the perimeter will now have to wait until the crime scene is released by the officer-in-charge – with no exceptions. Vehicle licence plate numbers should be recorded as it may assist in identifying witnesses to the event. (Establish a secure perimeter – job five: done.)

As additional back-up officers begin to arrive, you assign one to stay with the wounded victim to monitor his condition and gather whatever information he or she is able to regarding the victim's identity, the circumstances of the event and the identity of the offender, if known. A seriously injured person should be escorted to the hospital by an officer to receive any information the victim may disclose along the way and to gather the victim's clothing as evidence. (Victim security – job six: done.)

You assign another officer to stand guard over the bullet casings to ensure they don't disappear or get damaged until the arrival of a forensic identification officer. If any other officers are available, they should begin to canvass the crowd in an effort to identify witnesses. And now for a word of caution: never ask a group of people, "Is anybody here a witness?" The ensuing silence will be deafening. Many people, despite their good intentions, simply don't want to become involved in a situation where they may have to come to court and lose time off work.

Suggestion: When attempting to identify witnesses, you should ask, "Did anybody see what happened here?" People actually do want to help and knowing that they have information that will assist the police makes some people feel important. You will find that witnesses will be more forthcoming if they are approached in this manner. (Identifying witnesses – job seven: ongoing but underway.)

You obtain information from the witnesses identifying the person responsible for the offence, who left the scene prior to your arrival. You obtain a description of the suspect, his clothing, the vehicle he left in and his last known direction of travel.

Immediately have this information broadcast to other units and or police services with the appropriate cautions (e.g., violent behaviour and possibly armed with a firearm, etc.). (Identifying the suspect and taking steps to effect an apprehension – job eight: done.)

It is strongly recommended that you take the time to prepare a rough (not to scale) sketch of the crime scene in your notebook to depict the location of relevant things (e.g., victim, bullet casings, vehicles, blood stains, etc.). Note taking and crime scene sketches will be further discussed in Section 6.14.4 (Crime scene sketch – job nine: done.)

All you have left to do is to create a "scene security register" to record the identity and arrival time of everyone who entered the crime scene after your arrival, and continue your efforts to locate, identify and interview witnesses (don't forget to interview the owner of the premises who you met in the parking lot on your arrival).

(Scene security register – job ten: done.)

Upon the arrival of a supervisor who will relieve you and the senior investigators who will assume control of the scene, modestly accept their praise for the excellent manner in which you secured this crime scene. You have just made their jobs much easier.

6.10 SUSPECT PRESENT AT CRIME SCENE

On some occasions, the suspect will still be present upon your arrival at a crime scene. In fact, in many cases the suspect initially reports the crime to the police and patiently awaits their arrival. Other times, the suspect will have been detained by the victim or by bystanders at the scene. On still other occasions, you may catch the offender at the scene of a crime in progress.

In any of these situations (over and above your other responsibilities at a crime scene) you have the added task of effecting the arrest, if it is justified under a peace officer's powers of arrest contained in section 495(1) of the *Criminal Code*.[7] While the arrest of the suspect at the crime scene simplifies the investigation of the crime through the early identification of the offender, it by no means simplifies the subsequent investigation of the crime scene – the evidence necessary to prove the guilt of the accused beyond a reasonable doubt must still be gathered.

It is imperative that the suspect be removed from the crime scene as soon as possible. It is never advisable to transport a victim and a suspect together from a crime scene, although I once had to do just that with the victim and suspect of an attempted murder in a remote logging camp in Northern Ontario due to the urgent need to transport the victim for emergency medical assistance. In most cases, the availability of police backup and emergency medical services will remove the need for transporting victims, witnesses and suspects together.

Additionally, the *Ontario Major Case Management (MCM) Manual* provides the following instruction when a suspect is arrested at, or near, a crime scene:

---

[7]Criminal Code, R.S 1985., c. C-46, s. 495(1).

"Where a suspect is arrested, the officer shall, in addition to the initial search of the suspect, ensure measures are taken to avoid contamination of potential evidence. The following shall be considered:

(a)   in the event the suspect used a firearm, or has evidence on his/her hands, he/she shall not be allowed to wash his/her hands;

(b)   clothing and footwear may need to be seized for possible trace evidence; and

(c)   hair and biological samples may be needed for comparison purposes."[8]

Note that this final measure is only done in certain cases (e.g., crimes of violence). The collection of hair and biological samples would never be undertaken by the first responding officer and is usually only seized in conjunction with a search warrant.

Never allow any suspect who has been removed from a crime scene to re-enter the scene for any reason without the consent of the officer in charge of the investigation to prevent further contamination of the crime scene. If a suspect who meets the police at the door of a crime scene was involved in a crime of violence, trace biological evidence may be later found inside the crime scene. By removing the suspect quickly from the crime scene, the suspect can no longer claim that it might have been deposited there after the arrival of the police and is therefore not evidence implicating him or her in the crime with which he or she was charged.

6.11   MEDIA RELATIONS AT THE CRIME SCENE

In urban areas, it is not uncommon that one of the first arrivals at a crime scene will be the media. In their quest to inform the public of newsworthy events and to meet stringent publishing deadlines that police officers aren't subject to, the media desperately scrambles to get enough facts or footage to fill their newspaper or the evening television news in a very competitive industry.

We will discuss media relations during a major investigation at length in Chapter 12: Major Case Management; however, I first wish to address how to deal with the media at the actual crime scene. I have seen many police officers make false and outlandish statements or disclose far too many facts about their cases when a microphone is unexpectedly thrust in their face and they find themselves on camera.

By their behaviour, you would think that many police officers consider the media as the enemy or at the very least, regard the media as a major inconvenience. This perception is borne largely out of a misunderstanding of the role played by the media in a free and democratic society and of what a powerful ally the media is in reaching out to large numbers of the public in a short time.

If we expect the media to assist us when we request their assistance on public appeals, we'd better be prepared to assist them in their efforts to do their jobs. The first thing to remember in dealing with the media is – never, ever lie to them. I am reminded of a true story in which a uniformed police officer was interviewed on camera in front of a residence that was a crime scene. As the police officer explained to the reporter that nothing of great significance had happened, the television camera, capturing the scene

---

[8]Ministry of Community Safety and Correctional Services: *Ontario Major Case Management (MCM) Manual* (Oct. 1, 2004), p. 40.

over the officer's shoulder, recorded not one, not two, but three obviously full and very suspicious body bags being carried out of the residence to waiting hearses. "Are you certain there is nothing going on here, Officer?"

The second thing that you never want to do with representatives of the media is ignore them. When you give the media nothing – you give them nothing to lose. The media relations difficulties that occurred during the Green Ribbon Task Force investigations regarding the murders of Leslie Mahaffy and Kristen French (1991–94) are well documented. An aggressive media, when faced with a lack of co-operation from the investigators, simply conducts their own investigation – but to much different standards than the police. This created an adversarial situation between the police and the media and had a devastating effect on the investigation.[9]

The third and final issue to be addressed is favouritism in dealing with the media. Always ensure that all media are simultaneously provided with the same information and that no one media outlet receives special treatment over any other, such as more details or receiving the information first.

An officer sitting in front of a crime scene can fully expect the media to appear on the scene and begin to ask questions regarding the nature and details of the investigation. He or she needs to be guided by the respective departmental policy regarding media releases, but might give one or more of the following responses:

"I'm not authorized to make any media release at this time."

"I can only confirm that we are investigating a major incident, but we are still in the early stages of the investigation and aren't yet able to confirm any facts for you."

"A press conference will be held at [time] at [location], at which time a senior officer (or media officer) will attempt to answer your questions." When using this last option, make absolutely certain that there is, in fact, a press conference scheduled.

6.12 CREATING A CRIME SCENE INVESTIGATION PLAN

An officer (the "scene investigator" – who may be the Case Manager or any other officer to whom he or she delegates this duty) assigned the task of supervising the examination of a major crime scene (e.g., homicide or sexual assault, etc.) bears the responsibility of ensuring that this crucial task is carried out in the most effective way. Remember that we don't just snoop around looking for clues like your favourite television detectives do (they only have 45 minutes to solve their crime, we have all the time in the world – so let's take our time and put it to good use).

Before rushing into a major crime scene examination, the scene investigator should, in consultation with the forensic identification officer(s) and any other experts that may be appropriate, formulate a strategy called a scene investigation plan.

"The scene investigation plan shall include:

(a)   areas to be searched;

(b)   items to be searched for;

---

[9]Campbell (1996).

(c)   specialized investigative techniques/equipment to be employed;

(d)   sequence of examinations;

(e)   personnel requirements;

(f)   potential hazards; and

(g)   legal search requirements."[10]

A scene investigation plan is similar to an aircraft pilot filing a flight plan prior to take-off. The pilot does so to create an official record of the details of the proposed flight. The creation of a scene investigation plan creates an understanding in everyone's mind about: what will occur; when it will occur; what the objective is; when corrective action is necessary if deviation from the plan occurs; all necessary tasks; and those accountable for conducting the tasks.

Having a plan is only half the battle – there is no sense in having a plan that no one follows. The involved members of the investigative team must ensure that the plan is adhered to. That isn't to say that the scene investigation plan is so rigid that, once prepared, it can never be changed – quite the contrary.

If new information does come forward, it is the responsibility of the crime scene investigator to amend the plan to ensure the most effective examination of the crime scene as possible and to communicate the change to all personnel involved in the search. The scene investigation plan need not be in the form of a formal document but the "scene investigator" should, at a minimum, record what has been decided in his or her notebook.

If a crime scene is relatively straightforward and non-complex in nature, or if there are few investigating officers involved, a formal scene investigation plan might not be necessary. However, the examination of any crime scene will be far more organized and efficient if the investigating officer has at least mentally addressed those issues contained in a comprehensive scene investigation plan, as noted above.

6.13 LEGAL SEARCH REQUIREMENTS

The law of search and seizure continues to be one of the fastest evolving areas of Canadian criminal jurisprudence. Entire books have been written on this topic. Experience and training is a must in developing an adequate understanding of all issues relating to the search of crime scenes. In this section, we are limited to a brief examination of some of the central issues dealing with crime scene examination.

Generally speaking, there are no legal search requirements to search a crime scene unless the offender is known to have some control over it or property interest in it. If a member of the public reports that his or her residence or business has been broken into, he or she is consenting to your entry onto the premises. The offenders have no proprietary interest (right of ownership, etc.) in the property and therefore can have no reasonable expectation of privacy in the actions by the police that occur on the premises they victimized.

Police officers have a common law authority (and to some extent a statutory right under provincial law such as the *Police Services Act of Ontario*)[11] to investigate crime

---

[10]Ministry of Community Safety and Correctional Services: *Ontario Major Case Management (MCM) Manual* (undated), p. 49.

[11]*Police Services Act*, R.S.O. 1990, c. P. 15 ss. 4(2).

and enforce the law. Although crime scene examination is not specifically authorized by statute law, courts have consistently held that the investigation of crime scenes is one of the fundamental duties of the police in the investigation of crime. The Coroner's powers of entry, inspection and seizure[12] are discussed in Chapter 11: Sudden Death and Homicide Investigation.

Common law also authorizes first responding police officers at violent crime scenes to enter without warrant to perform a cursory search for victims, offenders and weapons to ensure officer safety, where legitimate concerns exist. This unwritten authority does not include searching for evidence and expires when officer safety concerns have been satisfied. Additionally, section 487.11 of the *Criminal Code*[13] grants police officers the warrantless authority to enter buildings, premises or places to seize evidence in respect of offences against the *Criminal Code* (or to install, maintain, remove, monitor or have monitored a tracking device) under exigent circumstances (i.e., emergency or urgent need).

Since about the mid 1980s it has become common practice to obtain search warrants authorizing the search of murder scenes in Ontario – a practice that is not consistently followed in the rest of Canada.

Clearly, the vast majority of people are murdered by intimate partners, former intimate partners, family members or close acquaintances. Where there is even the remotest possibility that the offender has (or could have) any reasonable expectation of privacy with respect to the premises being searched – for any crime – a search warrant is an absolute necessity.

Police officers must develop an understanding of the legal search requirements (the need, if any, to obtain a search warrant) prior to examining a crime scene, although there will only be a necessity to do so in the most serious of cases, or when the offender could be said to have a proprietary interest or expectation of privacy. Where it is a crime scene that requires a search warrant, always obtain a warrant where it is feasible and practicable to do so.[14]

6.14 CRIME SCENE SEARCH METHODS

The search methods employed at any crime scene will be driven by the nature of the crime, the complexity of the evidence and the individual circumstances of the crime scene. This section explains some accepted crime scene procedures that can be adapted to fit almost any crime scene.

6.14.1 Initial Entry of Crime Scene

As previously mentioned, first responding police officers at violent crime scenes (e.g., homicides) are authorized by common law to enter the scene, without warrant, to perform cursory searches for victims, offenders and weapons – but NOT for evidence. Logically, you would not expect to find a victim, suspect or weapon in every kitchen cupboard or bedroom dresser drawer. An extensive warrantless search of a crime scene will likely be held to be *prima facie* unreasonable.

---

[12]*Coroners Act*, R.S.O. 1990, c. C. 37 ss. 16(1)-(3).

[13]*Criminal Code*, R.S. 1985, c. C.46, s. 487.11.

[14]*Hunter v. Southam Inc.* (1984), 2 S.C.R. 45, 14 C.C.C. (3d) 97, 11 D.L.R. (4th) 641.

The number of officers involved in an initial search will be determined by such factors as:

- the number of officers present;
- the immediate priorities of the crime scene; and
- the need to ensure officer safety.

All officer(s) conducting such a search (the fewer the better) should establish and follow one route of ingress and egress (route in and route out) to be followed by all subsequent attending personnel, such as additional police officers, ambulance, Coroner, etc. While the warrantless initial search does not allow searching for evidence, there is nothing in law to prevent a police officer, when conducting such a search, from being observant while he or she is inside the crime scene.

6.14.2 Establishing a Security Perimeter

Once the crime scene has been cleared of victims, witnesses and suspects, the scene must be secured against unauthorized entry to prevent the possibility of contamination of evidence. This is accomplished by stringing yellow crime scene tape to create a largely symbolic but very effective boundary to enclose the area in which the crime occurred and in which physical evidence is known to be, or will most likely be found.

How large does a scene security perimeter have to be? While there are no hard and fast rules regarding the sufficiency of a scene perimeter, the basic rule of thumb is "bigger is better". You can always reduce the size of a perimeter, if necessary – but you may not be able to increase it in size at a later time.

The size of the perimeter must be tailored to the individual requirements of the scene:

- What relevant areas are involved?
- What is the nature and the severity of the crime?
- By what route did the offender(s) approach and depart from the crime scene?
- Do any special areas containing evidence (e.g., footwear, tire impressions, discarded evidence) require protection?
- What access points reasonably need to be protected to prevent unauthorized entry to the crime scene?
- How does the **law of diminishing return** apply? The law of diminishing return implies that as search effort continues further away from the actual location where a crime occurred, the amount of physical evidence recovered can be expected to diminish as distance from the scene increases.

As it may be difficult, if not impossible, to answer all of these questions at the time of your first arrival, it is better to err on the side of caution and, if anything, establish a perimeter that is initially too large rather than too small.

Crime scene tape is relatively inexpensive. Hundreds of kilometres of crime scene tape were manufactured today, so use it – they'll make more tomorrow.

6.14.3 Crime Scene Search Techniques

Not every officer involved in the securing and guarding of every crime scene will be eventually involved in the examination of the scene. The first initial responding officers may be relieved by designated criminal investigators. Some officers will only be involved in the continuous guarding of the scene (for hours, days and even weeks) until such time as the Case Manager orders the crime scene to be released. Assignment for the responsibility to conduct the search of the crime scene will be determined by the following factors:

- The need to limit the number of personnel at the crime scene;

- The nature and severity of the crime;

- Availability of personnel;

- The degree of expertise required; and

- Departmental policy.

Again, the actual search techniques employed at a crime scene will be determined by the nature of the crime and the location involved. An outside crime scene may be searched far differently from a crime scene within a building. Certain areas of a crime scene may require far more intensive search efforts than others and may justify an "inner perimeter" being established within the "outer perimeter".

It should go without saying that the larger the area to be searched, the larger the number of searchers needed to adequately conduct the search. The area may be so large (e.g., a city park or a forest) as to require the utilization of non-police searchers such as civilian volunteers, under the close supervision of a trained police search co-ordinator.

Large areas may be searched using a "Line Search" in which searchers are positioned equidistantly on a line and walk (or crawl on hand and knee, if necessary) from one point to another. If the area is very large, as in the case of a farmer's field, the area to be searched should be divided into a "grid" comprising an arrangement of squares or rectangles of equal size. Once a "grid" is completely searched in one direction, the area should be re-examined using a line search pattern conducted at right angles to the initial search. A "grid" is probably one of the easiest ways to graphically illustrate the progress of an ongoing search of a large area and can also be used to record exactly where certain exhibits were located.

Another common search technique is to search using ever expanding concentric circles around a central location of interest, always moving in a spiral pattern using the law of diminishing return to decide when to stop.

These same search methods can be utilized on a smaller scale when searching inside buildings, including houses. These patterns can be utilized when examining photographs of the crime scene, even years after the scene has been released. As new investigators are brought into unsolved investigations, they must familiarize themselves with the appearance of the crime scene as it appeared, sometimes many years before. The same "search" methods may be employed when viewing the photographs that are taken at crime scenes years later, when all that exists of the crime scene is the photographic evidence.

6.14.4 Recording the Crime Scene

It is essential that the circumstances of the search, especially a large area involving many searchers, be adequately recorded to document the areas that were searched, when and by whom, etc., to avoid duplication of effort and to document where evidence was located, and by whom. This is best accomplished by breaking the search area into identifiable sectors (e.g., by rooms if in a building, or using a grid system if the search involves a large area or where there are multiple search areas).

Don't immediately begin walking around the crime scene, randomly picking up evidence. We have already discussed the benefits of employing a methodical search pattern. The first search technique I recommend is to photograph your entire crime scene before anything is disturbed. If the crime scene involves a major crime, I strongly recommend that the scene also be videotaped prior to the collection of any exhibits. Videotaped evidence of the crime scene is compelling evidence that allows the trier of fact to personally view the scene, exactly as the police did.

Next, before anything is disturbed, the crime scene must be measured to allow a diagram to be prepared for investigative and court purposes. The crime scene diagram will also depict relevant exhibits and would allow the scene to be completely recreated, if necessary. In addition to the overall room dimensions (length and width) exhibits must be located by taking two measurements, at right angles, to a fixed object such as a wall, corner, doorway, etc. Unlike the not-to-scale sketch the investigator may record in his or her investigative notebook, the crime scene diagram is drawn to scale.

As long as the search area does not undergo significant structural renovations, these fixed objects (permanent features) can always be used to place the exhibits in a position that recreates their original locations, as closely as possible. We never take measurements from a particular piece of furniture, for example, because if the furniture is ever moved, as is often the case, the original location of the exhibit could only be approximated. In the case of outdoor crime scenes which lack any permanently fixed features, wooden or metal stakes may be placed in the ground to serve as reference points. A Global Positioning System (GPS) is now often used to permanently record the location of relevant items in outdoor venues.

6.14.5 Collection of Exhibits

With the scene secured, the scene investigation plan prepared, and the scene properly recorded, we may now turn our attention to the actual collection of physical evidence. Techniques of collection, handling, packaging and labelling of evidence will be fully discussed further in Chapter 7: Forensic Sciences.

FIGURE 6.2 | Crime Scene Search Patterns

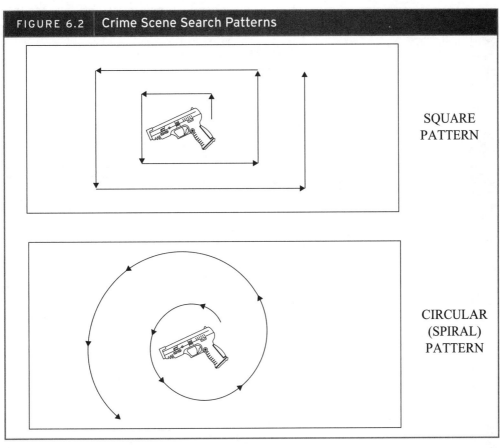

SQUARE
PATTERN

CIRCULAR
(SPIRAL)
PATTERN

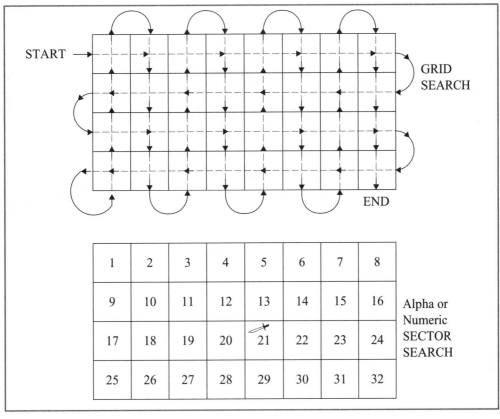

GRID
SEARCH

Alpha or
Numeric
SECTOR
SEARCH

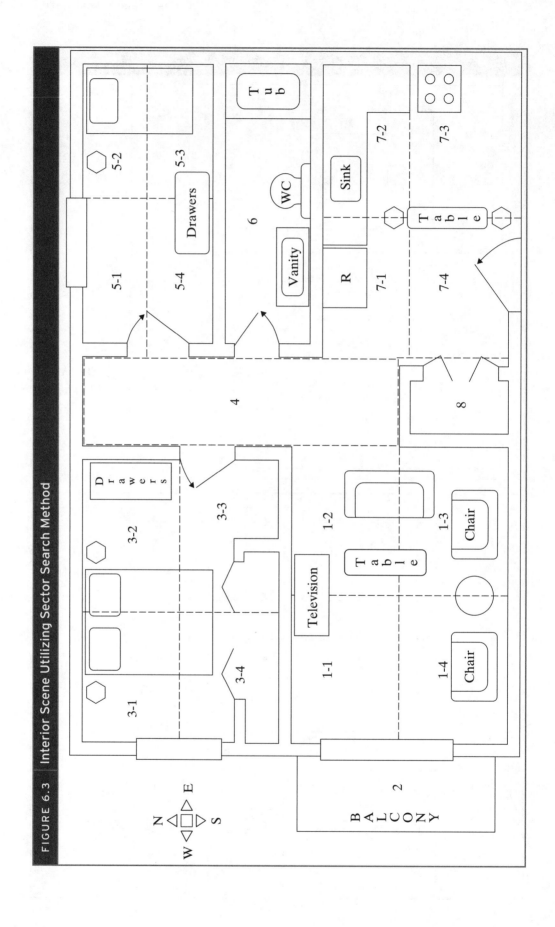

FIGURE 6.3   Interior Scene Utilizing Sector Search Method

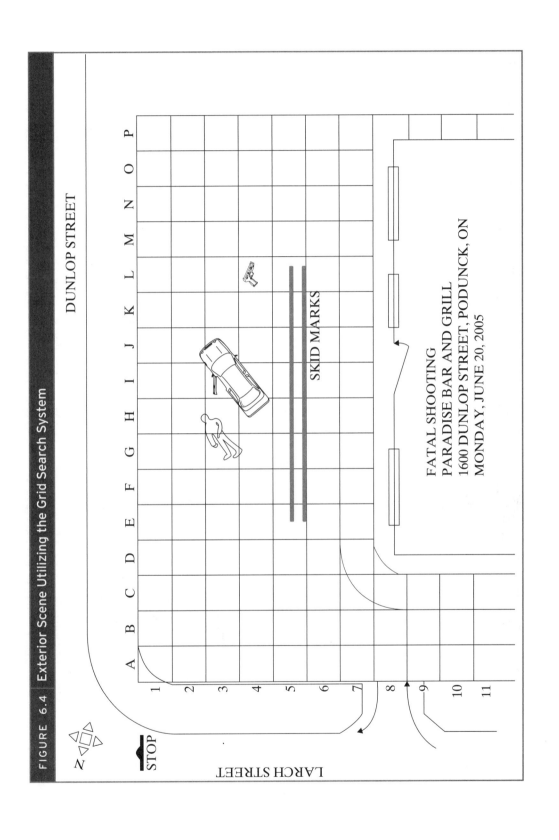

FIGURE 6.4 Exterior Scene Utilizing the Grid Search System

DUNLOP STREET

LARCH STREET

STOP

N

SKID MARKS

FATAL SHOOTING
PARADISE BAR AND GRILL
1600 DUNLOP STREET, PODUNCK, ON
MONDAY, JUNE 20, 2005

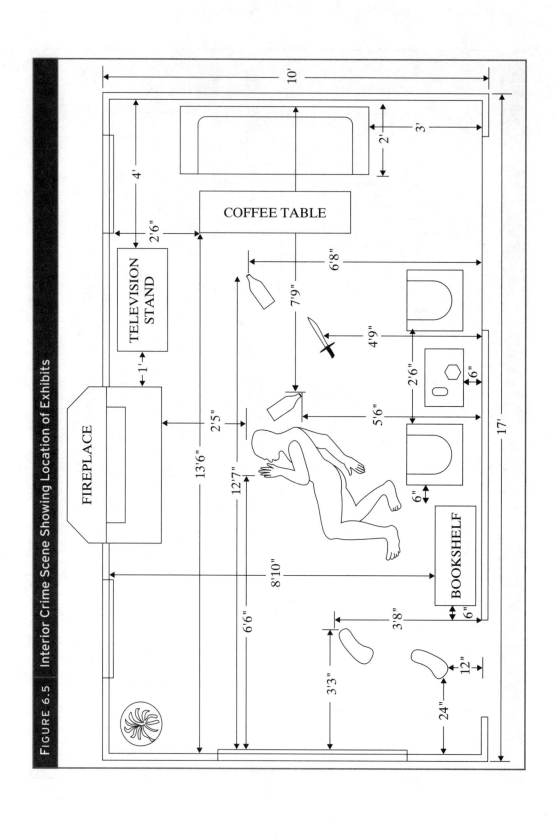

FIGURE 6.5   Interior Crime Scene Showing Location of Exhibits

Remember that Locard's Exchange Principle tells us that even police officers will leave traces of their presence at crime scenes. "Officers shall, whenever possible, utilize protective clothing to prevent the possible transfer of trace evidence or, where practicable, change clothing between crime scenes, etc."[15]

An experienced investigator will be familiar with the types of physical evidence that may be encountered at various types of crime scenes and must now examine the scene for anything that is material (relevant) to the investigation. Sounds easy enough, doesn't it? But what is relevant at a later stage of an investigation might not be so obvious in the early stages of an investigation before all of the facts of the case are known.

"All items of potential evidentiary value shall be identified, catalogued, documented, seized and preserved, regardless of whether immediate relevance to the investigation is established."[16] Adopting a search philosophy such as the preceding quote from the *Ontario Major Case Management (MCM) Manual* will virtually guarantee that all relevant evidence is appropriately gathered.

Always involve as few people as possible in the actual collection of exhibits and you will reduce the number of people that are required to testify in court. An "exhibit officer" should be appointed who may be an investigator or a forensic identification officer assigned to the case. As officers search their assigned areas of responsibility, and as pieces of evidence are located, an exhibit officer will first photograph the exhibit *in situ* (Latin, meaning "in its original location") and take measurements of its location (see Section 6.14.4 above on recording the crime scene) before gathering it.

6.15 OFFICER SAFETY CONSIDERATIONS AT A CRIME SCENE

If you suspect there may be hazardous material of any description at a crime scene that constitutes an unacceptable chemical or biological hazard to investigators, the Case Manager must be notified right away. Precautions should always be taken to ensure officer safety (e.g., the wearing of full "Haz-Mat" gear, including respirators) if necessary, at a crime scene. Such protection was used during the 1991 Milwaukee police search of serial murderer Jeffrey Dahmer's apartment, due to the amount and degree of decomposition of human remains and the presence of toxic chemicals that Dahmer used to dissolve his victims' bodies.

On occasions where the offender is still at large, physical security may need to be provided for the searchers while the crime scene is being searched. On more than one occasion, police officers have found themselves under hostile gunfire directed at them by a suspect who unexpectedly returned to the crime scene. This situation was recently underscored by the tragic murder of three members of the Mayerthorpe detachment and one member of the Whitecourt detachment of the Royal Canadian Mounted Police in the rural hamlet of Rochfort Bridge, Alberta on Thursday, March 3, 2005.

---

[15]Ministry of Community Safety and Correctional Services: *Ontario Major Case Management (MCM) Manual* (Oct. 1, 2004), p. 40.

[16]Ibid., p. 41.

6.16 SEARCH - THEN SEARCH AGAIN

"Unfortunately for the personnel who conducted this search, it is not their dedication, tenacity and professionalism that [are] remembered by most, but rather the regrettable misfortune of the missed videotapes."

Sergeant Gary Beaulieu, Niagara Regional Police Service,
referring to the unsuccessful search of Paul Bernardo's residence
for the six incriminating videotapes containing evidence
of sexual offences committed against Tammy Lynn Homolka,
Leslie Erin Mahaffy and Kristen Dawn French.[17]

It is not my intention to criticize anyone involved in the investigation of the crimes committed by convicted serial rapist and murderer, Paul Kenneth Bernardo. Any serious student of law enforcement should make every effort to read the Bernardo Investigation Review (Campbell, 1996) quoted throughout this text as an example of what can go wrong during a major investigation, despite the best efforts of a competent and dedicated investigative team.

Despite searching Bernardo's residence for 71 days and recovering some 943 pieces of evidence, police searchers failed to discover the hidden incriminating videotapes depicting Bernardo and his accomplice, Karla Homolka, sexually assaulting many of their victims. The tapes were later removed from the house by Bernardo's former attorney. Much later, the incriminating tapes were turned over to the police after Bernardo changed attorneys.

It has been a distinct privilege for me to speak personally with some of the original investigators who candidly described many of the events that occurred during that controversial case. It is clear that much more can be learned from one such problematic investigation than from any ten investigations where everything progressed smoothly.

The lesson of searching, then searching again, reminds me of one of my own cases. In the summer of 1996, the badly decomposed body of a teenaged female was discovered in a remote, forested area in Central Ontario. The victim's body had been reduced to skeletal remains and had been spread over a fairly large area by animals.

We followed accepted crime scene procedures, faithfully and meticulously searching for an entire week, but found only a portion of the body. Prior to releasing the crime scene, I was fortunate to attend a "case conference" (before it was ever known as such) with representatives from the Office of the Chief Coroner and with other involved agencies. It was suggested to me that a forensic anthropologist, specializing in human skeletal anatomy, should visit the scene to assess what, if any, further investigative steps might be conducted at the body recovery site.

I vividly recall standing in the middle of my crime scene (which had been searched extensively for an entire week) the next day with Dr. Jerry Melbye, of the University of Toronto, Forensic Anthropology consultant to the Office of the Chief Coroner. I pointed down at the ground at a gently curved, twig-like object and remarked to Dr. Melbye that, even to my untrained eye, the object on the ground resembled a human rib.

---

[17]Campbell (1996), p. 218.

Dr. Melbye confirmed that the "twig" was indeed a human rib, making my next decision a very simple one: "We'll search it again!" The next time, however, the scene was searched in conjunction with 40 archaeology students under the supervision of Dr. Dean Knight, of Wilfred Laurier University. During the next week, the students systematically searched approximately 1,500 square metres of bush divided in a grid system and recovered a substantial portion of the victim's body.

The murderer had previously been convicted of first-degree murder some 18 months prior to the discovery of the victim's body due to some excellent police work by the Durham Regional Police Service. The Supreme Court of Canada later refused to grant him leave to appeal his conviction.

The lesson to be learned here is not only to "search – then search again," but also that there is considerable merit in using a different group of individuals, with a different outlook, to conduct the second search. It is a fact of human nature that the original search team would have a lower expectation of discovery of new evidence while repeating their original search than an independent search team would.

According to Recommendation 15 of the *Campbell Report*: "The officers who conduct major searches should be selected based on their experience and expertise, with an effort to combine officers, and other persons selected to assist, with different perspectives [e.g., drug investigators who are accustomed to searching for concealed evidence].[18] A second team of searchers should be sent in after the first group has exhausted all apparent possibilities."[19]

BOX 6.4	Investigative Relevance

While the potential benefits of a second search team are self-evident, it must be acknowledged that doing so involves many more people in the chain of continuity of the scene and that of any new evidence that is found. In hindsight, do the (undeservedly) much-criticized Green Ribbon Task Force (Bernardo) investigators now wish they had employed a second set of searchers to search above the bathroom ceiling light fixtures for the incriminating videotapes? I expect they do.

6.17   RETENTION OF DEATH SCENES UNTIL CONCLUSION OF AUTOPSY

In the case of all homicides and suspicious death investigations, the Case Manager should consider the potential risks and benefits of "maintaining security of every homicide scene until the conclusion of the autopsy [to ensure that the most informed decisions in relation to the search of the scene may be made on the basis of all circumstances of the case]."[20]

An autopsy is a very informative, scientific procedure that yields considerable information regarding the cause and sometimes also the manner of death. Some investigators feel that evidence recovered from a crime scene is mutually exclusive from what is learned during an autopsy; however, I could not disagree more.

---

[18]*Ontario Major Case Management (MCM) Manual*, p. 49.

[19]Campbell (1996), p. 322.

[20]Ministry of Community Safety and Correctional Services: *Ontario Major Case Management (MCM) Manual* (Oct.1, 2004), p. 41.

A more thorough and effective examination of a crime scene is possible in the context of all available information from all available sources. Information from the autopsy, such as the number of defence wounds, the nature of the weapon(s) that caused certain wounds, etc., can be extremely valuable in re-constructing the events of the crime at the crime scene. Always remember that if information from one source doesn't agree with the theory of how the crime occurred – maybe it's the theory that is flawed.

I once investigated a homicide involving a fatal shooting that occurred at a residence in Northern Ontario. The scene was poorly illuminated and the only surviving witness was unreliable due to considerable emotional distress and intoxication by alcohol. The deceased had been found dead in the kitchen of the residence with no evidence to suggest that she had been wounded elsewhere in the residence. The shooter had fled the scene prior to the arrival of the police and had subsequently turned herself in to a police officer she knew personally, but had exercised her right to remain silent.

Information indicated that, prior to turning herself into the police the suspect had placed a long distance telephone call to her family in Southern Ontario. A hastily arranged interview of the family conducted by the police in that area resulted in learning of a confession made by the suspect and the unexpected disclosure that she had fired a single shot through the front door of the residence after she had been refused entry.

Upon re-examination, a very small (.22 calibre) hole that had not been previously noticed was located in the front door in the poorly lit porch of the residence. Knowing that the firearm involved was a semi-automatic, I had been earlier troubled by the absence of a spent shell casing in the kitchen (semi-automatic firearms automatically eject spent cartridges from the breech once a round is expended).

With information now indicating that the shot had been fired through the door from inside the porch, a 30-second search of the porch floor resulted in the discovery of the spent .22 shell casing. The front door was also removed as evidence (to the great displeasure of the property owner). Information from one interview allowed us to identify and seize two crucial pieces of physical evidence (door and bullet casing) and to more accurately re-construct the events of the crime.

Although none of the information came to the investigation from the autopsy, the same principle applies. Never be in too much of a rush to release your crime scene until you have as much information from available sources as you can get, allowing you to make the most informed search of your crime scene as possible. It is far easier to search for evidence when you know what to search for.

6.18 RELEASE OF THE CRIME SCENE

A very common fault in the examination of crime scenes is to hastily release the custody of the crime scene to the owner, or a person in authority. Don't be rushed into making the decision to release the crime scene (only the Case Manager has the authority to make that decision) until you are assured that "all practicable search methods and investigative techniques in relation to the scene have been exhausted."[21]

---

[21]Ministry of Community Safety and Correctional Services: *Ontario Major Case Management (MCM) Manual* (undated), p. 49.

The decision to release a crime scene is one that must be tempered with practicality. The maintenance of crime scene security can be very expensive, in terms of officer salaries and overtime. Sometimes there will be a compelling need to release a crime scene situated in a commercial institution (e.g., a bank robbery) to allow the victim to restore his or her business to normal. Other times releasing an outdoor crime scene (e.g., a busy street or intersection) may be necessary to restore the orderly movement of traffic or commerce in the area.

While the authority to release the crime scene is exclusively that of the Case Manager, the decision to do so should be made in collaboration with the forensic identification officer and any other members of the investigative team that the Case Manager feels are appropriate. Crime scene examination is just one of many areas of law enforcement where many heads are better than one. In every crime scene I've attended, I've never failed to learn something from another officer, sometimes a very junior officer.

6.19 "STAGED" CRIME SCENES[22]

"Staging" a crime scene means the intentional alteration of a crime scene for the purpose of misleading the police investigation by diverting suspicion from the most logical suspect(s). Staging is usually done to convey either a different "manner of death" or a different motivation for the crime.

Staging is almost always done by an offender. This can be obvious in the case of a murder where the offender stages the crime scene to convey a different manner of death, such as attempting to make a homicide appear to be suicide or an accidental death. The killer is attempting to mislead the police investigation by pointing suspicion away from the most logical suspect.

Perhaps the staging might be the result of actions taken by the alleged "victim," as in the case of a residential or commercial break, enter and theft. In these cases, the "victim" may actually stage a crime scene where no actual crime occurred to make it appear as if a crime did occur. I once had such a case in which an employee of a motel, who was a former police officer, broke a window at the rear of the motel, ransacked the owner's office, forced the door off a small office safe and stole a large sum of money and jewellery.

The "victim" may in reality be the victim of a minor break-in who attempts to make the crime look worse than it actually was, to inflate an insurance claim. In such cases, as with arson, the individual involved is attempting to defraud his or her insurance company is an offender, and not a victim at all.

The only example of staging a crime scene that is not done by an offender would be in the case of a person or persons who, discovering that a family member has committed suicide, intentionally alter the crime scene in order to convey a different manner of death prior to calling the police. This might be done for reasons surrounding the protection of the reputation of the deceased or his or her family honour due to their perception of the stigma of suicide.

---

[22]Much of the information in this section comes from personal conversations with D/Sgt. J.A. Van Allen, Criminal Profiling Unit, Behavioural Sciences Section, O.P.P. General Headquarters, Orillia (2003).

I suppose that in the strictest definition of "Obstructing a Peace Officer in the execution of their duty," family members in this situation would be guilty of committing an offence under the *Criminal Code*.[23] I do not feel that it is in the public interest to view such actions as criminal or to take any enforcement action against them. Empathy for the family of any deceased person is justification for compassion, and they should not, in my opinion, be considered as offenders.

6.19.1   Significance of Evidence of Staging at a Crime Scene

Ask yourself, "What does an offender have to gain by staging a crime scene?" Simply, offenders stage crime scenes out of fear of being identified as the offender due to their association with the victim or to the crime scene (e.g., the husband that murders his wife and attempts to make the death appear to be an accidental fall, or the employee of a gas station that stages a robbery). As they would be the most logical suspects, they attempt to divert suspicion away from themselves.

Evidence of staging at a crime scene usually appears fairly obvious to a cautious and methodical investigator, for example broken pieces of glass fallen to the outside, indicating that the force was applied to the window from the interior – not from the exterior as it would be done in the case of a genuine break-in. This is where investigators have the advantage as offenders stage crime scenes as they think they should appear, not as experienced criminal investigators know they appear.

When evidence of staging is detected at a crime scene, it indicates that there is a very close association between the victim and the offender. Physical evidence of staging can be very detectable, either due to the offender's youth, lack of criminal sophistication or because they are under considerable stress following the commission of the crime and may be in a hurry to escape.[24]

After having cautioned you about tunnel vision and warning you several times to "Let the evidence tell the story – don't make the evidence fit the story," I don't want you to view this as a contradiction of what you have already been told. Evidence of staging must be recognized for what it is and not be confused with other evidence at the scene, even though both are valuable, as they allow the investigator to reconstruct the events that occurred at the crime scene. Evidence of staging is evidence only of the intentional alteration of the crime scene that will be in addition to evidence of any actual crime, if one did, in fact, occur.

Evidence of staging allows you to draw conclusions about who might be responsible for the staging and their motive for doing so. Evidence of staging, if present, can concentrate your investigative efforts to where the focus should properly be placed.

The lesson learned with respect to staging of crime scenes is, "Things are not always as they appear to be!"

---

[23]*Criminal Code*, R.S. 1985, c. C-46, s. 129(a).

[24]Personal conversation with J.A. Van Allen.

6.20 EMOTIONAL IMPACT OF CRIME SCENE INVESTIGATION

Upon my arrival at a previously mentioned triple homicide scene, I learned that five police officers and one civilian ride-along passenger had previously entered the crime scene. This is far too many people to be in a crime scene by any standard – especially the civilian, for whom there was no valid reason to be granted entry to a murder scene.

When I inquired about any observations the five officers had made regarding the injuries to the three deceased persons, all five were at a loss to provide any meaningful details. Subsequent examination by the forensic identification personnel revealed there was extensive (and clearly visible) blunt trauma to one victim's head and ligatures in place around the necks of all three victims.

All of these details had been overlooked by five investigators and a civilian, presumably due to being overwhelmed by the nature and extent of the occurrence. Police officers are only human. What bothers other people emotionally can bother us too. But, it is our job to investigate crime and to search crime scenes. We owe it to the victims to perform this function with professionalism at all times.

Crime scenes involving crimes of violence are full of vivid evidence of the violence that some people are capable of toward others. Newer officers are sometimes immediately struck by the sight of a dead victim or the extent of the evidence of physical trauma at the crime scene. The sight of extreme injuries and severed human tissue is something that police recruit training does not prepare you for.

If you find that the circumstances of a crime scene are overwhelming you (e.g., scenes of violent death, child victims, etc.) take a moment or two and compose yourself. Take several deep breaths, calm down and remind yourself who you are and of your sworn duty to enforce the law. Gain control of the crime scene – never let the crime scene control you.

BOX 6.5	Investigative Relevance

The emotional effects of police work do not end at the end of your shift. Very few officers are totally immune to the effects of exposure to traumatic situations – and many experienced officers have suffered from symptoms of Critical Incident Stress. It is absolutely essential to discuss any troubled feelings that you may have with your loved ones or with co-workers, especially with those co-workers who have experienced similar traumatic situations.

Most police services have Employee Assistance Programs (EAP) in place to assist their members deal with personal crises, including the effects of Critical Incident Stress and Post Traumatic Stress Disorder. These programs operate under conditions of strict confidentiality. It is never a sign of "weakness" to take advantage of the benefits of such a program. Remember that you are far more valuable to your police service, your family and your community if you are mentally and emotionally well.

SUMMARY

- "Crime scene" means any location where a crime was actually committed, where evidence of a crime is located or where evidence is known to have been previously located, any of which provides a potential link between the victim(s), crime(s) or to the offender(s).

- The "Burning Bridges" theory states that every time anything is done at a crime scene, it represents another "bridge" burned. Whatever has been changed at a crime scene can never be restored to its original condition.

- Locard's Exchange Principle tells us that, "When any two objects come into contact, there is always a transference of material from each object onto the other."

- The initial actions taken by the first officer at a crime scene will profoundly impact the final outcome of any investigation.

- "Securing" a crime scene means the continuous stabilization and protection of the crime scene against entry by unauthorized persons and against contamination until a methodical and effective examination of the scene can occur.

- When establishing a security perimeter at a crime scene, it is better to isolate a larger area rather than a smaller one to protect all possible evidence.

- A crime scene investigator should, in consultation with the forensic identification officer(s) and any other experts that may be appropriate, formulate a strategy called a scene investigation plan.

- Although common law authorizes the police to enter violent crime scenes without warrant to search for victims, suspects and weapons, an extensive warrantless search of a crime scene will be held to be *prima facie* unreasonable.

- A crime scene should be released only when all practicable search methods and investigative techniques in relation to the scene have been exhausted.

- Where practicable, a crime scene involving a homicide or suspicious death should be retained until after the conclusion of the autopsy to allow for the most informed search of the crime scene possible.

- "Staging" of a crime scene means the intentional alteration of a crime scene for the purpose of misleading the police investigation by diverting suspicion from the most logical suspect(s) and indicates a close association between the victim or the crime scene and the offender.

DISCUSSION QUESTIONS

1. What are the responsibilities of the first officer at the scene of a crime scene involving an alleged homicide at a private residence? For what limited purposes may the first officer enter the scene without a search warrant?

2. What significance does Locard's Exchange Principle have for investigators tasked with investigating a crime scene? What implications can Locard's Exchange Principle have regarding contamination of a crime scene and what steps can an investigator take to prevent contamination?

3. Once a crime scene has been secured and the perimeter has been evacuated, what issues must an investigator consider in establishing a crime scene investigation plan? Who else might the investigator consult when preparing a crime scene plan?

 # WEB-LINKS

www.icsia.com/

International Crime Scene Investigators Association. A forum for crime scene investigators to express ideas, exchange information and seek the advice of others and related links.

www.mpss.jus.gov.on.ca/english/pub_safety/centre_forensic/forensic_links.html

Government of Ontario, Ministry of Community Safety and Correctional Services. Centre of Forensic Sciences. Services provided and related links.

www.rcmp.ca/fls/home_e.htm

Royal Canadian Mounted Police. Forensic Laboratory Services. Directory of regional RCMP forensic laboratories and services provided.

www.fbi.gov/hq/lab/labhome.htm

U.S. Federal Bureau of Investigation Laboratory services with links to Forensic Science Communications.

Chapter 7

Forensic Sciences

"Our duty is to believe that for which we have sufficient evidence, and to suspend our judgement when we have not."

John Lubbock, Baron Avebury, English politician (1834-1913).[1]

Learning Outcomes

After reading this chapter, students should be able to:

- Explain the fundamental principles of forensic identification.
- Explain the difference between **class characteristics** and **accidental characteristics**.
- Give examples of and describe at least five forensic sciences.
- Describe the range of testing services provided by the Centre of Forensic Sciences.
- Distinguish between the various possible forensic findings.
- Explain why it is dangerous for an investigator to act on the unwritten opinion of a forensic scientist.

7.1   FORENSIC DISCIPLINES

"Forensic science" refers to the application of scientific principles in the detection, investigation and prosecution of criminal matters. The term usually conjures up images of police officers on their hands and knees in a crime scene dusting for fingerprints, or a civilian analyst in a laboratory looking through a microscope at iridescent blue slime of unknown origin.

Space constraints prevent me from discussing each of the various disciplines that exist under the general heading of forensic science. Forensic science is by no means a single

---

[1] John Lubbock quote retrieved January 2, 2005, from www.brainyquote.com/quotes/j/

field and includes far more than merely those scientific disciplines usually associated with the processing of trace evidence at crime scenes. It also consists of contributions made by disciplines that include:

- Psychology — study of the functions of the human mind
- Psychiatry — study of mental disease and its treatment
- Anthropology — study of structure and evolution of humans
- Odontology — study of structure and diseases of the teeth
- Osteology — study of structure and function of bones
- Pathology — study of bodily diseases and their symptoms
- Entomology — study of the behaviour of insects
- Botany — study of plants
- Palynology — study of pollen and spores
- Meteorology — study of atmospheric conditions
- Firearm and tool mark examination — study of ballistics, and examination of tools and the marks made by them
- Toxicology — study of poisons
- Biology — study of living organisms
- Biochemistry — study of chemicals in living organisms
- Molecular biology — study of molecules in living organisms
- Radiology study of x-rays, especially in medicine
- Polygraph — measurement of physiological changes
- Digital imaging enhancement — digital enhancement of photographic images
- Forensic data recovery — restoration of data from computers
- Accounting — study of accounts and transactions

Recent advances in forensic science and technology have resulted in a significant windfall for criminal investigators and continue to be responsible for proving the guilt or innocence of untold numbers of suspects, world-wide. Unfortunately, many investigators have developed an over-reliance on forensic science to "solve their cases for them" due to its awesome persuasive powers in the courtroom and because of its reputation for being infallible.

Despite the recent media appeal surrounding forensic science, the collection of evidence at crime scenes consumes a relatively small portion of an investigator's day-to-day workload. Only a small percentage of evidence that is collected at crime scenes is eventually analyzed by a forensic scientist, and only a portion of all evidence analyzed is ever presented in court as exhibits. Many cases are successfully resolved in court without any scientific evidence ever being tendered.

Knowledge of various types of evidence, evidence gathering and testing techniques and the significance of possible scientific conclusions will enhance an investigator's ability to collect and present evidence. In my opinion, forensic science remains the tool most responsible for bringing law enforcement out of the dark ages, but it is only one weapon in the investigator's arsenal to search for the truth – and as with every other tool, one that is not without its limitations. "[I]t is essential that investigators have an understanding of what the forensic laboratory can and cannot do."[2]

7.2   CENTRE OF FORENSIC SCIENCES (ONTARIO)

The Centre of Forensic Sciences (CFS) is a government operated forensic laboratory within the Public Safety Division of the Ontario Ministry of Community Safety and Correctional Services. The CFS is situated within the ministry headquarters at 25 Grosvenor Street, Toronto, and maintains the Northern Regional Forensic Laboratory (NRFL) at 500-70 Foster Drive, Sault Ste. Marie, ON to service northern Ontario.

The CFS may be reached any time at:

The Director, Centre of Forensic Sciences, Toronto, ON
TEL: (416) 314-3200
FAX: (416) 314-3225
After Hours: (416) 314-3200

Similarly, staff of the NRFL may be reached at any time at the following:

The Manager, Northern Regional Forensic Laboratory, Sault Ste. Marie, ON
TEL: (705) 945-6551
FAX: (705) 945-6569
After Hours: (705) 945-6550

Some Ontario police services in the Ottawa area and those outside of Ontario utilize the services of the Royal Canadian Mounted Police (RCMP) forensic laboratories at:

1200 Vanier Parkway, Ottawa, ON
TEL: (613) 998-4843
or any of the RCMP regional forensic laboratories listed at:
www.rcmp.ca/labs/labs.e_htm

7.3   ROLE OF THE FORENSIC LABORATORY

The Centre of Forensic Sciences (CFS) in Toronto maintains the following sections:

• biology (including the DNA section);

• chemistry;

• document examination;

• firearms and Toolmark examination;

• photoanalysis;

---

[2]Centre of Forensic Sciences (1997), p. 10.

- toxicology; and

- pathology.

CFS provides their services at no cost to official investigative agencies and defence counsel in criminal cases. While forensic laboratories such as the CFS may not be capable of performing some of the "media magic" that is seen weekly on television, they do excel in providing several services, as detailed in the following sections.

7.3.1   Identification of Substances

Through a variety of sophisticated scientific examinations, such as microscopy, microspectrophotometry (MSP) and thin-layer chromatography (TSC), to name a few, forensic analysts are able to identify virtually any substance other than suspected seized drugs, which are the responsibility of Health & Welfare Canada laboratories. If an unknown substance is located at a crime scene that is "reasonably free from contamination,"[3] and it may be relevant to the case and cannot be identified through other methods, it should be collected, securely packaged and submitted for examination.

Liquid that is recovered from under baseboards or flooring at the scene of a fire might be analyzed to be gasoline or some other type of petroleum accelerant, proving the fire was of an incendiary origin (arson). The identification of substances that are foreign to the location where they are recovered may provide the investigator with a clue to the identity of an offender if the origin of the substance can be determined.

Often, it may be just as useful for the investigator to learn what a substance isn't as it is to identify what a questioned sample is. I once recovered an unknown white substance from the basement of an apartment building in which I had reason to believe that a stolen house safe had been peeled open. Suspecting that the material found on the basement floor might be trace evidence of the fire-retardant lining from between the layers of the safe, used to protect the contents, I carefully gathered and submitted a sample of the substance to the CFS.

When the results were returned, I learned that the substance was merely gypsum residue from sheet-roc, a very common building material. This finding did not prove that the stolen safe wasn't opened in that particular location but nor did it prove that it had been opened there. It didn't help solve the search for the truth of the case but was still useful as an investigative aid by indicating to me that I had to keep searching if I was to find the truth.

7.3.2   Revealing Additional Information Regarding Submitted Items

Forensic science can assist the investigator by developing additional information that may not be apparent or macroscopically visible, meaning visible with the human eye. An example of this would be the ability to restore engraved serial numbers on items such as firearms, home appliances or motor vehicles, etc., that have been obliterated to prevent their identification.

---

[3]Ibid., p. 11.

Early in my career, I investigated a break and enter at a bank where the offenders unsuccessfully attempted to cut their way through the bank vault door using stolen oxyacetylene welding equipment. The investigation eventually led to a single suspect and resulted in a search warrant being executed at his residence.

Two very new (but very ordinary) battery-operated, handheld camping lanterns were among the items seized from the suspect's residence and were submitted to the CFS for expert examination. Forensic analysis revealed that there were very small globules of metal adhering to various portions of both camping lanterns.

The analyst was able to conclude that both lanterns must have, at one time, been in close proximity to welding or similar metal-cutting operations. The metal on the lanterns could not be matched to the metal from the vault door and was only circumstantial in nature – but powerful circumstantial evidence, as it would have allowed a court to draw the inference that the lanterns had been used in the break and enter and that the owner was guilty. No such inference was ever drawn in this case as the accused pleaded guilty to the offence.

On another occasion, I submitted a pair of scissors that was alleged to have been used during an aggravated assault. A CFS biologist located a small piece of tissue, about the size of the head of a pin, lodged between the two blades. The tissue was determined to be similar in all respects to living tissue, although due to its small size, it could not be determined whether it was human or animal. With the DNA technology that exists today, it would likely be possible to match the sample to the victim herself.

7.3.3 Detection of Drugs/Poisons

While the CFS does not conduct analyses to identify illicit drug seizures, the Toxicology section analyzes and calculates amounts of alleged drugs or poisons contained in bodily samples. During the fall of 1994, I was assigned to investigate the sudden and suspicious death of an adult male who was found deceased in the front seat of his car, which was parked at a highway rest stop. When first discovered by the police, the man showed signs of recent, superficial trauma to his face that, quite properly, resulted in the initial suspicion of involvement of foul play in his death.

Upon examining the scene, I observed an empty plastic drinking glass on the floor of the car containing a few drops of green, liquid residue and a partial container of automotive anti-freeze on the floor behind the driver's seat. Toxicological analysis of post mortem blood samples indicated a level of ethylene glycol, the active ingredient in anti-freeze that was more than four times higher than the lethal limit.

While homicides by poisoning are statistically rare in Canada,[4] the CFS is able to detect toxic substances and their metabolites in samples collected from both living and deceased victims. Toxicological samples must be taken as soon as possible as some drugs continue to metabolize within the body, even after death.

7.3.4 Comparing Objects and Substances

The comparison of similarities and differences of objects and substances can establish whether or not they share a common origin. The characteristics of questioned samples,

---

[4]Statistics Canada: *The Daily*. Wednesday, September 29, 2004.

such as offender DNA samples collected from a crime scene, and known samples, such as a voluntary biological sample collected from a sexual assault suspect, can be compared to establish that both samples did or did not come from the same source, in this case the suspect.

Samples of material, such as material from a victim's clothing from a fatal hit-and-run motor vehicle accident, may be compared to paint samples from a suspect vehicle. A homicide suspect's shoes might be compared to soil samples from the scene where a victim's body was disposed of. The broken tip of a screwdriver or a knife recovered from the scene of a break and enter or violent crime can be compared to a similar tool or weapon found in the possession of a suspect.

For there to be any scientific validity for the analyses conducted, the forensic scientist must perform his or her testing from the position of absolute objectivity. The laboratory examiner must rely on scientific evidence alone and not be influenced by the circumstances of the investigation or external pressure from the police or prosecution. Like the investigator, the role of the forensic scientist is simply to seek the truth.

7.4   FORENSIC IDENTIFICATION

Forensic identification is a broad term that describes the general application of scientific techniques utilized during the investigation and prosecution of crime. The core function of the criminal investigator involves the use of logic and deductive reasoning but does not directly involve scientific principles in the investigation of crime. Forensic identification employs scientific methods that support the role of the investigator.

Forensic identification may involve specially trained police officers who receive expert training in scientific techniques relating to evidence collection, photography, and physical comparison. Forensic identification also involves scientists trained in one or more of a variety of disciplines who, through a wide array of scientific techniques, identify suspects, victims and the origin of objects and substances. Forensic identification and its subsequent findings are used to establish facts during investigations and, in many instances, can establish the validity of physical evidence in court.

BOX 7.1	Investigative Relevance

According to R.A. Huber, in his article, titled "Philosophy of Identification," "when any two items contain a combination of corresponding or similar and specific oriented characteristics of such number and significance to preclude the possibility of their occurrence by mere coincidence, and there are no unaccounted for differences, it may be concluded that they are the same, or their characteristics attribute to the same cause."[5]

In simple terms, this means that if two or more objects share a sufficient number of identical features and there are no unexplainable differences between them, it may be concluded that the objects are the same,

---

[5]Huber (1972).

| BOX 7.1 | (Continued) |

or that similar characteristics may be regarded as sharing a common origin. For example, two bullets which do not have any unexplainable differences and that are found to have a sufficient number of identical markings caused by the rifling of a gun-barrel, can be deemed to have been fired from the same firearm. A footwear impression at the scene of a break and enter can be deemed to have been made by a shoe seized from a suspect, providing there are a sufficient number of accidental characteristics (see Section 7.6) between them and no unexplainable differences.

Forensic identification can match a specific tool to a tool-mark left at a crime scene and identify a suspect through handwriting comparison. It can exonerate an individual as being involved in a crime by excluding him or her as a potential source of certain evidence, such as through the use of fingerprint comparison or DNA technology.

7.5   QUESTIONED SAMPLES V. COMPARISON SAMPLES

Comparison samples from known sources, also referred to as control samples, need to be collected and forensically compared to questioned (suspect) samples of material for the items to have any evidentiary value.

For example, if a suspect is found with muddy soil adhering to his shoes, the soil, when dried, may be scraped off into a **druggist's fold** to prevent it from becoming dislodged during transport to a forensic laboratory (see Section 7.13.3 of this chapter: Packaging of Evidence). Soil on the bottom of a suspect's footwear might only prove that he or she walked through soil while wearing those shoes.

If the soil from the suspect's footwear (questioned sample) was compared to soil gathered from the location where the victim's body was buried (comparison sample) and was determined to be identical in composition, the evidence now places those shoes at a crime scene. "Wait just a minute," you object, "I read Chapter 2 and I know that doesn't prove the accused was wearing the shoes at the time the soil became attached to them. It only proves the shoes were at that location at one time," and you'd be absolutely correct. It's pretty compelling evidence though, isn't it?

And we're not finished yet. Microscopic examination of one of the suspect's shoes now reveals a single drop of blood (questioned sample). When that drop of blood is compared to the suspect's own blood (comparison sample), it is determined that the two samples could not have come from the same source. When the blood on the shoe (questioned sample) is compared to blood drawn from the victim (comparison sample) DNA analysis indicates that the blood on the shoe could only have come from the victim.

"Wait just a minute," you protest again. "That still doesn't prove that the suspect was wearing the shoes when the victim was bleeding and was buried in an unmarked grave," and again, you'd be absolutely correct. But, I wouldn't ever want my shoes to be implicated as having been in such close proximity to a bleeding victim and which could also be placed at the victim's burial site, would you?

Always remember to ensure that comparison samples are never packaged together with questioned samples to prevent the inadvertent cross-contamination of evidence from one exhibit to another.

7.6   CLASS CHARACTERISTICS V. ACCIDENTAL CHARACTERISTICS

Physical objects are identified through the comparison of class characteristics and accidental characteristics. Two or more objects of similar manufacture will display certain identical class characteristics. These characteristics include size, shape, and pattern. If a footwear impression is left at a crime scene by a suspect, it will, of necessity, be a certain size, shape and pattern.

If a suspect is apprehended and is found to be in possession of shoes similar to the size, shape and pattern of a footwear impression found at the crime scene, the shoes would be circumstantial evidence through which the suspect cannot be excluded as having made the questioned impression. The evidence proves that a certain make and model of shoe left the impression but does not prove that the suspect's shoes made the impression at the crime scene. Every shoe of the same size, model and manufacture shares identical class characteristics and are all capable of making the same impressions as the suspect's shoes. Statistically, this can be somewhat problematic, especially if the manufacturer made 25 000 pairs or more of that model and size of shoe. If the class characteristics of two objects do not agree, however, no identification is possible.

Once all class characteristics have been proven to match, the identification of any two objects then involves the examination of accidental characteristics. An accidental characteristic is any random cut, tear, or other distinctive defect, wear pattern or flaw that may be used to distinguish one similar object from another. Accidental characteristics result naturally through normal usage or damage over the course of time. The differentiation of an object, to the exclusion of all similar objects, depends on the identification of a sufficient number of accidental characteristics to satisfy a court that they could not possibly have occurred coincidentally.[6]

7.7   SCIENTIFIC INTERPRETATION OF EVIDENCE

Based only upon the scientific evidence that can be verified, a forensic scientist is limited to making one of the following findings:

1. that the known and questioned samples did, or did not have a common source;

2. that the known and questioned samples probably came, or probably did not come, from a common source; or

3. that the known and questioned samples could possibly have come from a common source.

---

[6]Cassidy (1980).

Scientific findings are what they are – nothing more and nothing less. Usually, the results of a forensic examination are less than the "positive match to a high degree of scientific certainty" that the investigator might have hoped for. A questioned sample which excludes a suspect as a donor can be every bit as vital to an investigation as a finding that includes a suspect as a source or possible source of the questioned sample[7].

7.7.1 Common Origin

The finding that a questioned sample and a known sample shared a common origin requires that the two samples or objects be identical in all respects (inclusionary finding). Conversely, the exclusionary finding that a questioned sample and a known sample did not come from a common source indicates either an absence of similar characteristics, or the existence of unexplainable dissimilar characteristics. This conclusive inclusionary or exclusionary finding is the most definitive finding possible.

7.7.2 Probable Origin

The finding that a questioned sample and a known sample probably came, or probably did not come from the same source is obviously a weaker opinion than a positive or negative finding of common origin. A finding of probable origin indicates that the two samples are consistent with being from the same source. Therefore, there is only a probable likelihood that the questioned sample shares, or probably does not share, the same source as the known sample. Either differences were found to exist between the two objects, or not enough similarities were detected to prevent a more conclusive finding.

7.7.3 Possible Origin

The final possible finding a forensic scientist might arrive at is that a questioned sample and a known sample could have shared a common origin. This type of finding indicates that while the questioned and the known sample were found to be consistent with each other, the questioned sample could also have come from another similar source. To explain the significance of this finding differently, the questioned sample cannot be excluded as having shared a common origin as the known sample.

BOX 7.2	Investigative Relevance

While some investigators believe that findings of "probable origin" and "possible origin" are of neutral value to the investigation, the finding of the laboratory examiner is limited to the evidence that can be demonstrated. A court may still weigh a finding of "probable origin" or "possible origin" cumulatively with corroborating evidence, of which the forensic analyst is most likely unaware, to determine the probative value of the forensic evidence concerning the guilt or innocence of the accused. The forensic analyst does not have that luxury.

---

[7]Kaufman (1998).

7.8   TRANSFER OF EVIDENCE

Trace evidence may be transferred either by way of primary transfer, that is through the direct contact of one object with another; for example a baseball bat used in an assault might be found to bear blood from the victim that was transferred through the direct contact between the baseball bat and the victim. Evidence may also be transferred by way of secondary transfer, such as soil samples found inside a suspect's vehicle that was deposited by the suspect's footwear. No direct contact occurred between the questioned soil sample in the car and the original location of the soil but the secondary transfer occurred from the shoes that picked up the soil from the original location.

Other ways that evidence may be transferred include through the sharing of a common environment, contamination or by way of random occurrence. Finding trace evidence of a suspect's blood, or his or her fingerprints, at the scene of violent crime is of no probative value if he or she shares that environment with others, such as a residence or workplace. Contamination of evidence can occur at a crime scene, due to improper handling after the evidence has been collected by the police, or in the forensic laboratory itself, where two objects are allowed to come into contact resulting in the inadvertent post-crime transfer of evidence from one exhibit to the other.

Similar evidence may also be explained through random occurrence, such as a chance event that cannot otherwise be explained. For example, if a single synthetic fibre was located on the clothing of an abduction victim that was similar to fibres from carpet in a suspect's residence, the questioned sample would be of negligible probative value as the presence of the fibre could be explained by random occurrence. Not all fibres in every garment or fabric are identical and a single fibre might have been included in the manufacturing process or was previously transferred from an unknown source.

"[C]hances of random association decrease as the number of matches increase." For example, if 50 fibres are found on a victim's clothing that are similar to a suspect's carpet, the probability is higher that the transfer occurred through direct transfer and proportionately less probability that the transfer occurred by random occurrence.[8]

7.9   ACCESSING EXPERT RESOURCES

If expert forensic resources or services not available at the Centre of Forensic Sciences are required during any investigation, the staff of the CFS or the Office of the Chief Coroner should be consulted as to who should be utilized to ensure that the correct science is applied to the investigation by the correct people. Numerous instances have occurred when an investigator believed that a certain expert resource was required only to learn that another discipline would have been better suited to the investigation.

The Office of the Chief Coroner may be consulted during any defined "major case," such as a sexual assault or non-familial abduction, but the following policy must be complied with during every major case investigation involving a death:

---

[8]Kaufman (1998), vol. 1, p.155.

"The Office of the Chief Coroner shall be consulted in the following circumstances:

(a)   when a Major Case Manager deems it necessary to obtain the services of an expert in relation to the body of a deceased person in the investigation of a major case death investigation;

(b)   in cases where a second autopsy is required or has been requested;

(c)   where a request is made to have a body exhumed; and

(d)   in cases of found human skeletal remains or an interred body, for advice and guidance on processing the body site to ensure the preservation of physical evidence."[9]

I cannot stress strongly enough the benefit of utilizing a multi-disciplinary approach during police investigations. There are numerous people with expertise in a wide range of technical or medical disciplines who are more than willing to assist if you require their services. One important factor is to confirm that they are in fact qualified experts.

The private-sector forensic community contains numerous self-proclaimed forensic consultants, of varying degrees of ability – don't be hesitant about requesting and checking with references as to the past services provided to investigative agencies by any expert you anticipate retaining. Crown attorneys, CFS staff and the Office of the Chief Coroner usually are aware of the best external resources based on past performance. Another very important matter that needs to be discussed prior to any expert resource being brought into an investigation is the fee that they intend to charge for their services. Don't unnecessarily expose yourself or your agency to any unexpected and potentially exorbitant fees without first determining what the requested services will cost.

7.10 SCIENCE V. SCIENCE

Science is science and, all other things being equal, the results of a particular forensic analysis should be the same regardless of which scientist conducts the analysis. It would be naïve to conclude that this is the case, however, when two doctors might diagnose a patient's condition quite differently. There is a certain amount of subjectivity involved in the interpretation of science.

If proper scientific protocols are not followed, the results have been referred to as "junk science." When miscarriages occur, it is not the fault of science but of the individual responsible for not utilizing science correctly. It has become commonplace for each side of a criminal trial to produce a parade of forensic "experts" to rebut the testimony of the other side.[10]

Forensic witnesses have been used to uncover bad science applied to police investigations as well as to create reasonable doubt by attacking the integrity of the investigation in the light of overwhelming scientific evidence. When any two witnesses fail to agree, it is always up to the trier of fact to determine how much weight should be placed on the testimony of a particular witness.

---

[9]Ministry of Community Safety and Correctional Services: *Ontario Major Case Management (MCM) Manual* (Oct 1, 2004). p. 42.

[10]Baden and Roach (2001).

When used improperly, or when the probative value of forensic evidence is incorrectly interpreted, forensic science can also be a "double-edged sword," a fact that has resulted in false findings and wrongful convictions[11]. The forensic scientist should never be on the side of the prosecution or the defence. The forensic scientist must remain on the side of science.

7.11   RELIANCE ON FORENSIC OPINIONS

In high-profile abductions, homicide investigations, or in any other case where there is a clear and present danger to public safety, it may be necessary to act on the verbal expert opinion of a forensic scientist regarding an analysis he or she has done on evidence. To avoid the possibility of any misunderstanding as to what exactly was stated, it is strongly recommended that, where it is practicable to do so, investigators act only upon a written opinion of a forensic scientist. Instances have occurred where the police have acted on their interpretation of a forensic finding only to have a discrepancy occur at trial between the police and the forensic scientist either as to what was actually said, or regarding the correct weight that should have been attached to the significance of the findings.

"No police officer or Crown counsel should take action affecting an accused or a potential accused based upon representations made by a forensic scientist which are not recorded in writing, unless it is impracticable to await a written record. Where a written record is not obtained prior to such action, it should be obtained as soon thereafter as is practicable."[12]

7.12   DISCLOSURE OF PHYSICAL EVIDENCE

Physical evidence can and does play a significant role in many criminal trials. There is no property in physical evidence in relation to the police, the prosecution or the defence. The police have a responsibility to collect it legally and in accordance with investigative best practices to prevent contamination and to ensure the chain of continuity. Evidence recovered, whether it incriminates or exculpates the accused, must be disclosed to the defence.

Section 605 *Criminal Code* speaks directly to the matter of both parties involved in a criminal trial being able to independently test the physical evidence entered as an exhibit by the other party. "A judge of a superior court of criminal jurisdiction or a court of criminal jurisdiction may, on summary application on behalf of the accused or the prosecutor, after three days notice to the accused or prosecutor, as the case may be, order the release of any exhibit for the purpose of a scientific or other test or examination, subject to such terms as appear to be necessary or desirable to ensure the safeguarding of the exhibit and its preservation for use at the trial."[13]

7.13   COLLECTION OF EXHIBITS

With the crime scene secured, the scene investigation plan prepared, and the scene properly recorded, we may now turn our attention to the actual collection of physical evidence. Remember that Locard's Exchange Principle tells us that even police officers will leave

---

[11]Kaufman (1998).

[12]Ibid., pp. 328-329.

[13]*Criminal Code*, R.S. 1985, c. C-46, s. 605.

traces of their presence at crime scenes. "Officers shall, whenever possible, utilize protective clothing to prevent the possible transfer of trace evidence or, where practicable, change clothing between crime scenes, etc."[14]

Disposable full-body protective clothing (aka: "bunny suits"), latex gloves and footwear protection, depicted in the following photograph, should be worn by all searchers at scenes of major crimes to help safeguard against possible contamination of the crime scene.

An experienced investigator will be familiar with the types of physical evidence that may be encountered at various types of crime scenes and must now examine the scene for anything that is material (relevant) to the investigation. Sounds easy enough, doesn't it? But what is relevant at a later stage of an investigation might not be so obvious in the early stages of an investigation before all of the facts of the case are known.

"All items of potential evidentiary value shall be identified, catalogued, documented, seized and preserved, regardless of whether immediate relevance to the investigation is established."[15] Adopting a search philosophy such as the preceding quote from the *Ontario Major Case Management (MCM) Manual* will virtually guarantee that all relevant evidence is appropriately gathered.

7.13.1 Labelling of Evidence

Upon seizing an exhibit, the investigator or "exhibit officer" must identify the item. Identifying an exhibit means to first describe the exhibit in a precise way to differentiate it from any similar item and, second, to mark it in such a way that he or she can later positively identify the exhibit as the item that he or she seized.

If a crime involves a firearm that is recovered at the scene, it is not sufficient to identify the exhibit as a "firearm" – there are many firearms in the world. What is it that differentiates this particular firearm from all others? Items may be described by class characteristics (size, shape, colour, manufacturer, etc.) and may also have specific identifiers such as model and serial numbers. The firearm that was recovered at the crime scene is more properly described as:

"Smith & Wesson™, Model 10, .38 special, 6-shot revolver, serial #: 10D123456"; or

"Remington, Model 870 Wingmaster™, pump-action, 12 gauge shotgun, serial #: 3456789"; or

"Sturm Ruger, Mini-14™, .223 calibre, semi-automatic rifle, serial #: 2345678."

The above descriptions would sufficiently distinguish these hypothetical weapons from any firearms of similar make, model and calibre/gauge. If the particular exhibit does not have an individualized serial number, it must still be identified using all available class characteristics (e.g., "Goodyear Fortera HL™, P245/65R17 radial tire and rim, colour: Black").

The next step in the identification of the exhibit is for the person seizing the item to affix his or her initials and the date seized on the object in such a way as to allow them to positively recognize the exhibit as the item that they seized, to the exclusion of all other items. This may be accomplished by permanently writing their initials, badge number and date on the item, such as a document, etc., as depicted in the following photograph.

---

[14]Ministry of Community Safety and Correctional Services: *Ontario Major Case Management (MCM) Manual* (Oct. 1, 2004), p. 40.

[15]Ibid., p. 41.

Photo 7.1 - Investigator, wearing protective clothing, seizing an exhibit.

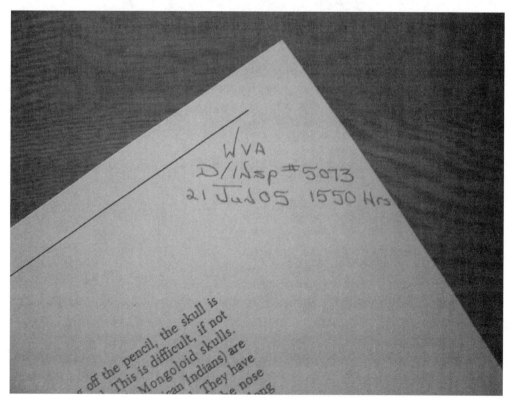

Photo 7.2 - Seized document marked for identification by initials, badge number and date.

There may be times when it is neither possible nor desirable to mark (or deface) the item. If marking the object for identification would permanently damage the item, or result in a possible loss of evidence, it is advisable to attach an exhibit tag (aka: property tag) to the item being seized. Most departments issue pre-printed tags that allow their officers to complete by filling in the case file number, time, date, description of item seized, location of seizure, and the signature of the seizing individual. One tag is used per exhibit. The tag can either be affixed directly to the exhibit or attached to or enclosed in a cellophane exhibit bag used to preserve the exhibit from contamination.

7.13.2 Completion of Property Tag

When completing a property/exhibit tag, it is important to refrain from the use of terminology either about the item itself or the location where it was seized that would call for the conclusion of any inference about what the item is or its significance as evidence. Microscopic and chemical analyses are required to prove that a hole in a garment of clothing was caused by a bullet. Until those analyses are completed, the hole is just a hole and should only be described as such. Similarly, human blood should only be described as "a reddish liquid [or substance] resembling blood" until proven to be blood by a person such as a biologist, who is qualified to identify it as blood and state whether in fact it is animal or human in origin.

To describe an item of apparel as having been worn by the "victim" presupposes that there is a victim when that is a matter that must be decided in court by the trier of fact.

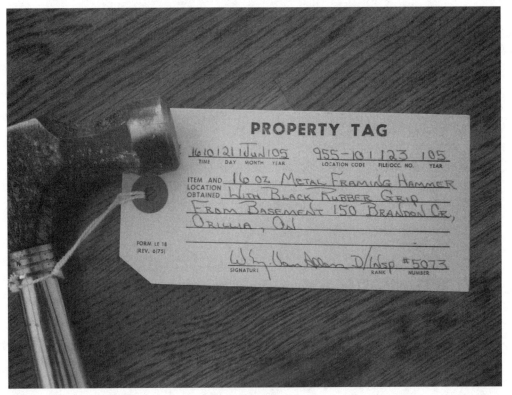

Photo 7.3 - Properly completed property tag affixed to an exhibit.

Photo 7.4 - Property tag enclosed in a bagged exhibit.

Similarly, stating that a certain object was seized from the residence of the accused concludes a certain degree of guilt can be attached to the person charged with the offence prior to receiving a fair and impartial hearing in court. If a particular item was seized from a person, he or she should be identified by name rather than by his or her particular role in the offence or investigation.

For example, a garment removed from the body of a live person ought to be referred to as:

"One pair of men's, grey, mesh/leather New Balance™ running shoes, Model: M2001GR, size: 10. Received from John Smith at Hooper General Hospital."

Evidence labelled in this manner does not make it readily apparent to anyone who reads the property tag whether John Smith is the victim, the accused, or perhaps another involved person. Such a label doesn't betray whether the shoes were seized voluntarily, incident to arrest or were removed from an injured person. No prejudice is caused to the accused when no conclusions can be drawn about the exhibit, especially conclusions that cannot be supported by evidence.

A blood-stained shirt seized from the accused's residence would more properly be described as:

"Long-sleeved, man's dress shirt, size: 16/34, Make: Arrow™, Colour: Light blue, bearing a small circular hole in the lower right front, surrounded by a reddish stain. Obtained from a laundry hamper in the master bedroom of 48 Smith Street, Thunder Bay, ON."

Proper Investigative Procedure

Exhibits must be identified in this manner in the following places: the seizing officer's notebook; the exhibit register; the property tag attached to the exhibit; a property report if any is required; any submission to a forensic laboratory; the general occurrence report; and any Crown brief for court purposes. Unless your police service has progressed to the stage to equip officers to electronically capture information at the source, this will be a lot of writing.

In most police services, these various documents serve quite different purposes and are submitted to different places and agencies. Considering the number of items seized by a police service every year, it is imperative that evidence be adequately catalogued. Doing so protects the integrity of items of evidence, protecting them against loss or confusion among similar items, thereby maintaining the chain of continuity.

7.13.3 Packaging of Evidence

To protect evidence against the risk of contamination or cross-contamination that will occur if exhibits come into contact with other exhibits, it is necessary to package the exhibits properly. Some exhibits, such as a firearm or knife, may need to be packaged in their original condition in a rigid container such as a cardboard box; blood stained garments or clothing may need to be air-dried prior to being packaged in plastic; wet leather footwear needs to be air-dried before being wrapped in paper bags to guard against mildew through exposure to moisture.

Human tissue samples and bodily fluids require refrigeration to prevent degradation through ordinary **putrefaction**. Chemicals and volatile substances such as gasoline are best packaged in glass "mason jars" that are used for laying up fruit preserves. Suspect and control samples of dry material in small quantities are often gathered in a folded piece of white paper in a druggist's fold, which involves placing the item or material into the fold of an ordinary piece of white paper that is then folded inward upon itself from all remaining edges to enclose the item and prevent it from falling out. The paper fold is then initialled and dated by the seizing individual and secured inside an envelope that is marked for identification with a description of the item and time, date and location obtained, and the signature of the individual who obtained the item.

Several properly packaged items of evidence may be carefully placed together into a larger container, such as a cardboard box, which is then sealed with a sequentially numbered self-adhesive evidence seal. When the cardboard box of exhibits arrives at a subsequent location (e.g., Centre of Forensic Sciences, Toronto) the chain of continuity will be intact as the exhibits inside the box can now be shown to have not changed in any respect since they were first packaged.

Whenever you are in doubt as to the best method to use to collect evidence at a crime scene, be guided by a forensic identification officer, if one is available. Where doubts still exist, consult a current version of *Laboratory Guide for the Investigator*, published by the Centre of Forensic Sciences, or contact the forensic laboratory utilized by your police service at the contact numbers listed in Section 7.2.

FIGURE 7.1   How To Make a Druggist's Fold

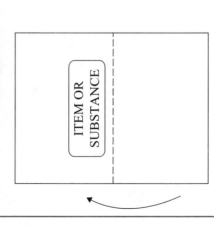

STEP 1: FOLD SHEET OF PAPER
IN HALF FROM BOTTOM
ALONG LINE AS SHOWN.

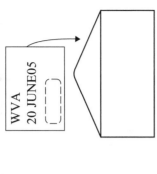

STEP 2: FOLD SHEET OF
PAPER INWARD FROM
EACH SIDE ALONG LINES
AS SHOWN.

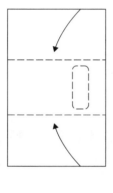

STEP 3:
FOLD PACKET
IN HALF
DOWNWARD
ALONG LINE
AS SHOWN.

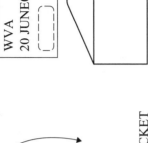

STEP 4: INITIAL
AND DATE DRUGGIST'S
FOLD BEFORE SEALING
IN ENVELOPE AND
LABELLING CONTENTS.

Adapted from:
*Laboratory Guide for the
Investigator*, fifth edition.
Ministry of Community Safety
and Correctional Services
Centre of Forensic Sciences.

Photo 7.5 - Proper packaging of a druggist's fold for laboratory submission.

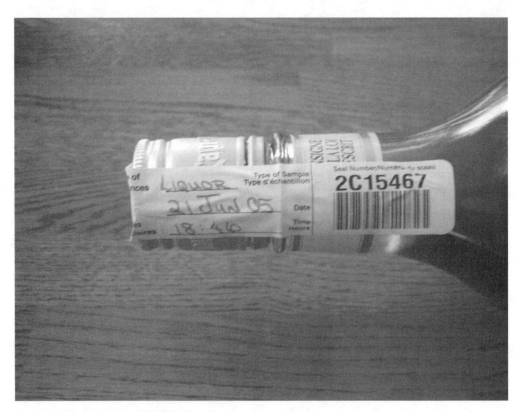

Photo 7.6 - Properly packaged exhibit with evidence seal.

7.14   FINGERPRINTS

"When bloody finger-marks or impressions of clay, glass, [et]c., exist, they may lead to the scientific identification of criminals."

Dr. Henry Faulds, British doctor (1843-1930)[16]

One of the first forensic sciences ever to be developed has also evolved into the most enduring. Dactyloscopy is the science of identification through comparison of friction ridge skin of the hands or feet - fingerprints. The primary usefulness of fingerprints as a means of personal identification is based on two main factors, their uniqueness and permanence.

Over the course of a lifetime, a person's physical characteristics, such as height, weight, the colour, length and style of his or her hair, facial appearance, etc., may change dramatically through the aging process or due to voluntary changes to one's appearance. A person's fingerprints at birth, however, are unique and never change throughout his or her lifetime except for the effects of deep permanent scarring. Any unnatural attempt to change the fingerprint pattern of one's fingerprints only makes them more unique.

Even with the recent advent of DNA technology, identical twins cannot be differentiated as each set of identical twins shares a common DNA profile.[17] The only reliable method of identifying identical twins is to revert to the infallible method of fingerprint comparison. While some scientists claim that the uniqueness of a single fingerprint cannot be established statistically, others citing the law of random probability claim that the odds of 2 people sharing a single fingerprint is approximately 1 in over 60 billion. If the latter school of thought is correct, with the world population standing at just over 6.4 billion at the time of this writing, those are very impressive odds.[18]

7.14.1   History of Fingerprints

The use of fingerprints as a non-scientific method of personal identification dates back to ancient times. Between the 8th and 14th century, thumbprints were commonly used on clay seals in ancient Babylon, China, Japan and Persia as a means of verifying the identity of parties to business transactions as well as on government documents.

In 1686, Marcello Malpighi (1628–1694), an anthropologist at the University of Bolgona in Italy, published an article on his study of ridges, spirals and loops on human skin. There was no opinion expressed in Malpighi's work of the potential usefulness of fingerprints in terms of personal identification. The Malpighian layer of skin was subsequently named in his honour for his work in this field.

The value of fingerprinting as a method of personal identification was initially scientifically recognized in 1823 and is attributed to Johannes Evangelista Purkinje (1787–1869), while a professor of physiology at the University of Breslau, Prussia. In 1856, Sir William Herschel (1833–1918) began using palm prints on documents relating

---

[16]Faulds (1880), p. 605.

[17]Skopitz (2002).

[18]US Census Bureau: *World Clock,* - January 9, 2005, 08:35 hrs EDT.

to employee pensions in India. Herschel's use of fingerprints was based more on necessity due to widespread illiteracy at the time, and the psychological effect of binding a party to a document through physical contact, than it was on scientific principles. Herschel is later credited with using fingerprints as a means to identify criminals after he became the Chief Magistrate in Jungipoor, India.

Dr. Henry Faulds (1843–1930), a Scottish surgeon, is credited with the first scientific declaration of the potential of fingerprints as a method of identifying criminals in a letter titled, "On the Skin Furrows of the Hand" in an 1880 issue of *Nature* magazine.

The first known criminal conviction based on fingerprint identification occurred in 1892. Juan Vucetich, an Argentine police official, was assigned to investigate the murders of two children in their home in Necochea, Argentina. A bloody fingerprint found on a doorway in the murder scene resulted in a positive match to that of the children's 26-year-old mother, Francesca Rojas[19].

When confronted with the evidence, Rojas confessed to having murdered her children to win the heart of a lover who did not want children. The facts of the case are strikingly similar to the October 25, 1994 murders of Michael and Alex Smith by their mother, Susan Smith in Union, South Carolina. Rojas, like Smith, was sentenced to life imprisonment.

The first recorded jury trial to consider fingerprint evidence involving the imposition of the death penalty occurred in England in 1902. Thomas and Ann Farrow were murdered in their shop in Deptford, London. A single fingerprint on a cash-box was identified by Scotland Yard detectives as belonging to one of two brothers known in the area. On May 23, 1905, Alfred and Albert Stratton were hanged for the Farrow murders.[20]

Until this time, measurements of physical characteristics were used to identify criminals. This anthropometrical system, known as Bertillonage, was invented in 1870 by Alphonse Bertillon (1853–1913) while employed at the Prefecture of Police, Paris, France. Bertillonage suffered a loss of credibility when, in 1903, two prisoners at the U.S. Federal Prison in Leavenworth, Kansas, were found to share identical measurements. The confusion surrounding prisoners William West and Will West was settled once and for all when a comparison of their fingerprints revealed them to be uniquely individual.

A fingerprint classification system developed in 1888 by Sir Francis Galton (1822–1922), a cousin of the famous naturalist Charles Darwin, was refined in 1901 by Sir Edward Henry (1850–1931). The Henry system of fingerprint classification is the system still in use by most of the world today.

In 1908, the National Fingerprint Bureau of the Dominion Police Force, which became part of the Royal Canadian Mounted Police in 1920, was mandated by Order in Council as the national repository for fingerprints of persons charged with indictable offences under the *Identification of Criminals Act*.[21] In 1924 the United States Congress established the Federal Bureau of Investigation (FBI) Identification Division as the central repository of fingerprints of convicted criminals in that country. In 2004, the Integrated Automatic Fingerprint Identification System (IAFIS) USA database contained approximately

---

[19]Evans (1996).

[20]Ibid.

[21]*Identification of Criminals Act*, R.S. 1985, c. I-1, s. 2(1).

46 million sets of criminal fingerprints as well as numerous others in various state-run AFIS systems.

7.14.2 Fingerprint Impressions

Fingerprint impressions fall into one of three categories:

1. Latent impressions – the most frequent form of impression. Formed by sweat on the skin of the hand coming into contact with a hard, smooth surface, such as glass, metal, or paper, etc. Soft or porous surfaces do not lend themselves well to the placement of fingerprint impressions, although it is possible to identify a latent impression on human skin if conducted within a short time. Latent impressions are invisible and must be developed using a number of developing processes.

2. Visible impressions – are far less frequent but, as the name suggests, are easily visible. They are formed by the surface of the finger, covered in blood, dirt, grease, etc., coming into contact with any surface. As they are visible, they are best photographed *in situ*.

3. Moulded impressions – the least frequent form of impression. Formed when a friction ridge skin is placed against a soft pliable surface, such as mud, grease, clay, etc.

Latent and visible fingerprint impressions degrade when exposed to environmental contamination such as precipitation in any form, direct sunlight, or accumulation of dust. If an impression is made on a hard surface that is protected from contamination, it could last an indefinite period of time[22]. Under suitable conditions, hard surfaces such as glass bottles, windows, mirrors, etc., and metal objects such as knives, firearms, and automobiles, often accept fingerprint impressions quite well. Soft or textured surfaces such as fabric, wood and leather do not accept fingerprints well, if at all.

In addition to the texture of the surface touched, the surface must also be of sufficient size for a full impression to be made on it. Small, irregular surfaces such as keys, certain tools, implements, doorknobs or the keys of computer keyboards may not have a sufficient surface area for an identifiable impression.

Fingerprint impressions are formed by perspiration from sweat glands on the friction ridge skin of the hands and feet. Human skin is composed of two main layers, the epidermis being the exterior layer of skin that covers the layer known as the dermis. Sebaceous glands within the dermis secrete perspiration and natural oils that lubricate the skin. Rubbing one's fingers on an oily part of the body, such as the face, will result in the transfer of oils to the fingers that will create fingerprint impressions when a surface is touched.

Latent fingerprints may be developed using a fine powder by dusting it in the traditional manner with a brush. The impression is then photographed to scale, lifted on cellophane tape and preserved on a clean material of contrasting background. Latent fingerprints may be developed on porous materials such as wood and paper utilizing processes involving iodine fuming or cyanoacrylate fuming (crazy-glue method) in a specially sealed chamber.

---

[22]Evans (1996).

On rare occasions, fingerprints have been enhanced on objects and developed on skin and wood utilizing Light Amplification by Stimulated Emission of Radiation (L.A.S.E.R.). Fingerprint impressions can also be developed on documents by spraying or immersing them in a Ninhydrin solution.

Early in my career, I recovered my first abandoned, stolen pickup truck, and was encouraged when I found a visible thumbprint in the middle of the exterior rear-view mirror on the driver's door. Thinking that the thumbprint might have been left by the offender while adjusting the mirror, and being far away from the nearest Identification Officer, I called for a tow truck to remove the vehicle to the garage to await the arrival of an identification officer who would lift the impression.

Imagine my disappointment when it unexpectedly rained heavily all the way back to the garage, totally obliterating any evidence of the thumbprint. After that day, I always carried a supply of exhibit bags of various sizes to protect my physical evidence from the elements.

7.14.3 Fingerprint Characteristics

Fingerprints are classified by comparing the various characteristics from the friction ridge skin patterns. The different characteristics used to analyze fingerprint impressions include:

1. ridge ending – the line of a ridge that ends within a pattern;

2. bifurcation – the line of a ridge splits to form other ridges;

3. island – a very short ridge; and

4. lake – the line of a ridge splits then rejoins.

A fingerprint impression will form one of three main patterns, of which there are sub-categories in each:

1. Loop – a pattern that features ridges that enter from one side, curve around a core pattern and exit the pattern from the direction in which they originated. A loop pattern will always feature one delta, which is a triangular shaped pattern within the pattern. Loops are the most common pattern and are encountered in about 60–70 per cent of fingerprints.

    Loops are further differentiated by the direction in which they are oriented. Radial loops point toward the inside of the wrist (the thumb side) and ulnar loops point toward the outside of the wrist (the little finger side).

2. Whorl – a pattern displaying two or more deltas, otherwise it is a loop. Approximately 25 per cent of fingerprints are classified as whorls.

3. Arch – any pattern that features ridges that enter from one side and exit toward the other side without either a core or a delta is an arch. If the pattern has one delta, it is a loop, if it has two deltas, it is a whorl. Arches may either be regular arches with smooth, easy curving ridges, or tented arches with sharper upward thrusting curves. Arches are the least common pattern encountered and are found in only about 5 per cent of all fingerprints.

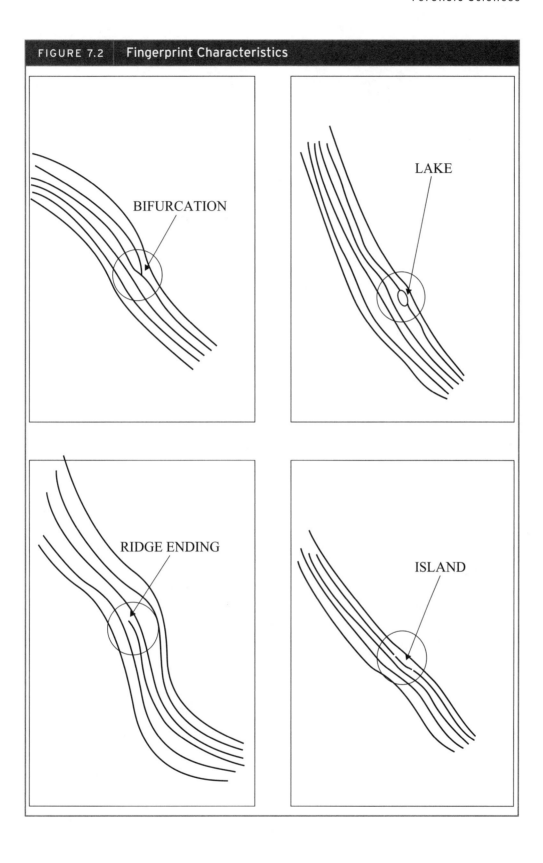

FIGURE 7.2   Fingerprint Characteristics

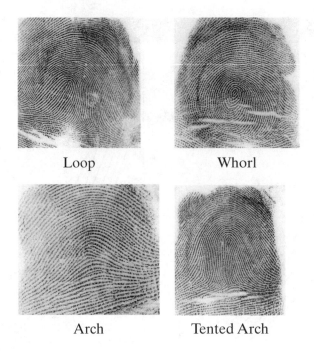

Loop   Whorl

Arch   Tented Arch

Illustration 7.1 - Fingerprint patterns.
Permission granted by Brian Dalrymple & Associates.

7.14.4 Evidentiary Value of Fingerprints

Fingerprints, while not as common as you might expect, are still an important source of physical evidence. Fingerprints can conclusively confirm the identity of a deceased victim or a suspect whose identity may be in question, or for the purposes of proving previous convictions. Fingerprints may provide the identity of a suspect for an unknown offender crime and may eliminate a person of interest from suspicion.

Fingerprint impressions usually corroborate some fact in issue, for example unlawful possession of an object or unlawful presence inside the premises where the crime occurred. Fingerprints may be used to disprove a suspect's alibi or may force him or her to engineer an explanation for the presence of their fingerprints. If the explanation given is false, the investigator may be able to disprove the alibi through other investigative means.

7.14.5 Limitations of Fingerprint Evidence

Fingerprint impressions can establish mere possession or presence, but the age of the impression cannot be determined. The presence of an impression does not prove when the particular impression was made. Nor does the existence of an identifiable impression prove the *mens rea* or the *actus reus* of the case. The existence of the impression is only circumstantial evidence.

Another obvious limitation of fingerprint impressions is that to identify a crime scene (questioned) fingerprint, you must have something to compare it to. If the identity of a suspect is known but he or she has no previous criminal convictions that are supported by fingerprints, you must attempt to obtain a comparison copy of their fingerprints, either voluntarily or covertly.

7.14.6 Comparison of Fingerprints

Comparison of fingerprints may only be certified by a designated fingerprint examiner. A fingerprint examiner is a person who has been designated by the Solicitor General of Canada for the purposes of proving the identity of a particular offender, or to prove that a particular offender was previously convicted of a certain offence. Both instances may be accomplished by direct testimony, or by way of certificate in either Form 44 or 45 of the *Criminal Code*, whichever is appropriate.[23]

The fingerprint examiner will compare the friction ridge characteristics of the fingerprint, which can contain up to 150 characteristics. The examiner may be required to attempt to compare a partial fingerprint impression, developed at a crime scene, to a full comparison set taken from the suspect, either previously or at the time of the investigation. It is always important to take the best set of impressions possible every time a person is fingerprinted, as those impressions may some day be used to make identification in a serious crime.

In 1918, Dr. Edmond Locard recommended that at least 18 concordant points of similarity were required to conclude that fingerprint impressions were made by the same person. There has never been any legal number of concordant points set by courts and many courts are willing to accept identifications of between 8–12 concordant points.

The fingerprint examiner will compare two fingerprints looking for a continuous agreement of ridge characteristics in an identical sequence. It is virtually impossible that there could be 8–12 concordant points shared by two fingerprints and still have differences between them. The fingerprint examiner's opinion must be one of absolute certainty or uncertainty (inclusionary or exclusionary).

7.15 OTHER FORMS OF IMPRESSION EVIDENCE

Other impression evidence, made by gloves or footwear worn by offenders, automotive or bicycle tires, tool marks, pattern wounds, bite marks, etc. (all questioned samples) may also be found at crime scenes. All of these impressions may yield class characteristics and accidental characteristics, which can be used to compare them to seized or recovered (known) items to compare their similarity.

Even if the physical object that created the impression cannot be located, an examination of the impression might yield information such as:

- the type of item that caused the impression;

- the origin, manufacturer and purchaser;

- the number of blows or impacts; or

- the direction of the force/motion.

Any of this information may yield clues as to the identity of the offender or may be used by an investigator to reconstruct the events of a crime. I once followed two sets of footwear impressions, one much larger than the other, in freshly-fallen snow leading away from a recovered stolen vehicle. The trail abruptly ended about a half-kilometre away, where it had been obliterated by a snowplow.

---

[23]*Criminal Code*, R.S. 1985, c.C-46, s. 667.

With limited information about the size, shape and pattern of the footwear impressions, a brief canvass of local shoe retailers resulted in a tentative identification of a women's snow boot, the sale of only four pairs of which could be associated to names of purchasers. Remarkably, one of the purchasers lived about 200 metres past the end of the trail of the suspect footprints. Within an hour, I had a signed statement from the girlfriend of the offender (the purchaser of the winter boots) who had been picked up after work by her boyfriend, who was driving an unfamiliar vehicle. After the vehicle had run out of gas, he had walked her to her residence – leaving their signatures in the snow in the form of their footprints. The offender pleaded guilty to avoid having his girlfriend testify against him.

7.16 DEOXYRIBONUCLEIC ACID (DNA)

Human cell research had been ongoing since the 1860s, when in 1953 the DNA molecule was first identified. It wasn't, however, until 1985 that the possibility was realized that the variable DNA patterns, which exist in every nucleated cell within the human body, could be used as an individual-specific identification system. Geneticist Sir Alex Jeffreys at Leicester University assisted the West Midlands Police in confirming the confession of 17 year old rape suspect, Robert Melias, the first person in history to be convicted on the strength of DNA evidence.

DNA is a molecule that makes up the 23 pairs of chromosomes in the nucleus of most cells in the human body. DNA consists of two intertwining strands that resemble a spiral shaped ladder referred to as a double helix. Sugar and phosphate molecules form the sides of the ladder while complementary nitrogenous base pairs, in the combinations of Adenine–Thymine and Guanine–Cytosine, form the rungs of the ladder. Each human has approximately 3 million base pairs, which carry his or her unique genetic information, with the exception of identical twins who always share an identical DNA profile.

The initial use of DNA by law enforcement agencies, which was almost exclusive to sexual assault cases, has now been expanded to other crimes of violence and any other case in which biological evidence may be transferred. Suspects have even been identified from DNA in the epithelial cells in their saliva recovered from the flap of an envelope or the back of licked postage stamps. DNA molecules may be extracted from samples of blood, semen, saliva, teeth, bone and the root sheath of hair follicles.

DNA profiles must be compared to the victim's profile as well as to the crime scene (questioned) sample to identify an offender, if a comparison sample of the suspect's DNA exists or can be otherwise obtained. Degraded DNA samples and samples containing mixtures of DNA must always be resolved during the testing process for there to be a suitable identification.

The primary value of DNA profiling, with its astounding ability to identify suspects and clear innocent persons, lies in its individuality and its permanence; as with fingerprints, a person cannot change his or her DNA. For law enforcement, DNA profiling has been the most significant technological advance to date and has resulted in many countries creating DNA databanks to collect biological samples from convicted offenders to be used for comparison with present and future unsolved crime scene samples.

SUMMARY

- The Centre of Forensic Sciences performs services for prosecutors and for defence counsel, which include: the identification of substances; the revealing of additional information regarding submitted items; the detection of drugs and poisons in bodily samples; and the comparison of objects and substances.

- "Forensic Identification" means that if two or more objects share a sufficient number of identical features and there are no unexplainable differences between them, it may be concluded that the objects are the same, or that similar characteristics may be regarded as sharing a common origin.

- Class characteristics are shared by similar objects and include size, shape and pattern. If the class characteristics of two items do not agree, no identification is possible.

- Accidental characteristics include random cuts, tears, defects, wear patterns and unique flaws that prove an object's individuality. If two objects display a sufficient number of accidental characteristics and there are no differences that cannot be explained, they can be deemed to be the same.

- The possible findings of a forensic examination include: Common Origin – the objects did or did not have a common origin; Probable – the objects probably did or did not have a common origin; or Possible – the objects may have had a common origin.

- The primary usefulness of fingerprints as a means of personal identification is based on two main factors, their uniqueness and permanence.

- The Henry system of fingerprint classification, developed in 1901, is the system still in use by most of the world today.

- Fingerprint impressions can establish mere possession or presence, but the age of the impression cannot be determined.

- Impression evidence may also be found at crime scenes that were made by gloves worn by offenders, footwear, automotive or bicycle tires, tool marks, bite marks, etc.

- DNA is a molecule that makes up the 23 pairs of chromosomes in the nucleus of most cells in the human body and which contains a person's uniquely identifiable genetic code, the exception being identical twins, who share a common profile between them.

DISCUSSION QUESTIONS

1. What is the most definitive finding that a forensic scientist could make after conducting a comparison of a questioned tire impression from a crime scene and a tire removed from a suspect's motor vehicle? Why?

2. Other than primary and secondary transfers, in what three manners may evidence be transferred from one object to another? What method does an investigator have control over, if any?

3. Why is it important for an investigator to refrain from the use of terms such as "gunshot," "accused," or "suspect" when labelling an exhibit to be submitted to a forensic laboratory for analysis?

4. What are the factors that contribute to the suitability and longevity of a latent fingerprint impression?

 # WEBLINKS

www.mpss.jus.gov.on.ca/english/pub_safety/centre_forensic/ forensic_links.html

Government of Ontario, Ministry of Community Safety and Correctional Services. Centre of Forensic Sciences. Services provided and related links.

www.rcmp.ca/fls/home_e.htm

Royal Canadian Mounted Police. Forensic Laboratory Services. Directory of regional RCMP forensic laboratories and services provided.

http://people.stu.ca/~mclaugh/index.html

The Forensic Science Resource Page at St. Thomas University, N.B. A forensic sciences database focusing on forensic anthropology and includes information on biology, chemistry, toxicology, entomology, pathology and the science of fingerprinting.

www.csfs.ca/

Canadian Society of Forensic Science. An organization created to maintain professional standards, and to promote the study and enhance the stature of forensic science. Forensic resources and educational opportunities.

www.ridgesandfurrows.homestead.com

Ridges and Furrows. A website containing research, resources and literature regarding the science of fingerprinting.

Chapter 8

Specialized Investigative Techniques

"All that is needed for evil to triumph is for good men [and women] to do nothing."

Edmund Burke, British (Irish-born) statesman and politician (1729-1797).[1]

Learning Outcomes

After reading this chapter, students should be able to:

- Describe the different types of physical surveillance that investigators conduct and give an example of a situation in which each method might be employed.

- Name the three primary roles on a physical surveillance detail and summarize the responsibilities of each of those roles.

- Explain both requirements that investigators must satisfy in order to establish the "investigative necessity" of utilizing the interception of private communications when applying for an authorization under s. 185(1) *Criminal Code*.

- Name the three physiological reactions monitored during a polygraph examination when assessing the credibility of a suspect, witness or person of interest.

- Name three types of behavioural analyses that are commonly used during the investigation of serial and predatory crime.

- Describe the three classifications of blood pattern evidence often found at scenes of violent crimes and explain the two important findings that may be determined from examining bloodstains.

8.1 INTRODUCTION

The majority of crimes are solved by the tried and true investigative techniques of interviewing witnesses, chasing down leads, systematic and meticulous crime scene examination and through the questioning of persons of interest. Over the years, however, criminal investigation has evolved from the concept of the "generalist" investigator, who conducted

---

[1] Edmund Burke quote retrieved April 28, 2003, from www.bartleby.com

every aspect of any investigation, to the diverse profession it is today, which often requires the use of expert investigative techniques to bring complex cases to a successful conclusion.

An important part of a criminal investigation is the appropriate use of specialized investigation techniques, such as **surveillance**, **photographic lineups**, undercover operations, psychological profiling, blood spatter interpretation and polygraph. Although often costly to utilize, certain cases will benefit from the use of these specialized techniques to gather evidence that might otherwise go undetected.

Cost is only one factor to assess when considering whether or not to use specialized investigative techniques. A responsible investigator must also recognize that society is more and more concerned with individual rights and with the protection of privacy.

Certain investigative techniques are highly intrusive and require the investigator to justify the necessity of employing such extraordinary evidence-gathering techniques. The limitations upon police evidence-gathering methods imposed by legislation and case law must always be complied with to avoid having evidence declared inadmissible on the grounds that an individual's constitutional rights were violated.

8.2 SURVEILLANCE

Surveillance is the continuous observation of a person, group of people, location or of some other situation, and may be conducted in either of two manners. Surveillance may be overt in nature, meaning that the subject who is being observed is aware of the surveillance, for example the openly visible closed circuit television (CCTV) camera in a variety store that is used to record all persons who approach the cash counter. The type of surveillance that we will concentrate on is the covert, or secret, methods of surveillance used to enhance an investigation and which, if successfully conducted, ensures that the subject under surveillance is not aware that he or she is being observed or monitored.

Investigators, alone or in teams, conduct surveillance in order to develop or corroborate criminal intelligence about an individual's or group's associations or activities, to uncover investigative leads or to gather evidence of acts taken in furtherance of crimes or the planning of crimes that may be used in criminal proceedings. Covert surveillance may also be conducted for the purpose of observing the anticipated commission of an offence or to prevent an offence from occurring.

Surveillance has been utilized to observe suspects return to scenes of crimes, to retrieve or dispose of evidence and to disprove a suspect's alibi. "Surveillance" includes both physical surveillance of an individual or the electronic interception of communications. Regardless of the particular target, surveillance that is covert, or secret, falls into one of the following four categories:

1. static (stationary – fixed);

2. physical (mobile – on foot or in vehicles);

3. photographic; or

4. electronic.

8.2.1 Static Surveillance

Static surveillance is the directed observation of a business, residence or other location. Surveillance in the form of a "stakeout" may be conducted to observe any activities in relation to a location where criminal activity is suspected, for example a residence from where it is believed that contraband, such as drugs or stolen property, is being trafficked or if information is received that a certain business will be victimized. A discreet observation post can be established in a vehicle or a nearby building with a vantage point of the target premises. This type of surveillance could also be done to gain knowledge of a suspect's associations, perhaps to identify others potentially involved in activity under investigation.

Surveillance of a target location that reveals a high volume of pedestrian traffic visiting for brief periods might result in a non-prosecution arrest and drug seizure involving no charges that, combined with other evidence (such as from a confidential informant) could be used as the basis upon which to obtain a search warrant for a suspected drug location. If reliable information indicates that a business is to be broken into, surveillance conducted from inside or outside the building might result in the apprehension of the persons responsible for that and other crimes.

Static surveillance is often very monotonous and unproductive, but it can also pay tremendous dividends, such as the time when investigators observed a suspect carrying an object that was later found to contain the severed head of a homicide victim. Static surveillance is never passive and requires more than just being in the right location. Communication between investigators assigned to the same surveillance detail is critical so that all members of the detail know what is happening. One investigator must be in command in order to adapt to any unforeseen circumstance that might occur.

Surveillance officers need to stay attentive and alert to their assignment at all times. Something as simple as lighting a cigarette or leaving a position of concealment could compromise the success of an operation or the safety of other officers. Considerable self-discipline is required for an investigator to sit in a vehicle or other location for lengthy periods of time and maintain their concentration.

8.2.2 Physical Surveillance

As with other forms of surveillance, the objective of physical surveillance is to gather as much relevant information as possible, without being seen – something which is far easier said than done. Depending on the nature of the case, there is a higher probability that officers assigned to physical surveillance details could witness a crime being committed. Physical surveillance is virtually impossible to conduct by oneself and requires the coordinated effort of a team of trained investigators.

Physical surveillance is typically utilized to gather evidence about suspected crimes, such as drug trafficking, breaking and entering, auto theft or armed robbery. Physical surveillance most often involves a team of between three to six investigators in separate vehicles but could also involve tailing a target on foot, or a combination of both.

A physical surveillance team must remain in constant communication and must be watchful for opportunities to collect physical evidence or to make an arrest, if required. Only one member of the team will closely observe the target at a time, and is referred to as the "eye". Another team member remains in a following position to assume the "eye" at any given moment. Team members change positions frequently to avoid being recognized by the target.

A target may be surveilled from behind, beside, in front, above or below. The key to conducting a successful mobile surveillance is the ability to adapt to any situation. If the target were to stop suddenly, the members of the surveillance detail must keep the observation going in all possible directions. When the target begins to move again, the first team member in the new direction of travel automatically becomes the "eye." The same procedure is followed if visual contact with the target is lost for more than a few seconds.

An "eye" should never stay with the target for very long, say more than two changes of direction. If it becomes necessary for one member to stay with the target for longer than that, disguises should be utilized to change one's appearance. Surveillance techniques will be discussed in more detail in a later section.

8.2.3 Photographic Surveillance

Photographic surveillance may be conducted alone or in conjunction with either static or physical surveillance. Still or video photography creates a permanent record of the observations of the surveillance in a form that is suitable for either investigative purposes or for presentation in court. Photographic surveillance can be conducted from inside a building or a vehicle, especially one that has been adapted with one-way windows for that purpose, or from an aircraft.

Photographic surveillance can even be conducted by installing covert camera equipment in vantage points in places where it would not be possible or practicable to assign surveillance officers. Photographic surveillance lends itself well to long-term investigations involving internal employee theft and organized crime investigations.

8.2.4 Electronic Surveillance

Electronic surveillance may also be used in conjunction with other surveillance and other investigative methods. Electronic surveillance may be in the form of a tracking device attached to a target vehicle to record routes travelled by a suspect, either as a stand-alone method or in conjunction with mobile surveillance. Tracking devices can be useful in circumstances where it would otherwise be difficult to observe a target without being detected by allowing the surveillance team to remain out of sight and follow the electronic signals from a discreet distance.

Tracking devices may also be inserted into items such as drug shipments, property that is vulnerable to imminent theft or ransom money to track its eventual destination. Electronic surveillance can also be in the form of intercepting private communications by the use of listening devices placed in a vehicle or room or through a wire tap on a subject's telephone. Interception of private communications is a complex issue that will be discussed in a separate section.

A person may be followed or physically observed at any time by police officers for reasons that amount to mere suspicion, far less than the standard of reasonable grounds, but the standard for electronic surveillance is much higher due to the subject's "reasonable expectation of privacy when in public."[2] An individual who travels freely in public forfeits their expectation of privacy when in public. In fact, the more intrusive the surveillance is, the more restrictions there are on the use of the technique.

A justice of the peace may, on the sworn application of a peace officer, issue a warrant for a police officer to install, maintain, monitor or remove a tracking device to gather information, on reasonable grounds that a suspect has committed or will commit any criminal offence.[3] A tracking device warrant is valid for a period not exceeding 60 days but may be extended by further warrants issued by the justice.[4]

A provincial court or superior court judge may issue a general search warrant to authorize a police officer to utilize a CCTV camera or similar recording device to observe any person for a designated offence that, on reasonable grounds has been or will be committed. The offence must be one that is referred to in section 487.01(5) of the *Criminal Code*.[5] Utilization of a tracking device or video surveillance may only be carried out without a warrant "if the conditions for obtaining a warrant exist but by reason of exigent circumstances it would be impracticable to obtain a warrant."[6] Exigent circumstances, although not defined, have been held to include circumstances that could result in imminent injury, death or the possible loss or destruction of evidence.[7]

8.3 PHYSICAL SURVEILLANCE TECHNIQUES

When following a subject, surveillance officers should make every effort to blend into their surroundings to avoid drawing the target's attention. If the target heads to a beach on a hot summer day, six investigators in business attire would expect to stand out as the result of their conspicuous appearance. The use of props, such as sporting equipment (e.g., tennis racquets, golf clubs or jogging equipment) and disguises will help investigators appear as if they are part of the landscape. The use of hats, wigs, sunglasses, changes of clothing (e.g., reversible garments or removable layers) can significantly change a person's appearance to avoid being recognized.

Surveillance officers should make use of all available barriers that still permit visual contact to be maintained. Aisles, foliage, signage and even crowds of people can hide an investigator from view while still maintaining observation. It is possible to turn your back to the subject and make use of reflective material such as mirrors and store windows to continue observing their movements. If the target leads you into a shopping mall, you must blend into the surroundings and appear to be a shopper.

If the target ventures into a rest room, a member of the surveillance team should consider following him or her to observe any possible meeting or exchange of goods, or overhear any conversation that might occur, providing it would not be hazardous to do

---

[2]*R. v. Wong* (1990) 3 S.C.R. 36, 60 C.C.C (3d) 460, 1 C.R.(4th) 1.

[3]*Criminal Code*, R.S. 1985, c. C-46, s. 492.1(1).

[4]*Criminal Code*, R.S. 1985, c. C-46, s. 492.1(2) and (3).

[5]*Criminal Code*, R.S. 1985, c. C-46, s. 487.01(5).

[6]*Criminal Code*, R.S. 1985, c. C-46, s. 487.11.

[7]*Criminal Code*, R.S. 1985, c. C-46, s. 529.3(2).

so. If the target enters a restaurant, a member of the team should follow as closely as possible without raising suspicion. It is often advisable to employ a female surveillance officer or two officers posing as a couple to avoid drawing attention in everyday social settings such as restaurants.

If a target climbs a set of stairs – you follow. If a target enters an elevator, attempt to follow or determine the floor they went to. A lone officer will not be able to stay close to a target for long without arousing suspicion but several skilful officers continually changing position and never appearing the same way twice to the target can follow a person indefinitely.

As with mobile surveillance conducted in vehicles, should the target stop for any reason, team members must cover off all possible directions by which the subject may leave. The closest member in the new direction of travel automatically becomes the "eye." If communicating by radio, only the "eye" and the team leader speak unless another member has some new relevant information.

If the target approaches an unknown individual, a decision will have to be made as to the feasibility of conducting a field interview regarding any conversation/transaction made by the subject, except where it is believed that the unknown person is an unidentified associate. At the very least, steps should be taken to identify every person the target has contact with during the period of the surveillance.

8.3.1   Roles and Responsibilities

Every surveillance detail must have a designated and experienced team leader who is responsible for directing and co-ordinating the efforts of the team. It is the team leader's responsibility to brief investigators assigned to the detail regarding all available information about the target, the area involved, strategy to be employed, radio frequencies, codes or signals, and assigning any individual responsibilities. The team leader is responsible for any tactical decisions, including the necessity to make an arrest, should circumstances dictate. The team leader should also oversee a debriefing of team members following every surveillance detail.

Every surveillance team should have a designated "**scribe**" who is responsible for recording the collective observations of the team. In addition to being an operating member of the team, the scribe records all times, dates and locations of observations, identities of persons, if known, or their detailed descriptions in writing and finalizes the results of the detail in a comprehensive written report. This final report may be signed by all participating members and may be accepted as the collective report of the team.

One member of the team should be designated as an exhibit officer whose responsibility it is to collect and preserve all evidence from the other members of the team at the end of the detail. The exhibit officer must ensure that all exhibits are properly packaged and labelled. The exhibit officer maintains an exhibit register listing all recovered items, and ensures that this information is included in the final surveillance report. Proper continuity, storage and processing of these exhibits may be the responsibility of the exhibit officer or could be delegated to another investigator. The use of still and/or video cameras is helpful when recording significant items of evidentiary value.

8.3.2 Evidence Gathering

If the target of a surveillance discards anything, such as notes, papers, packaging, food containers/napkins, etc., especially if fingerprint or DNA identification is relevant to investigation, it should be retrieved as soon as practicable, without drawing attention. Evidence gathering equipment, such as latex gloves and plastic exhibit bags should be carried by all members assigned to the detail.

8.3.3 Surveillance Equipment

In addition to the use of disguises and props to blend into the surroundings, vision equipment, such as binoculars/monocular and night vision equipment can also be useful for observing details from a distance or in low-light conditions. Recording equipment, such as notebooks and tape recorders, should be carried by all members of the detail.

Communication equipment is essential and should include two-way radios for each team member and cellular telephones, if available. Tracking equipment, such as Global Positioning System (GPS) and tracking devices known as "bird dogs," should be used in accordance with the previously described legal requirements.

8.3.4 Counter Surveillance

While some targets are sometimes completely unsuspecting and carry on their activities totally unaware that they are being followed, experienced criminals are often surveillance conscious and may employ a variety of **counter-surveillance** methods. Targets might suddenly stop, reverse their direction, change their appearance, enter premises and wait at the door to observe anyone who enters after them.

Targets will sometimes board a bus or other public conveyance and disembark just before getting under way to observe anyone who gets off with them in a manoeuvre referred to as "checking for heat." Targets occasionally drive the wrong way down a one-way street and have been known to approach and speak to people they suspect are following them.

Every member of a surveillance detail must expect the unexpected and be prepared to react to such a situation without registering a reaction or drawing attention. If you must walk past the subject, do so inconspicuously, without making eye contact with the target and allow another member to assume the "eye." If you are approached by the target, have a plausible excuse for being there. If you are accused of being a police officer – deny, deny, deny. Any member who is approached and engaged in conversation by the target has been compromised and should immediately cease his or her involvement in the detail.

If a member of the detail is approached by a target who then overhears radio transmissions from other members, the entire detail is compromised and should be discontinued. The decision to terminate the detail will be made by the Team Leader, alone or in consultation with the remaining team members.

Following every surveillance detail, the scribe will complete a comprehensive narrative report listing the date of the surveillance, the persons participating in the detail, the target(s), objective, reason for the detail, and a chronological summary of the collective observations of the team. The report will also detail any physical evidence that was collected and any other comments, such as counter-surveillance techniques employed by the target.

Following a review for accuracy, the report should be forwarded to the intelligence officer or Case Manager who authorized the surveillance detail for analysis. The authorizing officer will decide if the objective of the surveillance was achieved or if other surveillance and/or other investigative methods are required.

8.4 INTERCEPTION OF PRIVATE COMMUNICATIONS

There was a simpler time when the interception of private communication was limited to personal conversations or telephone conversations. There is now an abundance of methods that modern criminals can use to contact each other to discuss illicit matters and carry on their criminal affairs in our current high-tech world. Since the advent of electronic pagers, email, wireless messaging devices and satellite communications, law enforcement has had to continually develop strategies to respond to the investigation of technology-savvy law breakers in order to meet this challenge.

Electronic surveillance in the form of surreptitious eavesdropping on private communications has been held to constitute a search or seizure within the meaning of s. 8 of the *Charter of Rights and Freedoms*.[8] It is a criminal offence to intercept a private communication using "any electro-magnetic, acoustic, mechanical or other device" unless authorized by a judge of a designated court under either s. 184.2, where any party to the communication consents to its interception, or under subsection 186(1) *Criminal Code*, where no consent to intercept exists.[9]

"Private communications" implies that, at the time of the communication, the originator of the communication had a reasonable expectation that no one other than the intended recipient would receive it. For example, this could include a face-to-face conversation between two or more criminals in one of their residences, a car or other private place that is intercepted by means of an electronic listening device called a probe. A private communication would also include a pay-telephone call from a criminal to an associate whose residence telephone service has been "tapped" by a law enforcement agency.

Electronic surveillance utilizing a wire tap, room or car probe, or using a "body-pack" recorder, involves obtaining a judicially authorized, interception of private communications that may be used to gather evidence under very strict circumstances, which are set out in Part VI of the *Criminal Code*. Various criminal offences, including attempts, **counselling**, accessory after the fact and conspiracies to commit them, for which interception of private communications may be authorized, are contained in s. 183 *Criminal Code* and includes any offence where "there are reasonable grounds to believe is a criminal-organization offence, or any other offence that there are reasonable grounds to believe is an offence described in paragraph (b) or (c) of the definition 'terrorism offence'...."[10]

---

[8]*R. v. Duarte* (1990) 1 S.C.R. 30, 53 C.C.C. (3d) 1, 65 D.L.R. (4th) 240.

[9]*Criminal Code*, R.S. 1985, c. C-46, s. 184(1).

[10]*Criminal Code*, R.S. 1985, c. C-46, s. 183.

When applying for an authorization under s. 185(1) *Criminal Code*, a designated agent of the Solicitor General of Canada (or the designated agent of the Attorney General of Canada or any province) must establish that "other investigative procedures have been tried and have failed or it appears they are otherwise unlikely to succeed or the urgency of the matter is such that it would be impractical to carry out the investigation of the offence using only other investigative procedures." This requirement doesn't apply to the offences of instructing, participating in the activities of or committing offences for the benefit of a criminal organization as defined in s. 467.1 *Criminal Code*.[11]

The application made in support of an authorization is most often accompanied by the sworn affidavit of a specially trained investigator that sets out the grounds to establish why the interception of private communications is an investigative necessity.[12]

In exceptional circumstances, a police officer may intercept private communications without an authorization to do so where there are reasonable grounds to believe that it "is immediately necessary to prevent an unlawful act that would cause serious harm to any person or to property" and that one of the parties to the conversation is either the person who would commit the harm or be the victim of it.[13] An emergency 36-hour authorization to intercept private communications may also be applied for by a small number of specially designated police officers where because of urgent circumstances a normal authorization could not be obtained, but such authorizations are very rare.[14] Normally, the interception of private communications is authorized for a period not to exceed 60 days but may be extended by subsequent authorizations for further periods of not more than 60 days.[15]

In recognition of the privilege relating to solicitor–client communications, no authorization to intercept private communications may be issued for any place, including the law offices or residence of a lawyer, unless there are reasonable grounds to believe that the lawyer, an employee or a person residing in the lawyer's residence has been or will become a party to a designated offence.[16]

A judge may authorize the interception of the communications of known and unknown persons, whose communications would assist the investigation; for a 60-day period if they are satisfied that it "…would be in the best interests of the administration of justice to do so."[17] The covert installation and removal of surreptitious listening devices inside residences, cars etc., requires police officers to commit acts that would normally constitute unlawful acts. An authorization to intercept private communications, however, specifically authorizes police officers "to install, maintain or remove [the electronic devices used to intercept communications] covertly."[18]

During a drug-trafficking investigation several years ago, a particular suspect was known to conduct transactions on his yacht in the middle of a lake in the belief that his conversations were private and unheard by local law enforcement officers. We had, however,

---

[11]*Criminal Code*, R.S., 1985, c. C-46, s. 467.11 to 467.13.

[12]*Criminal Code*, R.S. 1985, c. C-46, s. 185(1).

[13]*Criminal Code*, R.S. 1985, c. C-46, s. 184.4.

[14]*Criminal Code*, R.S. 1985, c. C-46, s. 188(1)-(2).

[15]*Criminal Code*, R.S. 1985, c. C-46, s. 186(4)(e) and 186(7).

[16]*Criminal Code*, R.S. 1985, c. C-46, s. 186(2).

[17]*Criminal Code*, R.S. 1985, c. C-46, s. 186(1)(a).

[18]*Criminal Code*, R.S. 1985, c. C-46, s. 186(5.2).

installed a probe on his boat and had to surreptitiously re-enter the boat several times over the course of the boating season to maintain the device or to remove it when we became aware that the boat required servicing by a mechanic who might have inadvertently discovered the unusual apparatus. The probe was irreparably damaged on one occasion when either a mechanic or the owner forgot to replace a transom plug before re-launching and the vessel sunk in five feet of water, causing havoc with the boat's electronics – and ours.

The application for an authorization to intercept private communications and any documents in relation to the application are confidential and are placed in a sealed packet by the judge after the application is reviewed, whether or not an authorization is issued.[19] The only times that a packet may be opened are when an issue becomes relevant during the trial that requires that the contents of the packet be examined or when, after a prosecution has commenced, an accused applies for an order to receive copies of the contents of the packet to make full answer and defence to their charge(s).[20]

Prior to turning over copies of the contents of a sealed packet to any accused, the prosecutor is entitled to edit anything that might reveal the identity of a confidential police informant, compromise any ongoing investigation or endanger the safety of persons engaged in certain intelligence-gathering techniques or that would prejudice future investigations.[21]

Any person who is the object of an intercepted private communication must be notified of the interception in writing, usually within 90 days following the expiration of the authorization, whether or not the interception resulted in the laying of charges.[22] Where charges are laid, reasonable notice of intention to produce evidence obtained as the result of such interceptions must be given to all accused persons.[23] The Solicitor General of Canada and the Attorneys General of all provinces are required by law to prepare comprehensive annual reports detailing, among other things, the numbers of authorizations applied for, and issued or refused, in that year.[24]

BOX 8.1	Investigative Relevance

The area of law regarding the interception of private communications is extremely technical and complex and the use of electronic interception of private communications constitutes an extraordinary and highly invasive law enforcement method that far exceeds those used in typical investigations. While not necessarily a "last resort" investigative technique, it is a specialized investigative method that should be reserved for exceptional circumstances, when absolutely necessary.

Due to the considerable expense of utilizing electronic surveillance, it is a procedure that is reserved for major offences such as high-level drug trafficking, murder, organized crime investigations etc. Electronic surveillance should only be resorted to when, having regard to all the circumstances, conventional investigative methods have either been tried unsuccessfully or are unlikely to be successful and the success of the investigation depends upon its use.

---

[19]*Criminal Code*, R.S. 1985, c. C-46, s. 187(1).

[20]*Criminal Code*, R.S. 1985, c. C-46, s. 187(1.3) and 187(1.4).

[21]*Criminal Code*, R.S. 1985, c. C-46, s. 187(4)

[22]*Criminal Code*, R.S. 1985, c. C-46, s 196(1)

[23]*Criminal Code*, R.S. 1985, c. C-46, s. 189(5)

[24]*Criminal Code*, R.S. 1985, c. C-46, s. 195(1) to (5)

8.5   POLYGRAPH

"You can fool some of the people all the time, and all of the people some of the time, but you cannot fool all of the people all of the time."

Abraham Lincoln, 16th President of the United States (1809-1865).

People tell lies for any number of reasons. The telling of some lies may be relatively innocent. For example, who hasn't told a simple lie to avoid hurting the feelings of a friend or loved one when asked, "Do you think this shirt/coat/dress/hairstyle makes me look old/overweight/funny?" Unless we are totally insensitive to the feelings of the person, the safe and socially acceptable answer is something like, "Of course not... you look fine!" The telling of lies that we are concerned with are those that are far more sinister in nature than a social "white lie." When people lie to a police officer, it is usually to avoid prosecution or the imposition of other sanctions during the investigation of an offence.

Since ancient times, mankind has attempted to accurately determine guilt or innocence by successfully detecting whether a subject's account of an event or his or her knowledge of the event is truthful or deceptive. Various historical methods included torture, trial by ordeal, and occasional methods that employed pearls of common sense, such as the legendary biblical wisdom of King Solomon who threatened to equally divide a baby by cutting it in half when two women both claimed to be the baby's mother. The imposter agreed to the proposed arrangement while, out of love for her child, the baby's real mother withdrew her claim to spare her baby's life.

Historically, attempts to detect whether or not a person was lying largely depended on the interrogator's ability to induce a confession from the suspect. More recent attempts to induce suspects to tell the truth through the use of so-called "truth serums" in the form of pharmacological agents such as sodium amytal and sodium pentathol were unsuccessfully attempted. Overall, today we are probably only marginally better at detecting lies than our early ancestors were.

The **polygraph** is an instrument that measures a person's involuntary physiological responses while under stress, in this case, the stress of telling a lie and wanting to avoid being identified as the person responsible for the crime. The polygraph, mistakenly referred to by many as the lie-detector, is anything but a lie detector, even though a finding of truth or deception is incidental to the comparison of the subject's physiological responses between relevant and control questions. The value of the polygraph as an investigative aid or pre-employment screening device is considered contentious by its critics, due to the lack of any sound scientific basis for its results.[25]

Interestingly, the first use of the word "polygraph" had nothing whatever to do with the detection of deception and was a name that Thomas Jefferson gave to a copying device that he invented in 1790 to replicate words and writings. In 1885, Cesare Lombroso, an Italian anthropologist, monitored the blood pressure of three suspects during their questioning for a murder, evidently pronouncing them deceptive.

Just as the battle wages on as to the validity of polygraph results, so goes the battle as to who actually invented the polygraph. Both Dr. William Moulton Marston

---

[25]Maschke & Scalabrini (2000).

(1893–1947) and Dr. John A. Larson (1892–1983) are alternately credited with having invented the polygraph. It seems, however, that Dr. Marston invented the systolic blood pressure test, which contributed to the development of the polygraph in the 1920s by Dr. Larson, who patented the instrument as the Keeler Polygraph in honour of Leonarde Keeler, under whom he had studied and experimented with simultaneous measurements of blood pressure, respiration and pulse when questioning individuals. Credit for the invention of the polygraph must go to Dr. Larson, while Dr. Marston later went on to uncontested fame as the inventor of Wonder Woman, the DC Comic strip character.

8.5.1   How the Polygraph Works

The modern-day polygraph, as an instrument that assists with interrogative interviews, monitors and evaluates three physiological responses in the individual who is being examined:

1. blood pressure;

2. respiration; and

3. galvanic skin resistance at the fingertips, a function of perspiration.

When faced with any perceived threat, the human body involuntarily reacts in preparation to run or defend itself in the traditional "fight or flight" response. Our body produces adrenalin, our pulse rate quickens, as does our breathing in anticipation of the possible physical exertion that may be required to survive. It is some of these physiological reactions that the polygraph detects – not lies.

Often the subject's mere response to the offer of a polygraph examination may reveal certain information, on the assumption that an innocent person is less likely to refuse the test as they should have nothing to hide and no consequences to fear. Some subjects, after initially consenting to submit to an examination change their mind when faced with the reality of viewing the polygraph instrument. While nobody can be forced to submit to a polygraph test, an investigator should be wary of any person of interest or suspect who at any time refuses to be tested.

When a subject voluntarily agrees to submit to a polygraph examination during an investigation, he or she is requested to attend the examination well-rested and be free from the influence of drugs and alcohol to avoid effects of such agents on the central nervous system. This is done to ensure the individual's physiological responses are as normal as possible to yield the best possible test results.

A qualified polygraph examiner conducts a pre-test of the subject, during which the subject's legal rights are discussed, and inquiries are made as to his or her medical and psychological background as well as the subject's prior working knowledge of the polygraph instrument. Prior to the actual polygraph test being administered, the examiner will design a list of irrelevant and relevant questions regarding the incident(s) under investigation and review them with the subject.[26]

For the in-test phase of the examination, the subject is fitted with a blood pressure cuff, two rubber tubes called pneumographs around his or her chest, which are used to measure the individual's rate of respiration, and galvanometers to measure galvanic skin

---

[26]Ibid

resistance on two fingertips. Some modern polygraphs even detect muscle movement in the lower extremities of the body to monitor a subject shifting uneasily when asked a relevant question or movements intended to try to defeat the polygraph. Most polygraph tests are of a format referred to as the "Control Question Test," which combines the asking of relevant and control questions, in series that are repeated during the examination.

The post-test phase of the examination involves the examiner scoring the subject's test results and forming an opinion as to the truth or deception of the subject when he or she responded to the relevant questions. As the result of the subject's overall score, the examiner will render the findings as truthful, deceptive or inconclusive. The subject of the interview is then apprised of his or her respective "passing" or "failing" of the test. If, in the opinion of the examiner, the results indicate deception present in the subject's response, the examiner will embark upon a post-test interrogation in an attempt to gain an admission of deception or a full confession regarding the offences under investigation.

The American Polygraph Association (APA) claims 80–98 per cent accuracy during 80 research projects involving 6 380 individual polygraph tests. According to critics, however, the common physiological reactions that are measured by a polygraph are neither unique nor universal and might also be triggered by other normal human emotions such as hate, anger, and jealousy. This can potentially result in "false positives," a term applied when innocent individuals are determined to be deceptive or "false negatives," guilty individuals being mistakenly evaluated as having been truthful.

Persons of interest and suspects should never be cleared or charged purely on the basis of a polygraph examination – neither should the credibility of a witness who successfully passes a polygraph test be accepted implicitly without independent corroboration. In an attempt to reduce the secondary victimization of sexual assault victims, under no circumstances should a victim of a sexual assault be offered or administered a polygraph examination for the purposes of assessing the credibility of his or her statement."[P]olygraph examinations should not be used as a replacement for a full and complete investigation of potential suspects, and ... should not be used for anything other than investigative purposes."[27]

8.5.2 Admissibility of Polygraph Findings

"Whoever undertakes to set himself up as judge in the field of truth and knowledge is shipwrecked by the laughter of the gods."

Albert Einstein (1879-1955).[28]

Generally, neither the results of a polygraph examination nor the opinion of the polygraph examiner based on the test results are admissible as evidence in court. In the United States, the results of polygraph examinations may be admitted if both sides stipulate their use. In the 1998 United States Supreme Court decision of the *United States v. Scheffer* the exclusion at trial of an exculpatory polygraph test (favourable to the accused) was determined to have violated the accused's Sixth Amendment right to present a full defence as guaranteed by the US Constitution.[29]

---

[27]Kaufman (1998), p. 485.

[28]Albert Einstein quote retrieved April 28, 2003, from www.thinkexist.com

[29]*United States v. Scheffer*, 44 M.J. 22.

The Supreme Court of Canada has similarly ruled that polygraph tests are inadmissible, not because of their potential fallibility, but because they infringe upon established rules governing the admissibility of certain evidence. "The admission of [polygraph] evidence would offend well established rules of evidence, in particular the rule against oath-helping, which prohibits a party from presenting evidence solely for the purpose of bolstering a witness's credibility, the rule against the admission of past or out-of-court statements by a witness and the character evidence rule."[30]

Canadian courts have long struggled with the issue of the admissibility of confessions that result from polygraph examinations due to the issue of voluntariness and whether or not the subject of a polygraph test is deprived of an operating mind in light of the examiner's overwhelmingly persuasive explanations of the polygraph's infallibility, and the intimate rapport established between the examiner and the subject, both of which have been held on occasion to amount to inducements. In the 2000 Supreme Court decision of *Regina v. Oickle*, Mr. Justice J. Iacobucci stated for the majority, with respect to the use of post-polygraph confessions, "In short, merely confronting a suspect with adverse evidence – even exaggerating its accuracy and reliability – will not, standing alone, render a confession involuntary."[31]

The polygraph remains a useful investigative tool for eliminating persons of interest from suspicion and for obtaining admissions and confessions from suspects. The more the subject believes in the mystique and infallibility of the polygraph, the less inclined the subject is to believe that he or she is able to beat the instrument, even if the subject believes he or she has already successfully duped the examiner. The confrontation with "scientific" evidence of one's own complicity in a crime is a powerful factor in removing the subject's reluctance to confess his or her guilt.

8.6 FORENSIC ARTISTS

Forensic artists are another valuable investigative resource in a wide range of cases. A forensic artist should be considered to assist eyewitnesses in providing investigators with a likeness of an unknown suspect of a crime, whose face was observed during the offence. Composite pictures are sometimes hand-drawn or can be manually assembled by combining the witness's selection from a variety of acetate overlays, each containing a physical characteristic, such as noses, ears, chins, eyes, hairstyles, etc.

The use of computer generated imaging systems such as Smith & Wesson's Identi-Kit®, or Comfit®, a program developed by the Queensland Police in Australia, is becoming more widespread as police services embrace the new technology. Composite drawings are useful in that they allow investigators to visualize the suspect described by the witness and provide a picture that can be circulated to patrol officers and other enforcement agencies for comparison purposes.

Composite drawings may also be disseminated to the media for a public appeal for assistance in identifying the subject of the drawing. A well prepared composite drawing also helps to eliminate persons of interest or persons who randomly resemble a physical description provided by the witness.

---

[30]*R. v. Béland* (1987) 2 S.C.R. 398.

[31]*R. v. Oickle* (2000) 2 S.C.R. 3.

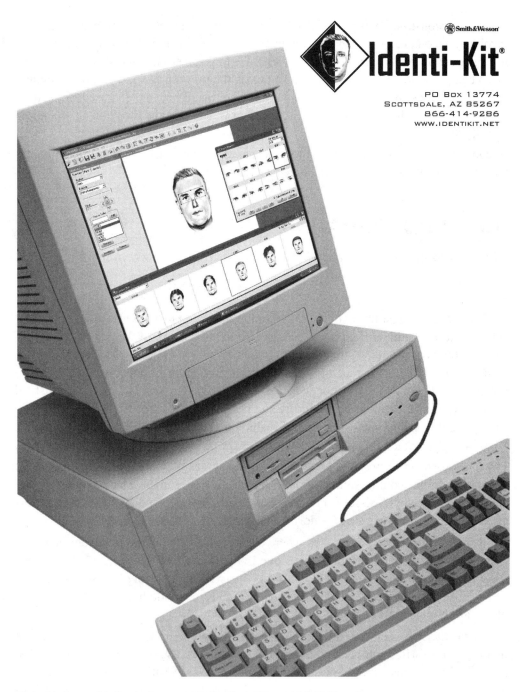

Photo 8.1 - Composite offender imagery using Smith and Wesson's Identi-Kit system. Reproduced with the permission of Smith and Wesson.

Forensic artists can also assist in advancing the age of the subject of a known photograph through the technique of age progression. As children age, their physical characteristics change rapidly. In the case of a child, missing or abducted for a considerable time, a forensic artist can advance the age of the child to provide a better sense of how the child may appear in real time. This same technique is useful for adults, both victims and suspects, in cold case investigations where due to the passage of time, or for any other reason, the subject's facial appearance might reasonably be expected to have changed.

Facial reconstruction is a specialized form of forensic artistry that is utilized in cases involving decomposed human remains in an attempt to identify the deceased. Working in conjunction with a forensic anthropologist, the forensic artist either sketches or develops a computer generated likeness, or replicates the missing facial tissue using modelling clay. It is possible to arrive at a reasonable likeness of how the deceased would have appeared in life, which may then be circulated or released to the media in an attempt to identify the deceased person.

Once a name can be associated to a deceased victim, positive identification techniques such as DNA, dental charts, or x-rays may be pursued.

8.7   PHOTOGRAPHIC LINEUPS

"We should all be reminded of the frailties of identification evidence."

Mr. Justice J.A. Finlayson, Ontario Court of Appeal.[32]

The successful resolution of an investigation involving unknown suspect(s) and any subsequent prosecution often depends upon the identification of the person(s) responsible for the commission of the crime by one or more eyewitnesses. It is crucial to the administration of justice that the identification procedure utilized is carried out by police investigators in a manner which is non-suggestive and which will withstand judicial scrutiny regarding the reliability and fairness of the identification. It is equally as important to clear innocent people of suspicion as it is to identify a guilty person(s).

Various methods of suspect identification are available for investigators to allow eyewitnesses to view possible persons of interest in an effort to identify the person(s) responsible for the commission of offences. Physical lineups involve having eyewitnesses separately view individuals, either one at a time or in a group including the person of interest standing with between six and eleven distracters.

Voice lineups may be conducted where the suspect was not viewed, rendering visual identification impracticable but where one or more witnesses overheard the suspect speaking. If a physical or photographic lineup is not practicable, a witness may be shown a video lineup that includes a suspect and multiple random distracters (for example, in a shopping mall or on a busy city street).

By far the most common method utilized is the photographic lineup, which is the method that we will focus on for the purposes of this text. The two main methods of displaying photographs to eyewitnesses for possible identification purposes include a photo spread containing approximately 12 photographs including one suspect photograph randomly placed with 6 to 11 photographs of similar physical characteristics that are displayed simultaneously or the same set of unmounted photographs known as the sequential photographic lineup.

The officer in charge of an investigation where a suspect has been arrested should contact the media and request that they not publish likenesses of the accused person(s) to reduce the possibility of contamination of possible witness identification when multiple eyewitnesses have still to be shown photographic lineups. Due to recent improvements

---

[32]Mr Justice J.A. Finlayson speaking in *R. v. McIntosh* (1997), CanLII 3862 (on. C.A.)

in police–media relations, the media will usually honour such a request due to the over-riding public interest – but won't wait forever.[33]

8.7.1   Simultaneous v. Sequential Photo Lineups

A growing body of psychological research into this issue unanimously favours the use of sequential presentation of photographs to an eyewitness over the simultaneous presentation of photographs mounted in a single photo spread. Photographs displayed sequentially to an eyewitness are considered individually by the eyewitness and therefore tend not to influence the identification of one another.

The research indicates that the "sequential-superiority effect" results in a higher ratio of accused identifications to mistaken identifications than do simultaneous photo lineups. Utilizing the sequential photo lineup, eyewitnesses were more conservative and also felt under less pressure to select a photograph.[34]

8.7.2   Preparation of a Photographic Lineup

For the identification of a suspect by a witness to be considered reliable, it must be conducted with absolute fairness to the suspect. If the presentation of a photographic lineup to an eyewitness is suggestive in any way, it may result in the misidentification of an innocent person, which only serves to compound the tragedy of any crime.

From the description of one or several eyewitnesses, a suspect may come to mind based on his or her known *modus operandi* or his or her physical resemblance to the description. If the suspect has a criminal record, a current mug-shot photograph can be used, providing it does not show that the person depicted in the photograph was in custody at the time it was taken. If no photograph exists of the individual, the suspect may consent to provide a voluntary photograph to assist in his or her elimination from suspicion. Quite often, a police photograph from a previous arrest is available. Some police services now have software applications that produce computer generated likenesses of individual photographs for use in preparing photographic lineups.

Ideally, to ensure fairness, the photographic lineup should consist of the suspect's photograph with up to eleven distracters of similar physical characteristics. Only one suspect should be shown in each lineup and he or she should resemble the other selected photographs with respect to age, build, complexion, hairstyle and facial characteristics as closely as possible.

Use as current a photograph as possible with the subject appearing the way he or she did at the time of the offence. If a suspect had a beard at the time of the offence, don't use a photograph of him clean-shaven to present to eyewitnesses. If a suspect has a moustache, every other picture should depict a person with a moustache. If the suspect is wearing a hat, every picture should show those subjects wearing hats. Any glaring differences between the selected photographs may be suggestive to the witness and will contaminate any subsequent identification.

---

[33]Ministry of Community Safety and Correctional Services: *Ontario Major Case Management (MCM) Manual* (Oct. 1, 2004), p. 34.

[34]Wells (2001).

Due to recent advances in digital imagery, it is now much easier to make photographs resemble each other. If one subject has a mole, blemish or distinctive feature such as a scar, tattoo, or body piercing, it may be superimposed on the other photographs to create additional similarity.

Ensure, to the extent possible, that the witnesses are not shown any single photographs of any suspect if you intend that they might view a photo lineup at a later date. Single photo identifications are extremely suggestive and will taint the reliability of any later identification. Other than obtaining an initial physical description from the witness, avoid having any conversation with him or her concerning the possible identity of a suspect.

8.7.3   Presentation of the Photographic Lineup

An eyewitness should only be shown a photographic lineup containing a suspect if he or she is physically and emotionally capable of doing so. Where possible, an investigator who is not familiar with the case and who is unaware of the identity of the suspect should present the photo lineup to the eyewitness, to avoid the possibility of the presenter influencing the eyewitness. Each eyewitness should be shown a photographic lineup independent of any other witness. If the same suspect is to be shown to several eyewitnesses, consider changing the order in which the suspect's photograph appears in the lineup.

An investigator assigned to present a sequential photo lineup to an eyewitness should instruct the witness of the following:

1. You will now be asked to view a series of [number] photographs in random order.

2. The picture of the person responsible for committing the crime may or may not be contained in this set of photographs.

3. It is as important to clear innocent people from suspicion as it is to identify guilty people.

4. View one photograph at a time and take as much time as you need to view each photograph.

5. Once you have viewed a photograph, you may not go back to it for another look.

6. If you identify a photograph, the procedure will be stopped and no more photographs will be shown.

7. If you identify a photograph, you will be asked to state in your own words how certain you are of your identification.

8. Regardless of whether an identification is made, the police will continue the investigation into this incident.

In serious cases, videotaping photo lineup procedures should be considered for the purpose of presenting potential identification evidence in court. Even if not videotaped, the procedure should be thoroughly documented, recording all information regarding all photographs contained in the lineup, the date and time of the viewing by the witness and information regarding all persons present at the time.

The photographic lineup should be preserved in the order it was displayed to the witness, who could be asked to date and sign the selected photograph. A photo lineup that results in the identification of a suspect should be preserved as an exhibit for court purposes.

8.8   UNDERCOVER OPERATIONS

Criminal organizations, large and small, are characteristically cautious about dealing with people who they do not know and trust. The types of offences committed by organized groups, such as drug-trafficking, theft-rings, gambling and racketeering have few, if any co-operative witnesses. The persons at the top, who direct these criminal operations, are usually well insulated from prosecution due to the distance they maintain from the day-to-day, hands-on operations of their underlings.

Sometimes, the only way to secure evidence against these individuals and to dismantle their operation is to infiltrate the organization using an undercover operative. This might involve the use of an **agent provocateur** (see Chapter 9), which can result in severe credibility issues at trial if the agent has an extensive criminal record. A viable solution to this problem is to employ the services of an undercover police officer to gain access to, and gather evidence of, the inner workings of a criminal enterprise.

Undercover police work is nothing similar to the romantic tripe portrayed in movies and on television. Undercover operations are difficult, time-consuming, costly, frustrating and fraught with danger for the officer's safety. Career criminals do not take kindly to anyone who interferes with their livelihood and may think nothing of disposing of rivals or perceived threats to their operations.

Criminal groups rarely welcome strangers into their midst, requiring the undercover police officer to establish a relationship with members of the group or to be introduced by a trusted associate of the group who has agreed to become an agent provocateur. If no introduction is possible, it may take a very long time to establish a relationship of trust.

The undercover officer's responsibilities will vary with the circumstances of the investigation; however, a good memory and the ability to assume a false identity and to maintain a convincing cover story are of paramount importance. If circumstances permit, a cover officer will attempt to provide security for the undercover officer from a distance and receive any evidence collected by the undercover officer during the course of the investigation.

Electronic surveillance in the form of the interception of private communications and photographic surveillance is often used in conjunction with undercover operations both to monitor the officer's safety and for evidence gathering purposes. Undercover operations have also been successful in clearing unsolved major crimes, such as homicides, etc., where the suspect remains at large, and will undoubtedly play a significant role with the recently increased priority of investigating terrorism.

8.9   BEHAVIOURAL ANALYSIS

Unlike the conventional investigative techniques used to link offenders to crimes using physical evidence, such as fingerprints or DNA or witness identification, behavioural profiling attempts to identify offenders through the interpretation of psychological clues that are evident from the offender's behaviour both during and after the offence. Everyone's uniquely individual personality directs their behaviour during every activity they do. How they dress and speak, even the types of vehicles they drive reveals something about their habits and personality traits to a trained profiler.

Behavioural analysis is not an exact science but is based more on the common sense comparison to factors that motivated the particular behaviour of the past offender(s). The cliché that all things happen for a reason also holds true for crime. Every crime requires the offender to make a series of decisions and choices, such as when to offend, which victim to select and how to commit the offence. While there are no absolutes, all behavioural clues can be used to profile the personality type and lifestyle of the likely suspect.

8.9.1   Psychological Profiling

Based on the known facts of a case, a behavioural analyst is able to make certain determinations as to why a particular offender committed a particular crime, involving a particular victim, at a particular place, in a particular manner. What an offender did or didn't do, anything that is said by him or her during the crime, the nature of the crime itself and any weapon used, all say something about the personality traits that motivated the offender's behaviour.

Behavioural analysis is commonly utilized during unknown offender investigations, including homicides and other sudden death investigations where the manner of death is not conclusive. Information gathered at the death scene and known facts about the deceased are analyzed to determine the most probable manner of death. Sexual offences, arsons, and abductions are examples of other crimes involving behavioural patterns that a trained profiler analyzes to form an opinion as to who the most probable offender might be.

When a suspect has been identified, their lifestyle and personality can be assessed to determine investigative and interview strategies that would likely be most successful. Behavioural analysis can also be used to develop trial strategies regarding jury selection, the order of witnesses to be called, presentation of key evidence and cross-examination strategies on the basis of the potential effect on the accused.

8.9.2   Organized and Disorganized Offenders

Information obtained from a crime scene reflects the offender's state of mind at the time of the commission of the offence. Offenders may be characterized as being either organized or disorganized personality types by the manner in which the crime is committed. A crime scene where the offender used a weapon of opportunity he or she found at the scene and left the crime scene in a state of disarray in their haste to escape would indicate a disorganized offender.

As children, disorganized offenders are likely to have been quiet and polite, tending to internalize their emotions. Disorganized offenders typically suffer from poor self-image and are socially incompetent around others. Disorganized offenders tend to be loners due to their inability to sustain relationships with members of the opposite gender. They tend to be of lower intelligence and, if employed, are more likely to work at menial jobs.

Organized offenders, by contrast, consider themselves to be superior to everyone around them. As children, organized offenders were likely well-known and tended to act out. Organized offenders are persuasive and likely have a history of failed relationships. The organized offender is capable of conning compliant victims to accompany him and would be more apt to personalize the victim by talking to him or her during the crime.

The organized offender is more likely to plan the offence, bring a weapon or restraints with him or her, and remove them from the scene after the crime. The organized offender would be more likely to move the victim's body after the crime to avoid apprehension.

Unlike the disorganized offender, the organized offender would follow the progress of the investigation in the media with considerable interest.[35]

8.9.3 Threat Assessment

Behavioural analysis is also employed to assess threat levels in situations such as criminal harassment involving unknown offenders, or political threats. **Threat assessment** is also utilized in individual or group situations that may have potential impact on public safety, such as the release of high-risk offenders back into the community or anonymous threats of violence. The linguistic patterns and other behavioural clues contained in a written or verbal threat can give insight regarding the unknown person behind the threat and shed light on whether the threat is credible or not.

8.9.4 Geographic Profiling

Another behavioural investigative aid used to assist investigators bring focus to an investigation is geographic profiling, developed in Canada by Dr. Kim Rossmo, a former police officer with the Vancouver Police Department. Dr. Rossmo studied Criminology at Simon Fraser University where he observed research being conducted by Paul and Patricia Brantingham. The Brantinghams theorized that an offender's potential range of crime locations could be predicted based upon the location of the offender's residence.

Rossmo reversed the Brantingham model and theorized that it was possible to determine the area where an offender lives by analyzing known locations involved in the crime. Rossmo developed a software application to conduct the analyses of data relating to multiple spatial locations involved in serial crimes such as armed robbery, sexual predatory offences, arsons and homicides.

Geographic profiling is based upon a psychological maxim known as the "least effort principle" that dictates that all people, including criminals, conduct their day-to-day affairs by expending the least amount of energy possible and while operating in areas that are familiar to them. Rossmo found that criminals maintain a "buffer zone" around their residence, in which they prefer not to offend in order to maintain a degree of anonymity.

Once outside their "buffer zone," the least effort principle begins to take effect and the offender begins to select suitable targets in familiar areas. The frequency of crime decreases as the distance from the offender's buffer zone increases due to the increased effort required to offend further outside of the area he or she feels most comfortable in. This observable reduction in crime frequency is referred to as "distance decay."[36]

Using data based on the latitudinal and longitudinal positions of at least five or six locations of crime events, the Rigel computer developed by Dr. Rossmo can provide a geographic profile of the area in which the offender most likely resides. Unlike normal techniques of attempting to identify an offender by various physical or biological classifications, geographic profiling provides a focused geographic area in which to intensify the search for the suspect.

---

[35]Ressler & Shachtman (1993).

[36]Rossmo (2005).

8.9.5 Violent Crime Linkage Analysis System (ViCLAS)

With over 60 police services plus the Ontario Provincial Police each providing policing services in clearly defined jurisdictions, and over 22 000 police officers in the province of Ontario alone, it would be a simple matter for predatory offenders to avoid detection by committing crimes in multiple jurisdictions. The significance of vital clues in combined investigations of similar crimes may be easily overlooked if the investigations are conducted separately by neighbouring police services. If a single offender is found to be responsible for two or more crimes in multiple jurisdictions, the cases must be investigated jointly to have the best opportunity to apprehend the offender.

A vital investigative tool that is used to link similar crimes in single or multiple jurisdictions is also based on behavioural principles. The Violent Crime Linkage Analysis System (**ViCLAS**) compares investigative data submitted by investigators on criteria offences such as homicides, sexual assaults, non-familial abductions and attempts to commit those offences, and missing persons where foul play is suspected.

ViCLAS captures information about the nature of the crime scene, the victimology, modus operandi and offender behaviour that, when analyzed, indicates the probability that two or more similar crimes may in fact be the work of a common offender. ViCLAS acts as a triggering mechanism that alerts police services to the possibility that a serial offender may be active within their respective jurisdictions.

Since February 1997, any Ontario police officer in charge of a designated ViCLAS criteria investigation is mandated to submit a ViCLAS form within 30 days of the start of the investigation and/or within 30 days of a material change or of acquiring additional information that is significant to the investigation.[37] This legal requirement was made as a direct result of the recommendation of Mr. Justice Archie Campbell in his 1996 review of the Paul Bernardo investigations.[38]

Behavioural analysis doesn't solve crimes but it does provide extremely valuable tools to the investigator with which to link similar investigations as well as focusing investigative efforts and shortening investigations through insight regarding the offender gained from the psychological clues he or she has left behind. Using behavioural analysis allows the police to apprehend the persons responsible for the commission of serial and violent crimes at an early stage of the investigation. Victimization can be reduced – not prevented, but reduced – by capturing offenders before they have an opportunity to re-offend.

8.10 BLOODSTAIN PATTERN ANALYSIS

During the commission of violent crimes, blood is often shed at the crime scene due to injuries to victims and also to assailants. Blood, like any liquid, reacts according to the laws of physics. When the forces of gravity and velocity act upon blood at a crime scene, they create stains of different shapes and patterns. Blood leaves telltale stains that can be interpreted to provide evidence of the sequence of events, the number of blows struck, the relative positions of the victim and the assailant in the scene as well as direction and

---

[37] *Police Services Act of Ontario*, O. Reg. 550/96, s. 2.

[38] Campbell (1996), p. 323

movement. This **bloodstain pattern analysis** can be used by the investigator to reconstruct the crime.

The volume of a person's blood represents approximately 8 percent of their total body weight. The average adult male has 5–6 litres of blood, while the average adult female has 4–5 litres of blood. A loss of 1.5 litres of blood is enough to incapacitate a person and a loss of 2.5 litres of an individual's blood supply may produce irreversible shock that can be lethal.

8.10.1 Presumptive Blood Tests and Blood Reagents

The amount of blood at a crime scene may be quite large, or may only be a few drops. When blood is located in quantities so small as to create uncertainty as to whether it is blood, or if the source of the blood is not self-evident, it may be necessary to conduct a "presumptive test" using products such as Hemastix® reagent strips or chemical agents such as Phenolophthalein® or orthotolidine to identify it as blood. Other reagents, such as Luminol® and leucomalachite green may be used to detect occult blood (not readily visible) or where an attempt has been made to clean up the blood at a scene.

Some of these products are time-sensitive, require the use of expert photography and are highly carcinogenic. They should only be used by a trained forensic identification officer under prescribed conditions. These products also contaminate small amounts of blood, destroying DNA evidence. The investigator in charge of the case, in collaboration with the forensic identification officer will have to assess the necessity and benefits of using such test procedures weighed against the potential loss of biological evidence they cause.

8.10.2 Bloodstain Characteristics – Directionality and Velocity

Freeflowing blood from a victim lying on the ground will flow from the wound(s) toward the lowest point of gravity where it will gather in pools in depressions on the ground, floor or natural hollows of the body, etc. The margins (edges) of the resulting flow pattern will be defined by gentle, flowing curves as the blood follows the path of least resistance, as determined by the force of gravity. If blood flows down a steep angle, it can form narrow run marks until it reaches a low point at which time it will begin to pool.

A single drop of any liquid, including blood, falls in the shape of a sphere due to its surface tension as it breaks away from the source. Free-falling blood, acted upon by gravity, will leave different stains depending on the angle at which it strikes a surface. The direction that a drop of blood was travelling can be determined by its shape.

For example, a perfectly round blood stain pattern from a drop of blood on a flat, horizontal surface indicates that the source of the blood was directly over that point when the spherical drop of blood struck the surface at the speed of gravity. Shape alone, however, doesn't tell us whether the source of the blood was from a bleeding wound or if it fell from the tip of a knife or other weapon, but a round bloodstain does indicate that the source was 90° above the resulting stain and travelling at low velocity.

A falling drop of blood striking a rough surface might not appear perfectly round due to the unevenness of surface at impact. Blood that is free-flowing or that falls in drops due to gravity alone creates stains that are referred to as "passive" stains.

A series of similar drops might give us additional information from which we might infer the source due to the quantity of the blood lost, etc. If the bloodstain shows distortion on only one side of the stain, this information can be used to determine the direction from which the blood was travelling.

A spherical drop of blood that strikes a surface at an oblique angle creates an elliptical, tear-shaped stain, the dimensions of which are determined by the angle and the velocity. An elliptical bloodstain has a round bulbous end and an elongated tail. It is easy to determine the direction of flight of the drop of blood that made the stain – although many people initially guess incorrectly until it is explained to them.

Imagine a spherical drop of blood in flight. When it strikes a surface at an oblique angle, the full width of the drop will strike the surface as it travels in the direction it was projected away from the source. A drop of blood striking a surface at an oblique angle becomes smaller and smaller as it travels. As the stain becomes narrower, it trails off to a point, indicating the direction it was travelling when the spherical drop of blood struck the surface.

A bloodstain created by a drop of blood propelled from its source at a velocity that exceeds the force of gravity is referred to as a "projected" bloodstain. The angle at which a drop of blood strikes a surface can be calculated from the ratio of its length to its width. The position of the source of several related "projected" bloodstains can be determined by a qualified bloodstain pattern analyst through a series of trigonometric calculations.

This type of bloodstain requires that the blood be projected toward the surface at a medium velocity, typically as the result of stabbings and beatings, etc. Blood can also be projected directly from a wound if an artery has been severed and the blood is under pressure. This type of pattern is referred to as "arterial gush."

The last type of bloodstain pattern encountered is referred to as a "transfer" pattern. This type of bloodstain occurs when a bloody object comes into direct contact with a surface. This type of stain may be in the form of a hand, fingerprint or footwear impression or may have been caused through direct contact with a bloody tool, weapon, hair or fabric.

The size of a bloodstain may also be used to determine the velocity at which it was travelling. Stains of more than one millimetre in diameter were travelling at a low to medium velocity, while stains of less than one millimetre in diameter were projected at a high velocity, and may appear as an aerosol mist. Such a misting pattern is generally characteristic of a firearm discharge.

Bloodstain pattern evidence is an extremely useful investigative tool for the investigation of crimes involving personal injury. While an expert examination should be conducted by a person who is qualified, bloodstains can reveal considerable information to an observant investigator. As blood dries relatively quickly, it is also useful to indicate whether or not a body has been repositioned after a crime if "passive" bloodstain patterns appear to defy gravity by pointing in any direction other than downward without a proper explanation.

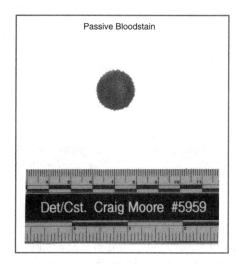

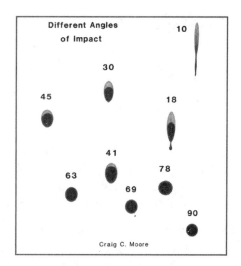

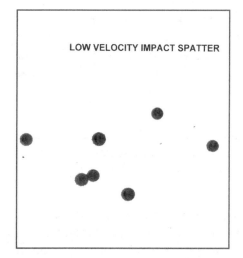

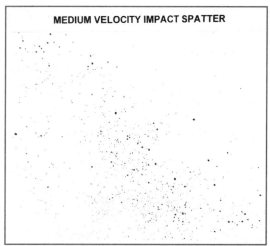

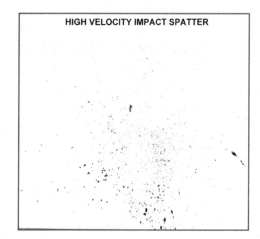

Illustration 8.1 - Diagram of passive drop of blood and projected drops of blood.
Permission granted by Craig C. Moore, Bloodstain Pattern Analyst, Niagara Regional Police Service.

SUMMARY

- Specialized investigation techniques, such as surveillance, photographic lineups, undercover operations, psychological profiling, blood spatter interpretation and polygraph are used in complex investigations to gather evidence that might otherwise go undetected.

- Cost and the inherent intrusiveness of certain techniques require that investigators justify the necessity of employing them. Limitations on their use must be complied with, to avoid having evidence declared inadmissible on the grounds that an individual's constitutional rights were violated.

- Surveillance is the continuous observation of a person, group of people, location or of some other situation, and is usually conducted covertly, meaning that the subject who is being observed is unaware of the surveillance. Surveillance may be static, physical, photographic or electronic.

- The interception of private communications has been held to constitute a search and seizure as referred to in s.8 of the *Charter of Rights and Freedoms* and may only be utilized where other investigative procedures have been tried and have failed or where it appears they are otherwise unlikely to succeed or the urgency of the matter is such that it would be impractical to carry out the investigation of the offence using only other investigative procedures.

- The polygraph measures certain involuntary physiological responses including blood pressure, respiration and galvanic resistance during interrogation to assess a person's credibility when answering questions relevant to their knowledge of an incident or participation in a crime.

- Forensic artists may be used to prepare composite drawings based on descriptions of suspects provided by eyewitnesses. They may also assist with age progression of photographs of missing persons or suspects and with the facial reconstruction of unidentified human remains.

- Psychological research indicates a higher ratio of successful identification to mistaken identification utilizing sequential photographic lineups rather than simultaneous lineups. A lineup should contain only one suspect and up to eleven distracter photographs displaying subjects of similar physical characteristics.

- Behavioural analysis, including the sub-specialties of criminal profiling, threat assessment, and geographic profiling, is an attempt to: link similar offences as having been committed by a common offender; profile personality types of unknown offenders; and predict the area where a suspect most likely resides based on an analysis of locations associated to the crime. All behavioural analysis is based on sound psychological theories that an individual's personality contains their urges and desires, thereby motivating their behaviour.

- Bloodstain pattern analysis is a useful investigative aid at a violent crime scene involving injury to a victim, suspect or both. Bloodstain patterns may be passive, transferred or projected and may be used to determine velocity and the directionality of the blood to assist investigators in reconstructing the events that occurred during the crime.

- Bloodstain pattern evidence can also be useful to indicate whether or not a body has been repositioned after a crime if "passive" bloodstain patterns appear to defy gravity by pointing in any direction other than downward, absent a proper explanation.

DISCUSSION QUESTIONS

1. Give examples of three different counter-surveillance techniques that the target of a mobile surveillance detail might employ in order to determine whether or not he or she is being followed. How might a team of investigators best deal with each of those situations?

2. What two legal requirements must investigators prove in order to establish the "investigative necessity" of employing the interception of private communications during investigations? Describe examples of how each might be shown.

3. Explain the difference between "passive," "transfer" and "projected" bloodstain patterns.

4. What is the correlation between the size of a "projected" bloodstain and the velocity with which it was projected? In what types of crime are low, medium and high velocity bloodstain patterns usually encountered?

5. Why are sequential photographic lineups recommended over simultaneous lineups? What is the recommended number of distracters that should be included in a photographic lineup?

 ## WEBLINKS

www.polygraph.org

American Polygraph Association website. Code of ethics, polygraph research validity statistics and related resources for polygraph technicians.

www.bloodspatter.com/BPATutorial.htm

Bloodspatter.com website. Comprehensive online tutorial explaining bloodsstain pattern characteristics and how bloodstain analysis is conducted to determine directionality from the source and angle of impact.

www.iabpa.org

International Association of Blood Pattern Analysts, an organization formed to promote education, standardize training standards for blood pattern analysts and encourage research in the field of bloodstain pattern analysis.

www.fbi.gov/hq/td/academy/bsu/bsu.htm

U.S. Federal Bureau of Investigation Behavioral Science Unit website. Description of services provided, research initiatives being conducted.

Chapter 9

Informant Management

"Justice depends not only on the substance of a criminal case, but upon the process by which the case is proved."

Los Angeles District Attorney's Office Special Directive 88-14.[1]

After reading this chapter, the successful learner should be able to:

- Differentiate between the terms "informant" and "agent."
- Differentiate between the various categories of informants.
- Give examples of the various factors that motivate informants.
- Differentiate between the terms "credibility" and "reliability."
- Explain the two methods by which an informant may be proven reliable.
- Explain the concept of **Crown privilege** as it relates to informants.
- Explain the **Innocence at stake** exception to "Crown privilege."
- Explain the dangers inherent in the use of **In-custody informers**.

9.1 INFORMANTS

Contrary to popular belief, induced in no small part through the public's current fascination with semi-realistic crime scene and forensic science television programs and movies, trace evidence and forensics do not solve every case. Much credit for solving criminal cases must go to the much-maligned investigative resource, the confidential police informant, who provides incriminating information to the police regarding suspect(s) and intimate details of crimes, criminals and criminal activity.

Throughout the years, informants have been referred to by many uncomplimentary names including fink, rat, snitch and stool pigeon. Despite their widely recognized value as an investigative aid, informants have long suffered reputations as traitors and turncoats. Even in real life, stereotypical police informants like those depicted in seedy

---

[1]Special Directive dated Nov. 17, 1988, quoted in Kaufman (1998), vol. 1, p. 576.

"cops and robbers" movies often don't enjoy the best of relations with the police officers who recruit them. However, by using the information provided by informants, investigators solve countless crimes, many of which might otherwise remain unsolved.[2]

Perhaps this distrust is due to the shroud of betrayal automatically bestowed on someone who becomes an informant. Although their information is relied upon as trustworthy, some informants are never really trusted and are often looked down upon as if they were some lower life form. After all, how do you (and for that matter, how could you) trust someone who has just betrayed somebody else?

It is said that "politics makes strange bedfellows." When police officers and criminals (or criminal associates) from opposing ends of the law enforcement spectrum suddenly begin working together for a common purpose, it is often compared to "sleeping with the enemy." However, criminal courts have long realized, and continue to appreciate, the necessity of confidential police–informant relationships in solving and preventing crime, in cases such as those that involve organized crime and cases where there are no witnesses, for example, drug cases.[3]

Confidential police informants are not always criminals or criminal associates, although they quite often are. Informants may be of any age, gender, walk of life and socio-economic standing. They can be upstanding members of the community: the spouses; intimate partners; sons; daughters; parents; relatives; associates; employers; employees; co-workers; business partners; landlords; or neighbours of the person(s) about whom they divulge their information.

In many cases, police officers are approached by someone with whom they have had past dealings; perhaps someone who was given a "break" on a traffic ticket, or someone who was charged with an offence but was treated fairly and with dignity. Either way, the officer will have made an impression upon this person and when he or she has information regarding criminal activity, the informant may seek out the officer in an attempt to repay the favour. This is just another perceptible benefit of treating all people fairly and with dignity.

An informant may eventually elect to waive the Crown (police informer) privilege, choose to become a witness and testify in subsequent judicial proceedings; or the informant may disclose the information on the condition of anonymity in order to protect his or her identity. While their standings in life, relationships to the suspect(s) and motives may differ, what all informants have in common is that they are capable of providing incriminating information to the police regarding crimes or criminal activity. The most important thing that informants have in common is their need for confidentiality to ensure that those about whom they provide information never learn of their co-operation and seek revenge against them.

9.1.1   Informant Typologies

There are a number of categories of confidential informant that differ in their nature, involvement, approach and motivation. Let's examine the types of confidential informant that may be encountered during the course of a criminal investigation.

---

[2]Madinger (2000). Also Roberts (2002); Weston & Wells (1997).

[3]*R. v. Scott* (1990), 3 S.C.R. 979.

9.1.2   The Self-Motivated Informant

The self-motivated informant is an unanticipated source who unexpectedly initiates contact with the police and discloses the belief that he or she possesses relevant information, material to an ongoing investigation or regarding alleged criminal activity that he or she wishes to bring to the attention of the police. The self-motivated informant might be a criminal, a law-abiding citizen or someone on the fringe of criminal activity either through voluntary association with criminals or by reason of employment, such as a hotel owner, bartender, taxi driver, etc.

The self-motivated informant might provide information regarding individual(s) who are planning a crime that has not yet occurred, or describe the method in which a crime was committed. He or she may also be able to provide the identity of the person(s) responsible for the crime. The type of information provided by this informant might be limited to a single crime and he or she might only be used on a one-time basis. If the informant proves to be reliable and if because of personal circumstances he or she has ongoing contact with the criminal element, the investigator might consider attempting to "recruit" the informant for ongoing informant activity.

Occasionally, the self-motivated informant seeks neither consideration nor compensation except, perhaps, for minor expenses. If one such individual were to contact the police and agree to give a statement and testify, he or she would be considered a witness. If, preferring to remain anonymous, he or she is reluctant to be identified or to testify, he or she is considered to be an informant and must be accorded the confidentiality they seek.

If the informant doesn't wish to deal directly with a police officer, he or she may prefer to provide their information confidentially through a local Crime Stoppers program so his or her identity is never revealed. Crime Stoppers tipsters have the option of collecting or declining cash awards for information leading to arrests and seizures of contraband. Unlike other informants who deal directly with investigators, the Crime Stoppers tipster never has to reveal their identity.

9.1.3   The Recruited Informant

A recruited informant is one who is approached first by the police. All good police officers have a network of regular "sources" who can be contacted on an as-needed basis to gain inside knowledge regarding a variety of issues. As with the self-motivated informant, recruited sources might include criminals, law-abiding citizens or individuals on the fringe of criminal activity, either through voluntary association with criminals or by reason of their employment, such as in the case of a hotel owner, bartender, or taxi driver. An informant might be recruited on a one-time basis for a single investigation or on a long-term basis, where the informant has continued exposure to a criminal individual, organization or to a location where criminal activity regularly occurs.

Once it is confirmed that the informant possesses information or is in a position to obtain information for the police (whether he or she is initially willing to do so or not) efforts may be taken to "persuade" him or her to co-operate and become an informant. Unless the informant is motivated purely by some sense of civic duty to co-operate, the investigator must assess the person's circumstances and provide the correct motivation for the individual to agree to co-operate in providing information to the investigation. More will be said on this issue in Section 9.2: Informant Motivation.

An accomplice may turn into a productive informant (or witness) if he or she can be successfully "flipped." In this situation, the police usually have some leverage over the accomplice and may convince him or her to co-operate with the investigation in order to avoid certain negative consequences (e.g., by laying or not laying charges against the accomplice or others, laying of lesser charges, etc.).

BOX 9.1	**Proper Investigative Procedure**

Never attempt to "persuade" an individual to become an informant, as is done many times on television and in real life, by threatening to expose him or her to others as an informant should they refuse to co-operate with you. It is one thing to threaten an individual with bona fide legal consequences – it is quite another to threaten their safety and physical well-being. Why would any individual agree to assist you now, or in the future, if they believe that you are untrustworthy and may betray them at any time? Informants are universally hated both in and out of jail and are continuously in danger of being assaulted, or worse. Threatening an individual with physical harm (real or imagined – directly or indirectly) is a coercive, unprofessional and unacceptable way of attempting to gain his or her co-operation.

9.1.4 The In-Custody Informer

The in-custody informer is "someone who allegedly receives one or more statements from an accused, while both are in [police] custody [or in a correctional institution], and where the statement[s] relate to an offence[s] that occurred outside of the custodial institution. [The prosecution must intend to call the in-custody informer as a witness in a judicial proceeding.]"[4]

The concept of jailhouse informants is not new by any means, but "in-custody informer" is a recent designation in Ontario that is reserved solely for informants who, while in custody (e.g., pre-trial or under sentence) gain information (i.e., alleged admissions or confessions) from another inmate relating to offences that occurred outside of the custodial institution. The in-custody informer is more than an ordinary informant as, for the in-custody informer to "earn" this status, the Crown Attorney must intend to call him or her as a witness to testify in a court proceeding. Therefore the in-custody informer is a witness who must waive the usual "Crown (police–informer) privilege" before being identified and giving testimony.

This official designation does not apply to incarcerated individuals who contact the police or are recruited by the police to provide information regarding an accused who was not, at any time, in custody with the informer regarding an offence that occurred outside of the custodial institution. Neither does the designation apply to an individual who is in custody and who contacts the police, or is recruited by the police to provide information regarding an offence that occurred inside the custodial institution, yet some of the same considerations and dangers apply as with in-custody informers. More will be said on the use of in-custody informers later in this chapter.

[4]Ministry of Community Safety and Correctional Services: *Ontario Major Case Management (MCM) Manual* (Oct. 1, 2004), p. 9 and Ministry of the Attorney General: *Crown Policy Manual 1-2 "In-Custody Informers,"* dated November 13, 1997 (Appendix "L"). *Quoted* in Kaufman (1998), vol.2 pp. 1350-1355.

The danger with in-custody informers and jailhouse informants (such as a prisoner who informs on a suspect who is out of custody for an offence that occurred either in or outside of jail) is that they are almost exclusively motivated by self-interest and are easily able to fabricate inculpatory evidence. Informants who are in custody can also be vulnerable to pressure, in the form of threats or other coercive methods, by unscrupulous investigators bent on solving a case – at any cost. Either scenario provides the recipe for a potential miscarriage of justice.

Many examples exist of persons being convicted and falsely imprisoned for crimes based on the false evidence of accomplices or cellmates who were either threatened with additional charges or heavier sentences if they did not "co-operate." Other jailhouse informants willingly fabricate false evidence in an attempt to gain consideration, such as having charges withdrawn, or to receive lighter sentences or early parole, etc.

Investigators must always remain vigilant about inadvertently divulging the facts of a case when dealing with in-custody informers and "jailhouse informants." A shrewd and manipulative inmate knows that his or her value as an informant or witness depends on the ability to match his or her story with the "official version" of the crime. Deceptive informants will be quick to pick up any fact available to them and incorporate it into their story.

For an informant's protection, whether the informant is an in-custody informer or merely an informant who is in custody, it may not be practicable to interview them inside the correctional facility, especially if the interview is to be videotaped. In such cases, it is necessary to remove a prisoner from the correctional facility and transport him or her to a secure location to conduct the interview.

It will first be necessary to obtain an order from a provincial court judge or a judge of a superior court for the release of the prisoner for the purpose of assisting a specified peace officer in the execution of his or her duty for a specified period of time. It must be noted that an application made by a prosecutor to a judge for an order for the release of a prisoner must include the written consent of the prisoner.[5]

9.1.5   The Opportunistic Informant

The "opportunistic informant" is motivated purely by self-interest rather than by any sense of civic duty or conscience. This category of informant always seeks some form of consideration or benefit, monetary or otherwise, in exchange for providing information to the police. While other types of informants may also be motivated by some form of benefit, the "opportunistic informant" initiates the contact with the police purely to seek or obtain a benefit or advantage for him or herself or for somebody associated to them.

The mere fact that the opportunistic informant seeks consideration does not render his or her information untruthful. However, the promise or hope of consideration to someone who is disadvantaged (e.g., either financially or through being incarcerated) can provide a powerful incentive to fabricate details of alleged "facts," admissions or confessions about a crime. Therefore, the need to establish credibility of the information and reliability of the informant through independent corroboration is never higher than when dealing with the opportunistic informant.

---

[5]*Criminal Code*, R.S. 1985, c. C-46, s. 527(7).

9.2   INFORMANT MOTIVATION

Regardless of which party (the police or the informant) initiates the contact, informants may be motivated for any of the following reasons, any of which could benefit either the informant or someone else:

Self-Interest

Financial reward

Pre-trial release from custody on bail or other form of conditional release

Withdrawal or dismissal of outstanding criminal charge(s)

Reduction of sentence or other criminal sanction (e.g., probation conditions)

Choice of location to serve an outstanding custodial sentence

Elimination of rivals or unwanted criminal associates

To divert suspicion from their own criminal activities

Revenge

Self-Preservation

Fear of harm from others

Threat of arrest and/or criminal charge(s)

Threat of incarceration

Witness protection program

Other Possible Motivational Factors

Desire to go straight

Guilty conscience

Genuine desire to assist the police

9.3   INITIAL INFORMANT EVALUATION

Whether the informant has initiated contact with the police or is being "recruited" as an informant, the investigator must assess the individual's motivation. An informant's motivation can often provide indicators of his or her reliability as well as the credibility of his or her information. People generally tend to do things that will result in the rewards or benefits the particular action brings for them. These may vary widely from one person to the next and one situation to the next.

If the informant initiated the contact, he or she may be very straightforward in relation to what, if anything, he or she expects to receive in exchange for the information. As with all informants, an investigator must be extremely cautious and refrain from promising anything to the informant that either exceeds the officer's authority to promise or that cannot be delivered.

For example, if an opportunistic informant contacts you seeking a monetary reward, inform him or her that you must first seek approval from your superiors. If the informant requests consideration regarding pre-trial custody or outstanding charges (for them or for somebody close to them), inform him or her that you will put the request forward to the Crown Attorney for consideration. You should always attempt to determine who will most likely benefit if the information is acted upon.[6]

BOX 9.2	Proper Investigative Procedure

Electronically record, or otherwise thoroughly document, the conversation of all parties regarding any request for consideration made by a potential informant, in writing. Civil lawsuits initiated by informants for "broken promises" allegedly made by the police are surprisingly common. A written or electronic record of what was actually stated will go a long way to protecting you and your police service against future civil actions. Advise the informant that it is necessary to document the facts for everyone's mutual protection.

Prior to taking any request from an informant for money or other consideration forward, the investigator must first be in a position to apprise his or her superiors or prosecutor regarding the nature of the information that is known by the informant. Of paramount importance is how the information became known to the informant. For example, you need to know if the information is known directly through personal knowledge (e.g., the informant witnessed it) or indirectly, such as in the form of third-party information (e.g., the information was told to the informant by another person).

If your informant learned the information from a third person, it must not be assumed to be reliable, and should only be used as a basis for reasonable grounds if it can be independently corroborated. Uncorroborated intelligence information might, however, point to sources of independent corroboration that may be used as reasonable grounds.

In the case of a potential informant being targeted for recruitment by the police, you must attempt to predict which individual(s) can most likely provide the needed information and, at the same time, might have a reason to co-operate with the investigation. The correct motivational approach under the particular circumstances must be made that addresses the individual's needs in order to "close the deal." By examining the personal circumstances and background of the individual, an investigator may gain insight regarding what factor would be most likely to motive him or her to become an informant.

The investigator must also analyze the potential risks and benefits to the investigation that might result from approaching an individual for recruitment as an informant, especially should he or she refuse to co-operate. If the unsuccessful recruitment of an informant will impact negatively upon the investigation in any way, the risk is too great and the effort to recruit the proposed individual should be abandoned.

Embittered or resentful associates, spouses, ex-spouses, love interests, former employees, etc., can all make excellent informants as they can usually be "turned" without the necessity of any financial compensation or consideration for charges. The investigator may only have to appeal to the individual's civic duty, conscience, or sense of revenge or

---

[6]Madinger (2000).

self-preservation in order to assist them in overcoming their feelings of loyalty toward the subject of the investigation. The appeal might be made either on emotional grounds or be on a logical basis, depending upon whichever might best motivate the particular individual.

9.4 INTELLIGENCE INFORMATION V. EVIDENCE

Informants may provide two types of information: intelligence and/or evidence. Intelligence information is secret information that is compiled for law enforcement or military purposes. Intelligence is information that either cannot be acted upon or does not prove anything. For example, a citizen approaches you and informs you of suspected criminal activity and may or may not know who is responsible for it. Another example of intelligence information would be that two unknown males in a white van have been selling new stereo equipment in the parking lot at the local tavern every night this week.

An example of evidence received from an informant might be to the effect that "John Smith has a marijuana growing operation in his basement. I was visiting him today and he showed me his plants and equipment and told me all about how he grows it and sells it." Information such as this constitutes reasonable grounds that, if reliable, can be used as the basis to obtain a warrant to search the Smith residence and seize the marijuana plants and cultivation equipment, etc.

9.4.1 Intelligence Information

Intelligence information might deal with a future crime that is being planned, allowing the police to proactively target the responsible individuals and prevent the substantive crime from occurring. Although crimes may already have been committed in terms of counselling offences or conspiracies to commit offences, timely enforcement can still prevent victimization and hold the offenders responsible for the attempt or a conspiracy to commit the intended offence. Intelligence information may also relate to previous criminal activity, but because the information has become old or outdated, it is no longer considered current and should not be acted upon unless it can somehow be verified by way of current information.

Intelligence information can still be very useful in that it might provide grounds for initiating a proactive investigation or may suggest the identity of a suspect for an unsolved case. Intelligence information should always be fully documented in the event it may lead to or become evidence at a later date, meaning that outdated information that is consistent with new information can become corroborative in nature and may be included in an investigator's reasonable grounds to arrest, charge or obtain a search warrant, etc. Another reason to record intelligence information (that can be corroborated) is that doing so may assist in proving the reliability (i.e., established past truthfulness) of the informant in the event he or she becomes involved in future informant activity.

9.4.2 Evidence

Credible information received from a proven and reliable informant (or, if the informant is unproven; information that can be corroborated and acted upon) is evidence, for example that the stolen property is stored at a particular location, or that the murder weapon is in a certain residence, etc. Evidence is information known to the informant by reason of being a direct witness to the event, having perceived the knowledge through one of his or her five senses, or by actually participating in the event, or by being directly told by a person who committed the crime, whether or not the informant is ever compelled to testify as to this knowledge in court.

If the confidential informant elects not to testify, his or her information (evidence) can still be used to further the investigation and the investigator who received the information may be required to testify regarding the information if necessary. This does not include revealing the identity of the informant – except in certain instances to be discussed later in this chapter.

9.5   EXCLUSIVITY OF INFORMATION

If the information is so exclusively known by the informant that acting upon the information could identify the informant, it should be considered intelligence information to avoid compromising the informant's identity. For example, an offender confesses to a close friend that he committed a theft. If the informant is the only person that the offender confessed to, by acting on the exclusively known information, the offender will automatically know who was responsible for informing.

A cunning offender who suspects an individual of informing might even test the person by supplying him or her with exclusive (but false) information in order to see if the fabricated information becomes known to the authorities. In the case of Crime Stoppers tipsters, who always remain anonymous, even the time and date of the call placed by the informant to the police might suggest to a criminal the identity of the informer.

The desire to use even exclusive information increases with the severity of the crime under investigation; however, any potential danger to the informant that might result from using the information must outweigh the benefit of using exclusively known information. An informant who remains adamant that he or she wishes to remain confidential and not testify as a witness must be accorded the confidentiality they seek.

9.6   INFORMANT CREDIBILITY

If the informant relates third-party information (information obtained from someone else), he or she will have no way of knowing whether or not the information he or she is providing is credible (true). The investigator must then assess the credibility of the informant (was the informant, in fact, told the information?) and whether or not the information itself is reliable (is what the informant related true?).

Always be aware of opportunities to independently corroborate what the informant has told you. Some informants are very good, while others are deceitful and manipulative. I once had an informant, who was an inmate in a jail, give me detailed information about being asked to arrange a contract murder for another inmate. The informant had an extensive history of informant activity on murders and conspiracies to commit murder and was fond of dropping the name of a now-deceased well-known senior investigator. It immediately struck me as odd that this person could be in the "right place" to become involved in so many similar cases – so many times.

I was never able to corroborate a single piece of information that the informant told me and one day, he informed me that he had been visited at the jail by a female associate of the suspect who displayed a large "flash roll" of money. A cursory examination of the inmate visitor's register revealed that the informant hadn't had any visitors on that date. I never again accepted any contact from that informant and, to this day, have serious reservations regarding the reliability of any previous information he provided to other investigators.

9.7   INFORMANT RELIABILITY

If information received from a confidential informant is to be used as a basis for reasonable grounds for an arrest, criminal charge, search warrant, or application to intercept private communications, the informant must be qualified as to his or her reliability. One method of indicating an informant's reliability is by confirming the accuracy of the information by corroborating information from another investigative source (i.e., the informant must be truthful because of independent corroboration identical to what the informant stated). If the information cannot be independently corroborated, the only other way to qualify the informant's reliability is on the basis of previous successful informant activity, either for you, another officer within your police service, or for any other police service.

If you have used the same informant on a previous occasion(s), state in your report that "the informant has previously [state month and year] provided me [or another police officer] with information that successfully resulted in an arrest and prosecution for [state offence] or that resulted in the seizure of [state dollar amount] worth of stolen property/drugs, etc., and resulted in a successful prosecution of [state name of accused] for [state offence and sentence]." Reliability of an anonymous repeat Crime Stoppers informant, whose identity is known to you only as an informant code number, may be established in the same manner by relating the details of previous successes achieved as a result of information provided by them.

If the informant is not previously known to you, simply ask the informant for details of any past informant activity he or she may have had where information he or she provided was successfully acted upon. Obtain the investigating officer's name and police service and contact them for the details of the previous case, including an opinion as to the informant's reliability on any such previous occasions.

Credible information – that is, information that can be corroborated that – is received from an informant of unproven reliability, meaning that the informant has never previously provided information, may still be used because the corroboration establishes the credibility of the information. While an unproven informant is not necessarily qualified, the information can still be acted upon and, if successful, used as a basis to prove the reliability of the informant on future occasions.

9.8   CURRENCY OF THE INFORMATION

Another important consideration in acting on informant information is the timeliness or currency of the information provided. If, for example, the informant states that he or she observed stolen television sets in a suspect's garage six months previously, would it be reasonable to assume that the television sets are still there now? I suggest that it would be highly improbable and therefore would not be reasonable to act upon.

While the outdated nature of the information might keep it in the category of intelligence information, it might be possible to request the informant re-establish, through personal knowledge, whether or not the stolen appliances are still in the same location, if doing so and acting on the new information would not compromise them in any way. There is a risk that by involving an informer in evidence gathering, Crown privilege relating to protecting their identity may be lost by changing their status from informer to agent provocateur (see Section 9.15: Crown (Police–Informer) Privilege and Section 9.16: Agents Provocateur, below).

Always establish when the information first became known to the informant and accurately document when you first became aware of the information.

9.9 POLICE-INFORMANT RELATIONSHIP

The police–informant relationship is an odd paradox involving both parties having to trust each other and, at the same time, often mistrusting each other. The investigator must always conduct him or herself in a professional and trustworthy manner while maintaining a cautious and reserved relationship with his or her informant, especially with informants of the opposite gender. Although the informant and the investigator may be working toward a common purpose (e.g., the arrest of a suspect or the resolution of a case), a police–informant relationship is never allowed to develop into a personal friendship.

Occasionally, investigators have identified with their informants and become involved in inappropriate relationships by placing too high an importance on the informant as being vital to the solution of the case. An investigator may lose his or her perspective and begin to rationalize a "friendship" with the informant as the result of believing "it's us against them." An investigator who becomes too close with an informant should be immediately removed from the case and possibly from that assignment, if warranted.

An informant may begin to identify with the investigator out of a misplaced sense of gratitude for feeling safer or believed in and may extend inappropriate offers (e.g., gifts or sexual favours) to the investigator. An informant must always remain an informant and, while you may discover (perhaps to your surprise) that you may share certain things in common, never allow them to become a part of your personal life and never become part of theirs.

BOX 9.3	Proper Investigative Procedure

It is one thing to view an informant as a human being, especially someone who is in need of assistance; it is quite another thing to identify with them as your friend. On occasion, I have given hand-me-down children's winter clothing that my children had outgrown to an informant on social assistance for his children. I have also regularly donated similar items to charitable organizations. Giving an informant a helping hand is appropriate – but engaging in a social relationship can easily impair an investigator's judgment and is inappropriate.

An investigator must take every reasonable precaution to maintain his or her professional reputation and integrity when dealing with informants. Due to the secretive nature of concealing the identity of confidential informants, investigators must often meet their informants in covert, out-of-the-way places. Clandestine meetings between lone officers and unsavoury informants have resulted in investigators becoming the subject of false allegations of discreditable conduct, including physical and sexual misconduct.

Investigators typically meet their informants in a wide variety of venues ranging from police vehicles, police offices, motel rooms, public places such as parks and parking lots, places of business, etc. A meeting with an informant may occur in any location where anonymity and the informant's confidentiality can be protected. Meeting at an informant's residence may be unavoidable; however, it should be discouraged if there is any likelihood of the informant's criminal associates unexpectedly becoming aware of the meeting and questioning the informant regarding the presence of the police.

If the informant will only agree to meet with a single investigator, arrange to meet in a public place, such as a mall parking lot or other crowded area, and arrange to have another investigator discreetly observe the meeting for your protection. At a minimum, make others, for example a colleague or supervisor, aware of the planned circumstances of the meeting, including notifying them when you are clear of the meeting. A lone investigator may consider tape recording the entire meeting with an informant, with the consent of the person being interviewed, for their mutual protection.

As with any other interview, good interviewing skills are essential. The investigator(s) should listen to every word that the informant is saying and must always be on guard against divulging information regarding the case. Be cautious about inadvertently expressing undue interest in any piece of information provided by the informant that might lead the informant to fabricate or exaggerate any one particular aspect he or she feels the investigator "wants to hear." Be aware of what information the informant may have gleaned from media releases concerning the crime or subject under investigation.

The public begrudgingly accepts the fact that sometimes their police force requires assistance of certain unsavoury individuals. What the public will not condone is when a confidential police informant breaks the law and the police service takes no enforcement action to hold the offender accountable. Regardless of how effective or valuable a confidential informant may prove to be, providing information to the police does not grant any informant a licence to abuse that relationship or to flout the law.

Every offence involves a victim and when confidential informants and agents are seen to receive preferential treatment over a victim, the public is quick to outrage at the thought that members of their police service "are in bed" with active criminals (at the expense of the citizens they are sworn to protect) If you suspect that an informant is involved in (unjustified) criminal activity, you should also suspect that they might also be giving you information to divert suspicion away from them. Never "turn a blind eye" to criminal acts that are committed by an informant. Your integrity and that of your police service hang in the balance.

9.10 JUSTIFICATION FOR ACTS OR OMISSIONS

The *Criminal Code* was amended in 2001 to justify specially designated peace or public officers who are engaged in the enforcement of an Act of Parliament or the investigation of criminal activity, and persons acting under the direction of such peace or public officers, "to commit acts or omissions that would otherwise constitute offences."[7] This amendment does not justify any acts or omissions that involve death or bodily harm to any person (intentionally or through criminal negligence) or any conduct that would violate the sexual integrity of any person.[8]

The legislation only allows acts involving loss or serious damage to property that are necessary to:

(i) preserve the life and safety of any person;

(ii) prevent the compromise of the identity of a public officer acting in an undercover capacity, of a confidential informant or a person acting covertly under the direction and control of a public officer (agent provocateur); or

(iii) prevent the imminent loss or destruction of evidence of an indictable offence; and which are personally authorized in writing by a competent authority or are designated by a senior official in exigent circumstances.[9]

For example, a designated "agent" or undercover investigator could be required to accompany criminals inside premises that had been broken into, to witness them committing a theft, or participate in the transportation of stolen property to determine where it is being stored. Both instances involve acts that the agent or undercover investigator may be unable to elude to avoid compromising his or her identity. The *Criminal Code* now justifies these actions and affords people engaged in the administration of justice protection against prosecution by being considered "parties to the offence."

While the *Criminal Code* amendments specifically do not apply to acts or omissions that would constitute offences under Part I of the *Controlled Drugs and Substances Act*; the CDSA also provides for the creation of regulations that authorize members of police forces and persons under the direction and control of such a member to commit acts or omissions "...that would otherwise constitute an offence under Part I of the regulations."[10]

9.11 DOCUMENTING INFORMANT MEETINGS

Some police services' policies provide that conversations with informants may be recorded in separate notebooks: one notebook per investigation, or one notebook per informant. Regardless of the method prescribed by your police service, it is vital that an abundant amount of notes be taken. It is virtually impossible to keep too many notes regarding:

• when and where you first met with the particular informant;

• the time, date and location of any subsequent meetings;

• who was present during any meeting with the informant;

• what consideration, if any, was requested or offered;

---

[7]*Criminal Code*, R.S. 1985, c. C-46, ss. 25.1 (8), (10).

[8]*Criminal Code*, R.S. 1985, c. C-46, s. 25.1 (11).

[9]*Criminal Code*, R.S. 1985, c. C-46. s. 25.1 (9).

[10]*Controlled Drugs and Substances Act*, R.S. 1996 C-19, (Police Enforcement) Regulation [SOR/97-234].

- exactly what the informant told you;

- how you determined how the informant knew the information;

- how you determined when the informant became aware of the information;

- whether the information was known to any other person;

- whether or not the informant could have learned the information from any other source (e.g. media coverage, etc.);

- whether or not the informant can be qualified as "reliable";

- steps taken, if any, to corroborate the information provided;

- any inconsistent information provided by the informant on different occasions;

- any information given by the informant that was found to be false; or

- record of any payments (cash awards or expenses) given to the informant.

9.12 INFORMANT CONFIDENTIALITY AND SECURITY

The rule of informant confidentiality is the result of society recognizing that citizens who assist the police by providing knowledge they have about crimes place themselves in danger from those against whom they provide information. To encourage the continued co-operation of citizens, informants must be protected from harm by criminals.[11]

This principle allows police officers to guarantee confidential informers that in exchange for their incriminating information about criminals and crimes, their identities will be protected throughout all stages of the investigation and any subsequent judicial proceedings.[12]

If you are assigned to "handle" an informant, or if you are initially approached or are successful in recruiting an informant, you must do everything within your control to guard his or her identity. It is permissible to make it known that you have received information from an informant without divulging the informant's identity. Every time you tell a colleague the identity of an informant, you lose total control over the informant's anonymity – his or her name is now "out there." You will not have the defence of saying, "I only told one person." If an informant trusts you to keep his or her identity confidential and you promised to do so, their trust in you will have been destroyed.

You can share any information you receive from any informant with another investigator on a case he or she is investigating by identifying your informant by a code name or number. If the witness can be proven reliable and if the information is credible, you may pass your informant's grounds for belief, which have become your grounds for belief, to the other investigator for his or her purposes. Never divulge the identity of your informant, unless your police service's policies and procedures require you to register

---

[11]*R. v. Hunter* (1987), 57 C.R. (3d) 1 (Ont. C.A.).

[12]*Bisaillon v. Keable* (1983), 2 S.C.R. 60.

your informant with a designated Informant Control Officer (see Section 9.13 below) and then share his or her identity only with that person.

Depending on the severity of any particular investigation involving the use of informants, ensure that an informant has the ability to contact his or her "handler" on very short notice. The decision to release your home telephone number to an informant is a personal one. You simply can't imagine the number of phone calls you will receive from informants on matters, large and small, personal and otherwise, until you give out your home telephone number.

There was a time when my wife was on a first-name basis with several informants as the result of having to perform "receptionist" duties at various times of the day and night. Divulge your residence telephone number judiciously, if at all, unless there is no other way for an informant to contact you when you are off-duty.

If you will be on vacation or otherwise unavailable and anticipate a possible development in your investigation, you may have to designate another contact officer for your informant during the period of your absence. This should be cleared with the informant in advance and only done if he or she agrees to deal with another officer. You should personally introduce the new contact to the informant so that they know who they will be dealing with.

You must have the utmost confidence that any such officer will guard your informant's identity as carefully as you have. You will be vouching for the officer's trustworthiness to your informant. Immediately upon your return to duty, debrief the interim "handler" and personally notify your informant of your return so that he or she may once again resort to you as the primary contact. Always show your informant the respect that you would show any other person and demonstrate to your informant that you consider his or her safety and security to be serious matters.

9.13   INFORMANT CONTROL

Larger police services have a designated Informant Control Officer, and processes incorporated into their policies and procedures to maintain a confidential master record of all informants. Such a system ensures the integrity of any payments made to informants and to ensure that a particular informant doesn't provide information for money to multiple officers. Once approved, in any future dealings, the informant is identified by a code number which is recorded in a secure master register.

Receipts are made out using the informant's code number to provide an accounting of the amount of awards provided to the informant. If your police service doesn't maintain such a system, there is nothing to prevent you from adopting your own system.

9.14   DECEPTIVE INFORMANTS

Informants have been known to provide horribly false information regarding crimes and suspects. Mild cases may result from an informant's honest but mistaken belief or speculation in certain information. Once you are aware that an informant has lied, you should immediately attempt to ascertain if the false information was provided in error or if it was knowingly provided by the informant.

Informants have been known to exaggerate details for effect to make themselves appear more knowledgeable, important or to exaggerate their status in the criminal community. Criminals and criminal-types may attempt to mislead and deceive an investigator to divert suspicion from themselves, to avoid prosecution for offences, or in an attempt to improve their situation in jail, to receive bail or parole considerations, for monetary consideration, or for the mere sport of it.

If you can prove that an informant has intentionally lied to you, you must consider terminating all agreements with him or her and, if justified, immediately conclude the police–informant relationship.

9.15 CROWN (POLICE-INFORMER) PRIVILEGE

The Crown has the "privilege" of concealing the identity of any person who supplies confidential information to a police officer about any charge before a court. It could even be said that the informer retains the privilege as the Crown cannot waive the privilege without the consent of the informer. Courts at all levels have historically recognized the valuable information provided to the police by confidential informants in the administration of justice.

Crown privilege not only prevents the disclosure of the informer's name but extends to the very nature of the information itself, the disclosure of which might tend to reveal the informer's identity.[13] In the case of anonymous informers, such as Crime Stoppers informers, when nothing else is known about the background or personal circumstances of the informer, there is an even greater danger to the informant by disclosing the information due to the possibility that the very details of the tip may tend to identify the person who made the call.[14]

BOX 9.4	Investigative Relevance

I once had an informant who provided me with information concerning her boyfriend, who was the main suspect in an armed robbery investigation. At my request, she agreed to testify in open court about three relatively insignificant details regarding her ownership of a vehicle, her ownership of an apartment building and the "suspect's" access to and usage of both.

In retrospect, the testimony did not significantly strengthen the case whatsoever; however, the informant agreed to testify to those limited facts. Prior to her testifying, I notified the Crown Attorney of the witness's informant activity and made it abundantly clear that he was to restrict his questioning of her to a carefully constructed script in order to protect her identity as an informant.

To my utter shock, during the examination-in-chief of the witness, the Crown Attorney questioned the witness (my informant) about several other things (including asking her to identify a handgun that was recovered at the crime scene). After the witness departed the court room, the Crown Attorney, in front of the accused and in open

---

[13]*R. v. Garofoli* (1990), 2 S.C.R. 1421.

[14]*R. v. Leipert* (1997), 112 CCC (3d) 193, 1 S.C.R. 281.

<table>
<tr><td>BOX 9.4</td><td>(Continued)</td></tr>
</table>

court, stated for the record that the previous witness had, in fact, been providing information to the police concerning the crime and would continue to do so.

By doing so, I had just witnessed a Crown Attorney unwittingly sign an informant's death warrant. This incident resulted in the witness being reluctantly accepted into the Witness Protection Program, administered by the Ministry of the Attorney General. Some good things did come out of this story as the witness eventually changed her life and is no longer a cocaine-using exotic dancer. The final outcome could have been tragic, had the police not intercepted the witness before her boyfriend's criminal associates found her.

The benefits of using the witness's testimony in this case obviously did not outweigh the potential risk to the informant. A valuable lesson was learned about the extent to which an investigator must go to protect the confidentiality of an informant and the potential disastrous results of not doing so.

9.15.1 "Innocence at Stake" Exception to Crown Privilege

The confidentiality of police informers is subject to the exception of a concept known as "innocence at stake," which recognizes that the need to prove the innocence of an accused must take precedence over the need to guarantee the confidentiality of an informant and their information. The accused must first put into evidence some reasonable basis that exceeds mere speculation to believe that **disclosure** of the information provided by an informer is necessary to prove his or her innocence (e.g., where the informant was an actual witness to the crime, or intentionally supplied false information to the police, acted as an agent provocateur, or planted the drugs or stolen property that is the subject matter of the charge, etc.).[15]

When the accused is successful in raising the issue of innocence at stake, the court will undertake the process of judicial editing to determine whether disclosure of some portion or all of the informant's information to the defence would be necessary to allow them to prove the innocence of the accused. Prior to any disclosure of privileged information to the defence, the Crown (Attorney) should be given the option of deciding whether or not to simply proceed on the remaining evidence (if any) or to request that the proceedings be stayed.

This procedure also extends to informant information used as a basis for reasonable grounds to obtain a search warrant and an application for an authorization to intercept private communications.

9.16 AGENTS PROVOCATEUR

An agent provocateur (agent) is different from an informant in two significant aspects. First, unlike the informant who assumes the passive role of an observer, an agent plays an active role in the investigation. Agents are used to make evidence purchases, to

---

[15]*R. v. Chiarantano* (1990) O.J. No. 2603 (C.A.), aff'd (1991) 1 S.C.R. 906.

introduce and vouch for undercover police officers, to "befriend" criminals and infiltrate criminal organizations, to gather evidence and even to become involved in providing justifiable opportunities to induce individuals to commit crimes. However, the efforts of an agent cannot be forceful and persistent enough as to be considered **entrapment** or untargeted and indiscriminate to such an extent as to be considered **random virtue-testing**.

Entrapment is the inappropriate inducement of a reluctant individual to commit a crime through excessively forceful and unrelenting persuasion by an agent provocateur.[16] Random virtue-testing only arises when a police officer presents a person with the opportunity to commit an offence "without a reasonable suspicion that: (a) the person is already engaged in the particular criminal activity, or (b) the physical location with which the person is associated is a place where the particular criminal activity is likely occurring."[17]

Second, and most importantly, an agent does not enjoy the police–informant privilege and must be identified in subsequent judicial proceedings, even if he or she is not called upon to testify.

Utilizing an agent always involves some form of consideration, either financial or in respect to outstanding charges or by way of witness relocation. Prior to the agent performing the duties that are required of him or her, it is essential that the terms, conditions and expectations of both parties to the agreement be explicitly set out in a Letter of Agreement. The Letter of Agreement forms a contract that is intended to protect the interests of all parties to the agreement.

9.17 HONOURING INFORMANT DEALS

Any time that any deal or agreement is struck with an informant, agent or accomplice, it is just as important for the police to honour the deal as it is to carefully document the agreement to specify responsibilities and expectations. Regardless of the overall success of the case, whether the agreement is to provide a monetary informant award, a one-time witness relocation or consideration with respect to a charge – a deal is a deal.

In 1993, members of the Green Ribbon Task Force and the Ontario Ministry of the Attorney General entered into a resolution agreement with Karla Homolka to testify against her former husband, Paul Bernardo. In exchange for a reduced sentence on charges of manslaughter in connection with the abduction and murders of Leslie Mahaffy and Kristen French, Homolka's testimony was the only evidence available against Bernardo on the murder cases. After the agreement was finalized, six incriminating video tapes implicating both Bernardo and Homolka that were recovered by Bernardo's first attorney were turned over to the police by Bernardo's second lawyer.

The agreement with Homolka, although vital to the success of the prosecution against Bernardo, was widely criticized in the media as a "deal with the devil" and resulted in the Attorney General appointing Mr Justice Patrick T. Galligan to conduct a review into certain matters, including:

---

[16]*R. v. Mack* (1988) 2 S.C.R. 903.

[17]*R. v. Barnes* (1991) 1 S.C.R. 449.

(a) whether the plea arrangement with Homolka was appropriate;

(b) whether advice given by crown counsel in the matter of another adolescent female sexual assault victim referred to as Jane Doe was appropriate; and

(c) whether it was feasible or appropriate to take further proceedings against Karla Homolka.

As distasteful as it was for many people, Karla Homolka was released from prison in July 2005, instead of serving a life sentence for two counts of first-degree murder. It is sometimes necessary to make unpalatable deals with "lesser" criminals in order to secure the convictions of a primary offender who might otherwise escape prosecution. It is difficult to see a criminal walk away with a "sweetheart deal" – but after all, a deal is a deal.

9.18 USE OF IN-CUSTODY INFORMERS

You will recall that an in-custody informer is defined as:

"Someone who allegedly receives one or more [incriminating] statements from an accused, while both are in [police] custody [or in a correctional institution], and where the statement[s] relate to an offence(s) that occurred outside of the custodial institution. [The prosecution must intend to call the in-custody informer as a witness in a judicial proceeding.]"[18]

The use of in-custody informers has become highly regulated to safeguard against the possibility of wrongful convictions, in light of past miscarriages of justice. Upon learning of the possibility of the involvement of an in-custody informer, the officer-in-charge of an investigation must determine whether or not the in-custody informer has made any request (on behalf of any person) for "consideration in exchange for his or her cooperation, including (but not limited to):

- financial benefits;

- beneficial treatment while in custody;

- early consideration for parole;

- outstanding charges reduced, stayed or withdrawn;

- a reduced sentence on outstanding charges;

- promises of 'best efforts' respecting any of the above; or

- any form of future indemnity."[19]

The Case Manager must make arrangements to have the in-custody informer interviewed at the earliest convenience. As previously stated, it may not be practicable to interview the informer inside the correctional facility, especially if the interview is to be videotaped. In such cases, it is necessary to remove a prisoner from the correctional facility and transport him or her to a secure location to conduct the interview.

It will first be necessary to obtain an order from a provincial court judge or a judge of a superior court for the release of the prisoner for the purpose of assisting a specified

---

[18]Ministry of Community Safety and Correctional Services: *Ontario Major Case Management (MCM) Manual* (Oct. 1, 2004), p. 9.

[19]Kaufman (1998), vol. 2, p. 1354.

peace officer in the execution of his or her duty for a specified period of time. It must be noted that an application made by a prosecutor to a judge for an order for the release of a prisoner must include the written consent of the prisoner.[20]

Any formal statement of an in-custody informer must be videotaped in accordance with the KGB guidelines as set out in Chapter 4: Interviewing Victims and Witnesses. "The KGB statement may take place within the custodial institution if it does not compromise the safety of the in-custody informer."[21]

An in-custody informer or agent provocateur (e.g., undercover police officer)[22] must never attempt to actively elicit (i.e., question or draw out, beyond merely listening to conversation with the suspect) evidence from a suspect or accused who is in custody, especially one who has elected to exercise his or her right to remain silent. The court will apply the test as to whether or not the evidence (the statement) would have been made "but for the intervention of the state or its agents."[23]

It is vital when dealing with an in-custody informer to refrain from discussing the details of the case or unconsciously affirming information provided by the in-custody informer. The interviewer(s) should gather information that would tend to confirm the in-custody informer's reliability (e.g., whether or not the informant made notes or records of the suspect's statement or whether or not any other person was present when the alleged statement was made, etc.).

The Case Manager of a case involving the potential use of an in-custody informer must notify the Crown Attorney immediately. "In cases where the Crown proposes to use an in-custody informer as a witness, an in-custody informer brief must be submitted to the ['In-Custody Informer'] Review Committee [a committee comprising 3–5 prosecutors, with trial or appellate experience, from various regions of the province] for a determination of whether there is a compelling public interest in presenting the evidence of the in-custody informer."[24]

SUMMARY

- A confidential police informant is any person who provides incriminating information to the police regarding suspect(s) and intimate details of crimes, criminals or criminal activity, but does not wish to testify as a witness and provides information on the condition of anonymity.

- Informers may initiate contact with the police or may be recruited by the police either to avoid arrest or being charged or on the basis of their ongoing contact with the criminal element or (due to their lifestyle or employment) their association with any location where criminal activity regularly occurs.

---

[20]*Criminal Code*, R.S. 1985, c. C-46, s. 527(7)

[21]Ministry of Community Safety and Correctional Services: *Ontario Major Case Management (MCM) Manual* (Oct. 1, 2004), p. 53.

[22]*R. v Hebert* (1990) 2 S.C.R. 151, 57 CCC (3d) 1, 77 C.R. (3d) 145.

[23]*R. v Broyles* (1991) 3 S.C.R. 595, 68 CCC (3d) 308.

[24]Ministry of Community Safety and Correctional Services: *Ontario Major Case Management (MCM) Manual* (Oct. 1, 2004), p. 10.

- Informers may be motivated by a variety of factors, including: their sense of civic duty; revenge; financial considerations (e.g., monetary awards); or consideration regarding outstanding criminal charges against themselves or others.

- An in-custody informer is "someone who allegedly receives one or more statements from an accused, while both are in [police] custody [or in a correctional institution], and where the statement[s] relate to offences that occurred outside of the custodial institution. The prosecution must intend to call the in-custody informer as a witness in a judicial proceeding."

- Informants must be assessed with respect to their credibility (i.e., is what the informant stated true?) and their reliability (i.e., has the informant given previous reliable informant information or is independent corroboration of the information available?).

- The investigator must always conduct him or herself in a professional and trustworthy manner while maintaining a cautious and reserved relationship with his or her informant, especially with informants of the opposite gender.

- Thoroughly document in writing (or electronically record) the conversations of all parties regarding any request for consideration made by a potential informant and never offer any consideration that exceeds your authority to offer.

- Never turn a "blind eye" to criminal acts committed by an informant – appropriate enforcement action should always be taken to ensure the integrity of the investigator and his or her police service.

- Always withhold the details of a case with an informant and avoid unconsciously confirming to the informant the accuracy of the information provided.

- The principle of informant confidentiality allows police officers to guarantee confidential informers that, in exchange for their incriminating information about criminals and crimes, their identities will be protected throughout all stages of the investigation and any subsequent judicial proceedings.

- Crown privilege not only prevents the disclosure of the informer's identity but extends to the very nature of the information itself, the disclosure of which might tend to reveal the informer's identity. Crown privilege is outweighed only by the need to prove the innocence of an accused under the principle of innocence at stake.

DISCUSSION QUESTIONS

1. Whether they are first to initiate contact with an investigator or are recruited, confidential informants may be motivated by a number of factors that may provide indicators of their reliability. What are some factors that motivate people to provide information to the police? What are the two methods of qualifying an informant as reliable?

2. It is vitally important for an investigator to thoroughly document the conversation during any meeting or contact with a confidential informant in his or her notebook. What are examples of the types of issues that an investigator should document?

3. The concept of "innocence at stake" recognizes the need to prove the innocence of an accused over the need to guarantee the confidentiality of an informant and his or her information. The court may order that a witness be identified or his or her information be disclosed if the accused puts credible evidence before the court of the necessity to do so in order to prove his or her innocence. What are some of the circumstances that could invoke the "innocence at stake" exception to the Crown privilege that normally protects informants?

WEBLINKS

www.canlii.org

Canadian Legal Information Institute. A searchable case law database.

Chapter 10

Major Crime Investigation

"The world is a dangerous place to live in not because of those who do evil, but because of those who watch and let it happen."

Albert Einstein (1879-1955).[1]

Learning Outcomes

After reading this chapter, students should be able to:

- Assess situations in order to determine legal search requirements to search a building, receptacle or place to seize evidence.
- Explain the exceptions that, if present, can permit the warrantless seizure of evidence.
- Analyze the facts in issue of a variety of selected criminal offences.
- Differentiate between Level I, Level II and Level III assaults.
- Summarize the exceptions that negate the defence of consent for any level of sexual assault charge.

10.1 SEARCH AND SEIZURE

A police officer's statutory and common law powers of search and seizure are some of the most powerful investigative tools that the officer has at his or her disposal. A properly obtained search warrant grants law enforcement officers, and persons assisting them, the authority to enter onto private property, and search for and seize specific items which will afford evidence with respect to the commission of a criminal offence.

Imagine that you are at home, enjoying a peaceful evening in the company of friends or family. Without warning, a group of uniformed men and women arrives at your door. The officer in charge informs you that they are in possession of a court order which allows them to enter your home to search for a particular item or items in relation to a criminal act they are investigating.

Despite your objections, you are powerless to refuse them entry in the face of their legal authority. You watch in disbelief as they invade the very place where, until this point,

---

[1]Albert Einstein quoted in Maschke and Scalabrini (2000).

you felt the safest. You look on as they systematically rummage through every room in your residence, examining your most personal belongings. As they continue searching, your liberty may be restricted – you are not free to come and go as you wish. You are now a prisoner in your own home.

Your children are upset and crying, fearful of the armed strangers who now control your family's home. Your partner is enraged at whatever action, real or imagined, you have committed to bring this most unwelcome invasion of your family's normal evening routine.

When the intruders have finished their search, your house is in complete turmoil and disarray. The officer in charge informs you that a variety of your possessions have been seized as evidence. At best, you are permitted to remain in your house after they leave, to deal with your irate family. At worst, you are placed under arrest, manacled, and led off to jail.

My point is this – whether or not a suspect is in fact guilty of any crime, having a group of strangers invade the privacy of their home is, short of being the victim of a violent crime, perhaps the most intrusive act that any private citizen might ever have to endure. The statutory authority authorizing police officers to perform warranted searches of private property is not treated lightly by the courts.

The authority to obtain search warrants carries with it a heavy burden of responsibility on the part of those so entrusted to ensure their actions are both justified and conducted in a reasonable manner. Every investigation leading up to the granting of a search warrant, including the content of the warrant itself and the circumstances of the search methods used in the execution of the warrant, may be subjected to the highest degree of judicial scrutiny.

If your actions in relation to executing a search warrant are found to be unjustified, you may be criticized, and your professional reputation damaged, perhaps irreparably – to say nothing of the potential for civil liability to you and your police service. Your evidence could be excluded and your case may be lost. The accused may be acquitted and you will likely suffer some professional embarrassment.

Worse, you may create bad case law that will place further investigative limitations on how every police officer in Canada does their job in the future. Most importantly, you will be placed in the unenviable position of having to explain to the victim of the crime why his or her case was lost due to mistakes that could have been avoided.

10.2 DO I NEED A SEARCH WARRANT?

"The house of everyone is to him as his castle and fortress, as well for his defence against injury and violence as for his [relaxation]." [2]

Sir Edward Coke, English jurist (1552-1634).

Volumes have been written about the continuously evolving area of criminal law that deals with police powers of search and seizure. Once again, space constraints preclude us from exhaustively examining every common law search authority, or those granted to police officers by various statutes, many of which are more likely resorted to during routine patrol duties. We will therefore examine some search and seizure authorities that are most commonly utilized during criminal investigations.

---

[2]*Semayne's Case (Semayne v. Gresham*, 5 Co. Rep 91a, 93a, 77 Eng. Rep. 194, 198 [K.B. 1604]).

You will recall from Section 2.16.1 that the *Charter of Rights and Freedoms* guarantees every individual in Canada the freedom against unreasonable search and seizure.[3] The primary rule that every police officer must always remember is that whenever it is practicable to obtain a search warrant a warrant must be obtained, or the search will be held to be *prima facie* unreasonable.[4]

Except for the warrantless search authorities that have been referred to in previous chapters, including: Search Incident to Arrest (Section 1.3.5), Plain View Seizure Rule (Section 2.14), Evidence Obtained by Consent (Section 2.17), Abandoned Evidence (Section 2.18), and Officer Safety Issues Relating to the Search for Weapons or Suspects (Section 5.13), physical evidence may be seized without a warrant only where there is an imminent danger that evidence of an offence will be lost, destroyed or removed.[5] This will be decided on a case-by-case basis depending on the individual circumstances of each case.

BOX 10.1	**Do I Need A Search Warrant?**

When you are in a search and seizure situation in which a known or unknown suspect has a proprietary interest, or could possibly have a reasonable expectation of privacy and are unsure of the legal search requirements, stop and ask yourself, "Do I need a search warrant?" It may be helpful to remember the mnemonic: S. E. P. I. C. O.

S – **Statute** – Is a warrantless search specifically authorized by statute or common law?

E – **Exigent Circumstances** – Will evidence be lost, destroyed or removed unless you act immediately?

P – **Plain View** – Are you lawfully positioned and inadvertently discover incriminating evidence?

I – **Incident to Arrest** – Is it a search incident to a lawful arrest?

C – **Consent** – Has person with lawful authority to consent to the search done so?

O – **Officer Safety** – Do reasonable officer safety concerns exist? This temporary search authority is rescinded when any legitimate safety concerns end.

If your situation does not fall within one of these exceptions, you almost certainly require a warrant. To proceed further without a search warrant may render any resulting seizure at risk of being excluded (see Chapter 13: Courtroom Procedures).

Therefore, to be considered proper, a search must be "reasonable." A reasonable search is:

1. authorized by statute; is reasonable and is carried out in a reasonable manner; or

2. judicially pre-authorized by a justice of the peace or judge; or

3. covered by one of the warrantless search exceptions described in the previous paragraph.[6]

---

[3]*Canadian Charter of Rights and Freedoms*, Being Part 1 of the *Constitution Act, 1982*, Enacted by the *Canada Act 1982* (U.K.) c. 11; proclaimed in force April 17, 1982, s.8.

[4]*Hunter v. Southam Inc.* (1984), 2 S.C.R. 45, 14 C.C.C. (3d) 97, 11 D.L.R. (4th) 641.

[5]*R. v. Grant* (1993) 84 C.C.C. (3d) 173 (S.C.C).

[6]*R. v. Collins* (1987) 33 C.C.C. (3d) 1 (S.C.C.).

A search begins the moment a police officer enters onto the premises to be searched and may be compromised if the initial entry itself is not conducted in a reasonable manner. In a landmark decision, the Supreme Court of Canada held that the police cannot effect a warrantless entry to "freeze" a premises until a search warrant is obtained.[7] "Either you have the right to enter and search without warrant or you don't. An artificial [distinction] between entry and search won't work."[8]

10.3 REASONABLE EXPECTATION OF PRIVACY

The stakes are high when the success of your case depends on the evidence gathered during a search. "Search" is a term that is broadly defined and is not confined solely to entry and search of a building or premises – a search may involve looking for evidence inside a motor vehicle, obtaining documentary information regarding a suspect, or employing an investigative technique in any other situation where the suspect has, or could be held to have, a "reasonable expectation of privacy."

BOX 10.2 | **Investigative Relevance**

An accused person who conceals physical evidence from a break and enter in a rented public storage facility would be held to have a reasonable expectation of privacy associated with that rental unit. An offender who commits a murder in the victim's residence has no such expectation of privacy, unless the suspect also resides at that location, such as in the case of a spouse, relative or tenant.

An offender who leaves bloody clothing or a weapon used in a homicide at the residence of a relative has no reasonable expectation of privacy if the relative consents to the seizure by the police. No offender can claim he or she has a reasonable expectation of privacy if he or she conceals evidence in a public place, such as a city park, as the evidence might be discovered at any time by anyone, including the police. An armed robber has no expectation of privacy if his or her image is recorded on videotape while committing a robbery in a convenience store.

If the suspect might possibly have a reasonable expectation of privacy in the item to be seized, or in the building, place or receptacle to be searched, or if the proprietary interest of the suspect isn't known or isn't clear to you at the time of the investigation, don't take any chances. When in doubt, always err on the side of caution and obtain a warrant, provided that it is practicable to do so.

The court will apply the standard of "reasonable expectation of privacy" in determining whether or not a search is reasonable. For example, if an individual conceals stolen property in the basement of his house, he would be deemed to have a reasonable expectation of privacy that the evidence would not be discovered and used against him. The sanctity of the home as a person's "castle and fortress" has been entrenched in Western law

---

[7]*R. v. Silveira* (1995) 97 C.C.C. (3d) 450 (S.C.C.).

[8]Sherriff (1997), p. 48.

since *Semayne's Case* in 1604, and extends the same protection to individuals who carry on illegal activities within the privacy of their homes as it does for law-abiding citizens.

Would an accused person have a reasonable expectation that his or her financial information would be kept confidential at the bank or financial institution where he or she conducts business? If you feel that you would have that expectation regarding your financial affairs at your bank – so would an accused person. The court will determine whether the **"reasonable person"** would claim that the use of an investigative technique was so intrusive that it should have been pre-authorized by an officer of the court.

10.4 SEARCH WARRANTS – SECTION 487 *CRIMINAL CODE*

Our society places a high value on the rights of the individual and at the same time recognizes that there are occasions when the rights of society, one of those being the right to effective law enforcement, sometimes supersedes the rights of the individual. One of the ways in which societal rights are exerted over individual rights is in the granting of powers of search and seizure to the law enforcement agents of the state. To ensure that individual rights are protected, our criminal justice system oversees the actions of law enforcement agencies with a view to providing fairness and guarding against overzealous law enforcement that might, intentionally or inadvertently, violate the rights of the individual.

The search warrant provisions of s. 487 *Criminal Code* are the most commonly used by investigators for obtaining judicial authorization to enter and search any building, place or receptacle for evidence of crimes. Evidence may be seized in relation to: an offence that has been committed; an offence that is suspected to have been committed; or to seize something that on reasonable grounds is intended to be used to commit an offence against the person for which an arrest may be made without warrant. A s. 487(1) search warrant may also authorize the seizure of offence-related property as defined in section 2 of the *Criminal Code*.[9]

The seizure of evidence authorized by s. 487 *Criminal Code* is contemplated as real or physical evidence, meaning tangible objects, but may also include searching a computer system for data and seizing a print-out of the data.[10] Section 487 search warrants are issued in Form 5 *Criminal Code* and are directed either to an individual or to police officers within a judicial district or province.

All police officers participating in the search don't have to be named on the warrant and the specific officer "named" need not be present during the search. If a search warrant is issued in one territorial division, such as the province of Ontario, but is intended for execution in another territorial division, for example British Columbia, it must first be endorsed in Form 28 *Criminal Code* by a justice in the territorial division (British Columbia) in which the warrant is to be executed.[11]

---

[9]*Criminal Code*, R.S. 1985 c. C-46, s. 487(1).

[10]*Criminal Code*, R.S. 1985 c. C-46, s. 487(2.1).

[11]*Criminal Code*, R.S. 1985 c. C-46, Part XXVIII (Part 28).

10.4.1 Information to Obtain a Search Warrant

The first step in obtaining a search warrant is to complete an Information to Obtain a Search Warrant in Form 1 *Criminal Code*. The information identifies the person applying for the warrant, referred to as the informant, and specifies the building, receptacle or place to be searched, the things to be searched for and the specific offences under investigation. The information also articulates the informant's reasonable grounds for belief in a nexus, or connection, between the things to be

---

BOX 10.3	Investigative Relevance

You are assigned to investigate the armed robbery of a credit union that was committed by a lone, male robber, wearing a black ski-mask and armed with a black semi-automatic handgun. The robber handed a teller a hold-up note and received $5 000 in a white canvas deposit bag. The robber was seen to make his getaway in a black pickup truck. You are aware that a federal parolee, who has served time for armed robbery, took up residence in your city two weeks before the robbery.

The parolee fits the general physical characteristics provided by witnesses to the robbery. You might suspect that the parolee might be responsible for the armed robbery and your suspicion may be well-founded; however, your suspicion does not, at this time, amount to reasonable grounds.

You conduct inquiries with the subject's parole officer and learn that, since his release from custody, the parolee has resided with his brother. You query provincial vehicle registration records and learn that the suspect's brother owns a black pickup truck similar to the description of the getaway vehicle reported by witnesses. You and other officers conduct surveillance and observe the parolee leaving and returning to the brother's residence several times each day, driving the brother's black pickup truck.

You receive reliable information from a confidential informer who indicates that the parolee was talking about planning to commit an armed robbery at an unspecified location only two days prior to the credit union robbery. Your informer states that the suspect also inquired where he could obtain a handgun and ammunition. Following the robbery,

the suspect was observed by the informer and others in a bar spending large amounts of money on food and liquor when, only two days before, he was borrowing money.

You make inquiries with the police agency that convicted him of his previous robbery and learn that the wording of the hold-up note in the previous robbery was identical to the note passed in the credit union robbery. Handwriting comparison between the two notes cannot be completed for several weeks. Immersing the recent credit union hold-up note in a ninhydrin solution has, however, developed a latent fingerprint impression, which when submitted to AFIS (Automated Fingerprint Identification System) is positively identified as belonging to the parolee.

When viewed collectively, all of the information is more than enough to meet the standard of "reasonable probability." A section 487 *Criminal Code* search warrant should then be obtained to search the brother's/suspect's residence and the pickup truck for:

1) the stolen money identified by amount, denomination and serial numbers if available;

2) the white canvas bank deposit bag;

3) the black ski-mask and any other clothing similar to that which was described by the witnesses;

4) the handgun and ammunition; and

5) any writing material including pens, note pads, etc., that may have been used to write the hold-up note.

searched for, the place, and the offence(s) under investigation.[12] The facts contained in the information to obtain the search warrant are sworn under oath or solemnly affirmed before a justice who, if satisfied that it is in the public interest to do so, may then grant the search warrant.

The standard of reasonable grounds, which must be met by the informant, is only one of "reasonable probability." The grounds must be credible, reasonable and must exceed mere suspicion. "Reasonable grounds" is a far lower standard than the standard of proof beyond a reasonable doubt which is necessary to convict an accused person. There is no universal definition of reasonable probability – each search warrant information will be judged in court on its individual merits, having regard to all the circumstances.

10.4.2 Building, Receptacle or Place to be Searched

When completing your information to obtain a search warrant, you must specify the exact address or location of the building, receptacle or place to be searched. The address must be as complete as possible so an uninvolved fellow officer would know exactly which premises to search. This is especially crucial when dealing with rural addresses and multiple dwellings.

I was once assigned to investigate a murder in an unfamiliar area. A local officer advised me of the lot, concession number and rural township of the address to be searched. Many hours later, we arrived at the location to execute the search warrant, only to discover the address I had been provided for the search location was incorrect. This resulted in a delay of several hours while a new search warrant was prepared for the correct address.

A serious error such as a wrong address on a search warrant will render the entire warrant defective. Had we gone ahead and executed the original warrant, it would have been the same as conducting a warrantless search and any evidence seized would have been excluded. The officer's mistake was an honest one and we all make mistakes, but it could have been an extremely costly mistake. After that investigation, to the extent that it was possible to do so, I always personally confirmed every last detail included in a search warrant before it was presented to a justice.

The term "building, receptacle or place" applies to most locations where you might ever expect to have to search, with the exception of seizing evidence from a person's body. The taking of bodily samples such as hair or impressions or seizing a bloody bandage worn by a suspect is not covered by s. 487(1) because "a person is not considered to be a 'building, receptacle or a place'."[13, 14]

The term "receptacle" refers to locations or things such as lockers in bus depots or airports, suitcases, briefcases, filing cabinets, etc. In addition to dwelling houses and other buildings, the term "place" includes "...places of fixed location, such as offices, shops or gardens, as well as vehicles, vessels and aircraft. It does not include public streets or other public places."[15]

---

[12]*Criminal Code*, R.S. 1985 c. C-46, s. 487(1).

[13]*R. v. Mutch* (1986) 26 C.C.C. (3d) 477 (Sask. Q.B.); *R. v. Legere* (1988), 43 C.C.C. (3d) 502 (N.B.C.A.); *R. v. Miller* (1987), 38 C.C.C. (3d) 252 (Ont, C.A.); *Laporte v. R.* (1972) 8 C.C.C. (2d) 343 (Que. Mun. Ct.).

[14]Hutchinson (1996).

[15]*R. v. Rao* (1984) 40 C.R. (3d) 1 ; 46 O.R. (2d) 80, 12 C.C.C. (3d) 97, 4 O.A.C. 162, 9 D.L.R. (4th) 542, 10 C.R.R. 275, (Ont. C.A.).

General warrants are now available to permit the seizure of bodily DNA samples[16] and for "handprints, fingerprints, footprint, foot impression, teeth impression or other print or impression of the body or any part of the body..."[17] as such seizures are not authorized by s. 487(1) and previous warrantless searches were held to constitute *Charter* violations (see Section 10.14: General Warrants, below).

10.4.3 Description of Things to be Seized

When listing the things to be seized, they must be described in as much detail as possible. A fellow officer with no knowledge of the investigation should be able to identify all of the listed items to be seized from their description on the search warrant, even if the investigating officer is not present. If applicable, every possible detail such as make, model, colour, size, serial number or other physical characteristics must be included to distinguish it from similar items. If only class characteristics are available, describe the item or class of item to be seized as precisely as possible.

Describing things to be seized can be a simple task when all of the details of the item are known, such as a stolen motor vehicle or television set, for which the owner can provide model numbers and serial numbers, etc. It can be somewhat more difficult in the case of a homicide investigation where investigators don't always know what it is they are searching for – until they find it, often before an autopsy has been conducted.

An investigator must utilize common sense and include items that, from experience, are routinely encountered at homicide scenes and allow "reasonable probability" to be inferred that those items will also be located at the scene to be searched. Stating what investigative techniques are anticipated to be employed in the search of a homicide scene, if known, will also indicate good faith on the part of the investigators.

BOX 10.4	Proper Investigative Procedure

Always describe every possible item that can reasonably be included on your search warrant information. If you are investigating the theft of 10 television sets in crates that were stolen from a warehouse, would it not be reasonable to assume that between the time of the theft and the time of the search, they might have been removed from their crates? If the television sets were described as "television sets in crates" the investigator may only reasonably search spaces large enough to conceal a crate.

If the investigator drafting the warrant includes descriptions of the remote control and the owner's manuals that were also inside the crates, investigators assigned to execute the warrant may then search much smaller areas that might conceal remote controls and paper manuals. If the crates bore shipping labels at the time of the theft, I would also include them on the warrant in the event that the suspect(s) had removed them from the crates in order to prevent them from being identified.

---

[16]*Criminal Code* R.S. 1985 c. C-46, s. 487.05(1).

[17]*Criminal Code* R.S. 1985 c. C-46, s. 487.092(1).

10.4.4 Reasonable Grounds for Belief

Drafting the search warrant information is a painstaking task, especially when it comes to the informant's grounds for believing that the things to be seized are in the building, receptacle or place to be searched and why they will afford evidence with respect to the offences under investigation. A search warrant information is a multi-page document that can reach several volumes in length in complex high-profile investigations. Search warrant preparation is an art and an investigator who is proficient in the drafting of warrants and the supporting applications is a valued member of any investigative unit.

An investigator who drafts a search warrant information must precisely state his or her reasonable grounds to justify the search. It is not sufficient merely to state, "My investigation has revealed that a blue car was seen leaving the crime scene." The informant must state how he or she knows this information to enable the justice who is asked to issue the search warrant to assess the credibility of the information.

For example, "On Tuesday, February 08, 2005, the informant personally interviewed Harry Johnson, Age 47, of 123 Smith Street, Podunck, Ontario. Mr Johnson provided a signed statement indicating that at approximately 12:30 a.m., Feb. 8, 2005, he observed a late-model blue car, make, model and licence number unknown, leaving the crime scene at a high rate of speed in a southbound direction on Memorial Avenue." The witness's information, if accepted as credible and believed to be truthful by the informant, now forms part of the informant's reasonable grounds for belief.

Hearsay information that cannot be used as evidence in court is allowable in a search warrant information but must be corroborated, or be otherwise shown to be reliable. Hearsay information may be obtained from a fellow police officer or from a witness or a confidential informer. In all cases, the information should be "sourced," meaning that every fact has to be attributed to the source from whom it was received and be clearly articulated as to how each particular source came to know the information that is attributed to them.

The confidential police informer who provides information should, of course, only be referred to as a confidential informer, or by an assigned informant number. An informer's reliability must also be "qualified" either on the basis of previous successful informant activity, or by way of independent corroboration of his or her information.

Where the information is known exclusively by the informer and the suspect/accused's knowledge that investigators have that information may help the suspect to identify the informer, the investigator should request that the issuing justice seal the search warrant information. Search warrant applications may be sealed by the court to protect the identity of confidential informers, undercover officers and the integrity of ongoing investigations.

A search warrant information must be a stand-alone document. A justice cannot cross-examine an informant on his or her application for a search warrant, nor may the informant verbally explain additional facts to the justice that are not part of the information to obtain the warrant.

All available grounds for belief must be truthfully and fairly disclosed in the information, not just those grounds that support the issuance of the search warrant. If information contained in the warrant is no longer current, it should be identified as such so that the justice may evaluate the information fairly. If a discrepancy exists between two facts, as is often the case during an investigation, both should be included in the information to obtain the warrant – not just those facts that favour the issuing of the search warrant.

Seized evidence may be declared inadmissible on account of any wilful non-disclosure or misrepresentation of the true facts of an investigation, unless there are sufficient remaining grounds upon which the warrant may survive without it.[18] If incriminating evidence of a witness is unreliable or if his or her evidence disagrees with evidence of another source, you must include these details in your search warrant information.

Wilful non-disclosure of evidence has resulted in several high-profile miscarriages of justice, such as in the cases of David Milgaard, Guy Paul Morin, Thomas Sophonow and more recently, in the 2005 exoneration of James Driskell in relation to the 1990 murder of Perry Dean Harder. The public interest and your long-term credibility in the eyes of your local judiciary are far more valuable than the granting of a single search warrant.[19]

10.5 TELEWARRANTS – SECTION 487.1 *CRIMINAL CODE*

Crime and criminals rarely keep normal office hours. Occasionally, a search warrant is required to be obtained and executed after-hours or on weekends. The *Criminal Code* provides that, "Where a peace officer believes that an indictable offence has been committed and that it would be impracticable to appear personally before a justice to make application for a [search] warrant...the peace officer may submit an information on oath by telephone or other means of telecommunication to a justice designated for the purpose by the chief judge of the provincial court having jurisdiction in the matter."[20]

In addition to an ordinary search warrant application, an information to obtain a **telewarrant** must also include the reason(s) why it is impracticable for the informant to appear personally before the justice. The information must still be sworn under oath; however, the oath may be in the form of a statement that, if transmitted electronically, "is deemed to be a statement made under oath."[21] Such a telewarrant or facsimile of a telewarrant issued by a justice has the same force in law as an original document.[22]

10.6 SEARCH WARRANT EXECUTION

The location of the building, receptacle or place to be searched and the items to be seized which are identified in the information to obtain the warrant must also appear on the face of the warrant itself. The informant's grounds for belief are not replicated on the face of the warrant, however, and the warrant should specify the times of execution, which should be limited, depending on the circumstances of the specific situation, but especially in situations involving searches of dwelling houses.

---

[18]*R. v. Bisson* (1994) 94 C.C.C. (3d) 94 S.C.C.

[19]Sherriff (1997).

[20]*Criminal Code*, R.S. 1985, c. C-46, s. 487.1(1).

[21]*Criminal Code*, R.S. 1985, c. C-46, s. 487.1(3) and (3.1).

[22]*Criminal Code*, R.S. 1985, c. C-46, s. 487.1(12).

Section 29(1) *Criminal Code* imposes the duty upon everyone who executes a process or warrant to have it in their possession and to produce it when requested.[23] Failure to do so has been held to constitute a violation of the guaranteed right to be free from unreasonable search and seizure.[24]

Unless authorized for execution by night, the search warrant must be executed between 6:00 a.m. and 9:00 p.m. This does not mean that the search must conclude before 9:00 p.m., only that it commences prior to that time. If circumstances require that the warrant be executed after 9:00 p.m., reasonable grounds requiring execution by night must be included in the information to obtain the search warrant and an endorsement for execution after that time must be included on the face of the search warrant itself.[25]

Any issue surrounding the reasonableness of the execution of a search warrant may also be examined by the court. Investigators executing search warrants must first knock and announce their presence and purpose, unless reasonable grounds exist to believe that to do so could result in the loss or destruction of evidence, or unless reasonable officer safety concerns exist. Unjustified force, at any time during the execution of a search warrant, could render a search a section 8 *Charter* violation.[26]

Serious and obvious defects on the face of the search warrant, such as an incorrect address, failure to specify the things to be seized or omitting the times of execution will render the warrant invalid.[27] Where only a part of a warrant is found to be defective and there are still enough remaining grounds to justify the warrant, the defective parts may be severed during a trial, following an application to quash the warrant.[28]

Search warrants authorize the search of the specified building, receptacle or place but this authority does not extend to the search of persons found on the premises at the time of the search, although reasonable concerns for officer safety may require a search of all occupants for weapons in limited but extreme instances. The search of an occupant of a building being searched must be incident to his or her lawful arrest. If the principal owner, tenant or occupier of a premises being searched is arrested, his or her right to retain and instruct counsel under s. 10(b) *Charter of Rights* may still be exercised in privacy, but the police are under no obligation to suspend or postpone the search until the prisoner has consulted with legal counsel.[29]

Often, investigators executing a search warrant will encounter evidence in the premises being searched that is not specified in the search warrant but is relevant to the case under investigation or that is evidence of another crime, or perhaps is something that has been used in a crime. Section 489(1) *Criminal Code* provides for the warrantless seizure of evidence located during the execution of a search warrant that is not named in the warrant. Sec. 489(2) of the *Criminal Code* signifies the "plain view seizure rule" in situations where a peace officer is "lawfully on the premises" whether executing a search

---

[23]*Criminal Code*, R.S. 1985, c. C-46, s. 29(1).

[24]*R. v. Bohn* (2000) 145 C.C.C. (3d) 320, 33 C.R. (5th) 265 (B.C.C.A.).

[25]*Criminal Code*, R.S. 1985, c. C-46, s. 488.

[26]*Genest v. The Queen* (1989) 1 SCR 59, 45 C.C.C. (3d) 385.

[27]*Genest v. The Queen*, supra.

[28]*R. v. Dobney Holdings* (1985) 18 C.C.C. (3d) 238 (B.C.C.A.).

[29]*R. v. Debot* (1989) 2 S.C.R. 1140, 52 C.C.C. (3d) 193.

or not. Any such evidence seized is required to be treated in the same manner as if it had been seized under the authority of a search warrant.[30]

If the execution of a search warrant requires the assistance of civilians whose expertise is essential to the identification or seizure of evidence, such as forensic identification technicians, forensic scientists, accountants, computer experts, mechanics or tradespersons, etc., they may be named on the face of the search warrant. Such persons, even if not named in the search warrant, must remain under the control of the peace officer who is accountable for the search.[31]

10.7 ENTRY OF DWELLING HOUSES TO EFFECT ARRESTS – FEENEY WARRANT

In 1997, the Supreme Court of Canada declared that, except in exigent circumstances,[32] police officers could no longer enter dwelling houses without judicial pre-authorization to effect arrests.[33] An arrest warrant in Form 7.1 – known as a **Feeney Warrant** – may be issued to enter a dwelling house to arrest a person if:

1. reasonable grounds exist to arrest the person without warrant for a *Criminal Code* offence or [the person] has contravened or wilfully failed to comply or is about to fail to comply with a court disposition; or[34]

2. a warrant for a federal offence exists for the person anywhere in Canada; or

3. grounds exist to arrest the person, without warrant, for any federal offence, other than those contained in the *Criminal Code.*

An investigator executing such a warrant must announce the entry unless, at the time of issuance, the justice is satisfied on "information on oath" that entry without prior announcement is necessary to prevent exposure of any person to imminent bodily harm or death or to prevent imminent loss or destruction of evidence.[35] Even after receiving such an authorization for entry without prior announcement, the officer may not enter the dwelling house unless reasonable grounds of the necessity to prevent exposure to imminent bodily harm or death or loss or destruction of evidence exist immediately before the entry.[36]

10.8 WARRANTLESS ENTRY OF DWELLING HOUSES – EXIGENT CIRCUMSTANCES

Where reasonable grounds exist to obtain a search warrant but emergency conditions make it impracticable to obtain a warrant, a peace officer may, in exigent circumstances,

---

[30]*Criminal Code* R.S. 1985, c. C-46.

[31]*R. v. B, (J.E.)* (1989) 52 C.C.C. (3d) 224 (N.S.C.A.).

[32]*Criminal Code,* R.S. 1985, c. C-46, s. 529.1.

[33]*R. v. Feeney* (1997) 2 S.C.R. 13, 115 C.C.C. (3d) 129, 7 C.R. (5th) 101.

[34]*Criminal Code,* R.S. 1985, c. C-46, s. 495(1)(a) and 672.91.

[35]*Criminal Code,* R.S. 1985, c. C-46, s. 529.4(1).

[36]*Criminal Code,* R.S. 1985, c. C-46, s. 529.4(2).

enter a building, receptacle or place and may seize evidence as if he or she were acting under a search warrant issued in accordance with s. 487(1) *Criminal Code*.[37] The exigent circumstances anticipated by this section are the same type as described in s. 529.3(2) *Criminal Code* and would include extreme situations involving imminent bodily harm, death or imminent loss, destruction or removal of evidence.[38]

A similar warrantless authority exists to enter a dwelling house for the purpose of arresting someone without a warrant where reasonable grounds for a warrant exist but it would be impracticable to obtain a warrant due to exigent circumstances and it is necessary to prevent imminent bodily harm, death or imminent loss or destruction of evidence.[39]

Exigent circumstances that justify a warrantless entry to effect an arrest under s. 529.3(1) *Criminal Code* do not excuse the officer(s) of the requirement of prior announcement of their entry. Reasonable grounds must exist, immediately before the entry, to believe that to announce their presence would expose themselves or any person to imminent bodily harm or death or would result in the imminent loss or destruction of evidence, to justify not complying with the prior announcement requirement.[40]

10.9 SEARCHES INVOLVING SOLICITOR - CLIENT PRIVILEGE

The procedures for searching law offices or seizing documents in the possession of a lawyer who claims solicitor–client privilege on behalf of a client, requires that the police officer not examine the seized documents, but seal them in a package which must then be turned over to the local sheriff. Within 14 days of the seizure, either party may apply to a judge to set a hearing date at which time the court will determine whether or not the documents should be disclosed to the police.[41]

10.10 SEARCHES OF MOTOR VEHICLES

Searches of motor vehicles typically present particular difficulty for investigators due to their inherent mobility. Although the reasonable expectation of privacy in relation to a motor vehicle is less than that of a dwelling house, the driver or owner of a motor vehicle still has an obvious expectation of privacy from intrusion resulting from police investigations. This reasonable expectation of privacy does not extend to the passenger of a motor vehicle who is not the owner of it. If reasonable grounds exist to arrest the driver, and/or the owner, if he or she is a person other than the driver and is an occupant of the motor vehicle, the common law warrantless authority to search the prisoner incident to arrest also extends to the motor vehicle.[42]

---

[37]*Criminal Code*, R.S. 1985, c. C-46, s. 487.11.

[38]*Criminal Code*, R.S. 1985, c. C-46, s. 529.3(2).

[39]*Criminal Code*, R.S. 1985, c. C-46, s. 529.3(1).

[40]*Criminal Code*, R.S. 1985, c. C-46, s. 529.4(3).

[41]*Criminal Code*, R.S. 1985, c. C-46, s. 488.1.

[42]*R. v. Belnavis*, (1989) 107 C.C.C. (3d) 195, 36 C.R.R. (2d) 32, 1996 C.R.R. Lexis 241.

The difficulty with searching motor vehicles is that by the time a search warrant is obtained, the vehicle may become mobile and may be far removed from where it was first observed. Exigent circumstances can be claimed where there are reasonable grounds to believe that evidence inside the motor vehicle may be lost or destroyed[43] or in circumstances of a motor vehicle which is either mobile, or is about to move.[44, 45]

BOX 10.5 | **Investigative Relevance**

I was once involved in a case in which a suspect transported bricks of cannabis resin by bus to a location where he had arranged for an accomplice to meet him and drive him by car to an unknown location. Surveillance was maintained at the location where the suspect was to disembark the bus. The accomplice arrived and the suspect was observed to get off the bus, place an overnight bag into the trunk of the vehicle and enter the front passenger seat.

Prior to that moment, while reasonable belief existed that illicit drugs would be in the accomplice's motor vehicle – that event was to occur in the future. Anticipatory or future grounds are not sufficient to obtain a search warrant. When the suspect disembarked from the bus, carrying the package, believed to contain the drugs, he could have been arrested and searched incident to the arrest, however, he might have escaped on the busy thoroughfare or possibly disposed of the drugs during a foot chase.

The conditions for making an arrest were far more controllable after the suspect

had entered the motor vehicle, however, it might then be said that he could have a reasonable expectation of privacy in his personal effects, now inside the vehicle – even though it was not his vehicle.

It was not practicable to obtain a warrant once reasonable grounds existed that the drugs were actually in the car, as the vehicle was about to become mobile. If we had then attempted to obtain a search warrant, who knows where the vehicle would have been by the time the warrant was issued?

Under legislation that existed at that time, both the driver and the passenger were arrested on reasonable grounds that they were in possession of narcotics for the purpose of trafficking. The trunk was opened, incident to the arrest, and the drugs were observed in the overnight bag. As a precaution, and in an effort to demonstrate good faith, the vehicle was towed to a nearby police station and kept under guard while a search warrant for the motor vehicle was obtained to seize the drugs.

If an officer routinely stops a motor vehicle and wishes to examine the glove compartment or trunk for evidence of a crime, absent reasonable grounds to arrest the driver/occupant that would justify a search incident to the arrest, the only lawful methods to search the motor vehicle are:

1. with the consent of the driver / owner; or

2. in exigent circumstances involving articulable reasonable grounds relating to the potential loss or destruction of evidence; or

3. on the authority of a search warrant.

---

[43]*R. v. Grant* (1993), 84 C.C.C. (3d) 97 (S.C.C.).

[44]*R. v. Rao*, (1984) 40 C.R. (3d) 1, 12 C.C.C. (3d) 97 (Ont. C.A.).

[45]Sherriff (1997).

A search warrant to search a dwelling house does not authorize the search of a motor vehicle situated on that property unless it is specifically named on the face of the search warrant as a "place to be searched." Investigators are reminded of the warrantless search authorities for motor vehicles that exist under federal legislation for weapons, ammunition, explosive substances, controlled substances in exigent circumstances,[46] and under provincial legislation for evidence in contravention of those respective acts.

10.11 RETURN TO A JUSTICE – SECTIONS 489.1(1) AND 490 *CRIMINAL CODE*

A police officer who seizes anything under the authority of any of the search warrant provisions of the *Criminal Code*, or without a warrant either incident to arrest,[47] or under the "plain view seizure rule" embodied in section 489, or in exigent circumstances as authorized by sections 117.02(1) or 487.11 *Criminal Code*, must make a return to a justice reporting that he or she has done so.[48] Making a report involves either producing the article(s) seized, and/or making a written report in Form 5.2 *Criminal Code*.

The justice may order the seized item be returned to the rightful owner, if he or she is known, unless the police or prosecutor shows that the item is required for the purposes of investigation, preliminary hearing, trial or other proceeding.[49] Such an order, if granted, is only valid for a period of not more than three months from the date of original seizure[50] and contains provisions that the person in whose custody the item is detained take "reasonable care to ensure that it is preserved."[51] A detention order may be extended for consecutive periods of three months unless, in the meantime, proceedings are instituted in which the item is required as evidence.

In complex, long-term investigations where no charges have been laid, extensions of detention orders beyond one year from the day of seizure must be ordered by a judge of a superior court.[52] Items may be detained for any length of time following a detention order, granted at the time of the initial return to a justice if the lawful owner (or a person lawfully entitled to possess it) consents in writing to its detention for that period.[53]

10.12 SEARCHES FOR WEAPONS, AMMUNITION AND EXPLOSIVE SUBSTANCES

If it is impracticable to obtain a warrant due to exigent circumstances, and a police officer has reasonable grounds to believe that a weapon,[54] imitation firearm, ammunition,

---

[46]*Criminal Code*, R.S. 1985, c. C-46, s. 117.02(1) and 117.04(2). *Controlled Drugs and Substances* 1996, C-19, s. 11.

[47]*R. v. Backhouse* (2005), Unreported case released March 3, 2005 Docket : C35171 (Ont. C.A.).

[48]*Criminal Code*, R.S. 1985, c. C-46, s. 489.1(1).

[49]*Criminal Code*, R.S. 1985, c. C-46, s. 490(1)(a).

[50]*Criminal Code*, R.S. 1985, c. C-46, s. 490(2).

[51]*Criminal Code*, R.S. 1985, c. C-46, s. 490(1)(b).

[52]*Criminal Code*, R.S. 1985, c. C-46, s. 490(3).

[53]*Criminal Code*, R.S. 1985, c. C-46, s. 490(3.1).

[54]*Criminal Code*, R.S. 1985, c. C-46, s. 2.

prohibited device or explosive substance[55] has been used in an offence, or will afford evidence of an offence that has been committed under the *Criminal Code*, he or she may search a person, vehicle or place other than a dwelling house without warrant, and seize that thing.[56]

If a peace officer has reasonable grounds to believe that any person is in possession of a weapon, prohibited device, ammunition or an explosive substance, and that such possession is not desirable in the interests of the safety of any person, a warrant may be obtained to search a dwelling house, building, receptacle or place to seize the thing.[57] If reasonable grounds exist to obtain a such a warrant to search any building, receptacle or place under section 117.04(1) *Criminal Code*, but due to exigent circumstances it is impracticable to obtain a warrant, a peace officer may enter a dwelling house, building, receptacle or place and seize weapons, prohibited devices, ammunition or explosive substances to prevent possible danger to the safety of any person.[58]

The "warrantless exigent circumstances" search provisions for weapons and ammunition contained in the *Criminal Code* are commonly resorted to in cases of persons threatening suicide, incidents involving persons suffering from mental disorders and often in cases of domestic dispute. A search of dwelling houses, buildings, receptacles or places for weapons, prohibited devices, ammunition or explosive substances conducted either with or without warrant also authorizes peace officers to seize any authorization, licence or registration certificate relating to the weapon, ammunition, explosive substance or prohibited device in the possession of the person.

10.13 APPLICATION TO JUSTICE FOR DISPOSITION – SECTION 117.05 *CC*

Where weapons, ammunition, prohibited devices or explosive substances are seized, with or without a warrant, a police officer must, within 30 days of the seizure, apply to a justice for an order of disposition with respect to the thing(s) seized. The justice will set a date for a hearing and direct that notices of the hearing be given to specified persons.[59]

At the hearing, which may be held ***ex parte*** (outside of the presence of the person who is the subject of the application), relevant evidence is heard and the justice may make an order prohibiting the person from the possession of weapons, ammunition or explosive substances for a period not exceeding five years and order that items seized be forfeited to the Crown or otherwise disposed of in a manner directed by the court.[60]

10.14 GENERAL WARRANTS

In 1997, amendments to the *Criminal Code* provided investigators with the legal means to obtain authority to seize evidence, obtain information and utilize investigative techniques

---

[55]*Criminal Code*, R.S. 1985, c. C-46, s. 84(1).

[56]*Criminal Code*, R.S. 1985, c. C-46, s. 117.02(1)

[57]*Criminal Code*, R.S. 1985, c. C-46, s. 117.04(1).

[58]*Criminal Code*, R.S. 1985, c. C-46, s. 117.04(2).

[59]*Criminal Code*, R.S. 1985, c. C-46, s. 117.05(1).

[60]*Criminal Code*, R.S. 1985, c. C-46, s. 117.05.

that had previously been held to constitute unreasonable search and seizures, but were not authorized under the search warrant provisions of s. 487(1) *Criminal Code*. General warrants may now be issued by *"a provincial court judge or a judge of a superior court of criminal jurisdiction"* to authorize investigative techniques, procedures, the use of devices or any thing in relation to a person or his or her property, which if not authorized, would result in a section 8 *Charter of Rights* violation.[61] The general warrant provisions specifically do not permit anything that would interfere *"with the bodily integrity of any person."*[62]

General warrants now authorize the seizure of intangible things such as information, biological samples for DNA analysis,[63] or to obtain comparison samples of a person's hand, foot or fingerprints, or teeth impressions.[64] General warrants also permit investigators to utilize investigative techniques including: the installation of tracking devices; surreptitious video surveillance installations;[65] to conduct perimeter searches; or to monitor a person's mail deliveries. The issuing judge must be satisfied on oath in writing that it is in the best interests of the administration of justice to issue the warrant and may place "such terms and conditions as the justice considers advisable to ensure that any search or seizure ... is reasonable."[66]

The process for obtaining and executing a general warrant is virtually the same as for a 487(1) *Criminal Code* search warrant except that general warrants may only be issued by a provincial court judge or a judge of a superior court of criminal jurisdiction. General warrants may also be obtained through the same telewarrant procedures as contained in s. 487.1 *Criminal Code*. A general warrant may be "backed" for execution in a different territorial division than the one in which it was issued if executing the general warrant would require entering upon private property in the other province, or involves DNA collection, tracking devices or a number recorder.[67] Any physical item seized as the result of a general warrant must also be the subject of a return to a justice under s. 490 *Criminal Code*.

10.15 ASSISTANCE ORDERS – SECTION 487.02 *CRIMINAL CODE*

A judge or justice who issues a warrant under the *Criminal Code* or who authorizes the interception of private communications or the installation of a number recorder, may also order that any person whose assistance is necessary to assist in the execution of the order provide such assistance as may be reasonably required. Assistance orders might be directed to employees of a telephone company to assist with the installation of surreptitious intercepting equipment or to search and compile customer billing records. Assistance orders may also be used to compel employees of Canada Post to assist with the interception of mail addressed by or to the subject of an investigation.[68]

---

[61]*Criminal Code*, R.S. 1985, c. C-46, s. 487.01(1).

[62]*Criminal Code*, R.S. 1985, c. C-46, s. 487.01(2).

[63]*Criminal Code*, R.S. 1985, c. C-46, s. 487.05.

[64]*Criminal Code*, R.S. 1985, c. C-46, s. 487.092(1).

[65]*Criminal Code*, R.S. 1985, c. C-46, s. 487.01(4).

[66]*Criminal Code*, R.S. 1985, c. C-46, s. 487.01(3).

[67]*Criminal Code*, R.S. 1985, c. C-46, s. 487.03(1).

[68]*Canada Post Corp. v. Canada (Attorney General)* (1995), 95 C.C.C. (3d) 568 (Ont. Ct. (Gen. Div.).

10.16 MAJOR CRIME INVESTIGATION

The remaining section of this chapter is dedicated to an overview of selected offences which are commonly encountered by criminal investigators. This is not an exhaustive list of "major crimes," nor anything else beyond a mere introduction to criminal investigation. This admittedly cursory treatment is necessitated both by the limitations of space, as well as the depth and duration of curriculum for the student. While there are indeed crimes, such as murder, which are far more likely considered to be a "major crime," sudden death investigation is covered at an introductory level in Chapter 11.

10.16.1 Theft

"Thieves respect property; they merely wish the property to become their property that they may more perfectly respect it."[69]

G.K. Chesterton, British author (1874-1936).

Facts in Issue for Theft

- Every one who

- fraudulently and without colour of right takes or converts

- to their own use or the use of another person

- anything, animate or inanimate

- with intent to deprive the owner of it

- or a person who has special property or interest in it

- of the thing, or property or interest.[70]

Theft is a frequently encountered criminal offence that covers a variety of crimes, the majority of which are not considered major crimes, including shoplifting, other forms of petty theft, pick-pocketing, thefts of gasoline from service stations, vehicle thefts, etc. What all thefts share in common is the unlawful taking or converting of property with the intention of depriving the owner, or a person having an interest in it, of the property. Theft is the most common property crime and is often assigned to entry-level investigators in order to gain experience before being entrusted to investigate more "serious" crimes.

In Canada, thefts are classified by the value of the property stolen and are categorized as being either under or over $5 000 in value. The item stolen can be anything, tangible or intangible; animate or inanimate, as long as someone can be shown to have a proprietory or special interest in the object that is stolen. As an offence, theft may be committed alone or in conjunction with other offences, ranging from break enter and theft to even murder.

---

[69]G.K. Chesterton: *The Man Who Was Thursday* (1908). Quote retrieved March 9, 2005, from www.amusingquotes.com/h/s/stealing_1

[70]*Criminal Code* R.S. 1985, c. C-46, s. 322(1)(a).

A person may even steal his or her own property from someone else who holds a "special interest" in it, such as in the case of someone who steals his car back from an auto mechanic who has a financial interest in the parts and labour costs incurred as the result of repairing the vehicle. Not all thefts require a direct taking of an item – theft may also be committed by conversion.

A person commits theft by conversion when changing something to their use, such as if a person was given something which they kept without colour of right (legal justification or excuse). An example of a conversion type of theft would be a person withdrawing money inadvertently deposited into their bank account or received from an automated teller machine (ATM) and refusing to return it to the bank.

While theft is often done secretively, it need only involve taking or converting something with a fraudulent purpose with an intent to deprive the owner of it. A person who presents him or herself at a car dealership as a prospective purchaser who wishes to take a demo model for a test drive, and then drives it directly into a container for shipping to a foreign country, commits theft, notwithstanding that the owner parted with the property voluntarily. The thief, although not acting secretively, took the car for a fraudulent purpose with the requisite *animus furandi*, meaning the intent to deprive the owner of the property.

Section 322 *Criminal Code* defines the general offence of theft and establishes that a theft is considered complete, "when, with intent to steal anything, he [or she] moves it or causes it to move or to be moved, or begins to cause it to become movable."[71] The punishment for theft is set out in section 334 *Criminal Code*, which states that if the value of the property stolen is over $5 000 or is a testamentary instrument (a will, codicil or other writing in relation to a person's will), the maximum penalty is a term of imprisonment not exceeding 10 years. If the value of the property stolen is not over $5 000 in value, the accused, if prosecuted by indictment, is liable to imprisonment for a period not exceeding 2 years or may be guilty of an offence punishable on summary conviction.

The *Criminal Code* sets out several other ways in which the offence of theft may be committed, including:

- s. 323 CC – theft from oyster beds;

- s. 324 CC – theft by a bailee of thing under lawful seizure by a peace or public officer;

- s. 326 CC – theft of electricity, natural gas or telecommunication service;

- s. 328 CC – theft by or from a person having special interest;

- s. 330 CC – theft by a person required to account for the proceeds of anything entrusted to them;

- s. 331 CC – theft by a person holding power of attorney;

- s. 332 CC – misappropriation of money or valuable security held under direction for the sale of real or personal property;

- s. 338(2) CC – punishment for theft of cattle; and

- s. 339 CC – theft of drift timber.

---

[71]*Criminal Code*, R.S. 1985, c. C-46, s. 322(2).

Other criminal offences resembling theft which do not necessarily involve an intentional conversion of the property taken to the use of the person taking it, are:

- s. 335 CC — taking a motor vehicle or vessel without the owner's consent with intent to drive/use/navigate or operate it; and

- s. 336 CC — criminal breach of trust by a trustee (converting, with intent to defraud, anything held in trust to a purpose not authorized by the trust).

During theft investigations, it is often not possible to prove the identity of the person responsible for committing the theft, even where the stolen property is recovered. If a person is found to be in possession of stolen property, a situation combining the elements of knowledge + consent + control, he or she may be charged with the offence of Possession of Property obtained by the Commission of an Indictable Offence, contrary to section 354(1) *Criminal Code*.

Where the person in whose possession recently stolen property is found elects not to provide an explanation of the circumstances of that possession, the Doctrine of Recent Possession (see Section 2.15), may be used to infer the accused's guilt for the theft.

A person may, however, not be convicted of the theft of an item and also of the possession of the same stolen item under the legal doctrine of *res judicata*, which protects people against being convicted for two offences arising out of the same set of facts or circumstances.[72]

Thieves can be motivated purely by greed to have certain property without obtaining it through legitimate means and/or if no other means to obtain it are available to them. Thefts are often motivated by the need to support a criminal lifestyle or addiction, in which case the stolen property is converted into cash for living expenses or is used to purchase drugs. The sooner that stolen property changes hands, the greater the probability the thief can avoid detection for the theft.[73]

Stolen property should be described in as much detail as possible and be thoroughly documented in the investigator's notebook, police reports, police service records management system and entered on the Canadian Police Information Centre (CPIC). The *modus operandi* used by the thief should also be documented; criminals, like all other people, are creatures of habit.

A similar *modus operandi* (M.O.) in multiple crimes might give investigators grounds to suspect that similar crimes are the work of a common offender. Clues from one investigation may be used to solve another. For this reason, circulating details of a major theft to canvass other investigators is often useful in identifying similarities so that information may be shared, resources may be combined and, if necessary, investigations may be integrated.

Investigators should exhaustively examine the scenes of even minor thefts for physical evidence that might identify the person(s) responsible for the theft, as large numbers of similar crimes are usually the work of a relatively small number of offenders. While some thefts are far more complex than others, there is no such thing as a "minor" crime.

---

[72]*R. v. Kienapple* (1975) 1 S.C.R. 729, 15 C.C.C. (2d) 524, 26 C.R.N.S. 1.

[73]Weston & Wells (1997).

10.16.2 Breaking and Entering

"Good swiping is an art in itself."

Jules Feiffer, American cartoonist
and screenwriter (b. 1929).[74]

Facts in Issue

- Every one who

- breaks and enters a place with intent to commit an indictable offence, or

- breaks and enters a place and commits an indictable offence, or

- breaks out of a place after committing an indictable offence, or

- breaks out of a place after entering with the intent to commit an indictable offence.[75]

Breaking and entering is another common property offence, but one which I consider to be more complex and deserving of inclusion in the classification of "major crime" due to the increased level of expertise and intent generally required over and above other property crimes to commit it and in the sheer impact it has on our society.

Before analyzing the facts in issue describing the different methods of breaking and entering and the two similar offences of breaking out of a place, we must first examine three key definitions: "break," "enter" and "place."

"Break" means "to open any part, internal or external, or to open any thing that is used or intended to be used to close or to cover an internal or external opening."[76]

We see that for the purposes of breaking and entering, the accused need not break a window or kick in a door or even gain entry to the "place" being broken into or out of. By merely opening a door or a window, a person would satisfy the Criminal Code definition of "break" for the purposes of this offence.

"Enter" means "(a) a person enters as soon as any part of his body or any part of an instrument that he uses is within any thing that is being entered; and (b) a person shall be deemed to have broken and entered if (i) he obtained entrance by a threat or artifice or by collusion with a person within, or (ii) he entered without lawful justification or excuse, the proof of which lies upon him, by a permanent or temporary opening."[77]

The definition of enter means that the accused need not be fully inside the "place" being entered to satisfy this definition. Once the mere tip of a screwdriver or other break-in tool enters a door jamb or window, or once the accused reaches any part of his or her body inside a window to unlock a door, etc., the accused will be deemed to have "entered."

An accused person will also be deemed to have broken and entered if he or she gained entry to any place by threat or by fraudulent means. Being granted entry as the result of

---

[74]Jules Feiffer quote retrieved March 12, 2005, from www.giga-usa.com/quotes/topics/robbery

[75]*Criminal Code*, R.S. 1985, c. C-46, s. 348(1).

[76]*Criminal Code*, R.S. 1985, c. C-46, s. 321.

[77]*Criminal Code*, R.S. 1985, c. C-46, s. 350.

threatening any occupant within or by entering under the pretext of working for a utility company or being a police officer, etc., satisfies the *Criminal Code* definition of "enter", whether or not any force was used to open or break any internal or external covering or permanent or temporary opening or whether any damage was caused to the thing.

An accused who enters any "place" in collusion, meaning with the agreement and voluntary assistance of someone inside the place, typically a disgruntled employee of a business, they are also deemed to have broken and entered.[78]

An accused who enters an industrial site or a house or structure under construction through a permanent or temporary opening, such as a fence or unfinished doorway to steal goods or building materials is deemed to have "broken and entered" if he or she entered without lawful justification. This is a **rebuttable presumption** of law, meaning that once the entry through a permanent or temporary opening is proved, the onus to prove the existence of a legal justification for entry now falls upon the accused.[79]

"Place" means all of the locations which it is possible to break into or out of and includes: "(a) a dwelling house; (b) a building or structure or any part thereof, other than a dwelling house; (c) a railway vehicle, a vessel, an aircraft or a trailer; or (d) a pen or an enclosure in which fur-bearing animals are kept in captivity for breeding or commercial purposes."[80]

The list of locations that satisfy the *Criminal Code* definition of "place" is quite comprehensive. A person can break and enter a dwelling house, which includes residences, apartments and mobile units, such as tents, recreational vehicles, etc., "designed to be used as a permanent or temporary residence and that is being used as such a residence."[81] Place also includes a building or structure of any description, other than a dwelling house, including garages, sheds, warehouses, businesses, etc., railway vehicles, boats, aircraft, trailers or pens for fur-bearing animals kept in captivity for breeding or commercial purposes.

If the location entered does not fit with the definition of "place," a person may not be charged with breaking into it. Anything that isn't a "place," such as an automobile or a mobile unit designed to be used as a permanent or temporary residence that was not being used as a residence at the time of the offence, is not included in the definition of "place." If an accused were to smash the window of an automobile and steal a compact disc player or other personal effects, he or she may be charged with the theft of the items but not with breaking and entering the vehicle – because a motor vehicle is not considered to be a "place." An exception would be in the case of a recreational vehicle, designed to be used as a temporary residence and actually being used as a temporary residence – not necessarily occupied – at the time of the offence.

By examining the facts in issue for the offence of breaking and entering, we see that there are four different ways by which a person might commit the offence of break and enter.

1. Breaking and entering a place with intent to commit an indictable offence:
This offence applies to an individual who breaks into a place and is either apprehended prior to committing any indictable offence or is unsuccessful in carrying out their purpose of committing an indictable offence once they have entered.

---

[78]*Criminal Code*, R.S. 1985, c. C-46, s. 350(b)(i).

[79]*Criminal Code*, R.S. 1985, c. C-46, s. 350(b)(ii).

[80]*Criminal Code*, R.S. 1985, c. C-46, s. 348(3)

[81]*Criminal Code*, R.S. 1985, c. C-46, s. 2

2. Breaking and entering a place and committing an indictable offence:

An accused breaks and enters, by any of the described methods, any location included in the definition of place and commits an indictable offence. Typically, the indictable offence committed is a theft; however, it may also include assault, sexual assault, arson, mischief, etc.

3. Breaking out of a place after committing an indictable offence:

An accused enters a place without legal justification (the proof of which lies upon the accused), commits an indictable offence, following which he or she breaks out of the place (using the reverse definition of breaking in). This offence applies to anyone who enters a business during business hours and once inside conceals him or herself until after the business closed. After committing an indictable offence, for example, a theft, the accused then "breaks out." The method of breaking out could be as simple as opening a door from the inside and walking away.

4. Breaking out of a place after entering the place with the intent to commit an indictable offence:

An accused enters a place without legal justification (the proof of which lies upon the accused), but is unable to commit the indictable offence he or she entered with the intention of committing. For example, an accused enters a business during business hours, and conceals him or herself with the intention of breaking open a safe or vault on the premises after the business closes and stealing the daily receipts. After being unsuccessful at breaking open the vault, the would-be thief then breaks out of the premises (using the reverse definition of breaking in). He or she could be convicted of breaking out after having entered with the intention of committing an indictable offence.

Either the actual commission of an indictable offence or the intention to commit an indictable offence is therefore a necessary element of these offences. When an indictable offence is committed, there is usually evidence of its commission and a charge would require that it be specified within the wording of the information.

For example, "John Smith, on or about the 12th day of March 2005, at the City of Barrie in the Central East Region, did unlawfully break and enter a certain place, to wit: a dwelling house situated at 1313 Mockingbird Lane, in the City of Barrie and did commit therein the indictable offence of theft contrary to paragraph 348(1)(d) of the *Criminal Code*." The wording of the information need not specify what is alleged to have been stolen – only that an indictable offence was committed.

Proving that a person either entered a place with the intention of committing an indictable offence or broke out of a place after committing an indictable offence or entered the place with the intention of committing an indictable offence, would be far more difficult were it not for the rebuttable presumption in s. 348(2) *Criminal Code*. This presumption in law may be relied upon once it is proved that an accused broke and entered or broke out of a place.

Such proof is, in absence of evidence to the contrary, proof that the accused either broke and entered with the intent to commit an indictable offence; or broke out either after committing an indictable offence or having entered with the intent to commit an indictable offence. The burden of proving he or she did not have any such intent to commit an indictable offence falls to the accused.

The complexity of the break and enter will reflect the skills necessary to commit the offence and will help to focus the investigation as to the identity of the offender(s). For example, did the accused defeat any intrusion alarm system? Was the volume of the property stolen such that it required transport above the capability of an offender acting on impulse alone?

The specialized nature, if any, of any property stolen may also focus on where the property may be disposed of, possibly leading back to the person(s) responsible for the crime. The amount of planning, preparation and criminal sophistication of the person(s) responsible for the offence is determined by factors such as whether or not the offender(s) brought the break-in tools to a scene or used tools found at the scene.

BOX 10.6 | Proper Investigative Procedure

When examining a break and enter crime scene, investigators should always take care to avoid contamination and to identify and preserve physical evidence. Tire marks, tool marks, footwear and fingerprint impressions are commonly encountered at break and enter crime scenes. Look for trace fibre evidence snagged on fences, window openings and other points of entry. It is not uncommon for an offender to injure themselves while committing an entry into the premises due to the amount of force that is usually required. DNA evidence from dried blood at or near a point of entry can circumstantially establish the offender's presence at a crime scene and may be used to infer his or her guilt for the break and enter.

10.16.3 Being Unlawfully in a Dwelling House

A section related to the offence of breaking and entering is the offence of "Being Unlawfully in a Dwelling House." This dual procedure offence, punishable by a term of imprisonment not exceeding 10 years, does not require that the accused commit a "break" for the purpose of entering a dwelling house. The offence does not apply to any location other than a dwelling house.

Facts in Issue:

- Every one who

- enters or is in a dwelling house

- without lawful excuse, the proof of which lies on them

- with intent to commit an indictable offence.[82]

The facts in issue provide for situations in which the accused unlawfully entered the dwelling house with the intent to commit an indictable offence, such as assault, theft, robbery, sexual assault, arson, etc. This charge also applies to cases where the accused formed the intent to commit the indictable offence after he or she was inside the dwelling house, or unlawfully remained in the dwelling house.

---

[82]*Criminal Code*, R.S. 1985, c. C-46, s. 349.

This offence contains its own rebuttable presumption by establishing that the evidence that an accused either entered or was in a dwelling house without lawful excuse "is, in the absence of any evidence to the contrary, proof that he entered or was in the dwelling house with intent to commit an indictable offence therein."[83] Although this offence is not intended to replace any lesser offences, such as trespassing, the arrest provisions of this offence might be resorted to in any situation where a suspect remains in the dwelling house of another person, without lawful excuse.

10.16.4 Possession of Break-in Tools

Facts in Issue:

- Every one who

- without lawful excuse (the proof of which lies on him or her)

- has possession of any instrument, suitable for the purpose of breaking into

- any place, motor vehicle, vault or safe

- in circumstances where it may be reasonably inferred

- that the instrument had been used or was intended to be used

- for such a purpose.[84]

Occasionally, patrolling uniformed officers locate persons under suspicious circumstances that suggest the person has been involved in a break-in or is intending to commit a break and enter. Such circumstances include finding a person with a criminal record for theft and or break and enter convictions behind a commercial location, in the early morning hours, without any reasonable explanation for his or her presence, and being in possession of crow-bars, electrical meters, screwdrivers, vise-grips and duct tape. If a break and enter hasn't already occurred, it is a safe bet that one has just been prevented.

The *Criminal Code* also provides us with an enforcement opportunity for any person found under such circumstances without lawful excuse, the proof of which lies on them. If a person has in his or her possession (knowledge + consent + control) any type of instrument that could be used to break into any place, motor vehicle, vault or safe that creates a reasonable inference that the instrument had been used or was intended to be used for such a purpose, he or she may be arrested.

The offence of possession of break-in instruments is an indictable offence, the maximum punishment for which is a term of imprisonment not exceeding 10 years. For the purposes of the charge of possession of break-in instruments, it doesn't matter that a motor vehicle is not a place – it is in addition to a place. If the person is found in a parking lot preparing to break into a vehicle, he or she may still be charged – not for the break and enter – but for the possession of the break-in instruments.

---

[83]*Criminal Code*, R.S. 1985, c. C-46, s. 349(2).

[84]*Criminal Code*, R.S. 1985, c. C-46, s. 351(1)

See s. 352 *Criminal Code* for a similar offence, punishable by a term of imprisonment not exceeding two years for possession of any instrument suitable for breaking into a coin-operated device or currency exchange device.

10.16.5 Using a Disguise in Commission of an Indictable Offence

The second part of s. 351 *Criminal Code* deals specifically with offenders who attempt to conceal their identity through the use of disguises or masks etc., and creates an additional indictable offence, punishable by a term of imprisonment not exceeding 10 years.

Facts in Issue:

- Every one who

- with intent to commit an indictable offence

- while his or her face is masked, coloured, or otherwise disguised[85]

The relatively high maximum punishment of imprisonment not exceeding 10 years for the offences of possession of break-in instruments and using a disguise, in my opinion, reflect Parliament's recognition that such actions are the hallmarks of more sophisticated criminality that reflect a high degree of *mens rea*, planning and a lesser degree of impulsivity on the part of the offender.

10.16.6 Robbery

"I am a brigand: I live by robbing the rich.
I am a gentleman: I live by robbing the poor."[86]

George Bernard Shaw, Irish dramatist, novelist and critic (1856-1950).

Facts in Issue:

- Every one who

- steals and

- uses violence or threats of violence to a person or property

- for the purpose of extorting whatever is stolen or

- to prevent or overcome resistance to the stealing, or

- steals from any person and

- wounds, beats, strikes or uses personal violence to that person

- immediately before, during or immediately after, or

---

[85]*Criminal Code*, R.S. 1985, c. C-46, s. 351(2).

[86]George Bernard Shaw (*Man and Superman*), quote retrieved March 12, 2005, from www.giga-usa.com/quotes/topics/robbery

- assaults any person
- with intent to steal from them, or
- steals from any person
- while armed with an offensive weapon or imitation thereof.[87]

The key elements of the offence of robbery can therefore be graphically illustrated using the following equation: theft + violence (personal or threatened) = robbery. It is this introduction of personal violence, threats of violence or the use of a weapon that, in my opinion, establishes robbery as a "major crime."

Robberies range in complexity from random purse-snatchings involving actual violence to victims of opportunity,[88] to highly organized bank/armoured truck robberies – but the only differences are the amount of property stolen and the potential for violence, relative to the individual circumstances. As seen from the facts in issue of robbery, the violence may only involve a threat of violence and may be in relation to property or to the victim or a person other than the victim.[89]

The threat of violence need only be an implied threat, such as a written hold-up note stating, "Give me all your money." Once the threat has been delivered, there is no further requirement for physical violence against the victim.[90]

If the robber does in fact steal from any person and either immediately before the theft uses personal violence to the victim or does so during or immediately after the theft, the offender may be charged with robbery.[91] This method of committing robbery requires both proof of the theft and the violence to the victim.

A complete offence of robbery occurs even if there is no theft when the robber assaults his or her victim, if at the time of the offence he or she had the intent to steal from the victim. Therefore, a charge of robbery could be laid where a robbery was intended and the accused was assaulted [as defined in s. 365(1) *Criminal Code*] but no theft occurred because the victim had nothing to steal or if the robber was prevented from stealing by the victim, bystanders or the arrival of police, etc.[92] It is important to note that this method of committing robbery requires only proof of the violence committed with the intention to steal.

The last method of committing a robbery is to steal from any person while armed with an offensive weapon or imitation thereof.[93] This method of robbery, referred to as "armed robbery," does not require that the weapon or imitation be used during the robbery or that there was any intent on the part of the robber to use the weapon or

---

[87]*Criminal Code*, R.S. 1985, c. C-46, s. 343.

[88]*R. v. Picard* (1976), 39 C.C.C. (2d) 57 (Que. Sess. Ct.).

[89]*Criminal Code*, R.S. 1985, c. C-46, s. 343(a).

[90]*R. v. Katrensky* (1975), 24 C.C.C. (2d) 350 (1975), 5 W.W.R. 732 (B.C. Prov. Ct.); *R. v. Pelletier* (1992), 71 C.C.C. (3d) 438, 44 Q.A.C. 168 (C.A.); *R. v. Lecky* (2001), 157 C.C.C. (3d) 351 (Ont. C.A.).

[91]*Criminal Code*, R.S. 1985, c. C-36, s. 343(b).

[92]*Criminal Code*, R.S. 1985, c. C-36, s. 343(c).

[93]*Criminal Code*, R.S. 1985, c. C-36, s. 343(d).

imitation – only that the accused was armed with an offensive weapon at the time of the robbery.[94] Section 2 *Criminal Code* gives the same meaning of offensive weapon as for weapon, however, this section also provides that an accused may be convicted for being armed with an imitation of a weapon, such as a starter's pistol or replica handgun, etc.

The punishment for the offence of robbery reflects the severity of the crime itself and sets out the maximum punishment for all robberies as life imprisonment. In cases where a firearm is used to commit a robbery, the law specifies the minimum punishment of a four-year term of imprisonment. A court may consider factors such as: the time of a robbery committed in relation to a dwelling house; whether the accused knew or was reckless as to whether the dwelling house was occupied; and the accused's actual use of violence as an aggravating factor when imposing sentence.

Although the *Criminal Code* does not define home-invasion robberies, this section does recognize this new crime trend and imposes a harsher sentence upon an accused in relation to offences of extortion, forcible confinement, breaking and entering or robbery, committed in relation to dwelling houses.[95]

Identification of the accused is of paramount importance in robbery cases. Obtain detailed descriptions of the offender(s) from victims or witnesses and circulate the description and M.O. to other investigators and other police services. Question the witnesses as to any words spoken by the offender(s), accent, the clothing worn, etc. If an escape was made on foot, consider the use of a canine team to attempt to track the fleeing offender and search the route for any discarded evidence.

Consider the use of composite drawings, mug-shot books and photographic lineups for witnesses who may be able to identify an offender. Check the use of police intelligence files, records of previous solved and unsolved robberies, as well as probation and parole records. There is a far higher probability that a complex robbery was committed by repeat offender(s).

If a mask or hat worn by the offender is recovered, consider that hair follicles or trace evidence of blood or saliva can be analyzed to yield the offender's DNA. Discarded evidence of sufficient surface characteristics as well as recovered hold-up notes may also be fingerprinted. Hold-up notes may also be subjected to handwriting comparison in the event that a suspect is identified at a later time. Handle all evidence using latex gloves and protect them from contamination.

If the offender(s) make their escape by a vehicle that can be described, the use of roadblocks can be effective in apprehending or containing the fleeing offenders. An investigator should also consider that if the offenders utilized a stolen vehicle to commit the robbery, it may be found abandoned a short distance from the robbery scene. Such a recovered vehicle should be towed and thoroughly examined for forensic evidence. The details of the original theft of a getaway vehicle may provide details regarding the person(s) responsible for the robbery.

---

[94]*Tremblay v. Quebec (Attorney General)* (1984), 43 C.R. (3d) 92 (Que. C.A.).

[95]*Criminal Code*, R.S. 1985, c. C-46, s. 348(1).

| BOX 10.7 | Proper Investigative Procedure |

Police officers – uniformed, plainclothes, on-duty or off-duty – should never enter high-risk robbery locations such as banks, convenience stores, gas stations, etc., without first surveying the interior to the extent that it is possible to do so, to assure themselves that the premises is not being robbed. More than one police officer has inadvertently walked into an armed robbery in progress, giving the robber the impression that he or she was responding to the robbery.

If an armed robbery is thought to be in progress, never – under any circumstances – attempt to enter any premises being robbed, or otherwise disrupt a robbery in progress. This may only result in your being taken hostage or becoming a casualty. Call for immediate backup and do your best to observe and contain the situation without putting yourself or any possible hostage inside the premises in danger.

An attempted takedown of an armed robber exiting the premises could result either in the robber(s) re-entering the premises and taking hostages or engaging you in a fire-fight, in which you may find yourself outnumbered and outgunned. Neither the banks, nor your police service, nor the public you are sworn to serve expect you to be wounded or killed over property, when less-violent arrests may be made in a manner and at a time of your choosing – with minimal or reduced risk to innocent bystanders, the offender(s) and the police. Property can always be replaced – lives cannot.

The tactics made famous in a classic scene of my all-time favourite police movie, *Dirty Harry*, starring Clint Eastwood – in which Inspector Harry Callaghan begrudgingly disturbs his lunch to single-handedly thwart an armed robbery by shooting up a neighbourhood and threatening a wounded robber at gunpoint – bear no resemblance whatsoever to real-life, accepted police procedure.

10.16.7 Assault (Level I, Level II and Level III)

"There are more pleasant things to do than beat up people."

Muhammad Ali, Former World Heavyweight Boxing Champion (b. 1942).[96]

Facts in Issue:

- Every one who
- intentionally
- applies force to another person
- without their consent
- attempts or threatens to apply force to another person
- by an act or gesture
- if the victim believes it can be done, or
- while openly wearing or carrying

---

[96]Muhammed Ali quote retrieved November 23, 2003, from www.quotationspage.com

- a weapon or imitation thereof

- accosts, impedes or begs.[97]

Assault is a wide-ranging crime that is classified under Canadian law as either Level I, Level II, or Level III, depending on the level of force used, the severity of injury to the victim, and whether or not a weapon was used in the commission of the respective offence. The facts in issue for Level I, listed above, can be committed in any of the three methods, only the first of which requires an actual application of force.[98]

Level I assault may also be committed if the accused attempts or threatens to apply force by an act or gesture, such as a raised fist or drawing a finger across one's own throat, if the victim believes that the accused has the ability to carry out their purpose. The final method in which Level I assault may be committed is if an accused person openly wears or carries a weapon or imitation of a weapon and accosts (approaches in a menacing manner), impedes (blocks, obstructs or hinders a person), or begs. This definition of assault applies to all other forms of assault, including all forms of sexual assault.[99] (See: Sexual Offences)

In addition to the intentional application of force to a person without his or her consent, a charge of Level II assault is warranted where the assailant "carries, uses or threatens to use a weapon or an imitation thereof"[100]. It is not necessary to prove that an assailant who carried a weapon or imitation of a weapon, used the weapon or imitation to commit the assault – only that he or she carried it. Nor is it necessary to prove that an assailant who threatens to use a weapon while committing an assault has the weapon in his immediate possession.[101]

A 1993 Yukon Territories case law decision established that a dog, and presumably other animals, can fulfill the definition of a weapon if such an animal were ordered to attack the victim, whether or not injury resulted.[102] In cases where a weapon was used in committing an assault, there is no requirement of proof that the weapon used actually caused the bodily harm.[103]

Whether or not a weapon is used in the commission of an assault, where the assailant causes bodily harm to the victim,[104] as defined in section 2 *Criminal Code*, the assault is considered as a Level II assault. The rule of thumb that I always used to determine "bodily harm" was whether or not the victim had to receive medical intervention as the result of his or her injuries. While a black eye may be painful and unsightly, it is transient in nature and will quickly heal – not bodily harm. Injuries that require sutures to close wounds, broken teeth, fractured bones, or concussions, etc., do require some degree of medical intervention and even though such injuries are not considered to be life-threatening, nor do they result in permanent effects, they are usually sufficient to be considered "bodily harm."

---

[97]*Criminal Code*, R.S. 1985, c. C-46, s. 265(1).

[98]*Criminal Code*, R.S. 1985, c. C-46, s. 265(1)(a).

[99]*Criminal Code*, R.S. 1985, c. C-46, s. 265(2).

[100]*Criminal Code*, R.S. 1985, c. C-46, s. 267(a).

[101]*R. v. Kelly* (1983), 37 C.R. (3d) 190 (B.C. Co. Ct.).

[102]*R. v. McLeod*, (1993) 84 C.C.C.(3d) 336 (Y.T.C.A.).

[103]*R. v. Richard* (1992), 72 C.C.C. (3d) 349, 110 N.S.R. (2d) 345 C.A.

[104]*Criminal Code*, R.S. 1985, c. C-46, s. 267(b).

Level III assault is the most serious form of assault and involves more serious injuries in which the assailant "wounds, maims, disfigures, or endangers the life of the complainant."[105] The injuries anticipated by this section involve far more severity than mere bodily harm and quite often involve permanent injury. I once charged and convicted an accused of Aggravated Assault where the evidence showed that he had repeatedly choked a victim to unconsciousness.

10.16.7.1 Consent

"Victims of [2002] sexual offences knew the accused in 80 percent of cases. About 10 percent were assaulted by a friend, while 41 percent were assaulted by an acquaintance. Just over one-quarter (28 percent) were assaulted by a family member, while the remaining 20 percent were victimized by a stranger."

Statistics Canada.[106]

During the course of routine human activities, it is common for individuals to voluntarily consent to situations where, had it not been for their consent, would have constituted assault. Amateur and professional sports, bar-room disputes, and consensual sexual relations, are all examples of instances in which varying degrees of physical contact or force are acceptable, providing the person to whom the force, however minor, is applied gives his or her consent.

Consent is often a contested issue during investigations and prosecutions of various types of assault. The court must then weigh the testimony of witnesses in order to determine their credibility in assessing whether or not the circumstances that are the subject matter of the trial were consensual or not. The defence of "consent" is not available to an accused where consent is obtained involuntarily, in any of the following ways:

1. through the application of force to any person, including the complainant;

2. through the threat of application of force to any person;

3. through deceit or fraud; or

4. through the exercise of authority.[107]

Additionally, for the purposes of Sexual Assault Levels I, II and III, no consent is obtained where:

5. consent is expressed by a person other than the complainant;

6. the complainant is, in any way, incapable of consenting;

7. the complainant is induced to consent due to the abuse of power, trust or authority;

---

[105]*Criminal Code*, 1985, c. C-46, s. 268(1).

[106]Statistics Canada: *The Daily*, Friday, July 25, 2003.

[107]*Criminal Code*, 1985, c. C-46, s. 265(3).

8. the complainant expresses a lack of consent in any way; or

9. the complainant, having consented to sexual activity, in any way expresses a lack of consent to continue the activity.[108]

Experienced investigators need to familiarize themselves with the various sexual offences contained in the *Criminal Code*, such as sexual assault, and sexual offences against children, including: luring children by means of a computer for the purpose of committing sexual offences;[109] sexual interference;[110] sexual exploitation;[111] and invitation to sexual touching.[112] Advanced interviewing techniques for child and adult sexual assault victims are beyond the scope of this textbook. Investigations of these types of offences may benefit from utilizing the services of an experienced sexual assault investigator or someone with expertise in working with child victims, in such cases.

Physical evidence in all assault cases and sexual offence cases is crucial and can vary significantly with the individual circumstances of the case. Always consider the possibility of the single or double transfer of physical evidence between the victim and the offender, the victim and the scene and the offender and the scene. Where consent is the key issue, identification of the suspect is stipulated. In those cases where identification of the suspect is central to the case, spare no effort in gathering evidence to prove the identification or to determine the validity of alibi evidence, if any.

The Ontario Sex Offender Registry (SOR) was established under *Christopher's Law*, so named in memory of 11-year-old Christopher Stephenson, who was murdered in 1988 by a paroled sex offender. The SOR is an automated database that assists police services by identifying all registered sex offenders living within a particular geographic area.

On December 15, 2004 Bill C-16, the *Sex Offender Information Registration Act*, was proclaimed in law and is intended to establish a National Sex Offender Registry to track registered sex offenders. Investigators are reminded that while sex offender registries are a useful investigative aid, dangerous sex offenders and murderers such as Paul Bernardo and Michael Briere had no previous criminal convictions at the time of their arrest for heinous crimes, and would thus not have been included in registries.

10.16.8 Arson

"The professional arsonist builds vacant lots for money."

Jimmy Breslin, American journalist (b. 1930).[113]

Facts in Issue:

- Every one who

- intentionally, or recklessly

---

[108]*Criminal Code*, 1985, c. C-46, s. 273.1(2).

[109]*Criminal Code*, 1985, c. C-46, s. 172.1(1).

[110]*Criminal Code*, 1985, c. C-46, s. 151.z

[111]*Criminal Code*, 1985, c. C-46, s. 153.

[112]*Criminal Code*, 1985, c. C-46, s. 152.

[113]Jimmy Breslin quote retrieved March 14, 2005, from www.en.thinkexist.com/keyword/arsonist

- by fire or explosion

- causes damage to property, whether or not he or she owns it

- knowing or being reckless as to the property being inhabited or occupied

- or causes bodily harm,[114] or

- intentionally or recklessly damages property that is not wholly owned by them

- by fire or explosion,[115] or

- intentionally or recklessly damages property owned by them, in whole or in part by fire or explosion

- that threatens the health, safety or property of another person,[116] or

- with intent to defraud causes damage by fire or explosion to property

- whether or not the property is owned by them, in whole or in part,[117]

- or causes a fire or explosion by negligence

- to property owned, in whole or in part, by them

- or controlled by them

- that causes bodily harm to a person

- or damage to property.[118]

Arson involves the intentional or negligent destruction of property or the injury or death of a person by fire or explosion. Various arson offences carry different punishments, depending on whether or not the accused owned the property that was damaged, totally or partially, or if at the time of the offence he or she had the intent to defraud any other person. The *Criminal Code* also creates the offence of having any incendiary (capable of causing fire) material, devices, or explosive substance for the purpose of committing an arson offence.[119]

The motivation for arson may be fraud, revenge, mental disorder, extortion, or for the purpose of concealing evidence of another crime, such as break and enter, sexual assault, or murder. Investigators should rely on assistance from firefighters, whose initial observations at the scene may be crucial in determining if the fire was accidental in nature, or incendiary. Determination of the cause of the fire is often the result of elimination of all possible accidental causes or through identifying multiple sources of ignition – a hallmark of arson.

---

[114]*Criminal Code*, 1985, c. C-46, s. 433.

[115]*Criminal Code*, 1985, c. C-46, s. 434.

[116]*Criminal Code*, 1985, c. C-46, s. 434.1.

[117]*Criminal Code*, 1985, c. C-46, s. 435(1).

[118]*Criminal Code*, 1985, c. C-46, s. 436(1).

[119]*Criminal Code*, 1985, c. C-46, s. 436.1.

An experienced arson investigator is trained to search for the origin of the fire, indicated by the area(s) of greatest charring in scenes that aren't totally consumed by the fire. Careful examination of the fire scene is necessary to locate possible trace evidence of incendiary devices, such as timing devices, wicks, fuses, or the use of accelerants, such as petroleum based flammable liquids used to ignite and intensify arson fires.

The background circumstances of the victim often shed light on the possible motivation of an incendiary fire. If the fire was revenge-motivated, the victim may be able to provide evidence of an ongoing dispute or disagreement in his or her personal life. The victim's financial stability or the history of the property itself may reveal evidence of an arson fire motivated by greed or profit. If the property was or had been unsuccessfully listed for sale, arson may have seemed like a viable option for a distressed owner.

If arson is committed with the intent to defraud, that intent may be inferred by the court against the holder or the beneficiary of a fire insurance policy in relation to the property in question.[120] Ascertain the details regarding any insurance policies to ascertain if the value of the policy accurately reflected the value of the property or whether or not the policy had been recently acquired or was increased in value shortly before the fire. A history of previous insurance claims of loss for fire or other reasons may also provide evidence of motive in some cases.

BOX 10.8	Proper Investigative Procedure

Unless a building is totally consumed by the fire, evidence of flammable liquids can be detected from telltale charring patterns created by the liquid flowing to the lowest point of gravity. Trace evidence of flammable liquids can be detected in small crevices between floorboards, underneath baseboards or in the backing of carpets. Seal such samples in an airtight glass jar (mason jars used for preserving fruits and vegetables are excellent for this purpose) and submit them to the Centre of Forensic Sciences (CFS). Samples of suspected incendiary substances may be identified through the process of gas chromatography and may provide additional avenues of investigation. In the event of suspected explosive substances or devices, check with an explosives disposal technician and the CFS prior to transporting any material that may be hazardous.

10.16.9 Missing Persons

Missing person investigation is an aspect of police work that too few people deem worthy of consideration as criminal investigation. Unlike the standard response of insensitive television investigators, however, there is no minimum statutory period of time a person must be missing before the police are allowed to commence an investigation.

People go missing in our society every day. Adults voluntarily choose to walk away from their lives because of dissatisfaction with a relationship, or their job, or to hide from some distressing aspect of their everyday life, such as a large debt, a responsibility, an addiction, or for many other reasons, including mental disorders. Children and

---

[120]*Criminal Code*, 1985, c. C-46, s. 435(2).

youths may voluntarily run away from home after a disagreement with one or both parents or guardians, or to avoid facing responsibility for a situation at school, etc.

Even voluntary missing person cases may involve crimes. People have falsified their own deaths in order to abandon unhappy relationships or to defraud life insurance companies to collect premiums. Some people are motivated to run away from crimes they have committed in order to avoid apprehension. Missing children may turn to drug trafficking, shoplifting or prostitution to support themselves after a being away from home for a short time.

Occasionally the first contact to the police, which may eventually lead to a major crime investigation, is a report that a person, either a suspect or a victim, has gone missing. The missing person report might be initiated by a loved one, family member, co-worker – or in cases where the missing person has met with foul play, by the person responsible for the disappearance, who wishes to appear uninvolved in the victim's demise by feigning concern for their safety.

Obtain the full particulars of the person making the report, a detailed physical description of the missing person and the clothing he or she was last seen wearing, if known. If the slightest possibility exists that the person did not go missing voluntarily, take detailed witness statements from relevant persons to record their knowledge of the incident. Obtain full background information regarding the missing person's demeanour and mental condition leading up to his or her disappearance.

Determine the last-known person to see the missing person alive and interview this person regarding the sighting. In the event of a missing person who lives alone and has not shown up for work or for some other appointment, a search should be made of his or her residence. If a person is missing voluntarily, he or she may take personal effects such as clothing, wallets, credit cards, automobile, etc. Monitor credit cards and financial accounts for banking activity.

Missing person investigations should never be taken lightly, even in the case of elderly Alzheimer's disease patients or chronic teenage runaways, both of whom are vulnerable to victimization or injury. All missing persons should be entered onto the Canadian Police Information Centre (CPIC) database at the earliest opportunity. If a photograph or detailed physical description of the missing person is available, consider a media release to request the public's assistance in locating the missing person.

In the event of a missing person under 18 years of age, when there is reason to suspect he or she has been abducted, assess the need to utilize an Amber Alert. Police services, in partnership with the Ontario Association of Broadcasters and the Ministry of Transportation may now alert the public to the possibility of abduction where specific criteria are met, and other provinces have similar schemes. Amber Alerts were developed following the 1996 abduction of nine-year-old Amber Rene Hagerman in Arlington, Texas, whose murder remains unsolved.

In the case of abducted or missing children, an immediate decision must be made as to the viability of conducting a search in the area in which the person disappeared from for the victim, evidence and/or the offender. Canvass known friends and classmates for clues as to a possible motive for running away or an intended destination. If the child has run away on a prior occasion, ascertain where he or she was located in that instance. School books, school lockers, writings and computer hard drives may be examined for leads as to associations, motives or intended movements.

In missing person cases in which foul play is suspected, while remaining hopeful, investigators must also turn their minds to the possibility that the missing person may not be found alive. As a precaution, secure personal effects from which fingerprint impressions of the missing person may be developed for future identification purposes. Dental charts and x-rays of all descriptions should be secured in the event they are needed to eliminate the missing person in future cases of found human remains. Properly preserved hairbrushes and toothbrushes and unlaundered undergarments have been used to identify the missing person's DNA profile.

Missing persons are always deemed to be missing from the location where they were last seen, which is not necessarily the area in which they normally reside. For example, if a person resided in City "A" and went missing during a business trip in City "B", he or she would be deemed to be missing from City "B". The City "B" Police Service would be the police service having jurisdiction of the case. Unfortunately, not all police officers agree or understand the established policy and refer the complainant to the police service where the person resided. Fortunately, most police services where the missing person resided will accept missing person reports if the proper police service fails to take action.

SUMMARY

- To be legal, a search, as defined by s. 8 *Charter of Rights and Freedoms* must be authorized by statute, be judicially pre-authorized in the form of a warrant, or fit one of the recognized exceptions that allow for warrantless searches and be both reasonable in nature and conducted in a reasonable manner.

- The mnemonic "S. E. P. I. C. O." outlines situations that allow for searches to be made without warrant.

    S – Statute - (warrantless search is authorized by statute)

    E – Exigent circumstances - (imminent death, bodily harm, or loss, destruction or removal of evidence would result)

    P – Plain View - (lawfully positioned and inadvertent discovery of evidence)

    I – Incident to Arrest - (in conjunction with a lawful arrest)

    C – Consent - (person having lawful authority consents to the search)

    O – Officer Safety – (searches for suspects, weapons, harmful to police).

- Locations to be searched and items to be seized must be specified on a search warrant, and search warrant information must have as much detail as possible so that an uninvolved officer would know exactly which premises is to be searched and precisely what items may be seized.

- Facts included in the grounds to obtain a search warrant must be attributed to the source from whom it was received and it must be stated how the source came to know the information that is attributed to them.

- General warrants may be issued by a provincial court judge or a superior court judge to authorize investigative techniques, procedures, the use of devices or any thing that does not interfere with bodily integrity in relation to a person or his or her property which, if not authorized, would result in a section 8 *Charter of Rights* violation.

- A police officer who seizes anything under a search warrant or without a warrant either incident to arrest or the "plain view seizure rule" (or in exigent circumstances as authorized by sections 117.02(1) or 487.11 *Criminal Code*) must make a return, in writing, to a justice reporting that he or she has done so.

- *Animus furandi,* meaning the intent to deprive the owner of the property, is an essential element of the charge of theft.

- The key elements of the offence of robbery can therefore be graphically illustrated using the equation: theft + violence (personal or threatened) = robbery.

- "Assault" is defined as the intentional, direct or indirect application of force to another person, without his or her consent.

- "Arson" involves the intentional or negligent destruction of property or the injury or death of a person by fire or explosion.

- Major criminal investigations, including abductions and homicides, often result following the report of a missing person. Every missing person report should therefore receive proper attention from the police service receiving the report.

DISCUSSION QUESTIONS

1. You are assigned to investigate an alleged theft of a boat, outboard motor and trailer from the driveway of a private residence. You obtain a list of the boat and its contents and a photograph of the property from the owner. Unable to locate any witnesses to the theft, you enter the boat, motor and trailer particulars on the CPIC system and file a report. One week later, the complainant calls you to advise that he has observed his boat sitting on the trailer inside the open garage at a small motor repair shop across town. Do you need a search warrant to enter onto the property to seize the vessel identified by the owner? Why?

2. If it is your decision to obtain a warrant, what information would have to be included on the information to obtain the search warrant and on the face of the warrant itself?

3. While on routine patrol, you observe two men struggling in a parking lot outside a local bar, well known for having disturbances. You observe one of the men holding a knife, which he throws away upon your arrival. The other man is found to be suffering from a non life-threatening wound to the arm and states that his attacker demanded his wallet. When the second man refused to give up his wallet, the first man stabbed him. You find the man you observed with the knife to be intoxicated by alcohol and arrest him. What offence(s) would you arrest him for?

4. Your partner locates the knife in the far corner of the parking lot as it begins to rain. Your partner asks you if a search warrant is required to seize the knife. What is your response? Explain the rationale for your answer.

 # WEBLINKS

www.ofm.gov.on.ca

Office of the Fire Marshal, (OFM) Ontario, providing fire prevention, investigative services and support to municipal fire departments and law enforcement agencies.

www.firearson.com

International Association of Arson Investigators (IAAI), an organization created to promote excellence and ongoing training for the arson investigation industry. Resources, publications, events, research links, etc.

www.ibc.ca

Insurance Bureau of Canada (IBC) providing vehicle information, publications, insurance industry access and investigative services to member agencies and accredited law enforcement agencies.

www.cpic-cipc.ca

Canadian Police Information Centre (CPIC). An RCMP-hosted nationwide automated database warehousing information relating to missing, charged or wanted persons, persons of special interest, and lost or stolen vehicles or property contributed by police services

Chapter 11

Sudden Death and Homicide Investigation

"The dead cannot cry out for justice; it is a duty of the living to do so for them."

Lois McMaster Bujold.[1]

Learning Outcomes

After reading this chapter, students should be able to:

- Distinguish between the terms "homicide" and "murder."
- Summarize the different classifications of **"manner of death."**
- Explain the "Burning Bridges" theory as it relates to death investigations.
- Describe the basic investigative sequence of a sudden death/homicide investigation.
- Contrast and compare indicators of homicide, suicide and accidental death.
- Give examples of physiological post-mortem changes and summarize the general reliability of their use in estimating time of death.
- Explain the role of the coroner in sudden and unexpected death investigation.

11.1   INTRODUCTION

There is no greater responsibility for any investigator than to be entrusted with the task of investigating the death of another human being. We live in a society that places a high value on the sanctity of human life. Every individual's right to life is enshrined in our *Canadian Charter of Rights and Freedoms*.[2] Yet, people die every day and will continue to do so – it is a natural and inevitable fact of life.

Accidents and deaths by natural causes claim a great many lives and, except for predictable and anticipated medical deaths that occur in hospitals, hospices or in the home, all sudden and unexpected deaths require investigation to determine the true circumstances

---

[1] Lois McMaster Bujold quote retrieved November 23, 2003, from www.quotationspage.com

[2] *Canadian Charter of Rights and Freedoms*, Being Part 1 of the *Constitution Act*, 1982,

of the individual's death. Accident investigation and Coroner's inquests can result in rec-ommendations to government, or to changes in legislation, labour practices or manufacturing standards to minimize the possibility of future similar deaths. Effective investigation of accidental deaths or deaths by natural causes can result in the payment of life insurance settlements and the awarding of survivor's benefits to entitled family and heirs that enable them to pick up the pieces of their lives and carry on.

It is possible for an offender to intentionally commit a murder and attempt to make it appear to be a death that was caused either by "suicide," "accident" or "natural causes." Two examples would be the intentional killing of an elderly relative to expedite an anticipated inheritance or the killing of an intimate partner to avoid a bitter divorce (see Section 6.19: "Staged" Crime Scenes). Every sudden and unexpected death must there-fore be investigated to either confirm or exclude the possibility of the involvement of criminal wrongdoing. Where criminal wrongdoing is found to be involved, every effort must be made to identify the offender and bring him or her to justice.

The offence of murder is, without doubt, the most serious offence in the *Criminal Code* and carries with it a minimum penalty of life imprisonment without possibility of parole for up to 25 years upon conviction for first-degree murder.[3] New police officers frequently respond as the first officers to scenes of death and must have a basic under-standing of the principles of death investigation and of relevant law to be able to recog-nize a suspicious death that potentially involves criminal wrongdoing, to be able to take the appropriate enforcement action.

11.2   CAUSES OF DEATH

There are any number of ways in which the deaths of human beings might occur. When we speak of the term **cause of death,** we are referring to the actual mechanism that resulted in the death, or WHAT killed the person. For example, the death might have resulted from trauma, disease or a variety of other conditions.

There are three internal systems of the human body that are necessary to sustain life. Interference with or disruption of any of these systems to any significant extent is capa-ble of resulting in death. The three vital internal systems referred to are:

Respiratory System: The respiratory system involves the throat, bronchial tubes, lungs and diaphragm, which draw oxygen into the lungs for supply to the tissues of the body. Asphyxia due to suffocation, strangulation or blockage of the airway, for even a short period of time, is sufficient to cause death (respiratory arrest).

Cardiovascular System: The cardiovascular system includes the heart and the net-work of arteries that circulate oxygenated blood from the heart to the tissues of the body and the veins that return blood, high in carbon dioxide, to the lungs for re-oxygenation. Interference with the heart's ability to circulate blood (cardiac arrest) or the severing of a major blood vessel resulting in acute blood loss (exsanguination) will be fatal in a rel-atively short period of time.

Central Nervous System: The central nervous system includes the brain, spinal cord and nerve tissues that transport the electrical pulses that control the activities of the

---

[3]*Criminal Code*, R.S. 1985, c. C-46 ss. 235(1), 745(a).

body. Blunt trauma to the head can cause destruction of brain tissue, or may result in a hemorrhage within the skull, causing pressure on the brain resulting in the suppression of normal brain activity. Severe trauma to the spinal cord can disrupt the activities of the body and may also result in death.

A police officer is not expected to be a medical expert; however, he or she should have a basic knowledge of anatomy and anatomical causes of death in order to recognize symptoms of death and more effectively communicate with medical professionals (e.g., paramedics, nurses, physicians, coroners, pathologists and forensic scientists) who are regularly involved in various stages of death investigations.

11.3 MANNER OF DEATH

"Life is pleasant. Death is peaceful. It's the transition that's troublesome."

Isaac Asimov (1920-1992).[4]

Deaths may be classified in one of five categories, which are used to determine the manner in which (or HOW) the deceased met his or her death:

1. *Homicide*: The legal definition of homicide is *"the killing of a human being [committed by another human being] by any means, directly or indirectly."*[5] The phrase, "by another human being," is implicit in the definition. The death of a backpacker mauled by a wild animal, or the death of a person falling off a ladder would not be considered homicides as the deaths were not caused by other human beings. Homicide can either be **culpable** (deserving of blame) or **non-culpable** (not blameworthy).[6] If the homicide is not culpable, it is not an offence.[7] In Canada, the term culpable homicide includes murder, manslaughter or infanticide.[8] "Homicide" is a broad term that is often confused with the term "murder" which means "the intentional killing of a human being."[9] The main difference between the terms of homicide and murder is the degree of negligence or specific intention to cause death, or the intention to cause bodily harm which results in death. Although the killing of a human being might be intentional, such as the use of lethal force against a suspect by a law enforcement officer or the killing of an assailant in self-defence by a member of the public, if the killing is legally justified (i.e., sanctioned by law) the death is considered to be a homicide, not a murder, due to the lack of criminal intent. All murders are homicides – not all homicides are murders.

2. *Suicide*: "Suicide" is defined as the intentional taking of one's own life by self-inflicted injury. Many times people die, unintentionally, by their own hands, such as in single-vehicle traffic accidents. Unless the person specifically intends to cause his or her own

---

[4]Isaac Asimov quote retrieved November 23, 2003, from www.quotationspage.com

[5]*Criminal Code*, R.S. 1985, c. C-46 s. 222(1).

[6]*Criminal Code*, R.S. 1985, c. C-46 s. 222(2).

[7]*Criminal Code*, R.S. 1985, c. C-46 s. 222(3).

[8]*Criminal Code*, R.S. 1985, c. C-46 s. 222(4).

[9]*Criminal Code*, R.S. 1985, c. C-46 s. 229.

death, it is not suicide. It is not a crime to commit suicide, nor, since 1972 is it any longer an offence under Canadian law to attempt to commit suicide. A police officer may apprehend a suicidal person under provincial legislation such as the *Mental Health Act of Ontario* if the officer has reasonable and probable grounds to believe that the person:

"(a) has threatened or attempted or is threatening or attempting to cause bodily harm to himself or herself...

and in addition the police officer is of the opinion that the person is apparently suffering from mental disorder of a nature or quality that likely will result in:

(d) serious bodily harm to the person...

and that it would be dangerous to proceed under section 16 [the laying of an information under oath before a justice of the peace to obtain an order of apprehension] the police officer may take the person in custody to an appropriate place for examination by a physician."[10] It is, however, a serious criminal offence for another person to "counsel, **aid or abet**" (to instruct or advise: to assist, incite or encourage) a person to commit suicide; an indictable offence that carries a maximum penalty of 14 years imprisonment.[11]

3. *Accidental Death*: This is a category that includes all sudden and unexpected death, absent the intention to cause death on the part of any participant in the event. A downhill skier crashes into a tree and succumbs to his or her injuries, a passenger in a boat falls overboard and drowns, a cyclist is fatally injured in a collision with a motor vehicle – these are all examples of accidental deaths.

4. *Natural Causes*: "Natural causes" include deaths that result from disease, illness, the effects of aging, or other medical condition. Many deaths by natural causes will occur expectedly in a hospital and will involve a patient under the care of a physician. Other natural deaths will occur expectedly at the decedent's residence, to which the patient returns home to die in comfort and privacy. Still other natural deaths will occur unexpectedly from previously diagnosed or undiagnosed medical conditions, such as cardiac arrest, aneurysm, stroke, etc.

5. *Undetermined*: This category is used to classify all deaths that cannot be conclusively determined to have resulted either by homicide, suicide, accident or by natural causes. The classification of any death as undetermined may result either from the lack of information upon which to determine an anatomical cause of death, or because the investigation could not establish sufficient information regarding the circumstances of the person's death to allow for a conclusive determination.

11.4   THE "BURNING BRIDGES" THEORY REVISITED

We first discussed the "burning bridges" theory as it relates to crime scene examination. Once any investigative procedure has been conducted at a crime scene, the scene can never be exactly restored to its original condition. This theory applies equally to death

---

[10]*Mental Health Act*, R.S.O. 1990 c. M.7, s. 17.

[11]*Criminal Code*, R.S. 1985, c. C-46, s. 241.

investigation scenes, but the investigator must be aware that there are three additional "bridges" that are burned during every death investigation.

The first "bridge" is burned when the body of the deceased is moved. Once moved, the body can never be replaced exactly in the original location in which it was found. The second "bridge" is burned when a body is autopsied. A medico-legal autopsy is a very complex and invasive procedure that involves the surgical dissection and examination of the internal organs and body cavities. While the body still remains after an autopsy, and although second autopsies are occasionally conducted, the body's condition will have been significantly and permanently altered as the result of the initial autopsy.

The third and final "bridge" is burned when the body of the deceased is buried or cremated. While it is possible to exhume a buried body for further examination, if new information about the death requires it, the body's condition will usually have changed significantly due to the effects of decomposition. Obviously, the destruction of the body that occurs during cremation renders the deceased's body totally unsuitable for any subsequent post mortem (after death) examination.

11.5   THE DEATH SCENE

There is no common denominator for comparing scenes in which death investigations begin. The death may occur in a variety of outdoor locations, or in a building of any description. The deceased may have little if any connection to the death scene or, in the event of a death involving murder, the scene in which the body is situated may not be the same location in which the death occurred.

Persons responsible for murder sometimes transport the body of their victim some distance from the murder scene to avoid being associated with the crime because of their association with either the victim or the murder scene (see Section 6.19: "Staged" Crime Scenes). Sometimes, as in the case of a missing person where foul play is suspected, a homicide investigation will have to be initiated without either a scene or a body.

If the body of the deceased is present at the scene, as it is in most but not all cases, the body may either be a recently deceased intact body, a severed body part, or the body may be badly decomposed. After time, all the soft tissue of the body decomposes and all that is left are the skeletal remains of the deceased, which may be either in place or can be disarticulated (separated at the joints) and spread over a wide area. The body may be in an outdoor location, exposed to the elements and to the effects of scavenging by animals, submerged underwater, or totally or partially buried, requiring expert archaeological excavation.

Despite my previous remarks about the investigator's added responsibility and the seriousness involved in death investigations, there is no significant difference between the basic methods used to conduct the examination of a death scene compared to any other type of crime scene. The only appreciable differences between non-death crime scenes and those that involve a death are the presence of a dead (complete or partial) body, the nature of evidence that is encountered and the expertise normally required to conduct the investigation.

The same crime scene examination methods apply in a death scene investigation as those discussed for crime scenes in Chapter 6, namely: securing the scene; establishing a perimeter; devising a comprehensive scene investigation plan; and adopting a methodical, systematic approach. Where there may be said to be differences is in terms of the advanced investigative procedures (e.g., search for trace evidence of blood, laser, ballistics, pattern wound, entomology, surveillance, etc.) and the undeniable need to adopt an interdisciplinary approach to all death investigations.

11.5.1   Presumption of Death

Simply stated, there is no death investigation until you have a dead victim, meaning one who has been pronounced dead by a qualified medical practitioner, or is presumed dead, or is legally proven to be dead. Prior to the pronouncement of death, the investigation may be classified as personal injury; or missing person, presumed dead; or missing person with foul play suspected, etc. There are medical conditions (e.g., hypothermia, electrocution, etc.) in which the victim may appear dead but may possibly be revived.

Any medical doctor may legally pronounce death – not nurses, not paramedics or ambulance attendants and certainly not police officers. You must either have a coroner (or other medical doctor) attend the scene to pronounce death or you must transport the victim, whether or not vital signs are absent, to a hospital for pronouncement of death. Removing the body of a deceased "burns a bridge" that permanently alters the death scene; however, your primary responsibility as a police officer is the preservation of human life.[12]

There are certain circumstances in which death of a human being may be presumed. Those situations, where any of the following conditions are present, include:

- decapitation (complete separation of the head from the torso of the body);

- transection (severing of the torso of the body into two or more pieces);

- gross (significant) decomposition;

- grossly charred (thermal burns) body;

- open head or torso with gross (significant) outpouring of cranial or visceral contents; or

- gross (significant) *rigor mortis* (i.e., a gradual and temporary post mortem stiffening of the muscles of the body) in a pulse-less, apneic (not breathing) patient.[13]

11.6   BASIC DEATH INVESTIGATION SEQUENCE

"Think dirty..."

Dr. James G. Young, M.D., Former Commissioner of Emergency Management,
Ministry of Community Safety and Correctional Services (Former Chief Coroner)
for the Province of Ontario.[14]

The fundamental principle of any proper death investigation involves the mindset to "think dirty." Visualize the worst-case scenario imaginable – having regard to all of the

---

[12]*Police Services Act*, R.S.O. 1990, c. P.15, s. 1.

[13]*Ont. Reg. 19*, R.R.O. 1990, pursuant to the *Ambulance Act*, ss. 44 & 45 as referred to in the Ontario Ministry of Health (MOH) Policy 4.4 *Transportation of Patients with Vital Signs Absent*.

[14]Dr. Jim Young, personal conversations with the author.

circumstances of the case, and in most cases, you will be close to the truth. "Thinking dirty" means to suspect that every death under investigation is a homicide, until homicide can be eliminated as the manner of death. This advice might appear to some to contradict the previous rule, "Let the evidence TELL the story, don't make the evidence FIT the story." However, the investigator must keep an open mind while regarding everything with a critical eye and in the end, it will be the evidence and the correct analysis of that evidence that will solve the puzzle for you.

Whether the deceased is an infant, an adolescent, an adult or is elderly – whether they died at home, school, at work, or outdoors – or whether they died alone or in the presence of family members, friends or others, treat every death as a homicide until you can eliminate homicide as the manner of death.

After eliminating the possibility of homicide, you should next examine the death from the perspective of a possible suicide until suicide can be eliminated as the manner of death. Once you can conclusively eliminate both homicide and suicide as the manner of death, what you will be left with is an accidental death or a death by natural causes. Both of these should be relatively simple to establish based on witness accounts, evidence of circumstances of the death and or the decedent's medical history.

Never be in too much of a hurry to work your way down the ladder of potential manners of death. The investigator who makes snap judgments based on "hunches" about the initial appearance of the scene or of a body is forgetting the cardinal rule: "Things are not always as they appear to be."

Never accept what other people, including other police officers, tell you as the truth unquestioningly. At some point, trust and good faith has to enter into dealings with others, but I have been proven wrong many times and have received much bad information from others over the course of my career.

On occasion, I have been provided with incorrect addresses of crime scene locations, incorrect identities of victims, wrong information regarding the nature of deaths, or of possible weapons involved, wrong information about whether weapons were present or absent at the scene – and the list goes on. In these cases the erroneous facts were received from well-intentioned but mistaken police officers who were careless, had misinterpreted certain information or had simply not confirmed the information that they passed along.

Police officers, like everyone else, are only human and therefore capable of error. The consequences of making errors during sudden death and homicide investigations are too great to risk making careless mistakes. Never hesitate to question any source of information, including information received from other police officers.

Always confirm information that is provided and look for corroboration of your facts. *"How do we know this?"* and *"Who else can confirm this information?"* should be frequently asked questions during death investigations. It is always better to risk hurting someone's feelings by questioning his or her information than to make a serious and perhaps irreversible error during any death investigation.

11.6.1   Identification of the Deceased

The identification of the deceased is a vital part of any death investigation. The victim may be identified at the scene by relatives or associates. The victim may be in a location such as a residence or workplace, motor vehicle, etc., by which his or her identity may be quickly established through association. The deceased may have documentary identification on his or her person which will lead to tentative identification, which can be confirmed by relatives.

The deceased may be found in a non-familiar location, without any identification, in a charred, dismembered, or badly decomposed condition that will require his or her identification through the use of forensic comparison of fingerprints, x-rays, dental records or DNA. It may take considerable time to establish the identity of the victim, but the earlier the victim's identity is known, the sooner the victimology can be investigated, (i.e., place of residence, marital status, family background, occupation, employment, lifestyle, financial history, medical history, criminal record if any, associates, etc.)

11.6.2   Determine Cause of Death

While physical evidence at the scene or the nature of the wounds or other circumstances of the body may give rise to plausible causes of death, such as multiple gunshot wounds where no weapon is recovered at the scene, etc., the pathologist is the only person who can verify the cause of death. A body found hanging by the neck may initially appear to be a suicide, but other injuries may prove that death occurred by another method prior to the victim's body being staged.

A body found in water might be initially taken to be a possible drowning until the absence of water in the lungs and evidence of ligature strangulation indicate that the victim was already dead when placed into the water. A body found dead in bed might be taken as a death by natural causes until toxicological analysis detects lethal concentrations of toxic poisons, giving rise to suspicion of homicide or suicide depending on the circumstances of the case.

Arrange for a post-mortem examination at the earliest opportunity and be prepared to brief the coroner and pathologist of the circumstances of the investigation to date, including the last known activities of the deceased and the results of the scene investigation. Scene photographs – or even better yet, a videotape recording of the scene, if available – should be shared with the pathologist to allow him or her to make the most informed post mortem examination of the deceased as possible.

Remember to "think dirty!"

11.6.3   Determine the Time of Death

Contrary to what you see on television and in the movies, the only accurate way to determine the actual time of death is to have a witness observe the pulse-less and non-breathing body of the deceased fall to the ground, look at his or her watch and record the exact time. Movie and television doctors have an uncanny ability to fix the time of death within a given half hour span of time only because movie detectives have just an hour and a half to solve the case and bring the accused to justice.

Rigor mortis (the gradual and temporary post-mortem stiffening of the muscles of the body); *livor mortis* (post-mortem settling of the victim's blood to the lowest point of gravity in the body); and post-mortem analysis of the victim's gastric (stomach) contents may all, in their own way, shed some light on the approximate time of death;

yet all are far too variable to establish the time of death to a high degree of scientific certainty. These and other post mortem changes will be discussed in further detail in a later section.

Sometimes it is only possible to prove that death occurred between the time the victim was positively last seen alive and the time the body was discovered. You must, however, take the circumstances of your investigation as you find them, regardless of how problematic the case may be.

In cases of homicide, establishing the time of death allows inferences to be made as to who had an opportunity to murder the victim and may eliminate certain persons of interest from the investigation or suspects from suspicion based on alibi evidence.

11.6.4 Reconstruct the Events

Reconstruction of the events leading up to, including and immediately following the death of the victim is accomplished in a number of ways. Through interviews of family and associates, investigators establish the last known person to see the victim alive. Through interviews, canvasses, tips from the public, credit card purchases, bank records, cellular phone records, etc., establish the last known movements and activities of the victim. A thorough and methodical examination of the scene of the death (or body discovery site) plus the results of the post-mortem examination will now probably start to provide insight as to the manner of death (homicide, suicide, accident, natural causes) if it hasn't already become evident through other investigative means.

11.6.5 Eliminate "Persons of Interest" from the Investigation

The concept of a person of interest is relatively new and we should review the definition. The *MCM Manual* defines a person of interest as: "A person whose background, relationship to the victim or the opportunity to commit the offence(s) [may] warrant further investigation but [at that time no other grounds exist] to suggest culpability in the commission of the [crime being investigated]."[15]

Start eliminating people from the investigation beginning with the next-of-kin, family members, intimate partners, people in past and present relationships with the victim. Continue through the list eliminating close friends, acquaintances, associates, neighbours, business partners, schoolmates, and others. Establish their alibis and corroborate what they say to eliminate them as possibly being involved in the death of the victim.

The cause of death, manner of death and reconstruction of events may already have provided a possible or known motive for the crime in the form of robbery, theft, sexual offence, etc. This, in turn, may provide additional information as to a person or persons who, having had the opportunity to kill the deceased, might have also had a motive. Many of these steps might seem to assume that the death is a homicide but remember,

---

[15]Ministry of Community Safety and Correctional Services. *Ontario Major Case Management (MCM) Manual* (Oct. 1, 2004), p. 10.

until we have eliminated homicide as the manner of death, we will continue to treat the investigation as such. We are still "thinking dirty."

11.6.6 Examine Similar or Related Events

Sometimes the solution to a crime is found within the context of another event or location, which will share a common (yet not readily apparent) denominator with the incident under investigation. Have any similar events/crimes recently occurred within the same jurisdiction or in neighbouring or nearby jurisdictions? Circulate the event utilizing CPIC (Canadian Police Information Centre) Zone Alerts or Provincial Alerts, if appropriate. Canvass other police services and examine your own service's files. In the event of a predatory crime, contact the provincial ViCLAS (Violent Crime Linkage Analysis System) centre to ascertain if they have any record of similar crimes.

Closer to the scene, were any vehicles stolen (or recovered, or abandoned) break-ins, noise complaints (e.g., screeching tires or gunshots, yelling, etc.), any prowler or suspicious person complaints? Did anything unusual occur at or near the scene? Were there any traffic stops, speeding tickets, parking infractions or motor vehicle collisions in the vicinity around the time of the events involving the death of the victim? These or any number of other incidents may give light to other pre-offence or post-offence activities of persons responsible for the death.

11.6.7 Gather Evidence to Corroborate the Facts of the Case

Start building your case like a bricklayer builds a house – one brick at a time. Whether a suspect is known or still unknown, with each and every fact always confirm and corroborate the findings of the case until you can prove every detail. Once you have exhausted all possible avenues of investigation, you will either be in the position to institute judicial proceedings against the person or persons responsible, or terminate the investigation.

11.6.8 Prepare Your Case for Court or Archiving

If criminal wrongdoing is involved in your investigation and you have reasonable grounds to believe an identifiable suspect is responsible, you will lay the appropriate charge(s), conferring with a Crown Attorney if necessary, and effect an arrest. Fully investigate the accused, gathering all relevant evidence (either for or against the guilt of the accused) and prepare a Crown Brief for delivery to the Crown Attorney.

In the event of a cold case, the complete case file (i.e., all interviews, evidence, photographs, search records, police officers' notes, investigative and forensic reports, etc.) must be properly organized and archived to allow the investigation to be re-opened at a later date, should new information come to light or a review of the case be deemed worthwhile. Nothing is worse than inheriting a case that is many years old and opening numerous "mystery boxes" of files only to have to sort through assorted and un-catalogued papers, photographs and reports in an effort to determine what happened and what, if anything, was ever done about it.

11.7   INDICATORS OF HOMICIDE

"In death investigations, there are no absolutes."

Vernon J. Geberth, former Lieutenant Commander,
New York City Police Department.[16]

There are many easily observable indicators that, if present upon the arrival of the police, should raise the possibility of the involvement of homicide to the investigator. The ability to recognize and to correctly interpret indictors of types of death may determine the course of the investigation.

As uniformed patrol officers are almost always the first to arrive at the scene of a death, it is vital that they be familiar with indicators of the various manners of death in order to assess a death scene and make appropriate notifications for necessary support services. Failure to recognize indicators of a homicide may result in the death being improperly classified as suicide, resulting in a murderer escaping prosecution for his or her crime.

11.7.1   Multiple or Unusually Located Wounds or Injuries

Without disturbing the body of the deceased, visually examine the observable areas of the body for the type and amount of wounds or injuries. The presence of multiple wounds and even the area of the body in which the wounds are located may indicate homicide. Multiple wounds and/or wounds located in an area of the body that would be unlikely, difficult or impossible for the deceased to have inflicted (e.g., the back, face, eyes, genitals, etc.) are indications that the wounds might have been caused by another person. The presence of blunt trauma may also indicate the involvement of an assailant and therefore homicide.

BOX 11.1	Investigative Hypothesis
Suspiciously located and or multiple wounds = assailant = homicide	

11.7.2   Defence Wounds

If the deceased displays evidence of defence wounds, such as blunt trauma, stab or incised wounds, to "defensive" areas of the body (e.g., arms and hands) it will indicate that the deceased attempted to fight off his or her assailant(s) in an effort to save his or her own life. Without disturbing the body, visually examine the neck, wrists and ankles of the victim for ligatures (anything used to bind or strangle the victim) or marks left by ligatures that were removed prior to the discovery of the body. Trace biological evidence may be detected under the deceased's fingernails if the victim scratched his or her assailant(s) during the offence.

---

[16]Gerbeth (1996).

BOX 11.2	Investigative Hypothesis
Defence wounds = assailant = homicide	

11.7.3   Disruption of the Deceased's Clothing

Without disturbing the body of the deceased, visually examine the clothing for evidence of disruption (i.e., clothing damaged, removed or replaced by the offender) such as trouser buttons and zippers undone, tears or holes in the fabric, garments that are out of place on inside-out, shoes missing, etc. In cases of sexual homicide (involving victims of any age or gender) an offender may attempt to hurriedly replace the clothing of the victim to conceal evidence of the sexual offence(s).

At the time of discovery, carefully note the condition of the deceased's apparel including tears, rips or stains, especially the knee, elbow and posterior (back) surface areas. Missing articles of clothing or accessories are sometimes kept by sexual offenders as trophies or souvenirs by which they recall or relive the memories of their crimes.

To the extent that it is possible to do so without disturbing the body, visually examine the pockets of apparel worn by male victims and the purses/handbags of female victims (e.g., lining turned inside out indicating the removal of items, presence or absence of a wallet, credit cards, ATM cards, etc.). Visually examine the deceased's fingers for horizontal white bands indicating the removal of rings and abrasions around the neck indicating the possible forcible removal of chains and necklaces.

BOX 11.3	Investigative Hypothesis
Disruption of victim's clothing = assailant = homicide	

11.7.4   Signs of Struggle at the Death Scene

Signs of disturbance at the death scene (e.g., pieces of furniture disturbed or overturned) may be the result of a violent struggle either prior to or at the time of the death or may have been caused by an injured (or intoxicated) but still conscious and stumbling victim. Check the victim for abrasions (scrapes) and contusions (bruises) in relevant areas such as the knees, elbows and shins, but pay particular attention to the possibility of homicide. Dried or fluid blood in the bathroom (e.g., vanity sink or bathtub) or in the kitchen (e.g., sink) except in clear cases of suicide, indicate that an assailant washed blood off him or herself or made an attempt to clean up the crime scene prior to departing.

BOX 11.4	Investigative Hypothesis
Signs of struggle = assailant = homicide	

11.7.5   Evidence of Additional Persons at the Death Scene

If physical evidence indicates that others were present around the time or a shortly before the death occurred, pay particular attention to the possibility of homicide. The number of glasses, liquor bottles, dishes or place settings, different brands of cigarette butts in ashtrays, etc., indicate that another person or persons were present some time before the death. Footprints or footwear impressions (if in blood, immediately check the bottom of the deceased's feet for blood) of different size or tread patterns indicate the presence of another person or persons some time prior to or possibly around the time of the death. In the case of a female victim who lived alone, check if the toilet seat is in the up or down position.

BOX 11.5	Investigative Hypothesis
Indications of other persons present at time of death = assailant = homicide	

11.7.6   Presence or Absence of a Weapon at the Scene

If the victim's wounds indicate that a weapon was involved in the death (e.g., knife, firearms or blunt instrument, etc.) and the weapon is not located at the scene, it is indicative that the assailant took the weapon away when he or she departed or another person did so afterwards.

If a weapon is present at the scene, the investigator must determine whether the weapon originated at the scene or was brought to the scene and left behind (intentionally or inadvertently) by an unknown offender. Determine the origin of any weapon located at the scene and whether it was stolen. The weapon, if possible, should be identified by serial number and all possible information concerning its manufacture, sale and ownership.

BOX 11.6	Investigative Hypotheses
Absence of weapon at scene = assailant = homicide	
Presence of weapon unfamiliar to the scene = assailant = homicide	

11.7.7   History of Domestic Instability

Statistically, the majority of people are murdered by intimate partners, former intimate partners, family members and acquaintances (85 percent). In fact, only 14 percent of all homicides are committed by strangers.[17] Homicide may be indicated where there is a

---

[17]Statistics Canada: *The Daily*. October 25, 2002; October 1, 2003; September 29, 2004.

history of domestic unrest involving the deceased. Interviews of family members, neighbours and associates as well as a search of police occurrence files should indicate the involvement of a possible motive (e.g., spousal abuse, infidelity, impending divorce proceedings, etc.) for homicide.

BOX 11.7	Investigative Hypothesis
	Domestic unrest = motive for homicide

11.7.8 Theft of Property

When property owned by the deceased is missing from the scene, it usually indicates theft. Cupboard doors and bureau drawers left open or overturned, with the contents disturbed, may indicate that an assailant searched for valuables around the time of or following the death. Articles of value removed from a death scene by an assailant are not merely indicative of homicide; if located they can be extremely valuable evidence for establishing a possible motive and circumstantially linking an offender to a crime scene.

BOX 11.8	Investigative Hypothesis
	Removal or attempted removal of property = theft = motive for homicide

11.7.9 Victim's Background

Often, a victim's lifestyle may contribute to his or her involvement in the crime that resulted in his or her death. Gang membership, involvement in the illegal drug trade and sex trade all increase a person's vulnerability to violence by placing him or her in situations having a higher statistical probability for violence. According to Statistics Canada homicide statistics for 2003, 52 per cent of adult homicide victims had a record of criminal convictions while approximately two thirds of persons accused of homicide had a criminal record.[18]

BOX 11.9	Investigative Hypothesis
	Criminal lifestyle of victim = high probability of victimization

11.7.10 Evidence of Forced Entry

Signs of forced entry to the death scene (e.g., windows broken or doors kicked or pried open) may indicate the presence of an intruder who entered the premises intent upon

---

[18]Statistics Canada: *The Daily*. September 29, 2004.

committing murder or some other offence, or who was surprised at the scene and committed murder either to facilitate his escape or to avoid leaving a witness capable of identifying him in the future.

BOX 11.10	Investigative Hypothesis
	Forcible entry = intruder = homicide

11.7.11   Expert Medical Opinion

The attendance of a medical doctor or a coroner at the scene of a death may yield valuable information concerning the circumstances surrounding the death. The opinion of the pathologist who conducts the medico-legal autopsy will often assist in establishing homicide as the manner of death by eliminating other possible anatomical causes of death.

Due to their experience and training, pathologists can identify certain post-mortem artifacts such as petechiae (reddish or purple dots visible on the eyes, lungs or skin that are pinpoint hemorrhages caused by pressure, sometimes in asphyxial deaths). A forensic toxicologist may identify poisons or toxic chemicals in post-mortem tissue samples.

BOX 11.11	Investigative Hypotheses
	Expert medical diagnosis of homicidal cause of death = high probability of homicide
	Expert medical elimination of non-homicidal causes of death = high probability of homicide

11.7.12   Motive

The famous Austrian psychiatrist Dr. Sigmund Freud (1856–1939) believed that love, aggression and sex are fundamental motivators of human behaviour in every individual.[19] While many of Freud's theories have been criticized, all homicides can usually be categorized into slightly different categories of motive, including:

11.7.12.1 Gain/Greed

Offences may involve murders that occur during the commission of thefts, robberies or life insurance fraud (and attempts to commit those offences), which may result in a direct gain to the assailant. Offenders may be attempting to support costly addictions or may be career criminals whose only means of support is through crime. Murders committed under these circumstances may be either inadvertent or intentional.

This category also includes offences of murder in which the offender seeks to avoid the loss of monies. This may involve the killing of business associates to elude

---

[19]Schmalleger & Volk (2005).

business losses, or the killing of past or present intimate partners to prevent divorce settlements.

What the offender hopes to gain by committing a homicide doesn't always have to be financial, however. The removal of a frustrating or aggravating factor (parent, sibling or authority figure) from the offender's life is sometimes what the offender seeks to "gain." To this extent, even political assassinations could be considered to be committed for "gain" in that, if successful, an incumbent unsympathetic to the assassin's political ideology is removed from a position of power.

11.7.12.2 Revenge

Offences motivated by revenge always involve some form of direct or indirect relationship or previous acquaintance between the participants (or, at a minimum, the perception of a relationship or acquaintance in the mind of the offender). Murders in this category may include the intentional killing of a former girlfriend/boyfriend/intimate partner (e.g., "If I can't have them, nobody will" or "They will be punished for ruining my life"), or of a former partner's new love interest, or both.

Murders in this category also include the intentional killing of past or present business associates (in partnerships or transactions gone awry) and incidents in which employees or former employees return to their workplace and lash out aggressively on past or present colleagues for some transgression, real or imagined.

Murders in this category also include incidents such as the April 20, 1999 Columbine High School shooting in Littleton, Colorado by teenagers Eric Harris and Dylan Klebold. Although many of the victims were not on the list of intended victims, the shooting appears to have been motivated out of revenge against many of their fellow students for alleged taunting incidents and against certain teachers for perceived grievances.

The victim–offender relationship may be indirect or even symbolic. Revenge homicides also include politically motivated terrorist attacks such as the September 11, 2001 World Trade Centre attack in which the victims were considered one and the same as the target of the attack, the United States. A Canadian example of a symbolic or indirect victim–offender relationship is the December 6, 1989 mass murder of 14 female students of École Polytechnique at the University of Montreal by Marc Lepine who lashed out at "feminists" who he believed had taken educational and job opportunities away from males. Lepine had himself been refused entry to the prestigious engineering school.

11.7.12.3 Sex

It is something of a misstatement to include sex as a "motive" for homicide. Sexual crimes are crimes of personal violence in which the offender(s) seeks to exert power, control, dominance and degradation over the victim – sex is merely the vehicle chosen by offenders to carry out their purpose.

Sexual homicides sometimes arise out of non-familial abductions of children, and are also committed against estranged spouses or intimate partners and sex-trade workers. Sexual homicides may also occur within the context of a date rape, an intimate relationship or a random attack or abduction. Victims (of any age) are often found in various stages of undress. Biological evidence can be vital to solving these cases if it is successfully collected before degradation occurs. Bite marks may also be located on sexual areas of the victim's body (e.g., breasts, buttocks, thighs) or on his or her shoulders and back.

11.7.12.4 Mental Disorder

The *Criminal Code* defines mental disorder as "a disease of the mind."[20] Mental disorders include a variety of conditions, ranging from those in which the offender may outwardly function normally in society to those where the offender suffers from psychotic delusions or hallucinations. Delusional offenders cannot be held criminally responsible by reason of their mental disorder in cases where the person either does not appreciate what they are doing or doesn't know that what they are doing is wrong.[21]

Homicides involving mental disorders might include offences committed by psychopathic offenders, who are always fully aware of what is happening around them. Or they may be committed by a psychotic offender suffering from the delusion that the victim was a monster or demon and killing him or her was in some way justified. It is in this type of case that the trier of fact may find that, at the time of the offence, the accused was "suffering from a mental disorder so as to be exempt from criminal responsibility by virtue of subsection 16(1)..."[22]

11.7.12.5 Thrill Killings/Copycat Killings

Sometimes the motive for a homicide may not be evident in the early stages of the investigation, such as the unexpected death of an adolescent male or female, or a highway sniper shooting. The disturbing phenomenon of thrill killings is not new. There is an alarming amount of documentation citing murders where the killer, working either alone or with an accomplice, killed merely for the "thrill" of doing so or to see what the experience of killing another human being was like.

Copycat killing was recently in the news when on June 25, 2003, two teenage stepbrothers in Tennessee fatally shot 45-year-old Canadian born Aaron Hamel, while they were emulating the video game *Grand Theft Auto III,* which depicts shooting at tractor trailer units and people.

Thrill killings and copycat killings may be difficult to identify as the victim–offender relationships vary from known victims to randomly selected victims. Media coverage has been blamed for glorifying killing (at least in the mind of the certain potential offenders). Albert Bandura, credited with developing the Social Learning Theory of Criminology, explains that all violence is learned by observing the behaviour of others and modelling one's behaviour to emulate inappropriate role models. Exposure to media violence, graphic coverage of similar crimes and violent video games can all lead certain individuals to commit violent copycat crimes. [23]

BOX 11.12	Investigative Hypothesis
	Existence of motive = high probability of homicide

---

[20]*Criminal Code*, R.S. 1985, c. C-46, s.2.

[21]*Criminal Code*, R.S. 1985, c. C-46, s.16(1).

[22]*Criminal Code*, R.S. 1985, c. C-46, s. 672.34.

[23]Schmalleger & Volk (2005).

11.8   SUICIDE

Suicide is defined as the intentional taking of one's own life by self-inflicted injury. Suicide may be encountered in the form of a single death or in the case of suicide by a criminal offender in conjunction with the murder(s) of one or more victims or merely for other crime(s) for which he or she wishes to avoid prosecution. Suicides are sometimes, although far less frequently, committed by two or more persons who, having formed a suicide pact, take their lives in a single incident.

In 1997 in Canada there were approximately 12 suicides per 100 000 of the population. While that sounds like a relatively small number, consider that in the same year only 10 deaths per 100 000 were attributed to fatal motor vehicle accidents and only 2 deaths per 100 000 of the population were due to homicides. Between 1997 and 1999, there was a 10 per cent increase in the incidence of suicide in Canada [24].

11.8.1   Indicators of Suicide

The primary indicator of suicide is an absence of indicators of homicide, accidental or natural death. There are several other indicators of suicide the investigator must also be aware of.

11.8.1.1 Age

According to the Centre for Suicide Prevention, next to accidental death, suicide is the second leading cause of death in people aged 10–24 and the fourth leading cause of death in people aged 15–44. The Canadian Institute for Health Information (Nov. 28, 2001) indicates that 33 per cent of all injury-related deaths in Ontario may be due to suicide.

11.8.1.2 Gender

Males commit suicide at almost four times the rate of females[25]; however, females attempt suicide at a rate of approximately 1.5 times more often than males. According to Health Canada, "[W]e found a significant correlation between a history of sexual abuse and the life-time number of suicide attempts and the correlation was twice as strong for women."[26]

11.8.1.3 Time of Year

Contrary to a widely held myth that most suicides occur around Christmas, according to the Canadian Mental Health Association, suicides occur more frequently in July and August than at any other time of the year.[27]

11.8.1.4 Suicide Notes

According to the Centre for Suicide Prevention, only 12–37 percent of all suicides leave notes. It is important, in cases where a note is found, that the original be compared to known handwriting samples of the deceased. Where suspicion exists as to the manner of death as a suicide, it would not be unrealistic to have the original note fingerprinted.

---

[24]Centre for Suicide Prevention.

[25]Statistics Canada: *The Daily*. Thursday, April 26, 2001. "The health divide: How the sexes differ."

[26]Health Canada (2002). "A report on mental illness in Canada", Canada. *Women's Health Planning Project Final Report* (2000).

[27]Canadian Mental Health Association – Centre for Suicide Prevention: *SIEC Alert 43 16: Are Suicide Rates Higher at Christmas?* (1995).

Genuine notes often give insight as to the motive of the suicide. The tone of the wording of the note may be apologetic for having caused family pain or for not having been "stronger" to face the circumstances that motivated the suicide. The note may provide instructions to survivors as to how they are to carry out the deceased's last wishes. A suicide note may also be accusatory or critical of others whom the deceased blames for his or her hopeless situation (e.g., parents, former lovers, employers, co-workers, etc.).

Suicide notes are sometimes removed or destroyed by family members or relatives who discover the body, in an effort to protect the deceased from the stigma of suicide or to attempt to collect death benefits payable on a life insurance policy that is void in the event of self-inflicted death.

11.8.1.5 Motive

Suicides (people who commit suicide) see their own death as the most viable option as a result of in a variety of factors including mental disorders; depression; terminal or debilitating illnesses; or out of a sense of self-hatred, rejection, guilt or hopelessness. While mental disorder increases a person's risk for committing suicide, any number of other reasons may contribute to the person's decision to end his or her life.

Chemical addictions (e.g., drugs or alcohol) place individuals at increased risk of suicide. As noted in the section dealing with gender, a history of sexual abuse places all persons, but especially females (at a factor of 2:1 over males) at an increased risk of suicide. A history of previous suicide attempts or a family history of suicide also places individuals at a heightened risk of suicide. Other personal/social factors include unmanageable debt, loss of employment, relationship break-up or instability and a sense of failure. These factors can all lead certain individuals to a level of destructive thinking from which the overpowering thought of suicide appears to be their only means of escape.

Some suicides are motivated by an attempt to induce guilt in the person or persons whom the deceased blames for their actions. Others are the result of despondency as the result of overwhelming loneliness (e.g., single lifestyle or following the loss of a spouse), while others seem to be prompted by similar suicides (i.e., copycat suicides).

11.8.1.6 Self-inflicted Wounds

The presence of wounds or injuries of a nature to suggest that they could have been inflicted by the deceased may be indicative of suicide. Wounds (e.g., knife or gunshot) must be consistent with the "handedness" of the deceased (i.e., a pistol shot to the right side of the head by a right handed victim rather than to the left side or back of the head).

Never underestimate the determination of a suicide to end his or her own life in terms of the amount of injury he or she causes. I once investigated a suicide involving a (right handed) man who was despondent over the passing of his wife some years earlier. He murdered his adolescent son and then cut his own (left) wrist with an electric circular saw. He then walked through the house, leaving a significant blood trail, and sat in the bathroom waiting to die. When the bleeding stopped, he took a length of chain and hanged himself by the neck in a stairwell.

The presence of multiple wounds to both of the deceased, and the extensive blood trail within the residence caused other investigators to suspect that foul play was involved in the two deaths. Yet, the father's wounds were consistent with having been self-inflicted. The wound on the inside of the left wrist would have been difficult (if not impossible) for an assailant to inflict and his wristwatch was located on his basement workbench where the injury was sustained. The father had removed the watch to facilitate inflicting the wound and, presumably, because he had no further need to tell time. Multiple wounds, including gunshot wounds – provided they are close-range wounds – do not preclude the possibility of suicide.

Self-inflicted incised (cutting) and stab (puncture) wounds may be accompanied by "hesitation wounds" which are superficial wounds in the area of the fatal wound made by the suicide prior to causing the fatal wound. Hesitation marks represent an attempt by the deceased to build up the courage to commit suicide.

It is often said that females very rarely commit suicide using firearms and even more rarely do they shoot themselves in the face or head. During my career, I recall investigating three separate suicides of women involving firearms (two of which involved disfiguring head wounds). In cases of either gender, examine the body for evidence of the removal of clothing or jewellery by the deceased prior to the suicide, either to safeguard them (e.g., wedding rings, pendants, etc.) or to facilitate the causing of the injury (e.g., removal of wristwatch prior to causing a laceration of the wrist).

11.8.1.7 Weapon Present at the Scene

The presence of the weapon or method used to cause death (e.g., knife, pills, rope, gun, etc.) may indicate suicide. Multiple methods of death (e.g., pills and suffocation; or pills and slashing wrists) are evidence of the determination of the deceased to take his or her own life and may be indicative of suicide.

Weapons and other means of death may also be removed by relatives and family prior to the arrival of the police in an effort to protect the family (or the deceased) from the stigma usually associated with suicide or to attempt to collect death benefits payable on a life insurance policy that is void in the event of self-inflicted death.

11.8.1.8 Suicide by Cop

"Suicide by Cop" is a phenomenon in which an individual (sometimes a criminal offender – but not always) chooses to end his or her life and selects unsuspecting law enforcement officers as a convenient mechanism of death. The title given to this occurrence is "catchy" and virtually guaranteed to attract media attention. However, it does not satisfy the definition of suicide as the death, although intentional, is not caused by a self-inflicted injury. "Suicide by Cop" is more appropriately classified as "victim precipitated homicide," which is defined as, "[A] killing in which the 'victim' was the first to commence the interaction or was the first to resort to physical violence." [28]

You will recall the *Criminal Code* definition of homicide which is "the killing of a human being by any means, directly or indirectly." [29] The "victim" may be a criminal who would rather die by a police bullet than face arrest and incarceration for a criminal offence for which they are under investigation. Non-criminal "victims" will typically set up a barricaded person scenario or an alleged hostage-taking scenario, knowing that it is likely to attract the desired response from the police.

---

[28]Schmalleger & Volk (2005).

[29]*Criminal Code*, R.S. 1985, c. C-46 s. 222(1).

I once investigated such an occurrence involving a chronic alcoholic, who was depressed over the recent separation from his wife. He telephoned 9-1-1 in a highly intoxicated condition and advised the police dispatcher that an intruder had broken into his residence but had since departed. The caller informed the dispatcher that he was armed with a rifle and wished to speak to a police officer about the incident.

The man's report made little sense to the very competent dispatcher who calmly tried to reason with the caller and attempted to have him exit the residence, without the firearm, to speak to the police officers, who now numbered approximately seven at various points around the house. After a considerable period of time, the man suddenly presented at the door of the residence and pointed a .30-30 rifle at a uniformed officer.

A nearby plainclothes detective verbally challenged the man who swung the rifle at the detective. The officer, fearing for his life and the life of the other officers present, dispatched the man with a single shot from his service revolver. The officer had no way of knowing that the man's rifle was unloaded at the time.

The officer was cleared of any wrongdoing and returned to duty. Many officers involved in similar incidents suffer from considerable stress and guilt. Officers in these incidents react as they have been trained to and are legally and morally justified in their actions. The involved officers are not responsible for having initiated the incident and must continue to rely on making split-second decisions based on the information available to them at the time that are typical of the law enforcement profession. Internal investigations always provide the same findings: "Justifiable shooting. Officer cleared of any wrongdoing."

11.9   INDICATORS OF ACCIDENTAL DEATH

The absence of indicators of either homicide or suicide is the most important indicator in establishing the likelihood of accidental death. Investigators must always remain alert as offenders may attempt to stage homicides to appear as accidental deaths. Usually, the circumstances of the death will be obvious at the scene during the event reconstruction process and may be verified by witnesses, if any are present. What activities was the deceased involved in just prior to his or her death? Is it possible for the accident to have occurred in the manner presented?

A middle-aged man was once found floating face-down in water in front of his cottage in Northern Ontario. The local police attended and observed the scene. The local Coroner, based on the findings of the police investigation, sent the man's body to a hospital some 60 miles away for an autopsy, stating the possible cause of death was either drowning or heart attack.

As the Crime Supervisor for that area at the time, I received a telephone call from a pathologist's assistant who postponed the autopsy, suspecting that the death may have been caused by electrocution. The pathologist's assistant diplomatically suggested that further investigation was warranted. A thorough re-investigation by a more experienced officer resulted in determining that, at the time of his death, the man had been using an electrical hand tool to grind the bottom of a metal boat, which was partially suspended on a metal stand in shallow water in front of his cottage and partly on land.

The power source, a tool shed, was improperly wired and the electrical extension cords, used to conduct electricity from the shed to the work site, were frayed. A reconstruction of the scene resulted in assessing three possible scenarios – all of which could have led to the man being accidentally electrocuted.

Although there was no foul play involved, the findings in such cases entitle the victim's survivors to double the life insurance settlement if the deceased had a double-indemnity policy that pays double benefits in the event of accidental death. While investigators are not in the business of collecting maximum life insurance benefits for surviving family, we are in the business of seeking the truth.

11.9.1 Autoerotic Deaths

One manner of accidental death that is often mistaken as suicide or homicide is the thankfully rare phenomenon of autoerotic deaths. Autoerotic deaths involve a person, typically a male, who induces oxygen deprivation to enhance their masturbatory sexual gratification. The victim may be found nude or with genitalia exposed. The victim may be dressed in fetish wear (e.g., rubber or leather, etc.) or in female attire.

Take note of any sexual paraphernalia at the scene such as pornographic literature, sex toys or homemade devices that involve bondage. The deceased may have set up a mirror to watch himself during the act and may have even used a camera to record the act. Once a state of hypoxia (a deficiency of oxygen to the brain) is achieved and before reaching unconsciousness, the deceased will "rescue" him or herself and may repeat the process over and over.

At some point, an unfortunate victim may wait too long to self-rescue or the "self-rescue" device malfunctions, resulting in the accidental death of the victim by asphyxia.[30]

11.10 INDICATORS OF NATURAL DEATH

An absence of indicators of homicide, suicide and accidental death will be the best indicator of natural death. The autopsy results will likely provide an anatomical cause of death for a diagnosed or undiagnosed medical condition. An investigation of the deceased's health history should be conducted for previous instances or symptoms of life-threatening illnesses.

11.11 DETERMINING TIME OF DEATH

As previously stated, the only accurate way to determine the actual time of death is to have a witness observe the pulse-less and non-breathing body of the deceased fall to the ground, look at their watch and record the exact time. Determining the time of death can be crucial in a (culpable) homicide investigation because it establishes a window of opportunity that is useful to assist investigators in eliminating persons of interest and suspects whose alibi indicates they did not have the opportunity to commit the offence.

---

[30]Geberth (1996).

Conclusively determining the exact time of death is never as easy or precise as it appears to be on television and in the movies. "...[I]t is utterly impossible to fix the exact hour and minute that life ceased unless you were there at the moment of death."[31] Next, we will examine a few of the methods used to determine times of death and their respective shortcomings.

11.11.1   Body Temperature

The normal body temperature of a human being is 37.0 degrees Celsius (98.6°F). After death occurs, a body will cool (or warm) to the ambient (surrounding) temperature. The general rule of thumb is that the body will cool approximately .833 degrees Celsius (1.5°F) per hour. There are many variables that affect a body's cooling rate.

The body of a small child will cool faster than an adult having more body mass. A body laying on a cold surface will cool faster than a body lying in bed, covered by blankets. A body that is totally nude will cool faster than a fully or partially clothed body. A body in an outdoor location in Ontario in November will cool faster than a body in an outdoor location in June in Florida.

With all of these variables, a correlation between body temperature change over a fixed period of time and the ambient temperature has to be established to determine the rate of change of body temperature at that particular ambient temperature. Attempting to determine time of death by body cooling rate relies on the assumptions that all bodies cool at the same rate and that the body temperature at the time of death was normal. Body temperature can be elevated due to drug use, exertion or infection. The resulting data is by no means conclusive proof of time of death to a high degree of scientific certainty.

11.11.2   *Rigor Mortis*

Rigor mortis is the temporary post-mortem stiffening of the muscles of the body. *Rigor mortis* usually begins to appear within 2–4 hours after death and appears first in the facial muscles, spreading downward throughout the body until it is fully fixed at around 12–18 hours. As the tissues of the body begin to decompose, the muscles of the body begin to relax between 24–36 hours after death.

Within 48–72 hours after death, *rigor mortis* will fully disappear. There are many factors that may affect the rate of onset and departure of *rigor mortis*, including: temperature; age of the victim; certain forms of poisoning; physical exertion by the victim prior to death; and asphyxia, making the estimation of time of death based upon analysis of *rigor mortis* open to doubt.[32]

Rigor mortis can still be useful to an investigator as it can "freeze" the position of a body stored or transported in a location different from that in which it is found. A body stored in a closet, steamer trunk (suitcase) or automobile trunk may be folded in a fetal position that, if "fixed," may not be consistent with the position where it is found. It can then provide the investigation with the valuable information that death did not occur at the discovery site.

---

[31]Geberth (1996). Also: Inbau, Reid, Buckley and Jayne (2001).

[32]Locke (1996).

11.11.3 Post Mortem Lividity (*Livor Mortis*)

As the pulse of a dying victim ceases, the heart no longer circulates blood throughout the body. Except in cases in which the victim has lost an extremely large volume of blood, this results in the blood inside the victim's body settling by gravity where, a short time after death, it begins to be visible as a bluish-purple staining of the skin in the lower-most portions of the body. Lividity is easily visible within 4 hours after death and becomes totally fixed around 12 hours after death. Unlike *rigor mortis, livor mortis* does not disappear or subside after death.

Any low area of the body that is in contact with a firm surface (e.g., floor) will appear white (referred to as an area of blanching) as no blood can settle in the capillaries (small blood vessels) of the skin due to the pressure of the body against that surface. While lividity is not conclusive in establishing time of death, it can be very useful in establishing that a body had rested for a significant time in a position other than that in which it was found. A body found lying face down in bed with significant lividity and visible areas of blanching on the victim's back should indicate to an investigator that the body had laid on its back for at least 12 hours against a firm surface before being re-positioned, face down.

11.11.4 Gastric Contents

The examination of the gastric contents of the victim's stomach (i.e., the degree of digestion of food) was once thought to be an accurate scientific method of determining the time of death. It is now recognized that digestion may be delayed by physical or psychological stress for a significant time prior to death. "Two equally competent observers looking at the same stomach contents may get very different impressions and therefore arrive at very different conclusions regarding the time of death… This makes it basically an almost useless method [of estimating time of death]."[33]

11.11.5 Decomposition

Once death occurs, the tissues of the body begin to break down naturally due to the process of putrefaction (decomposition). Tissue begins to swell and gases are formed within the gastrointestinal tract. "This particular method of determining time of death is very inaccurate because of the variables involved."[34] As with other post mortem changes, how quickly a body decomposes is affected by various factors, such as whether or not the body is in an indoor or outdoor location, the amount of clothing worn by the deceased, the mass of the body itself and the ambient temperature, humidity and moisture.

Putrefaction appears in several ways. The veins in a body may begin to darken a dark blue or purple (not to be confused with post-mortem lividity) and is referred to as "marbling" due to its resemblance to the coloured streaks in a piece of marble. The skin may take on a greenish appearance and begin to slough (separate or slip away) from the body.

---

[33]Excerpt from the testimony of Dr. Frederick Jaffe, former Assistant Pathologist for Toronto Western Hospital and former Regional Pathologist for the Province of Ontario, testifying at the appeal of Steven Murray Truscott at the Supreme Court of Canada, October 1966. Quoted in Sher (2002), p. 436.

[34]Geberth (1996).

Swelling of the abdomen occurs due to the formation of gases within the abdominal cavity. A decomposing body begins to emit unpleasant, pungent odours that often result in the discovery of a dead body when neighbours report strange smells emanating from the residence of someone who has not been seen for some time, or may lead to the discovery of a body in an outdoor location.

After a period of time, post mortem chemical reactions convert the fatty tissues of a body exposed to moisture or water into **adipocere**, a white, soap-like substance. A body found in either an indoor or outdoor location with hot temperatures and dry conditions may quickly dehydrate. Through the process of **mummification** the tissues of the body lose their moisture and become hard and leathery.

BOX 11.13 | **Investigative Relevance**

If a pathologist or other medical expert expresses an "opinion" as to the time of death, purely on the single basis of either body cooling rate, *rigor mortis*, *livor mortis* or degree of putrefaction, it should be treated only as a ballpark estimate for investigative purposes only, and should never be relied upon as evidence. Nor should time of death based on any of these factors be used as the single-determining reason to eliminate a person of interest from an investigation or as reasonable grounds to charge any suspect because of the many variables that impact on the reliability of estimated time of death.

11.11.6 Forensic Entomology

Entomology is the study of insects. Insects are often the first to discover an unattended body, whether it is indoors or outdoors. The females of indigenous insect species lay their eggs in the exposed orifices (ears, eyes, nostrils and open wounds) of a deceased victim. The eggs hatch and the larvae feed on the tissues of the body, significantly speeding up the decomposition process.

An entomologist can examine samples collected at the scene (i.e., all stages of development including live adult insects, maggots, and pupae) to identify the species and may even possibly express an estimation of the time of death or, at a minimum, how long the body has been at the location of discovery. As the developmental stages of known species of insects are quite unique, entomology has evolved into one of the more reliable methods of establishing time of death (or time elapsed since a body was disposed of at that location).

Collection of post mortem samples for entomological examination should best be left to a trained forensic identification officer if it is not possible to have the entomologist personally attend the body site. The collection and preservation process is complex and is best carried out by a trained identification officer in collaboration with the entomologist. If you don't have an entomologist in your area, your Regional or Chief Coroner, or your Medical Examiner's Office should be contacted for guidance.

11.11.7 Conventional Investigative Techniques

Sometimes it is only possible to prove that death occurred between the time the victim was positively last seen alive and the time the body was discovered. This information must be gathered from a variety of sources including witnesses, such as neighbours, etc., who last saw the victim alive or heard any signs of life. If the witness is wearing a wristwatch, is it running or did it perhaps stop due to impact damage (freezing the time when the watch's movement stopped)? Employment attendance records, mail opened or newspapers collected, and whether the lights are on or off within the residence of a deceased victim may all give some indication as to a span of time when death might have occurred.

11.12 THE ROLE OF THE CORONER

In Ontario, the Coroner has a statutory authority to investigate sudden and unexpected deaths and certain specified categories of deaths, the circumstances of which warrant further investigation. In other Canadian provinces, medical examiners fulfill a similar function. In Ontario, the legislation that grants coroners authority to perform their duties is the *Coroners Act*.

11.12.1 The Coroners Act

Under the *Coroners Act*, every person who becomes aware of a death in one of the following categories is required to report the circumstances to a police officer or a coroner.

"Every person who has reason to believe that a deceased person died,

(a)   as a result of
    (i)   violence,
    (ii) misadventure,
    (iii) negligence,
    (iv) misconduct, or
    (v)   malpractice;

(b)   by unfair means;

(c)   during pregnancy or following pregnancy in circumstances that might reasonably be attributable thereto;

(d)   suddenly and unexpectedly;

(e)   from disease or sickness for which he or she was not treated by a legally qualified medical practitioner;

(f)   from any cause other than disease; or

(g)   under such circumstances as may require investigation, shall immediately notify a coroner or a police officer of the facts and circumstances relating to the death, and where a police officer is notified he or she shall in turn immediately notify the coroner of such facts and circumstances."[35]

Additionally, deaths that occur in provincial institutions, psychiatric facilities, nursing home, or homes for the aged must be reported to the coroner. In addition to the usual

---

[35]*Coroners Act*, R.S.O. 1990, c. C.37, s. 10(1).

investigation, the coroner must also order that an inquest be held into the circumstances of the death if it involves: inmates of a psychiatric facility; persons at an adult or young offender correctional institution; or someone who is in police custody, or if the death occurred on a construction project or at a mine.

In order to conduct the necessary investigation into a death, the Office of the Chief Coroner, not having any dedicated investigative resources apart from the medical doctors who are appointed as coroners, must rely upon the investigative capacity of the police in the jurisdiction in which the death occurred.[36] The Chief Coroner may also request the assistance of the Criminal Investigation Branch (CIB) of the Ontario Provincial Police, if appropriate, to assist with an investigation or an inquest.[37]

11.12.2 Investigative Powers of a Coroner

The statutory investigative powers under the *Coroners Act* granted to all coroners may also be delegated by the coroner to police officers or medical practitioners not designated as coroners, and authorizes these three classifications of persons to:

- view or take possession of any dead body;

- enter and inspect (which is different than the enter, search and seizure powers contained in s. 487 of the *Criminal Code*) any place where a dead body is found and any place from which the coroner has reasonable grounds to believe the body was removed from;[38]

- inspect any place where the deceased person was, or in which the coroner has reasonable grounds to believe he or she was, before his or her death;

- inspect and extract information from records or writings relating to the deceased; and

- seize anything that there are reasonable grounds to believe is material to the investigation.[39]

Subsection 15(1) of the *Coroners Act* authorizes a coroner to issue a warrant to seize a dead body. While there is no specific statutory authority for a coroner to issue a warrant to "enter," "inspect" or "seize" evidence, common practice (in Ontario) has been for the coroner to issue a warrant, in writing, notwithstanding the absence of documentation specifying the grounds for reasonable belief. Presumably, this practice began in an effort to formalize the delegation of the coroner's authority to police officers, as the grounds for believing that those actions are material and necessary, must be the personal belief of the coroner – not of the police officer executing the coroner's delegated powers.

A police officer may not presume to be exercising the powers of a coroner under the *Coroners Act* when the coroner has no knowledge of the case nor any personal belief of the necessity to "enter," "inspect" or "seize" anything, material or otherwise, and where there has not been any directed delegation of his or her powers to the police officer(s).

---

[36]*Coroners Act*, R.S.O. 1990, c. C.37, s. 9(1).

[37]*Coroners Act*, R.S.O. 1990, c. C.37, s. 9(2).

[38]*Coroners Act*, R.S.O. 1990, c. C.37, s. 16(1).

[39]*Coroners Act*, R.S.O. 1990, c. C.37, s. 16(2).

BOX 11.14	Investigative Relevance

A police criminal investigation must never "piggy-back" on the coroner's investigation to circumvent the requirements of obtaining judicial pre-authorization for search and seizure. There must be a separation between the role of law enforcement to investigate crime and the role of the coroner to investigate certain classes of deaths.[40]

11.12.3 Post Mortem Examinations

The *Coroners Act* provides that "A coroner may, at any time during an investigation or inquest, issue a warrant for a post mortem examination of the body, an analysis of the blood, urine or contents of the stomach and intestines, or such other examination or analysis as the circumstances warrant."[41]

The term "post-mortem examination" is often used to refer to the autopsy procedure which must be authorized by a warrant issued by the coroner, but also applies to any other examination of a deceased body. The autopsy, which is conducted by a qualified pathologist, is a medico-legal procedure in which all internal and external aspects of the body of the deceased are visually, surgically or microscopically examined in an attempt to determine the anatomical cause of death. The more intact a body is and the freer it is from the effects of decomposition, the greater the likelihood of successfully determining the cause and manner of death.

The autopsy should always be witnessed by an investigator and can be one of the most informative stages of a death investigation. The need for interdisciplinary co-operation and teamwork in sudden death investigations is unconditional and requires that all participants (e.g., police, coroner, pathologist and forensic scientists, etc.) freely and fully share all information (that may legally be disclosed) at their disposal.

Once the body has been identified, it is weighed, measured and disrobed, if necessary, and photographed (front and back). All visible wounds or injuries should be measured, described and photographed to scale. If appropriate, x-rays should be taken prior to any dissection (to identify bullets, broken knife tips or fractures). In cases involving the possibility of sexual assault, a Sex Assault Kit should be conducted to preserve biological evidence. In cases of violent assault, fingernail scrapings should be taken from the deceased.

An external examination of the head, eyes, ears, mouth, trunk, extremities and genitalia is conducted and any trauma is described, photographed and recorded. A surgical dissection of the body follows with all internal cavities being examined. Organs are removed, examined and weighed. Blood and bodily fluid and tissue samples are taken and submitted for chemical, biological and toxicological analyses. Following this procedure, the pathologist, if possible, may express an opinion as to the cause and manner of death. When his or her post-mortem examination report is completed, it is forwarded to the coroner.

---

[40]*R. v. Colarusso* (1994) S.C.R. 20.

[41]*Coroners Act*, R.S.O. 1990, c. C.37, s. 28(1).

The pathologist's expertise may be useful in determining whether or not a deceased was dead or alive when certain wounds were inflicted and in the event of multiple wounds which, by themselves or together, would have been sufficient to cause death. A conditional cause of death may be dependent upon subsequent toxicological analysis, such as in cases where it is believed that toxic substances were ingested.

11.12.4 Purpose of a Coroner's Inquest

In cases where the coroner believes it is necessary in the public interest to do so, or where a coroner's jury may make useful recommendations to avoid future deaths in similar circumstances, the coroner may call an inquest. A coroner's inquest is a "quasi-judicial" hearing (i.e., almost judicial in appearance and function, but not totally), presided over by a coroner and open to the public. Witnesses are called to testify under oath (or solemn affirmation) and the trier of fact is the coroner's inquest jury, comprising 5 members (instead of the 12-member juries in criminal proceedings) who return their findings based on a majority decision. The objective of a coroner's inquest is to determine:

- who the deceased was (identity);
- how the deceased came to his or her death;
- when the deceased came to his or her death;
- where the deceased came to his or her death; and
- by what means the deceased came to his or her death.[42]

A coroner's inquest is never allowed to make any determination of criminal responsibility for a death and, "if during an inquest, a person is charged with an offence under the Criminal Code arising out of the death, the coroner shall discharge the jury and close the inquest..."[43]

11.13 COMMON INJURIES IN DEATH INVESTIGATIONS

There are many life-threatening injuries that are encountered during death investigations. Let's now examine some of the more common injuries that investigators come across.

11.13.1 Gunshot Wounds

Determining the distance between the wound and the firearm, if present, may indicate whether or not the wound was self-inflicted. A comparison of the measurement from the trigger to muzzle of a rifle or shotgun, to the measurement of wound to index finger (or toe, etc.) of a deceased person may also reveal whether or not it was even possible for the deceased to discharge the weapon. Be observant for devices at the death scene that may have been utilized by the deceased to extend his or her reach to allow for the discharging of the weapon.

---

[42]*Coroners Act*, R.S.O. 1990, c. C.37, s. 31(1).

[43]*Coroners Act*, R.S.O. 1990, c. C.37, s. 27(2).

Powder burns and soot will be present around the margins of a close-range wound. The number and location of gunshot wounds (e.g., heart, mouth, temple) may also indicate whether the wound was self-inflicted. Testing a recovered firearm with similar ammunition will indicate similar burn patterns to determine the distance involved.

11.13.2 Stab Wounds

Stab wounds may be caused by edged or sharp instruments and are puncture or piercing type wounds rather than cutting wounds (stab wounds are deeper than they are long). Stab wounds may be single or multiple and may be located in any area of the body. Stab wounds are rare (but not unheard of) in suicides and cases of accidental death. The absence of the weapon at the scene is a strong indicator of homicide, unless other indicators of suicide are present. Further investigation may reveal that the weapon was removed by family members prior to the arrival of investigators, for reasons previously stated.

11.13.3 Incised Wounds

Like stab wounds, incised wounds may be caused by edged or sharp instruments, but are more cutting in nature than puncture wounds (incised wounds are longer than they are deep). They may be found anywhere on the body, but especially on the face, neck, wrists, hands, and arms and in some cases, in sexual areas of the body (e.g., breasts and genitalia). It is possible to determine the directionality of the wound as the wound will be deeper at the beginning than at the end.

11.13.4 Asphyxial Deaths

Asphyxial deaths involve the obstruction of adequate oxygen to the tissues of the body, which may or may not involve blockage of the respiratory passages. The following are examples of commonly encountered asphyxial deaths.

11.13.4.1 Drowning

The majority of drowning cases are accidental. Children left unattended and adults under the influence of an intoxicant are common victims of bathtub drowning. Able-bodied adults who are not under the influence of intoxicants do not commonly drown in bathtubs. The autopsy should be able to determine the presence of water in the lungs, indicating that the victim was alive upon entering the water.

11.13.4.2 Suffocation

Asphyxia by suffocation may be accidental, suicidal or the result of homicide. The very young and people who are obese or are under restraint in police custody may die from positional suffocation through compression of the diaphragm, if they are unable to breathe. Homicidal suffocation may result in bruising around the mouth and face where an object was held forcefully against the nose and mouth to cut off the victim's breathing. Fibres and foreign matter may be found in the mouth and airway of the victim. Petechial hemorrhages (small pinpoint red or purple subcutaneous bleeding) may be observed on the conjunctivae (white portions of the eyes), lungs, neck, etc.

11.13.4.3 Hanging

In cases of suicide, the bruising on the victim's neck created by the ligature will be high on the neck and will point upward and to the rear at a sharp angle, consistent with the direction of the ligature against the weight of the victim's body. Petechiae may also be present on the neck and lower limbs of a suspended victim. Look for other indicators of suicide.

11.13.4.4 Ligature Strangulation

Unlike hanging, the ligature bruising to a victim's neck, resulting from homicidal ligature strangulation, will be lower on the neck and will be horizontal, consistent with the direction of the force applied by the assailant. Check for bruising on the victim's back that might indicate force exerted by the assailant in a "push – pull" movement.

11.13.4.5 Manual Strangulation

Manual strangulation (strangling a victim by using hands only) will result in severe bruising to the victim's neck and possibly underneath the chin due to the amount of force applied. If the autopsy is conducted a short time after death, consider returning to the morgue to re-examine the body, as bruising can continue to develop after death. A period of time may allow for a more complete and accurate examination of the trauma to the victim.

11.13.4.6 Blunt Trauma Injuries

A variety of injuries caused by external blunt force may be experienced on their own or in conjunction with other injuries. These include abrasions, contusions and fractures. Abrasions involve a scraping or wearing away of the layers of the skin and depending on their age, may appear as raw and oozing fluid or dry, having formed a scab over the damaged tissue.

Contusions, better known as bruises, are caused by subcutaneous hemorrhaging (bleeding beneath the skin) that doesn't involve a breaking of the skin. Contusions appear discoloured (e.g., blue, black, purple, yellow or green depending on their age) and, if recent, may also involve a localized swelling of the tissue.

Fractures involve a breaking of bone or cartilage of the body that may range from very minor to misshapen or, in the case of a compound fracture, protruding through the skin.

11.13.5 Fire Deaths

Fire deaths may be either asphyxial or the result of thermal injuries. In both cases, it is necessary to prove that the victim was alive at the time of the fire. Victims who were alive at the time of the fire will have evidence of soot in their trachea and lungs, as well as thermal burns to their airways from breathing super-heated air, and carbon monoxide in their blood.

SUMMARY

- Every sudden and unexpected death must be thoroughly investigated to either confirm or exclude the possibility of the involvement of criminal wrongdoing.

- Police officers who respond to death scenes must have a basic understanding of the principles of death investigation and of the relevant law to be able to recognize a suspicious death (i.e., a death involving possible criminal wrongdoing) and to take the appropriate enforcement action.

- Every death should be treated as a homicide until homicide can be eliminated as the manner of death.

- The term "cause of death" refers to the actual mechanism that resulted in the death, or WHAT killed the person (e.g., asphyxia, exsanguination, blunt trauma).

- The term "manner of death" refers to HOW a person died (e.g., homicide, suicide, accidental death, natural causes).

- The difference between homicide and murder is the degree of negligence or specific intention to cause death, or the intention to cause bodily harm that results in death. All murders are homicides – not all homicides are murders.

- Three "bridges" that are burned during every sudden death investigation are: when the body is moved; when the body is autopsied; and when the body is buried or cremated.

- Estimating time of death by evaluating post-mortem changes (e.g., *rigor mortis*, *livor mortis*, body temperature cooling and decomposition) may shed light on the approximate time of death, but there are far too many variables for such an estimation to be considered reliable to a high degree of scientific certainty.

- A forensic entomologist may estimate time of death or how long a body has been at a location from examining insect samples (from various stages of development) collected from a dead body.

- In Ontario, the Coroner has a statutory authority to investigate sudden and unexpected deaths and other specified categories of deaths.

- The investigative powers of a coroner (e.g., to view and take possession of dead bodies, to enter and inspect premises where bodies are or were located, and to seize things material to the investigation) may be delegated by the coroner to police officers or medical practitioners.

- In cases where the coroner believes it is necessary in the public interest to do so, or where a coroner's jury may make useful recommendations to avoid future deaths in similar circumstances, the coroner may call an inquest.

- Interdisciplinary co-operation and teamwork in sudden death investigations is essential and requires that all participants (e.g., police, coroner, pathologist and forensic scientists, etc.) freely and fully share all information (that may legally be disclosed) at their disposal.

DISCUSSION QUESTIONS

1. In addition to the usual "bridges burned" at a typical crime scene, what additional three "bridges" are burned during every homicide investigation?

2. While only a medical doctor may pronounce death, there are certain circumstances in which death of a human being may be presumed by lay persons, including police

officers. In what circumstances may a police officer presume the death of a human being?

3. What are some of the dangers involved in attempting to estimate time of death by analyzing post-mortem physiological changes?

4. What is the difference between a post-mortem examination and a coroner's inquest? What are the objectives of each?

WEBLINKS

www.ihia.org

International Homicide Investigators Association. International organization of homicide and death investigation professionals whose purpose is to promote inter-agency and inter-disciplinary co-operation and partnerships in the field of death investigation

www.mpss.jus.gov.on.ca/english/pub_safety/office_coroner/about_coroner.html

Office of the Chief Coroner, Ontario (Ministry of Community Safety and Correctional Services).

www.e-laws.gov.on.ca/home_E.asp?lang=en

Government of Ontario. Provincial statutes including the *Coroner's Act*.

www.mpss.jus.gov.on.ca/english/pub_safety/centre_forensic/forensic_links.html

Government of Ontario, Ministry of Community Safety and Correctional Services. Centre of Forensic Sciences. Services provided and related links.

www.rcmp.ca/fls/home_e.htm

Royal Canadian Mounted Police. Forensic Laboratory Services. Directory of regional RCMP forensic laboratories and services provided.

http://nddb-bndg.org/main_e.htm

Government of Canada. National DNA Databank. Case histories, statistics and related legislation.

SUGGESTED READING

Geberth, Vernon J: *Practical Homicide Investigation: Tactics, Procedures, and Forensic Techniques, Third Edition.* Boca Raton, Florida: CRC Press, 1996.

Chapter 12

Major Case Management

"[A] skilled commander seeks victory from the situation and does not demand it of his [or her] subordinates."

Sun Tzu[1]

Learning Outcomes

After reading this chapter, students should be able to:

- Describe the circumstances, which if present, benefit investigations from the utilization of Major Case Management (MCM) methodologies.

- Describe the potential benefits of employing MCM methodologies to investigations and how the utilization of MCM might vary between complex and non-complex cases.

- Compare the three functions included in the **command triangle** and give examples of the responsibilities of each function.

- Explain the benefits of merging investigations of crimes committed by a single offender or group of offenders and give examples of when this might be done.

- Describe the purpose of **case conferencing** giving examples of various disciplines, agencies or individuals who might participate in a case conference.

- Give examples of considerations involved in planning a "neighbourhood **canvass**"

12.1 WHAT IS MAJOR CASE MANAGEMENT?

"[M]otivation, investigative skill, and dedication are not enough. The work of the most dedicated, skilful, and highly motivated investigators and supervisors and forensic scientists can be defeated by the lack of

---

[1]Hanzhang (2000).

effective case management systems and the lack of systems to ensure communication and co-operation among law enforcement agencies."[2]

Mr Justice Archie Campbell, *The Campbell Report.*

"Major Case Management" (MCM) is a philosophy that promotes the use of investigative best practices and systems, discussed throughout this textbook, to ensure the efficient and effective administration of every aspect of any major police investigation. Among other things, MCM focuses on: accountability; proper investigative techniques; information sharing and management; inter-disciplinary coordination; the proper use of science and technology during investigations; and ensuring that people have the correct amount of training and experience to conduct the tasks which they are assigned.

The fundamental principles of MCM were originally developed to respond to situations such as multi-jurisdictional serial investigations, homicides and civil disasters of any description. It has since been accepted that the utilization of relevant MCM methodologies will also benefit any complex or high-profile police investigation involving multiple victims, multiple accused, multiple crime scenes, multiple offences, or multiple investigative agencies, where it is feasible to do so.

In 1992, under the auspices of the Canadian Police College (CPC) Ottawa, a nation-wide collaboration of senior Canadian investigators identified desirable areas of expertise and established recommended procedures for senior investigating officers. In 1993, I was fortunate to attend the inaugural MCM course at CPC. The value of MCM was further identified to address the well-documented problems that had occurred during the Paul Bernardo serial rape and murder investigations.[3]

Between 1997 and 2003 I served as the Project Director of a team of senior police and officials of the Ministry of the Solicitor General (as it was then known) that was responsible for the implementation of the *Campbell Report* recommendations. The project's efforts culminated in the design and implementation of a province-wide MCM system for use by all Ontario police services in the investigation of serial predator crimes in single and multiple jurisdictions.

12.2 FUNCTIONS AND RESPONSIBILITIES

"It is also necessary to know the strong points of your various commanders so that you may ask them to do tasks for which they are best suited."

Sun Tzu[4]

Every aspect of any major case investigation falls under the umbrella of what the Canadian Police College first defined as the "Command Triangle," an investigative oversight authority comprising the three main functions of:

1. Case Management: Overall strategic command of the investigation in accordance with established policies and procedures, liaison with other involved law enforcement

---

[2]Campbell (1996), p. 2.

[3]Ibid., pp. 319-326.

[4]Hanzhang (2000).

agencies, victims and the media. Accountable to executive bodies for all aspects of the investigation.

2. Primary Investigation: Identification and procurement of the necessary resources to conduct an investigation. Prioritization, assignment and supervision of investigative tasks, including witness interviews, suspect classification, ground searches, canvasses, search warrant preparation, crime scene investigation, collection of evidence, analyses of evidence and arrests.

3. File Coordination: Collection, management, retrieval, analysis, dissemination and security of all information collected during the investigation. Prioritization of investigative leads for follow-up action. Responsible for completion of necessary court briefs and documents.

In a straightforward and non-complex investigation, the relevant responsibilities of these three functions may be performed by a single investigator. As investigations increase in complexity, such as the involvement of multiple victims, multiple accused, or multiple agencies, each Command Triangle function will be performed by one or more individuals, as required. Whether a case involves 5 witnesses or 500 witnesses, the relevant functions described above must be conducted by investigators with the correct amount of training and experience to conduct the job effectively.[5]

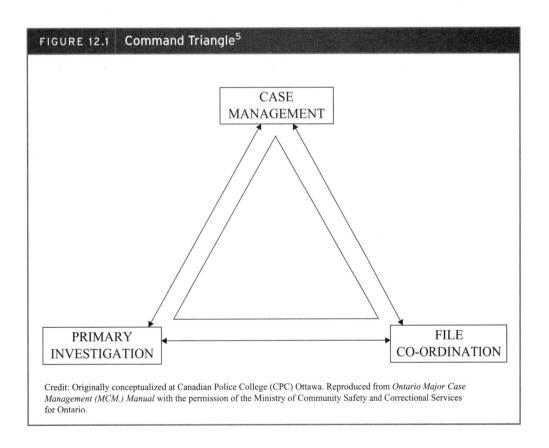

FIGURE 12.1   Command Triangle[5]

CASE MANAGEMENT

PRIMARY INVESTIGATION

FILE CO-ORDINATION

Credit: Originally conceptualized at Canadian Police College (CPC) Ottawa. Reproduced from *Ontario Major Case Management (MCM.) Manual* with the permission of the Ministry of Community Safety and Correctional Services for Ontario.

---

[5]*Ontario Major Case Management (MCM) Manual*, p. 14. (This subject material was initially conceptualized and taught by the Canadian Police College, Ottawa).

12.3 MERGING LINKED INVESTIGATIONS

"There were times during the separate investigations of the Scarborough rapes and the St. Catharines rapes and murders that the different police forces might as well have been operating in different countries.[6]

Mr Justice Archie Campbell, *The Campbell Report*.

When a case involves multiple law enforcement agencies, the coordination of the relevant functions described in the "Command Triangle" becomes critical, in order to guard against relevant information or suspects being overlooked. Information-sharing between the investigations is vital as leads from one case could be instrumental in solving other cases in different jurisdictions.

Unified command and accountability are the main benefits that result from linking similar investigations within a police service or when cases involving multiple law enforcement agencies are linked. One person, having overall command of linked cases, has the authority to ensure that everything is done for the greater good of the overall investigation. Unified command can prevent the rivalry, competition and private agendas that have historically occurred during independent investigations. In Ontario, the practice of linking cases involving multiple police services has become quite commonplace following high-profile problematic cases, such as those of Paul Bernardo and Guy Paul Morin.

Merging linked investigations under single command is necessary both to ensure effective co-ordination and to prevent duplication of effort between agencies. More importantly, linking investigations often results in the quicker apprehension of the person(s) responsible for the crime(s). Merging investigations from different jurisdictions should be considered whenever there are reasonable grounds to believe that the same offender or group of offenders is responsible for a series of crimes. Cases are often merged as the result of linking by forensic methods, including DNA or fingerprints, tire impressions or tool-mark comparison.

Grounds for believing that similar cases were likely committed by a common offender may also be inferred on the basis of behavioural links, such as ViCLAS or Behavioural Profiling, or by conventional investigative methods such as witness identification. Linking similar investigations is desirable in all types of cases but is mandatory in Ontario when the linked offences are among those listed as "Major Case" criteria offences, including:

"(a)   homicides as defined in subsection 222(4) *Criminal Code of Canada*, and attempts;

(b)   sexual assaults, and all attempts [including] sexual interference, sexual exploitation and invitation to sexual touching;

(c)   occurrences involving non-familial abductions and attempts;

---

[6]Campbell (1996).

(d)   missing person occurrences, where circumstances indicate a strong possibility of foul play;

(e)   occurrences suspected to be homicide involving found human remains; or

(f)   criminal harassment cases in which the offender is not known to the victim."[7]

12.4 CASE CONFERENCING

"The agencies co-operated, some of the time. But even such co-operation as there was is not the same thing as joint action. When agencies co-operate, one defines the problem and seeks help with it. When they act jointly, the problem and options for action are defined differently from the start. Individuals from different backgrounds come together in analyzing a case and planning how to manage it."

The 9/11 Commission Report.[8]

Major case investigations can often involve agencies from different backgrounds or disciplines, having different objectives. An unsolved serial homicide investigation may involve multiple police agencies, different Crown Attorneys, the Centre of Forensic Sciences, the Office of the Chief Coroner and other expert agencies and individuals. These agencies all have distinctly different roles to play during an investigation and, to some extent, a division of responsibility needs to be maintained due to their different objectives.

For example, police officers lay charges but Crown Attorneys decide which prosecutions are in the public interest. The role of the police investigator is to determine criminal liability, if any, in a death investigation, while the objective of the Coroner is to determine only the "Who, Where, When, How and By What Means" issues of a death investigation. While contributing greatly to the understanding of how and why an event occurred, forensic scientists have no vested interest in the results of the investigation or the prosecution. The forensic scientist's role, on the other hand, is to apply and interpret science correctly and independently within the context of the investigation.

When all of these investigative agencies are assembled during the early stages of an investigation, cultures may either clash or, in the spirit of co-operation, produce a combined result that is greater than the sum of the individual agencies. When various professions come together to form an Investigative Consultant Team, cross-disciplinary expertise is shared across differing perspectives in what has become commonly known as "case conferencing."

Case conferencing may be formal or informal in structure and may consist of nothing more than regular liaison with a designated forensic scientist or Crown Attorney. When such individuals are designated as case advisers, they are available for ongoing consultation. Such an individual retains a working knowledge of the case from which they may render periodic or continuing assistance to an investigation.

---

[7]Ministry of Community Safety and Correctional Services: *Ontario Major Case Management (MCM) Manual* (Oct. 1, 2004), p. 7.

[8]Final Report of the National Commission on Terrorist Attacks upon the United States, p. 400.

The probability of an investigation falling victim to "tunnel vision" is greatly reduced when different perspectives provide an enhanced clarity of issues that highlight the potential pitfalls of certain strategies. Legal problems can be identified in advance and forensic issues may be examined in order to set up protocols to collect and submit the best possible evidence – in the correct sequence. Having input from all involved agencies in areas of common interest allows the Case Manager to develop and execute more well-informed investigative strategies.

On occasion, there may be sensitive issues regarding an investigation that cannot be fully shared with non-police members of an Investigative Consultant Team. **Holdback evidence**, the existence and identity of confidential police informers or agents and issues surrounding officer safety, such as the use of an undercover officer, may have to be withheld from certain members of such a team of advisers. Usually, however, the vast majority of information can be shared with all members during ad hoc or regularly scheduled ongoing meetings of an Investigative Consultant Team.

While we may be good at what we do, it is not possible to be expert at everything. Sharing information and expertise makes everyone better at fulfilling their individual responsibilities. When you have a problem with your car, you most likely take it to an auto mechanic. If you have a medical problem, it is prudent to seek advice from a doctor or other health care professional. Case conferencing uses this very same principle to apply the expertise of others to planning and problem solving during major case investigations.

If an official investigative consultant team is formed, meetings of all necessary individuals or agencies should be scheduled at regular intervals and minutes of the meetings should be accurately recorded. It may later become important to know who participated in a certain meeting, what was discussed, what became known to the team and when, and (most importantly) what suggestions or recommendations were made to the case manager. The police service(s) involved always maintain tactical control of the investigations, but they should be guided by the consensus of the team.

12.5   INFORMATION MANAGEMENT

"[Paul] Bernardo's name was added to the investigation at least eight times. No system existed to check for prior entries of a name at that time other than a manual search. If information is submitted to a central database and it is possible to search for other entries of similar information, links can be made even if the information is contained in a different file."[9]

Excerpt of the internal report of the Metropolitan Toronto Police
examining the Toronto Police investigative response to the Scarborough Rapes.

A problem that occurs during every major case investigation is how to deal with the large volume of information that is generated by and collected throughout the case. Witness interviews, tips from the public, officers' notes, occurrence reports, vehicle checks,

---

[9]Campbell (1996), p. 298.

criminal records, suspect information, search warrants and investigative assignments can be amassed at an astounding rate.

The problem of information management is further compounded when a **public appeal** or a neighbourhood canvass results in the generation of thousands of new pieces of information. In the absence of systems in place to handle the large amount of new information that is collected over a very short period of time, it is easy for an investigation to become quickly overwhelmed.

Boxes, filing cabinets and entire rooms can be filled to capacity. When this occurs, new investigators assigned to the case are unable to familiarize themselves with the "facts" of the investigation.

No individual can possibly remember thousands of separate pieces of information or recall the original source of every lead. When information overload occurs, critical information can be rendered valueless if it cannot be managed, retrieved, and analyzed. If every investigator assigned to a case is out doing what investigators do, which is collecting more information and more evidence, with no system in place to organize and analyze it, any focus the investigation had in the early stages will be lost in very short order.

Fortunately, it is a simple matter to design and implement systems to manage the flow of information to avoid information overburdening from occurring. An effective information management system is required from the outset of every investigation to ensure that no piece of information or evidence is lost and that similar pieces of information are linked, so that proper investigative action may be taken. Information management systems can be one of two types, either manual or automated.

Manual systems, referred to as **hard copy file management**, comprise paper-based systems that are used to manage documents. Hard copy systems therefore require that every piece of information be reduced to writing and be catalogued in some way. Categories of information are sorted by type, such as tips, statements, assignments, etc. and are sequentially entered on separate registers. An investigator is assigned to index relevant information using an alphabetical system.

BOX 12.1	Proper Investigative Procedure

A witness at the scene of a robbery, John Smith, provides a statement, which is the 14th written interview obtained during the investigation. The Statement Register will indicate statement #14 was taken from Smith, John and will contain the witness's date of birth, address and telephone number. An index card is started for Smith, John with the same personal information, along with a brief summary of what the witness said. The index card will be filed alphabetically with the witness's surname placed before his given name.

For instructional purposes, let's say that, when interviewed, Smith provides information indicating that an acquaintance of his, one Donald Brown, was also present and observed the alleged robbery. Brown evidently left the scene prior to the arrival of the police. Smith also reports seeing a red pickup truck leave the scene of the event immediately following the robbery.

An alphabetical index card will be started in the name of Brown, Donald with an entry indicating that his name was mentioned in the statement #14 of Smith, John. Investigators will now want to interview Donald Brown to confirm his presence at the time of the robbery and obtain any information he might

| BOX 12.1 | (Continued) |

possess. An "assignment form" is completed, assigning Investigator Woods to interview Donald Brown.

The "Locate and Interview" Donald Brown assignment will then be sequentially entered in the Assignment Register, also recording the name of the investigator assigned. The assignment number is also placed on Donald Brown's index card. An alphabetical index card is started for "Red Pickup Truck" cross-referencing it to "Statement #14 of Smith, John."

Two days later, Investigator Woods interviews Donald Brown, who also reports having observed a red pickup truck in the area of the event. The assignment form is completed and the statement of Donald Brown is sequentially recorded (#32) in the Statement Register. A file coordinator or investigator reads the Brown statement and determines whether or not further investigation is required. If not, the Brown statement is filed, a summary of the information received is recorded on his index card and the assignment is marked "Closed" and filed appropriately.

If any new information requiring investigation had been gained as a result of the Brown interview, the process would repeat itself. This may initially sound like a lot of additional work for the sake of 2 routine interviews, but imagine if this case goes on for 2 more years and involves 1 698 additional witnesses. At that point, a person of interest who owns a red pickup truck comes to the attention of the investigation. Everyone looks at each other and asks, "Who was it that mentioned the red pickup truck?"

Without any hard copy record system in place, the prospect of randomly searching through 1 700 statements would be somewhat daunting. But because a hard copy system was established to organize the case files, we simply search for and retrieve the index card labelled "Red Pickup Truck." On the card, we observe that references to a similar vehicle appear in the statements of John Smith, #14 and that of Donald Brown, #32. The system provides "providence" for every piece of information by allowing investigators to trace the origin or source of every piece of information. If the system is carefully maintained, it becomes virtually impossible to lose any piece of information.

The other type of information management system is one that is automated, or computerized. Automated systems range from simple to extremely complex. *Xanalys Investigation Manager*™ (formerly known as *PowerCase*™) by Xanalys LLC is the software application that is currently utilized by the Ontario Major Case Management (MCM) System; however, because of licencing restrictions, its use is restricted to defined criteria major cases.[10] Several other applications are commercially available or have been adapted on an individual case basis by using MS Excel or MS Access databases.

Ad hoc computerized information management systems (those systems which are improvised for a specific investigation) are vulnerable to a variety of problems. Not all personnel may be familiar with data entry or retrieval, and the capacity of the system might overload as data continues to pour into the investigation. Adoption of a more powerful system to handle the capacity of the information after any extended period of time creates its own difficulties. It is labour-intensive to re-enter information from a redundant system to a new system – a luxury that few major investigations can afford.

If one major case investigation using an ad hoc system is later linked with another investigation, it creates information sharing difficulties if one agency is not utilizing the

---

[10] O. Reg. 354/04, s. 3–4, *Police Services Act*, R.S.O. 1990, c. P. 15.

same system or a compatible system. Ad hoc systems are marginally better than having no system at all.

Typically, when ad hoc automated information management systems have been utilized for specific major investigations, the complete case file is archived at the conclusion of the investigation and its value is lost. Data stored on such a system is usually never downloaded into a mainframe database and cannot be applied to future investigations. Automated police records management systems (RMS) are used to warehouse investigative data but few if any such systems, despite their claims, possess the functionality necessary to manage all of the aspects of a major case investigation.

The Ontario Major Case Management System is the first system of its kind to connect all police services in a jurisdiction, using a wide-area network and centralized database to capture and compare compatible investigative data from similar crimes. The Ontario MCM system facilitates the sharing of information when investigations are linked by using standard software that officers are trained in, province-wide. Another tremendous advantage is that even once a case is solved, investigative data remains in the database to be used to compare against other solved and unsolved cases.

12.6 CHRONOLOGY OF INVESTIGATION

When large amounts of information begin pouring into an investigation, it is not long before it becomes difficult for any one person to maintain an accurate working knowledge of information in terms of "who said what" and "what happened when." If the case files have been well-organized, it is possible to produce a summary of the investigation – but to do so is a painstaking and time-consuming task.

Often, when an arrest occurs unexpectedly, a search warrant may be urgently required or the case must be quickly summarized in the form of a bail brief. An experienced investigator will anticipate the possibility of having to prepare legal documents such as search warrants and court briefs on short notice and will ensure that a running chronology of the investigation is regularly maintained throughout the course of the investigation.

The method by which a chronology is developed and maintained is largely a matter of personal preference. A chronology can be prepared in the form of daily or weekly progress reports or may be compiled in a "living document" to which any information of an evidentiary value (inculpatory or exculpatory) is added to as it occurs.

The type of information that I would maintain in a case chronology would include:

1. A summary of the offence(s), including the date, time, location, when and by whom it was reported.

2. Victimology, including a description of injuries if the case involves violence.

3. A summary of witnesses and their observations including victims, police officers and independent witnesses; Include all witnesses, even those who would not be called to testify due to rules of evidence. Remember that hearsay evidence that can be corroborated is admissible for the purpose of developing reasonable grounds to obtain a search warrant. Include summaries of witnesses that are not in agreement with other witnesses or facts of the case. It is the investigator's job to gather and present evidence and let the justice or judge assess the credibility of conflicting witnesses.

4. A summary of police investigative techniques employed and the results.

5. A summary of physical evidence, including the details of where it was found, who found/seized it and the status or results of any forensic testing.

The benefits of maintaining an investigative chronology are many. The main benefit is as a time-saving mechanism that allows for complex search warrants and Crown briefs to be generated in a matter of hours instead of days or weeks. Another benefit is in terms of accuracy. If all information is properly sourced it allows an investigator tasked with drafting a search warrant to confidently state when and from whom a certain piece of information was obtained. Another benefit of a chronology is its sheer versatility. Any investigator, armed with a properly maintained summary, can rapidly confirm all of the information and adopt it as grounds for a search warrant, regardless of how many people produced the chronology.

12.7 OPERATIONAL PLANNING

"If you fail to plan...plan to fail."

Popular maxim.

As we have seen throughout this textbook, criminal investigation is an aspect of policing that involves a great number of possible specialized techniques and police operations. Given the high-profile nature of many criminal investigations, there is a proportionately high risk of failure, injury and civil liability. One method commonly used by experienced investigators to increase the probability of success of any large-scale police operation is **operational planning**.

An operational plan is a document that should be prepared prior to any noteworthy high-risk police operation involving specialized investigative techniques. Operational planning may be applied to single incidents such as one-time mobile surveillance details, stakeouts or evidence raids. Operational planning is more often utilized in regards to long-term operations employing extraordinary resources such as task force investigations, especially those involving multiple police agencies.

Operational planning promotes the effective use of resources by encouraging investigators to identify the objectives of the proposed investigative technique and to ensure efficient execution of the operation in accordance with those identified objectives. Operational planning involves the development of tactical options and the identification of possible obstacles to the success of the operation, in order that the risks may be managed, to the extent possible.

An operational plan is a permanent record that survives beyond the actual operation and serves as an official record of the original intention of, and rationale for, the operation. The operational plan provides an overview of the operation that reflects the consideration and planning that was undertaken prior to the operation, identifies police resources that contributed to the effort and outlines the command and approval authorities that were set in place.

An operational plan can be a very useful document when an operation results in the high-profile arrest of an individual, to demonstrate that the arrest was in fact planned and was not random in nature. In the event of a death or serious injury occurring during a police operation, the operational plan will serve as an official record of the due diligence undertaken by investigators and their police service when the case is scrutinized by a Coroner's Inquest or Special Investigations Unit (SIU) investigation.

Operational planning involves five different stages:

1. planning;

2. briefing;

3. execution;

4. debriefing; and

5. follow-up.

Every operational plan should attempt to address all possible "Who?, What?, When?, Where?, Why? and How?" issues of the proposed operation.

Who? – Who is the target of the operation? Supply the personal information of target(s) and suspect(s) including their names, aliases, dates of birth, fingerprint serial numbers (FPS) and photographs, if available, as well as the information of key known associates. Who will be involved in the operation? Who will be in command?

What? – What is the type, purpose and objective of the intended operation? What do you hope to accomplish? What other investigative efforts have been taken to this point? What alternative operations, if any, are available? What threats to the success of the operation are known to exist? What evidence or results are anticipated? What resources are necessary to ensure the success of the operation? What is the cost of conducting the operation?

When? – When will the operation be carried out? When will any related briefings or debriefings be conducted?

Where? – Where will the operation be conducted?

Why? – Why is it necessary to conduct the proposed operation in the intended manner? Why is it necessary to conduct the proposed operation at all?

How? – How will the operation be conducted? How long will it take to complete the operation? How have contingencies (unforeseen events) been addressed? How will media releases be conducted? How will financial expenditures be accounted for?

12.7.1 Threat Assessment

If circumstances which might have an adverse impact upon a police operation can be anticipated during the planning stage, strategies need to be developed to diminish – not necessarily prevent – the threat, thereby improving the probability of success. Threat assessment should be part of any operational planning stage and should involve those members performing "Command Triangle" functions as well as any other individuals the Case Manager deems necessary. For our purposes, threats may be classified into one of three different categories: low, medium or high-level, and are categorized as follows:

1. Low-level Threat: Circumstances that exist which may be successfully managed through the use of standard operating procedures and available resources.

2. Medium-level Threat: These threats may be impossible to overcome utilizing even extraordinary measures. The operation may result in considerable property damage or personal injury to targets, police personnel or members of the public. The possibility of exposure to civil liability and or media attention is very high. Senior management should be briefed regarding medium-level threat situations and the proposed measures to obtain approval or consensus to proceed with the operation or consider alternative options, if any.

3. High-level Threat: Circumstances indicate a significant threat of extreme property damage, severe injury, death or overall likelihood of failure of the operation. Necessary executive approval to proceed with operation must be sought or consider aborting operation.

12.7.2 Factors Considered in Threat Assessment

"Move when it is advantageous to you. Concentrate or disperse your troops according to circumstances."

Sun Tzu[11]

What situations might render a proposed police operation more hazardous than another, and what circumstances might tend to have more impact than others? Let's examine a number of circumstances that may require the deployment of extra resources or might necessitate the development of alternative strategies.

- *Number of targets or bystanders:* The sheer number of targets will impact the number of personnel required. More personnel will be required to execute an arrest at an outlaw motorcycle club rally than at a professional business conference or sporting event. If a situation exists that requires the evacuation of a large number of people, crowd management and or traffic control officers should be deployed to ensure an orderly movement of people. If a mass arrest situation is required, systems will have to be developed to process and transport arrestees.

- *Motivation of targets or sympathetic bystanders:* Individuals attending biker events and rock concerts have a different motivation than political protestors. Is there a common theme or cause that brought these individuals together. How fervently committed are the targets to the cause? How sympathetic will bystanders likely be to the targets in view of police intervention? All crowd management situations are potentially hazardous due to the anonymity offered to an individual. A "crowd mentality" sometimes causes individuals to behave in ways that they would not normally act. A calm, professional, show of force is often sufficient to discourage unruly behaviour in most law-abiding people, but all possible

---
[11]Hanzhang (2000).

steps should be taken to ensure the safety of the public and the police. The deployment of canine units or undercover personnel is effective in managing crowd situations.

- *Criminal sophistication of the target(s):* Is there a heightened risk that the target(s) might escape? If the operation involves entry to premises, what is the possibility that it is booby-trapped? Will the entry and arrest likely be recorded by counter-surveillance video cameras? Is there an increased risk of loss, removal or destruction of physical evidence? Due to the nature of the offence(s) under investigation, are hazardous materials expected to be on the premises? Ensure that sufficient resources are on site to contain and manage such risks.

- *Violent background of the target(s):* Has the target individual or organization previously demonstrated or threatened to use violence against anyone, including the police? Is there information which suggests the presence of weapons or explosives? Tactical units should be deployed to minimize the threat of injury to the target(s) and to officer safety. Consider alerting a trauma centre and have ambulance personnel or paramedics on stand-by near the site to tend to the injured.

- *Anticipated resistance to the operation:* Are the involved premises fortified against intrusion? Are political agitators present who typically use a variety of weapons from marbles, rocks and pointed sticks to clubs and incendiary devices? Would a change of timing likely reduce the probability of anticipated resistance?

- *Obstacles:* What physical obstacles are present that might impact approach and entry to a site of a proposed operation? Consider the effects of climate, topography, bridges, bodies of water and distance in planning the operation.

- *Available police resources:* How many personnel are available to you? Do they have the appropriate skill sets necessary to conduct some of the expert tasks required? If not, are those experts available to you? Consideration should be given to postponing or aborting the operation if these conditions are not met.

- *Anticipated duration of operation:* What is the anticipated length of time it will take to conduct the operation? What logistics are necessary to transport, relieve and feed personnel at the site if the operation lasts for several hours?

12.7.3 Operational Plan Briefings/Debriefings

Once an operational plan has been finalized, if executive approval is necessary or even desirable due to expense, scope or anticipated threat involved with conducting the operation, the plan should be formally presented to the required executive body for necessary approval. Copies of operational plans should never be submitted through normal office channels in order to restrict the number of personnel having advance knowledge of the proposed operation. A prudent investigator ensures that briefings of senior command personnel are conducted when multiple agencies are to be involved in the operation, or extraordinary expense, or if there is likely to be exposure to danger or liability.

The next important briefing to occur involves the personnel assigned to conduct the operation itself. To preserve the integrity of the operation, participating personnel should be assembled at the briefing location without being given any prior information regarding their assignment. Once briefed, personnel are restricted both in their movements and their outside communications to ensure the security of the operation.

Consider the use of photographs, maps, plans of buildings, etc., to familiarize everyone with the location and target(s) of the operation. Every participating member must be given a clear understanding of the objective of the operation, all aspects of his or her respective role, who he or she reports to and any other relevant information.

Following the operation, wherever possible, all participating personnel should meet to critique what occurred, whether the objectives were met, what worked well and what could have been done to improve the efficiency or success of the operation. Even a successful operation might have been conducted in a more efficient manner and suggestions can be incorporated into future operational planning.

12.7.4 Follow-up of Operation

An operational plan should also anticipate the possible ramifications of the operation, in terms of arrests, charges, seizure of evidence, etc., and also detail which individuals or units within a police service will be responsible for the law enforcement activities that result. High-profile investigations can create a great deal of work for personnel, who may resent the unanticipated increase to their workload.

If more than one police service is involved in an operation, who will lay the charges? Who will process and store the seized evidence? Who will prepare the court documentation, etc? If these details were specified in the operational plan, involved parties need only refer to their copy to confirm what was agreed to.

A representative from every police service or unit that will be impacted by a high-level operation should participate in the operational planning and agree to accept the workload that results from the operation. Press conferences, if any, should be conducted jointly in the location(s) specified in the operational plan.

12.8 CANVASSING

Canvassing is a specialized form of interviewing technique that attempts to identify potential witnesses from an identifiable group of people. Canvasses are often conducted of residents of a neighbourhood, street or apartment building, or patrons or employees of a mall. Motorists or service providers who commonly utilize a specific route that may have placed them in the area of a crime at or near the time of the incident under investigation may also be canvassed. Canvassing differs from a "public appeal" in that public appeals randomly target the general public, seeking information about the event under investigation.

A canvass may be conducted in various ways, including, but not limited to:

1. door-to-door interviews in a neighbourhood, street, or apartment building;

2. surveys of pedestrians or motorists at an established check-point;

3. establishing a visible presence aimed at soliciting information from a certain group of people who habitually frequent the location where a crime occurred, such as a public park, place of entertainment or shopping mall; or

4. interviewing employees at a large workplace, office building or factory, etc.

Canvassing is an investigative technique that does not benefit every type of investigation. For example, if the body of a homicide victim is located in a remote forest or parkland location that does not typically attract large numbers of people, canvassing may not be a viable investigative technique. An investigator in charge of any serious case should always stand at the crime scene, and slowly turn in a circle while asking him or herself, "Who might have seen what happened here?" in order to determine whether or not conducting a canvass might be beneficial.

If the investigator sees several windows of apartment buildings with a potential view of the scene, or if the scene is situated on a high-volume traffic route, he or she should consider whether or not anyone may have been looking out one or more of those windows or whether anyone in a passing vehicle may have seen something of relevance to the investigation.

The investigator must then assess the feasibility of conducting a canvass. I am not suggesting that canvasses should only be conducted in densely populated urban settings – quite the contrary. The primary consideration in utilizing a canvass should be whether or not the potential exists to identify possible witnesses and, if so, whether the use of the canvassing technique is justified.

Canvassing may be beneficial to investigations either where the suspect/accused has been identified or where the identity of the offender remains unknown. A word of caution when conducting canvasses in unknown suspect cases; canvassers should always be instructed to remain mindful that any person they canvass might turn out to be the person responsible for the incident under investigation.

In any event, conducting a proper canvass can be very labour-intensive and expensive. "Any canvass, once undertaken, must be diligently followed through to its natural conclusion to ensure that all possible sources of information have been contacted."[12] There are several things that may be done to maximize the effectiveness and success of a canvass, including:

1. assigning adequate human resources to carry out a canvass based on a realistic assessment of the area and the number of people to be canvassed;

2. canvassers must be well-briefed about the crime and about what questions need to be asked of the persons canvassed;

3. conducting follow-up visits when no answer is received at a particular door of an apartment or residence during the original canvass;

4. all persons within any given residence must be identified and canvassed independently;

---

[12]Ministry of Community Safety and Correctional Services: *Ontario Major Case Management (MCM) Manual* (undated), p. 44.

5. names of boarders and visitors who were present at the time of the incident under investigation must be recorded – more than once suspects have been identified through conducting a neighbourhood canvass – and

6. ensure that potential witnesses identified by canvassers are interviewed.

Prior to conducting any canvass, all relevant information should be provided to the canvassers. In cases involving an identified offender that attracts significant media attention, the investigator in charge of the case should consider contacting the media to request that the identity and photograph of the offender not be published. Widespread media publicity about the offender may negatively impact a possible future identification by any subject of a canvass. The media usually responds favourably to reasonable requests from the police considering the public interest, but they will not hold off indefinitely – time will be of the essence in conducting a canvass in this situation.

As with most areas of criminal investigation, the potential success of any operation increases in direct proportion to the amount of advanced planning and preparation. Canvassing is no exception to this rule.

12.8.1 The Canvass Plan

Every canvass undertaken should be the assigned responsibility of a single co-ordinator, someone with expert knowledge or demonstrated experience in conducting canvasses. The co-ordinator may or may not be the investigator in charge of the case. Where the co-ordinator is someone other than the investigator in charge, the two must remain in close consultation regarding all aspects of the proposed canvass. In formulating the canvass plan, the Case Manager, in conjunction with command triangle personnel and the canvass co-ordinator, should be able to provide the following information:

1. Define the goals and objectives of the proposed canvass. What do you intend to accomplish through the canvass?

2. Define the area(s) to be canvassed. Obtain an adequate supply of maps of the area(s) to be canvassed. Keep the areas to be canvassed realistic in terms of resource availability and the estimated time you anticipate will be necessary to conduct the canvass.

3. Determine whether there is a need to establish a separate canvass command post. The comings and goings of potentially large numbers of police officers/volunteers involved in the canvass can quickly overwhelm the day-to-day operations of even large police stations. Consider the use of a secure public building, such as a community hall, arena or vacant office building near the area(s) to be canvassed. Is there sufficient parking?

4. Determine the sequence of the areas to be canvassed. Targeted areas should be determined in "bite-sized chunks" utilizing the "law of diminishing return." Concentrate canvassing efforts on areas that produce high returns over areas that produce low returns, using a pattern of concentric circles surrounding the crime scene.

5. Determine the questions to be asked during the canvass. It is necessary to prepare a standardized canvass questionnaire to ensure that all canvassers ask the same

questions. The use of a standard questionnaire also ensures that all information is eventually returned to the canvass co-ordinator for evaluation. It may be necessary to go through several drafts of the questionnaire before the correct list of questions is selected. Once the canvassers start knocking on doors, it may be too late to include another question. Due to the labour-intensive nature of canvasses, assume that you have only one opportunity to conduct the canvass. Canvassers should record all responses on the questionnaires and sign them prior to handing them in at the completion of their duties.

6. Identify, acquire and allocate the necessary resources to conduct the canvass. The investigator in charge of any investigation must be prepared to justify the extraordinary resource demands involved in conducting a canvass to his or her superiors. Lack of human and physical resources may restrict the selection of areas to be canvassed. There is little point in undertaking a canvass if it would take an inordinate amount of time for available resources to complete it. Even though a particular case may warrant a canvass, resources are not always available – unfortunately, we don't live in a perfect world.

    Fortunately, a properly organized canvass can be conducted using less than expert investigative resources as door-to-door canvassers. Uniformed police officers, auxiliary members, cadets, etc., can all be pressed into service for this duty, providing they are properly briefed and supervised.

    If the canvass will take a full day or perhaps several days to complete, consider the need to schedule rest periods and meals for the canvassers. Arrange for refreshments and washroom facilities for canvassers, unless the canvass can be completed in a relatively short period of time. Arrange to have a sufficient number of questionnaires, clipboards, pens, etc., on hand to issue to the canvassing personnel.

    Civilian volunteers are not recommended for use as canvassers, as they lack the investigative instincts that uniformed members of police services quickly develop. Suspects responsible for certain crimes have also been known to involve themselves, as searchers, etc., during an investigation to avoid suspicion and to gain intelligence on the progress and status of the investigation.

7. Determine whether or not the upcoming canvass would benefit from prior media attention. The investigator in charge of the case must consider whether or not to publicize the canvass in advance. Doing so can have the effect of reaching out to cooperative witnesses, who will ensure that they make themselves available to be canvassed. If unco-operative witnesses or an unknown suspect resides in the area(s) to be canvassed, it might also warn such persons of the impending canvass and allow them the opportunity to be absent when the canvass occurs. Considering that the objective of a canvass is to identify potential witnesses, the benefit of advanced media attention for co-operative witnesses usually outweighs the risk of alerting possible suspects.

8. Arrange to have interviewers available to conduct follow-up interviews and forensic identification personnel available in the event of physical evidence being located. Especially when utilizing non-investigative resources to conduct the actual canvassing, any potential witness with relevant information should only be identified by competent interviewers. Individuals or teams of interviewers should be assigned to conduct interviews or photo line-ups with identified witnesses, either

immediately upon being identified by canvassers, or at a pre-arranged time, as decided by the investigator in charge of the investigation.

9. Arrange to have forensic identification personnel either on-site or on standby to respond to reports of located physical evidence to ensure the proper handling of evidence and provide the proper chain of continuity. If physical evidence is located during the course of a canvass, it should be secured in the location in which it was found, and the investigator in charge of the case should be notified as soon as possible.

The above list sets out only the minimum requirements that need to be included in a canvass plan and should in no way be considered an exhaustive list of issues that could be included, given the individual circumstances of each case in which canvassing might be utilized.

12.8.2 Briefing and Debriefing Canvassers

The briefing and subsequent debriefing of the canvass team might be the single most important factor to be considered when conducting a canvass. An investigator with intimate knowledge of the case should be assigned to brief the canvassers on the important details of the case, except for hold-back evidence that needs to remain confidential. There is no point in sending out a small army of canvassers if they lack at least a basic understanding of the case they are involved with.

A properly planned canvass that is not properly executed is doomed to fail. A full and complete briefing of the basic facts of the case will help to give the canvassing personnel a sense that they are about to participate in an important and worthwhile operation and will result in increased attention to detail on the part of the canvassers.

Canvassers also need to have a clear understanding of precisely what is expected of them, in terms of their precise area(s) of assignment, how they are to carry out their duties and to whom they should report any significant developments that might occur during the canvass. A de-briefing at a pre-arranged time will also identify important information obtained, or identify any problems that were encountered so that they may be addressed.

During the de-briefing, the canvass co-ordinator must: ensure that the names, etc., of all personnel participating in the canvass have been recorded; collect all completed questionnaires; identify any area(s) that were not canvassed; identify areas that require follow-up; record the details of any physical evidence collected during the canvass; and collect copies of notebook entries made by all canvassers. Once the canvass is complete, all records pertaining to the canvass should be forwarded to the officer responsible for overall file co-ordination.

12.9   VICTIM ISSUES

Certain victims may unwittingly contribute to their own victimization, in minor ways, such as through routine daily activities which have the effect of increasing the risk of victimization. Walking alone at night in a high-crime area would be an example of how a victim could contribute to his or her victimization by making him or herself an easy target of opportunity for a mugger.

No victim, however, asks for or deserves to be the victim of a crime unless he or she is the initial aggressor who is later injured in self-defence by the person they provoked. A victim who was intoxicated by alcohol or drugs at the time of the offence, or who voluntarily accompanied an acquaintance and was later victimized by him or her, is no less a victim than someone who was abducted by a stranger.

A primary victim is considered to be an individual against whom a crime was directly committed. Crime also impacts the family members of both surviving and deceased victims. The family members, including spouses, children or parents of primary victims are referred to as secondary victims.

Assistance to victims of crime is one of the core responsibilities that Ontario police services are mandated to provide under the *Police Services Act*.[13] Victims are sometimes made to feel as though they were directly responsible for what happened to them as the result of the treatment they receive from the health care profession, law enforcement and the courts. Genuine victims have already been victimized once by the offender – it is the responsibility of those employed in the administration of justice to treat victims of crime in such a way as to minimize the possibility of post-crime victimization during the investigative and court processes.[14]

When dealing with primary victims, first impressions mean absolutely nothing. Investigators must realize that no two victims will necessarily respond in the same way to having been victimized. I have personally observed bona fide victims of brutal sexual assaults react calmly, while others reacted hysterically. I have also personally observed inexperienced or insensitive investigators mistakenly assess victims as not being credible because they arbitrarily believed the victim's reaction should have been opposite of what it actually was.

Investigators should never impose their own judgments on how they believe a victim should appear. We are all very different individuals – with different personalities and different coping mechanisms. There are no guidelines on how a victim of any crime "should behave."

BOX 12.2	Investigative Relevance

What all victims have in common is that, during the crime, a certain amount of control over their lives was taken away from them. Investigators, from initial uniformed responders to the most senior investigators, can assist victims to regain that lost control and begin to cope with what has happened to them. As these feelings of loss of control may continue for some time following the crime, it is advisable, to the extent possible, to involve the victim in the investigation so that the victim feels that he or she does have a role to play.

If a person has been the victim of a crime involving personal violence, he or she may feel violated and fear for his or her safety, especially if the crime occurred within the victim's own residence. It is important to offer assurances to the victim that he or she is out of harm and can rely on the police, family, relatives and caregivers to keep him or her safe. A victim should only be subjected to an in-depth interview if he or she is physically and emotionally able to and chooses to participate in the interview. Granting the victim the choice to decide whether or not to be interviewed is sometimes the first step in helping the victim regain control of his or her life.

---

[13]*Police Services Act*, R.S.O. 1990, c. P.15, s. 4(2).

[14]Schmalleger & Volk (2005).

12.9.1 Victim – Police Relationship

An effective relationship between the victim of a crime and the police is one of ongoing communications and support that encompasses several different areas. To the extent that it is possible, every effort should be made to limit the number of investigators who have ongoing dealings with the victim of a crime. On rare occasions, a personal bond can form between a victim and an investigator, involving inappropriate conduct or behaviour that would threaten the professional nature of the victim–police relationship.

An investigator may develop sympathetic feelings toward a victim that evolve into personal feelings. A victim may develop similar feelings for an investigator as the result of perceived kindnesses or out of gratitude for assurances of his or her safety. If a Case Manager becomes aware that a professional relationship between a victim and an investigator may become compromised, immediate steps should be taken to reassign the primary victim liaison officer to prevent any possible discredit to the investigator or to the police service.

12.9.2 Security and Protection

Protection of the victim should always be of paramount concern. In many cases there may not be any apparent security concerns with respect to the victim, but victims should always be asked whether or not they are concerned for their personal safety. This is especially true in cases involving domestic assault, or threatening and criminal harassment involving a current or former relationship between the victim and the offender.

Where the offender has previous convictions or complaints of assaultive behaviour against the victim, or where the victim has threatened the victim with bodily harm or death, the investigator should request that the prosecutor consider a **show cause** hearing to justify the continued detention of the accused for reasons of public safety as authorized by s. 515(10)(b) *Criminal Code*.

If the accused is released from custody pending trial, or escapes from custody, an assigned investigator should assist the victim to develop necessary precautions to ensure the victim's safety. Considerations for a victim's safety plan will include, among other things, the need for an unpublished telephone listing, possible change of residence, physical security measures such as locks, alarms or police guard, transportation, employment and child care arrangements.

12.9.3 Communication and Control of Information

The best way to ensure a victim feels included in an investigation is to keep him or her well-informed about as many aspects of the investigation as possible. A victim should always personally hear about a material development in the case, rather than hear or read about it in the media. Regular contact should be established to inform the victim about the progress of the investigation – even if there are no significant developments to report. If releasing certain information to a victim would compromise the integrity of the investigation, explain why the information cannot be shared with him or her.

Discussing such topics as the laying of charges will familiarize the victim with certain legal issues and discussing the need for media releases will show respect for the victim's privacy. Victims should always be kept aware of the status of pre-trial custody, release, bail conditions, escapes, future court appearances and court dispositions with respect to the accused.

An assigned investigator should notify the primary victim, "who [has] suffered physical or emotional loss as a result of the commission of the offence,"[15] of his or her opportunity to prepare a Victim Impact Statement to be introduced in court for any offence at the time of sentencing. In the event of the death of the primary victim, a spouse, common-law partner, relative, legal guardian or dependant of the primary victim may prepare a Victim Impact Statement.[16]

Following the finalization of court proceedings, the victim should be personally notified of the disposition, sentence, any relevant term of probation, or acquittal of the accused. Notification of the victim should not end with the trial disposition. The victim should also be made aware of any appeals launched by the accused, or any parole hearings or judicial reviews with respect to the accused.

12.9.4 Referral and Compensation

There are numerous agencies designed to assist, support and compensate victims of crime. Among them, the Victim Crisis Assistance and Referral Services (VCARS) is an agency comprised of volunteers working in conjunction with the police to provide round-the-clock support and counselling for victims of crime. The Victim Witness Assistance Program (VWAP) is a province-wide, court-based program in Ontario that provides orientation and support to victims and witnesses during their involvement with the criminal justice system. Both programs are partially funded through the Victims' Justice Fund as the result of victim surcharges imposed by courts in addition to other dispositions at the time of sentencing.[17]

The Criminal Injuries Compensation Board may, on application of a victim, award financial compensation for medical or emergency expenses arising out of the injury or death of a victim, including loss of wages, pain and suffering, etc.[18] Other agencies such as shelters and Children's Aid Societies may also provide assistance and support to victims of crime. Investigators should be aware of all services available to victims in their area and refer the victim to any appropriate service.

Investigators should be aware of and comply with the provisions of the *Ontario Victims' Bill of Rights* with respect to the treatment of and notifications to victims of crime.[19]

12.10 MEDIA RELATIONS

We previously examined the issue of media relations in relation to the attendance of journalists and reporters at crime scenes (see Section 6.11). The media can be a powerful resource during a major case investigation. Whether or not the media turns out to be

---

[15]*Criminal Code*, R.S. 1985 c. C-46, s. 722(4)(a).

[16]*Criminal Code*, R.S. 1985 c. C-46, s. 722(4)(b).

[17]*Provincial Offences Act*, RSO 1990, c. P.33, s. 60.1(4) and *Criminal Code*, R.S.C. 1985, c. C-46, s. 737.

[18]*Compensation for Victims of Crime Act*, RSO 1990 c. C. 24.

[19]*Victims' Bill Of Rights*, S.O. 1995, Chapter 6.

your enemy or your ally depends largely on the relations that you develop and maintain throughout the course of your investigation. The benefits of good media relations during a major case investigation cannot be underestimated.

Let's review the three fundamental principles of effective police–media relations:

1. Never, ever, lie to the media by knowingly providing them with information you know to be false. The information will be attributed to you and your integrity could be compromised for doing so.

2. Never ignore the media's request(s) for information. The media has a job to do and if they are put in the position of having to conduct their own investigation, they will do just that – though usually, to a far different standard from that to which police investigations are conducted.

3. Never demonstrate favouritism to any particular media outlet by exclusively granting information that would allow them to gain advantage with respect to the story over their competitors. Allow all media outlets the identical opportunity to publish information contained in media releases.

Cynicism among investigators toward journalists for merely doing their job of keeping the public well-informed of crime-related issues is both undeserved and short-sighted. The purpose of the media is not to compete with the police, nor is it their purpose or their intention to interfere with a police investigation – they simply wish to report the facts. They are in competition with other media outlets to be the first to report the news and occasionally, as a result, the media is fairly or unfairly accused of sensationalizing a case in an attempt to gain favour with a large share of viewers or readers.

Once information regarding a case is provided to the media, police control over the information and the manner in which it is presented is forfeited. If information is inaccurately reported, specific and legitimate concerns should be addressed with the individual media outlet involved. The role of the police is not to judge media reporting or their evaluation of what is or is not newsworthy.

We live in an age of instantaneous information-sharing, and as investigators we must acknowledge three fundamental issues:

1. Policing is a profession that attracts a great deal of media attention due to the very nature of our duties.

2. Media reporting can have an enormous impact on an investigation.

3. An objective journalist may take a critical view of certain aspects of a police investigation. Do not take such reporting personally – policing is a profession that regularly attracts such scrutiny from stakeholder groups.

If investigators wish to maintain any control over the information that is released to the media and the portrayal of that information by journalists, they must be prepared to be in a partnership, of sorts, with the media. In my opinion, the police actually share a responsibility with the media to keep the public informed regarding crime trends and specific events. Benefits to the police for co-operating with the media are numerous. For example:

1. Public awareness that the police are actively investigating an incident may result in individuals reporting relevant information that might be useful in solving the case.

2. Public education encourages citizens to take proactive measures to protect themselves against possible victimization resulting in crime reduction.

3. Public confidence in local police services is enhanced when the efforts being taken by police to combat crime are visible.

Every police service should have at least one trained media liaison officer who should be utilized as a resource in designing and delivering media releases regarding major occurrences. Larger police services that recognize the benefits of good media relations sometime employ entire units for this purpose. Various forms of media, such as newspaper, radio and television all have different needs and trained media officers will be sensitive to those needs in their advice to you.

Interaction between the police and the media usually occurs in one of the following ways:

1. Formal dissemination of a written media release dealing with a certain event or investigation. This type of release is well suited to radio and print media and alerts all media to the fact that a newsworthy event has occurred. A written media release is a one-way flow of information that can be disseminated simultaneously to all media outlets in a given area. Information is easy to control and the accuracy of the information is assured.

2. A scheduled press conference to which members of the media are invited and presented with certain facts by designated spokespersons who deliver prepared statements and may or may not answer specific questions. Press conferences are excellent opportunities to share media attention among multiple agencies involved in an investigation. Press conferences can also be used to emphasize visual images such as seized evidence, photographs or other graphics. A press conference is suitable for all forms of media but especially television. Press conferences typically reach out to the largest number of viewers, due to the numbers of media outlets who participate in the coverage.

   The biggest danger involving press conferences is, ironically, police officers themselves. In dealing with the media, police officers should refrain from expressing personal opinions about the nature of the crime, a suspect's character or his or her guilt or innocence. When you answer questions from the media, your replies should be brief and factual. If a question is improper, or if the release of the information might jeopardize the investigation, professionally decline to answer, stating a legitimate reason for not responding. When responding to the media, limit your response to the known facts of the case. If a question can't be answered because you don't have the information, simply state that you don't have that information.

3. One-on-one interviews may occur at any time, or at any location, during an investigation. This type of interview may involve any type of media; however, it frequently involves the electronic media.

4. Public appeals, such as for information regarding a case or the whereabouts of a certain individual, may be conducted utilizing any form of media. Be prepared for a high volume of response to a public appeal and ensure that you are prepared to manage and respond to the flood of tips that may be generated. Crime Stoppers

re-enactments and the announcement of the creation of telephone hotlines are examples of a public appeal for information. A public appeal may also be part of a scheduled press conference (see Section 12.10.2: Public Appeals).

5. Special news features are sometimes conducted to reach large numbers of viewers and provide them with specific information concerning a case. A special news feature may also involve a request for the public to provide information but is mostly utilized to communicate information about a case. Television programs such as *America's Most Wanted* and locally produced programs can be used to communicate information to the public, witnesses, other possible victims and even suspect(s).

BOX 12.3 | **Proper Investigative Procedure**

Bear in mind that suspects routinely follow the progress of the investigation of their crimes in the media. Regardless of the type of media event being utilized, always demonstrate professionalism and confidence that the case will be solved – and always assume that your suspect is listening to you. Behavioural profilers may be able to provide assistance in drafting specific press releases to create a desired impact or to provoke a desired response from an unknown offender.

It is possible to be entirely truthful with the media while portraying quite different messages. For instance, evaluate the effectiveness of the following alternative exchanges between a reporter and an investigator:

1) **Reporter:** "Officer, do you have any suspects?"

   Officer: "We have absolutely no idea who committed this crime."

Or, alternatively:

2) **Reporter:** "Officer, do you have any suspects?"

   Officer: "We are still in the preliminary stages of our investigation. We are looking into a number of persons of interest in the case and we are interviewing possible witnesses who may have information that is relevant to the investigation. We've received a number of tips from the public, and we will continue to thoroughly investigate every lead until we identify the person(s) responsible for this crime."

Both responses say the exact same thing, which is, "We have absolutely no idea who committed this crime," but the latter response communicates a far more positive message to the listener, whether the listener is a member of the public or the person(s) responsible for the crime.

Always secure and file copies of all media releases, transcripts, press clippings and media footage with the case file in order to show precisely what information was released by the investigation. The Case Manager should authorize all media releases in any form.

12.10.1 Release of Personal Information

Every police service has established policies and procedures governing the release of information to the media. It is important to be familiar with and to comply with those policies when drafting media releases or when responding to questions during media interviews.

In the early stages of an investigation prior to charges being laid, the time, date and location of an alleged offence under investigation may be released along with a general description of the offence. Matters touching upon the specific evidence of the case should be avoided where possible. Surviving victims should only be described by gender, age, their towns or cities of residence and by their relationship to the case.

Information, including photographs, of a homicide victim or missing person should only be released with the permission of the victim's next-of-kin. In a sexual assault investigation or any investigation involving a child victim, neither the victim's identity nor any personal information that might tend to identify the victim should be released to the media.

A police chief or Commissioner of the OPP, or his or her designate, may release personal information with respect to any individual who has been charged with, convicted, or found guilty of an offence under any federal or provincial statute. A reasonable belief must exist that the person whose information is released poses a significant risk of harm to the community and that the disclosure will have the effect of reducing the perceived risk.

The personal information of a suspect or accused that may be released includes:

1. the individual's name, date of birth and address;

2. the offences with which he or she has been charged or convicted and any sentence imposed;

3. the outcome of any court proceedings;

4. whether the accused is in custody or at large;

5. in cases where the individual has been released from custody, any terms or conditions of his or her release; and

6. date of release or impending release from custody of an individual on parole or temporary absence pass.[20]

Investigators should never allow or arrange for individuals who are suspected of or charged with offences to be paraded or posed in front of the media in the practice colloquially referred to as a "perp walk." The media may attempt to photograph accused persons being transported into and from court facilities, but this practice too should never be facilitated by the police.[21]

A police service may not publish the name of a young offender except under the authority of an order signed by a youth court judge that establishes that "there is reason to believe that the young person is a danger to others; and publication of the information is necessary to assist in apprehending the young person."[22] Such an order authorizing the publishing of the identity of a young offender includes the release of photographs, physical descriptions, etc., but expires five days after it is issued.[23]

---

[20]O. Reg. 265/98, s. 2-3 Amended to O. Reg. 81/00, *Police Services Act*, R.S.O. 1990, c. P. 15.

[21]Ministry of Community Safety and Correctional Services *Ontario Major Case Management (MCM) Manual* (Oct. 1, 2004), p. 31.

[22]*Youth Criminal Justice Act*, S.C. 2002, c.1 in force April 1, 2003, s. 110(4).

[23]*Youth Criminal Justice Act*, S.C. 2002, c.1 in force April 1, 2003, s. 110(5).

12.10.2 Public Appeals

One investigative strategy used to reach out to members of the public and request their assistance is to conduct a public appeal. Public appeals may involve one or more media, alone or in combination, such as radio, television, print media, Amber Alerts, billboards, handbills, etc., but all methods involve the direct solicitation of relevant information from potential witnesses.

Public appeals can be very effective in identifying previously unknown witnesses that have relevant information regarding an investigation. A public appeal may take the form of a television re-enactment, a case study or a simple billboard beside a high-volume thoroughfare that asks, "Have you seen _____?," or "Do you know the whereabouts of _____?"

A public appeal can quickly turn into a "double-edged sword" if a case manager fails to anticipate and takes steps to manage the large number of tips from the public that can be generated. In a high-profile case, a case manager should obtain prior approval for the necessary resources to conduct a public appeal. The senior police service media liaison representative should be consulted to determine the appropriateness of a public appeal in terms of both benefits and media to be utilized.[24]

A plan to conduct a public appeal should be developed that clearly states the planned objective and duration of the appeal, the proposed media to be utilized, the wording of the appeal and the necessary resources to conduct the appeal. Public appeals utilizing the regular police switchboard to handle incoming tips can quickly overwhelm the system and the call-takers. It is recommended that respondents be urged to contact a dedicated number such as a "hot-line" set up for the express purpose of the appeal and that appropriate staff, including civilian volunteers or auxiliary police, are in place to handle calls the moment the appeal goes "live."

Call-takers should be briefed about the case so they have some knowledge of the facts. Investigators also need to be involved in order to supervise the incoming tips and to prioritize tips for investigative follow-up.

SUMMARY

- Major Case Management (MCM) promotes the use of investigative best practices and systems to ensure the efficient and effective administration of every aspect of a police investigation. MCM focuses on accountability, proper investigative techniques, information sharing and management, inter-disciplinary co-ordination, science and technology, and training.

- While originally developed to respond to multi-jurisdictional serial investigations, homicides and large-scale civil disasters, MCM methodologies will also benefit any

---

[24]Ministry of Community Safety and Correctional Services: *Ontario Major Case Management (MCM) Manual* (Oct. 1, 2004), p. 32.

complex or high-profile police investigation involving multiple victims, multiple accused, multiple crime scenes, multiple offences, or multiple investigative agencies.

• The "Command Triangle," comprising the functions of case management primary investigation and file co-ordination, oversees all aspects of any major investigation.

• When reasonable grounds exist to believe that similar offences are the work of a common offender, those cases, whether they involve one or more police services, should be merged to provide unified command and to promote effective information sharing between investigations.

• "Case conferencing" involves various relevant professions such as police, coroners, prosecutors, technical experts and forensic scientists coming together to provide formal or informal cross-disciplinary expertise on matters relating to an investigation to allow a case manager to make better informed decisions about an investigation.

• Manual (hard-copy, paper based) or automated (computerized) information management systems are necessary to manage, retrieve and analyze the large volumes of information that are collected during major police investigations.

• A chronology of a case that is maintained throughout the course of an investigation will serve as a useful summary for urgently required search warrants and other legal documents such as bail briefs.

• Operational planning promotes the effective use of resources by encouraging investigators to identify the objectives of the proposed investigative technique and to ensure efficient execution of high-level police operations in accordance with those identified objectives. Operational planning also involves the identification of low, medium or high-level threats to an operation and enables investigators to take precautions, where possible, to mitigate impediments to the success of any operation.

• Canvassing is a specialized interviewing technique that attempts to identify potential witnesses from an identifiable group of people, such as residents of a neighbourhood, street or apartment building, or patrons or employees of a mall. Motorists or service providers who utilize a specific route that may have placed them in the area of a crime at or near the time of the incident under investigation may also be canvassed.

• A comprehensive canvass plan should be developed to identify the objectives of a canvass, necessary resources, sequence of areas to be canvassed, questions, the desirability of media involvement, briefing/debriefing of canvassers and follow-up investigation of tips prior to embarking on a canvass.

• Investigators should be aware of and comply with the provisions of the *Ontario Victims' Bill of Rights*, or equivalent provincial legislation, with respect to the treatment and compensation of victims of crime.

• Effective relations with victims of crime include ongoing support, communication, sharing of information, security/protection and referral involving a minimum number of investigators throughout any police investigation.

- Media coverage can have an impact upon any major police investigation. Whether the media turns out to be a useful resource or an obstacle depends largely on the relations that are developed and maintained throughout the course of the investigation.

- Public appeals can be very effective in identifying previously unknown witnesses that have relevant information regarding an investigation. A public appeal may take the form of a television re-enactment, a case study or a simple billboard beside a high-volume thoroughfare but must be managed properly due to the large number of tips that can be generated from the public.

DISCUSSION QUESTIONS

1. What are the three functions comprised by the "Command Triangle"? What respective responsibilities pertain to each? What type of cases or circumstances might result in the assignment of multiple personnel to the three Command Triangle functions?

2. What types of similar investigations lend themselves to being merged? What rationale might justify the linking of investigations in the same or in different jurisdictions? What benefits could be expected to result from the merging of similar investigations?

3. What are the circumstances that should be considered when assessing the level of threat to the success of any operation during the planning stage of formulating an operational plan?

4. What are some of the various methods employed by investigators when dealing with victims of crime in an effort to minimize the possibility of post-crime victimization?

5. What are the three fundamental principles that ensure good media relations in respect to police operations?

 ## WEBLINKS

www.attorneygeneral.jus.gov.on.ca/english/about/vw/vcars.asp

Ontario Ministry of the Attorney General – Victim Crisis Assistance and Referral Services (VCARS). Description of the provincially funded police-based community volunteer program, offering 24/7 support and referral services to victims of crime or disaster. List of available VCARS locations in Ontario.

www.attorneygeneral.jus.gov.on.ca/english/about/vw/vwap.asp

Ontario Ministry of the Attorney General – Victim/Witness Assistance Program (VWAP). Description of the provincially funded court-based program that provides information and support to adult and child victims and witnesses of crime throughout all aspects of their involvement with the criminal justice system. List and contact information of VWAP locations in Ontario.

www.attorneygeneral.jus.gov.on.ca/english/about/vw/cicb.asp

Ontario Ministry of the Attorney General – Criminal Injuries Compensation Board. Description of compensation that may be awarded to primary or secondary victims of violent criminal offences that occurred in Ontario, that resulted in personal injury or death.

www.attorneygeneral.jus.gov.on.ca/english/about/vw/ovc.asp

Ontario Ministry of the Attorney General – Office for Victims of Crime (OVC). Permanent advisory body to the Ministry of the Attorney General on matters of victim's services and the Victims Justice Fund.

Chapter 13

Courtroom Procedures

"Injustice anywhere is a threat to justice everywhere."

Martin Luther King Jr, US civil rights activist (1929-1968).[1]

Learning Outcomes

After reading this chapter, students should be able to:

- Compare and contrast the powers of arrest for both a civilian and a police officer.

- Explain what is meant by the term "statute of limitations," and distinguish between the statute of limitations for indictable and summary conviction offences.

- Explain the significance of the mnemonic "R.I.C.E." in relation to the public interest, which if met, prohibit arrest without warrant by a police officer.

- Explain the procedure for taking an individual, arrested without warrant for an indictable offence committed in a different province, before a justice.

- Explain the limitations on the number of expert witnesses for any party to a judicial proceeding who intends to call to provide opinion evidence.

- Distinguish between "conscriptive" and non-conscriptive evidence and explain the significance of each as it relates to the fairness of a trial.

13.1 INTRODUCTION

"The first thing we do, let's kill all the lawyers."

Dick the Butcher in *Henry VI*, by William Shakespeare (1564-1616).[2]

The legendarily disdainful reputation with which the legal profession is often regarded is graphically demonstrated in the preceding Shakespearian quotation. Yet, imagine the

---

[1]Martin Luther King Jr: "Letter from Birmingham Jail, April 16, 1963."

[2]William Shakespeare: *Henry VI, Part II*, Act IV, Scene ii, Lines 83-84.

chaos that could threaten our free society without a legal system involving laws, courts and lawyers as a mechanism for resolving disputes between individuals. The adversarial nature of our criminal justice system is intended to ensure that both sides in criminal proceedings receive the best possible representation in order to ensure fairness in all aspects of the proceedings.

While the investigator's duty is always to seek the truth, truth is not always the final result in the arena of the courtroom. If proving an allegation would involve undue prejudice (unfairness) to the accused, the court must arrive at a verdict of not guilty. Often, a verdict of "not guilty" is misinterpreted to mean "innocent." While a verdict of "not guilty" does sometimes equate with a finding of innocence, it can alternatively mean that there was simply insufficient evidence upon which the court could convict to the legal standard of beyond reasonable doubt.

Whether the investigator believes a particular verdict to be right or wrong, the result is still justice. It is the investigator's duty to enforce the law and to seek the truth – not to dispense justice. Justice is determined in the courtroom. Police officers must always conduct themselves according to the rules of law and must always respect the verdict of a court. An unjust verdict may be appealed, but that is a decision for the Crown – not the investigator – to make.

I learned a very valuable lesson early in my policing career that I would like to share with you and that is, "Good defence lawyers make good police officers." Actually, the same is true of good Justices of the Peace, good Judges and good Crown Attorneys, but any lessons learned from them usually tend to be "easy" lessons. When you are on the witness stand and the weaknesses of your case are being critically exposed during vigorous cross-examination by an experienced defence counsel, it should give cause for an investigator to consider, "What more could I have done to make my case stronger?" or "Next time, I'll do things differently."

Contrary to popular belief, most embarrassment experienced by police officers in court is not the responsibility of defence counsel. If defence counsel successfully exposes reasonable doubt in your investigation, the responsibility for any ensuing embarrassment rests entirely with the investigator. You can avoid or at least reduce embarrassing moments in court through adequate preparation of your case and by following the interdisciplinary, ethical and systematic approach recommended throughout this textbook.

Let's imagine that you have now arrived at the stage where you have conducted your investigation to the best of your ability, and have solved your case. If the resolution of the case has resulted in the laying of criminal charges, you will undoubtedly find yourself compelling the attendance of the accused in court – where all aspects of a criminal investigation come together.

13.2 POWERS OF ARREST

We first examined a police officer's warrantless powers of arrest in Section 1.3.5, dealing with the objectives of an investigation and the development of reasonable grounds. You should familiarize yourself with these powers, which are set out in subsection 495(1) *Criminal Code*. Remember that in court you may be required to articulate what your reasonable grounds for arrest were in order to prove that the arrest you conducted was in fact lawful.

"A peace officer may arrest without warrant:

(a)   a person who has committed an indictable offence or who, on reasonable grounds, he [or she] believes has committed or is about to commit an indictable offence..."

For a police officer to arrest an individual for an indictable offence contained in any federal statute (or a dual procedure offence which, for the purposes of arrest is treated as indictable), the officer must either have witnessed the commission of the offence, or have a reasonable belief, exceeding mere suspicion, that the suspect committed the offence. This authority also allows a police officer to arrest an individual for the purpose of preventing the commission of an offence when the officer has reasonable grounds to believe the person is about to commit an indictable offence.

(b)   "a person whom he [or she] finds committing a criminal offence..."

A police officer may arrest any individual he or she finds committing a summary conviction, dual procedure or indictable offence contained in any federal statute. Finally,

(c)   "a person in respect of whom he [or she] has reasonable grounds to believe that a warrant of arrest or committal, in any form set out in Part XXVIII in relation thereto, is in force within the territorial jurisdiction in which the person is found."

The police officer may arrest the individual, if the officer has reasonable grounds, such as a confirmed Canadian Police Information Centre (CPIC) report or some other current and reliable information that a warrant for the arrest or committal of a person exists within the territorial jurisdiction, meaning the region or province where the person is found.

You will remember the previous definition of "reasonable grounds" as: a set of facts or circumstances, which if true, would lead an ordinary, prudent and cautious individual to have a strong belief which exceeds mere suspicion. The standard of reasonable grounds is a significantly lower standard than *prima facie* evidence and a far lower standard than proof beyond a reasonable doubt.

Police officers must often rely on the hearsay evidence of others and other available evidence, for their reasonable grounds to arrest individuals. A police officer must remain objective when formulating reasonable grounds and must consider all available evidence. Investigators must never be selective in their determination of which evidence to rely upon and which evidence to disregard unless the discounted evidence is clearly unreliable.[3]

Peace officers may also receive into custody any individual who has been lawfully arrested, without warrant, by a citizen under the authority of section 494 *Criminal Code*, which reads:

"1.   Any one may arrest without warrant:

(a) a person whom he finds committing an indictable offence; or
(b) a person who, on reasonable grounds, he believes

(i) has committed a criminal offence, and
(ii) is escaping from and freshly pursued by persons who have lawful authority to arrest that person."[4]

---

[3]*Chartier v. Quebec (Attorney General)* (1979) 2 S.C.R. 474, 48 C.C.C. (2d) 34, 9 C.R. (3d) 97.

[4]*Criminal Code*, R.S. 1985, c. C-46, s. 494(3).

This authority allows citizens to arrest individuals, without warrant, for committing any indictable offence, if the citizen actually witnessed the individual commit the offence. A citizen may also arrest a person if he or she did not actually witness the offence being committed but has a reasonable belief, exceeding mere suspicion, that the individual is escaping from and is "freshly pursued" by someone who does have the lawful right to arrest him or her. This is the classic scenario where an individual is being chased down a street by a victim yelling, "Stop! Thief!," or is being chased by one or more police officers.

2. "Any one who is:

(a) the owner or a person in lawful possession of property, or

(b) a person authorized by the owner or by a person in lawful possession of property, may arrest without warrant a person whom he finds committing a criminal offence on or in relation to that property."

Property owners and persons in lawful possession of property (or persons who are authorized by the owner or person in lawful possession of property) may arrest any person they witness committing any offence against a federal statute on or in relation to the property. This might include the owner or tenant of a house, or the owner of a business or his or her employees, family members or any person(s) designated by the owner to safeguard the property (such as a security guard or watchperson).

Additionally, citizens may also "detain" (arrest) any person whom they witness either committing, or about to join in, continue or renew a breach of the peace, and deliver that person to a peace officer.[5]

Police officers effecting an arrest must always be mindful of the requirements of subsections 10(a) and 10(b) of the *Charter of Rights and Freedoms* relating to a peace officer's duties to promptly advise any person arrested of the reason for his or her arrest and to inform the person of his or her legal right to retain and instruct counsel without delay.

13.3 WHEN NOT TO ARREST – THE IMPORTANCE OF R.I.C.E.

Certain limitations are placed on a police officer's warrantless powers of arrest. These limitations are set out in subsection 495(2) *Criminal Code* which states:

"A peace office shall not arrest a person without warrant for (a) an indictable offence mentioned in section 553..."

Section 553 sets out offences which are the exclusive or **absolute jurisdiction** of a provincial court judge to try. Even though these offences are dual procedure or hybrid offences, if the prosecutor were to elect to proceed by indictment, the accused may not elect to be tried in a higher court, due to the designation of the offence as being the absolute jurisdiction of the provincial court.

The rationale for the absolute jurisdiction designation is to keep the lower-end offences at the provincial court level. Trials of this scope are numerous and are well within

---

[5]*Criminal Code*, R.S. 1985, c. C-46, s. 30.

the capability of a Provincial Court judge to try without a jury. This list includes committing, counselling, conspiracies or attempting to commit the following offences:

- Theft under $5 000 (other than theft of cattle)
- False pretences under $5 000
- Possession of property under $5 000 obtained by commission of an indictable offence
- Fraud under $5 000
- Mischief to property under $5 000 – see subsection 430(4) CC, or the commission of any of the following offences:
- Keeping a gaming or betting house
- Betting, or bookmaking
- Placing bets
- Offences dealing with lotteries and games of chance
- Cheating at play
- Keeping a common bawdy-house
- Fraud in relation to fares (transportation fraud)
- Breach of recognizance
- Breach of probation order, or
- Possession of schedule II drugs in amounts less than the maximum amounts specified in schedule VIII of the *Controlled Drugs and Substances Act* (<30g. of Cannabis [Marijuana] or < 1 g. of Cannabis resin).

A peace officer shall not arrest, without warrant, for any of the following offences:

1. any designated section 553 *Criminal Code* offence, listed above;
2. any dual procedure (hybrid) offence; or
3. any summary conviction offence

in situations where the public interest may be satisfied by not arresting the individual, especially if the following needs, described by the mnemonic "R.I.C.E," have been met, namely:

R   Reasonable grounds, Court: No reasonable grounds exist to indicate that the accused, if not arrested, would fail to appear in court.

I   The identity of the individual has been satisfactorily established.

C   Continuation or repetition of the offence: Prevention of the repetition of the offence, or another offence does not require the individual's arrest.

E   Evidence: The arrest or continued detention of the person is not justified by the need to secure or preserve evidence of the offence.[6]

---

[6]*Criminal Code*, R.S. 1985, c. C-46, s. 495(2).

13.4 COMPELLING THE ATTENDANCE OF THE ACCUSED IN COURT

If a police officer arrests an individual without a warrant for an indictable, dual procedure or summary conviction offence (where R.I.C.E. is not satisfied), or continues the lawful arrest of a citizen, the accused must be charged within a maximum period of 24 hours or be released from custody.[7] Whether the individual is issued an appearance notice, requiring him or her to appear in court in lieu of arrest, or released conditionally, or held pending a bail hearing, all judicial proceedings commence with the swearing or affirmation of an information in Form 2 before a justice.[8]

A charge must be laid within the statute of limitations (the time limit following an offence during which a charge must be laid) allowed for that type of offence. It should be noted that while there is no statute of limitations for indictable offences, a summary conviction offence must be laid within six months after the offence, unless both the prosecutor and the accused consent to the extension.[9] Dual procedure (hybrid) offences may be laid more than six months following the offence as they are treated as indictable offences for the purposes of determining the statute of limitations.

Arrest is not the only way to compel the attendance of the accused to court. A police officer may issue an Appearance Notice in Form 9 *Criminal Code* instead of arresting a person who has not yet been charged for a section 553 CC (absolute jurisdiction) offence, a dual procedure (hybrid) or summary conviction offence, where R.I.C.E. has been satisfied.[10]

A police officer may arrest a person without warrant for a section 553 CC (absolute jurisdiction) offence, a dual procedure (hybrid) offence, or a summary conviction offence where the public interest considerations of R.I.C.E have not been satisfied. For example, a person arrested for operating a motor vehicle while his or her ability to drive was impaired by alcohol contrary to section 253(a) *Criminal Code* may be returned to a police station for the purposes of administering breathalyzer tests. The arrest of the allegedly impaired driver would be justified due to the public interest requirement to ensure that evidence of his or her impairment could be established (secured or preserved). Once the breathalyzer tests are administered, however, that public interest requirement will have been met, continued detention is no longer justified on the grounds of securing evidence.

Once the public interest considerations of R.I.C.E., plus the additional consideration of safety and security of the victim or any witness to the offence have been assured, any person arrested for a section 553 CC indictable offence (absolute jurisdiction), dual procedure offence or summary conviction offence must be released by way of appearance notice or later issued with a summons, as soon as practicable.[11]

The *Criminal Code* places additional responsibility upon the Officer in Charge of a police station or detachment to effect the release of persons arrested without warrant for

---

[7]*Criminal Code*, R.S. 1985, c. C-46, s. 503(1)(a).

[8]*R. v. Southwick, ex p. Gilbert Steel Ltd.*, (1968) 1 C.C.C. 356, 2 C.R.N.S. 46 (Ont. C.A.).

[9]*Criminal Code*, R.S. 1985, c. C-46, s. 786(2).

[10]*Criminal Code*, R.S. 1985, c. C-46, s. 496.

[11]*Criminal Code*, R.S. 1985, c. C-46, s. 503(1)(a).

section 553 indictable (absolute jurisdiction), dual procedure (hybrid) offences, summary conviction offences and any other offence punishable by a term of imprisonment not exceeding five years, as soon as practicable. Interim release options available to an Officer in Charge include a summons (Form 6 CC), Promise to Appear (Form 10 CC), or a Recognizance entered into before an Officer in Charge (Form 11 CC).[12]

When a person has been issued with an Appearance Notice or was released from custody on a Promise To Appear or a Recognizance entered into before an Officer in Charge, an information (Form 2) charging the alleged offence should be laid as soon as practicable, or at least before the returnable court date set on the release form. Otherwise the method of release will be invalidated.[13]

A police officer or an officer in charge must release unconditionally any person arrested without warrant on reasonable grounds that he or she was about to commit an indictable offence, if the officer is satisfied that the continued detention of the person is no longer necessary to prevent the commission of the indictable offence.[14] If a person is arrested with or without warrant and is not released by the arresting officer, or by the officer in charge, the arrested person must be released from custody or taken before a justice within 24 hours.[15]

If the person responsible for the commission of an offence cannot be conveniently located or is avoiding service of a summons or has absconded (fled from) the jurisdiction of the court, a warrant to arrest the person may be issued by a justice in Form 7, if it is in the public interest to do so.

13.5 ARREST WITHOUT WARRANT – OUT OF PROVINCE INDICTABLE OFFENCE

A person may be arrested without a warrant for indictable offences committed in Canada, outside of the territorial jurisdiction in which the person is found. If an arrest warrant exists in British Columbia for an armed robbery that occurred there and the person is subsequently found in Ontario, the person may be arrested without warrant upon the expressed indication of the agency holding the arrest warrant to return the prisoner.

In such a case, the prisoner must be taken before a justice in the territorial jurisdiction in which he or she was arrested and remanded into custody for a period up to six days to allow the police from out of the province to execute their warrant.[16] A warrant issued in one province must be first endorsed in Form 28 *Criminal Code* prior to execution in the new territorial jurisdiction.[17]

---

[12]*Criminal Code*, R.S. 1985, c. C-46, s. 493.

[13]*Criminal Code*, R.S. 1985, c. C-46, s. 505.

[14]*Criminal Code*, R.S. 1985, c. C-46, s. 503(4).

[15]*Criminal Code*, R.S. 1985, c. C-46, s. 497(1).

[16]*Criminal Code*, R.S. 1985, c. C-46, s. 503(3).

[17]*Criminal Code*, R.S. 1985, c. C-46, s. 528.

13.6 SUPERIOR CRIMINAL COURT – ABSOLUTE JURISDICTION OFFENCES

Only a judge of a superior court may release an accused from custody or try an accused charged with committing, attempting or conspiring to commit one of the following offences as set out in section 469 *Criminal Code*:

1. Sec. 47 CC Treason;

2. Sec. 49 CC Alarming Her Majesty;

3. Sec. 51 CC Intimidating parliament or a legislature;

4. Sec. 53 CC Inciting to mutiny;

5. Sec. 61 CC Seditious offences (illegal acts to overthrow a government);

6. Sec. 74 CC Piracy; or

7. Sec. 75 CC Piratical acts.

Also, for committing or conspiring to commit the offence of Murder, Sec. 235 CC, or for committing any of the following offences:

8. accessory after the fact to murder or treason;

9. bribery by the holder of a judicial office; or

10. an offence under Sections 4–7 *Crimes Against Humanity and War Crimes Act.*

The most commonly encountered offences, which are the absolute jurisdiction of Superior courts of criminal jurisdiction, are the offences of murder, conspiracy to commit murder and accessory after the fact to murder. The offence of attempted murder is not in this class of offences and, subsequently, an accused charged with this offence also has the option to elect to be tried by a judge of the Provincial Court.[18]

13.7 JUDICIAL INTERIM RELEASE

"Where law ends, tyranny begins."

William Pitt, Earl of Chatham, British statesman (1708-1778).[19]

Where a prisoner has been arrested, either with or without warrant, and is not released from custody by the police, he or she must be taken to appear in front of a justice within 24 hours of his or her arrest. The justice is required to release the individual on his or her undertaking to appear in court unless the prosecutor "shows cause" why the continued detention of the individual is necessary or why the accused should be made to comply with certain conditions, known as conditional release.[20] An accused arrested with or without warrant for a section 469 CC offence (absolute jurisdiction of a superior criminal

---

[18]*Criminal Code*, R.S. 1985, c. C-46, s. 554(1).

[19]William Pitt, Earl of Chatham quote retrieved April 26, 2005, from www.bartleby.com

[20]*Criminal Code*, R.S. 1985, c. C-46, s. 515.

court) must also appear before a justice within 24 hours but will be remanded in custody to be dealt with by a superior court judge.

At any time before or during an interim release or "show cause" hearing, a justice may, on the application of the prosecutor or the accused, remand the accused to custody for a period of up to three "clear" days. "Clear days" is a term meaning excluding the first day and the last day. An accused person remanded on Monday for three clear days would have to appear again on or before Friday of the same week as the Monday and the Friday were not included in the three day remand. An accused may be remanded for longer than three clear days if he or she consents to the remand.[21]

13.7.1   Show Cause Hearings

Where the prosecutor feels that the continued detention of an accused person in custody is necessary, he or she may attempt to "show cause" why the accused should not be released for one or more of the following reasons:

1. Detention is necessary to ensure the person will attend court.

2. Detention is necessary to ensure the protection or safety of the public (including any victim or witness) having regard to the likelihood that the accused, if released, would commit a criminal offence or interfere with the administration of justice.

3. Detention is justified in order to maintain public confidence in the administration of justice due to the severity and circumstances of the offence, the probability of conviction, and the potential for a lengthy term of imprisonment if convicted.

While the *Criminal Code* places the onus on the prosecutor to "show cause" why the accused should not be released from custody, it is still the responsibility of the police to gather the evidence that will be relied upon to show cause and provide it to the prosecutor, who will introduce it in court.

The *Criminal Code* describes the types of admissible evidence that may be introduced by a prosecutor during a show cause hearing and includes the following:

"(i) ...that the accused has previously been convicted of a criminal offence;

(ii) ...that the accused has been charged with and is awaiting trial for another criminal offence;

(iii) ...that the accused has previously committed an offence under section 145 [Escape lawful custody, Fail to attend court, Fail to appear for the purposes of the *Identification of Criminals Act*, or Fail to comply with the conditions of an undertaking]; or

(iv) to show the circumstances of the alleged offence, particularly as they relate to the probability of conviction of the accused." And also:

"(d.2) The justice shall take into consideration any evidence submitted regarding the need to ensure the safety or security of any victim of or witness to an offence, and

---

[21]*Criminal Code*, R.S. 1985, c. C-46, s. 516(1).

(e) The justice may receive and base his [or her] decision on evidence considered credible or trustworthy by him [or her] in the circumstances of each case."[22]

Evidence that demonstrates the probability that the accused, if released, might fail to attend court might include evidence regarding his or her lack of stability or attachment to family and to the community. Investigators should gather all information relating to an accused that would assist the court in making a finding that could lead to an order for release or detention, including:

1. Criminal record: If the accused is convicted for the offence charged, is there a strong likelihood of conviction and punishment in the form of a period of imprisonment? Does the accused have a history of failing to appear in court or breaching the conditions of previous releases?

2. Residence: Does the accused have a fixed residence where he or she has lived for any length of time or does the accused relocate frequently from place to place or depend on others for housing?

3. Employment: Does the accused have an occupation and was he or she employed at the time of the offence? What is the accused's previous employment history?

4. Family Status: Does the accused have family or relatives in the area that would be able – and willing – to provide support (financial, moral or emotional), or be responsible for the accused if he or she is released from custody? If so, are they trustworthy?

5. Personal history: Is the accused suffering from any known disorders or addictions which, if left untreated, might tend to place him or her at risk of re-offending if released? Does the accused have a stable environment to return to, if released from custody?

6. Offence: Is there evidence of planning and premeditation in the offence charged?

7. Victims/Witnesses: Is there evidence of any threats of violence, or previous violence or threats of violence toward any victim or witness in this case?

8. Investigation: Is there any evidence that the accused, if released, could destroy or tamper with evidence in the case or otherwise interfere with the investigation or the administration of justice?

Witnesses may be called to give sworn evidence at a show cause hearing and may include hearsay evidence, "provided it is credible and trustworthy."[23] As an investigator I often testified at show cause hearings, to summarize the findings of an investigation, including the events of the case, the findings of other investigators and the anticipated evidence of civilian witnesses.

Where the prosecutor successfully shows cause why an individual should not be released from custody, the justice will order that the accused be detained in custody until he or she is dealt with according to law.[24] Where an accused is charged with a

---

[22]*Criminal Code*, R.S. 1985, c. C-46, s. 518(1).

[23]*R. v. Powers* (1972), 20 C.R.N.S. 23, 9 C.C.C. (2d) 533 (Ont. H.C.).

[24]*Criminal Code*, R.S. 1985, c. C-46, s. 515(5).

Superior Court absolute jurisdiction (s. 469 CC) offence, the justice must remand the accused in custody for one week at a time until he or she is dealt with by a Superior Court Judge.[25]

If a prosecutor does not show cause justifying the individual's continued detention, the individual may be released on his or her undertaking before the justice and may be required to comply with appropriate conditions that include:

1. reporting to police or other persons at stated intervals;

2. remaining within the jurisdiction of the court or other jurisdiction;

3. notification to police of change of address or employment;

4. abstention of communication with victims or witnesses or to refrain from attending designated locations;

5. deposit of his or her passport, if any;

6. any other condition considered necessary to ensure the safety and security of victims or witnesses; and

7. prohibition of possession of weapons, ammunition or explosive substances if the offence involved personal, threatened or attempted violence, terrorism, criminal harassment, or designated *Controlled Drugs and Substances Act* offences.

Accused persons who are remanded in custody or ordered detained in custody until being dealt with by law may also be required to abstain from communicating with victims or witnesses or other designated persons, as the justice deems appropriate.[26]

13.7.2 Reverse Onus – Show Cause Hearings

There are instances where the onus (responsibility) is placed on the accused to show cause why his or her continued detention is not necessary. Among others, some of the more common reverse onus situations include those where an accused is charged with:

1. an indictable offence other than s. 469 CC offence (superior court absolute jurisdiction) while at large awaiting appeal [see s. 679, 680 CC];

2. designated offences involving criminal organizations;

3. a designated terrorism offence;

4. an indictable offence other than s. 469 CC offence (superior court absolute jurisdiction), while not ordinarily a resident of Canada;

5. failing to attend court or to comply with the conditions of a summons, appearance notice, promise to appear, recognizance before an officer in charge or a recognizance or an undertaking given to a justice while at large for another offence; or

6. an offence punishable by life imprisonment under sections 5–7 of the *Controlled Drugs and Substances Act.* [27]

---

[25]*Criminal Code*, R.S. 1985, c. C-46, s. 515(11).

[26]*Criminal Code*, R.S. 1985, c. C-46, s. 516(1).

[27]*Criminal Code*, R.S. 1985, c. C-46, s. 515(6).

Even though the onus is placed on the accused to establish why he or she should not be further detained, an investigator must still gather relevant evidence, if any, as for a normal show cause hearing to assist the prosecutor rebut evidence introduced by the defence.

13.8 ARRAIGNMENT, CROWN ELECTION, PLEA AND ELECTION BY ACCUSED

When an accused charged with a criminal offence appears in court, the charge(s) against the accused will be read to him or her, usually by a court clerk. The reading of the charge to the accused in court is referred to as the "**arraignment**." Prior to the accused being asked to indicate his or her plea to the charge, if the charge is a dual procedure offence, the court clerk or the judge will ask the Crown Attorney how he or she elects to proceed on the charge, either by indictment or by summary conviction.

If we sat in a courtroom, the actual proceedings would sound something like this:

John Smith answers to his name and stands before the court when his name is called from the docket.

Court:	"Are you John Smith?"
Accused:	"Yes, I am."
Court:	"John Smith stands charged that he, on or about the 25th day of May, 2005, at the City of Orillia in the Central East Region, did unlawfully break and enter a certain place, to wit: a building situated at 25 Godfrey Drive, with intent to commit an indictable offence contrary to paragraph 348(1)(e) of the Criminal Code of Canada. Do you understand the charge against you?"
Accused:	"Yes, I do."

As the offence of breaking and entering with intent to commit an indictable offence in relation to a building, other than a dwelling house, is a dual procedure offence, the court must now seek the Crown Attorney's election as to whether or not to proceed on the charge by indictment or by summary conviction.

Court:	"How does the Crown elect to proceed in this matter?"
Prosecutor:	"By summary conviction, please Your Honour [or Your Worship]."

Summary conviction offences or dual procedure offences, where the Crown elects to proceed by summary conviction, will be tried in Provincial Court. If the offence is an indictable offence that is designated as being the absolute jurisdiction of the Provincial Court under s. 553 *Criminal Code*, the trial will still be conducted in the Provincial Court, but the accused will be liable to the greater penalty provided by way of trial by indictment.[28]

Once the accused is aware of the Crown's election, the accused will be asked how he or she pleads to the charge, either "Guilty" or "not guilty." Where the accused does not answer or refuses to enter a plea, the court will enter a plea of "not guilty" and proceed

---

[28]*Criminal Code*, R.S. 1985, c. C-46, s. 536(1).

as if the accused had requested a trial.[29] The only time an accused is allowed to enter a different plea is if he or she pleads "not guilty" to the offence charged, but "guilty" to another offence, with the prior consent of the prosecutor.[30]

Court: "Mr Smith, how do you plead to this charge?"

Accused: "Not guilty."

In any case where the charge is an indictable offence other than an offence listed in s. 469 *Criminal Code* (absolute jurisdiction of Superior Court Judge) or a dual procedure offence where the Crown elects to proceed by indictment, the accused would then be asked in which court he or she elects to be tried. As the charge against John Smith is neither an s. 469 nor an s. 553 *Criminal Code* offence, had the Crown elected to proceed by way of indictment, the following words would be read to the accused by a justice of the peace or by the judge:

Court: "You have the option to elect to be tried by a judge without a jury and without having had a preliminary inquiry; or you may elect to have a preliminary inquiry and to be tried by a judge without a jury; or you may elect to have a preliminary inquiry and to be tried by a court composed of a judge and jury. If you do not elect now, you shall be deemed to have elected to have a preliminary inquiry and to be tried by a court composed of a judge and jury. How do you elect to be tried?"[31]

Accused: "By judge and jury."

If the accused refuses to elect a court in which to be tried, his or her trial will be conducted by a superior court composed of a judge and jury.[32]

13.9 ADJOURNMENTS

When an accused initially appears on a charge, it may take several court appearances for the judicial proceedings to be finalized. Various motions may be brought before the court by either party to the proceedings, dealing with matters of custody, or mental competency of the accused to stand trial, etc. Once the plea of the accused is taken and the preliminary inquiry or trial commences, it may still take several sittings of the court before the charge(s) are finally dealt with. These breaks in the trial are referred to as adjournments.

On occasion, one party may request that a scheduled appearance be adjourned due to the availability of a witness or to grant additional time to prepare for a hearing. The other party may consent or object to the adjournment. The justice or judge will then determine whether or not the proceedings or any party to the proceedings are unfairly prejudiced and whether or not, having regard to all the circumstances, it is in the public interest to grant the adjournment.[33]

---

[29]*Criminal Code*, R.S. 1985, c. C-46, s. 606(2).

[30]*Criminal Code*, R.S. 1985, c. C-46, s. 606(4).

[31]*Criminal Code*, R.S. 1985, c. C-46, s. 536(2).

[32]*Criminal Code*, R.S. 1985, c. C-46, s. 471.

[33]*Criminal Code*, R.S. 1985, c. C-46, s. 571.

13.10 APPEARANCE BY THE ACCUSED

In criminal proceedings against individuals charged with summary conviction offences, the accused may appear personally or be represented by counsel or by agent (person acting on behalf of the accused). An accused may be ordered to appear personally by the court and a warrant may be issued for the arrest of the accused. Where an organization is charged with a summary conviction offence, the organization must appear represented by counsel or by an agent. A court, once satisfied that a summons was served upon an organization, charged with a summary conviction offence that is not represented, may proceed with the trial *ex parte* (in the absence of the accused).[34]

In proceedings involving indictable offences, the accused may file with the court an appointment of a designated counsel to appear on his or her behalf during any part of the proceedings, except when the oral evidence of a witness is taken, or during jury selection. An accused charged with an indictable offence must also be present for the purposes of entering a plea of guilt and the passing of sentence, unless the court orders otherwise. A court may at any time order the accused to be personally present by issuing a summons or a warrant for the arrest of the accused.[35]

Where an organization is charged with an indictable offence, they must appear and plead to the charge by counsel or by agent.[36] The notice of an indictment that is served upon an organization must advise that if the organization fails to appear and enter a plea, a plea of not guilty will be entered by the court and the trial will proceed *ex parte*.[37]

Except when the evidence of a witness is being taken, for both summary conviction and indictable offences where the accused is in custody, he or she may appear in court by means of closed-circuit television or by any means that allows for simultaneous visual and oral communication between the court and the accused.[38] A court may have an accused removed from the court for interrupting the proceedings during any part of the trial, if necessary.

13.11 JOINDER OF ACCUSED – JOINDER OF COUNTS

If more than one accused is charged with the same offence, they may be charged jointly on the same information in Form 4 *Criminal Code* (a **joinder of accused**). The main benefit to charging multiple accused jointly is to limit the number of preliminary inquiries and trials. An adult accused should not be joined on the same information as an accomplice who is a young offender.

One or more accused persons may be charged with multiple charges on the same information if all of the counts apply jointly to them all. The exception to this rule prohibits a charge of murder from being joined to any other charge for an indictable offence

---

[34]*Criminal Code*, R.S. 1985, c. C-46, s. 800.

[35]*Criminal Code*, R.S. 1985, c. C-46, s. 650.01.

[36]*Criminal Code*, R.S. 1985, c. C-46, s. 620.

[37]*Criminal Code*, R.S. 1985, c. C-46, s. 621.

[38]*Criminal Code*, R.S. 1985, c. C-46, s. 650 and s. 800(2.1).

except where it arises out of the same circumstances as the charge of murder or without the accused's consent.[39]

If a court believes that it is in the public interest to do so, it may order that where more than one accused is charged with the same offence, that one or more of them be tried separately. Likewise, where an accused is charged with more than one offence, the court may order that the accused be tried separately on one or more of the counts.[40]

13.12 CHANGE OF VENUE

Prior to trial for an indictable offence, a prosecutor or the accused may request a **change of venue** (location) to a different territorial jurisdiction in the same province where:

(a)   it would be expedient to the ends of justice; or

(b)   a jury cannot be convened at the location where the trial would normally have been held.[41]

An example of a case where the venue was changed was the trial of convicted serial rapist and murderer Paul Bernardo. Due to the scope and magnitude of the proceedings, the intense media scrutiny, security considerations and the anticipated duration of the trial, the murder and rape trials were held in Toronto where the court facilities could support a trial of that complexity.

Other grounds for requesting a change of venue would be necessary to ensure a fair and impartial trial[42] or where a jury would be unable or reluctant to render a verdict due to fear of retaliation.[43]

The venue of a trial may also be changed to a different territorial jurisdiction in the same province if the court orders that the accused's trial be held in one of Canada's official languages and that services for conducting the trial in the language best understood by the accused is not available in the jurisdiction where the trial would normally be held.[44]

13.13 DISCLOSURE

"Crown counsel is under a duty to disclose [to the defence] all information in his or her possession relevant to the guilt or innocence of the accused...whether favourable or unfavourable to the accused...which is not clearly irrelevant."[45]

The Honourable G. Arthur Martin, O.C., O.Ont., Q.C., LL.D.

---

[39]*Criminal Code*, R.S. 1985, c. C-46, s. 589.

[40]*Criminal Code*, R.S. 1985, c. C-46, s. 591(3).

[41]*Criminal Code*, R.S. 1985, c. C-46, s. 599(1).

[42]*R. v. Turvey* (1970), 1 C.C.C. (2d) 90, 12 C.R.N.S. 329 (N.S.S.C.).

[43]*R. v. Lafferty* (1977), 35 C.C.C. (2d) 183 (N.W.T.S.C.).

[44]*Criminal Code*, R.S. 1985, c. C-46, s. 531.

[45]The Attorney General's Advisory Committee on Charge Screening, Disclosure and Resolution.

The modern investigator must realize that while there may or may not be privilege in some of the findings of a criminal investigation, there is never any ownership in it. This means that, once a criminal charge has been laid, evidence gathered during the course of an investigation doesn't belong solely to the police or to the Crown. If evidence can be said to be owned at all, it is the property of the effective administration of justice in a free and democratic society.

Disclosure of evidence allows accused persons to make full answer and defence to charges against them by making all relevant evidence – inculpatory as well as exculpatory – available to the defence prior to the commencement of trial. The benefits in disclosing evidence include:

1. It helps to ensure against the possibility of wrongfully convicting persons by allowing accused persons the opportunity to investigate and rebut false or erroneous evidence.

2. It allows for the resolution of non-contentious issues of evidence that a well-informed defence may stipulate (agree to).

3. Accused persons may elect to waive preliminary hearings or shorten the duration of their trials.

4. Accused persons may plead guilty to offence(s) against them when they are made aware of the strength of the evidence against them.[46]

The 1993 *Report of the Attorney General's Advisory Committee on Charge Screening, Disclosure and Resolution Discussions* recommended that the responsibility of the Crown to disclose evidence to the accused extends even beyond the original police investigation. After initial disclosure of a case is made to the defence, the Crown is still required to disclose any evidence during or after a trial or appeal that would tend to demonstrate the innocence of the accused or reasonable doubt of his or her guilt.[47]

An accused person who is unrepresented is entitled to disclosure in the same way as if he or she were represented by legal counsel but should be informed of his or her right to obtain disclosure by either the Crown or the court. Most, if not all, disclosure requests to the Crown are made in writing by counsel for the defence. Requests for disclosure must be made and responded to in a timely manner.[48]

The 1993 *Martin Report* recommended that the defence is entitled to disclosure of the following types of evidence, including:

1. a copy of the charges contained in the information or indictment;

2. a complete synopsis prepared by the investigating police agency setting out the circumstances of the alleged offences committed by the accused;

3. written statements or "Will Say" statements of all persons, including statements of co-accused persons, interviewed during the police investigation, whether or not the Crown intends to call them as witnesses (this includes any police notes or reports from which they were prepared or in relation to interviews where no statements were taken);

---

[46]*Martin Report*, 1993.

[47]*Martin Report*, 1993.

[48]*Martin Report*, 1993.

4. the original copy of electronically recorded statements, which the defence may listen to in private. Copies or transcripts of such electronically recorded statements may be disclosed at the discretion of the Crown;

5. the criminal record of the accused;

6. a copy of any written statements of the accused, including transcripts, corresponding police reports or notes (or the opportunity to view or listen to the original copy of an electronically recorded statement in private);

7. copies of any police occurrence report and supplementary report;

8. copies of forensic, medical or laboratory reports relating to the offence;

9. copies of documents, photographs, audio or video recordings of anything other than a statement of a person;

10. copies of search warrants and lists of seized items;

11. copies of judicial authorizations to intercept private communications;

12. upon request, copies of criminal records relating to proposed Crown or defence witnesses;

13. all information relating to the visual identification of the accused where identity is an issue; and

14. any material relevant to the credibility of any proposed Crown witness.

The 1991 Supreme Court of Canada landmark ruling in the *Stinchcombe* decision set out similar guidelines for disclosure of relevant inculpatory or exculpatory evidence in the possession of the Crown.[49] The *Stinchcombe* decision and the recommendations of the *Martin Report* have since been entrenched in s. 603 *Criminal Code*.[50] As yet there is no statutory authority for the defence to disclose relevant defence evidence to the Crown.

As the investigating police agency is the source of the disclosable evidence, the obligation of the Crown to evaluate and disclose relevant evidence to the defence can only be met if the police fully disclose the findings of the case to the Crown in a timely fashion. Investigators must make full and timely disclosure of their case to the Crown Attorney and, for greater certainty, should maintain detailed records of what evidence was disclosed to the Crown and when it was disclosed.

13.14 PRELIMINARY INQUIRY

If the accused elects trial by a judge of the Provincial Court, the court will set a date for trial or may proceed directly if both parties are ready. If the accused elects to be tried by a judge of the Superior Court sitting alone or sitting with a jury, the court will set a date for a preliminary inquiry. If the accused refuses to make an election, he or she will be deemed to have elected trial by judge and jury and a preliminary inquiry will be scheduled.

---

[49]*R. v. Stinchcombe* (1991) 3 S.C.R. 326, 68 C.C.C. (3d) 1, 9 C.R. (4th) 277 (7:0).

[50]*Criminal Code*, R.S. 1985 c. C-46, s. 603.

Unlike a trial, the purpose of a preliminary inquiry is not to determine the guilt or innocence of the accused. The purpose of a preliminary inquiry is to determine whether or not there is sufficient evidence to warrant committing the trial proceedings before a judge and jury. Preliminary inquiries are held at the Provincial Court level. A prosecutor may use a preliminary inquiry to test the strength of the witnesses and evidence of a case while the defence may use a preliminary inquiry to obtain a better sense of disclosure regarding the Crown's case.

If the judge finds, as the result of the preliminary inquiry, that there is enough evidence for a properly instructed jury to convict, the accused will be committed to stand trial before a court of competent jurisdiction. If, in the opinion of the judge, there is insufficient evidence to convict, the accused will be discharged.

The accused may be sent directly to trial without a preliminary inquiry if the prosecutor prefers a "direct indictment," but this procedure may only be done with the consent in writing of the Attorney General or Deputy Attorney General.[51]

13.15 OATH / AFFIRMATION

"Insight, untested and unsupported, is an insufficient guarantee of the truth."

Bertrand Russell, British philosopher and logician (1872-1970).[52]

Any person who is 14 years of age or older and who understands the nature and quality of an oath sworn on the Bible, or a solemn affirmation, may give testimony during a judicial proceedings. Instead of taking a (religious) oath, any person may testify after affirming to tell the truth in the following words:

"I solemnly affirm that the evidence to be given by me shall be the truth, the whole truth and nothing but the truth."

If a witness is under the age of 14 or if his or her mental capacity is challenged, a court must conduct inquiries before allowing the witness to testify, in order to determine:

1. the witness's ability to understand the nature of an oath or a solemn affirmation; and

2. the witness's ability to communicate the evidence.[53]

If the court finds that the witness does appreciate the nature of an oath or affirmation and is able to communicate the evidence, the witness will be sworn or affirmed.[54]

If a witness is under the age of 14 or if his or her whose mental capacity is challenged, and he or she is deemed not to understand the nature of an oath or affirmation but is able to communicate the evidence, the witness may be permitted to testify if he or she promises to tell the truth.[55] A witness who is deemed not to understand the

---

[51]*Criminal Code*, R.S. 1985, c. C-46, s. 577.

[52]Bertrand Russell quote retrieved May 19, 2005, from www.cs.wustl.edu~plezbert/quotes

[53]*Canada Evidence Act*, R.S.C. 1985, c. C-5, s. 16(1).

[54]*Canada Evidence Act*, R.S.C. 1985, c. C-5, s. 16(2).

[55]*Canada Evidence Act*, R.S.C. 1985, c. C-5, s. 16(3).

nature of an oath or affirmation and is not able to communicate will not be permitted to testify.[56]

If a witness is unable to testify orally only by reason of a physical or mental handicap, the court may order that the witness be permitted to give his or her evidence in any way that would make the evidence intelligible.[57] Such instances might involve a witness who is deaf and non-speaking giving his or her evidence by writing out answers or through an interpreter skilled in sign language, etc.[58]

13.16 EXPERT WITNESSES

"Extraordinary claims demand extraordinary evidence."

Carl Sagan, US scientist, educator and author (1934-1996).[59]

In our increasingly complex profession, we rely heavily upon recent advances in scientific and technological search methods to locate and identify evidence. Investigators and prosecutors must rely on witnesses who have expertise that exceeds that of the average witness to testify in relation to matters of evidence. Forensic scientists from a variety of disciplines, criminal behavioural analysts, technical engineers and medical experts are among those witnesses who are regularly called upon to give opinion evidence dealing with certain aspects of a case.

Any party to criminal or civil proceedings who intends to call expert witnesses to testify on his or her behalf is limited to five such witnesses, without the prior permission of the court or judge or the person presiding over the proceedings.[60] An investigator may be in charge of a case that involves the anticipated evidence of a fingerprint examiner, a criminal behavioural analyst, a pathologist, a document examiner, a biologist who will testify regarding DNA evidence, and a firearm and tool mark examiner. The investigator should realize that the prosecution will exceed the maximum allowable number of expert witnesses and bring this to the attention of the prosecutor to make a motion to the court for permission to exceed the statutory limitation.

13.17 STRUCTURE OF CRIMINAL PROCEEDINGS

We have seen throughout this textbook that our court system is based on the adversarial system involving a prosecution pitted against one or more accused, who are usually, but may not always be, represented by defence counsel. If the accused pleads guilty to the offence(s) charged, the court will hear evidence, which has been stipulated (agreed to) by the accused, as read by a prosecutor. The accused may be convicted on that evidence without the necessity of calling any witnesses or without the production of any exhibits.

---

[56]*Canada Evidence Act*, R.S.C. 1985, c. C-5, s. 16(4).

[57]*Canada Evidence Act*, R.S.C. 1985, c. C-5, s. 6.

[58]*R. v. Carlick* (1999), 42 W.C.B. (2d) 326 (B.C.S.C.).

[59]Dr. Carl Sagan quote retrieved May 19, 2005, from www.cs.wustl.edu~plezbert/quotes

[60]*Canada Evidence Act*, R.S.C. 1985, c. C-5, s. 7.

If an accused has been arraigned and has entered a plea of not guilty, a trial date will be set. If the offence charged is one for which the accused may elect trial by a superior court judge, sitting without a jury, the trial will be presided over by a judge as the "trier of fact." If the accused elects trial by judge and jury, a judge will still preside over the trial but the jury becomes the "trier of fact."

In a jury trial, both parties to the proceedings will make opening arguments prior to the calling of evidence to highlight their positions regarding the case for the members of a jury. Opening arguments are not considered evidence and differ significantly on crucial points such as identity of the accused or the facts in issue of the charge(s).

As all charges are prosecuted by the Crown, the Crown bears the onus of proving the case in every trial and will put forth the case for a conviction. The Crown introduces evidence first by way of oral testimony of witnesses and through the production of physical and circumstantial evidence. If the prosecution evidence does not establish a *prima facie* case, the judge may direct a verdict of not guilty.

When a witness is called to testify in a judicial proceedings, he or she will be asked questions by counsel for whichever party called him or her in what is referred to as "examination-in-chief." Following the examination-in-chief, the witness will be asked questions by the opposing party in a procedure known as "cross-examination."

When the Crown has introduced all of their evidence to prove the facts in issue, the prosecution will rest their case. Following the case for the prosecution, the accused is then permitted to make full answer and defence to the charge(s), either personally or by way of counsel for the defence.[61]

In a jury trial, following the introduction of all of the evidence, each party will offer summations to the jury in the form of verbal addresses to summarize their interpretation of the evidence as it relates to the guilt or innocence of the accused. If, following the case for the prosecution, the defence elects not to call any evidence, the prosecution will proceed with their summation, followed by summation for the defence.[62] If the defence does call evidence on behalf of the accused, the defence will offer their summation to the jury and the prosecution will deliver their summation last.[63]

13.18 TESTIFYING IN COURT

In most cases – though not always – when an investigator is called upon to testify in court it will be as a witness for the prosecution. Police witnesses are usually called chronologically in order of their involvement in the investigation to help prove the facts in issue of a case through their findings and observations, to introduce seized evidence and to corroborate civilian witnesses. First-responding uniformed officers usually precede more experienced investigators as witnesses to lay the foundation for the case. Police officers testify either in relation to the facts of a case or, in a minority of cases, offer opinion evidence if they may be qualified as expert witnesses by reason of experience and training.

---

[61]*Criminal Code*, R.S. 1985, c. C-46, s. 650(3) and 802(1).

[62]*Criminal Code*, R.S. 1985, c. C-46, s. 651(1).

[63]*Criminal Code*, R.S. 1985, c. C-46, s. 651(3).

Police witnesses were once widely regarded as being more credible than civilian witnesses by reason of presumed fairness, impartiality and training, though I no longer believe this to be true in all cases. There have been several high-profile cases where it was subsequently proved that police witnesses gave false testimony – sometimes knowingly – for the purposes of obtaining a conviction. Extensive media coverage of such cases has left the public to conclude that police witnesses are not infallible and, in several cases, have led the public to question the truthfulness and motive of police testimony.

Only when police officers establish individual reputations of honesty, credibility and professionalism within their own jurisdictions, are they regarded as unbiased witnesses by prosecutors, defence counsel and judges. A police witness who expects to be believed as a witness must always strive to give the court sufficient indicators of truthfulness, in his or her words and actions. Once that reputation is established, it should be guarded and must never be abused or taken for granted.

Testifying in court is an art that brings together all aspects of an investigation from note taking, to interviewing witnesses, to crime scene examination, to continuity of evidence and the investigator's dealings with accused persons. Even if an investigator has exceptional investigative skills, he or she must master the art of articulating his or her observations and actions on the witness stand to see the case through to its conclusion.

The more well prepared an investigator is to testify, the more confident he or she will be about the case. Leading up to a court case, investigators should carefully review their notes several times for the purpose of refreshing their independent recollection of the events. Separate the relevant dates using elastic bands and mark the pages containing important entries with paper clips. A police witness must also present a professional appearance in court.

13.18.1 Attire in Court

If your departmental policy requires that you attend court in uniform attire, it should be clean and neatly pressed with your shoes polished. If you are assigned to plainclothes duties, you should appear in court in conservative business attire – I prefer a dark business suit and white shirt/blouse for investigators and a matching necktie for males. If you wear a necktie to court, wear it as a tie is meant to be worn, with the shirt-collar button fastened and the knot of the tie centred over the collar button – not pulled down below an unbuttoned collar.

The investigator attending court should be well-rested, if possible, and neatly groomed. While on the witness stand or anywhere in the courtroom, the professional investigator should understand that he or she is a key player in the proceedings and for that reason is always closely watched by spectators, witnesses, attorneys, the accused and the judge and jury (if a jury is involved in the proceedings). A professional appearance portrays the message that if you take care with your appearance, you probably also take care to perform your duties well.

Issued sidearms, handcuffs, and Oleoresin Capsicum (OC) spray should always be concealed on a belt under your attire. Investigators' hair should be clean and neatly combed/brushed. Male officers should be clean-shaven or with facial hair neatly trimmed. In my opinion, visible tattoos and body piercing do nothing to enhance a police officer's professional appearance – cover them up or remove them.

13.18.2 Courtroom Demeanour

Investigators should always maintain good posture and not fidget while seated or when standing in a courtroom. If you are attending court after a night-shift and are tired, it is better to wait outside the courtroom until your name is called. A courtroom is a solemn place and a judicial proceedings is a solemn event – talking, laughing or joking with others while the proceedings are in progress give the appearance that a person doing so doesn't take the matters before the court seriously.

Behaviour such as yawning portrays lack of interest in the proceedings, while head-shaking in the negative, in response to something said during the proceedings, may give the impression that the investigator is biased regarding the outcome of the proceedings. Police officers should only enter and depart a courtroom during recesses in the case. If an officer is required to enter or leave for any reason, they should stand, facing the front of the courtroom, and nod respectfully to the judge immediately before exiting or after entering a courtroom when proceedings are in progress.

Attorneys should be addressed by name, as "Mr" or "Ms," or by "Sir" or "Ma'am." Justices of the Peace are addressed as "Your Worship," while judges of the Provincial or Superior Court are addressed as "Your Honour." An investigator should never directly address a member of a jury, nor should he or she ignore the jury while answering questions during examination-in-chief or cross-examination.

If you have read and have accepted the concepts that I have expressed throughout this entire textbook, you need not be anxious about any courtroom proceedings. If you are sincere and unbiased, you will easily project those qualities – if you have to try to appear to be sincere or unbiased your bias and insincerity will be obvious.

It is common knowledge that most people are fearful about speaking in public and yet that is exactly what testifying in court is. While on the witness stand, having "butterflies" in your stomach is perfectly normal. If you feel nervous prior to or during your testimony, take several slow deep breaths and compose yourself. Be aware of tightness in the muscles of your arms, shoulders, jaws or neck and concentrate on relaxing those areas. If nervousness causes your knees to tremble, lean against the edge of the witness stand to steady yourself.

You will be first asked to state your name for the court record. Speak in a voice loud and clear enough to be heard by someone sitting in the back row of the courtroom. State your name, rank, badge number and police service as follows:

Court: "Please state your name for the court."

Witness: "Constable Lynn Smith, Badge # 12345, Orangeville Police Service."

You will then be sworn or affirmed according to your personal preference prior to testifying.

During examination-in-chief, and cross-examination, pay very close attention to the questions that are asked. If either counsel asks more than one question before giving you a chance to reply, ask them to clarify the question. Only answer questions that were asked and don't hesitate to ask counsel to repeat or reword any question if you don't understand the question.

Take as much time as you need to formulate your answers. If you don't know the answer to any question, state, "I don't know." When the time comes that you have to refer to your investigative notes, remember that you have to request permission from the court to do so. Refer to the proper procedure for requesting permission in Section 3.2.12: Permission to Refer to Notes in Court. Once permission to refer to your notes has been granted, only glance at your notes when necessary – don't read from them unless you need to read a lengthy series of numbers or a statement.

Remember that you are not allowed to testify about what another police officer or witness told you. The following example reflects an exchange between a Crown Attorney and a police officer in which the officer testifies without giving hearsay evidence:

Crown: "Officer, were you on duty on May 26, 2005 and did you have any involvement in the matter before the court?"

Officer: "Yes [Sir or Ma'am], I did."

Crown: "Please tell the court about your involvement in this case."

Officer: "As the result of receiving a radio dispatch, I patrolled to 49 Parker Boulevard, arriving at 4:17 p.m., Thursday, May 26th, 2005."

Crown: "What was the nature of the dispatch to 49 Parker Boulevard, Officer?"

Officer: "The call was in relation to an alleged complaint of assault."

Crown: "And, what did you find there, officer?"

Officer: "A person met me at the door and was identified as John Doe, age 22, of that address."

Crown: "Officer, did you make any observations about Mr Doe's physical appearance?"

Officer: "Yes [Sir or Ma'am], I noticed that Mr Doe was bleeding heavily from a laceration above his right eye and he appeared to be in a great deal of pain."

Crown: "Officer, what happened next?"

Officer: "As the result of a conversation I had with Mr Doe, I entered the residence and located Henry Smith seated at the kitchen table. I placed Mr Smith under arrest for Assault Causing Bodily Harm at 4:22 p.m. and read him the standard police caution and his rights to counsel and to legal aid from my notebook."

Crown: "Do you see the person that you arrested in court today?"

Officer: (Witness points) "The man sitting against the wall with a green shirt and black pants."

Crown: "For the record, the officer has indicated the accused, Your Honour."

This entire exchange has occurred without the officer stating what anyone told him or her directly. The officer has testified about having had conversations but only paraphrased the nature of the conversations and stated what was done as the result of those conversations. Any statements made by the accused constitute exceptions to the Hearsay Rule and may be admissible if it can be proved they were made voluntarily (see Section 2.11.2: Exceptions to the Hearsay Rule).

13.18.3 Repeating Profanity while Testifying

If counsel for either the prosecution or the defence ask you a question that requires you to express an answer that will contain profanity, such as when repeating the statement of an accused, you should first warn the court and request the permission of the court prior to repeating profanity in the courtroom. You will never be refused; however, if the courtroom contained a gallery of schoolchildren on a field trip observing a judicial proceedings as part of their class, the presiding judge may appreciate the opportunity to caution the spectators and chaperones or to clear the spectators. I recommend using the following approach at all times prior to repeating profanity:

Counsel:	"Officer, did the accused make any statement to you at the time of his arrest?"
Officer:	(turning to the judge) "Your Honour, I would seek the court's direction prior to answering counsel's question. My answer will contain profanity."
Court:	"I'm certain that we've all heard the words before, officer. Please answer the question."
Officer:	"When I placed the accused under arrest he stated, '(verbatim substance of the accused's statement)'."

The use of profanity has become commonplace in our society and rarely offends anyone accustomed to day-to-day courtroom events. However, warning the court about the imminent use of profane words shows your respect for courtroom decorum (proper conduct) and will be appreciated by the judge.

13.18.4 Cross-examination by Defence Counsel

"All's fair in love and war."

Popular maxim.

During my policing career, I was cross-examined by a wide variety of defence counsel. Some defence attorneys defended their clients and, at the same time, treated me with dignity and respect. I was also cross-examined by defence attorneys who, during the course of conducting their defence, could be described as antagonistic, argumentative and condescending. My very first cross-examination went rather poorly for me when a defence attorney took advantage of my four months of police service and began making disparaging remarks about virtually everything I testified to.

I contributed to the disaster (as counsel undoubtedly hoped I would) by taking his remarks as a personal attack and reacting defensively. I knew that as I walked off the witness stand my inaugural performance as a police witness had not helped the prosecution in the least. I had a job to do and so did defence counsel, but he had done his job far better than I had done mine. I vowed to myself that day that I would never again "take the bait."

My attitude while testifying had been anything but professional and I had broken the cardinal rule of testifying: "Never engage a defence attorney in an argument." Being argumentative with defence counsel only portrays that you perceive them to be your adversary. The defence is the adversary of the prosecution – not of the witness. You must be the unbiased, impartial investigator who is only interested in seeking the truth and in fairly gathering and presenting evidence – both for and against the accused.

When defence counsel becomes argumentative, recognize it for what it is – a simple defence strategy. Your defence when faced with such treatment is simply to remain calm and professional and treat all parties with the same respect that you would like to be treated with. If counsel continues to attack you, in the face of your professional demeanour, they risk alienating themselves before the judge or the jury.

After all – "All's fair in love and war."

13.18.5 "Officer, Would it be Fair to Suggest...?"

Some of the most common questions asked of police witnesses during cross-examination begin with the phrase, "Officer, would it be fair to suggest...?" Hearing these very words should at least put the officer being questioned on guard for what is about to follow. If the question that follows is, "Officer, would it be fair to suggest – that the world is flat?", the correct answer would be, "No [Sir or Ma'am], I believe [due to my previous education or personal experience] that the world is round."

My point is, that "just because someone says it's so – doesn't make it so." For example, let's examine the following exchange:

Defence: "Officer, you testified during examination-in-chief that my client was intoxicated. Would it be fair to suggest that my client's condition was consistent with a person who had only consumed two bottles of beer that evening?"

Officer: "No [Sir or Ma'am], your client was slurring his words, his eyes were bloodshot and glassy, he was unable to keep his balance when walking and he smelled strongly of an alcoholic beverage. From my personal observations of his physical condition, and my experience in dealing with intoxicated persons, I believe he had consumed more than two bottles of beer."

Another strategy I have witnessed defence counsel successfully execute is to "suggest" that because an experienced police officer had not recorded something in his or her notes that the event must not have happened. The exchange went something like this:

Defence: "Officer, I know that you have testified as to your observations but you have no notes regarding that particular observation and I think that you would agree that because you would have made notes of such an important detail as this, that the fact you have no note of it suggests that it didn't happen. Is it fair to suggest that, officer."

Officer: "I guess so."

In the above exchange (a true story) a senior officer on one hand testified under oath that he had witnessed an event that occurred and then agreed with the attorney's circular logic that if "X" had happened the officer would surely have noted it. Therefore because no notes existed, "X" could not have happened.

The officer, who had an independent recollection of the event, simply didn't know how to explain the absence of notes on the subject and disagreed with something he had already testified to. He felt that if he didn't agree with defence counsel he would have appeared incompetent for not having recorded such an important detail in his notes. I suggest the officer should have answered to the effect:

Defence: "Officer, I know that you have testified as to your observation but you have no notes regarding that particular observation and I think that you would agree that, because you would have made notes of such an important detail as this, that the fact you have no note of it suggests that it didn't happen. Is it fair to suggest that, officer?"

Officer: "No (Sir or Ma'am) that would not be a fair suggestion. I am testifying from memory about the events that day. I take notes for the purpose of refreshing my memory and whether I chose not to include that detail in my notes or simply didn't have time to record every detail of the event, I still have a clear and specific recollection of that point."

If defence counsel's suggestion which follows the phrase, "Officer, would it be fair to suggest...?" is in fact a fair suggestion, the officer should, in all fairness, respond accordingly. For example:

Defence: "Officer, you testified during cross-examination that my client's eyes were bloodshot and glassy. Would it be fair to suggest that the blood-shot and glassy appearance of my client's eyes were possibly symptomatic of an allergic reaction due to hay fever?"

Officer: "Yes [Sir or Ma'am], that's possible, especially given the time of year. I have seen such symptoms in allergy sufferers as well as in persons intoxicated by alcohol."

(The officer may wish to add that hay fever doesn't make a person stagger, slur their words or smell strongly of an alcoholic beverage.)

If what counsel proposes is a fair suggestion, answer honestly, qualifying your answer if necessary, but don't feel compelled to go along with a proposal that you feel is erroneous having regard to all the circumstances.

13.19 PRODUCTION OF A PRISONER

Occasionally, it becomes necessary to have a prisoner removed from a jail or prison to testify in court or for investigative purposes, such as to conduct an interview. A judge of a superior court may order in writing that a prisoner be brought before the court. If the prisoner is being produced for investigative purposes, the prisoner must consent, in writing, to the transfer. A prosecutor may apply for an order for the production of a prisoner for a specified period of time where the judge is satisfied that the order is necessary. A provincial court judge may exercise the authority of a superior court judge for the purpose of this procedure where the person in custody is within the jurisdiction of the judge.[64]

---

[64]*Criminal Code*, R.S. 1985, c. C-46, s. 527.

13.20 PRODUCTION OF COPIES OF DOCUMENTARY EVIDENCE

Entering evidence in the forms of documents is often necessary in order to prove the facts in issue of a case. Documentary evidence may take the form of cancelled cheques, bank statements, certificates of analysis, government records, contracts, or a multitude of other documents. Often an investigator is limited to obtaining copies of the original document for evidentiary purposes.

The *Canada Evidence Act* sets out that no copy of any document is to be admitted into evidence at a trial unless the party who intends to introduce the document gives reasonable notice of their intention to introduce the document to the person against whom it is to be introduced. The *Canada Evidence Act* does not specify precisely what "reasonable notice" is deemed to be. Presumably, in complex fraud cases involving large numbers of documents, "reasonable notice" might be held to be six months or more. The Act does, however, state that "the notice shall not in any case be less than seven days."[65]

13.21 SPECIAL CONSIDERATIONS INVOLVING TESTIMONY OF VICTIMS

The presiding judge in a trial or preliminary inquiry relating to any sexual or morality offence listed in s. 486(2.1) *Criminal Code* may order that a victim or a witness to such an offence, if under the age of 18 years, be allowed to testify outside the courtroom or behind a screen or device that would block his or her view of the accused. This procedure is followed in cases where the judge feels that such measures are necessary to obtain a full account of the testimony of the child victim or witness.

A judge may allow any witness, regardless of his or her age, to testify outside the courtroom or behind a screen or device that would block his or her view of the accused in a trial where the accused is charged with intimidation of designated offences committed in relation to a criminal organization. The judge may order these measures if he or she feels that it is necessary in order to obtain a full account from the witness or for his or her safety.

An accused person who is charged with any level of Sexual Assault or with an offence in which alleged violence was used, threatened or attempted against any person may not personally cross-examine a witness who at the time of the proceedings is under 18 years of age without the permission of the court.

The presiding judge may also make an order directing that the identity of a victim, witness or justice system participant (or any information that could disclose their identity) not be published in any document, media or broadcast where an accused is charged with any offence listed in subsections 486(3), (4), (4.1) or (4.11) *Criminal Code*. Any person who fails to comply with such a publication ban is guilty of an offence punishable by summary conviction.[66]

---

[65]*Canada Evidence Act*, R.S.C. 1985 c. C-5, s. 28.

[66]*Criminal Code*, R.S. 1985, c. C-46, s. 486.

13.22 INCLUDED OFFENCES

Where an accused is charged with an offence and the full offence is not proved, but the evidence proves the accused attempted to commit the offence, the accused may be automatically convicted of the attempt to commit the offence without relaying the charge.[67] In certain other instances, where an accused is charged with an offence but the evidence fails to prove the full offence or an attempt to commit the full offence, the accused may still be convicted of an **included offence**, or an attempt to commit an included offence, without relaying the charge.[68]

For example, the *Criminal Code* specifies that a person charged with murder may be acquitted of the charge of murder and convicted of the included offences of manslaughter or infanticide if the evidence proves the commission of those offences.[69] Included offences are also held to be any offence that the accused had to commit as part of the full offence that is charged but not proved. An example would be a charge of Level I Sexual Assault, for which the facts in issue are:

- the application of force to another person

- intentionally

- without their consent

- directly or indirectly

- in sexual circumstances

- that violated the sexual integrity of the complainant.

If the evidence failed to prove that the assault occurred under sexual circumstances that violated the sexual integrity of the complainant, but the remaining facts in issue were proved, the accused could still be convicted of the included offence of Assault Level I as that offence was committed in the commission of the offence that was charged.[70]

13.23 INTRODUCING PHOTOGRAPHIC EVIDENCE

In court proceedings involving charges of Theft, Robbery, Breaking and Entering, Possession of Property obtained by Indictable Offence, False Pretences and Fraud, recovered property that is returned, ordered to be returned or forfeited may be photographed and entered into evidence. The photograph may be entered into evidence if accompanied by a certificate stating that the photograph is a true photograph of the property and that it was taken by or taken under the direction of a police officer.

An affidavit of a police officer or other person must accompany the photograph and certify that the property was not altered in any way between the times it was detained until it was photographed. Photographic evidence, in absence of evidence to

---

[67]*Criminal Code*, R.S. 1985, c. C-46, s. 660.

[68]*Criminal Code*, R.S. 1985, c. C-46, s. 662(1).

[69]*Criminal Code*, R.S. 1985, c. C-46, s. 662(3).

[70]*R. v. Foote* (1974), 16 C.C.C. (2d) 44, (N.B.S.C. App. Div.).

the contrary is admissible and will have the same evidentiary value as the property would have had.[71]

13.24 EXCLUSION OF EVIDENCE

No discussion of courtroom proceedings would be complete without an explanation of how evidence is dealt with in court when it is determined that the *Charter* rights of the accused have been violated. Where an accused person believes that his or her rights or freedoms have been infringed upon or otherwise denied, the accused may apply to a court for appropriate "judicial remedy."

For example, such situations might involve an incriminating statement where the accused's rights to counsel under subsection 10(b) were denied, or where real evidence was improperly seized in contravention of the accused's rights against unreasonable search and seizure guaranteed by section 8 of the *Charter of Rights*. Where the court finds that incriminating evidence was obtained as the result of a *Charter* breach, the remedy sought by the accused will most likely be to have the evidence excluded (meaning that it will be declared inadmissible).[72] Where no evidence was obtained but if proceeding with a trial in the face of a *Charter* breach would bring the administration of justice into disrepute, the appropriate remedy may be to stay the proceedings (a procedure whereby a charge is discontinued by the Crown for a period of up to one year and if not recommenced during that time, must be re-laid).[73]

It is still possible that evidence could be admitted in cases where it is determined that an accused's *Charter* rights have been violated. The test that will be used by the court to determine whether the evidence should be admitted or excluded is whether or not the introduction or exclusion of the evidence obtained as the result of a *Charter* breach could bring the administration of justice into disrepute, meaning that to admit the evidence would render the trial unfair.[74] Factors that are used by courts to determine whether or not admission of improperly obtained evidence should be excluded include:

1. the type of evidence that was obtained;

2. how and when the evidence was discovered;

3. the *Charter* right of the accused that was denied or infringed upon;

4. the severity of the *Charter* breach;

5. whether or not the *Charter* breach was intentional;

6. the existence of exigent circumstances;

7. whether or not the evidence would likely have been found through other investigative methods;

---

[71]*Criminal Code*, R.S. 1985, c. C-46, s. 491.2.

[72]*Canadian Charter of Rights and Freedoms*, Being Part 1 of the *Constitution Act, 1982*, Enacted by the *Canada Act 1982* (U.K.) c. 11; proclaimed in force April 17, 1982, s. 24.

[73]*Criminal Code*, R.S., 1985 c. C-46, s.579.

[74]*R. v. Collins* (1987), 1 S.C.R. 265, 33 C.C.C. (3d) 1, 56 C.R. (3d)193.

8. the severity of the offence (the more serious the charge, the more likely that the admission of tainted evidence could bring the administration of justice into disrepute);

9. the necessity of the evidence to prove the charge (whether or not the exclusion of the evidence would render the charge impossible to prove); and

10. whether or not other remedies are available to the accused.[75]

13.24.1 Conscriptive vs. Non-conscriptive Evidence

When determining the impact of evidence on the fairness of a trial, a court will first assess whether or not the evidence is **conscriptive** or **non-conscriptive**, based largely on how the evidence was obtained. The best way to explain this difference is that conscriptive evidence involves the participation of the accused in its creation or discovery, meaning that the accused is involuntarily "conscripted" (compelled) to supply evidence against himself.

An example of conscriptive evidence might involve an accused voluntarily providing a self-incriminating statement or providing a blood sample to police after being denied his *Charter* rights to counsel. Conscriptive evidence which did not exist prior to the *Charter* violation, and which would not otherwise have been discovered, such as an illegally obtained confession, will almost always be deemed to be inadmissible.

Conscriptive evidence also includes real evidence that is discovered as the result of conscriptive evidence such as a murder weapon being recovered as the result of a conscriptive confession made by a suspect (derivative evidence). Non-conscriptive evidence is evidence where the accused does not participate in its creation or discovery. The admission of conscriptive evidence would almost always be deemed to affect the fairness of the trial, whereas non-conscriptive evidence is usually seen to not affect the fairness of the trial.

If the evidence is determined to be conscriptive in nature, the court must determine if the evidence could have been discovered in a non-conscriptive way, had the Charter breach not occurred. If, on a balance of probabilities, conscriptive evidence would have been discovered anyway by non-conscriptive means, the admission of the evidence would probably not render the trial unfair if the evidence were admitted. The court must still assess the severity of the *Charter* breach and whether or not the admission or exclusion of the evidence would bring the administration of justice into disrepute.

If conscriptive evidence would, on a balance of probabilities, not have been discovered by non-conscriptive means, the court will normally exclude the evidence.[76]

SUMMARY

- A peace officer shall not arrest, without warrant, for a section 553 *Criminal Code* offence, a dual procedure (hybrid) offence, or a summary conviction offence, where

---

[75]*R. v. Collins*, supra.

[76]*R. v. Stillman* (1997), 1 S.C.R. 607, 113 C.C.C. (3d), 5 C.R. (5th) 1.

the public interest described by the mnemonic "R.I.C.E." may be satisfied by not arresting the individual.

- The *Criminal Code* places the onus on the prosecutor to "show cause" why the accused should not be released from custody and, under certain circumstances, places the onus on the accused to "show cause" why his or her continued detention is not necessary.

- All relevant evidence – inculpatory as well as exculpatory – in the possession of the prosecutor and the police must be made available to the defence prior to the commencement of trial through the disclosure process.

- The purpose of a preliminary inquiry is to determine whether or not there is sufficient evidence to warrant the trial proceedings to a judge and jury.

- Any party to criminal or civil proceedings is limited to five expert witnesses testifying on their behalf. To exceed that number, they must obtain the prior permission of the court, judge or the person presiding over the proceedings.

- A judge of a superior court may order in writing that a prisoner be brought before the court. If the prisoner is being produced for investigative purposes, the prisoner must consent, in writing, to the transfer.

- A party involved in any judicial proceedings who intends to introduce a copy of a document must give reasonable notice of their intention to introduce the document to the person against whom the evidence will be introduced. Such notice shall not be less than seven days.

- "Included offences" are held to be any offence(s) that the accused had to commit as part of the full offence that is charged but are not proved or are specified as included offences by statute.

- Conscriptive evidence involves the participation of the accused in its creation or discovery, meaning that the accused is involuntarily "conscripted" (compelled) to supply evidence against him or herself. The accused does not participate in the creation of non-conscriptive evidence.

- The admission of conscriptive evidence which would not have been discovered by alternative non-conscriptive methods and would bring the administration of justice into disrepute will be excluded at trial.

DISCUSSION QUESTIONS

1. Police in Ontario arrest a person without warrant on reasonable grounds he or she committed an armed robbery in Halifax, Nova Scotia. Halifax police indicate by telephone calls and written CPIC messages that they are willing to return the suspect to stand trial. What procedure should be followed to keep the suspect in custody until the arrival of the Halifax police to execute their warrant? For how long may such an individual be held?

2. A prosecutor may "show cause" why an individual charged with an offence within the same territorial jurisdiction may be detained in custody until he or she is dealt with by law. What three reasons could form the basis for a prosecutor to show cause? If a prosecutor required a remand to prepare for a show cause hearing, how long could the remand be granted without the consent of the accused?

3. In what situations may a child witness, under the age of 18 years, testify from behind a screen or a device that prevents them viewing the accused? Why might the judge consider it necessary to give such an order?

WEBLINKS

www.aidwyc.org/

Association in Defence of the Wrongfully Convicted website. Founded in 1993, AIDWYC is a non-profit, public interest volunteer organization dedicated to preventing and rectifying wrongful convictions. Features include summaries of alleged wrongfully convicted individuals and related news articles.

www.lexum.umontreal.ca/index_en.html

University of Montreal, Faculty of Law website. Searchable Supreme Court of Canada decision database, with links to federal and provincial legislation, periodicals and law libraries. Site features a wide variety of national and international legal resources.

www.canlii.org/

Canadian Legal Information Institute website. Searchable case law database and links to courts, appeal courts and various tribunals, boards and committees.

Appendix

This section includes a representative sampling of frequently used investigative and case management forms, which were developed by investigators from a variety of police services over the last several years.

It is not possible to include every variation of form that has ever been used, nor is it possible to design one generic form which will fulfill the needs of every investigation for every police service. With a little imagination, however, the fundamental principles used to capture information on these forms can be easily adapted to the specific requirements of any case.

The main purpose of utilizing electronic or hard copy investigative and case management forms is to create an information management system so that individual pieces of information do not get overlooked and "fall through the cracks" when the flow of information threatens to overwhelm an investigation.

Even if an information management system isn't perfect – it's better than no system.

ASSIGNMENT FORM

ASSIGNMENT NUMBER:
NATURE OF ASSIGNMENT:
DATE OF ASSIGNMENT:
OFFICER(S) ASSIGNED:
SUBJECT OF ASSIGNMENT:
BACKGROUND INFORMATION:
ACTION TAKEN:
OFFICER'S SIGNATURE: **DATE:**
CLOSED BY: **DATE:**

ASSIGNMENT REGISTER

Assignment Number	Subject Of Assignment	Date Of Assignment	Officer Assigned	Diary Date	Closed Date and by Whom

CANVASS FORM

INVESTIGATION: _____

CANVASSING OFFICER: _____

TIME AND DATE: _____

ADDRESS CANVASSED: _____

NAME OF OWNER OR TENANT: _____

NAME AND ADDRESS OF PERSONS PRESENT AT TIME OF CANVASS:
(including date of birth, telephone numbers and description of vehicles if relevant)

_____

_____

_____

_____

_____

NAME, ADDRESS OF OTHER PERSONS PRESENT AT TIME OF INCIDENT:

_____

_____

_____

REMARKS: _____

_____

_____

FOLLOW-UP INVESTIGATION REQUIRED: YES ☐   NO ☐

CANVASS SUPPLEMENTARY FORM

CANVASSING OFFICER: _____

ADDRESS: _____

TIME AND DATE: _____

ADDITIONAL INFORMATION: (including knowledge of either the incident or of the participants of event, nature of observations, need for interview by investigators and any other relevant information)

_____

_____

_____

_____

_____

_____

_____

_____

_____

_____

_____

_____

_____

_____

_____

_____

_____

_____

_____

_____

_____

_____

CONSENT TO SEARCH

DATE: _____ TIME: _____

LOCATION: _____

In order to co-operate with an investigation being conducted by the

_____ Police Service,

I, _____ (Name)

of _____ (Address)

do hereby authorize _____ (officer) of the

_____ Police Service to search my

_____

_____

(detailed description and location of place, dwelling, vehicle, etc. to be searched)

and its contents, which are owned or controlled by me and to remove any items pertinent to their investigation, providing a detailed receipt is furnished to me for any items that are removed by the police.

I have been advised that any items taken by the police may be used in their investigation, subjected to possible forensic testing and may be introduced as evidence in a court proceeding.

No promise, nor inducement, nor threat, nor coercion of any kind has been made to or against me by the police and I have been advised of my right to refuse to consent to this search and of my right to withdraw my consent to search at any time.

I have been advised of my right to retain and instruct legal counsel prior to the signing of this document and make this consent voluntarily and of my own free will.

_____   _____
Signature of Person Consenting   **Witness Officer**

CROWN DISCLOSURE REGISTER

NAME OF ACCUSED: _____   PAGE NO: _____

OFFENCE(S): _____

FILE NUMBER: _____

ITEM NO.	DESCRIPTION OF ITEM	DISCLOSURE DATE / OFFICER	CROWN COUNSEL OR PERSON PROVIDED WITH DISCLOSURE
	_____ _____ _____		
	_____ _____ _____		
	_____ _____ _____		
	_____ _____ _____		
	_____ _____ _____		

DOCUMENT REGISTER

#	Description	Location Obtained	Officer	Date	Search Warrant	Return To Justice	Date	Photocopied	Forensic Testing	Crown Brief

Exhibit Register

Page No. (___)

| | | Occurrence No. | |
| | | Exhibit Officer: | |

Exhibit Number	Time and Date Collected	Location where found and Detailed Description of Exhibit	Continuity of Exhibit Name Date

<u>INTERVIEW REPORT</u>

Page 1

	Occurrence No:
Name: **Date of Birth:**	**Dr. Licence #:**
Residence Address:	**Residence Telephone:**
Name of Employer:	**Occupation or Position:**
Business Address:	**Business Telephone:**
Interviewed By: **(Name, Rank, Badge #)**	**Unit / Department:**
Date of Interview: **Time Commenced:**	**Time Concluded:**
Location of Interview:	**Condition of Person Interviewed:**

_____

_____

_____

_____

_____

_____

_____

_____

_____

_____

_____

_____

_____

_____

_____

_____

_____

_____

_____

_____

_____

_____

_____

_____

_____

INTERVIEW REPORT

PAGE (___)

	Occurrence No:
Name:	Date of Interview:

_____

_____

_____

_____

_____

_____

_____

_____

_____

_____

_____

_____

_____

_____

_____

_____

_____

_____

_____

_____

_____

_____

_____

_____

_____

_____

_____

_____

CRIME SCENE SECURITY REGISTER

OFFICER'S NAME: _____   RANK: _____   BADGE # _____

OCCURRENCE: _____   LOCATION: _____

TIME COMMENCED: _____   TIME RELIEVED: _____

DATE	TIME OF ENTRY	NAME	REASON	TIME OF DEPARTURE	REMARKS

STATEMENT REGISTER

NUMBER	NAME	ADDRESS	DATE	TAKEN BY	INTERVIEW REPORT	KGB VIDEO	WILL SAY AND/OR SUMMARY	TYPED

TIP SHEET

NUMBER: _____

DATE RECEIVED: _____ TIME RECEIVED: _____

RECEIVED BY: _____

RECEIVED FROM:
(NAME AND ADDRESS: _____

HOW RECEIVED: TELEPHONE (__) WALK-IN (__) OTHER _____

TELEPHONE NUMBER: (_____) _____ - _____ EXT. _____

SUBJECT OF INFORMATION:

_____

_____

_____

_____

_____

_____

_____

_____

_____

_____

_____

_____

_____

_____

_____

_____

REQUIRES FOLLOW-UP INVESTIGATION: YES (__)   NO (__)

ASSIGNED FOR FOLLOW-UP TO: _____

ASSIGNMENT NUMBER: _____

WITNESS WILL SAY

Page No.

Name of Witness: _____

Date of Birth: _____

Address: _____

Residence Telephone Number: _____

Business Telephone Number: _____

_____

_____

_____

_____

_____

_____

_____

_____

_____

_____

_____

_____

_____

_____

_____

_____

_____

_____

_____

_____

_____

_____

_____

90–10 Rule	A fundamental principle of witness interviews in which the subject being interviewed should do 90 per cent of the talking during the interview, while the interviewer does only 10 per cent of the talking.
Absolute Jurisdiction	A classification of offence designated as the exclusive entitlement of a particular level of court to try, or to deal with matters of interim judicial release and trial.
Accidental Characteristics	Any random cut, tear or other distinctive defect, wear pattern or flaw that may be used to distinguish one similar object from another.
	(See antonym: **class characteristics**)
Accused	A person against whom a charge is formally laid. Alternatively referred to in court as a defendant.
	(See synonym: **defendant**)
Acquittal	The release of an accused from a charge by a verdict or finding of not guilty in a court of law.
	(See antonym: **conviction**)
	(See: **verdict**)
Actus Reus	Latin = guilty act: an act prohibited by statute law.
Adipocere	After a period of time, post-mortem chemical reactions convert the fatty tissues of a body exposed to moisture or water into adipocere, a white, soap-like substance.
Admission	A written or verbal acknowledgement of a specific circumstance, fact or partial fact of a lesser nature than a full confession, made by a suspect or accused person to a witness, especially a police officer. An admission may assist in proving one or more of the facts in issue of a case or provide circumstantial evidence (e.g., knowledge of event, location, knowledge of the victim or the skills necessary to commit the offence(s) under investigation).
	(See: **facts in issue; confession**)
Agent Provocateur (Agent)	One who is in the employ of the police who takes an active role in the investigation to gather evidence or to facilitate the commission of offences through the justifiable offering (on the basis of reasonable suspicion) of the opportunity for individuals to commit crimes. The term "agent" is broadly considered to include undercover police officers; however, it

mostly refers to non-police officers in the employ of the police. Crown privilege that applies to informants does not extend to agents.

(See: **informant**; **Crown privilege**)

Aiding or Abetting	To assist or to encourage a person to commit an offence. The person who aids or abets is a party to the offence and guilty of the full offence. It is a criminal offence to aid or abet a person to commit suicide although it is not an offence to attempt to commit suicide. (See: **party to an offence**; **suicide**; **counselling**.)
Alibi	Latin = elsewhere: a written or verbal claim or proof that when an offence under investigation occurred, a subject was in a different location and therefore could neither have participated in, nor been responsible for, the alleged crime(s).
Amnesia	A temporary or permanent medical condition resulting in the partial or total loss of one's memory, due to psychological disturbance, brain injury, illness, shock, fatigue or repression. Also sometimes induced by anesthesia.
Animus Furandi	Latin = the specific intent to steal: an essential element of the offence of theft (s. 322(1) *Criminal Code*) involving the intent to deprive the owner of his or her possession of the property.
Arraignment	The official reading of the charges of an information or an indictment to the accused in court.
Arson	The intentional or reckless damage of property by fire or explosion.
Assault	The direct or indirect intentional application of force to another person without their consent.
Balance of Probability	Burden of proof used in civil court to establish a person's civil liability in suits involving claims of loss or damage. After hearing the evidence, the trier of fact in a civil proceeding may be convinced (or at least 51 per cent certain) of the likelihood or probability of a defendant's liability and make a judgment in favour of the plaintiff (claimant). Burden of proof is a far lower standard of proof than the criminal standard of proof beyond a reasonable doubt. (See: **reasonable doubt**)
Behavioural Analysis	The examination of behavioural clues and factors that motivate behaviour of particular offenders.
Best Evidence Rule	The evidentiary rule that requires that the best evidence available be presented to the court. With certain exceptions, if an original is available, a copy is not acceptable as evidence.
Bloodstain Pattern Analysis	The investigation of bloodstains of different shapes and patterns resulting from the forces of gravity and velocity. This analysis is used to recreate the events of a crime, such as the

number of blows struck and the relative positions of the participants of an event.

Burning Bridges Theory

Every time any investigative process is conducted at a crime scene, it represents another bridge burned, in that whatever has been changed can never be exactly restored to its original condition. For example, if an exhibit is moved, it can never be put back in exactly the same place; or if chemicals are used as a test for the presence of blood, this will prevent future DNA testing.

Canvassing

A specialized form of interviewing technique that attempts to identify potential witnesses from an identifiable group of people. Canvasses are often conducted of residents of a neighbourhood, street or apartment building, patrons or employees of a mall, motorists, pedestrians or service providers.

Case Conference

"[One-time or ongoing] consultation with appropriate representation from all involved agencies [e.g., police services, coroner, Crown attorney] and any other experts [e.g., forensic scientists, medical experts, technical experts] who may assist in [an] investigation. This includes obtaining interdisciplinary input at the earliest opportunity to assist in developing investigative strategies, establishing priorities and ranking the sequence of any necessary investigative procedures." (Definition from the Ontario Major Case Management [MCM] Manual)

Case Law

Law that is created by previous court decisions. Case law decisions may be reported in a variety of legal publications (e.g., *Supreme Court Reports*, *Canadian Criminal Cases*). According to the rule of precedent, lower courts are bound by the decisions of higher courts in similar situations. Equal or higher courts may take a case law decision into consideration, but are not required to do so.

(See: **rule of precedent**)

Cause of Death

Identification of the mechanism involved that explains how a death occurred (e.g., asphyxia due to strangulation, exsanguination [loss of blood] due to multiple stab wounds, etc.). Not to be confused with manner of death, which explains the way in which the death occurred.

(See: **manner of death**)

Caution

A formal warning given by a peace officer to a person under arrest or detention or a person suspected of or charged with an offence, to inform the person of his or her legal right not to respond to questioning or not to make a statement unless he or she voluntarily wishes to do so. The formal statement caution also warns the suspect or accused that should he or she choose to make any statement, the statement may be recorded and used as evidence against him or her in any future judicial proceeding.

(See: **supplementary caution; person in authority**)

Chain of Continuity   The systematic management of physical evidence to ensure the safety and integrity of each individual item and track the movement of pieces of evidence to prove that a particular item was in a specific place at a specific time in a particular condition. The chain of continuity also tracks all persons who handled or controlled the item at any given point in time.

Change of Venue   Changing the location of a trial to a different territorial jurisdiction within the same province where necessary in the interests of justice or because a jury cannot be convened in the location where the charge originated.

Circumstantial Evidence   A detail or circumstance (or a series of them) that is consistent with the guilt of the accused and inconsistent with any other rational explanation; it does not directly prove a fact but may be used to infer one or more facts in a criminal proceedings.

Class Characteristics   Identical physical attributes, such as size, shape and pattern that are shared by items of similar manufacture or origin.

(See antonym: **accidental characteristics**)

Command Triangle   An oversight authority of an investigation comprising the functions of primary investigation, file co-ordination and case management.

Common Law   A system of traditional laws that originated in England in the Middle Ages and was later adopted in North American law. Common law refers to those laws that are based on customs, traditions and judicial precedent as opposed to written statutes.

Compellable   The degree to which a Crown or defence witness can be legally forced to testify (e.g., no spouse is compellable to disclose any communication made to them by their spouse during their marriage except for specified sexual offences involving children, sexual assaults, abandonment or abduction of children, bigamy and polygamy offences).

(See: **competence**)

Competence   The legal appropriateness or suitability of a witness to be heard on matters relating to the trial. For a Crown or defence witness to testify, he or she must be deemed to be both competent and compellable. A witness may be competent but not compellable. A spouse is always a competent witness for the defence.

(See: **compellable**)

Confession	A written or verbal acknowledgement of a fault, wrongdoing or the facts in issue of a crime made by a suspect or accused person to a witness, especially a police officer.
	(See: **admission**; **facts in issue**)
Confession Rule	A legal maxim requiring that before any statement made by a suspect or accused can be admitted into evidence, it must first be proven beyond a reasonable doubt by the Crown to have been made voluntarily and be free from threats or inducements.
	(See: **confession**)
Consciousness of Guilt	Circumstances of the post-offence conduct of an accused (e.g., flight from a crime scene or the destruction or concealment of evidence) that may be used by the trier of fact to make a logical inference of the guilt of the accused for the offence charged. No probative value can exist where the conduct might have been caused by some other reason (e.g., fleeing from another offence or in recognizing that sometimes innocent people also flee from the scene of a crime).
Conscriptive Evidence	Conscriptive evidence is obtained in breach of the accused's Charter rights and involves the participation of the accused in its creation or discovery, meaning that the accused is involuntarily conscripted (compelled) to supply evidence such as a confession that is used against him or herself.
	(See antonym: **non-conscriptive evidence**)
Consent	The voluntary and informed permission given by an individual to conduct an examination, search or some other action that would normally require prior judicial authorization (e.g., a search warrant). To be a valid consent, the guidelines of the decision of *R. v. Wills* must be followed, namely:
	1. actual consent, express or implied;
	2. consenter must have legal right to consent;
	3. consent must be voluntary and not coerced;
	4. person must be aware of nature of police conduct;
	5. person must be aware of right to refuse to consent; and
	6. person must be aware of consequences of action.
Contamination of Evidence	Contamination of evidence or of a crime scene may occur, due to exposure to environmental factors (e.g., wind or precipitation) or through the introduction of foreign material or trace evidence, not connected to the crime. Contamination, even in the slightest degree, impairs the integrity of the evidence or of the crime scene, reducing its evidentiary value or destroying the evidence completely.
	(See: **crime scene**; **securing a crime scene**)

Conviction	A finding of guilt in a court of law.
	(See: **acquittal**; **verdict**)
Corroborate	When an independent piece of evidence or an independent fact confirms and supports another piece of evidence or fact. Corroborative evidence strengthens the belief in the related evidence and has the effect of enhancing its credibility due to its independent but confirming nature. If similar information comes from different sources, it is more likely to be reliable.
Counselling	Instructing, teaching or advising a person to commit an offence and includes procuring, soliciting or inciting. If the offence counselled is committed, the person who counsels is a party to the offence and to any other offence committed in consequence of the counselling. It is an offence to counsel an indictable offence that is not committed (e.g., attempting to hire a hit man to conduct a contract killing that is not committed). It is also an offence to counsel a person to commit suicide.
	(See: **suicide**; **aiding and abetting**; **party to the offence**)
Counter Surveillance	Steps taken by the target of a physical surveillance detail to avoid, detect or defeat effective observation of them, such as suddenly stopping, reversing their direction, changing their appearance, or entering premises and waiting at the door to observe anyone who enters after them.
Crime Scene	Any location where any one of a series of events involved in the commission of a crime occurred, including:
	• the location where a crime was actually committed;
	• a location where evidence of the crime is located; or
	• a location where evidence of the crime is known to have been previously located,
	any of which are capable of providing a potential link between the victim(s), the crime or to the offender(s).
	(See: **staged crime scene**)
Cross-examination	The questioning of a witness by counsel for the opposing party regarding matters testified about during the witness's examination-in-chief.
	(See antonym: **examination-in-chief**)
Crown Brief	A document that combines all of the findings and evidence of the case to be used as the basis for prosecuting offenders when charges have been laid and to provide disclosure of the case to the defence.
Crown Privilege	The long-held legal principle that the Crown must claim privilege (i.e., the right to withhold from the court and defence) for any information provided to police by a confidential

police informer, and the identity of the informer. Crown privilege must yield to the claim of innocence at stake by an accused person.

(See: **innocence at stake**)

Culpable Homicide　　Homicide that is deserving of blame; blameworthy. Culpable homicide is murder, manslaughter or infanticide per s. 222(4) *Criminal Code*.

(See: **homicide; non-culpable homicide; murder**)

Deductive Reasoning　　To arrive at a particular conclusion through logical inference, reasoning and analysis.

Defendant　　A person against whom a charge is formally laid in a court of law. Alternatively referred to as an "accused."

(See synonym: **accused**)

Disclosure　　The legal obligation on a prosecutor to make known all relevant information, whether favourable or unfavourable to the accused, about a case in his or her possession relevant to the defence.

DNA (Deoxyribonucleic Acid)　　A molecule found in the 26 pairs of chromosomes within the nucleus of human cells that has been referred to as the "fingerprint of life." Every human being inherits half of his or her DNA from each parent (except for mitochondrial DNA which is found throughout the body, not only in nucleated cells and is only inherited from the mother). DNA determines a person's physical characteristics (e.g., gender, height, hair colour, etc.) and is a valuable investigative aid in identification of persons through recovered biological material.

Druggist's Fold　　A method for packaging small quantities of evidence (e.g., soil samples, paints samples, hair and fibres, glass particles, etc.) that involves placing the item or material into the fold of an ordinary piece of paper that is then folded inward upon itself from all remaining edges to enclose the item and prevent it from falling out. The paper fold is then initialled and dated by the seizing individual and secured inside an envelope that is marked for identification with a description of the item and time, date and location obtained and the signature of the individual who obtained the item.

Elements of an Offence　　The three necessary elements that must be proven for every criminal offence, including:

i) identity of the accused (as the person who committed the offence);

ii) *mens rea* (criminal intent); and

iii) *actus reus* (the prohibited act).

(See: *mens rea; actus reus;* **facts in issue**)

Entrapment	The inappropriate inducement of a reluctant individual to commit a crime that he or she would not otherwise have committed, through excessively forceful and unrelenting persuasion by an agent provocateur. (See: **agent provocateur**)
Episodic Memory	The type of memory through which a witness acquires, encodes and later recalls incidents or events. (See: **procedural memory**)
Ex Parte	A hearing or application that is conducted outside of the presence of the person who is the subject of the hearing or application.
Examination-in-chief	The direct questioning of a witness by counsel for the party that called the witness. (See antonym: **cross-examination**)
Exclusion of Evidence	The refusal by the court to admit evidence obtained as the result of a breach or violation of the accused's *Charter* rights where to admit the improperly obtained evidence could bring the administration of justice into disrepute.
Exculpatory	Evidence in the form of physical evidence, direct testimony, circumstantial evidence or denial, etc., that tends to exonerate or free a suspect or an accused person from blame. (See antonym: **inculpatory**)
Exigent Circumstances	Where reasonable grounds exist to obtain a search warrant but emergency conditions make it impracticable to obtain a warrant, a peace officer may enter a building, receptacle or place and may seize evidence as if he or she were acting under a search warrant where there is a reasonable belief of imminent loss, removal or destruction of evidence, or imminent bodily harm or death to a person.
Expert Evidence	Oral testimony by witnesses who are individually qualified by the courts as experts on the basis of education or experience. They are permitted to testify as to their conclusions on matters within their expertise and to state the reasons for their opinions. In criminal trials, expert evidence may be given by physicians, forensic scientists, fingerprint examiners, breathalyzer technicians, engineers, etc. (See: **opinion evidence**)
Facts in Issue	The essential elements of any offence that must be proven to form the basis for a finding of guilt in court (i.e., a *prima facie* case which involves sufficient evidence that, if not contradicted, will result in a conviction or finding of guilt). (See: *prima facie*)
Feeney Warrant	An endorsement on a Form 7.1 *Criminal Code* arrest warrant that authorizes peace officers to enter into dwelling

houses to make arrests in all cases except those involving exigent circumstances.

Field Interview

The preliminary questioning of a victim, witness or bystander at or near the scene of a crime to identify participants in an event and to determine the essence of their involvement in an incident under investigation. Field interviews differ from investigative interviews in the amount of planning and structure involved in them. Field interviews that determine the significance of a subject's involvement usually result in a more formal attempt to obtain a full statement at a later time.

Forensic Identification

[W]hen any two items contain a combination of corresponding or similar and specific characteristics of such number and significance to preclude the possibility of their occurrence by mere coincidence, and there are no unaccounted-for differences, it may be concluded that they are the same or their characteristics attribute to the same cause.

Hard Copy File Management

Paper-based information management systems that are used to manage and retrieve documents that require every piece of information to be reduced to writing and catalogued in some way.

Hearsay Evidence

Oral testimony of a witness that is third person in nature and not from the witness's direct knowledge (i.e., the witness heard [and then repeats] words spoken by another person, who is not called to testify).

(See: **hearsay rule**)

Hearsay Rule

"The long-standing evidentiary rule is that hearsay [evidence] cannot be used in court. Rather than accepting testimony based upon hearsay, the trial process asks that the person who was the original source of the hearsay information be brought into court to be questioned and cross-examined."

"Exceptions to the hearsay rule may occur [e.g., spontaneous utterances, dying declarations, admissions or confessions, business records or when there are sufficient indicators of the statement's reliability and due to circumstances of necessity] when the person with direct knowledge is dead or is otherwise unable to testify." (Definition from the Pearson Education On-line Glossary of Terms)

(See: **hearsay evidence**)

Holdback Evidence

Sensitive issues or information regarding an investigation that cannot be fully shared with non-police members of an investigative team or be released to the media. Holdback evidence might include details only known outside the investigation by the offender, the existence and identity of confidential police informers or agents, and issues surrounding officer safety, such as the use of an undercover officer.

Homicide	The killing of a human being by any means, directly or indirectly (s. 222(1) *Criminal Code*). Not synonymous with the term "murder."
	(See: **culpable homicide**; **non-culpable homicide**)
Impression Evidence	Impressions such as fingerprints, gloves or footwear worn by offenders, automotive or bicycle tires, tool marks, pattern wounds, bite marks, etc., that may be found at crime scenes.
In Situ	Latin = in its original location.
Included Offence	Included offences are designated by statute, but are also held to be offences that the accused had to commit as part of the full offence that is charged but not proved.
Inculpatory	Evidence in the form of physical evidence, direct testimony, circumstantial evidence or an admission or confession, etc., that tends to incriminate or blame a suspect or an accused person.
	(See antonym: **exculpatory**)
In-custody Informer	Someone who allegedly receives one or more (incriminating) statements from an accused, while both are in (police) custody (or in a correctional institution) and where the statement(s) relate to offences that occurred outside of the custodial institution. The prosecution must intend to call the in-custody informer as a witness in a judicial proceeding.
Inducement	Any promise of favour or hope of advantage held out to a suspect or an accused person by a person in authority for the purpose of persuading the suspect or accused to make an admission or confession that would tend to incriminate him or herself as evidence.
	(See: **admission**; **confession**; **person in authority**)
Informant (Informer)	Any person who voluntarily or for some consideration (financial or otherwise) provides incriminating information to the police regarding outstanding crimes or alleged criminal activity.
	Also a person who, having reasonable grounds for belief, initiates under oath or by solemn affirmation a document referred to as an "information" to lay a charge or initiate a legal process (e.g., search warrant, etc.).
Informed Consent	See: **consent**
Innocence at Stake	A legal principle that recognizes that the need to prove the innocence of an accused must take precedence over the need to guarantee the confidentiality of an informant or their information.
	(See: **Crown privilege**)
Interrogation	The formal examination of a suspect or an accused person by questioning. The primary objective of an interrogation is to

obtain an admission or confession from the suspect or accused to establish their guilt in the matter under investigation

(See: **interview**)

Interview	A conversation conducted with a person from whom information relating to the event under investigation is sought. An interview may result in the taking of a statement in writing or by audio or video recording if it is determined that the subject being interviewed has relevant knowledge of the case under investigation. (See: **interrogation**)
Investigator Bias	The improper selectivity, suppression or ignorance of evidence for any reason, such as pressure to solve a high-profile case.
Irrebuttable Presumption	A presumed truth in law that cannot be disproved by any means (e.g., "presumption of innocence," or a slot-machine being found in a house conclusively establishes the house as a common gaming house [s. 198(2) CC]). (See antonym: **rebuttable presumption; presumption of innocence**)
Joinder of Accused (or Joinder of Counts)	The joining of multiple charges and/or multiple accused on an information or indictment to avoid separate trials.
Law of Diminishing Return	As search for evidence continues further away from the location where a crime occurred, the amount of physical evidence recovered can be expected to diminish as the distance away from the scene increases.
Leading Question	A question that suggests or invites the answer (e.g., "Was the car that you saw a black car?" suggests that the colour of the vehicle was in fact black). This technique is to be avoided at all costs when interviewing witnesses as it may influence the witness's memory and obtain a response from other than memory. (See antonym: **open-ended question**)
Livor Mortis	Also referred to as post-mortem lividity or lividity. A dark blue or purplish staining of the skin caused by the blood of a pulse-less victim settling by gravity to the lower-most portions of the body.
Locard's Exchange Principle	A universally recognized scientific principle developed (circa 1928) by Dr. Edmond Locard, French anthropologist and criminologist, relating to the inevitable transfer of trace evidence that occurs when any two substances come into contact with each other. (See: **trace evidence**)
Manner of Death	A classification of the way a death occurs as opposed to the cause of death which explains how the death occurred. Manner

of death includes: Homicide; Suicide; Accidental causes; Natural causes; and Undetermined.

(See: **cause of death**)

Mens Rea   Latin = guilty mind; criminal intent to commit an offence.

Modus Operandi   The particular method in which an offender commits a crime. Offenders may demonstrate a particular preference for certain methods; this may be used to identify similar offences that were committed by the same individual(s).

Mitochondrial DNA   See: **DNA**

Mummification   The post-mortem dehydration of a body exposed to hot and dry conditions causing the tissues of the body to lose their moisture and become dry and leathery.

Murder   Culpable homicide includes:

(a) the intentional killing of a human being; or

(b) the intentional infliction of bodily harm the assailant knew was likely to cause death and being reckless as to whether death occurred or not that results in the death of the victim;

(c) meaning to cause death or bodily harm to a person, by accident or mistake causing the death of another human being regardless of the lack of intention to cause death or bodily harm to that person; or

(d) doing anything for an unlawful object that the assailant knew was likely to cause death and the death of any person results regardless of the lack of intention to cause death or bodily harm. (s. 229 Criminal Code)

Section 231 *Criminal Code* differentiates between first-degree and second-degree murder.

All murder is homicide. Not all homicides are murders.

(See: **homicide; culpable homicide; non-culpable homicide**)

Non-conscriptive Evidence   Evidence that is not obtained as the result of a breach of the accused's *Charter* rights that the accused did not participate in the creation or discovery of the evidence.

(See antonym: **conscriptive evidence**)

Non-culpable Homicide   Not deserving of blame (e.g., accident or justifiable homicide). Homicide that is not culpable is not an offence (s. 222(3) *Criminal Code*).

(See: **homicide; culpable homicide; murder**)

Objectivity   An investigative mindset that is based purely on observable facts and is not influenced by the investigator's personal prejudices or emotions.

Open-ended Question

A question asked by an interviewer that minimizes the possibility of suggestion to the subject being interviewed and calls for a more complete and expanded reply (e.g., "What colour was the car that you saw?")

(See antonym: **leading question**)

Operational Planning

Operational planning involves the development of tactical options and the identification of possible obstacles to the success of any operation, in order to manage risks, to the extent possible. Operational planning promotes the effective use of resources by encouraging investigators to identify the objectives of the proposed investigative technique and to ensure efficient execution of the operation in accordance with those identified objectives.

Opinion Evidence

Oral testimony given by a witness that is from personal belief or a presumption that is not based on fact. Generally inadmissible in court, except where the issue is universally common knowledge (e.g., the effects of intoxication by alcohol) or where the witness is uniquely able to provide knowledge of a fact.

(See: **expert evidence**)

Party to an Offence

Everyone who actually commits an offence or who does anything to aid (assist) a person to commit an offence (or omits to do anything to hinder it) or who abets (encourages) a person to commit an offence is a party to the offence and is guilty of the full offence.

(See: **aiding and abetting; counselling**)

Person in Authority

Any person formally involved at any stage of the investigation, arrest, detention, examination or prosecution of a person suspected or charged with an offence and who the accused believes to have such authority.

Any statement made by a suspect or accused to a person in authority must be shown to have been made voluntarily and without threats or inducements before it can be admitted into evidence. Peace officers, jailers, educators, parents of young offenders and members of the medical profession have all been considered to be persons in authority.

(See: **inducement**)

Person of Interest

A person whose background, relationship to the victim, or opportunity to commit the offence may warrant further inquiry but at that time no other grounds exist to suggest culpability (i.e., criminal liability, blameworthiness) in the commission of the crime being investigated.

A person of interest is not a "suspect" and should never be identified as such.

(See: **suspect**)

Photographic Lineup	The displaying of approximately 12 sequential photographs (including 1 suspect photograph randomly placed with 11 photographs of persons with similar physical characteristics) to eyewitnesses for possible identification purposes.
Physical Evidence	Real evidence (e.g., a tangible item such as a firearm or article of clothing, etc.). (See: **real evidence**)
Plain View Seizure Rule	A common law doctrine that permits the warrantless seizure of inadvertently found evidence in circumstances that make it entirely impracticable to obtain a search warrant. Three conditions must exist for a plain view seizure to be considered valid: <ul><li>the police must be lawfully positioned;</li><li>the finding of the evidence must be inadvertent; and</li><li>the evidence must implicate the accused in some criminal activity.</li></ul>
Polygraph	The polygraph, mistakenly referred to as a lie-detector, is an instrument that measures a person's involuntary physiological responses while under stress, such as the stress of telling a lie and wanting to avoid being identified as the person responsible for a crime.
Prejudice	In legal terms, prejudice refers to the harm or injury that might be caused to the fairness of the trial by reason of the admission of certain evidence that could cause the trier of fact to give undue weight to that particular piece of evidence. To be admissible in a criminal proceeding, the probative value of a piece of evidence must outweigh any potential prejudice to the fairness of the trial. (See: **probative**; **trier of fact**)
Presumption of Innocence	An irrebuttable presumption (something that is presumed to be true) of Western criminal law which holds that any person charged with any offence has the right to be presumed innocent until proven guilty, beyond a reasonable doubt, in an open and impartial court. In Canada, this right is guaranteed by s. 11(d) of the *Canadian Charter of Rights and Freedoms*. (See: **irrebuttable presumption**; **rebuttable presumption**)
Prima facie	Evidence that, if not contradicted, is sufficient to prove one or more fact in issue of a case or result in a finding of guilt. (See: **facts in issue**)
Privilege	Immunity against forced disclosure that is granted to certain evidence made under circumstances of assured confidentiality, (e.g., spousal communication, solicitor–client privilege, etc.).

Probative	The evidential value of a piece of evidence and its ability to afford proof of a fact of a case. Although a piece of evidence may have probative value, it may not be admitted unless the probative value outweighs any potential prejudice to the fairness of the trial. (See: **prejudice**)
Procedural Memory	The repetitive learning of a skill (e.g., tying one's shoes, learning the alphabet, etc.). (See: **episodic memory**)
Propping	"Propping" involves the strategic placement of artifacts intended to be observed by the suspect in and around an interrogation room to impress upon the suspect the gravity of the offence and the strength of the evidence against them. Propping may include conspicuous signage, photographs, wall-charts and file cabinets bearing the suspect's name on the drawer-fronts, etc. (See: **interrogation**; **suspect**)
Proxemics	The study of personal space as it relates to ordinary human relations, and the interrogation technique based on this study.
Public Appeal	The direct solicitation of relevant information from the public involving one or more media, alone or in combination, such as radio, television, print media, Amber Alerts, billboards, handbills, etc.
Putrefaction	The process of decomposition involving the post-mortem breakdown of tissues of the body.
Random Virtue-testing	The inappropriate inducement of one or more persons to commit a crime without a reasonable suspicion that the person is already engaged in the illegal activity (e.g. drug trafficking) or that the location involved is one in which the illegal activity is likely to be occurring.
Real Evidence	Physical evidence (e.g., a tangible item such as a firearm or article of clothing, etc.). (See: **physical evidence**)
Reasonable Doubt	A disbelief or uncertainty to a high degree of moral certainty. Beyond a reasonable doubt is the standard of proof used in Canadian criminal courts to establish criminal culpability (i.e., guilt). Where the trier of fact (i.e., judge or jury as the case may be) is, after hearing the evidence, left with a reasonable doubt that the accused committed the offence as charged, that doubt must be resolved in favour of the accused and the accused will be acquitted or found not guilty. (See: **presumption of innocence**; **balance of probability**; **civil standard of proof**)

Reasonable Expectation of Privacy
A legal concept used to determine the privacy interest of an accused person. For a party to a conversation, "reasonable expectation" means a justifiable belief that no one other than the intended recipient would hear the conversation. A conversation held in public could not justify a reasonable expectation of privacy as anyone nearby might overhear it. Reasonable expectation of privacy also relates to whether or not an accused has a justifiable belief that real property would not be discovered and used against him or her in court.

Reasonable Grounds
A set of facts or circumstances which, if true, would lead an ordinary, prudent and cautious individual to have a strong belief (e.g., as to the identity of the accused or as to whether or not a suspect has committed a breach or violation of statute law) and which exceeds mere suspicion.

Reasonable grounds also refers to the standard imposed upon peace officers as the basis of formulating grounds upon which to make an arrest, swear to an information to obtain a search warrant or lay a charge before the courts, etc.

Reasonable Person
A legal standard involving a fictitious prudent and cautious person who always exercises good judgment and does not act recklessly or based on emotion. Used to determine negligence in civil court proceedings and in criminal courts to evaluate the objective reasonableness of arrests, searches and seizures of evidence.

Rebuttable Presumption
A presumption that proves a fact in issue of a charge that may be contradicted or disproved by evidence to the contrary. The *Criminal Code* presumes, in the absence of evidence to the contrary, that a person who breaks and enters a place has the intent to commit an indictable offence. This presumption may be rebutted if the accused enters evidence that demonstrates a lack of such intent (e.g., the accused testifies that he broke into a cottage in winter as he was lost and it was necessary to do so to ensure his survival from the elements, etc.) (s. 348(2)(a) CC).

(See: **irrebuttable presumption**; **presumption of innocence**)

Res Judicata
A legal doctrine that protects people against being convicted for two offences arising out of the same set of facts or circumstances.

Rigor Mortis
A gradual and temporary post mortem stiffening of the muscles of the body that begins 2–4 hours after death and is complete within 12–18 hours. At 24–36 hours after death, *rigor mortis* begins to subside and disappears completely within 48–72 hours.

Robbery
A theft or attempted theft involving the use of personal or threatened violence before, during or after the theft to

overcome resistance or to escape. Also, a theft committed while the offender is armed with an offensive weapon.

Rule of Precedent   Lower courts are bound by rule of precedent or case law (i.e., the previous decisions of higher courts in similar matters). Equal or higher courts may take decisions of lower courts into consideration, but are not required to do so.

(See: **case law**)

Scribe   A member of an investigative team who is assigned to record all times, dates and locations of observations, identities of persons, if known or their detailed descriptions of a search or a surveillance detail in written form. The scribe finalizes the results of the detail in a comprehensive written report.

Securing a Crime Scene   The continuous stabilization and protection of the crime scene against entry by unauthorized persons and against contamination until a thorough and methodical examination of the scene is conducted.

(See: **crime scene; contamination**)

Show and Tell Statement   A cautioned and video-recorded statement of a suspect or accused person involving a re-enactment of the offence at the crime scene or to retrieve hidden evidence at location(s) known only to the suspect.

(See: **crime scene; suspect; accused; interrogation**)

Show Cause Hearing   A judicial interim release hearing to determine whether or not the continued detention of a prisoner is justified under the circumstances of the case.

Spontaneous Utterance   An unanticipated, unsolicited incriminating verbal statement made by a suspect or person in custody to a witness (especially a police officer) admitting or confessing some responsibility for the crime under investigation, prior to the administering of the standard caution. The caution should be administered to the suspect or prisoner as soon as possible after such a statement is made. A spontaneous utterance is an exception to the hearsay rule, as witnesses are permitted by the courts to testify as to such statements they heard being made by an accused.

(See: **hearsay rule**)

Staged Crime Scene   The intentional alteration of a crime scene for the purpose of misleading the police investigation by diverting suspicion from the most logical suspect(s); usually done to convey either a different manner of death or a different motivation for the crime.

(See: **crime scene**)

Subpoena   Latin = under penalty. A court order (in Form 16 CC) issued by a Justice under s. 699 CC that compels a Crown or defence witness to appear at a stated time and place to give evidence concerning the charge before the court. Under the terms and conditions of the subpoena, the witness may also be required

	to bring to court certain specified items or documents that are relevant to the case and are in his or her possession. (See: **warrant for a witness**)
Suicide	The intentional taking of one's own life by self-inflicted injury.
Supplementary Caution (Secondary Caution)	A formal warning given by a peace officer to a person under arrest or detainment or a person suspected of or charged with an offence (following the standard caution) for the purpose of removing any previous threat, promise or inducement made to the prisoner/suspect/accused by a person in authority. (See: **caution; person in authority**)
Surveillance	The continuous overt or secret observation of a person, group of people, location or of some other situation, often conducted to gather evidence or intelligence information.
Suspect	A person [whom] an investigator reasonably believes may possess a degree of culpability [i.e., criminal liability, blameworthiness] in the commission of the criminal offence being investigated and there [exists] some incriminating information linking the person to the crime. (Definition from the Ontario Major Case Management (MCM) Manual.) (See: **person of interest; witness; accused; defendant**)
Telewarrant	An electronically transmitted search warrant issued by a justice in a centralized location to accommodate the weekend and after-hours operational needs of law enforcement agencies.
Theft	The fraudulent taking of property with the intent to deprive the owner, or a person with a special interest in it, of the possession of the property.
Threat Assessment	The analysis and classification of anticipated factors that might adversely impact a police operation or may result in harm to an individual. Threat assessment is utilized to identify threats and to develop strategies to diminish – not necessarily prevent – the threat, thereby improving the probability of success or safety.
Tombstone Information	The unique information that distinguishes one occurrence from another and includes the incident number, time, date, location and personal identifiers of the main persons involved.
Trace Evidence	Various types of physical evidence used to draw associations between the location of the evidence and the source of the evidence that may be circumstantial evidence at a trial (e.g., rug fibres found on the clothing of a victim that are related back to an accused's vehicle or residence, or microscopic blood spatter transferred from a victim onto a suspect's clothing). (See: **Locard's Exchange Principle**)

Trier of Fact	The party in a criminal trial with the responsibility of determining the facts of a case from the evidence and for arriving at a verdict. The trier of fact is the *judge* in a court composed of a judge sitting without a jury, while the trier of fact is the *jury* in a court composed of a judge and jury. Even in a jury trial, it is still the responsibility of the judge to determine the admissibility of evidence that may be put before the jury.
Tunnel Vision	A single-minded and overly narrow focus on a particular investigative or prosecutorial theory, so as to unreasonably colour the evaluation of information received and one's conduct in response to that information. (Definition from Kaufman 1998, p. 479.)
Verdict	A legal finding of guilty (a conviction) or not guilty (an acquittal), rendered by a court of law.
	(See: **acquittal**; **conviction**)
ViCLAS	The Violent Crime Linkage Analysis System (ViCLAS) is an investigative tool utilizing a computerized database to link similar crimes in single or multiple jurisdictions as having possibly been committed by a common offender, based on behavioural principles.
Voir Dire	A judicial hearing, often referred to as a trial within a trial, for the purpose of determining the admissibility of a verbal or written statement made by a suspect or an accused person. During a trial involving a jury, a *voir dire* is conducted by the judge in the absence of the jury. If, as the result of the *voir dire*, the statement is held to be admissible, the jury is returned to the courtroom and the statement is then introduced into evidence.
Warrant for a Witness	A court order (in Form 17 CC) issued by a Justice under s. 698 or 705 *Criminal Code* that authorizes the arrest of a Crown or defence witness who will not attend court unless compelled to do so or is evading service of a subpoena or was served with a subpoena and failed to attend court as required.
	(See: **subpoena**)
Will Say (Statement)	A point-form summary prepared to assist the assigned Crown Attorney in quickly reviewing the main points of testimony that a witness is capable of testifying to. A Will Say includes evidence, in any form, regarding any of the facts in issue of the case (e.g., verbal statements by a suspect that the witness overheard and any physical evidence that the witness has knowledge of).
Young Offender	A person who is between 12 and 17 years of age, inclusive, at the time he or she commits an offence for which he or she is charged under the *Youth Criminal Justice Act* or any preceding legislation.

Bibliography

American Polygraph Association. *Polygraph Validity Research Statistics*. Retrieved January 23, 2005, from www.polygraph.org

Arcaro, Gino. (2004). *Criminal Investigation: Forming Reasonable Grounds* (4th ed). Scarborough: Thompson Canada.

Baden, Michael, and Marion Roach. (2001). *Dead Reckoning: The New Science of Catching Killers*. New York: Simon & Schuster.

Beaven, Colin. (2001). *Fingerprints: The Origin of Crime Detection and the Murder Case that Launched Forensic Science*. New York: Hyperion Publishing.

www.bloodspatter.com. Homepage. Retrieved January 29, 2005.

Brazoria County Sheriff's Department. "Blood Spatter Interpretation: General Rules to Consider." Retrieved January 29, 2005, from www.brazoria-county.com/sheriff/id/blood/

British Broadcasting Corporation. "Faulds, Henry" (biographical information). Retrieved January 9, 2005, from http://www.bbc.co.uk/history/historic_figures/faulds_henry.shtml

Campbell, Mr. Justice Archie G. (June 1996). *Bernardo Investigation Review: Report of Mr. Justice Archie Campbell*. Toronto: Ontario Ministry of the Solicitor General and Correctional Services (now the Ministry of Community Safety and Correctional Services), Queen's Printer for Ontario.

Canadian Institute for Health Information. "Canadian Suicide Statistics." Retrieved October 9, 2004, from www.secure.cihi.ca

Canadian Legal Information Institute. Homepage. Retrieved March 21, 2005, from www.canlii.org/ca

Canadian Mental Health Association. *Suicide Statistics (Ontario and Canada)*. Retrieved September 3, 2004, from www.ontario.cmha.ca

Canadian Police College, Ottawa. *Major Case Management: Team Commander's Course*. Retrieved March 21, 2005, from www.cpc.gc.ca/courses/

Carpenter, R. Scott. "Forensic Science Resources: Criminalistics and Trace Evidence." Retrieved January 25, 2004, from www.tncrimlaw.com/forensic/

Cassidy, Michael J. (1980). *Footwear Identification*. Ottawa: Public Relations Branch, Royal Canadian Mounted Police, Ministry of Supply and Services Canada.

Centre of Forensic Sciences. (1997). *Laboratory Guide for the Investigator* (5th ed). Toronto: Ministry of Community Safety and Correctional Services, Public Safety Division.

Cornwell, Patricia. (2003). *Portrait of a Killer: Jack The Ripper, Case Closed*. New York: Berkley Publishing Group.

www.crimelibrary.com. Homepage. Retrieved October 2, 2004.

Darden, Christopher A. *In Contempt*. (1996). New York: Harper Collins.

http://Dictionary.law.com. Homepage. Retrieved August 11, 2004.

www.e-laws.gov.on.ca. Homepage. Retrieved April 17, 2005.

www.elisabethkublerross.com. Homepage. Retrieved September 17, 2004.

Euale, James, et al. (1998). *Principles of Evidence for Policing.* Toronto: Emond Montgomery.

Evans, Colin. (1996). *The Casebook of Forensic Detection: How Science Solved 100 of the World's Most Baffling Crimes.* New York: John Wiley and Sons.

www.evidentcrimescene.com. Homepage. Retrieved January 29, 2005.

Fauld, Henry. (1880). "On the Skin Furrows of the Hand." *Nature* magazine, October 28, 1880. Retrieved January 9, 2005, from www.eneate.freeserve.co.uk/page3.html

www.forensicartist.com. Homepage. Retrieved January 31, 2005.

Geberth, Vernon J. (1996). *Practical Homicide Investigation: Tactics, Procedures and Forensic Techniques* (3rd ed). Boca Raton, FL: CRC Press.

Government of Canada, Department of Justice. "Hearsay Evidence and Exceptions to the Hearsay Rule." Retrieved July 28, 2004, from www.canada.justice.gc.ca

Government of Ontario. "Amber Alerts in Ontario." Retrieved March 20, 2005, from www.gov.on.ca/opp/amberalert/english/

Greene, Richard (with Florie Brizel). (2002). *Words that Shook the World: 100 years of Unforgettable Speeches and Events.* New York: Penguin Putnam.

Hanzhang, Tao, General. (2000). *Sun Tzu's Art of War: The Modern Chinese Interpretation.* Trans. Yuan Shibing. New York: Sterling.

Hillsdon Smith, John. (1981). *Clock and Calendar: The Technical Approach to Crime Scene and Sudden Death Investigations.* Ontario Ministry of the Solicitor General, Public Safety Division, Forensic Pathology Branch.

Hopper, Carolyn. (2003). *Practicing College Learning Strategies* (3rd ed). New York: Houghton Mifflin.

Horton, Fabien. (2000). "Electronic Evidence, Continuity of Evidence." Retrieved January 23, 2004, from www.sinch.com.au/articles/2000/FHorton1.htm

Huber, R.A. (1972). The Philosophy of Identification. *RCMP Gazette*, vol. 34 nos. 7, 8.

Hutchinson, Scott C. (1996). *Issues in Search and Seizure Law in Canada.* n.p.

Inbau, Fred E. *et al.* (2001). *Criminal Interrogation and Confessions* (4th ed). Gaithersburg, MD: Aspen.

International Association of Blood Pattern Analysts. "Blood Spatter Principles and Terms." Retrieved January 28, 2005, from www.iabpa.org

www.interviewing.net. "Verbal and Nonverbal Cues of Deception." Retrieved September 17, 2004, from www.interviewing.net

Jeffreys, Alec and Robert Melias. "First DNA Conviction." Retrieved January 10, 2005 from www.home.iprimus.com/au

www.jurisdiction.com. Homepage. Retrieved July 28, 2004.

Kaufman, The Hon. Mr Fred. (1998). *The Commission on Proceedings Involving Guy Paul Morin* Toronto: Ontario Ministry of the Attorney General. Toronto: Queen's Printer for Ontario.

Kelly, John, ed. (2000). *National Crime Faculty Guide to Investigative Interviewing* (3rd ed). Hampshire, UK: National Crime Faculty, Environmental Research Team, Crown Copyright.

'Lectric Law Library. Homepage. Retrieved January 24, 2004 from www.lectlaw.com.

LexUM. Homepage and database of the Faculty of Law, University of Montreal. Retrieved January 6, 2004, from www.lexum.umontreal.ca

Locke, Laron. (1996). *Factors Used in Estimating the Time of Death: Post Mortem Changes*. Paper presented to the Homicide Investigation Seminar, April 1996, hosted by the Medical-Legal Research and Education Association and Harvard Associates in Police Science.

Loftus, Elizabeth F. (2003). "Repressed Memory." *American Psychologist*, November 2003.

Lowenstein, David. (2004). "Children's Memory: Fact or Fiction?". Retrieved January 28, 2004, from www.clubtheo.com/momdad/html/dlmemory.html

Madinger, John. (2000). *Confidential Informant: Law Enforcement's Most Valuable Tool*. Boca Raton, FL: CRC Press.

Martin's Annual Criminal Code. (2005). Toronto: Canada Law Book.

Martin, Dianne L. (2005). "Lessons about Justice from the Laboratory of Wrongful Convictions: Tunnel Vision, the Construction of Guilt and Informer Evidence." *University of Missouri-Kansas City Law Review*, 70/4: p. 847.

Maschke, George W. and Scalabrini, Gino G. (2000). "The Lie Behind the Lie Detector." Retrieved January 24, 2005, from http://antipolygraph.org

www.milestonesinc.com. Biographical data, Dr. William Moulton Marston. Retrieved January 22, 2005, from www.milestonesinc.com/assessments/dr.marston.htm

www.missing.puellula.org. Biographical data, Amber Rene Hagerman. Retrieved March 20, 2005.

Moody, Janette W. and J. Ellis Blanton, *et al*. (1998). "A Theoretically Grounded Approach to Assist Memory During Information Requirements Determination." *Journal of Management Information Systems,* Vol. 15, No. 1, p.79.

National Commission on Terrorist Attacks. (2004). *The 9/11 Commission Report (Final Report of the National Commission on Terrorist Attacks Upon The United States)*. New York: W.W. Norton & Company.

New South Wales Police (unofficial website). "Fingerprint Patterns." Retrieved January 9, 2005, from www.policensw.com/info/fingerprints/finger07

Ontario Attorney General's Advisory Committee on Charge Screening, Disclosure and Resolution Discussions. (1993). *Report of the Ontario Attorney General's Advisory Committee on Charge Screening, Disclosure and Resolution Discussions (The Martin Report)*. Toronto: Queen's Printer for Ontario.

Paciocco, David M. and Lee Steusser. (1996).*The Law of Evidence*. Concord, ON: Irwin Law.

www.pearsoned.ca. Homepage. Retrieved July 28, 2004.

Pennsylvania Office of the Attorney General. History of the Polygraph. Retrieved January 22, 2005, from www.attorneygeneral.gov/cld/articles/poly

Ressler, Robert H. and Shachtman, Tom. (1993). *Whoever Fights Monsters*. New York: St. Martin's Press.

Ridges and furrows (2005). Information about fingerprints. Retrieved January 9, 2005 from www.ridgesandfurrows.homestead.com/fingerprints.html

Roberts, Tim. (2002). *The Human Factor: Maximizing the Use of Police Informants*. London (UK): New Police Bookshop, Benson Publications.

Rossmo, Kim. (2005) "Geographic Profiling." Retrieved January 28, 2005, from www.geographicprofiling.com/geopro/krossmo.pdf

Royal Canadian Mounted Police. Homepage. Retrieved October 17, 2004, from www.rcmp.ca

Royal Society of New Zealand. "DNA History". Retrieved January 10, 2005, from www.rsnz.org/topics/biol/dna50/history.php

Sapir, Avinoam. (2000). *Scientific Content Analysis*. Phoenix: The Laboratory for Scientific Interrogation (LSI).

Schmalleger, Frank and Volk, Rebecca. (2005). *Canadian Criminology Today: Theories and Applications* (2nd ed). Toronto: Pearson Education Canada.

Select, Assess and Train. Homepage. Retrieved September 16, 2004, from www.selectassesstrain.com

Sher, Julian. (2002). *Until You Are Dead: Steven Truscott's Long Ride into History* Toronto: Random House of Canada.

Sherriff, Steve. (1997). *Convicting the Guilty: A Strategic Manual of Law and Technique for Dedicated Investigators and Prosecutors Combating Major Crime*. n.p.

Simon Fraser University News. (1996). Dr. Kim Rossmo and Geographic Profiling. Retrieved January 28, 2005, from www.sfu.ca/mediapr/sfnews/1996/June6/rossmo.html

Skopitz, Kimberly. (2002). "History of Fingerprints." Retrieved January 9, 2005, from www.kyky.essortment.com/fingerprinthist_rmmv.htm

Slemco, J. "Bloodstain Pattern Analysis Tutorial." Retrieved January 29, 2005, from www.bloodspatter.com/BPATutorial.htm

Statistics Canada. (2004). *The Daily*. Retrieved December 27, 2004, from www.statcan.ca

www.suicideinfo.ca. (2004). *Research Regarding Suicide*. Retrieved October 4, 2004.

Turpin, Silvana. (2002). *Communications in Law Enforcement* (2nd ed). Toronto: Pearson Education Canada.

United States Department of the Census. World POPClock Projection. Retrieved January 9, 2005, from www.census.gov/cgi-bin/ipc/popclockworld

United States Department of Justice Technical Working Group on Eyewitness Evidence. (1999). "Eyewitness Evidence: A Guide for Law Enforcement." Retrieved January 29, 2005, from www.ncjrs.org

University of Alabama Center for Teaching and Learning. "Principles of Memory." Retrieved January 28, 2004, from www.ctl.ua.edu/CTLStudyAids/StudySkillsFlyers/MemorySkills/

University of Ottawa. Biographical data, David Paciocco. Retrieved August 21, 2005, from www.commonlaw.uottawa.ca/faculty/prof/dpaciocco/desce.htm

Washington University St. Louis, Department of Anatomy and Neurosurgery. "Neural Systems." Retrieved January 28, 2004, from www.thalamus.wustl.edu/Neural_Systems_03

Webs to Awareness. Homepage. "The Body Language of Proxemics." Retrieved September 16, 2004, from http://members.aol.com/katydidit/bodylang.htm

Wells, G. (2001). "Sequential versus Simultaneous Photographic Lineups: Sequential-superiority Effect." Retrieved January 29, 2005, from www.psychology.iastate.edu/faculty/gwells/Youaskedaboutsequential.htm

Weston, Paul B. & Wells, Kenneth M. (1997). *Criminal Investigation: Basic Perspectives* (7th ed). Upper Saddle River, NJ: Prentice Hall.

Index